W9-BEF-007

Stuffed Tomatoes in Olive Oil, page 213

Frico, page 92

Ham Fritters in the Andalusian Style, page 361

OPPOSITE: *Olives Stuffed with Ground Beef in Piquant Tomato Ragout, page 216*

*Chickpeas and Hazelnuts with
Three Peppers, page 163*

Red and Black Caviar Canapés, page 24

Zucchini and Bell Pepper Frittata from Murcia, page 109

Fougasse, page 273

Prosciutto and Peaches, page 394

Tabbouleh, page 238

*Catalonian Spinach Empanadas
with Raisins and Pine Nuts,
page 325*

*Octopus and Radicchio Salad from
Sardinia, page 406*

Brīk with Tuna and Egg, page 330

OPPOSITE: *Spicy Carrot Salad from Morocco, page 199*

Fried Feta Cheese and Black Olives with Oregano, page 90

Stuffed Grape Leaves with Rice, Currants, and Pine Nuts, page 228

Turkish-Style Stuffed
Mussels, page 416

Gorgonzola and Walnut
Canapés, page 31

Olive Oil–Bathed Artichokes from Syria, page 196

Pizza con Pancetta, page 303

*Pan-Fried Shrimp with
Dill, page 144*

Muḥammara, page 59

Puff Pastry Crescents with Saffron Chicken and Almonds from Spain, page 285

Red Bean and Onion Salad with Dill, page 165

Baby Clams in
Piquant Tomato Sauce,
page 150

Pearl Onions in Sweet-and-Sour Sauce in the Style of Monaco, page 175

Cheese and Potato Cigars of the Tunisian Jews, page 334

Croûtes of Cotechino Sausage and Marsala Wine, page 52

Mediterranean-Style Fried Small Fish, page 372

Sicilian Red Radishes with Fresh
Peppered Pecorino, page 244

 Pork and Pine Nut Meatballs in
Romesco Sauce, page 133

Little Foods of the Mediterranean

ALSO BY
CLIFFORD A. WRIGHT

ON COOKING

Real Stew

Mediterranean Vegetables

A Mediterranean Feast

Italian Pure & Simple

Grill Italian

Lasagne

Cucina Rapida

Cucina Paradiso

CONTRIBUTOR

"Harold l'Américain" in
Saveur Cooks France

ON POLITICS AND HISTORY

Facts and Fables

After the Palestine-Israel War

Little Foods of the Mediterranean

500 FABULOUS RECIPES FOR ANTIPASTI, TAPAS, HORS D'OEUVRE, MEZE, AND MORE

CLIFFORD A. WRIGHT

THE HARVARD COMMON PRESS • BOSTON, MASSACHUSETTS

THE HARVARD COMMON PRESS
535 ALBANY STREET
BOSTON, MASSACHUSETTS 02118
WWW.HARVARDCOMMONPRESS.COM

©2003 by Clifford A. Wright

All rights reserved. No part of this publication may be reproduced or transmitted in any form or by any means, electronic or mechanical, including photocopying, recording, or any information storage or retrieval system, without permission in writing from the publisher.

Printed in the United States

Library of Congress Cataloging-in-Publication Data

Wright, Clifford A.

   Little foods of the Mediterranean : 500 fabulous recipes for antipasti, tapas, hors d'oeuvre, meze, and more / Clifford A. Wright.

     p. cm.

   ISBN 1-55832-227-2 (pbk : alk. paper) — ISBN 1-55832-226-4 (hc : alk. paper)

   1. Appetizers—Mediterranean Region. 2. Snack foods—Mediterranean Region. 3. Cookery, Mediterranean. I. Title.

   TX740.W75 2003

   641.8'12'091822—dc21   2003014623

Special bulk-order discounts are available on this and other Harvard Common Press books. Companies and organizations may purchase books for premiums or resale or may arrange a custom edition, by contacting the Marketing Director at the address above.

10 9 8 7 6 5 4 3 2 1

www.cliffordawright.com

BOOK DESIGN BY DEBORAH KERNER/DANCING BEARS DESIGN
PHOTOGRAPHY BY DUANE WINFIELD
FOOD STYLING BY MEGAN FAWN SCHLOW

FOR MY YOUNGEST SON,

SERI NICHOLAS KATTAN-WRIGHT,

WHO WONDERED WHEN WE WOULD AGAIN EAT "BIG" FOOD

Contents

Acknowledgments

The people I could thank who gave me inspiration or who helped in some way with the research for and writing of this book number in the hundreds, because these recipes have been collected over the past twenty years and represent countless journeys to the Mediterranean in search of the familiar, the unfamiliar, the hidden, and the known. The great bulk of the research for this book derives from my archival-like notes from the writing of my book *A Mediterranean Feast*. However, this book is not a sequel to that book, but a companion.

There are several people whom I would like to thank who have been steadfast in their support of this book in particular and of my efforts in general to provide my readers a deeper understanding of the foods they eat. Specifically, three women form the bedrock of the books I love to write. My agent, Doe Coover, not only has my interests at heart, but also has heart for my interests. My editor, Pam Hoenig, has been more than just my editor for the past decade: I feel she may be more aptly described as my co-conspirator. My girlfriend,

Sarah Pillsbury, my joyous companion, not only cooks but eats too and eats my Mediterranean food while wholeheartedly suspending her Minnesota culinary upbringing. She believes in me and promotes me tirelessly, for which I am humbly grateful.

I would also like to thank my children, Ali, Dyala, and Seri, for they literally ate all the food in this book, and now that they are grown and have been eating Mediterranean food all their lives their contributions are truly critical and appreciated. I believe the reason my children eat everything (and I mean everything) is that from the day they were born the were offered real food from real places and were never given saccharin "kid food."

Thanks also to my publisher, Bruce Shaw, for his support of my efforts and to Valerie Cimino, managing editor; Jodi Marchowsky, production editor; Carole Berglie, copyeditor; Skye Stewart, marketing director; and everyone else at The Harvard Common Press for being such enthusiastic fans of mine and for making such fine books.

Introduction

My first taste of Tuscan *crostini* was so magical that I made the second bite smaller in the hope of prolonging the experience. Perhaps it was the sublime simplicity of the three canapés that so intrigued me: a *crostini* with chicken liver pâté, one with shrimp pâté, and one with crushed white beans. The ambience was restoratively perfect as we gazed at grape arbors draped with leaves dappled yellow, which stretched toward the Tuscan hills before our open terrazzo. Our restaurant, the Osteria alla Piazza in Castellina in Chianti near Siena, called them *i nostri crostini,* "our canapés," an appellation so personal, so welcoming, that I just knew the food to follow would be memorable. The suave waiter made us feel we were in secure and professional hands. This beautiful perch overlooking the vineyard, at a table with crisp white cloth, was quiet and relaxing as we continued with our *passatempo,* a little food had before an antipasto. At this moment, it dawned on me why these little foods were important in a culinary experience. It wasn't so much that they "opened the appetite," as it was that they were

a reassuring affirmation that we were in the caring hands of a good cook who wanted us to be happy with the expectation of even greater things to come. It was both a preview and an end in itself, if that was to be our fate. And this, I realized, is what the little foods of the Mediterranean were all about: they can be both a beginning and an end in themselves.

Around the Mediterranean these small foods are known as hors d'oeuvre, *amuse-gueules, amuse-bouches, passatempo,* antipasti, tapas, *mazza,* meze, *zakuski, qimiyya,* and *ādū,* not to mention a host of inviting snacks and street foods. These little foods of the Mediterranean are becoming better known in America, where all of them are assumed to be appetizers. An appetizer is a food usually served before a meal as a means of stimulating the appetite, although Joe Moore in *The Quotable Cook* calls appetizers the little things you keep eating until you lose your appetite. For me an appetizer is a preview, a taste of things to come. Every recipe in this book is an appetizer, but many of these recipes are much more, and much less, because throughout the Mediterranean it is not a shared culinary tradition that the appetite needs an opening, a stimulation. In many cultures, especially in countries of North Africa and the Middle East, the notion of an appetizer is foreign.

This book is not what it appears: a book of appetizers. It is an introduction to the way people eat in the Mediterranean. The entire psychology of eating is different in the Mediterranean from how it is in the United States. Here we eat to live and in the Mediterranean they live to eat. Here we feed at the trough of the "all-you-can-eat" restaurant, while in the Mediterranean they would ask, "Why would you want to eat all you can eat?" Here we guzzle a beer or knock back several martinis on an empty stomach, and in the Mediterranean they are likely to sip wine that complements food. Here a man is admired if he is a human garbage disposal, while in the Mediterranean a man is more likely to be a gourmet, savoring each nibble of food as if he were kissing a woman's neck. Here a woman will brag to her date that she doesn't cook, while in the Mediterranean women know the way to a man's heart. And men know the way to a woman's heart. Having said that, I understand that this volume will be used both as an appetizer book and as a book on the Mediterranean style of eating, and you can feel comfortable with both approaches.

Small foods or appetizers get eaten in two ways: either sitting or standing. If you are throwing a cocktail party and guests are milling about with glasses and napkins and small plates in their hands, then you will want to avoid at all costs their need for forks. One of the best ways to do this is to choose finger foods or foods that can be speared with disposable frilly cocktail toothpicks. If your guests are fewer in number and are sitting, a world of foods can open up to you and many more dishes can be served. The best kind of cocktail party is the one where no plates are required and servers pass through the crowd with savory bites on platters for guests to try, popping them in their mouths in one or two bites and wiping their hands on small cocktail napkins.

It's unclear when appetizers got their start but there are enough references from the classical age of Greece to see that it is early indeed. Of course, it should be understood that what we think of appetizers today are a truly recent invention and that historically people ate differently in different places at different times. Certainly in Homer's *Odyssey* we hear (I:163–168) of a housekeeper who brings "appetizers aplenty." In Athenaeus's *The Deipnosophists* (II:58 (253)) from the third century A.D., appetizers called *propoma* (literally "preliminary drink") are served, and among the ingredients used in these "fore-drinks" the roots of mallow are mentioned. Later, the description (II:59-60 (261)) of a "complete appetizer" served by a character called Alexis is, well, appetizing: "There was set before us a platter with a marvelous smell of the Seasons, shaped like the hemisphere of Heaven's vault. For all the beauties of the constellations were on it— fish, kids, the scorpion [an allusion to Pisces, Capricornus, and Scorpio] running between them, while slices of eggs represented the stars." Another appetizer served were turnips done in vinegar and mustard (IV:133 (113)). A character in Athenaeus at one point describes an appetizer tray (IV:132 (107)): "For the cook sets before you a large tray on which are five small plates. One of these holds garlic, another a pair of sea urchins, another a sweet wine sop, another ten cockles, the last a small piece of sturgeon." And he tells us (IV:133 (111)), "For the ancients employed dishes to whet the appetite, such as olives in brine, which they call kolymbades." Other sources tell us of fruits and vegetables being served as appetizers and, of course, olives.

The idea of appetizers may have its root in Roman times. Although our evidence comes from fragments, it seems that the Roman *gustatio* or *gustus* was the eating of appetizers, especially the roots of vegetables, fish, and eggs. This eating of appetizers culminated in the *cena*, the dinner proper. Martial's description of the *gustus* reads as a foretaste of dinner, as appetizers and not just a cataloging of simple foods. Pliny, too, describes what appears to be an appetizer table filled with lettuce, "three snails each," two eggs, emmer-gruel with *mulsum* (honeyed wine), olives, beetroot, gourds, onions, and a "thousand other delicacies." Petronius's mention (Satyricon: 31, 9) of *promulsidari* is a description of a platter of hors d'oeuvre.

Even though the Roman *gustatio* seems like it is the precursor to the modern Italian antipasto, a word that means "before the meal," this word *antipasto* does not appear for the first time until the sixteenth-century writings of Agnolo Firenzuola. Very early on in Italy these *antipasti*, before that word was commonly used, were called *primo servizio di credenza*, which means something like "first service of food on the sideboard."

As I mentioned before, the "appetizers" weren't exactly what we today think of as appetizers because they were eaten with the prevalent theory of dietetics in mind. Galen's theory of dietetics, which postulated four fundamental elements of the world related to the four constituent elements of the human being that had to be in balance with each other for good health, remained important well into the Middle Ages. Then it finally succumbed to the more accurate theories of nutrition and medicine that resulted from modern science. People ate differently both in ancient Greece and in medieval France. For example, in medieval France, judging from a few fourteenth-century menus, banquets were served in successive courses of groups of dishes, which were placed on the table simultaneously, and each guest ate only what was within reach. But the course that we could call an "appetizer" was fixed in a culinary concept that was informed through and through by the theory of dietetics, which required the stomach to be "opened" by certain foods where they could then become "cooked." These "openers" were often fresh fruit or salads with vinaigrette dressing. The knowledge we have of French dining habits during medieval times comes from some of the extant cookbooks and menus of the time. Following the medieval concept of dietetics, which was based on Galen's now discredited theory of humors, there was a distinction between foods that were *aperitivus* and foods that were *appetitivus*. The first set of foods was meant to open the stomach to allow food for digestion. These foods might be lettuce, mint, almonds, ginger, or cinnamon. But other foods were used to stimulate the appetite once the stomach was opened. These were, for example, rabbit, black cherries, mustard, or roast beans. Little delicacies were served at the French court, called *menu drois*, which meant the more delicate parts of slaughtered game from the hunt that were reserved by rights (*droits*) to the hunter. This phrase came to mean specifically the liver and giblets, which were cooked and served with vinaigrette or egg sauce and spices such as cinnamon, cloves, ginger, and saffron as an hors d'oeuvre.

The Italians of the same time ate more or less similarly to the French, but it's difficult to determine from the extant menus if any of their courses would count as today's appetizer. For example, in the textbook *Banchetti, compositioni di vivande et apparecchio generale* published in 1549, the head chef at the court of the Dukes of Este in Ferrara, Cristoforo di Messisbugo, describes some copious and splendid feasts, including one held by Cardinal Hippolyte of Este for fifty-four guests. The dining lasted for seven hours, and after the ninth course of oysters, oranges, and pears, the guests thought the meal was over, but the tablecloth was changed and the feast went on. The menu was enormous: eighteen courses with eight dishes each. The first course, which we would think of as an appetizer, but which was merely the first of many courses, consisted

of trout patties; a hundred spiced hard-boiled eggs cut in half; sturgeon roe and pike spleens fried with orange, cinnamon, and sugar; boiled sturgeon with garlic sauce; sixty fried sea bream; grain soup; Catalan-style flaky pastry pizza; and small fried fish from the Po River. The dishes were served on large platters spaced at intervals along the table and some were presented on individual plates. Many of the extant menus from the Middle Ages are similar. That is, rather than appetizers per se, the menu was of multiple courses each consisting of many dishes. For example, the fourteenth-century French cookbook *Le Ménagier de Paris* describes a dinner for a "meat day" served in thirty-one dishes and six courses. The first course consists of slices of bread soaked in grenache wine (a sweet Greek wine), veal pies, *pinparneaulx* pies (a little fish), black puddings, and sausages. This first course was not identical to our contemporary appetizer. The Italian historian Giovanni Rebora points out that as the equipment for the table changed, so did the syntax of the meal, which gave up salad as first course. It was replaced by a "starter" that for a time in Tuscany was called *camangare*—that is, *capo del mangiare* (beginning or head of the meal), and in Liguria and other regions was known as *incisame* (cut into), and also referred to the *incominciame* (beginning).

W. Montgomery Watt, emeritus professor of Islamic Studies at the University of Edinburgh, Scotland, suggested that the order in which we moderns eat, starting with appetizers and moving on to various courses that end in dessert, might be attributable to the high culture that existed during the golden age of Islamic Spain in the ninth century. A high standard of taste developed for the upper layers of society in Muslim Spain. One of the greatest influences was a singer and bon vivant named Ziryāb, who lived in Córdoba from 822 to 857, and who had sung as a youth before the famous caliph Hārūn al-Rashīd in Baghdad. Ziryāb was an extraordinary individual, a man of science as well as an arbiter of fashion and taste in general. He is said to have introduced an order in which different dishes were to be served at a banquet. In the tenth century, the royal courts of the caliphs in Baghdad, where Ziryāb had earlier performed, were famous for the lavishness of their tables, as intimated by the famous Arab poet and historian al-Mas'ūdī (d. 946) in his *Meadows of Gold*. He describes dishes, such as olives or salted fish, that are meant to "tempt the palate" or "whet the appetite."

HORS D'OEUVRE

❖

In the English-speaking world we have appetizers, inherited for the most part from French cuisine, where hors d'oeuvre are small savory foods served before the meal. In fact, the expression *hors d'oeuvre* means "outside the work"—that is, outside (or before, in this case) the menu. The hors d'oeuvre probably evolved into what it is today when the style of eating in France changed after François Pierre de La Varenne published his *Le cuisinier françois* in 1651. Meals were served in courses, each

Escoffier on Hors d'Oeuvre

"I regard cold hors d'oeuvre as quite unnecessary in a dinner; I even consider them counter to the dictates of common sense, and they are certainly injurious to the flavor of the soup that follows."

—AUGUSTE ESCOFFIER, *GUIDE CULINAIRE*

course containing several dishes. The first course was not an appetizer, but merely the first course. Throughout the meal small foods, foods outside of the main menu and usually cold, would come to the table for diners to eat while they digested or waited for the more substantial dishes. Over time hot hors d'oeuvre arose, then called *entrées volantes* or *petites entrées*, and were added to the cold ones. From the seventeenth until perhaps the nineteenth century, the setting of the French table and the serving of the meal followed a regulated and proscribed pattern. Courses were served and the foods were placed on the table in an orderly fashion by size and arranged symmetrically. Small dishes were set outside of the main body of dishes for each course, and these were the hors d'oeuvre. So hors d'oeuvre were always served spatially outside of the meal and not temporally outside the meal, as it is done today as an opener or starter.

Traditionally, hors d'oeuvre were served only at luncheons, were always served cold, and only with meals that didn't include soup. *Larousse Gastronomique* instructs that hors d'oeuvre must be presented elegantly. An appetizer should never fill one up. Michel Bouzy claimed in his *Les poissons, coquillages et crustacés*, published in 1929, that the hors d'oeuvre is gastronomically correct only at luncheons, never at dinner, except in the case of oysters or caviar. The French do not have bars that resemble the tapas bars of Spain, where little dishes of foods are served with drinks. But today one will often find wine bars where some hors d'oeuvre, usually very simple ones, will be served. Elizabeth David, in her *French Provincial Cooking*, informs us that:

the English visitor to France cannot fail to observe that the artistry with which the French present their food is nowhere more apparent than in the service of the hors-d'oeuvre. So far from appearing contrived, or zealously worked on, each dish looks as if it had been freshly imagined, prepared for the first time, especially for you. Now, since the main object of an hors-d'oeuvre is to provide something beautifully fresh looking which will at the same time arouse your appetite and put you in good spirits, this point is very important and nothing could be less calculated to have the right effect than the appearance of the little bits of straggling greenery, blobs of mayonnaise and wrinkled radishes which show all too clearly that the food has been over handled and that it has been standing about for some hours before it was time to serve it.

These are sage words that should be remembered as you go about preparing the recipes. A guest's first introduction to your cooking is the

> ### Hors d'Oeuvre or Hors d'Oeuvres?
>
> Today one describes hors d'oeuvre only in the singular, but in the eighteenth century Vincent La Chapelle spoke of the plural *hors d'oeuvres* in his *Cuisinier moderne*, published in 1733.

hors d'oeuvre. Your guests will tend to enjoy whatever is coming next because they now have the confidence that you have thought about their happiness and they will be in the right frame of mind. Composing a selection of appetizers requires both an imagination and a sense of proportion. You will come to see the truism of "less is more." Let me give you an example: very thinly sliced *coppa* (an Italian pork cold cut) overlapping in concentric circles on a round platter with some decorative black olives in the middle will often have more bang for the buck than a complicated choux pastry filled with lobster whatnot that you may or may not cook properly.

The number of possible appetizers, combinations, fillings, stuffings, shapes, and so forth seems endless. Choosing the dishes for this book was excruciating because, as soon as I finished testing a recipe or finished writing a chapter, I would think of a thousand other preparations. I have tried to choose dishes that come from all Mediterranean traditions in somewhat equal balance. First, let me review what these various traditions are and explain them a bit.

ANTIPASTO

✦

An antipasto is not the course before the pasta, but rather it means the food served before the meal, *pasto*. The wide range of Italian *antipasti* today was not seen fifty years ago. Historically, appetizers—that is, *antipasti*—did not play a very important part in the regional cooking of the Italian peninsula, unlike other European countries, especially France. *Antipasti* were nonexistent in the south and were always more evident in the cuisines of the north. *Stuzzichini*, deriving from the verb "to pick" or "to poke," is another Italian word for starters or appetizers, as is *passatempo*, which actually is a very little tidbit eaten with a drink before *antipasti*. *Principii* is yet another name, and in Tuscany it was once customary to eat these tidbits after the soup course.

The absence of *antipasti* in traditional Sicilian cuisine is thought to be an Arab legacy because the small foods eaten by others as *antipasti* are treated more like the Middle Eastern meze by the Sicilians. Appetizers or *antipasti* are found in Sicilian restaurants today, but at home what Sicilians eat are more accurately called *grape 'u pittitu*, "openers of the mouth," which are better translated as snacks, tidbits, munchies, or yummies. One Sicilian food writer refused to open his book with an appetizer section because he didn't want to give the impression that Sicilians needed stimulation to relish a meal. In Sardinia, too, *antipasti* are not traditional in the gastronomy, where several slices of local prosciutto, especially those made from wild boar, might be typical as a kind of snack, but not so much as an "appetizer."

Called *sfizi*, *merende*, *antipasti*, or *assàggi* throughout Italy and *ciccheti* in Venice, these appetizers, like their Spanish tapas counterparts, are best shared so that one can experience a variety of flavors and textures. Interestingly, in Italy, only Venice seems to have a tradition similar to the Spanish tapas bar. They are called *cicchetteria* or *bacari*, where one goes to get a "shade"—that is, a drink. I'm not sure about the origin of the expression *andiamo per una ombra* (let's go for a "shade"), but it means "let's get a glass of wine or *prosecco* at the local *bacari*," where you can also eat tapas-like foods called *ciccheti*, or little nibbly things. I once went to one called Al Leon d'Oro at Cannareggio 2345, where I drank too much Aurum, a very strong orange-flavored grappa type of drink that I imbibed with some little dishes. *Ciccheti* is derived from the French word *chiqueter*, "to dribble" or "to crumble." The word comes from the Piedmont, perhaps from the Provençal word *chiquet*, "little glass." In the last twenty years a variety of new drinking establishments have opened up in Italy that serve small foods. In Rome, pubs—that is, real English or Irish pubs—are very popular with young Italians. Wine bars are now ubiquitous, too, and they serve little foods occasionally.

Carlo Middione, author of *The Food of Southern Italy*, makes the suggestion that, because *antipasti* are so diverse, they make a perfect *assàggio* meal, "a meal of tastes," a kind

The Basic Little Foods

Entertaining in a Mediterranean style means entertaining with the quintessential Mediterranean little foods such as olives or roasted almonds. Having a good number of attractive polychromatic platters of various sizes and shapes to offer various foods to guests as they arrive or are sitting around is one of the easiest ways to make people feel welcome and to provide a variety of what can be called tidbits before appetizers, also known in French as *amuse-bouches*, *amuse-gueules*, or *amusements* or in Italian as *passatempi*. It is very typical at American parties to serve cubes of cheese before appetizers. I'm not in favor of serving cheese as a tid-bit because I think it is too rich and heavy for that purpose and people tend to overeat. Save cheese for after dinner, when it provides a nice conclusion to a meal and people are more inclined to take small tasting slivers. Although olives and nuts are almost always found as basic Mediterranean tidbits, others are typical, too, depending on the class people come from. On the rich man's table you are likely to find beluga, sevruga, or osetra caviar served on ice, along with the finest *foie gras de canard*, as well as smoked Scottish salmon and raw shellfish. On the middle-class table you'll find cold cuts, and on the poor man's table you'll find marinated anchovies, vegetables, and various bread preparations.

In the Mediterranean, many people cure their own olives. The Spanish might pit some green olives, stuff them with lemon peel, and marinate them in fine sherry, water, olive oil, and thyme. The Sicilians might toss cracked green olives with finely diced celery, olive oil, vinegar, basil, and oregano, and the Greeks might toss them with rosemary and olive oil. Pitted olives can be stuffed with much more than pimientos, anchovies, or almonds. You could try blue cheese, or prosciutto, or cream cheese.

Here's a list of some foods that can be served with cocktails and don't require any, or very little, preparation.

- Black and green olives
- Stuffed olives
- Lupini beans
- Roasted salted almonds

of tasting menu consisting of a variety of small bites. "A meal comprised of several *antipasti*," says Middione, "not only rewards the palate, but also educates, letting the eater savor more or less of many different dishes."

TAPAS

In Spain, an appetizer, called an *entremés*, or *apertivo*, is a complement to a meal. Although an *entremés* can be the same little food

- Hazelnuts
- Pistachios in the shell
- Steamed shrimp with mayonnaise or lemon
- Raw oysters on the half shell
- Raw clams on the half shell
- Steamed mussels with lemon
- Smoked salmon with lemon
- Canned sardines in olive oil, arranged on a small plate or placed on top of bread
- Canned tuna in olive oil, flaked and arranged on a small plate or placed on top of bread
- Salted anchovy fillets, rinsed and soaked in milk for an hour before serving
- Caviar
- Foie gras
- Pâtés and terrines
- Chopped salted anchovies and chopped hard-boiled egg
- Boiled whole artichoke with a dipping sauce, *avgolemono*, vinaigrette, drawn butter, or olive oil
- Radishes dipped in salt
- Sweet gherkins

- Cold cuts such as *jamón Serrano, prosciutto di Parma, coppa, capicollo, soppressata, mortadella*, Genoa salami, etc.
- Fresh sugar snap peas
- Fresh young fava bean pods (let guests open the pods themselves)
- Blanched fresh green beans
- Celery sticks
- Fennel bulb sticks
- Sliced lettuce hearts
- Sliced cucumbers or cucumber sticks
- Carrot sticks
- Raw sliced broccoli stems
- Cherry tomatoes

The Spanish sometimes serve sautéed almonds as a *tapa*. In a small skillet, heat a little olive oil over medium heat, then cook some whole almonds until a little darker, salt, and serve.

that a *tapa* is, it is served differently. It is literally the appetizer coming before the first course. But a *tapa* is something altogether different. Tapas are tiny plates of food served in bars all over Spain to accompany drinks. Tapas are not so much a kind of food as a Spanish way of eating. It seems as if any kind of food can be a *tapa*, so long as it comes out of the kitchen in a small plate. A step into a Spanish tapas bar is a wonderful experience even if you

Olives

The olive is the most famous drupe of the world and the quintessential little food of the Mediterranean. A drupe is a one-seeded indehiscent fruit having a hard, bony endocarp, a fleshy mesocarp, and a thin exocarp that is flexible or dry or almost leathery. What this means in practical gastronomic terms is that the olive is inedible in its raw state; it must be treated to be eaten. The most common way of treating an olive is by pressing it for oil or brining (or salting in some cases) it for a table fruit. Green olives are unripe olives and black olives are ripe olives, but both are edible when brined. There is a huge variety of olives available in the market and the best are those sold loose in bins, not those sold in cans. Loose olives are mostly sold in smaller Italian, Greek, Middle Eastern, or Mediterranean markets, in some specialty stores, via the Internet, and in a select number of supermarkets. The variety that is most common is the Kalamata olive from Greece, although the Manzanilla of Spain and the Ascolana and Gaeta of Italy are also common in American markets. I couldn't even begin to give you a list of the olives to seek out—there are too many. All I can do is encourage you to keep trying different olives because not only do the olive varieties taste different, but also the various brines make them taste even more different. Olives may be found whole, with their stem perhaps; stoned (that is, pitted); stuffed; cut in half; sliced; or cracked. When buying olives, buy them whole at first, and it is expected and permissible that you should be able to taste the olive before buying it. Taste as many olives as you like, then choose your favorite. Olives don't need to be stored in the refrigerator as long as they stay in their brine, although I do refrigerate my olives but bring them to room temperature before serving. Serve them in platters and bowls, and don't forget to set out a little bowl for the pits.

don't speak Spanish. It's lively and animated, as Spaniards like to talk, and you may be approached by patrons wishing to practice their English. Spaniards go to tapas bars before lunch and before supper to meet friends, to converse, and to watch. It's hard to think of a tapas bar as an eating establishment because it functions more like a conversation establishment. Conversation ranges from the mundane to the philosophical, and the food ranges from the simple toasted almond to the complex *callos* (A Tapa of Stewed Tripe and Sausage in the Style of Seville, page 131). You will be able to taste snippets of a huge variety of foods just as you would hear snippets of conversation, perhaps about the lottery, bullfighting, the local team, or the local politics.

The word *tapa* means "lid." It was thought that the plate acted like a lid on top of the mug or glass (to keep out dirt, dust, and insects) in bars that originally offered food, probably to attract customers. Anna MacMiadhacháin, in her *Spanish Regional Cookery*, speculates that the dishes are a legacy of the Arab presence in Spain, when, she says, the serving of alcohol was forbidden except with food. This explanation doesn't make too much sense because the Koranic prohibition against alcohol is total. On the other hand, Muslims were drinking wine over the ages in spite of the prohibition, as we know from the centuries of delightful poetry in Arabic about the glories and virtues of wine. Although tapas might have roots in the Arab era, they are today not philosophically related to the similar seeming *mazza* or meze (page 12) of the eastern Mediterranean. Tapas, unlike *mazza* or meze, are not meant to replace dinner.

Originally, tapas were small plates of food that were set down for customers without charge, but shortly restaurants and bars came to charge for the food. Tapas are also never served at home; they are always foods served at eating establishments. Eating tapas is part of the *tapeo*, the tradition of stimulating the appetite with friends while trysting and drinking an apéritif. The art of the *tapeo*, Alicia Rio, a Spanish food writer, tells us, "is like a baroque, sybaritic game, as it pleases the five senses by means of multifarious smells, friendly pats on the back, the sight and beauty of the streets. It induces states of inspiration and delight, it gives rise to witty banter on trivial topics and the interchange of snippets of juicy gossip."

Tapas can be grouped into three main categories, according to how easy they are to eat: *cosas de picar*, *pinchos*, and *cazuelas*. *Cosas de picar* (meaning "things to nibble") basically refer to finger food, the most famous being the olive—the quintessential Spanish and, in fact, Mediterranean finger food. If a utensil (like *banderillas*, decorated toothpicks that get their name because they look like the darts used in a bullfight) is required to eat the food, the *tapa* is called *pinchos*. *Cazuelas* (little dishes) are tapas that usually come in sauce—for example, *albóndigas* (Chicken, Beef, and Ham Meatballs in Gravy; page 127) or Shrimp and Garlic from Granada (page 146). All regions of Spain have tapas, although Catalonians have not traditionally eaten tapas (gastronomically they had closer ties to the French and Italians) and do so now only because of the unification of modern Spain. The Basques call their tapas *pintxos*, from the Spanish word *pinchar*, "to prick," because at one time, they were served with toothpicks to pick them up. The Spanish proverb *comiendo, comiendo el apetito se va abriendo*—appetite increases with constant eating—might give you a better idea of what lies behind the culinary experience of Spain.

· ❁ ·

Tapas Bar

In Spain, tapas bars are called *tasca* and it is difficult to convey the exuberant liveliness of a tapas bar because they are not just about drinking wine and fine sherry and not just about eating little foods. A tapas bar is more of a window into the Spanish soul and the Spanish gastronomic mentality. They are egalitarian places where people of all classes will congregate. Children are welcome. Tradition has it that the art of tapas had its beginning in Andalusia. Some of the most memorable tapas bars I've been to were indeed in Andalusia, especially in Seville. I remember the low yellow light, the wood tables and wood walls, and sawdust on the floor, but not everywhere. Elegant men, beautiful women, scruffy students, a tourist here and there, old folks and young ones, they all are denizens of the *tasca*. The raucous conversation surrounds you, conversation about the bullfight, the soccer team, national politics, a business deal, the exams, the lottery, and it goes on and on, fine dry sherries drunk with countless tapas. Pedro Soleras, a journalist with *El País* in Madrid, offered that "the tapa, invented in an age less obsessed with productivity, is a trick for spinning out your drinks without getting drunk."

THE MEZE TABLE

◆

Meze (or *mazza*, as it is transliterated from Arabic) is universally described as Middle Eastern appetizers. *Mazzat* (plural) are little tidbits served on little plates and they certainly bear a resemblance to appetizers or tapas. In fact, there is nothing wrong in serving them as appetizers. *Mazza* are called meze in Greek and Turkish, *qimiyya* in Algeria, and *ādū* in Tunisia. But, for the record, it is incorrect to speak of the Middle Eastern meze table as appetizers. To think of these small dishes as appetizers is to misunderstand the Arab culinary sensibility. For the Arab, the notion of a food needed to "open the appetite" is completely foreign, although the influence of Western cuisine is to be felt and today one can find traditional appetizers, called *muqabbilāt* from the word for "appetite," *qabaliyya*. But in the traditional cuisine the Arab simply starts eating; one is hungry and the stomach enzymes are ready to go to work. An appetizer just slows the process down, so says the Muslim, and the Prophet Muhammad is said to have had this view as well. A meze table can be the entire dinner, thus it is more appropriate to compare meze to the Scandinavian smorgasbord, to which it is more philosophically related. Meze are part of the culinary culture ranging from

Greece clockwise around the Mediterranean until you reach Morocco on the Atlantic.

In Turkey and Greece, meze are also eaten in the same manner and with the same purpose. These are not snacks, a category of food served on toast points or croutons covered by the Turkish word *tırıt*. One of the most familiar and common of Turkish and Greek meze are black and green olives or a salty white goat or sheep's cheese such as feta. Nuts are popular, too—pistachios or salted almonds. Very simple fried shrimp with a little lemon juice or fried mussels are popular in Turkey as meze, as are sausages such as *sucuk* (pronounced *soo-juk*) or cured beef such as *pastırma*. So, too, among hot dishes is the wide variety of *böreks*, little cheese or meat pastries wrapped in a flaky or phyllo dough, well liked, as is the equally expansive range of *köftes*, ground grilled meat either in the form of meatballs or molded around a skewer. In Greece, too, meze are small samplings of food to be had with drinks. *Krasomezedes* are meze that go with wine (*kraso*), while *ouzomezedes* go well with ouzo. Diane Kochilas, in her book *The Food and Wine of Greece*, suggests three categories of *mezedes* (plural): hot or cooked meze, dips and spreads, and salads, pickles, and vegetable meze. All of these Greek meze can also become *orektiko*, appetizers, during a traditional sit-down dinner. Among the hot Greek meze are the famous *tyropittakia* (Cheese Pie in Phyllo Pastry; page 271) and Spanakopita (page 268), among the dips are the equally famous Tzatziki (page 56)—and everyone has heard of Greek salad. Meze will be found in

restaurants, tavernas, and ouzeries, where ouzo is served.

The eating of small plates of food with drinks is also an old custom in Cyprus. Most men were farmers or cattlemen and they drank only on special occasions. These were usually feasts, *xefandomata*, celebrating religious days, birthdays, weddings, or deaths. As they sit around drinking and eating, men—never women or children—tell jokes and philosophize about life, or complain about their crops or the weather. The meze themselves are cooked by the housewives and served in small quantities, always cut up into small serving pieces. Wine flows copiously, or they drink *zivania*, a grappa-like drink made from the distillation of grapes, usually homemade. Various grilled parts of a pig are favorite meze, as is the famous *zalatina*, a dish in which the head and trotters are preserved together in their natural gelatin, flavored with lemon and orange juice. The dish is then cut up with the tongue, ears, and eyes and put in bowl with its stock, red chiles, and rosemary. The Cypriots make pickles from vegetables called *ksidhata*, and they also pickle various small birds as well as rabbits. Many Greeks will tell you that there are two kinds of meze: those eaten with drinks and those eaten without. A short glass of ouzo, or a glass of red wine or even a beer might accompany many a meze.

The origin of meze is unknown, but food writers have offered a plethora of speculative derivations. The Turkish writer Ayla Algar believes the word derives from the Persian *maza*, meaning "taste" or "relish." Another writer offered the explanation that the word comes from the Italian *mezzano*, meaning an intermediary course of foods, introduced by Genoese merchant-traders in the fourteenth-century Middle East to refer to certain foods. On the other hand, the word *meze* does derive from the root word for "to suck," which also gives the word for "acidulous." An Arab writer claims that meze is a colloquial expression meaning "what," as in the exclamation *mazza haza* (what is this?). Other Arabs have told me that explanation is nonsense. And might the word have any connection with the Hebrew word for unleavened breads, *mazzot*? Probably not.

ZAKUSKI: LITTLE BITES FROM THE BALKANS

Because of the Ottoman Empire's long stay in a good portion of the Balkans, the Turkish culinary influence is quite evident. The Turkish meze is known as well in Albania, Bosnia, Bulgaria, Macedonia, Serbia, Croatia, and Romania. In the Balkans, distinct from Turkish meze, which is not necessarily eaten with a drink, are two types of meze: those to be eaten with distilled drinks and those that are not. In all cases, lively conversation goes along with meze eating. Another word for meze used among the Slavs of the Balkans is *zakuski* (or *zakouski*), a Russian word used by Serb-Croats, Slovenians, Bulgarians, and Macedonians that means "little bites." Sometimes, but not always, they are served as a starter to a meal as opposed to the true nature of meze, which is a *speise-an-sich* (food-in-itself), to paraphrase a German philosophical concept. As with the Turkish and Arab traditions, a Balkan meze table will include maybe six, seven, or eight dishes. Some examples are: slices of *kashkaval* cheese or chunks of wet feta cheese, pickled vegetables, salamis, boiled eggs, head cheese, and other kinds of brawn made from sheep's or pig's trotters, veal feet, or stuffed pig's stomach. Canapés are common, too, topped with *tarama* (fish roe), anchovies or sardines, *lakerda* (dry salted bonito slices), and fish or cheese spreads such as *aygotarahon*, the dried gray mullet roe enjoyed in Greece, too. Cheese makes a wonderful meze (if consumed in moderation) served plain or perhaps grilled or fried. In Croatia, cured ham is as popular as it is in Italy, where they call it *pröšut* (from the Italian prosciutto). All over Yugoslavia one can find *köftes*, tiny meatballs that are grilled or fried in oil and served on small skewers or cocktail toothpicks. Nuts and olives are also popular. Stuffed grape leaves are as common in the Balkans as they are in Greece and Turkey.

As you work your way through this book, at the very least I hope we can join together and wish banishment upon the stale pretzel, canned peanuts, generic store-bought hummus, bag of potato chips, and cubes of cheddar cheese that so often pass as appetizers in American homes.

CONSTRUCTING A MENU OF SMALL FOODS OR APPETIZERS

There are several decisions you need to make first. Here are the possibilities:

- A standing cocktail party not to be followed by dinner
- A standing or sitting party to be followed by a sit-down dinner
- A traditional Mediterranean meze dinner or tapas party

In the first possibility, you must decide how many people will be invited and how long they will stay. If you are serving appetizers to be followed by a main course, it is best to choose the main course first and then find an appropriate appetizer. Finally, if you are choosing a selection of dishes to be presented as traditional Spanish tapas or as an Arab, Greek, or Turkish meze, then you must select dishes that will provide variety and substance. You also need to balance dishes between hot and cold, dry and saucy, and spicy and savory. There are an optimal number of dishes for each of these scenarios. Too many dishes become an assault on people's stomachs and foods begin to clash.

Too few dishes leave people bored and hungry. If you are serving appetizers while guests are standing, to be followed by a sit-down dinner, then four dishes are optimal. If you are serving a cocktail party that will last a good number of hours without a sit-down dinner, then eight dishes would be appropriate. If you are serving a meze dinner for eight people, then eight to ten dishes are appropriate.

For more specific recommendations on building menus using the recipes in this book, take a look at Suggested Party Menus starting on page 478 for a wide range of variously themed get-togethers.

And in the end they loved one to thee shall become they food and water, submissive and obedient and beautiful as well; they meze and wine too . . .

—MEVLANA JALALUDDIN-I RUMI, *MESNEVI*, POEMS AND COMMENTARY (1207–1273)

Canapés, Crostini, Bruschetta, Little Sandwiches, and Croûtes

This chapter is filled with all those little things that can be popped in your mouth and are served on or in bread. They're called canapés, *crostini*, *bruschetta*, and *croûtes*, and they include a variety of little sandwiches such as *panini* (page 47) or Casse-Croûtes (page 48). These preparations are always eaten as a passed appetizer while one is standing. If you like, you can get even more elegant than I suggest in the recipes and cut out minuscule rounds of bread, about an inch in diameter—it's more work, but very fancy.

CANAPÉS

A canapé is a small piece of bread, toast, or cracker that is topped with a savory preparation. Usually the crust is removed from a rather dense-textured rectangular loaf of bread and cut into any number of shapes, such as rounds, diamonds, hearts, triangles, and/or squares. Canapés are almost always served before dinner as an accompaniment to cocktails while guests are still standing and are meant to be eaten in one or two bites, ideally. They are usually cut into bite-size pieces about 1½ inches square or round and are topped with a wide variety of foods both hot and cold.

It is important when making canapés that the bread not become soggy. The best way to avoid this is to make them at the last minute or to spread them lightly with butter, which sets up a bit of a moisture barrier, or to use stale bread, which can absorb a bit of liquid without losing its texture, or and this is most typical, to lightly toast the bread. Canapés made with toast or crackers should not be prepared more than one hour before you will serve them.

The range of canapés you could make is limited only by your imagination. The ones I've chosen for this book are either standard ones found in the Mediterranean or some interesting and unusual ones. But nearly any leftover food from the many recipes throughout the book can be put atop a piece of bread and, voilà, you've got a canapé.

Canapés are most attractive when garnished. Some garnishes you can use on the finished canapés are chopped hard-boiled eggs, cooked and finely diced beets; pimientos; chopped parsley, tarragon, chervil, basil, dill, or chives; finely chopped or sliced cucumber; sliced lemon; capers; sliced gherkins; chopped olives; truffles; mushrooms; or anchovies. Canapés are also nice when spread with a compound butter (page 22) before the topping goes on. Some examples of compound butters, besides those in this book, made simply by blending the butter with one or two other ingredients are almond butter, chive or shallot butter, maître d'hôtel butter (finely chopped parsley and a little lemon juice), crab butter, walnut butter, green butter (made with spinach, chives, and tarragon), mushroom butter, pistachio butter, and smoked salmon butter.

What Bread to Use? Crust or No?

For canapés I use either a dense rectangular loaf of bread or a thin, long French baguette. In either case, the diameter of the piece of bread (which I slice ¼ inch thick) after I cut it is about 2 inches. For the rectangular loaf, I usually remove the crust because it is easy, while I usually leave the crust on the baguette. But one can also buy cutting rings of different sizes at kitchen supply stores to make more professional-looking canapés.

Lobster Canapés with Lobster Butter

Although this is an extravagant canapé, I assure you that it is not only worth the effort but you can then take all those broken lobster shells and make a very nice lobster stock out of them. This is what the great French chef Escoffier, who was originally from the mountainous area of Provence, recommended.

Two 1-pound live lobsters
¼ cup (½ stick) unsalted butter, at room temperature
Salt to taste
1 large hard-boiled egg, shelled and finely chopped
¼ cup mayonnaise, preferably homemade (page 466)
Twenty-four ¼-inch-thick slices French baguette, lightly toasted

1. Pour about an inch of water into a large pot that will fit both lobsters and bring to a boil. Put the lobsters in and cook until bright red, 15 to 17 minutes. Drain and let cool. Crack open the shells and remove all the meat, placing the meat from the arms and legs, as well as the tomalley and coral, in one bowl. Remove the meat from the claws and tail, slice it thinly, and reserve it separately. Put the arm and leg meat in a food processor with the butter and salt and run until blended.

2. Stir the egg and mayonnaise together. Spread each toast piece with the lobster butter, then a little egg mayonnaise, and place some lobster slices on top. Serve.

Makes 24 slices; 8 servings

Canapés of Lobster and Allioli

In the Basque country, where some of the finest cooking in the Mediterranean can be found, there is a dizzying variety of small bites served at tapas bars. This emparedados de langosta e allioli *is a favorite, with a Catalan influence derived from the garlic mayonnaise—and very simple, too.*

2 tablespoons extra-virgin olive oil
1 large garlic clove, crushed
Thirty-six ¼-inch-thick slices French baguette
One 1½-pound live lobster
¾ cup Allioli (page 466)
¼ cup finely chopped fresh parsley leaves
1 tablespoon hot Spanish paprika

1. In a large skillet, heat the olive oil and garlic together over medium-high heat. Discard the garlic when it begins to sizzle and turn light brown. Place the bread slices in the skillet and cook until crusty light brown on one side only, then remove and set aside. Do this in batches if your skillet is not large enough.

2. Bring an inch of water to a boil in a stockpot, then place the lobster in and cook until bright red, 15 to 17 minutes. Remove the lobster, let cool, and crack open the shells to remove all the meat. Slice the larger pieces of meat and set aside in the refrigerator until needed. Save any tomalley and coral for another use.

3. Spread some *allioli* on the nonfried side of the bread slice and place a piece of lobster on top. Top with a pinch of parsley and a sprinkle of paprika and serve.

Makes 36 canapés; 12 servings

Lobster Tomalley Canapés

Whenever you are cooking lobster, always remove the tomalley and coral, and you can use the tomalley for this delicious canapé. It's a quick way to serve an hors d'oeuvre. Or I will use the butter to toss with linguine. Usually you make this when you are preparing lobster for another dish. One would not buy two lobsters simply to make this.

Tomalley from 2 cooked lobsters (page 20)
¼ cup (½ stick) salted butter, at room
   temperature
Salt to taste
A few drops fresh lemon juice (optional)
Twenty-four ¼-inch-thick slices dense white
   French baguette, toasted lightly, or six
   ¼-inch-thick slices dense rectangular loaf
   bread, crusts removed, if desired, cut into
   1-inch squares, and toasted lightly

1. In a small bowl, blend the tomalley and butter together with a fork. Taste and add salt and/or lemon juice if desired. Transfer to a sheet of aluminum foil, fold one end over, and roll back and forth to form a cylinder. Twist the ends and refrigerate until needed. The butter will keep in the refrigerator for 10 days or indefinitely in the freezer.

2. Spread the lobster tomalley butter on the bread within an hour of serving.

Makes 24 canapés; 8 servings

Shrimp and Egg Canapés with Mustard Butter

These Italian canapés di scampi *are most easily made with precooked very tiny shrimp sold either frozen or in a can. If you do make it with either frozen or canned shrimp, make sure you drain and dry them thoroughly. Preferably, though, you will find this delicacy attaining greater culinary heights by using fresh shrimp of about 120 count per pound. If you make these ahead of time, refrigerate for no more than two hours. The compound butter used here is made with mustard and is especially good with ham* canapés, *too.*

Mustard Butter

½ cup (1 stick) salted butter, at room
   temperature
1½ tablespoons dry mustard
1 teaspoon Worcestershire sauce
⅛ teaspoon cayenne pepper

Canapés

Sixty ¼-inch-thick slices French baguette
2 large hard-boiled eggs, shelled and finely
   chopped
¾ pound very small peeled cooked shrimp
Salt to taste

1. Make the butter. Place the butter in a food processor and blend it with the mustard, Worcestershire, and cayenne. Transfer to a sheet of aluminum foil, fold one end over, and roll back and forth to form a cylinder. Twist the ends and refrigerate until needed, but bring to room temperature first. The butter will keep for

A Duo of Delicious Butters

Compound butters are butters blended with other ingredients. They are useful to have in your refrigerator for many purposes, including making sandwiches and canapés, tossing with cooked vegetables or pasta, or placing on top of a grilled steak.

Hazelnut Butter

Compound butters are often used in French cooking and provide a nice complexity of flavor to otherwise simple preparations. This *beurre de noisette* is called for in some recipes, but it is also nice spread on toast.

¼ cup hazelnuts

¼ cup (½ stick) salted butter, at room temperature

Salt to taste

A few drops of fresh lemon juice

1. Preheat the oven to broil. Place the hazelnuts on a baking sheet and bake until golden, 4 to 5 minutes. Remove from the oven immediately, pour the nuts into a bowl, and let cool. Peel off the brown skin by rubbing the nuts in a kitchen towel.

2. Place the hazelnuts in a food processor and grind until fine. Add the butter, salt, and lemon juice and process to combine. Transfer the mixture to a sheet of aluminum foil, fold one end over, and roll back and forth to form a cylinder. Twist the ends and refrigerate until needed. It will keep for a month in the refrigerator and longer in the freezer.

Makes ½ cup

up to a month in the refrigerator and indefinitely in the freezer.

2. Spread the bread slices with the mustard butter, sprinkle some chopped egg on top, and arrange a few shrimp to cover the slice. Season with salt and serve or refrigerate until needed.

Makes 60 canapés; 20 servings

Shrimp and Lemon Canapés

This is another Italian version of the previous preparation, here using lemon. In Provence, a canapé such as this one could also be garnished with a caper.

Sixty ¼-inch-thick slices French baguette

½ cup mayonnaise, preferably homemade (page 466)

¾ pound very small peeled cooked shrimp

Anchovy Butter

Anchovy butter is one of the oldest of compound butters. The anchovy has traditionally been the food of the poor in the Mediterranean, and its simplest use in this form has been to toss it with linguine, spread it on a canapé, or place a pat on a grilled fish steak.

½ cup (1 stick) unsalted butter, at room
  temperature
¼ cup finely chopped fresh parsley leaves
8 salted anchovy fillets, rinsed and patted dry

2 large garlic cloves, mashed into a
  paste in a mortar
2 teaspoons fresh lemon juice
Freshly ground white pepper to taste

1. Place all the ingredients in a food processor and process until smooth and well blended.

2. Transfer to a sheet of aluminum foil, fold one end over, and roll back and forth to form a cylinder. Twist the ends and refrigerate until needed. It will keep in the refrigerator for up to a month and indefinitely in the freezer.

Makes ½ cup

8 very thin slices Meyer lemon, each cut into
  eighths, leaving the peel on
Salt to taste

Spread the bread slices with the mayonnaise. Place some shrimp on top and flank with 2 triangles of the sliced lemon. Season with salt and serve or refrigerate.

Makes 60 canapés; 20 servings

Clam Salad Canapés

In Spain, this tapa *is called* emparedados de ensaladilla de almejas *and is made with the carpet-shell clam, called* almejas *in Spanish,* cloisses *in Catalan, and* palourde *in French, all places where one might find variations of this canapé. When making this, remember not to prepare the canapés too far ahead of time, otherwise the bread will become soggy. Prepare them about half an hour in advance at the most.*

24 littleneck clams (about 3½ pounds),
   washed well, soaked in cold water to cover
   with 1 teaspoon baking soda for 30 minutes,
   and drained
½ cup water
1 green bell pepper, seeded and finely chopped
1 medium-size onion, finely chopped
¼ cup pitted and finely chopped green olives
Sweet Spanish paprika to taste
Salt and freshly ground black pepper to taste
¾ cup mayonnaise, preferably homemade
   (page 466), or Allioli (page 466)
Forty-eight ¼-inch-thick slices French baguette
1 large garlic clove, cut in half

1. Put the clams in a pot filled with the water, turn the heat to high, cover, and steam until all the clams have opened, about 5 minutes. Discard any that remain tightly shut. Remove the clams from their shells and chop. In a medium-size bowl, mix the clams with the bell pepper, onion, and olives and season with paprika, salt, and black pepper. Transfer to a strainer, set over a deep bowl, and let drain for 1 hour in the refrigerator. Return to a bowl and stir in the mayonnaise.

2. Toast the bread slices until very light brown, then rub one side with the cut garlic half. Place a heaping teaspoon of clam mixture on each slice of bread, push down slightly, and serve.

Makes 48 canapés; 16 servings

Red and Black Caviar Canapés

Whether it's crostini col caviale *in Italy,* canapé de caviar *in France, or* haviari kanape *in Greece,* caviar canapés are always well received because not only are they extravagant but the contrast of colors makes them quite appealing. If your budget allows it, use beluga caviar instead of the lumpfish caviar.

2 tablespoons salted butter, at room temperature
Sixteen ¼-inch-thick *crostini* (page 37)
1 tablespoon black lumpfish caviar
1 tablespoon red salmon caviar
1 tablespoon very finely chopped onion
   (optional)
1 tablespoon very finely chopped hard-boiled egg
   (optional)
1 thin slice Meyer lemon, cut into 16 wedges
2 teaspoons very finely chopped fresh parsley
   leaves

Lightly butter the *crostini*. Place a small amount of black caviar on one half of the *crostini* and a small amount of red caviar on the other. If you wish, place some onion and egg between each section of caviar. Place a small wedge of lemon on top, sprinkle with the parsley, and serve.

Makes 16 canapés; 6 servings

Don Quixote and Caviar?

In Cervantes's great novel *Don Quixote*, food plays a significant role in the lives of Don Quixote and his sidekick, Sancho. In one episode, we find Sancho spreading salt, onions, walnuts, hunks of cheese, ham bones, and caviar on "grass bread."

Hors d'Oeuvre and Caviar in Venice

In the eighteenth century, appetizers were not really factored into a meal, so Venice was ahead of the times when state dinners started serving *ordover*, a Venetian translation of the French hors d'oeuvre. These *fuori d'opera* (hors d'oeuvre) were varied, but that fact was legislated by the Venetian Republic, which arrived at the number 11 for the number of hors d'oeuvre put on the table of the hundred Arsenale workers invited for a state dinner at the Palazzo Ducale. If the feast of San Girolamo fell on the day of the dinner, the *ordover* included salted tuna and caviar.

Beluga Caviar Canapés

This kind of extravagant canapé might have been found at the state dinner of the Venetian doges in the eighteenth century. If you're like me, beluga caviar is a very rare and special treat, and you will want to eat it as plain as possible. As many connoisseurs point out, beluga caviar goes particularly well with plain, fresh creamery butter.

Twenty-four ¼-inch-thick slices French baguette, lightly toasted
Fresh unsalted butter to taste, at room temperature
4 to 6 tablespoons beluga caviar

Spread the toast with the butter, as little or as much as you like. Spoon a little of the caviar on top and serve.

Makes 24 canapés; 8 servings

Anchovy Canapés in the Style of Nice

In the nineteenth-century Provençal cookbook of J.-B. Reboul, La cuisinière Provençale, *these canapés are called* medaillons d'anchois à la Niçoise. *They seem so simple, yet every bite of this hors d'oeuvre exudes the flavors of the Mediterranean. For bright sunny-yolked eggs, place the eggs in boiling water for 9 minutes exactly, then remove and let cool quickly. It's best to slice the eggs with an egg slicer.*

¼ cup (½ stick) unsalted butter, at room temperature
3 tablespoons tomato paste
Twenty-eight ¼-inch-thick slices Italian bread or French baguette, about 2 inches in diameter, cut in half, with or without crust
4 large hard-boiled eggs, shelled and sliced
28 pimiento-stuffed rolled anchovies
15 to 20 imported black olives, pitted and chopped
2 tablespoons finely chopped fresh parsley leaves
28 small 3-leaved sprigs fresh parsley

In a small bowl, mix the butter and tomato paste until the butter is red. Butter the bread and lay a slice of egg on top, then a rolled anchovy. Garnish each slice with a sprinkling of olives and chopped parsley. Finally, stick in a tight sprig of parsley and arrange attractively on a serving tray.

Makes 28 canapés; 10 servings

Anchovy Paste Canapés

Everywhere in Italy you will find mashed anchovies served on canapés, melted on vegetables, blended into sauces, or tossed with linguine. The unexpected secret to these canapès alla pasta di acciughe, *so delicious and pretty, are the little triangles of lemon, so don't skip them. The miniature tomatoes called for here are smaller than cherry tomatoes.*

Twenty-four ¼-inch-thick slices French baguette
½ cup mayonnaise, preferably homemade
    (page 466)
4 large hard-boiled eggs, shelled and sliced
1 Meyer lemon, washed, dried well, very thinly
    sliced, and each slice cut into small wedges
6 tablespoons anchovy paste
12 miniature tomatoes, cut in half
Salt and freshly ground black pepper to taste
2 tablespoons extra-virgin olive oil

Spread the bread with the mayonnaise. Lay a slice of egg on each, then 2 little triangles of lemon flanking it. Smear a small amount, about ¼ teaspoon, of anchovy paste on top of the egg, then place a tomato half on the anchovy paste. Salt and pepper lightly and drip several drops of olive oil on top. Arrange on a serving platter and serve.

Makes 24 canapés; 8 to 10 servings

Corsican Anchovy and Fig Canapés

Anchoïade may seem an unusual appetizer, although the question is asked in L'inventaire du patrimoine culinaire de la France*'s "Corse: Produits du terroir et recettes traditionnelles" (a cataloging of traditional foods of the regions of France) whether* anchoïade *(or anchiuata) is an hors d'oeuvre or an* amuse-gueule *had before an apéritif. A canapé with the same name is known all over Provence, and it can be made in a variety of ways, but always has anchovy in it. Some people put a little chopped onion on top.*

8 salted anchovy fillets, rinsed well and chopped
1 large garlic clove, chopped
½ pound ripe figs, flesh scooped out of peels
Twenty ¼-inch-thick slices French baguette
2 to 3 tablespoons extra-virgin olive oil,
    as needed

Put the anchovies and garlic in a mortar and mash together with a pestle. Add the figs and continue to pound until mushy. Brush the slices of bread with the olive oil, spread some anchovy-fig relish on top, and serve.

Makes 20 canapés; 8 servings

Sardine Canapés in the Italian Style

This simple and popular canapé makes a party giver's task so easy. It takes nothing to put these together, and if you use a good-quality Italian, Spanish, Portuguese, or Moroccan canned sardine in olive oil, it's a memorable taste.

Sardines

The sardine fishing off Sardinia was once so plentiful that the island gave its name to the fish. Although sardines can grow to 8 inches, the best ones, and the ones used for canning in olive oil, are the smaller ones. Sardines are a favorite food in all of the Mediterranean and are prepared grilled, fried, or canned in oil. In the Middle Ages, the sardine catch was famous off Provence and Sicily, where a special net called a *spiruni* was used for the sardine, which was sold as "blue-fish."

Sardines have always been considered poor people's food, as we see in the story of the Spanish soldier who found himself at the Zaragoza market between two campaigns in 1645 and stood amazed at the piles of fresh tuna, salmon trout, and hundreds of other fish from the sea or the nearby river. But what did he buy in the end, with the coins in his purse? A few *sardinas salpesadas* (sardines packed in salt), which the landlady at the corner tavern grilled for him, a banquet that he washed down with white wine.

2 tablespoons unsalted butter, at room
   temperature
Sixteen ¼-inch-thick *crostini* (page 37)
One 4¼-ounce can imported sardines in olive
   oil, drained
16 drops fresh lemon juice

Lightly butter all the *crostini*. Divide the contents of the sardine can into 16 pieces, discarding the backbone of the fish. Arrange the pieces on the *crostini* and splash each one with a drop of lemon juice. Serve within 1½ hours.

Makes 16 canapés; 6 servings

Sardine Canapés in the Algerian Style

Sardines are a popular fish off Algeria, and although they are most typically grilled, this canapé uses canned sardines with a bit of hot chile paste to give a real kick to the preparation.

Sixteen ¼-inch-thick slices French baguette
2 tablespoons Harīsa (page 468)
One 4¼-ounce can imported sardines in olive
   oil, drained

1. Lightly smear each slice of bread with the *harīsa*.

2. Divide the contents of the sardine can into 16 pieces, discarding the backbone of the fish. Arrange the pieces on the bread. Serve within 1½ hours.

Makes 16 canapés; 6 servings

Tuna, Egg, and Cheese Canapés from Tunisia

In Tunisia, this canapé is served as a meze but is called salāṭa al-balankīṭ, *meaning "bathed" salad, which implies that it is thought of as a salad even though it is served on bread. The Dutch cheeses called for are not a conceit, but typical in Tunisia, a country not known for its cheeses, where a lot of European Community cheeses are imported.*

1 long French baguette
3 tablespoons extra-virgin olive oil
2 tablespoons white wine vinegar
1 tablespoon water
2 teaspoons Harīsa (page 468)
2 large hard-boiled eggs, shelled, sliced, and cut in half lengthwise
One 3-ounce can imported tuna in olive oil, drained and crumbled
1 ounce Dutch Edam or Gouda cheese, cut into small dice
1 ounce Gruyère cheese, cut into small dice
14 pitted black olives, cut in half
28 salted or brined capers, rinsed or drained
Salt to taste

1. Slice the bread into twenty-eight ½-inch-thick slices and leave on a tray for a day to become stale. It's important the bread be stale so that when you dip it into the liquid, it doesn't become soggy.

2. On a dinner plate, stir together the olive oil, vinegar, water, and *harīsa.* Dip one side of each bread slice into this sauce. Arrange the bread slices on a serving platter and top with a

slice of egg, a small piece of tuna, and a few bits of the cheeses, then garnish with the olive halves and capers. Season with salt and serve.

Makes 28 canapés; 10 servings

Chicken Salad Canapés in the Style of Castile

This tapa *is known as* emparedados de ensaladilla de pollo, *an* emparedados *being a little sandwich or canapé. I once ate these at a bar in Madrid accompanied with a glass of Rioja and thought them a good match.*

2 teaspoons extra-virgin olive oil
½ pound boneless skinless chicken breast, trimmed of any fat and cut into ¼-inch dice
Salt and freshly ground black pepper to taste
One 4-ounce jar pimientos, drained well and finely chopped
½ cup peas, cooked in water to cover until tender and drained
¾ teaspoon freshly ground cumin seeds
¼ cup mayonnaise, preferably homemade (page 466)
Twenty-four ¼-inch-thick slices French baguette

1. In a small skillet, heat the olive oil over medium-high heat, then scatter the chicken pieces over the bottom of the skillet. Season with salt and pepper. It will stick, but leave it for 1 minute, then turn with a metal spatula and cook another minute, until golden. Remove the chicken to paper towels and let drain.

2. In a medium-size bowl, combine the cooked chicken, pimientos, peas, cumin, and 2

tablespoons of the mayonnaise. Cover with plastic wrap and refrigerate for 1 hour.

3. Spread the remaining 2 tablespoons mayonnaise on the bread slices, top with the chicken salad, and serve.

Makes 24 canapés; 8 servings

Spanish Canapés

The Spanish word *emparedados* covers a range of items served as tapas, from little sandwiches to canapés. There are thousands of canapés; some that I've run across in my travels in Spain, almost exclusively in tapas bars, are *emparedados* with *jamón de York*, with tomato and béchamel sauce, with zucchini, with ham and cheese, with tuna, sardines or crayfish, with veal brains, with mushrooms and pimientos, and the list can go on.

Dumpling Canapés of Chicken, Sausage, and Mushrooms with Garlic Mayonnaise

This delightful party appetizer has a number of influences running through it, from a simple quenelles ordinaires from Provence made with flour to a Turkish spice blend to a Spanish tapas.

¼ pound boneless skinless chicken breast
2 sweet Italian sausage links (about 6 ounces), casings removed
3 ounces mushrooms

2 ounces Canadian bacon
8 pitted black olives
16 pimiento-stuffed Spanish green olives
4 thick slices Italian bread, crusts removed, soaked in tepid water for 1 minute, and squeezed dry
1 teaspoon freshly ground coriander seeds
1 teaspoon freshly ground cumin seeds
Salt and freshly ground black pepper to taste
2 large egg whites, beaten until stiff peaks form
Forty-eight ¼-inch-thick slices French baguette, or loaf bread, crusts removed, cut into 1½-inch squares
½ cup mayonnaise, preferably homemade (page 466), or Allioli (page 466)
1 small jar cut-up pimientos, drained

1. Place the chicken, sausages, mushrooms, Canadian bacon, black and green olives, Italian bread, coriander, cumin, and salt and pepper to taste in a food processor and process until well blended, doing this in batches if necessary and by pulsing the machine. Stir in the egg whites. Transfer to a bowl.

2. Bring a medium-size saucepan of water to a gentle boil. Form the dumplings with 2 spoons and not your hands because the mixture will be too sticky, drop into the simmering water, and cook until firm, about 8 minutes. Remove with a slotted ladle and set aside to cool.

3. Slice the dumplings thin. Place the slices of dumpling on thinly sliced bread squares with a dollop of mayonnaise, and top with a little piece of pimiento.

Makes about 48 canapés; 16 servings

Duck and Chicken Liver Canapés

In the Languedoc region of France, ducks are a much appreciated food and you are likely to find them appearing everywhere, from the cassoulet of Toulouse to this scrumptious canapé.

6 tablespoons (¾ stick) unsalted butter
4 duck livers, trimmed of membranes and very finely chopped
4 chicken livers, trimmed of membranes and very finely chopped
2 tablespoons finely chopped fresh parsley leaves
4 salted anchovy fillets, rinsed and chopped
Salt and freshly ground black pepper to taste
1 tablespoon all-purpose flour
¼ cup water
1½ tablespoons fresh lemon juice
Twelve ¼-inch-thick slices dense Italian or French bread, cut in half diagonally to form triangles

1. In a large skillet, melt ¼ cup (½ stick) of the butter over medium-high heat, then cook the duck and chicken livers and parsley until they turn color, 2 to 3 minutes, stirring. Add the anchovies and season with salt and pepper. Stir in the flour and, once it is blended in, add the water, bringing it to a boil as you stir. Remove from the heat and stir in the lemon juice.

2. In another large skillet, melt the remaining 2 tablespoons butter over medium heat and fry the bread triangles on one side.

3. Spread the liver mixture over the fried, crunchy side of the triangles of bread. Serve immediately.

Makes 24 canapés; 8 servings

Ducks in France

One doesn't simply buy duck in France. In the Languedoc, Périgord, the Lot, and Gascony in the south, and Normandy and Brittany in the north, where ducks are very much appreciated, there are varieties of ducks. The Rouen and Nantes ducks are considered the best. Duclair ducks are a variety of Rouen duck. The Barbary duck, whose flesh is mediocre, is mated with the Rouen duck to produce the mulard duck, which is bred specifically for the production of foie gras. The Rouen duck has such a fine taste and color because it is smothered and not bled like other fowl. This allows its flesh to stay red and has a special taste. The Nantes duck is also a delicious bird, but smaller. The Muscovy duck, prized for its red flesh and lesser amount of fat, is a duck that originates in tropical America and has nothing to do with Moscow.

Black Sausage, Raisin, and Pine Nut Canapés

This delicious tapa canapé called emparedados de morcilla is an Aragonese-Catalan preparation. To make it properly and to have it be memorable, you will need to procure the very best blood sausage. An excellent morcilla sausage can be ordered through www.donajuana.com. Theirs is made with pork, cooked rice, beef blood, paprika, garlic, and spices. Rudolf Grewe, a scholar of medieval Hispano-Muslim cuisine, believed that the North African merguez sausage was the ancestor of the morcilla *sausage. Another blood sausage used in Catalonia is called* botifarra negra.

2 teaspoons extra-virgin olive oil
½ pound fresh or cooked *morcilla* sausage
2 tablespoons golden raisins, soaked in tepid water 15 minutes and drained
2 tablespoons pine nuts
Twenty-eight ¼-inch-thick slices French baguette

1. In a medium-size skillet, heat the olive oil over medium heat, then cook the sausage, if fresh, until it browns and has given off a lot of its fat but is still slightly pink in the middle, about 10 minutes. If it is cooked, cook just until heated through. Remove the sausage from the skillet, pour off the fat, slice open the sausage, remove the meat from the casing, and crumble it. Return the sausage meat to the skillet and cook for a minute, then add the raisins and pine nuts and cook until cooked through, about 5 minutes, stirring.

2. Spoon a small amount on the bread slices, arrange on a platter, and serve.

Makes 28 canapés; 10 servings

Feta Cheese Canapés

I'm not sure if this is an actual Greek kanape, *but it is a delicious tidbit that I once had at a reception and enjoyed for its simplicity. The feta cheese needs to be washed of as much salt as possible and creamed until smooth.*

½ pound imported Greek or Bulgarian feta cheese, soaked in water for 2 hours and drained
¼ cup heavy cream
1 tablespoon unsalted butter, at room temperature
32 *crostini* (page 37)
8 gherkins, each sliced into 4 pieces, or 8 black olives, each sliced into 4 pieces

In a medium-size bowl, mash together the feta cheese, cream, and butter until creamy or do this in a food processor. Spread this mixture on the *crostini* and garnish with a gherkin slice or olive piece.

Makes 32 canapés; 12 servings

Gorgonzola and Walnut Canapés

This Italian antipasto called tramezzini al gorgonzola e noci *can be served as an open-faced canapé or you can lay a slice of bread on top to enclose it and form a sandwich. You can use any cooked ham, what the Italians call* prosciutto cotto, *but I think Black Forest ham is particularly good.*

3 tablespoons unsalted butter, at room temperature
Sixteen ¼-inch-thick slices Italian or French baguette, about 2 inches in diameter, cut in half, with or without crust
Salt to taste
6 ounces imported Italian gorgonzola cheese, at room temperature
16 walnut halves, chopped
3 ounces thinly sliced Black Forest ham, chopped

Lightly butter each slice of bread and sprinkle with a little salt, then spread some gorgonzola on top. Sprinkle with some of the walnuts and arrange a couple of pieces of chopped ham on top, pushing both down into the cheese. Serve at room temperature.

Makes 32 canapés; 10 servings

A Train Station in Milan

I've always associated gorgonzola and walnuts with a train station in Milan. It was 1968 and I was rushing to catch a train to Venice, but was starving and had time only for a quick bite at the railroad bar, filled with people from all countries, tripping over their luggage. The station bars served a variety of prepared sandwiches, as well as pizzas and other take-away foods. In those days I didn't speak a word of Italian and simply pointed at these little triangular sandwiches I later learned were called *tramezzini*. I had a few, but the one with creamy soft and slightly pungent gorgonzola and some chopped walnuts was really good and tided me over to Venice.

Roquefort and Gruyère Canapés

Roquefort cheese comes from the caves around the town of the same name in the Aveyron region of Haut Languedoc. Roquefort is made exclusively from sheep's milk and is unique in that the curds are mixed with fine bread crumbs that have been allowed to develop a green mold, the basis of the "blue" of the blue cheeses, of which Roquefort cheese is the most famous. This appetizer is called brissauda *in the old language of Provence. It's rich, but in small bites, just right.*

1 thin long French baguette, quartered crosswise, then each quarter cut in half lengthwise
3 tablespoons extra-virgin olive oil
2 ounces Roquefort cheese, at room temperature, crumbled
3 ounces Gruyère cheese, cut into thin shavings
Salt and freshly ground black pepper to taste

1. Preheat the broiler. Place the bread crust side down on a broiling tray and put under the broiler until crisp, about 1½ minutes.

2. Remove from the broiler and drizzle the oil evenly over the bread. Spread half the bread with Roquefort and arrange the Gruyère shavings on the remaining bread. Place the broiling tray under the broiler and, once the cheese melts, about 1 minute, remove. Season the Gruyère breads with salt and pepper and the Roquefort with pepper only. Cut each bread piece in half and give each person one with each cheese.

Makes 8 servings

The Aphrodisiac Roquefort

Giovanni Giacomo Casanova de Seingalt is arguably the most famous of Venetians, along with Marco Polo. Casanova, an adventurer, author, international gambler, and spy, was most famous for his amorous conquests and he believed Roquefort cheese was an aphrodisiac. "Lithe as a doe she spread the tablecloth, set two places and then served some Roquefort cheese with a wonderful glazed ham. Oh what an excellent pair are Roquefort and Chambertin [a wine] for stimulating romance and bringing a budding love affair to quick fruition."

Pistachio Canapés from Italy

This canapé sounds unusual, but it is not only a treat, it is a slightly old-fashioned northern Italian tidbit. Use only natural raw salted pistachios and not dyed ones.

¼ cup ground pistachios
4 ounces cream cheese, softened
Sixteen ¼-inch-thick slices Italian or French bread

In a small bowl, beat the pistachios and cream cheese together. Spread the mixture on the bread slices and serve.

Makes 16 canapés; 6 servings

Horseradish Canapés

In Verona, Italy, some cooks liked to use horseradish instead of pepper, and one finds horseradish in the cooking of Friuli-Venezia Giulia as well. These very simple canapés are slightly spicy from the horseradish, but not overly so. Decorate the top with a small leaf of watercress if you like.

3 ounces whipped cream cheese
¼ cup peeled and grated fresh horseradish
3 tablespoons sour cream
½ cup finely chopped fresh watercress
Thirty ¼-inch-thick slices French baguette

In a medium-size bowl, mix the cream cheese, horseradish, sour cream, and watercress until well blended, keeping to the side some watercress leaves for garnishing the tops, if desired. Spread about 1 teaspoon of the mixture on each slice of bread and serve.

Makes 30 canapés; 12 servings

Pistachios in Italy

Pistachios were first brought to Sicily by the Arabs in the ninth or tenth century. There Arab notions on artificial pollination were extensively put into practice, boosting the cultivation of pistachio nuts and palm trees. Pistachios are much used in Italian sweets, but in savory dishes too, especially those of Sicily. The English word *pistachio* comes from the Arabic word for pistachio, *fustaq*, through the Sicilian.

Canapés à la Provençale

These delicious morsels will remind you of a gay time by the shore in some little coastal village of Provence. They should be eaten relatively hot.

18 pitted black olives
3 tablespoons unsalted butter, plus softened
  butter for spreading
½ cup fresh bread crumbs
¼ cup finely chopped onion
1 garlic clove, finely chopped
3 medium-size ripe tomatoes, cut in half, seeds
  squeezed out, grated against the largest holes
  of a grater, and skin discarded
Salt and freshly ground black pepper to taste
2 teaspoons finely chopped fresh parsley leaves
Eighteen ¼-inch-thick slices French baguette
9 salted anchovy fillets, rinsed and cut in half

1. Bring a saucepan of water to a boil and cook the olives for 2 minutes to remove any salty or briny taste. Drain, cut each in half, and set aside.

2. In a medium-size skillet, melt 2 tablespoons of the butter over medium heat, then brown the bread crumbs, 4 to 5 minutes, stirring. Remove from the pan and set aside.

3. In the same skillet, melt the remaining 1 tablespoon butter over medium-high heat, then cook the onion and garlic until soft, 2 to 3 minutes, stirring frequently so the garlic doesn't burn. Reduce the heat to medium-low, add the tomatoes, season with salt and pepper, and cook until it forms a thick paste, 7 to 8 minutes, stirring. Turn the heat off and stir in the parsley.

4. Preheat the oven to 475°F.

5. Lightly butter all the bread rounds on both sides, then place in a large skillet and brown lightly on both sides over medium heat, 4 to 5 minutes. Spread all the bread rounds with some tomato sauce, then arrange 2 olive halves on each. Lay half an anchovy fillet on top of the olives. Sprinkle about 1 teaspoon or less of the browned bread crumbs on top, place all the rounds on a baking sheet, and bake until very hot, 3 to 4 minutes.

Makes 18 canapés; 8 or 9 servings

Cucumber Canapés with Salted Sardine Mayonnaise

A canapé does not always have to be made out of bread. Slices of vegetables, especially cucumber, work quite well as a vehicle to carry spreads and toppings. Salted sardines are only sold in Italian markets. They are packed like salted anchovies and they must be rinsed and then the fillets peeled off the backbone. Alternatively you can use anchovies.

8 salted sardine fillets, rinsed
½ cup mayonnaise, preferably homemade
  (page 466)
Sixteen to twenty ⅛-inch-thick slices peeled
  cucumber

Pound the sardine fillets in a mortar until mushy, then stir in the mayonnaise. Spread over the cucumber slices, refrigerate for 30 minutes, and serve.

Makes 16 to 20 canapés;
4 to 6 servings

Salted Anchovies and Salted Sardines

These two products are imported from Italy, Greece, France, and a few other countries. I think the best are those imported from the Augustino Recca firm of Sicily and sold in approximately 1-pound cans that cost about $14. They are exclusively sold in Italian markets. Once I open a can for use, I store the remainder by covering it with plastic wrap, using a rubber band to secure it, and place it in the refrigerator, where it will keep indefinitely.

Cucumber Canapés with Scallions and Mascarpone

These little bits are great as a passed antipasto at a cocktail party. They are simple yet satisfying because of the mascarpone.

6 tablespoons mascarpone cheese
¼ cup ricotta cheese, preferably homemade (page 88)
3 scallions, 2 finely chopped and 1 sliced ½ inch thick
Pinch of cayenne pepper
Sixteen to twenty ⅛-inch-thick slices peeled cucumber
32 to 40 pine nuts

In a small bowl, mix the mascarpone, ricotta, chopped scallions, and cayenne. Spread over the cucumber slices and garnish each slice with a piece of scallion and 2 pine nuts.

Makes 16 to 20 canapés; 4 to 6 servings

Cucumber Canapés with Ricotta and Pancetta

One reason slices of cucumber are perfect canapés is that they are a bland vegetable. So, as in this preparation, you load them up with richer ingredients. These are nice as a passed appetizer.

2 tablespoons mascarpone
6 tablespoons ricotta cheese, preferably homemade (page 88)
2 tablespoons *labna* (strained yogurt; page 56)
16 to 20 thin slices *pancetta*
Sixteen to twenty ⅛-inch-thick rounds peeled cucumber

1. In a small bowl, mix the mascarpone, ricotta, and strained yogurt.

2. Place the *pancetta* in a large skillet, turn the heat to medium, and cook until crispy or microwave between 2 sheets of paper towel until crisp.

3. Spread the cheese mixture on each slice of cucumber and top with a piece of *pancetta*.

Makes 16 to 20 canapés; 6 to 8 servings

Cucumber Canapés with Tapenade and Walnuts

I usually make this very simple canapé when I have leftover tapenade. The walnut on top gives a flavor and style familiar in Languedoc.

5 tablespoons Tapenade (page 58)

Sixteen to twenty ⅛-inch-thick rounds peeled
cucumber

16 to 20 walnut halves

Spread the tapenade on the cucumber slices,
then garnish each with a piece of walnut and serve.

Makes 16 to 20 canapés; 6 to 8 servings

Cucumber Canapés with Coriander Pesto and Hard-Boiled Egg Slices

*This vegetable canapé sounds unusual but it
actually has a nonintrusive taste—perfect as a
passed appetizer at a cocktail party.*

2 large garlic cloves, peeled

½ teaspoon salt

1 cup loosely packed fresh coriander (cilantro)
leaves

½ cup mayonnaise, preferably homemade
(page 466)

Sixteen to twenty ⅛-inch-thick rounds peeled
cucumber

3 large hard-boiled eggs, shelled and cut into as
many slices as you have cucumbers

1. In a mortar, pound the garlic with the salt
until mushy. Add the coriander and continue
pounding until it has a pesto consistency. Whip
in the mayonnaise.

2. Spread the coriander pesto on the cucumber slices, garnish with a slice of egg, and serve.

Makes 16 to 20 canapés;

6 to 8 servings

Fried Pumpkin, Onion, and Dill Pancakes

This Turkish meze is called mücver, *which means
"croquette," but they are formed into patties and
fried in oil. Typically, they are eaten at room temperature, but I like to serve them hot with a little
Cacık (page 56) on the side. I find it easiest to
grate all the pumpkin and onion with the grating
attachment of my food processor. The soft white
cheese called for could be any of the Mexican
cheeses sold in packages, such as* queso fresco, *or
you could use Syrian cheese, farmer cheese, cow's
milk feta cheese, or even cottage cheese.*

2 pounds peeled and seeded pumpkin flesh,
shredded

2 medium-large onions, grated

6 ounces soft white cheese, crumbled

½ cup all-purpose flour

4 large eggs

Leaves from 2 bunches fresh dill, finely chopped

2 teaspoons salt

½ teaspoon freshly ground black pepper

1 cup extra-virgin olive oil

1. In a large bowl, toss the pumpkin, onions,
cheese, flour, eggs, dill, salt, and black pepper
together and mix well.

2. In a large skillet, heat 2 tablespoons of the
olive oil over medium-high heat, then place 5
heaping tablespoonfuls of the pumpkin mixture
into the skillet, press down with a metal spatula
to flatten it into a pancake shape about 3 inches
in diameter, and cook until brown on both
sides, 4 to 6 minutes, turning once. Remove
from the pan and drain on paper towels. Cook

The Cuisine of the Monzù

Beginning in the eighteenth century, but especially in the nineteenth century when Sicily and Naples merged into a single kingdom under the House of Bourbon-Sicily to form the Kingdom of the Two Sicilies in 1816, nobles and prelates of both Sicily and Naples began to hire French-trained chefs or to send their young chefs to France to learn the principles of haute cuisine. These professional chefs were known as the *monzù*, a corruption of the French word *monsieur*. These chefs developed the secrets of aristocratic cuisine and many famous *antipasti* of today can be traced to them since traditionally modest households would not be having cocktail parties, an activity popular among the aristocracy. It seems likely that both Mozzarella in Carozza (page 94) and Crostini alla Napoletana (below) may be preparations from the cuisine of the *monzù*.

another batch of 5 before adding another 2 tablespoons of oil. Cook without crowding the skillet. Remove and continue cooking the remaining pumpkin in batches.

3. Transfer to a large platter and serve on a buffet table.

Makes about 40 patties; 12 to 14 servings

CROSTINI

Crostini are toasted Italian canapés. The bread can be cut into small rounds, squares, triangles, or diamonds, lightly buttered or oiled, and toasted or baked until crispy. Then various compound butters can be spread on them and garnished with anything you like, although tiny shrimp or pieces of prosciutto are favorites. *Crostini* made in southern Italy, such as Crostini alla Napoletana (opposite), tend to resemble pizzas in some ways, while *crostini* from Tuscany, such as *crostini alla chiantigiana* (Tuscan Chicken Liver Crostini; page 38) are quite famous.

Crostini alla Napoletana
All the typical ingredients of a Neapolitan pizza go on top of this crostini *from Naples, not surprisingly.*

3 tablespoons unsalted butter, at room temperature
1 loaf Italian or French bread, cut into twenty ¼-inch-thick slices, each slice about 4 inches in diameter
1¼ pounds fresh buffalo milk (preferably) mozzarella, sliced
20 salted anchovy fillets, rinsed
1½ pounds ripe tomatoes, seeded and sliced
Salt and freshly ground black pepper to taste
2 to 3 teaspoons dried oregano, to your taste
Extra-virgin olive oil for drizzling

1. Preheat the oven to 450°F.

2. Butter each slice of bread lightly. Grease a baking sheet with butter and arrange the slices of buttered bread on it. On each piece of bread place a slice of mozzarella and an anchovy fillet and cover with a slice or two of tomato. Sprinkle with some salt, pepper, and oregano to taste. Drizzle olive oil over each and place in the oven until the cheese is melted and the top is beginning to bubble, about 15 minutes. Serve hot.

Makes 20 crostini; 8 to 10 servings

Tuscan Chicken Liver Crostini

This famous antipasto called crostini di fegatini is a balanced blend of chicken livers, vegetables, wine, capers, and anchovies, which becomes a smooth, spreadable pâté covering crisp fried pieces of bread. It is also known by other names—crostini all chiantigiana (from Chianti), crostini neri (which is from San Gimignano), and crostini alla Toscana, a name used elsewhere in Italy. The roots of this chicken liver spread may go back to the peverada found in the anonymous Tuscan cookbook from the fourteenth century called Libro della cocina, made by pounding livers with toasted bread, saffron, and spices, and moistened with vinegar or wine. As cuisine and dietetics were considered handmaidens in fourteenth-century nutritional thinking, and Italian dietetics of the time were thoroughly informed by Arab medical science, it originally was thought of as healthy. Some years ago while conducting research in the Biblioteca Nazionale Marciana in Venice, I was perusing the Liber tertius Almansori aut libal-

doni, one volume of the great works by the tenth-century Muslim physician Rhazes, as he was known in the West (his name was Abū Bakr Muḥammad ibn Zakarīyā al-Rāzī), and noticed that he prescribed the eating of spleen and liver because they were nutritious. Rhazes work was first published in Milan in 1481 and was very influential, although we can never be sure if some cook somewhere understood this.

Since this is an appetizer, in Tuscany you would eat this crostini with an aperitivo such as Fernet–Branca or a glass of Vernaccia di San Gimignano.

3 tablespoons extra-virgin olive oil

5 tablespoons unsalted butter

½ cup finely chopped onion

¼ cup finely chopped carrot

1 large garlic, finely chopped

½ stalk celery, finely chopped

1 tablespoon finely chopped fresh parsley leaves

½ pound chicken livers, trimmed of any membranes

¼ cup dry white wine

1 tablespoon tomato paste

⅓ cup hot water

Salt and freshly ground black pepper to taste

2 tablespoons salted or brined capers, rinsed or drained and chopped

2 salted anchovy fillets, rinsed and chopped

Thirty-six ¼-inch-thick slices French baguette

1. In a medium-size skillet, heat the olive oil and 2 tablespoons of the butter over medium-high heat until the butter melts, then cook the onion, carrot, garlic, celery, and parsley until

mushy looking, about 5 minutes, stirring. Add the chicken livers and cook for 3 minutes. Pour the wine into the skillet, reduce the heat to low, and let the wine evaporate, about 5 minutes, stirring occasionally. Dissolve the tomato paste in the hot water and add to the skillet. Stir, season with salt and pepper, and cook for 20 minutes.

2. Transfer the mixture to a food processor, add the capers and anchovies, and process until smooth. Taste and correct the seasonings if necessary and add a tablespoon of water if it is too thick (it should be spreadable).

3. In a large skillet, melt the remaining 3 tablespoons butter over medium heat and cook the bread slices in a single layer, cooking in batches if necessary, until crispy brown on one side. Remove the bread and spread the chicken liver mixture on the crisp side of the slices. Serve warm if you can.

Makes 36 crostini; 12 servings

Veal Scaloppine alla Milanese, Tomato, and Mozzarella Crostini

These little morsels should be made with veal scaloppine, although veal shoulder pounded thin will work fine too. Typically, you make this crostini *when you have leftover cooked breaded veal scaloppine, which is believed by Neapolitans to have been invented by them, even though they also call it* alla Milanese *(from Milan).*

Twenty-four ¼-inch-thick slices French or Italian bread, about 3 inches in diameter
All-purpose flour for dredging
Salt and freshly ground black pepper to taste

Tuscan Crostini

The number of traditional *crostini* one can have in Tuscany is remarkable. Here are some possibilities: *crostini di caccia*, made with the livers of small birds such as doves, blackbirds, or figpeckers soaked in red wine, mashed with capers, and cooked in butter with lemon juice, onion, meat extract, nutmeg, cloves, and vin santo (a dessert wine); *crostini di milza*, or spleen *crostini* cooked in butter and olive oil with white wine, beef broth, anchovies, and capers; and *crostini con i funghi*, made with porcini mushrooms cooked with garlic, a little onion, and parsley in olive oil. In Siena they make *crostini di fegatini* with rabbit livers cooked with onion, capers, and vin santo. A very simple *crostini* is called *bianco-neri* and is made with some beef extract whipped with butter until creamy and bathed in a sauce of melted butter and Parmesan cheese.

---

2 cups dry bread crumbs
1 large egg
½ pound veal scaloppine, pounded thin and cut into 24 pieces total
1 cup olive oil
1 large ripe tomato, cut into 12 slices and each slice cut in half
24 small fresh basil leaves
Extra-virgin olive oil for drizzling
½ pound fresh mozzarella cheese, cut into 12 slices and each slice cut in half

1. Arrange the bread slices on a large rectangular or round baking sheet that will accommodate all of them in a single layer.

2. Put the flour in a medium-size bowl and season with salt and pepper. Put the bread crumbs on a piece of waxed paper. Beat the egg in a wide bowl. Toss the veal pieces in the flour, then pat them all to remove the excess flour. Dip in the egg, then dredge well in the bread crumbs. Arrange on a tray and refrigerate for 30 minutes if time allows.

3. Preheat the oven to 400°F.

4. In a large skillet, heat the olive oil over medium-high heat, then cook the veal until crispy brown on both sides, 1 to 2 minutes. Remove with tongs and place on top of the bread. Season with salt and pepper. Place a like-sized slice of tomato on top, then a basil leaf, a drizzle of olive oil, and finally the mozzarella. Bake until the cheese is completely melted, about 8 minutes.

5. Remove from the oven and serve when it is cool enough to hold in your hand.

Makes 24 crostini; 12 servings

Veal Marrow Crostini from Lazio

This wonderfully simple yet delicious preparation is an old recipe called crostini con merollo *that I learned from one of Ada Boni's cookbooks. In the dialect of Rome,* merollo *refers to marrow. It's easiest to get the marrow out of bones when they are at room temperature. Use a narrow spoon or butter knife and a paring knife to extract the marrow.*

1½ cups veal marrow (from about 5 pounds of
    bones), at room temperature
Twenty ¼-inch-thick slices French baguette
Salt to taste

1. Preheat the oven to 400°F.

2. Spread some veal marrow on each slice of bread, not too liberally. Arrange the bread slices on a baking sheet and bake until the marrow has melted, about 7 minutes.

3. Remove from the oven and season with salt. Serve immediately.

Makes 20 crostini; 8 to 10 servings

Learning to Cook Italian Food

People who love Italian food probably have some of Marcella Hazan's books, so they are quite surprised to hear that, although I admire her work, she was not the doyenne of Italian cuisine for me as she was to so many others. I began to cook Italian food in the 1960s, and the four most important sources for me were my family, my travels in Italy, the Italian restaurant where I worked on Long Island, and Ada Boni, the most important Italian cookery writer of the twentieth century. So much of what I learned about the basics of Italian cookery came from two of her books, which were my bibles, *The Talisman Italian Cookbook* and *Italian Regional Cooking.*

Provolone and Pancetta Crostini

Who can deny the great taste of bacon and cheese? Pancetta is an Italian cured bacon and provolone is a good melting cheese. Make sure the provolone is mild and not the sharp variety. The crispy pancetta on top of the melted cheese makes this crostini hard to stop eating.

Twelve ¼-inch-thick slices French baguette, lightly toasted
Twelve ¼-inch-thick slices mild provolone cheese, cut the same size as the bread slices
12 very thin slices *pancetta*

1. Arrange the toasted bread on a serving platter. Arrange the cheese slices on a baking sheet or microwave-safe tray and cover each with a slice of *pancetta*. Microwave until the cheese is bubbling or place under a preheated broiler until the cheese is bubbling, 2 to 3 minutes.

2. Remove with a metal spatula, place on top of a bread slice, and serve immediately.

Makes 12 crostini; 6 servings

Variation: Replace the provolone with soft, young *pecorino pepato*; microwave the *pancetta* until crispy and place on top of the bread slices, then place the cheese slices on top and bake in a preheated 400°F oven until the cheese is bubbling.

Crostini di Mortadella e Fontina

Although this crostini sounds simple enough—just layering mortadella and fontina—you do need to be careful when you construct it because the bread can fall apart when you dip it in the egg. Let the crostini drain after cooking and serve warm.

Sixteen ¼-inch-thick slices French or Italian bread, about 4 inches in diameter, crusts removed and each cut into 2 triangles
8 salted anchovy fillets, rinsed and cut in half
2 ounces fontina Val d'Aosta cheese, cut into 16 thin slices and folded or cut into triangles
2 ounces mortadella, cut into 16 thin slices and folded or cut into triangles
Freshly ground black pepper to taste
¾ cup olive oil
4 large eggs
¼ cup freshly grated Parmigiano-Reggiano cheese

1. On each triangle of bread, place an anchovy half, a slice of fontina, and a slice of mortadella; sprinkle with pepper and place a plain triangle of bread on top to make a sandwich. Press down.

2. In a large skillet, heat the olive oil over medium-high heat.

3. In a medium-size bowl, beat the eggs and Parmigiano together. Dip each sandwich in the egg carefully on all sides, then fry in the oil until golden, 1 to 2 minutes, turning with tongs. Drain on paper towels and serve hot or warm.

Makes 16 crostini; 8 servings

Fontina Val d'Aosta Crostini

This sounds like it's not much more than melted cheese, but if you use the excellent fontina Val d'Aosta you will see that this crostini is much more than that. If you use fontina Valbella or Swedish fontina, you just will not have the same experience. Read more about fontina Val d'Aosta on page 287.

Twelve 2-inch-square thin slices fontina
    Val d'Aosta cheese
Twelve ¼-inch-thick slices stale French or Italian
    bread, cut into 2-inch-square pieces

1. Preheat the oven to 350°F.

Elegant Antipasti

These extraordinary *antipasti* are complex (I don't provide recipes) and typically found in higher end restaurants in Italy serving innovative food: *portobello gratinato*, wood oven–roasted portobello mushrooms and lobster with *fontinella* cheese; *crostini al prosciutto*, homemade *bruschetta* topped with prosciutto and goat cheese; *costolette*, grilled pork ribs; *manicotti pescatore*, seafood-stuffed rolled crêpes with spicy marinara sauce; *frittelle d'aragosta*, pan-seared lobster cake with fresh tomato and porcini cream sauce; *olive Ascolana*, fried olives stuffed with crab meat; and stuffed porcini mozzarella, made with homemade mozzarella cheese.

---

2. Put a slice of cheese on each slice of bread and set on a baking sheet. Place the bread in the oven until the cheese begins to bubble, about 10 minutes. Serve immediately.

Makes 12 crostini; 6 servings

Artichoke and Mozzarella Crostini

This crostini *is typical of the area around Naples and on the island of Capri, and is meant to resemble the popular* pizza con carciofi, *or pizza with artichokes.*

½ pound fresh mozzarella cheese, chopped
4 large cooked fresh or canned artichoke
    bottoms, chopped
8 pitted black olives, chopped
1 medium-size ripe tomato, peeled, seeded,
    and chopped
2 tablespoons extra-virgin olive oil, plus more
    for drizzling
16 salted anchovy fillets, rinsed, and 6 chopped
    and 10 cut in half
1 tablespoon finely chopped fresh oregano leaves
Salt and freshly ground black pepper to taste
Twenty ¼-inch-thick slices French or Italian
    bread, about 3 inches in diameter
¼ cup salted or brined capers, rinsed or drained
    and cut in half if large

1. Preheat the broiler.
2. In a medium-size bowl, mix the mozzarella, artichoke bottoms, olives, tomato, olive oil, chopped anchovies, and oregano and season with salt and pepper. Place about 1 tablespoon

How to Serve Crostini

You can get as fancy as you want, but I like to keep it simple, although I will garnish *crostini* a bit more than described in the recipes. Wherever appropriate, you can add a little sliver of thinly sliced lemon, a leaf of parsley, a caper, a piece of red bell pepper, and so on. Think of color more than taste, although don't go too wild. Arrange the assembled *crostini* attractively on a serving tray that can be passed to a group of standing people. Remember that they are probably holding a glass, so make it easy to pick up one of the *crostini* and a cocktail napkin. Leave enough room between each *crostini* so those with two left thumbs can pick them up without knocking everything around. Fantail the cocktail napkins so people can pick them up easily, too, and not fumble.

of this mixture on each slice of bread. Arrange the bread on a broiler tray or baking sheet and place a half anchovy fillet on top along with 1 or 2 capers. Drizzle very lightly with olive oil and place under the broiler until the cheese is bubbling, about 2 minutes. Serve immediately.

Makes 20 crostini; 8 to 10 servings

Porcini Mushroom and Béchamel Crostini

This very old-fashioned antipasto comes from an Italian cookbook on entertaining from the

1950s. You will not see this crostini ai funghi made anymore, partly because it's too rich for modern diet-conscious tastes. But there's nothing wrong with it; it's luscious and a perfect vehicle for the extravagance of porcini mushrooms.

5 tablespoons unsalted butter
3½ ounces fresh porcini mushrooms, thinly sliced, then coarsely chopped
1 tablespoon fresh lemon juice
2 tablespoons all-purpose flour
⅔ cup beef broth
⅔ cup dry white wine
Salt and freshly ground black pepper to taste
1 large egg yolk
Twelve ¼-inch-thick slices Italian or French bread, about 2 inches in diameter

1. In a small or medium-size nonstick skillet, melt 1 tablespoon of the butter over medium-high heat and cook the mushrooms with the lemon juice until golden, about 5 minutes, stirring or tossing.

2. In a medium-size saucepan, melt 2 tablespoons of the butter over medium-high heat, add the flour, and cook, stirring, to form a roux without letting it color. Slowly pour in the broth and wine, whisking constantly. Reduce the heat to medium and let the sauce thicken until quite dense, about 10 minutes, stirring or whisking frequently. Season with salt and pepper and add the mushrooms. Stir in the egg yolk and remove from the heat.

3. Meanwhile, melt the remaining 2 tablespoons butter in a large skillet over medium heat and fry the bread slices on one side until

golden. Arranged the bread slices on a platter, spread the mushroom sauce over them, and serve immediately.

Makes 12 crostini; 6 servings

Crushed White Bean Crostini

Tuscan crostini con i fagioli cannellini is made with white cannellini beans, although any dried white bean is fine. It's a very simple preparation, so that means the quality of the olive oil you use will be critical. Don't try and fancy it up; just make sure the beans are well cooked and crushable and that you use a good extra-virgin olive oil.

1 cup dried cannellini beans (about ½ pound), picked over, soaked in water to cover overnight, and drained
Salt to taste
2 tablespoons extra-virgin olive oil, plus more for drizzling
1 large garlic clove, crushed
2 large fresh sage leaves
Forty ¼-inch-thick slices French baguette, lightly toasted
Freshly ground black pepper to taste

1. Place the drained beans in a large saucepan with cold water to cover by several inches. Bring to a boil with the salt, olive oil, garlic, and sage and cook until tender, about 1¼ hours, replenishing the water if it evaporates too much. Drain well and transfer to a bowl. Mash the beans slightly. Taste and add more salt if necessary.

2. Arrange about 1 tablespoon or a little less of the warm beans on top of each bread slice. Drizzle with olive oil, sprinkle with some pepper, and serve immediately.

Makes 40 crostini; 20 servings

BRUSCHETTA

❖

Bruschetta (pronounced *broo-SKET-TA*) sure seem like the same thing as *crostini*, but they're not. A *crostino* (singular) is nothing but a toasted canapé or crouton for soup while a *bruschetta* is a thick slice of a large round rustic bread loaf that is rubbed with oil and grilled or *abbrustolito* (roasted), hence the word. *Bruschetta's* home is in the regions of Lazio and the Abruzzi, but is now found all over Italy.

Andalusian Bruschetta with Olive Oil and Garlic

In Andalusia, tostada de pan con aceite y ajo is the kind of snack fieldworkers would make for themselves during the day in the arable lands surrounding Córdoba. Make these tostadas while you have the grill fired up for pinchon moruno (Grilled Pork Kebabs from Andalusia; page 424).

1 round country-style Italian, French, or Spanish bread, sliced ⅜ inch thick
Extra-virgin olive oil to taste
Salt to taste
2 large garlic cloves, crushed slightly and cut in half

1. Prepare a hot charcoal fire or preheat a gas grill for 15 minutes on high.

2. Put the slices of bread on a grill or griddle and, with a brush, dab each slice with some olive oil, then sprinkle with salt. Grill until golden or to your taste, then rub both sides with the garlic. Serve immediately.

Makes 8 servings

Bruschetta with Tomatoes and Basil

This Neapolitan bruschetta *is a bit larger than a typical antipasto* bruschetta *or* crostini*, so you may want to make more of them, and smaller, or cut them in half.*

3½ pounds very ripe tomatoes, peeled if desired, seeded, chopped, and drained well

¼ cup finely chopped fresh basil leaves

Coarse salt and coarsely ground black pepper to taste

Twelve ¾-inch-thick slices Italian or French country bread, about 3 x 4 inches

¼ to ½ cup extra-virgin olive oil, to your taste

1. Preheat the oven to 350°F.

2. In a medium-size bowl, mix the tomatoes and basil and season with salt and pepper.

3. Arrange the bread slices on a baking sheet and place in the oven until the bread is hard on top but not brown, about 5 minutes.

4. Remove from the oven, spoon the tomato mixture equally over each slice of bread, and drizzle with the olive oil. Serve.

Makes 12 servings

Bruschetta with Fresh Ricotta and Spinach

This bruschetta *is made with country bread rather than a baguette, providing a deeper, earthier taste. Country breads are usually made into large rounds, so you would slice off a piece of country bread and cut it up into the portion size you like. The size I suggest here may be a bit substantial for an antipasto, so feel free to make them a bit smaller. Although ubiquitous in America, in Italy* bruschetta *is mostly found in Lazio, Tuscany, and Abruzzo; it's not traditionally a pan-Italian thing.*

10 ounces fresh spinach, heavy stems removed and washed well

3 tablespoons unsalted butter

6 tablespoons extra-virgin olive oil

1 garlic clove, crushed

Salt and freshly ground black pepper to taste

Eight ¾-inch-thick slices French or Italian country bread, about 3 x 4 inches

1 pound fresh ricotta cheese, preferably homemade (page 88)

1. Preheat the oven to 350°F.

2. Put the spinach in a large saucepan with only the water adhering to its leaves from its last rinsing. Cover the pot and wilt the spinach over medium-high heat, 4 to 5 minutes, turning occasionally. Drain well, using the back of a wooden spoon to squeeze out all the water. Chop coarsely.

3. In a medium-size skillet, heat the butter, 2 tablespoons of the olive oil, and the crushed garlic until the butter melts over medium heat.

Add the spinach and cook for 5 minutes. Season with salt and pepper. Set aside and keep warm.

4. Meanwhile, coat the slices of bread with the ricotta cheese. Drizzle 1¼ teaspoons of the olive oil over each slice and season with salt and pepper. Set on a baking sheet and place in the oven until the oil starts bubbling, about 10 minutes. Remove from the oven and cover each slice with the spinach. Return to the oven and bake for 2 minutes, cut in half, then serve immediately.

Makes 16 servings

LITTLE SANDWICHES

The little sandwiches of the Mediterranean are famous. Whether it's the street food of Tunisia, such as the sandwich known as a Casse-Croûte (page 48), or the Provençal Pan Bagna (page 50), they are all easily turned into starters. In Italy, little sandwiches are often called *tramezzini*. Open-faced sandwiches are called *tartine* and they are eaten often as snacks.

Catalan Bread with Oil and Bread with Tomato

One finds pa amb oli *everywhere in Catalonia, as a* tapa *in bars and restaurants, in homes, and eaten by children.* Pa amb oli *and* pa amb tomàquet *are made with slices of bakery-fresh bread held on the end of a long fork over a fire. Then the bread is coated with olive oil and a sprinkle of sugar, or it is brushed with oil and rubbed with garlic. Or, for* pa amb tomàquet, *a very ripe tomato can be cut in half, the seeds and excess liquid squeezed out, then the slice of bread rubbed with the tomato, leaving a pinkish stain. Olive oil is drizzled on along with a sprinkling of salt—and there you have it. This theme of smeared bread also finds a home in Valencia, where I once was served a delicious* pan de pueblo con all i oli *at the Casa Navarro Restaurant in Valencia. They spread some toasted country bread with mashed garlic and fruity olive oil, along with a little Allioli (page 466), or garlic mayonnaise, and it was just great.*

Eight ½-inch-thick slices Italian or French country bread
1 large ripe tomato, cut in half and seeds and liquid squeezed out
Extra-virgin olive oil
Salt to taste

Toast or grill the bread slices lightly first, then rub both sides with a cut tomato half, drizzle a little olive oil on both sides, salt to taste, and serve.

Makes 8 servings

Andalusian Spiced Mushrooms on Fried Bread

This delectable tapa *called* setas con pan frito *is spicy and excellent with sangria or some red*

Panini

One curiosity about Italian cookbooks is that they don't have recipes for *panini*, little bread sandwiches. The reason for this, and the reason there are no "recipes" for *panini* in this book, is that you don't need a recipe. *Panini* are just too simple. If you were to put any of the toppings of the canapés or *crostini* in this chapter into a small soft roll, you would have a *panino*. *Panini* are usually made as snack material, but you could also serve them as cocktail appetizers. The most typical *panini* are those with ham and cheese or prosciutto and mozzarella. But the combinations are truly endless, and if you want to start experimenting, remember that you use soft rolls, buttering, oiling, or "mayonnaising" them before putting in other ingredients. Some combinations you could try are: shrimp and onion, roasted red bell pepper, roasted or fried eggplant, various cold cuts such as prosciutto, mortadella, *coppa*, *capicollo*, salami, and *soppressata*, and cheese such as mozzarella, provolone, *scamorza*, gorgonzola, and provola, with or without lettuce, tomato slices, and onion. You could use fried artichokes, or roasted yellow pepper, or asparagus, or hearts of palm—you'll only be limited by your imagination. If you were to make these *panini* with regular slices of white bread with the crusts cut off, you would then have *tramezzini*.

wine. It's delicious on top of the fried bread, which absorbs some of the richness of the mushrooms. I like to serve it with drinks before my guests and I sit down for dinner.

3 tablespoons pork lard
1 pound white mushrooms, quartered
¼ cup fresh lemon juice
1 teaspoon freshly ground cumin seeds
1 teaspoon paprika
Salt and freshly ground black pepper to taste

Twenty ¼-inch-thick slices French baguette or
    Italian country bread

1. In a medium-size skillet, melt 1 tablespoon of the lard over medium heat, then cook the mushrooms, lemon juice, cumin, paprika, salt, and black pepper until most of the mushroom liquid has evaporated and the mushrooms are soft, about 25 minutes.

2. Meanwhile, in a large skillet, melt the remaining 2 tablespoons lard over medium-high

What to Drink with Tapas?

In Spain, a bar where you could not eat is unheard of. Eating and drinking is part of the Spanish national character. The most fun place to have a drink and a bite is a *tasca*, a place where you have tapas, a drink, and a tryst. In a *tasca*, you can order a *cava*, a sparkling wine, or perhaps a Rioja. Whatever you order, you'll never encounter the fussiness of the French when it comes to wine. Trust the barman and have a *vino de la casa*. At home, drink Spanish wine or have a fine sherry with your *tapa*, such as a *fino* with its amber color and aroma of almonds. Or have a beer. You probably don't think of beer as a Spanish drink, but it has been ever since young Spaniards after the Franco era searched for the "modern." Drink and be merry.

heat, then cook the bread slices until light golden on both sides.

3. Arrange the fried bread slices on a serving platter. Cover with the mushrooms and serve.

Makes 8 tapas servings

Fried Cheese in Pita Sandwiches

This preparation is fantastically simple, yet because it is so well received, I am always asked for "the recipe." It consists of four ingredients. You

will need Syrian white cheese, which is available in Middle Eastern markets. A Mexican queso ranchero *or* queso fresco *will also work very well. These are usually wrapped in plastic and sold in supermarkets. You will also need* labna, *strained yogurt, which you can make yourself or buy at a Middle Eastern market, and you will need small fresh pita bread loaves. One should be able to eat these starters in one or two bites.*

1 tablespoon unsalted butter
1 pound Syrian white cheese or Mexican *queso ranchero* or *queso fresco*, cut into ¼-inch-thick, 2-inch squares
1 cup *labna* (strained yogurt; page 56)
Eight 6-inch-diameter pita breads, warmed and cut into sixths

1. In a large nonstick skillet, melt the butter over medium-high heat, lay down the cheese squares, and cook until crispy brown, about 3 minutes. Then turn with a metal spatula and cook the other side until crispy brown, about 2 minutes.

2. Meanwhile, spread a little strained yogurt on each piece of pita bread, opened at the fold, then lay a fried cheese square on top, and close. Serve immediately as a passed appetizer.

Makes 10 servings

Casse-Croûtes

Even in Tunisia people still use the French name casse-croûtes, *which is colloquial French for a snack, to refer to the little street food sandwiches called* shatīra al-Tūnisiyya *in Arabic.*

They are made with soft rolls cut open and stuffed with canned tuna, harīsa *dissolved in a little water, chopped tomatoes, black olives, capers, a little Tunisian Salad (page 241), pickled carrots, olive oil, and vinegar. They are very tasty and can sometimes contain other ingredients, such as sliced bell peppers, parsley, cucumbers, sliced cooked potatoes, and very thin slices of lemon. Children eat these sandwiches as a snack after school, bought from the vendor who goes through the residential neighborhoods of Tunis selling them. Use small rolls or long soft rolls or the Tunisian* tabbuna *bread, a griddled ½-inch-thick flatbread without pockets sometimes sold frozen in Greek markets as* pide *bread (page 432).*

2 teaspoons Harīsa (page 468)

1 tablespoon extra-virgin olive oil, plus more for drizzling

½ green bell pepper, seeded and cut into very thin strips

8 small soft rolls (about 3 inches long) or 4 long soft rolls (about 6 inches long), split open

1 small plum tomato, chopped

One 3-ounce can imported tuna in olive oil, flaked apart

¼ cup Tunisian Salad (page 241)

10 pitted black olives, chopped

4 very thin slices Meyer lemon, cut in half

2 tablespoons chopped fresh parsley leaves (optional)

¼ cucumber (optional), peeled, seeded, and thinly sliced

½ small potato (optional), boiled in water to cover until tender, drained, peeled, and thinly sliced

1. In a small bowl, stir the *harīsa* and olive oil together until dissolved.

2. Arrange the bell pepper slices on the bread, cover with a little chopped tomato, the tuna and its oil, Tunisian salad, olives, slices of lemon, and parsley, cucumber, and potato, if using, and finally drizzle the *harīsa* over everything. Drizzle a little more olive oil if desired, then, making sure the stuffing stays in, press the rolls down with the palms of you hand until flattened a bit. Slice the longer rolls and cut the shorter rolls in half and serve.

Makes 8 servings

* 🐚 *

Eating in Tunisia

I had been in Tunisia a while and there was one food I kept seeing but hadn't had a chance to try because it seemed like street food, which it was. These were the *casse-croûtes*. Finally, the bus I was traveling on made a pit stop at the tony seaside town of La Marsa, north of Tunis, and a little hole-in-the-wall cookshop was making *casse-croûtes*. I had to fight my way through hordes of schoolchildren picking up their afternoon snack, when I was handed my *casse-croûte* stuffed into a soft roll and scrumptious from a confusion of flavors.

Pan Bagna

In Provence, especially Nice, pan bagna *(or* bagnat*) is a street food that can easily be turned into this hors d'oeuvre. The name* pan bagna, *which means something like "bathed bread," implies that the bread becomes soaked, which it does. It is a curious method: a roll is stuffed with tomatoes, olives, garlic, fresh fava beans, and sometimes canned tuna, and all this is sprinkled with olive oil and vinegar. The roll is closed up, then it rests under a weight that flattens it considerably. This Provençal snack has much in common with the Tunisian Casse-Croûtes (page 48).*

6 small soft rolls (about 2½ inches long) or one
   8-inch soft roll, cut in half lengthwise
2 garlic cloves, mashed in a mortar until mushy
½ cup cooked and skinned fresh fava beans
   (from about ½ pound fava bean pods)
6 imported black olives, pitted and chopped
2 tablespoons chopped pimiento
1 small ripe tomato, thinly sliced
1 tablespoon extra-virgin olive oil
1 teaspoon red wine vinegar
Salt and freshly ground black pepper to taste

1. Spread the bread on both sides with the mashed garlic, then lay the fava beans, olives, pimiento, and tomato on top. Drizzle with the olive oil and vinegar and season with salt and pepper. Then close the two halves together, wrap tightly in aluminum foil, and place a heavy weight on top for about 30 minutes.

2. If using the 8-inch roll, slice it into 8 portions and serve.

Makes 6 to 8 servings

Pistachio and Emmentaler Cheese Sandwiches

Although this is a rich and filling canapé, found in the Alpes-Maritime in France and the Piedmont in Italy, once it's sliced and served it becomes a delectable morsel, perfect while having a pre-dinner drink. Make sure you chop the pistachios and don't grind them because you want them to be visible once the baguette is sliced.

6 ounces Emmenthaler cheese, 4 ounces
   shredded (about 1 cup) and 2 ounces cut into
   tiny dice (about ½ cup)
¼ cup (½ stick) unsalted butter, at room
   temperature
3 tablespoons heavy cream
¼ cup chopped pistachios
One 16-inch-long French baguette, split open
   lengthwise and some of the white part inside
   removed

1. In a medium-size bowl, mix the grated cheese with the butter and cream. Fold in the diced cheese and pistachios. Stuff both the tops and bottoms of the rolls, push back together tightly, cover tightly with plastic wrap, and refrigerate for 3 hours.

2. Slice about ¼ inch thick, arrange attractively on a platter, and serve at close to room temperature.

Makes 10 servings

CROÛTE OR CROUSTADE

✦

A croustade or *croûte*, or *croste* in Italian, is a hollowed-out bread tartlet. It is made from a rectangular loaf of dense white bread whose crust has been removed. The loaf is then cut up into 1½-inch-thick cubes, which are made crisp either by brushing them with butter or oil and baking them in the oven or by frying them in oil. A little incision is made and some of the dough is removed to form a well for a stuffing.

To make *croustades* or *croûtes*, take a rectangular loaf of day-old unsliced dense white bread and remove the crust so the loaf has straight sides. Cut the loaf into 1½-inch-thick slices, then cut each slice into 4 cubes. Cut a square in the center of each cube, about ¼ inch deep, using a small paring knife or, better, a curved grapefruit knife, and remove the bread to form a well. Now, you can either brush the croustades with melted butter or olive oil and bake them for 30 minutes at 300°F or deep-fry them in vegetable or olive oil heated to 375°F until golden, which will take less than a minute. Once they have cooled, remove the pre-cut center with the tines of a small fork and pick out the soft white center from the cube and from the lid.

Croûtes Cardinal

These croûtes *are a kind of* croustade *(see above), although the word* croûte *actually applies more broadly to a range of doughs that could be used, such as brioche dough or bread slices. The appellation* cardinal *refers to a Catholic cardinal. Presumably, only the well-appointed cardinal (with his peaked red hat) would be able to afford this expensive and elegant hors d'oeuvre, which can be found in France and northern Italy.*

One 1¼-pound live lobster
2 tablespoons unsalted butter
1 cup Béchamel Sauce (page 468)
2 tablespoons chopped black truffle
20 *croûtes* (see opposite)
2 tablespoons dry bread crumbs

1. Bring about an inch of water to a boil in a large pot. Put the lobster in, cover, and steam until bright orange, 17 to 18 minutes. Remove from the pot and let cool. Crack the shell and remove all the meat, including the meat from the legs and fantail. Chop the tail and leg meat together with any coral and tomalley that you find in the lobster and mix it with the butter, blending well. Chop the remaining lobster meat and reserve it separately. Refrigerate until needed.

2. Preheat the broiler. Make the béchamel sauce. Stir the lobster, truffle, and 1 tablespoon of the lobster butter into the béchamel and cook until heated through. Stuff the *croûtes* with the mixture using a small baby or demitasse spoon, then sprinkle with the bread crumbs and dot with the remaining tablespoon of lobster butter. Place them on a broiler tray, brown under the broiler, about 1½ to 2 minutes, and serve immediately.

Makes 20 croûtes; *10 servings*

Making Croûtes

Remember that the *croûtes* on pages 48–53 will be, at 1½ inches cubed, a wee bit too big for bite size. Guests will probably have to take two bites and that means you don't want to have the stuffing falling all over the place, so don't overstuff them.

Croûtes of Cotechino Sausage and Marsala Wine

Cotechino *sausage, also seen spelled as* cotechino*, is a thick, squat sausage popular in soups, stews, and with earthy legumes like lentils. It is a sausage usually found in Italian markets in this country. This old-fashioned* croste *recipe from Emilia-Romagna was popular in the 1950s and is adapted from a recipe by Waverly Root, author of* The Food of Italy *and many other books.*

12 to 16 *croûtes* (page 51)

Olive oil for brushing

2 tablespoons pork fat or pork lard

1 tablespoon extra-virgin olive oil

6 ounces cooked or raw cotechino sausage, skinned and cut into tiny dice, or mild Italian sausage, casing removed and crumbled

¼ cup sweet Marsala wine

2 tablespoons unsalted butter

1 tablespoon fresh lemon juice

¼ cup finely chopped fresh parsley leaves plus extra for garnish

1. Make the *croûtes*, brushing them with olive oil instead of butter.

2. In a medium-size skillet, render the pork fat or melt the lard with the olive oil over medium heat until the pork fat, if using, is crispy, 3 to 5 minutes; then cook the sausage until it turns color, about 5 minutes. Remove with a slotted spoon to paper towels to drain, set aside, and discard all the fat from the skillet. Pour the Marsala into the skillet and cook until reduced to about 2 tablespoons of liquid, stirring to scrape up any browned bits from the bottom of the pan. Return the sausage to the skillet, add the butter, and heat for 2 minutes, stirring. Add the lemon juice and parsley, stir, and remove from the heat.

3. Preheat the oven to 350°F.

4. Spoon the sausage mixture into the wells of the *croûtes* and set them on a baking sheet. Place in the oven until crispy, 15 to 20 minutes. Serve hot.

Makes 12 to 16 croûtes*; 6 servings*

Croûtes of Calf's Brain

This antipasto, called croste con cervella *in Italian, is a great one to use when you want to introduce people to calf's brains. They'll pop the whole* croustade *in their mouths and get the complex taste of creamy brains, crunchy golden roasted bread, and scallions all in one bite, as they should.*

1 pound calf's brain

¼ cup white wine vinegar

3 tablespoons unsalted butter

1 or 2 scallions (white and light green parts
   only), finely chopped
Salt and freshly ground black pepper to taste
24 *croûtes* (page 51)
Extra-virgin olive oil for drizzling

1. Soak the brain in cold water to cover for 1 hour. Drain, rinse, and place the brain in a saucepan, then cover with cold water and the vinegar and bring to just below a boil. Poach gently until firm, about 20 minutes, then remove from the cooking water and set aside.

2. In a large skillet, melt 2 tablespoons of the butter over medium heat and cook the scallions until soft, 1 to 2 minutes, stirring. Add the brains and season with salt and pepper, then cook for 5 minutes, breaking them up slightly with a wooden spoon and turning them occa-sionally. Remove the mixture to a cutting board and chop coarsely.

3. Add the remaining 1 tablespoon butter to the skillet and melt over high heat until it is just beginning to turn brown, then return the brain to the skillet, toss to coat with the butter, and turn the heat off. Check the seasonings.

4. Preheat the oven to 400°F.

5. Spoon a bit of the brain stuffing into each of the *croûtes*, pushing it down tightly, arrange on a baking sheet, and bake for 5 minutes. Remove from the oven and drizzle a little olive oil over the *croûtes*. Serve hot or warm with a sprinkling of parsley on top.

Makes 24 croûtes; *12 servings*

· 🧠 ·

Dips, Spreads, and Pâtés

What is a cocktail party without a dip? This is true in America and it's true in the Mediterranean. This chapter has some old classics, like Hummus (page 68) and Baba Ghannouj (page 60), and a whole bunch of new dips and spreads. When you think about it, calling hummus and baba ghannouj old classics is revealing of how international our food tastes have become because thirty years ago one couldn't have said that. But now you'll have a chance to make some old Mediterranean classics such as Tapenade (page 58), a savory blend of black olives, capers, and anchovies from Provence, or the flavorful Eggplant, Yogurt, and Walnut Salad-Dip from Turkey (page 64).

One can dip bread or vegetables into these dips, spreads, or pâtés, making for such a convivial feeling among guests. In the Mediterranean, small pieces of bread, either French-type bread or Arabic bread, would be used, or raw vegetables such as celery, carrots, broccoli stems, or cauliflower florets, and you can do the same. Try some of the recipes you may never have encountered before, such as Biṣāra (page 70), Brandade of Haricot Bean (page 72), or Swiss Chard Stalk and Tahini Dip (page 73), and I'll wager that your guests will be happy and your repertoire expanded.

Cacık and Tzatziki

Cacık (*pronounced* jajuk) *is a yogurt and cucumber dip common throughout Turkey. In Greece it is known as* tzatziki *and in Cyprus they call it* talattouri. *Although it is a meze that can stand on its own, one often finds it used as a kind of relish for any number of prepared foods, especially grilled kebabs and* köfte *(grilled ground meat).*

1 large cucumber, peeled, seeded, and shredded
Salt
3 large garlic cloves, mashed in a mortar with 1 teaspoon salt until mushy
2 cups full-fat plain yogurt (see Note)
1 tablespoon chopped fresh dill
¾ teaspoon dried mint
1 tablespoon extra-virgin olive oil

1. Toss the shredded cucumber with a light sprinkling of salt. Leave for 30 minutes. Drain the cucumber, squeezing out all the liquid.
2. Stir the garlic paste into the yogurt and beat with a fork until smooth. Stir in the cucumber, dill, mint, and olive oil until it has the consistency of a thick soup. Refrigerate for 1 hour and serve cold.

Note: If the yogurt you usually buy is not thick, stir some *labna* into it (strained yogurt; see opposite).

Makes 3 cups

Yogurt and Cayenne Dip from Turkey

This preparation, called açili esme, *is a simple blend made with yogurt and garlic, a spiced-up* cacık *(previous recipe). You eat it with pieces of bread and scallions, but I also loved to dip* köfte *(pages 427 and 430) into it.*

1 teaspoon salt
4 large garlic cloves, peeled
¾ cup full-fat plain yogurt
6 tablespoons *labna* (strained yogurt; see below)
½ teaspoon cayenne pepper
1 teaspoon chopped fresh dill
Extra-virgin olive oil for drizzling
Whole scallions for garnish
French bread

Labna, or Strained Yogurt

Yogurt, a Turkish word, is a semisolid cultured or fermented milk containing the bacteria *Bacillus bulgaricus* and *Streptococcus thermophilus*. These organisms present in the "starter," given warmth, will ferment whole or skimmed fresh milk overnight. *Süzme yoğurt* is the Turkish word for *labna*, the Arabic word for strained yogurt. To make your own, pour yogurt into a linen towel or several layers of cheesecloth, tie off, and hang from a kitchen sink faucet to drain overnight. A quart of yogurt will make between 2 and 3 cups of *labna*, depending on the original content of the yogurt and how long you drain it.

1. In a mortar, pound the salt and garlic together until mushy.

2. In a small bowl, blend the mushy garlic with the yogurt, *labna*, cayenne, and dill. Drizzle with a small amount of olive oil and serve with scallions and good French bread.

Makes 4 servings

Smooth Feta Cheese Dip with Spices

This Turkish recipe called beyaz peynir ezmesi *is adapted from Özcan Ozan, chef-owner of the Sultan's Kitchen in Boston. This kind of spicy feta cheese dip is also popular in Greece, where* htipiti me piperia *is made with fresh chiles and feta cheese blended smooth. Please see Sources (page 496) for suggestions on where to find Aleppo pepper.*

1 pound Greek, Bulgarian, or Turkish feta cheese
4 large garlic cloves, finely chopped
2 teaspoons hot or sweet Hungarian paprika
2 teaspoons red Aleppo pepper
3 tablespoons extra-virgin olive oil
2 teaspoons dried mint
2 medium-size ripe tomatoes, sliced
Imported green and black olives for garnish

1. Break the feta cheese into chunks and soak in warm water for 30 minutes, changing the water every 5 to 10 minutes. This will reduce the saltiness of the final preparation. Drain the cheese and crumble further.

2. Place the feta cheese, garlic, paprika, red Aleppo pepper, and olive oil in a food processor and process until smooth. Transfer to a shallow

bowl, cover, and refrigerate for at least 20 minutes.

3. Serve the cheese at room temperature, drizzled with olive oil, sprinkled with the dried mint, and garnished with the sliced tomatoes and olives. Spread on some flatbread to eat.

Makes 6 servings

Smooth Walnut and Feta Cheese Dip

This Turkish dip called cevizli beyaz peynir *is ideally served as a meze with crisp toasted pieces of pita bread.*

½ pound imported feta cheese
2 tablespoons extra-virgin olive oil
¼ cup whole milk
1 cup walnut halves or pieces
¼ cup heavy cream
⅛ teaspoon cayenne pepper
Salt to taste
1 teaspoon Hungarian paprika

1. Soak the cheese in water to cover for 24 hours, changing the water one time, to remove salt. Drain and break into chunks.

2. Put 1 tablespoon of the olive oil and 3 tablespoons of the milk in a blender with one-third of the cheese and ⅓ cup of the walnuts and process for 10 seconds. Scrape down the sides and blend again. Add the remaining 1 tablespoon oil, a little more of the milk, half the remaining cheese, and ⅓ cup of the walnuts and process again for a few seconds, scraping down the sides if necessary. Add the remaining milk,

History of Tapenade

Although capers are native to the Mediterranean, it is likely they were brought to Provence from Crete by the Phocaeans, Greeks from Asia Minor who settled near Marseilles in the sixth century B.C. The caper plant was known as *tapeneï* in Provençal, and the flower buds, the part of the caper used for culinary purposes, were the *tapeno*, which were preserved in amphoras filled with olive oil since vinegar was not used at that time. The capers became mushed together in the amphoras to form a kind of pâté of crushed *tapeno*, the ancestor of the modern tapenade. This is why it is today known by the word for "caper" rather than "olives," which is actually, in volume, the greater constituent ingredient. In the second century A.D., vinegar came to be used more in preserving and so too garlic, the great universal medication in the medieval period when the Greek physician Galen's medical theories were prevalent.

⅓ cup walnuts, and cheese and the heavy cream and cayenne; season with salt, and process until a smooth paste.

3. Refrigerate 1 hour before serving. Transfer to a plate and spread the dip around. Sprinkle the top with the paprika and serve.

Makes about 2 cups

Tapenade

A tapenade is a seasoned Provençal condiment made of mashed black olives, capers, salted anchovy, preserved tuna, and olive oil. Traditionally, it has only been used for spreading on bread as a snack or appetizer or as an accompaniment to raw vegetables. A simpler version of tapenade is known in Italy as caviale di olive, *or olive caviar. The word* tapenade *derives from the Provençal word* tapéno, *meaning "capers."*

Keep the tapenade stored in the refrigerator covered by an ⅛-inch-deep layer of olive oil to preserve it, where it will keep for several months.

14 ounces oil-cured black olives, drained and pitted

¼ pound salted anchovy fillets (about 12 whole anchovies, 24 fillets), rinsed

One 3-ounce can imported tuna in olive oil

½ cup salted capers (about 2 ounces), rinsed

An Apéritif with Tapenade

A typical hors d'oeuvre enjoyed in Provence is a dab of tapenade spread on a square of toasted bread and enjoyed with a small glass of Pernod.

1 garlic clove, peeled

1 teaspoon prepared mustard

1 tablespoon cognac

⅛ teaspoon dried thyme

⅛ teaspoon dried summer savory

⅛ teaspoon freshly ground coriander seeds

1 loaf French bread, cut into slices, toasted, and rubbed with a cut garlic clove on one side

6 to 8 tablespoons extra-virgin olive oil

Place all the ingredients except the bread in a food processor with 6 tablespoons of the olive oil and process until smooth. Taste and add more olive oil if necessary. Do not add salt because all the ingredients are salty enough. Serve with the garlic-rubbed toasts.

Makes about 3 cups; 12 servings

Muḥammara

Arabs will reflexively tell you that the famous muḥammara *comes from Aleppo in Syria. This blend of walnuts, red bell peppers, pomegranate molasses, and bread used as a dip or a spread is indeed from Aleppo, but one can find it toward the north and east, too, especially in southeastern Turkey and toward the Caucasus. Some cooks add onions to theirs. I collected this recipe the last time I was in Aleppo and I like to serve it with warm Arabic bread or as an accompaniment to grilled steaks, grilled fish, grilled kebabs, or just dipped into with Arabic bread. The red Aleppo pepper called for can usually be found in Middle Eastern markets. In Turkey, they call it* kırmızı biber. *It can be ordered off the Internet, too (see Sources, page 496).*

¼ pound walnuts

2½ tablespoons tomato paste

¾ cup fresh bread crumbs (from about 1 thick slice French or Italian bread, crust removed)

3 tablespoons extra-virgin olive oil

1½ tablespoons pomegranate molasses

1 teaspoon coarsely ground red Aleppo pepper

2 red bell peppers, roasted (page 415), peeled, seeded, cut into strips, and set in a colander to drain for 15 minutes

1 teaspoon freshly ground cumin seeds

1 teaspoon sugar

Place all the ingredients in a blender and process into a paste, stopping the blender and scraping it down when necessary. Refrigerate, but serve at room temperature. It will keep, refrigerated, for up to 2 weeks.

Makes 2 cups

Tahini

In Middle Eastern cooking, tahini, a sesame seed paste, is an essential ingredient and must be in your pantry. It is used for the making of hummus and other dishes. Tahini, which is sold in jars like peanut butter, can always be found in Middle Eastern markets and in many supermarkets. The paste of sesame seeds usually will separate from its oil as it rests in your pantry so you need to give the thick paste a few stirs to mix the oil and seed together again.

Baba Ghannouj

This famous eggplant and tahini puree is a dip obligatory on every meze table in the Middle East. Along with hummus, baba ghannouj *is probably one of the best-known Arab preparations in America. The key to making* baba ghannouj *is getting the right proportion of tahini to lemon juice and of the tahini-lemon juice mix to eggplant; you don't want to overpower the eggplant, as sometimes happens. You can make your* baba ghannouj *even more distinctive by grilling the scored eggplants so they take on a smoky taste from the charcoal fire. Serve with warmed Arabic pita bread, cut into wedges.*

4 medium-size eggplants (about 4 pounds)
9 tablespoons fresh lemon juice
½ cup tahini (sesame seed paste; page 59), stirred if oil has separated out
4 large garlic cloves, peeled
1¾ teaspoons salt

Garnishes
Extra-virgin olive oil
2 tablespoons finely chopped fresh parsley leaves
Imported black olives
Pomegranate seeds (optional)

1. Puncture or score the eggplants all over with a fork or knife. Preheat a gas grill on high for 20 minutes or prepare a charcoal grill and grill the eggplant whole until the skins are black and blistered, about 40 minutes. Or preheat the oven to 425°F and roast in a pan for 40 to 45 minutes. (Some Arab cooks blister the eggplants over a gas burner flame, but I have always found

---

Serving Baba Ghannouj

Baba ghannouj shouldn't really be thought of as a dip. It's more of a scoop. Traditionally it is served on a platter, not in a bowl. The eggplant is spread, not too deeply, on a large platter and then diners pick up bite-size portions by scooping with a piece of Arabic flatbread.

---

that way messy, although it may be quicker.) Carefully remove the skins and spoon out the soft pulp just as soon as you can handle the eggplant. Puree the pulp in a food processor, then squeeze or drain out some of the bitter liquid from the eggplant by letting it sit in a strainer over a bowl or the sink for an hour.

2. In a small bowl, slowly mix the lemon juice and tahini. Pound the garlic and salt together in a mortar until it is a paste, then stir into the tahini mixture. Stir this into the eggplant puree. Taste and add water to thin—*never* thin with more lemon juice.

3. Pour the mixture onto a serving platter and garnish with a drizzle of olive oil, the parsley, some black olives, and pomegranate seeds, if using.

Makes 6 to 8 servings

The Monk's Salad

This Lebanese meze is called bādhinjān al-rahab, *the monk's salad, a dish obviously popular with and derived from the Christian com-*

munity. It can be thought of as a tahini-less baba ghannouj *and as a result is even lighter in taste. This dish is called a salad because that's how all vegetable dishes served at room temperature are thought of in Lebanon.*

4 eggplants (about 4 pounds), each slit down the middle

3 large garlic cloves, peeled

2 teaspoons salt

¼ cup fresh lemon juice

1 green bell pepper, peeled, seeded, and sliced into half rings, or 4 scallions, chopped

1 medium-size ripe but firm tomato, seeded and chopped

2 tablespoons finely chopped fresh parsley leaves

Seeds from ¼ pomegranate

½ teaspoon red pepper flakes (optional)

2 to 3 tablespoons extra-virgin olive oil, to your taste

3 large loaves Arabic flatbread (pita bread), warmed and cut up

1. Preheat the oven to 425°F. Place the eggplants on a baking sheet and bake until the skin blisters black, about 45 minutes. Remove from the oven and, when cool enough to handle, scrape out the pulp into a strainer and leave to drain for 30 minutes.

2. In a mortar, mash the garlic with the salt until mushy.

3. In a large bowl, mix the garlic and eggplant pulp together, beating it with a fork. Add the lemon juice and mix it in well. Spread the eggplant mixture on a round serving platter and garnish the perimeter and top with the pepper

or scallions, tomato, and parsley. Sprinkle the pomegranate seeds and red pepper flakes, if using, on top, then drizzle with olive oil and serve with pita bread.

Makes 8 servings

 ## Eggplant Puree in the Greek Style

This Greek version of the Middle Eastern baba ghannouj *is also served as a meze and called* melitzanes salata *(or* melitzata salata*), or eggplant salad. It is served at room temperature*

> ### Pita Bread
>
> Pita bread, also known as Arabic bread, Syrian bread, Arab flatbread, pocket bread, or just flatbread, is a highly perishable product, meaning it dries out in about an hour. Don't just reach and buy a package of pita bread; feel and squeeze it first. If it doesn't feel soft, it's already going stale and you can forget it. I find that most pita bread sold in supermarkets arrives stale. I don't know why this is, but as a result I only buy pita bread at Middle Eastern or Greek markets that I shop at only once I've asked what time their bread guy delivers. Buy as much pita bread as you need and freeze it as soon as you get home. When serving pita bread, always serve it slightly warm and preferably put it back into its plastic bag. Never let pita bread sit out, otherwise it will go stale quickly.

A Lunch on Santorini

A blazing midday sun was shielded by a vast blue awning at the Restaurant Neptune in the little village of Oia on Santorini in the Cyclades. We were tired and staring at the startling blue sea below our perch in this whitewashed terrace village was mesmerizing. We were hungry, too, and knew we would be in good hands with Antonis Karvounis, who is the chef and owner and committed to real Greek food. It all looks like a Greek island on Santorini, except for the Greeks. We were in Santorini for one day and outside of the waiters, the bus driver, and the men with donkeys for the tourists, we neither met nor saw any Greeks—not even in the shops. Santorini is totally given over to tourists. But we ate well, and nontouristically, that afternoon, having a variety of meze. We had *faba santorini*, the famous yellow fava beans of Santorini that are pureed with a slight taste of split green pea, drizzled with olive oil, and sprinkled with some chopped red onions. Our Eggplant Puree in the Greek Style (page 61) was a little thicker than Baba Ghannouj (page 60) and sprinkled with sesame seeds. We also enjoyed Grilled Marinated Octopus (page 440) and that familiar but-good-every-time Spanakopita (page 268), but made with puff pastry, not phyllo. Being tourists, we drank beer (although Greeks do drink beer, even though we tourists love to think of them as drinking ouzo and throwing plates).

with pieces of warm pita bread. This preparation can be very personalized, as some cooks blend in other ingredients, such as paprika or mustard or dried wild marjoram. In Epirus, in northwestern Greece where many almond trees grow, cooks like to add ground almonds and sliced hard-boiled eggs to the salad. This meze is also known in Yugoslavia as ajvar.

4 pounds eggplant
Salt
1 large onion, cut up
2 medium-size ripe tomatoes, peeled and seeded, 1 cut up and 1 cut into eighths

4 large garlic cloves, chopped
Two 1½-inch-thick slices fresh Italian or French bread, ground to coarse crumbs in a food processor
1 tablespoon finely chopped fresh mint leaves
1 tablespoon finely chopped fresh wild marjoram (*rigani*), marjoram, or oregano leaves
2 tablespoons finely chopped fresh parsley leaves
Freshly ground black pepper to taste
½ cup plus 2 tablespoons extra-virgin olive oil
3 tablespoons white wine vinegar
1 tablespoon fresh lemon juice
1 green bell pepper, seeded and cut into rings
2 teaspoons sesame seeds

1. Preheat the oven to 425°F. Place the eggplant on a baking sheet and bake until blistering black on its skin, 40 to 45 minutes. Remove from the oven and let cool. Once the eggplant is cool enough to handle, remove all its flesh from the skin, transfer to a colander, salt, and let drain for 30 minutes. Place the drained eggplant in a food processor; add the onion, cut-up tomato, garlic, bread crumbs, mint, marjoram, and parsley and process until smooth, doing this in 2 batches if necessary. Season with salt and pepper. With the machine running, slowly pour in the olive oil, vinegar, and lemon juice through the feed tube, processing until thickened.

2. Refrigerate for 2 hours before serving, but serve at room temperature garnished with the tomato wedges, bell pepper rings, and sesame seeds.

Makes 10 servings

Eggplant, Yogurt, and Garlic Dip from Syria

Baṭarsh *is from the town of Homs and is a kind of* baba ghannouj *made with yogurt and garlic instead of tahini. Although I call for grilling the eggplants, you can also place them in an oven on a baking sheet and bake at 425°F until blackened, about 40 minutes. Serve with Arabic pita bread for dipping.*

3 large eggplants (about 6 pounds)
4 large garlic cloves, peeled
2 teaspoons salt
2 cups full-fat plain yogurt

4 to 6 tablespoons *labna* (optional; page 56), as needed
Fresh mint leaves for garnish
Pomegranate seeds for garnish

1. Preheat a gas grill on high for 20 minutes or prepare a hot charcoal fire. Place the eggplants on the grill until the skins are blackened and the inside pulp is very soft, about 45 minutes, turning to blacken evenly. Remove from the grill; when they are cool enough to handle, cut in half. Scrape out all the pulp and transfer to a strainer to drain the bitter juices from the pulp for at least 30 minutes.

2. Transfer the eggplant to a large bowl and beat vigorously with a fork. In a mortar, pound the garlic with 1 teaspoon of the salt until mushy. Stir the yogurt, garlic, and the remaining 1 teaspoon salt into the eggplant. Continue beating with a fork for 1 minute. (If you use a food processor in this step, make sure you use only short bursts so the eggplant doesn't turn into a puree.) Check the seasoning and add a little *labna* if your yogurt is too thin. Transfer to a serving platter. Garnish with fresh mint leaves and pomegranate seeds.

Makes 8 servings

Anatolian Creamy Eggplant and Almond Salad

This Turkish salad served as a meze is called nazuktan *and is typical in central Anatolia. It is made in a number of different ways. Some cooks stir in pomegranate molasses, a taste I like in this recipe. It can be found in Middle Eastern markets.*

1½ pounds eggplant

½ cup blanched whole almonds

¼ cup *labna* (strained yogurt; page 56)

1 tablespoon extra-virgin olive oil

2 large garlic cloves, finely chopped

Juice from ½ lemon

2 teaspoons pomegranate molasses

Salt to taste

3 tablespoons finely chopped fresh mint leaves

1. Preheat the oven to 425°F. Place the eggplant in a baking dish with a little water or on a rack and roast until the skin blisters black, 45 to 50 minutes. Remove from the oven and, when cool enough to handle, peel off the skin and stem and remove as many seeds as you can.

2. While the eggplant is roasting, place the almonds on a baking sheet and bake until golden, 6 to 7 minutes. Transfer to a plate to cool. Set aside 6 whole almonds and grind the rest coarsely in a food processor.

3. Chop the eggplant and place in a colander to drain for 20 minutes. Transfer the eggplant to a large bowl and stir in the strained yogurt, chopped almonds, olive oil, garlic, lemon juice, and pomegranate molasses, and season with salt.

4. Transfer to a serving platter, sprinkle with the mint, and garnish with the whole almonds.

Makes 4 to 6 servings

Eggplant, Yogurt, and Walnut Salad-Dip from Turkey

This meze, which resembles baba ghannouj, *is called* yoğurtlu patlıcan salatası *in Turkish,*

indicating that the yogurt and eggplant are thought to be the primary ingredients and that it is a salad. We can think of it as a salad-dip. Serve with any of the garnishes suggested, but you can also eat it with pieces of pita bread, scallions, or romaine lettuce leaves.

1 large eggplant (about 1½ pounds)

2 green bell peppers

2 small hot green chiles

Juice of ½ lemon

¼ cup ground walnuts

½ cup plus 2 tablespoons full-fat plain cow's milk yogurt

A Turkish Menu

A Turkish *restoran* is a step up from a *lokanta* (the Turkish version of a Greek *taverna*). There you will find drinks served and that means you'll find *mezeler* (the Turkish plural of *meze*) because one always has food with drinks. The range of meze can be quite wide and is always delicious because Turkish cooks use only the freshest local and seasonal ingredients, even in tourist areas. Under the most comprehensive menu, and not all restaurants are this thorough, *mezeler* will be the first item, under which you will find subcategories such as *soğuklar*, cold meze; *zetinyağlı*, foods cooked in lots of olive oil; *dolmalar*, stuffed vegetables; *sarmalar*, stuffed leaves; *salatalar*, salads; as well as *ördövr*, hors d'oeuvre; and *başlangıçlar*, starters.

2 tablespoons extra-virgin olive oil

3 large garlic cloves, peeled

1 teaspoon salt, and more to taste

1 tablespoon white wine vinegar

Tomato slices for garnish

Imported black olives for garnish

Hot Hungarian paprika or Turkish red pepper
for garnish

1. Preheat the oven to 425°F. Place the eggplant, bell peppers, and chiles in a baking dish with a little water and roast until the skins blister black on all, about 25 minutes for the small chiles and 40 minutes for the eggplant and bell peppers. Remove from the oven and, when cool enough to handle, peel off the skin from all, scraping with a knife if you have to. Remove the stem and seeds from the peppers. Put the eggplant flesh in a strainer, pour the lemon juice on top, and leave for 20 minutes to drain. Squeeze out any excess moisture from the eggplant.

2. Place the eggplant in a medium-size bowl and mash with a fork. Stir in the walnuts and blend well. Stir in the yogurt and olive oil and blend again. Mash the garlic in a mortar with the salt until mushy, then add the roasted peppers and mash them into a paste. Stir this mixture into the eggplant, stir in the vinegar, and blend. Place in the refrigerator and serve cold by spreading it on a large platter and placing the tomatoes around the edge, then the olives closer to the center, and finally sprinkling the paprika or red pepper over everything.

Makes 6 servings

Eggplant Compote of the Tunisian Jews

Ajlūk al-bādhinjān is said to be typical of the Tunisian Jews and is adapted from a recipe of Edmond Zeitun's, the author of a Tunisian cookbook called 250 recettes classiques de cuisine tunisienne, *published in 1977. He tells us that in Tunisia, as in other meze-eating cultures such as in Greece, Turkey, and all of the Middle East, drinks are usually had with meze. In Tunisia non-Muslims and lapsed Muslims drink* bukha, *an eau-de-vie made from figs.*

2 cups water

2 medium-size eggplants (about 2½ pounds),
peeled and cut up

1 red bell pepper, roasted (page 184), peeled,
seeded, and cut in half

3 tablespoons fresh lemon juice

3 tablespoons extra-virgin olive oil

2 garlic cloves, mashed with ½ teaspoon salt in a
mortar until mushy

½ teaspoon Harīsa (page 468)

1 teaspoon freshly ground caraway seeds

1 teaspoon freshly ground coriander seeds

12 imported black olives

4 small loaves Arabic flatbread

1. Bring the water, lightly salted, to a boil and cook the eggplants and bell pepper until soft, about 20 minutes. Drain and squeeze the water out of them in a colander. Transfer to a medium-size bowl and mash with a fork or potato masher. Beat the puree with a fork, then stir in 2 tablespoons of the lemon juice, 2 tablespoons of the olive oil, the garlic paste, *harīsa*,

Turkish Red Pepper

In various recipes I call for Turkish red pepper. This is a ground red chile blend used in Turkish cooking. Every spice house will have a slightly different blend, but it is basically a combination of dried red chiles and dried bell peppers. In Turkey you would have to be even more specific for there are pepper blends with different pungencies, such as Maraş red pepper and Urfa red pepper, named after towns. A similar pepper mix is Aleppo pepper from Syria. These pepper mixes are coarse, not blazingly hot, aromatic, and deep red. Although you should be able to find Turkish red pepper and Aleppo red pepper at Middle Eastern markets, I find it easier to order it from a Web site, such as www. kalustyan.com, www.zingermans.com, www.turkishdeli.com/index2.html, or www.penzeys.com.

caraway, and coriander. Beat again, check the seasonings and correct, and transfer to a small serving platter.

2. Garnish the top with the remaining 1 tablespoon each olive oil and lemon juice, and the olives. Serve and eat with heated Arabic flatbread.

Note: Alternatively, you can bake the eggplants at 425°F. until their skins are crispy black and the insides soft, about 1 hour. After removing the flesh, salt lightly and let sit in a colander to drain for 30 minutes. If you roast the bell pepper at the same time, it will take about 35 minutes for the skin to blacken and get crispy.

Makes 4 to 6 servings

Pumpkin Compote in the Style of the Tunisian Jews

Winter squash from the New World entered the Mediterranean via Spain, and from there it traveled to North Africa, Italy, and Turkey more or less simultaneously in the sixteenth century. In

Tunisian Jewish Food

Given the contemporary Arab-Israeli conflict, one doesn't think of Jews living in Arab countries. But we should remember that this tragic conflict is modern and that Jews have lived in Tunisia both before the Arab conquest in the seventh century A.D. and after for twelve centuries under Muslim rule as *dhimmi*, protected people of the Book. Only after the 1967 Arab-Israeli War did a majority of Jews finally emigrate, many to Israel and to France. Today there are about 2,000 Jews in Tunisia. Although Tunisian Jewish food is similar to the cuisine of Tunisia in general, certain specialized dishes, usually made around the major Jewish holidays and guided by *kashrut*, Jewish dietary law, continue to be made, such as the compotes known as *ajlūk* (page 65, this page, and page 74).

Tunisia, winter squashes became popular vegetables in everything from couscous to this ajlūk, *a colloquial word from northern Tunisia meaning a kind of compote that is served as part of a Tunisian* ādū, *another colloquial word meaning a meze. This recipe, called* ajlūk al-qaraᶜ, *is said to be typical of Tunisian Jews and is adapted from Edmond Zeitun, the author of a Tunisian cookbook.*

1 pound pumpkin or winter squash, peeled, seeded, and cut up
3 tablespoons fresh lemon juice
3 tablespoons extra-virgin olive oil
2 garlic cloves, mashed with ½ teaspoon salt in a mortar until mushy
½ teaspoon Harīsa (page 468)
1 teaspoon freshly ground caraway seeds
1 teaspoon freshly ground coriander seeds
12 imported black olives
4 small loaves Arabic flatbread

1. Bring a medium-size saucepan of lightly salted water to a boil and cook the pumpkin or squash flesh until soft, about 12 minutes. Pass through a food mill or process until smooth in a food processor and return to the saucepan. Heat for 1 or 2 minutes to evaporate a bit of the remaining liquid.

2. Beat the pumpkin puree with a fork, then stir in 2 tablespoons of the lemon juice, 2 tablespoons of the olive oil, the garlic paste, *harīsa,* caraway, and coriander. Beat again, check the seasonings and correct, and transfer to a small serving platter. Garnish the top with the remaining 1 tablespoon each olive oil and lemon juice, and the olives. Serve and eat with heated Arab flatbread.

Makes 4 to 6 servings

Variation: Replace the pumpkin with zucchini.

Pumpkin Puree with Tahini

This recipe, called qaraᶜ bi'l-ṭaḥīna, *is popular among Lebanese, Syrians, and Palestinians, who make it as a meze. This is the pumpkin version of what is usually made with chickpeas (hummus). I think you will find it lighter and more intriguing, not to mention enjoying its extraordinarily inviting color. Tahini is sesame seed paste that can usually be found in supermarkets and certainly in Middle Eastern markets.*

5 pounds pumpkin flesh, peeled, seeded, and cubed
½ cup tahini, stirred if the oil has separated out
4 large garlic cloves, mashed in a mortar with 2 teaspoons salt until mushy
½ cup fresh lemon juice
1 to 2 tablespoons finely chopped fresh parsley leaves, to your taste
Extra-virgin olive oil
½ teaspoon freshly ground cumin seeds
Seeds from ½ pomegranate

1. Place the pumpkin cubes in a large saucepan and cover with water. Turn the heat on, bring to a gentle boil, and continue to boil until soft, about 40 minutes. Drain well and pass through a food mill. Return the pumpkin to the saucepan and cook over medium-high heat until

Impressing with Meze

I have traveled throughout the Middle East, but some of the best Arabic restaurants I've been to are in London, where there is a large Arab community. Restaurants seem to compete with each other by impressing their customers with the variety and range of meze they offer. Remember that meze are not appetizers, nor are they like tapas. Meze are little foods that one eats not before anything, although you can, but what might be the entirety of the meal. A dizzying array of meze will come out of the kitchen in a random and haphazard way, depending on what finishes cooking when and what the waiter remembers to bring. Some restaurants might offer up to fifty different meze, and given that a party of four might order eight to twelve different ones at the most, it's an agonizing decision because when you see that many meze offered, you know that the restaurant will deliver on its promise.

all the liquid is nearly evaporated, about 25 minutes. Transfer to a food processor and process until creamy. Transfer to a medium-size bowl.

2. Stir the tahini into the pumpkin and mix well. Stir in the garlic mixture and lemon juice. Mix well and transfer to a serving platter. Garnish with the parsley, a drizzle of olive oil, and the cumin. Decorate the outside edges of the platter with the pomegranate seeds and serve with Arabic flatbread to scoop up the dip.

Makes 6 servings

Hummus

This chickpea and tahini dip is always part of an Arab meze table. But it has become so popular that it is also considered a must-have dip for any party in America. The word hummus *means "chickpea" in Arabic. Tahini is a sesame seed paste that one stirs into the mashed chickpeas. If you want to make a smoother hummus, run the cooked chickpeas through a food mill or process in the food processor for a longer time. You can also make this with canned chickpeas; although very good, you will not get the full earthy taste that comes from the dried chickpeas.*

3 cups dried chickpeas (about 1½ pounds), picked over, soaked overnight in cold water to cover mixed with 1 teaspoon baking soda, and drained, or 6 cups canned chickpeas, drained, reserving the liquid

¾ cup extra-virgin olive oil

8 large garlic cloves, peeled

1 tablespoon salt, or more to taste

½ cup tahini, stirred if the oil has separated out

½ cup fresh lemon juice

Freshly ground black pepper to taste

Garnishes

¼ cup pine nuts

⅓ cup finely chopped fresh mint leaves

Whole fresh mint leaves

½ teaspoon sumac (page 427)

Seeds from ¼ pomegranate (optional)

1. Place the chickpeas in a pot of lightly salted water to cover by 2 inches. Bring the water to a boil over high heat until it foams, 5 to 10 minutes. Remove the foam with a skimmer and continue to boil, partially covered, until tender, 1 to 3 hours, depending on the age of the chickpeas, so keep checking. Add boiling water to the pot to keep the chickpeas continuously covered, if necessary. Drain and save 1½ cups of the cooking water. Return the cooked chickpeas to the same pot filled with some cold water so you can rub the skins off the chickpeas with your fingers (many of them will rise to the surface).

2. Process the drained chickpeas with ½ cup of the olive oil and 1 cup of the reserved chickpea cooking water in a food processor until creamy.

3. In a mortar, pound the garlic with 1 tablespoon salt until it is a creamy mush. In a small bowl, beat the tahini and lemon juice together slowly. If it is too thick, add water—*never* more lemon juice. Stir the tahini-and-lemon-juice mixture into the garlic and salt. Stir this mixture into the chickpea puree, adjust the salt, and season with pepper. Check the consistency; if it is too thick, like oatmeal, then add some of the remaining reserved chickpea cooking water until it is smoother, like Cream of Wheat. Check the taste and adjust the seasonings if necessary. If you do need to adjust them, the

process must be repeated—in other words, mash some more garlic with salt or mix 1 tablespoon tahini with 1 tablespoon lemon juice.

4. In a small skillet, cook the pine nuts in 1 tablespoon of the olive oil over medium heat until light brown, stirring, about 4 minutes. Remove from the heat and set aside.

5. Spoon the hummus onto a large round serving platter, not a bowl. Warm the remaining 3 tablespoons extra-virgin olive oil. Make spiral or fan-shaped furrows in the hummus and fill with the warm olive oil. Sprinkle the toasted pine nuts around. Garnish the edges with mint leaves and sprinkle the chopped mint on top. Sprinkle the sumac over and serve with warm Arabic flatbread or pita bread.

Note: Other garnishes used are whole cooked chickpeas, black olives, cayenne pepper, red Aleppo pepper, paprika, or ground cumin.

Makes 6 servings

Hummus with Olive Oil

This interesting hummus called ḥummuṣ bi'l-zayt *is made in the Syrian city of Homs. Instead of preparing it with tahini and lemon juice as is typical, you use olive oil, allspice, and a little cumin. In this recipe, I call for canned chickpeas, but you can use dried chickpeas, too— just follow the instructions in step 1 above.*

Two 15-ounce cans chickpeas, drained, reserving
  the liquid
½ cup extra-virgin olive oil
½ teaspoon freshly ground allspice berries
½ teaspoon salt
¼ teaspoon freshly ground cumin seeds

1. Place the chickpeas in a food processor and
process. With the machine running, slowly pour
the olive oil in through the feed tube and
process until thickened. If the hummus is too
thick, run the processor again and add the
reserved liquid until it has the consistency of
Cream of Wheat. Add the allspice, salt, and
cumin and process again for a few seconds.

2. Transfer to a serving platter and serve at
room temperature, garnished with the same
garnishes as in the Hummus recipe (page 69).

Makes 4 servings

Bisāra

Bisāra *is an Egyptian fava bean puree
made with abundant fresh green herbs and
spices, and eaten in the same manner as Lebanese and Palestinians would eat hummus, as
part of a meze table with Arabic pita bread.
Bisāra is flavored quite differently from hummus, with its fresh mint, coriander, and dill.
The kind of fava bean used is a dried fava bean
that has been peeled of its skin and crushed,
called* fūl madshūsh. *The best dried fava beans
for this preparation are the ones called yellow
fava, found in Middle Eastern markets in this
country.*

¾ pound skinned and crushed dried fava beans
4 medium-size onions, 2 chopped and 2
  thinly sliced
10 large garlic cloves, chopped
Leaves from 1 bunch fresh dill, chopped
Leaves from 1 bunch fresh coriander (cilantro),
  chopped
Leaves from 1 bunch fresh parsley, chopped
Leaves from 1 bunch fresh mint, chopped
1 teaspoon freshly ground cumin seeds
2 tablespoons chopped fresh *mulūkhiyya*
  (see below; optional)
1 teaspoon freshly ground coriander seeds
¼ teaspoon cayenne pepper
2 teaspoons salt, or to taste
¼ teaspoon freshly ground black pepper
5 tablespoons clarified butter or extra-virgin
  olive oil
Extra-virgin olive oil

Mulūkhiyya or Jew's Mallow

Jew's mallow (*Corchorus olitorius* L.), also
called jute or *mulūkhiyya*, and transliterated
in dozens of different ways, is a popular
mucilaginous vegetable in Egypt. The leaves
are eaten fresh or dried, usually in soups or
stews. Occasionally, farmer's markets will
have fresh Jew's mallow, which they might
sell as "okra leaf" or "meloukia." The leaves
should look crisp, full, dark green, and fresh.
Middle Eastern markets may sell frozen Jew's
mallow as well as dried. Incidentally, almost
no one knows it by the name Jew's mallow.

Bişāra and the Boys

Marsa Matruh is a dusty coastal town in the western part of Egypt near Libya, where I spent some time years ago after being befriended by a gaggle of young men whose lives circulated around the butcher shop of Khaled Abdel-Karim, who was about twenty-five years old. In the evening, we would sit on chairs outside his shop, which spilled onto the street, and chat and banter. The street was filled with life like a scene from a Naguib Mahfouz novel. The wafting smells of kebabs enticed and the frothy green mugs of freshly squeezed sugarcane juice sweetened our throats, and somebody would run down the street to bring back some fragrant Bişāra (page 70), which we would scoop up with small pieces of *khubz al-malih*, a piping hot and fresh rod of bread direct from the oven. It was the size and length of a large thin cucumber and would disappear in an instant.

8 lime or lemon wedges
Arabic flatbread

1. Place the fava beans in a large stockpot with the chopped onions, garlic, dill, fresh coriander, parsley, and mint and cover with 6 inches of water. Bring to a boil and continue to boil until the beans are tender, 1½ to 2 hours, skimming the surface of foam as it appears and replenishing the water if necessary if the beans are still hard. Drain the beans and herbs, saving at least 1 cup of the cooking water.

2. Place the beans in a food processor or blender and process until almost completely smooth, about 1 minute. Return the puree to a smaller saucepan and heat over medium heat with the cumin, *mulūkhiyya*, if using, ground coriander, cayenne, salt, and pepper until the puree tastes well blended and flavorful, 7 to 8

minutes, adding the reserved water if necessary to keep it from drying out and to achieve the same consistency as hummus.

3. Meanwhile, in a large skillet, melt the clarified butter or olive oil over medium-high heat. Add the sliced onions and coat with the fat. Continue turning the onions as they change from white to yellow to brown. Once they turn brown, 10 to 20 minutes, continue to cook until some turn dark brown, another 2 minutes. Remove the skillet from the burner and quickly transfer the onions to a paper towel-lined platter to cool and drain. Once they are cool, they will become crispy.

4. Transfer the *bişāra* to a shallow serving platter, drizzle with olive oil, and garnish with the fried onions. Serve with the lime or lemon wedges and Arabic flatbread.

Makes 8 servings

Fresh Fava Bean Puree in the Moroccan Style

In Morocco, this puree served as a meze is called rafìssa al-fūl *or* rafìssa "de fèves fraîches" *and can be served as a dip for warm or deep-fried pieces of pita bread. A* rafìs *is an interesting dish made of wheat flour, dates, honey, butter, and other ingredients with a history. We have a record of a Tunisian sheik of Qairouan (then the capital city) in the fourteenth century who once a year shared in a celebratory* rafìs *with the students of his* zawiyya, *a hospice and theological school. A recipe preserved from the fifteenth century tells us how to make* rafìs: *"take pieces of bread smaller than an olive and mix with dates and honey until it looks like it will break apart. Work the mixture for a long time with the hands not over a fire until you get a* rafìs." *But this* rafìssa *is nothing of the kind; it is a puree.*

3 pounds fresh fava beans in their pods, shelled
2 garlic cloves, mashed in a mortar with 1
  teaspoon salt until mushy
¼ cup extra-virgin olive oil
¼ teaspoon sweet paprika
½ teaspoon freshly ground cumin seeds

1. Place the fava beans in a steamer and cook until soft, about 10 minutes. Drain, then pinch off the peel and place the beans in a food processor with the garlic paste. With the machine running, pour the olive oil in through the feed tube. Stop for a moment and add the paprika and cumin. Continue running the processor until the beans are smooth.

2. Spread the puree on a flat, round platter and serve with portions of pita bread. You can garnish the platter with black olives and small pieces of chopped tomatoes.

Makes 6 servings

Brandade of Haricot Bean

The famous brandade de morue, *salt cod whipped to a cream, which is usually associated with Nîmes in southern France, is the inspiration behind this "poor man's" brandade made with beans,* la brandade de haricots. *In Marseilles, they like to sprinkle* poutarge, *that is,* bottarga, *salted and pressed dried tuna roe, on top and eat it with toast points. When I have leftovers or when I make a double recipe, I spread the bean brandade over a canapé for a nice passed appetizer at a party. Don't forget to garnish the canapé with a quarter of a black olive or a piece of walnut.*

1 cup (about ½ pound) dried haricot beans,
  picked over and rinsed
6 tablespoons extra-virgin olive oil
1¼ cups whole milk
2 tablespoons fresh lemon juice
1¼ teaspoons salt
¾ teaspoon finely ground white pepper
1 tablespoon freshly grated *bottarga* or 4 salted
  anchovy fillets (optional), rinsed and chopped

1. Place the beans in a medium-size saucepan and cover with water by 4 inches. Turn the heat to high, bring to a boil, and continue to cook at a boil until very tender, about 1 hour. Drain, saving ½ cup of the cooking liquid.

2. Transfer the beans to a food processor and process for 15 seconds. With the machine run-

Les Crudités

Although served throughout France, *les crudités*, crisp raw vegetables eaten as an hors d'oeuvre, are famous in Provence, where small farms produce a bounty of vegetables. Examples include very firm tomato slices dressed with a little olive oil, lemon, and seasoning and a sprinkle of parsley; "thinly sliced cucumbers, radishes left as God intended them and not dressed to look like water lilies," as Elizabeth David put it; raw Florence fennel bulb, celery, very young raw broad beans to be eaten *à la croque au sel*—that is, simply with salt; thin rings of red, yellow, and green bell peppers; raw carrots (*carottes râpées*), the very finely grated outer part only, dressed with a very small amount of finely chopped shallot, olive oil, lemon juice, salt, and a pinch of sugar; *céleri-rave rémoulade*, a shredded raw celeriac dressed with mayonnaise, mustard, salt, and vinegar. Some other vegetables that make great crudités are julienned broccoli stems, green beans, red cabbage wedges, cauliflower florets, slivered lettuce hearts, split scallions, and zucchini sticks. And all of these vegetables can be dipped in a variety of sauces, from a vinaigrette or romesco or taratur sauce to mayonnaise or *allioli*.

The Greeks know *crudités* as well, calling them *etima orektika*, or "ready appetizers." They may consist of ready-to-eat products such as jarred taramasalata or salamis or sliced ham. But almost always plain and stuffed olives will play a part, perhaps pickles, and sliced cucumbers, radishes, various cheeses, canned anchovies, and fresh butter and bread for making canapés.

ning, slowly pour in the olive oil and milk in a steady stream through the feed tube until the mixture is thickened. Stir in the lemon juice. The consistency should be like that of hummus. Season with the salt and white pepper. Check the consistency and add ¼ cup of cooking liquid or more if necessary to make the mixture a little thinner than hummus. Correct the seasonings. Stir in 2 teaspoons of the *bottarga* or 2 anchovy fillets, if using.

3. Transfer to a serving platter or shallow bowl

and sprinkle the top with the remaining 1 teaspoon *bottarga* or 2 anchovy fillets.

Makes 3 cups

Swiss Chard Stalk and Tahini Dip

There is such a variety of vegetable preparations served as part of a meze in the cuisines of Lebanon and Syria that the ingenuity of the cook never fails to amaze me. Called silq bi'l-ṭaḥīna, *this dip is a wonderful way to use up those thick Swiss chard stems, which many people discard. You can use white or red Swiss chard stalks, or both, if you want to fool around with the color. Serve with pieces of warm Arabic pita bread.*

1 pound Swiss chard stalks (save the leaves for another preparation)

1 teaspoon salt

6 garlic cloves, peeled

½ cup tahini, stirred if the oil has separated out

½ cup fresh lemon juice

Extra-virgin olive oil

¼ cup pine nuts, toasted in 1 tablespoon olive oil in a small skillet over medium heat until golden, 1 to 2 minutes

1 tablespoon finely chopped fresh mint leaves

1. Place the Swiss chard in a pot of boiling water to cover or steam until soft, about 20 minutes. Drain well and chop. In a mortar, mash the salt and garlic together until a paste.

2. Place the chard in a food processor and process until smooth. Add the tahini and garlic paste and process until incorporated. Pour the lemon juice into the feed tube as the processor is running until absorbed. Correct the seasoning if necessary.

3. Transfer the dip to a serving bowl or platter, spreading it out with the back of a spoon, and make furrows with the flat side of a knife in a fan shape. Drizzle with a little olive oil and garnish with the fried pine nuts and mint.

Makes 6 servings

Carrot Compote of the Tunisian Jews

This recipe, called ajlūk al-jazar, *is said to be typical of Tunisian Jews and is adapted from one of Edmond Zeitun's, the author of a Tunisian cookbook. It is a delightful meze with lettuce leaves or warm Arabic bread. Don't forget the olives, not only for taste but also for appearance.*

2 cups water

6 large carrots, cut up

1 potato (about ½ pound), peeled and quartered

3 tablespoons fresh lemon juice

3 tablespoons extra-virgin olive oil

2 garlic cloves, mashed with ½ teaspoon salt in a mortar until mushy

½ teaspoon Harīsa (page 468)

1 teaspoon freshly ground caraway seeds

1 teaspoon freshly ground coriander seeds

12 imported black olives

4 small loaves Arabic flatbread

1. Bring the water to a boil and cook the carrots and potato until soft, about 25 minutes. Drain in a colander and press out any excess water. Transfer to a medium-size bowl and mash with a fork. Beat the puree with a fork, then stir in 2 tablespoons of the lemon juice, 2 tablespoons of the olive oil, the garlic paste, *harīsa,* caraway, and coriander. Beat again, check the seasonings and correct, and transfer to a small serving platter.

2. Garnish the top with the remaining 1 tablespoon each olive oil and lemon juice, and the olives. Serve in small bowls and eat with heated Arab flatbread.

Makes 4 to 6 servings

What Is Brandade?

Brandade is a mashed salt cod blended with olive oil and a little garlic until it is a smooth cream. The French word *brandade* derives from the Provençal *brandado*, which in turn comes from the past participle of *brandar*, "to shake" or "stir," in Old Provençal, which has its ultimate derivation from the word *brand*, a word of Germanic origin meaning "sword." The origin of *brandade* is most likely related to the bipolar trade of salt from nearby Aigues-Mortes with the cod being caught off Iceland, Greenland, and Newfoundland by northern fishermen, especially those from Iceland, Norway, Scotland, England, and Brittany. The fishermen needed to have salt aboard their ships in order to preserve the freshly caught cod, a fish that is exported to and does not exist in the Mediterranean. The cooks of Nîmes, which was the major entrepôt in southern France, along with Marseilles in the eighteenth century, were likely responsible for the invention of *brandade*. Adolphe Thiers (1797–1877), the president of the Second French Republic and a noted historian, called *brandade* a "masterpiece of the human race." The Nîmois author Alphonse Daudet (1840–97) founded the club *Le Brandade*, and after receiving his last rites, wished to write an ode to *brandade* that was to be read during the annual tastings of the club.

Brandade de Morue

This preparation composed of beaten salt cod became popular in the United States during the 1990s as restaurant chefs and food writers began to explore Provence, discovering all kinds of culinary gems. Unfortunately, it is rarely made properly. Its birthplace is Nîmes, in Languedoc, so we can't say that it is Provençal, although it is known in Provence (and many consider Nîmes to be in Provence). I learned how to make it in two places: Venice and Nîmes. In Venice it is called baccalà mantecato, *or "whipped salt cod," and is as popular as it is in Languedoc and Provence. It is also known in Corsica and Catalonia. Chef Michel Kayser of the Michelin one-star Restaurant Alexander, just outside of Nîmes, taught me how to make it, too. Properly made, the salt cod is whipped and beaten until emulsified with the olive oil and other ingredients. But that is a bit difficult to do, although a food processor makes the task much easier than it used to be with only the mortar and pestle. It is important that the soaked cod be thoroughly drained before beating.*

Leftover brandade has many wonderful uses. You can use it as a stuffing for a feuilleté de brandade nîmoise, *a vol-au-vent stuffed with brandade and a very small piece of anchovy, as I had it once at the Grill Room in Nîmes. Or you could make croquettes with some béchamel sauce and bread them, or spread* brandade *on a canapé, or stuff it into a crepe with some Gruyère cheese on top and bake it* au gratin. *If you have a half-pound of* brandade *left, you can make a* soufflé de brandade, *by mixing the* brandade *with ¾ cup hot milk, 2 teaspoons cornstarch, 1 tablespoon butter, 3 egg yolks, 4 stiffly beaten egg whites, and a pinch of salt.*

1 pound boneless salt cod, soaked in cold
   water to cover for 3 days, changing the water
   twice a day
About 1 cup extra-virgin olive oil or sunflower
   seed oil
¾ cup plus 2 tablespoons milk
1 teaspoon salt
1 garlic clove, peeled
Freshly ground black pepper to taste
1 tablespoon very finely chopped parsley leaves

1. Place the salt cod in a medium-size saucepan and cover with cold water. Bring to just below a boil slowly over medium heat, never letting the water come to a boil, then turn off the heat and leave for 20 minutes. Drain very well. This is very important. Pat dry with paper towels.

2. Making sure it is dry, place the salt cod in a food processor. Mix the olive oil and milk. With the machine running, slowly pour in the milk and olive oil through the feed tube. Stop every once in a while and look at the consistency of the salt cod. It should not be stringy; if it is, continue processing. When finished, it should look like whipped cream and be a light,

fluffy white foam. If there are any solid pieces of salt cod, continue processing.

3. Put the salt and garlic in a mortar and pound together with a pestle until the garlic is completely mashed. Stir the garlic into the salt cod and, once the mixture is velvety, season with black pepper, and stir in the parsley.

4. The basic way to serve *brandade* is to spread it on a shallow plate and eat it by spreading small amounts on toast points. For other possibilities, see the note above.

Makes 6 cups

Kibbe Nayya

One of my favorite meze is Kibbe nayya (kubba nā'), *the Lebanese version of steak tartare. It is hard to find this dish prepared properly because it can only be made with the highest quality prime lamb tenderloin and the ratio between the meat and the bulgur must be perfect. It is said that it is a specialty in Zahle in Lebanon. In southern Lebanon, fresh basil and a little marjoram are pounded into the onions first. To make this properly, ask the butcher for lamb tenderloin, then remove any and all the fat and sinews—that's important—and grind the meat in a food processor. As with the principal underlying steak tartare, only the tenderloin can be used for this dish. The bulgur should expand when it absorbs the water but still be firm, yet soft enough to eat. It should not lose its color or become mushy.*

¼ cup raw fine bulgur (no. 1)
1 small onion, peeled

Raw Sea Urchin

I first ate raw sea urchins in Mondello, a suburban summer resort outside of Palermo in Sicily, and quite fell in love with them. Years later I was able to get some of my own sea urchins skin diving off of Marzamemi on Sicily's extreme southeast coast. We had to handle them very carefully because we were not prepared and had to use our bare hands, which is not a smart idea. Undaunted, we got a few and cracked them in half using a Swiss army knife with a not-long-enough blade. But it was all worth it. The *ricci di mare*, as they are known in Italian, are a true delicacy in Sicily. Many Sicilian gourmets will tell you about the aphrodisical properties of sea urchins. The meat of a sea urchin is considered by connoisseurs to be some of the finest shellfish eating. One sea urchin per person may be enough; it depends on how much you like them.

Hold the sea urchin with one hand, using a heavy glove or kitchen towel to protect your hand. Drive a chef's knife into the hard shell, cutting horizontally, and split the shell in half. There is very little meat inside, but it is heavenly. Serve with only a squirt of lemon juice.

1 pound boneless lamb tenderloin, trimmed of all fat and silverskin and cubed

1 teaspoon salt

Freshly ground black pepper to taste

1½ tablespoons freshly ground allspice berries

½ teaspoon freshly grated nutmeg

⅛ teaspoon ground cinnamon

¼ teaspoon cayenne pepper

1 teaspoon freshly ground cumin seeds

¼ cup ice water

Extra-virgin olive oil

3 tablespoons pine nuts, toasted in 1 tablespoon olive oil in a small skillet over medium heat until golden, 1 to 2 minutes

1 medium-size onion, cut into wedges

4 scallions

Arabic flatbread (pita bread), warmed

1. Cover a strainer with cheesecloth and place the bulgur on top. Place the strainer in a pot filled with cold water and soak the bulgur for 10 minutes. Pull up the sides of the cheesecloth, encasing the bulgur, and squeeze out all the water. Place in a large bowl.

2. Place the onion in the food processor and run until creamy, scraping down the sides when necessary. Add the lamb and run until it is pasty-creamy. In a small bowl, mix the salt, black pepper, allspice, nutmeg, cinnamon, cayenne, and cumin.

3. In a large bowl, mix the drained bulgur, lamb, and 1½ tablespoons of the spice mix, saving the rest for another purpose. Transfer this mixture to the food processor, in batches if necessary, and process until smooth and pasty.

Add the ice water as the processor is running to make it smooth. The mixing is important. The kibbe should glaze smoothly when spread with a knife blade, without being too soft; then it is ready to be served.

4. Spread the mixture on a serving platter, making fan-shaped furrows in it with the edge of a knife. Drizzle olive over it and garnish the edges and top attractively with the toasted pine nuts and the onion wedges. Serve with the scallions and flat bread.

Makes 8 servings

Pâté of the Two Sicilies

This mushroom pâté from Naples is adapted from one that was attributed to F. Santasilia di Torpino, a local cook, and is typical of the kind of dish created in the 1800s by the monzù, *the French-trained or influenced chefs of aristocratic families in Naples or Sicily. I have adapted it from the one found in Jeanne Caròla Francesconi's* La cucina napoletana *as* pâté delle due Sicilie. *The Kingdom of the Two Sicilies was a short-lived merger of the kingdoms of Sicily and of Naples under the House of Bourbon-Sicily in 1816. By 1861 the kingdom had ceased to exist once Italy was united.*

2½ tablespoons unsalted butter
1 pound button mushrooms, sliced
1 teaspoon dried *herbes de Provence*
Salt to taste
½ cup dry Marsala wine
1 tablespoon salted Pantelleria capers, rinsed
6 black Gaeta olives, pitted and chopped

⅔ cup heavy cream
Toast points

1. In a large skillet, melt the butter over low heat, then cook the mushrooms with the *herbes de Provence* and a little salt. Once the mushrooms' liquid has been released and then almost evaporated, about 30 minutes, increase the heat to medium, add the Marsala, and cook until it evaporates, 7 to 8 minutes, stirring occasionally. Add the capers and olives and cook 3 to 5 minutes.

2. Place the mixture in a food processor and process in bursts until it looks like a pâté. Return to the skillet and add the cream. Continue to cook over medium heat until thick, 4 to 5 minutes. Transfer to a small terrine, packing it in, and let cool. Refrigerate for at least 2 hours.

3. Serve with toast points.

Makes 8 servings

Mushroom and Eggplant Terrine from Provence

This terrine aux champignons *is elegant but has a rustic taste. It is best served in small slices with a little fresh creamery butter and crusty French bread.*

¾ pound eggplant, peeled and diced
Salt
10 large eggs
1 large garlic, finely chopped
½ teaspoon dried *herbes de Provence*
1 teaspoon freshly ground white pepper
1 cup heavy cream, whipped until stiff peaks form

Carpaccio

Carpaccio, a famous antipasto from Venice, is a restaurant invention and almost exclusively made in restaurants and is not traditionally made in the home. The recipe was invented in 1950 by the Venetian restaurateur and hotelier Giuseppe Cipriani for a client who was under doctor's orders to eat a particular diet. The name was suggested to him by an exhibition then being shown in Venice of the works of the Venetian artist Carpaccio, who painted many famous cityscapes and was known for his deep reds. The dish is made with very thinly cut slices of beef or filet mignons and is dressed with a sauce made from mayonnaise, cream, mustard, Worcestershire sauce, Tabasco sauce, and salt. If you decide to give it a try, remember that the meat needs to be a whole piece of tenderloin that is semi-frozen as you shave it into thin slices.

18 ounces button mushrooms, brushed clean and coarsely chopped
¾ cup dried porcini mushrooms (about ½ ounce), soaked in tepid water 10 minutes, drained, rinsed, and chopped
2 tablespoons extra-virgin olive oil
Juice from ½ lemon

1. Lay the eggplant pieces on some paper towels and sprinkle with salt. Leave them to drain of their bitter juices for 30 minutes, then pat dry with paper towels. Place the eggplant in a food processor and process until smooth. Transfer the eggplant to a large bowl and mix with the eggs, garlic, *herbes de Provence*, 2 teaspoons salt, and the white pepper. Stir in the whipped cream.

2. Place the button and rehydrated mushrooms in a large, hot, dry skillet without any fat or water over medium heat and let the mushrooms sweat their liquid, about 15 minutes. When they are dry, add 1 tablespoon of the olive oil and cook until golden, 3 to 5 minutes, stirring a few times. Drain if necessary and set aside.

3. Preheat the oven to 375°F. Once the mushrooms are cool, stir into the eggs with the remaining 1 tablespoon olive oil and the lemon juice. Butter a round 8-inch terrine that is 3½ inches deep and pour in the egg mixture. Place the terrine in a bain-marie or baking casserole and fill with water to go halfway up the sides of the terrine. Place in the oven and bake until brown and a skewer inserted in the center comes out clean, about 1¼ hours. Remove from the oven and let cool for 1 hour.

4. Place a round plate on top of the terrine and flip it over to unmold. Serve in thin slices.

Makes 14 servings

Blackbird Pâté from Corsica

One of the most celebrated charcuteries found in Corsica is *pasticciu di meruli*, a blackbird pâté served as an appetizer. If you could find blackbirds, you could make this, although quail meat might be fine, too. Freshly killed blackbirds are plucked, cleaned, and singed before being left to hang in cold storage for three days. The meat of the birds is removed, coarsely chopped, and mixed with an equal amount of pork tenderloin, pork fat, and pork liver. The meat is laid in a terrine, covered with a Corsican eau-de-vie, juniper berries, salt, and pepper, and allowed to rest for 24 hours in the refrigerator. Then the mixture is removed from the refrigerator, the juniper berries are disposed of, and the mixture is processed in a food processor. The bottom of the terrine is covered with pork lard and the mixture placed on top, and on top of that is placed a top crust to make the terrine *en croûte*. Then it gets cooked for 2¹/₂ hours in a bain-marie. It is served with slices of bread, the pâté spread over them and accompanied by a glass of eau-de-vie.

Terrine of Duck and Rabbit Livers

This terrine, called terrine de foies de canard et lapin, *is inspired by the great number of terrines I've had in the Languedoc. I doubt you'll be able to just walk into the supermarket and pick up duck and rabbit livers, so what I do is save the livers over time as I buy and cook rabbits and ducks, then throw them into a freezer bag. It's worth it.*

12 ounces duck livers

6 ounces rabbit livers

2 cups milk

¾ pound duck breast, with skin and fat, sliced into strips

18 ounces pork fatback

Grated zest from ½ orange

2½ teaspoons paprika

1 teaspoon canned or bottled green peppercorns, drained

⅛ teaspoon ground ginger

⅛ teaspoon freshly ground allspice berries

½ teaspoon dried thyme

½ teaspoon finely chopped fresh rosemary

1 small bay leaf, finely crumbled

4½ teaspoons Armagnac

14 slices French baguette, crusts removed

½ cup finely chopped shallots

1 garlic clove, crushed

1 large egg white

¼ cup light cream

2¼ teaspoons fine salt

Leaves from 1 sprig fresh tarragon

Leaves from 1 sprig fresh sage

Leaves from 3 sprigs fresh oregano

Leaves from 3 sprigs fresh thyme, with their flowers, if possible

1. Remove any sinews from the duck and rabbit livers. Place in a wide bowl and cover with the milk. Let soak for 2 hours in the refrigerator, then drain, discarding the milk. Slice the livers into strips.

2. Arrange the livers over the bottom of a terrine and cover with the strips of duck breast and 6 ounces of the pork fat, cut into strips. Sprinkle evenly with the orange zest, paprika, green peppercorns, ginger, allspice, thyme, rosemary, bay leaf, and Armagnac. Cover with the slices of bread and sprinkle on top of that the shallots and garlic. Pour the egg white and cream, beaten together, over the bread. Cover with plastic wrap and refrigerate overnight.

3. Place a medium-size metal mixing bowl in the freezer. Place liver mixture in a food processor and process in bursts until smooth. Transfer to the frozen metal mixing bowl and whip in the salt vigorously with a wooden spoon until the mixture is velvety.

4. Preheat the oven to 350°F. Line the bottom and sides of an appropriately sized terrine with 6 more ounces pork fat, cut into thin slices, and pour the liver mixture in. Cover the top with the remaining fat, sliced, and cover with the leaves of the sprigs of herbs. Cover and set in a deep, large baking casserole. Fill the casserole with water so it comes three-quarters of the way up the terrine. Place in the oven for 50 minutes,

---

Finocchiona

Salume is what the Italians call cold cuts, the easiest of *antipasti* to serve. *Finocchiona* is a Tuscan salami made from finely ground pork flavored with wild fennel seeds, garlic, salt, and pepper. It is aged seven months to one year before being sold. Its texture is soft and best when sliced not too thin and eaten with saltless Tuscan bread. It is 10 inches in diameter and often appears as part of the classic Tuscan antipasto platter along with Tuscan Chicken Liver Crostini (page 38), olives, other types of salami, marinated mushrooms (page 455), prosciutto, and *fett'unta*, the Tuscan name for *bruschetta*.

---

never letting the water temperature go above 175°F, which it will reach in about 35 minutes; then remove from the oven and let cool completely in the water bath.

5. Place a large plate over the terrine and invert quickly, holding the plate and terrine tightly. Remove the terrine and let cool further if still warm. Remove and discard the fat before serving.

Makes 8 servings

Cheesy Mouthfuls

I could live on the Saganaki (page 91) alone, that delicious Greek meze of broiled cheese. With a squirt of lemon and a glass of ouzo and, ideally, a perch overlooking an azure Ionian Sea—this has got to be what heaven is like. When it comes to serving little foods based on cheese, everyone is happy because cheese is always a winner. I prefer keeping the amount of cheese I use for appetizers on the reasonable side because cheese will fill you up and that is not always what you want. Whether it's the delightful puffs from Burgundy (page 85) or those of Parmigiano-Reggiano (page 85), they are satisfying as small bites with lots of flavor and it's not necessary to stuff yourself. One of my other favorites is Mozzarella Fritta (page 94), which I always drape some big, fat anchovies over.

Mozzarella alla Caprese

This famous antipasto is served in nearly every restaurant in the region of Campania in Italy, as well as the island of Capri, which claims it as its own, but also in nearly every Italian restaurant in America. It's all very simple and, for that reason, is difficult to pull off successfully. The secret is in the shopping: you'll need great tomatoes, great mozzarella, and fresh, fresh, fresh basil. Also, never refrigerate the tomatoes. Carmelo tomatoes are a particular cultivar that I like to use because of its sweetness; they are most likely found in a farmer's market, although it's perhaps even easier to find some seedlings and grow your own Carmelos in a pot on your balcony or in your garden.

1 pound ripe Carmelo tomatoes, peeled, if desired, and sliced
1 pound fresh buffalo milk mozzarella, sliced
Salt to taste
20 large fresh basil leaves
¼ cup extra-virgin olive oil

Arrange the tomatoes in a circle on a round serving platter, interspersed with slices of mozzarella. Salt, then arrange the basil leaves on top. Drizzle with olive oil and serve.

Makes 8 servings

Rolled Yogurt Balls

This meze, rolled balls of thick strained yogurt, is popular in Syria and Lebanon, where it is called labna daḥarīj. *The name derives from the words for strained yogurt (*labna *or* labny*)*

*and the verb to roll (*daḥarīj*). First, yogurt is strained to make* labna, *then formed into balls and preserved in oil. If you don't have a local Middle Eastern market and need to make your own* labna, *line a strainer with cheesecloth, pour the contents of a 1-quart container of whole plain cow's milk yogurt into it, rest over a deep bowl in the refrigerator, and leave to drain for 12 hours. The yogurt that remains in the strainer is the* labna. Zaᶜtar *is a thyme-based spice mix found in Middle Eastern markets, or you could easily make the mix yourself (see Note).*

¾ pound *labna* (strained yogurt; see headnote)
½ to 1 cup extra-virgin olive oil, as needed
¼ cup *zaᶜtar* (see Note below)
Toasted Arabic flatbread, broken into pieces

1. Roll the *labna* into balls a wee bit smaller than the size of golf balls. Arrange them on a plate or tray and place in the refrigerator, uncovered, overnight.

2. Once they are firm, arrange in a wide-mouthed glass jar or a small glass baking dish and cover with olive oil. Close the lid, or cover with plastic wrap, and store in the refrigerator. They will keep indefinitely as long as they are covered with olive oil.

3. When you want to serve them, sprinkle some *zaᶜtar* on a plate and roll the balls in it to coat all sides. Arrange on a small serving platter and spoon some olive oil over them. Serve with the toasted flatbread.

Note: To make *zaᶜtar*, mix 1 cup finely crumbled dried thyme, ¼ cup sesame seeds, 1 tablespoon sumac, and ½ teaspoon salt, or more to taste. Store as you would any spice.

Makes 14 balls; 8 to 10 servings

Burgundian Cheese Puffs

Les gougères are traditional hors d'oeuvre from Burgundy, but are sometimes eaten after the main course and before dessert. Some cooks claim that this pastry originates in Sens, but it is prepared in other parts of France, too. It is made with pâte à choux or ordinary cream puff pastry. The puffs can also be filled (see variation below).

1 recipe Basic Beignet Dough for Baking (page 476)
4 ounces Gruyère cheese, diced

1. Prepare the beignets through step 3 of the basic recipe, blending the Gruyère in with the nutmeg. Preheat the oven to 400°F.

2. Butter a baking sheet and drop large table-spoonfuls of the dough in rows on the sheet 1½ inches apart. Bake until golden brown, 22 to 25 minutes. Do not be tempted to peek in the oven; if you must, crack the oven door open slowly, otherwise, the puffs may collapse. They will look and seem done at 15 minutes, but they are not; continue to bake until they are firm when pressed down on top with your finger. You can serve them hot as is, or let them cool, then stuff them. Or freeze them for later use.

Makes 50 to 60 gougères

Gougères with Creamy Cheese Sauce • In a medium-size heavy saucepan, heat 2 cups milk until bubbles form around the edge, then add a slice of onion, 6 black peppercorns, and 1 bay leaf and leave it to steep off the heat for 10 minutes, covered. Make a thin béchamel sauce by melting 2 tablespoons unsalted butter in another heavy saucepan and incorporating 2 tablespoons all-purpose flour to form a white roux. Slowly whisk in the hot milk by pouring it in through a strainer, discarding the onion, bay leaf, and peppercorns. Bring to a boil and season with salt and pepper and a pinch of freshly grated nutmeg. Reduce the heat to low and simmer for 10 minutes. Stir in 2 tablespoons crème fraîche and ⅔ cup shredded Gruyère cheese. Stir until it melts and is smooth. Check the seasoning. Slice the puff pastries open, stuff with a spoonful of the sauce, and serve hot.

Parmesan Puffs

I like to serve this Italian passatempo, a small tidbit to "pass the time," while people are still standing, just as they arrive. Cook them about 5 minutes before the first guest arrives and keep them warm in the oven.

6 cups olive oil, olive pomace oil, or a mixture of olive and vegetable oil for frying
3 large egg whites, beaten until stiff peaks form
1 cup freshly grated Parmigiano-Reggiano cheese
½ teaspoon freshly ground aniseeds
Pinch of salt

1. Preheat the frying oil in a deep fryer or an 8-inch saucepan fitted with a basket insert to 375°F.

Parmesan Cheese

In my recipes I always call for Parmigiano-Reggiano cheese rather than Parmesan cheese. Only the large wheels of cheese stamped with the words "Parmigiano-Reggiano" are the real Parmesan. Parmigiano cheese was born long ago in the mist of time. We know it existed in the time of Boccaccio because he describes in the *Decameron* the imaginary land of Bengodi, a mountain of grated Parmigiano with macaroni and ravioli cooked in capon broth. Already by the fourteenth century Parmigiano was a prestigious cheese. It seems that the double designation of the cheese Parmigiano (from Parma) and Reggiano (from Reggio) can be traced back to the time of Charlemagne in the eighth century. In other countries, including the United States, Parmesan cheese has come to mean a grated cheese usually sprinkled on spaghetti, but according to the Court of Justice of the European Union, only the cheese from a specific region around Parma can be legally called Parmigiano-Reggiano. When you buy Parmesan cheese, buy the real thing because the difference in taste is significant.

2. In a medium-size bowl, mix the egg whites, cheese, aniseeds, and salt. Drop the mixture by spoonfuls into the hot oil and cook until light golden, 1½ to 2 minutes. Remove using a skimmer and drain on paper towels. Let the frying oil cool completely, strain through a porous paper filter, if necessary, and save the oil for a future use.

Makes about 12 puffs

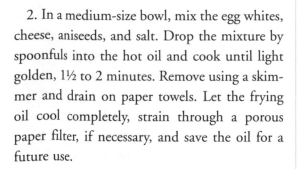

Spanish Baked Cheese Marbles

This Spanish tapa is called delicias de queso, *or cheese delights, and is made with cream cheese*

or a semi-hard cheese that grates and melts well, such as Gruyère, Gouda, Edam, or Emmentaler.

6 ounces whipped cream cheese or other soft creamy cheese
¾ cup all-purpose flour
¼ cup (½ stick) unsalted butter, at room temperature
Salt to taste
Dry bread crumbs for dredging

1. Preheat the oven to 350°F.
2. In a medium-size bowl, mix the cream cheese, flour, butter, and salt until well blended and it forms a homogenous dough. Pinch off

marble-sized pieces of dough and roll them into a ball between the palms of your hands. Dredge the cheese balls in the bread crumbs, then lay them on a greased baking sheet. They can be refrigerated at this point for several hours if necessary.

3. Bake until golden, about 20 minutes, turning once. Serve hot.

Makes 50 to 55 balls; 8 servings

Gruyère Half-Moons

These little half-moons are known as mezzalune al Gruyère *in Italian and they make a great tidbit to pass at a party.*

1¼ cups all-purpose flour
½ cup (1 stick) unsalted butter, at room
    temperature
6 ounces Gruyère cheese, shredded
Pinch of salt
1 large egg

1. Pour the flour onto a work surface or into a bowl and make a well in the center. Work the butter, cheese, salt, and egg into the flour to form a dough. Wrap the dough in waxed paper and let rest in the refrigerator for 30 minutes.

2. Preheat the oven to 400°F.

3. Remove the dough and roll it out on a flour-strewn counter with a rolling pin until ⅛ inch thick. Cut as many 2-inch disks as you can and cut each disk in half to form a half-moon. Continue to gather and roll out the remaining dough until it is all used. Butter a baking sheet, then sprinkle flour on top and shake so the

whole tray has a light dusting of flour. Place the half moons on the sheet and bake until golden on top, about 10 minutes. Serve hot or cold.

Makes 6 to 8 servings

Broiled Fresh Ricotta Cheese

This Sicilian preparation called ricotta frisca 'nfurnata *is made with fresh ricotta cheese that has been drained completely and is thick and dense like an unsalted ricotta salata. The ricotta is cut about 1½ inches thick and placed in a small baking pan, one in which it fits snugly, and baked until a beautiful golden brown.*

Four 1-inch-thick slices very well drained
    fresh ricotta cheese, preferably homemade
    (page 88)
Salt to taste

1. Preheat the oven to broil.

2. Fit the ricotta slices into a small baking pan or, preferably, 4 individual baking ramekins. Season with salt. Place under the broiler until golden and slightly blackened on top, 4 to 5 minutes. Serve immediately in their ramekins with a small spoon and some pieces of bread as an antipasto before a sit-down dinner.

Makes 4 to 8 servings

Sardinian Grilled Cheese

This antipasto is called casu cotto, *"cooked cheese." It is a bit tricky to do because you want the cheese grilled but not melting through the grilling grates, and grilling grates*

Homemade Ricotta

Ricotta is quite easy to make at home, but time-consuming. I use a mixture of cow's milk and goat's milk. You could use all cow's milk and your ricotta will be fine. The difference between homemade and commercially made is quite significant. Homemade is richer and deeper in flavor.

2 quarts whole milk (preferably raw)
2 quarts goat's milk (preferably raw)
1 quart buttermilk
1 quart rich, whole goat's or cow's milk
   yogurt

2 cups heavy cream (preferably not
   ultrapasteurized)
6 tablespoons white wine vinegar

1. Pour all the ingredients into a large stockpot and place a candy/deep-fry thermometer in so it is not touching the sides of the pot. Turn the heat to low and leave until the temperature reaches 194°F. Using a skimmer, remove the curds and transfer to a cheesecloth-lined strainer set over a pot. Place in the refrigerator and leave to drain for 2 hours.

2. Transfer to an airtight container to store. It will stay fresh for a week.

Makes 2 quarts

can be different widths on different grills. An alternative, and much easier, method is to place a greased cast-iron pan or griddle on your grilling grate and let it get very hot, about 45 minutes of preheating over a very hot fire. In any case, you will need a long-handled grill spatula and you should have the slices of bread ready to go before you do this because everything cooks very quickly. It's best to cook two pieces of cheese at a time. If you try to cook more at once, you will not be fast enough to avoid it melting and dripping through the grate. The best way to serve this antipasto is when you've got the grill going

for some other food and people are milling about and can eat as soon as you whip the grilled cheese off the grill.

1 pound young pecorino Sarde cheese or
   scamorza cheese
Extra-virgin olive oil for drizzling
20 slices crusty Italian bread

1. Preheat a gas grill for 15 minutes on high or prepare a hot charcoal fire. If you have a cast-iron griddle, lay it on the grilling grate and preheat it for 45 minutes.

2. Cut the cheese into ⅜-inch-thick slices, cutting away any outer protective layer of wax, and trim into the same size as the bread slices. Drizzle some olive oil over one side of the bread and over both sides of the cheese slices.

3. Grill the bread briefly, so it's just hot. Set the bread aside on a serving platter. Oil the spatula. Place the cheese down on the grill and, as you begin to see the sides starting to melt, in as little as 10 seconds, scrape it up with the spatula and flip it over to cook the other side, also for a few seconds. Remove from the grill and place on the slices of bread. Go ahead and serve it immediately while you continue to cook the rest. If you are cooking on a hot griddle, you will have a little more leeway.

Makes 8 servings

Sardinian Cheese

There are more than a hundred different pecorinos, which is the predominant cheese made in Sardinia. Cheese making in Sardinia reaches back into prehistoric times and for centuries the two cheeses most prominent were known as *casu cotto* or *semicotto* and *fiore sarde*. The so-called *pecorino Sarde* is usually sold as a young semi-hard cheese about six months old; it is excellent for grilling or roasting, as it becomes soft in an appetizing way.

Grilled Feta Cheese in Grape Leaves

This Turkish meze called yaprak sarması *is an interesting dish, which diners will really like. It's very simple to do and perfect to prepare before you grill something more substantial for dinner.*

1 pound imported Greek or Bulgarian feta cheese, soaked overnight in water, drained, and cut into rectangular pieces
32 grape leaves packed in brine
Six to eight 10-inch wooden skewers
Extra-virgin olive oil
1 lemon, cut into 8 wedges

1. Prepare a hot charcoal fire or preheat a gas grill on high for 15 minutes.

2. Rinse the brined grape leaves and arrange them in front of you with the underside of the leaf (the duller green side) facing upward and the stem end near you. Place the rectangle of cheese just above where the stem is and fold over once to cover the cheese. Fold the side leaf flaps over and continue rolling the leaf. Arrange two 10-inch wooden skewers parallel to each other, about ½ inch apart, and double-skewer the wrapped cheese onto them, putting 8 to 10 bundles on each set of skewers.

2. Drizzle some olive oil over the leaves and grill until the leaves get crispy black in places and the cheese seems to be melting, 5 to 10 minutes, turning once. Serve immediately with a lemon wedge.

Makes 8 to 10 servings

Feta Cheese

The cheese we all think of as Greek cheese is feta cheese, but feta cheese may have been originally Italian. The word *feta* does not exist in classical Greek; it is a New Greek word, originally *tyripheta*, or "cheese slice," the word *feta* coming from the Italian word *fette*, meaning a slice of food. Although cheeses are mentioned frequently in the writings of the ancient Greeks, it is never clear what kind of cheese they are talking about. The description of cheese making in Homer's *Odyssey* (Book 9: 278–79) sounds more like the Sicilian cheeses known as *tuma* or *canestrato* than it does a brined cheese like feta. In the anonymous fourteenth-century Venetian cookbook *Libro per cuoco*, there are two recipes that call for *formazo di Candia*, a cheese made in the then Venetian island of Crete, which may be the first feta cheese. One recipe specifically calls for the cheese to be washed, as you would feta. Greek feta cheese is a soft, white cheese made by mountain shepherds from goat's or ewe's milk, whose curd, once solidified from rennet, is placed in wooden barrels or boxes to drain and is then rubbed with salt and sold in a salted brine. In the United States, feta cheese is made from cow's milk. In Turkey, a feta-like cheese is called *beyaz peynir*.

Fried Feta Cheese and Black Olives with Oregano

Feta is a brined cheese originally from Greece, but is also made and eaten in Turkey, Bulgaria, the various Yugoslavian republics, France, Denmark, Germany, and the United States. This preparation is inspired by a meze I once had in Greece. The best feta is the rich, milky feta that is imported from Greece or Bulgaria. Domestic feta and most other feta cheeses are made from cow's milk and not the traditional sheep's milk. As a result, it is blander, but if bland is your thing, then go ahead and use it.

6 ounces imported Greek or Bulgarian feta cheese
2 tablespoons extra-virgin olive oil
12 imported black olives, pitted
1 teaspoon dried oregano
Romaine lettuce leaves or *crostini* (page 24)

1. Soak the feta cheese in cold water for 2 hours to remove some of the salt. Drain and dry by patting with paper towels. Break the cheese into bite-size pieces.

2. In a medium-size skillet, heat the olive oil over medium heat, then add the broken-up pieces of feta cheese, olives, and oregano. Cook until the feta cheese starts to melt, then remove the skillet from the heat, transfer its contents to a serving platter, and serve immediately, picking up pieces of cheese with the lettuce leaves as a wrapper or placing them atop *crostini*.

Makes 4 servings

• ❀ •

Serving Cheese for Starters

Everyone loves cheese, but as an appetizer or starter you need to be careful not to over-stuff your guests, who will automatically have a tendency to eat too much. I've always been against the mountains of tasteless cheese chunks served as a kind of crudité at American cocktail parties, but a little taste of melted cheese is something else. When serving any of the recipes in this chapter, remember that a little goes a long way and you might be able to stretch the yield beyond what I suggest.

Saganaki

Athenaeus, the second-century Greek food writer (c. 170–c. 230), relates in his book The Deipnosophists *that Pherecrates, author of* The Slave-Teacher, *waxed poetic about "melted cheese sizzling." One can still find "melted cheese sizzling" in Greece today, especially in the form of a favorite meze called* saganaki, *which is the name of the dish and the name of the small two-handled pan used to make it. Serve* saganaki *with a glass of ouzo and lemon wedges for the cheese. Some cooks like to sprinkle dried oregano on the cheese, but I like it this way. Kefalotyri cheese can be found in Greek and some Italian markets. If you can't find it, use provolone instead.*

½ pound *kefalotyri* cheese, cut into wedges
3 x 2 x ¼ inch

All-purpose flour for dredging
½ cup olive oil
Freshly ground black pepper to taste
Lemon wedges for garnish

1. Soak the cheese in water for 30 minutes. Drain, pat dry with paper towels, and dredge in flour, tapping off any excess.
2. In a small cast-iron skillet, heat the olive oil over medium heat until it begins to smoke. Add the pieces of cheese and cook until golden brown, about 2½ minutes in all, turning only once. Remove from the oil using tongs, drain on paper towels, sprinkle with pepper, and serve with lemon wedges.

Makes 3 to 4 servings

Variation: Place under the broiler until bubbling.

Breaded Fried Kashkaval Cheese of the Greek Jews

This popular meze called kashkaval pane, *or breaded* kashkaval *cheese, is notable among the Jewish population of Thessaloniki (Salonika) in Greece. Typically, you would eat it with a glass of ouzo.*

3 tablespoons all-purpose flour
1 large egg
¼ cup whole milk
1 tablespoon unsalted butter
2 tablespoons extra-virgin olive oil
Six ½-inch-thick slices *kashkaval* cheese (page 92)
Lemon wedges for garnish

1. Put the flour in a small bowl and beat in the egg until well blended. Slowly whisk in the milk until the batter is smooth. Refrigerate for 1 hour.

2. In a medium-size skillet, melt the butter with the olive oil over medium-high heat. Once the bubbles have subsided, but before any smoking occurs, dip the cheese slices in the cold batter and cook until the bottom is light brown, 3 to 4 minutes. Turn with a metal spatula, quickly and carefully, otherwise the batter crust may come off. Cook until the other side is light brown, another 3 to 4 minutes, and remove to a serving platter or plate with the spatula and serve with a wedge of lemon.

Makes 2 to 4 servings

Kashkaval Cheese

The famous mountain cheese of Wallachia, the region of the lower Danubian plain of Romania, was originally called *cascaval*. *Cascaval* is an ewe's milk cheese repeatedly boiled like the Italian *caciocavallo*. In fact, it was exported to Italy, where it got that name, and to Istanbul, at least as far back as 1675. We know that it was also exported from Roumelia, today's Thrace in northern Greece, in the form of small balls and where it came to be known as *kashkaval*. One usually finds *kashkaval* in Middle Eastern or Greek markets.

Frico

One of the wonderful little antipasto inventions is the frico *of the northeastern region of Italy known as Friuli-Venezia Giulia. Even though it's simple, it's a bit tricky to make. Of course, once you've made one successfully, it does seem so easy. A* frico *is nothing more than a crisp-fried cheese wafer made in a small pan with grated cheese. The cheese used for making it is a three-month-old* Montasio, *a cow's milk cheese with a buttery, creamy taste that melts very well. The difficult part of making a crisp* frico, *which is called locally* frico croccante, *is knowing when to remove the wafer from the pan. If it cooks too long and becomes golden brown, it will be bitter.* Montasio *cheese can be found in cheese stores and gourmet markets. If you can't find it, you can try using freshly grated Parmigiano-Reggiano cheese, grating from a large, not-dried-out chunk.*

Extra-virgin olive oil
1 pound *Montasio*, Asiago, or Parmigiano-
 Reggiano cheese

1. Rub some olive oil on a paper towel, then use the paper towel to grease a small nonstick skillet about 7 inches in diameter. Alternatively you can use a spray can of oil. Turn the heat to medium and, once the skillet is hot, begin grating the cheese over the skillet until the bottom is covered with cheese in a single layer. Turn the heat to low and cook until very light golden, 1 to 2 minutes, then begin to peel the wafer up in one piece using a rubber spatula and flip to the other side for 30 seconds.

2. Remove the wafer from the skillet and serve at room temperature. If you want to stuff them, place each *frico* over a clean empty tomato paste can or shot glass, and fold the sides down to form a cup. Let cool before removing and filling. Otherwise, just leave them flat.

Makes 30 frico; *8 servings*

Stuffings for Frico

There are a million, but give these a try:

- A piece of prosciutto
- A small chunk of tomato
- Mousse (chicken, lobster, crayfish, ham, tomato, smoked salmon, broccoli, etc.)
- Mayonnaise
- Cream cheese (possibly mixed with smoked salmon or other ingredients)
- Foie gras
- Spinach puree

Fried Mozzarella in Tuna Sauce

This recipe from Campania, the region in which one finds Naples, is called mozzarella in salsa di tonno *and is one from the early part of the century that was collected by Ada Boni, the famous mid-twentieth-century Italian cookbook writer. It is not a dish you are likely to come across very often, but it is very nice as an antipasto or even as a main course.*

3 tablespoons extra-virgin olive oil
2 ounces dried porcini mushrooms, soaked in tepid water for 20 minutes, drained, and chopped
1 large garlic clove, finely chopped
1 pound ripe tomatoes, peeled, seeded, and finely chopped
Salt and freshly ground black pepper to taste
One 3-ounce can imported tuna in olive oil
1 pound fresh mozzarella cheese, cut into ½-inch-thick slices
½ cup all-purpose flour for dredging
1 tablespoon unsalted butter

1. In a medium-size skillet, heat the olive oil over medium heat, then cook the drained mushrooms and garlic until golden and wilted and sticking slightly, about 3 minutes, stirring. Add the tomatoes, season with salt and pepper, and cook until some of the liquid is evaporated, 3 to 4 minutes, stirring. Add the tuna and its oil, stir to break it up, then turn the heat off, check the seasonings, and leave in the skillet, keeping it warm until needed.

2. Dredge the mozzarella slices in the flour on all sides, including the edges, and set aside. In a large skillet, heat the butter over medium-high heat and, once it has melted and stopped bubbling and is beginning to turn brown, lay down the mozzarella slices and cook until the bottoms are light brown, in a few minutes. Turn carefully, making sure you use a metal spatula to scrape up the browned bottom. Cook until it looks like it's beginning to melt.

3. Transfer to a serving platter, cover with the warm tuna sauce, and serve immediately.

Makes 4 servings

Mozzarella Fritta

This is the easy version of mozzarella in carrozza. *Here you must bread the mozzarella twice in order for the cheese not to escape when it is frying. This recipe is the much-abused one that results in those nasty mozzarella sticks you've seen in American restaurants. Taste these and you'll wonder why they can't get it right, since it's so easy.*

½ pound fresh mozzarella cheese, cut into
    8 slices
All-purpose flour
2 large eggs, beaten
Dry plain bread crumbs for dredging
1 cup olive oil
1 large garlic clove, crushed
8 salted anchovy fillets, rinsed
Extra-virgin olive oil for drizzling
2 tablespoons finely chopped fresh parsley leaves

1. Dredge the mozzarella slices in flour on both sides, patting off any excess, then dip the slices in the eggs and dredge in bread crumbs until fully and evenly coated. Dip again in the eggs and again in the bread crumbs and set aside.

2. In a large skillet, heat the olive oil with the garlic clove over medium-high heat and remove and discard the garlic as it begins to turn light brown. As the oil begins to smoke, place the breaded cheese slices in the oil and cook until golden, about 2 minutes. Turn carefully with tongs and cook for another 2 minutes. If any cheese starts to escape, remove the slices immediately.

3. Place the mozzarella on a plate and lay an anchovy fillet on top of each piece. Drizzle some olive oil over the top and sprinkle with the parsley. Serve immediately.

Makes 4 to 8 servings

Mozzarella in Carrozza

This is a favorite Neapolitan antipasto in both Italy and in America—or at least it once was. It's simplicity itself: a kind of Italian croque monsieur, *a slice of fresh mozzarella between two slices of bread, dipped in eggs and fried in olive oil.* Carrozza *means "carriage" and in this preparation the bread carries the mozzarella as a "carriage." Some cooks dip the mozzarella in egg, then dip the bread in milk, then flour, then the egg.*

Twenty-four ¼-inch-thick slices dense French or
    Italian sandwich bread, crusts removed and
    each slice trimmed to form 2 triangles
1 pound fresh mozzarella cheese, cut into
    twelve ⅜-inch-thick slices the same shape as
    the bread slices
Salt to taste
12 salted anchovy fillets (optional), rinsed and
    cut in half
3 large eggs, beaten
3 cups olive oil for frying

1. Arrange half the bread slices on a work surface and place a slice of mozzarella on top of each. Season with salt. Lay an anchovy half on top, if using. Cover with the other triangles of bread and press down, then dip into the eggs,

On Mozzarella

Mozzarella, the most famous Italian cheese along with Parmesan (page 86), is a *pasta filata* or stretched curd cheese (also known as a plastic curd or strung curd cheese). Other Italian cheeses of this type are provolone, *scamorza*, and caciocavallo. Although it has traditionally been associated with the region of Campania, mozzarella is made everywhere in Italy, especially Molise, Calabria, and Sicily, but huge production occurs in America, too. Skimmed or whole milk from cows or buffalo (traditionally called *fior de latte* or *mozzarella*, respectively, but now both called mozzarella) is heated and the whey is drained from the curd. Then the curd is immersed in the whey, and then in warm water and then it is worked by stretching, folding, and molding while it is still in a malleable condition. At this point the various mozzarella cheeses begin to diverge from the lowly rubbery plastic-wrapped product they call mozzarella in the supermarkets, which is ubiquitous in the form of mozzarella sticks or as pizza cheese, to the heavenly tender and soft fresh mozzarella dripping in its milk. Fresh buffalo mozzarella, *mozzarella di bufala*, is prized even more by connoisseurs; although the differences are subtle, buffalo milk is a bit earthier. Even fresh mozzarella can be found in lesser or greater densities and more or less dry or wet. When buying mozzarella, you always want to buy fresh mozzarella, but if using it for pizzas, buy the less wet kind if possible. Although increasingly available in supermarkets, fresh mozzarella is always found in Italian markets. The rubbery supermarket mozzarella has no place in good cooking under any circumstances.

---

soaking all sides. Make sure the edges are pressed together to seal in the cheese.

2. In a large skillet, heat the olive oil over medium-high heat until it begins to smoke. Fry the sandwiches in batches so the skillet isn't crowded, until light golden, about 3 minutes in all. Remove with tongs, drain on paper towels, and serve hot.

Makes 12 sandwiches; 12 servings

Golden-Fried Bread with Fontina Cheese Sauce

This Italian antipasto is called pandorato alla crema di formaggio, *which means literally "goldened bread with cheese cream." It is quite rich, and therefore you may want to make the pieces even smaller than I call for here. On the other hand, people will gobble them up anyway. When making the sauce, be sure to pay attention to what you are doing when you add the egg yolks, otherwise they might congeal. They can be shallow-fried or deep-fried, whatever is more convenient for you. This preparation can also be made with Gruyère cheese, in which case the taste will be a little stronger. If serving the* pan-dorato *as a passed antipasto, then spread the cheese so it remains on the top; otherwise, spread it over the bread completely.*

2 cups olive oil for shallow-frying or 6 cups olive oil for deep-frying
Six ½-inch-thick slices dense Italian country bread, each slice about 5 x 3 inches, crusts removed, and cut in half diagonally
1 cup milk
All-purpose flour for dredging
2 large eggs, separated, whites beaten until frothy but not forming peaks
¼ pound fontina Val d'Aosta or Gruyère cheese, cut into small pieces
2 tablespoons unsalted butter

1. Preheat the oven to "warm" (about 150°F). Preheat the frying oil in a large skillet over medium-high heat if shallow-frying or in a deep fryer or an 8-inch saucepan fitted with a basket insert to 375°F if deep-frying.

2. Dip the bread in the milk, then in the flour, and finally in the egg whites. Fry the bread slices in the hot oil until golden brown on both sides, 2 to 3 minutes, turning once. Arrange the fried bread slices in a baking dish and keep warm in the oven.

3. Put the cheese in a bowl and cover with the milk leftover from dipping the bread for 1 hour to reduce the salty or briny flavor. Drain, then place the cheese in the top of a double boiler set

over simmering water. Once the cheese begins to melt, whisk the egg yolks in one at a time, beating constantly until it looks like a thick cream and lowering the heat if it looks too hot. Remove from the heat and stir in the butter. Spread this cream over the fried bread and serve immediately.

Makes 4 to 6 servings

Greek Rarebit

This meze called prochira tyropittakia *does not mean "rarebit," but that's what it is—a cube of bread dipped into the cheese-and-egg mixture, then fried in olive oil or hot butter. It requires a nice cold glass of white wine. There are a number of variations of this dish, such as* tyrakia tighanismena, *fried cheese that puffs up to a golden ball. These puffs are best served on small individual plates as part of a sit-down meze party.*

6 cups olive oil, olive pomace oil, or vegetable oil for frying
1 cup finely grated *kefalotyri* cheese (page 361)
1 cup finely shredded *graviera* or Gruyère cheese
2 large eggs, beaten
Pinch of freshly ground black pepper
Twelve ½-inch-thick 1-inch squares French or Italian bread, crust removed

1. Preheat the frying oil in a deep fryer or an 8-inch saucepan fitted with a basket insert to 375°F.

2. In a medium-size bowl, stir the cheeses into the beaten eggs and sprinkle with the pepper. Dip the squares of bread into the cheese-and-egg

mixture and deep-fry several at a time (don't crowd them) until golden brown, about 1½ minutes. Remove with a slotted spoon, drain on paper towels, and serve hot. Let the frying oil cool completely, strain through a porous paper filter, if necessary, and save the oil for a future use.

Makes 12 puffs; 6 servings

Ricotta Fritters

Frittelle di ricotta are ricotta fritters *from the northern Italian region of Emilia-Romagna and they truly require homemade fresh ricotta. In the Middle Ages,* fritelle *or* frictelle *were small fritters that were popular and sold by street vendors. Today, these simple fritters are considered a* passatempo, *a kind of small cocktail snack had with a drink before any formal dining begins.*

1 cup fresh ricotta cheese, preferably homemade (page 88)
¾ cup all-purpose flour
Salt to taste
1 large egg
1 tablespoon Marsala or dark rum
6 cups olive oil, olive pomace oil, or canola oil for frying

1. In a medium-size bowl, blend the ricotta, flour, salt, egg, and Marsala together with a fork. Cover with plastic wrap and let sit for 30 minutes in the refrigerator.

2. Preheat the frying oil in a deep fryer or an 8-inch saucepan fitted with a basket insert to 375°F. Deep-fry several soup spoonfuls of the

ricotta dough at a time without crowding the fryer until golden, 4 to 5 minutes, turning if necessary. Drain on paper towels and serve hot or warm. Let the frying oil cool completely, strain through a porous paper filter, if necessary, and save the oil for a future use.

Makes 4 to 6 servings

Caciocavallo and Anchovy Fritters from Sicily

These popular fritters are called sfince cu' caciu. *The cheese used here is caciocavallo, a hard southern Italian cow's milk cheese usually made in the shape of a gourd and tied off at the top to another gourd. As the cheese ages, it is used for grating. Caciocavallo is usually found in Italian markets but can be replaced by a mild provolone. These fritters are addictive and usually served as a snack, but they also make a great passed antipasto at a cocktail party.*

1 package active dry yeast (2½ teaspoons or 7 grams)
2 cups tepid whole milk
2½ cups all-purpose flour
1 teaspoon salt
Freshly ground black pepper to taste
16 salted anchovy fillets, rinsed and chopped
6 ounces caciocavallo or mild provolone cheese, cut into small dice
6 cups olive oil or olive pomace oil for frying

1. In a medium-size bowl, dissolve the yeast in the milk and leave for 5 minutes. Add the flour and salt and incorporate to form a very thick

Gorgonzola

One of the oldest and most famous of the Italian cheeses, gorgonzola is said to have been made since A.D. 879 in the Po Valley, its name coming from the town of the same name. Gorgonzola is a rich, creamy, pungent, blue-veined cheese made from whole cow's milk whose true name is *Stracchino di Gorgonzola*. Gorgonzola is a cheese associated with transhumance, which saw the shepherds driving their cattle down from the high Alps in the autumn to the plains below, where the cheese would be made. The name came about because the cows would be tired from their long trek and *stracco* means "tired" in Lombard, giving the name *Stracchino*. The mold that makes the blue veins in gorgonzola is *Penicillium glaucum*. When buying gorgonzola, buy only the real thing and taste it, too, before buying it. It shouldn't taste like blue cheese salad dressing; it should taste like something you would want to eat alone or with a little bread and a slice of apple.

batter that can still flow very slowly. Cover with a kitchen towel and leave to rise for 1 hour.

2. Stir the pepper, anchovies, and cheese into the dough and let rise another 2 hours.

3. Preheat the frying oil in a deep fryer or an 8-inch saucepan fitted with a basket insert to 350°F. Drop large spoonfuls of the dough into the hot oil (do not crowd them) and fry until golden, about 4 minutes, turning. Remove with a slotted spoon, drain on paper towels, and serve hot or warm. Let the frying oil cool completely, strain through a porous paper filter, if necessary, and save the oil for a future use.

Makes 40 fritters; 20 servings

Gorgonzola and Egg Fritter

The pungency of the gorgonzola makes this little fritter a real favorite, although it is rich. This is nice to serve while people are standing and drinking some champagne, asti spumante, or prosecco.

6 cups olive oil, olive pomace oil, or vegetable oil for frying
3 large egg yolks
1 to 2 ounces gorgonzola cheese, to your taste
1 tablespoon finely chopped fresh parsley leaves
Dry bread crumbs for dredging

1. Preheat the frying oil in a deep fryer or an 8-inch saucepan fitted with a basket insert to 375°F.

2. In a small bowl, mix the egg yolks, gorgonzola, and parsley. Spread the bread crumbs on a sheet of waxed paper or a plate. Form the fritter mixture into small patties with a spoon and dredge them in the crumbs without handling them too much. Drop several at a time (don't crowd them) into the hot oil and cook until light golden, about 2 minutes. Remove

with a slotted spoon and drain on paper towels. Serve hot. Let the frying oil cool completely, strain through a porous paper filter, if necessary, and save the oil for a future use.

Makes about 8 fritters; 4 servings

Taleggio Cheese and Buckwheat Flour Fritters from Lombardy

This antipasto, called a frittelle, *from the mountainous region of Lombardy in northern Italy, is best made with a strong, creamy cow's milk cheese such as Taleggio. These fritters will be dark brown in appearance when they're cooked. Cut the recipe in half if you need to, as this recipe yields quite a bit. When you cook the fritters, make sure the batter has been refrigerated first so that they can be dropped into the oil in heaping teaspoonfuls. Don't make them any bigger than called for, otherwise they will taste pasty.*

2 cups buckwheat flour
1 cup unbleached all-purpose flour
4 teaspoons salt
About 2¼ cups water
6 cups olive oil or olive pomace oil for frying
6 ounces Taleggio cheese, diced (see opposite)
2 tablespoons grappa

1. In a large bowl, sift together the flours. Add the salt, then enough water to make a stiff batter. Cover with a cloth and leave for 1 hour.
2. Preheat the frying oil in a deep fryer or an 8-inch saucepan fitted with a basket insert to 300°F.

Taleggio

Taleggio is a relatively new cheese. It is a surface-ripened whole-milk *Stracchino* (page 98) with a moldy rind that was first made in the Taleggio Valley of Lombardy just after World War I. It is an 8-inch square cheese about 2 inches high that weighs about 3½ pounds. Today it is mostly made in the provinces of Bergamo, Brescia, Como, Cremona, Milan, and Pavia. The cheese is straw yellow and the flavor is slightly sweet and aromatic. It is considered a table cheese, but because it melts so well, you will find it on pizzas and in risotto.

3. Stir the cheese and grappa into the batter. Deep-fry heaping teaspoonfuls of batter in the oil, several at a time (don't crowd them), until golden brown, about 8 minutes. Remove with a slotted spoon, drain on paper towels, and serve immediately. Let the frying oil cool completely, strain through a porous paper filter, if necessary, and save the oil for a future use.

Makes 10 servings

Provolone and Mortadella Bombs

There are a number of dishes in Sicilian cuisine, and Italian cuisine in general, that are called bombe, *or bombs. These fritters are called* bummi *in Sicilian, a name that refers to the way bombs were made in the late nineteenth century—round*

Buckwheat

Buckwheat (*Fagopyrum esculentum*) is not a cereal but an annual grass whose seeds resemble grain. It entered Italy in the fifteenth century, where it came to be known as *saraceno*, derived from either the belief that it was an Arab (Saracen) introduction or from its color, which is dark like the Arabs. In the Middle Ages, peasants used buckwheat for the same reason they used rye, spelt, millet, panic, or sorghum: they produced higher yields than wheat. Buckwheat spread and we know that an evening meal for a farmhand on a demesne (royal estate) in Saxony in 1569 consisted of buckwheat gruel, rutabaga, and buttermilk. But the origin of buckwheat is obscure. Its name in Latin languages suggests an Arab provenance. There is a legend that Joost van Gistele brought it back with him from his journey to the Holy Land in 1485, and an inscription on a gravestone in Zuiddorpe near Axel in the Netherlands still to be seen in 1779 seems to confirm this story. But recent archeological research casts doubt on an Arab introduction. From pollen analysis it has come to light that buckwheat grew in the Netherlands and northwest Germany long before the beginning of our era. The first documentary evidence is of four *malder boicweyts* (barrels of buckwheat) supplied in 1394 in Middelaar, near Mook (Netherlands) to the Duke of Gelre (Silcher). Buckwheat can be found in many supermarkets, and always in a whole food market.

with a fuse coming out of them, the kind anarchists would toss at monarchists. These bombs only explode in flavor: they are light and puffy and deliciously addictive. Serve them as a passed appetizer with sparkling wine or white wine.

½ pound boiling potatoes
1¼ teaspoons active dry yeast
¾ cup tepid milk
2 teaspoons salt
1½ cups all-purpose unbleached flour
3 ounces provolone cheese, finely chopped
3 ounces mortadella, finely chopped (page 360)
6 cups olive oil, olive pomace oil, or peanut oil
   for frying

1. Place the potatoes in a medium-size saucepan and cover with several inches of cold water. Turn the heat to high and, once it comes to a boil in about 20 minutes, reduce the heat to medium-high and continue to boil until a skewer glides easily to the center of the potato, about 20 minutes more. Drain and, when cool enough to handle, peel, and pass through a food mill or strainer into a large bowl.

2. Dissolve the yeast in the milk, about 5 minutes. Pour the milk into the potatoes, add the salt, and stir well. Add the flour and knead the dough until it is a soft mass and elastic. Cover with a kitchen towel for 1 hour.

3. Knead the cheese and mortadella into the dough, cover with the kitchen towel, and let it rise for another hour.

4. Preheat the frying oil in a deep fryer or an 8-inch saucepan fitted with a basket insert to 375°F.

5. Form the dough into balls a little smaller than golf balls and fry several at a time (don't crowd them) until golden, about 4 minutes. Drain on paper towels and serve hot or warm. Let the frying oil cool completely, strain through a porous paper filter, if necessary, and save the oil for a future use.

Makes 24 fritters; 10 servings

Oil for Frying

The most common oil used for deep-frying in the Mediterranean is olive oil, although vegetable oil is popular too, and in Turkey they use lots of sunflower seed oil. But when you see in a recipe that "6 cups olive oil for frying" is called for, just remember that does not mean some very expensive extra-virgin olive oil. "Olive oil" is the actual name used for a quality of oil as determined by the International Olive Oil Council, a United Nations agency. It will say so on the label, although sometimes you may see "pure olive oil," which is the same thing. Pomace olive oil is made from pits and other olive by-products and is an oil I use a lot for deep frying because it is inexpensive. Whatever you buy for deep-frying foods, it should not be expensive.

Kefalotyri Cheese Croquettes

This Greek meze is called kroketakia, *or "croquette," simply enough. The* kefalotyri *cheese is a hard, light yellow grating cheese made from either sheep's or goat's milk and usually found in Greek markets, but you could replace it with a young pecorino cheese. Although these croquettes seem ideal as a passed appetizer, I also like to serve them for a sit-down dinner or meze party.*

3 cups grated *kefalotyri* cheese (page 361)
1 teaspoon baking powder
½ teaspoon salt
5 large egg whites, beaten until stiff peaks form
2 tablespoons all-purpose flour (optional)
6 cups olive oil or olive pomace oil for frying

1. In a medium-size bowl, mix the cheese, baking powder, and salt. Slowly add the cheese mixture to the egg whites, beating constantly. The mixture should be very thick. If it isn't, add some or all of the flour.

2. Preheat the frying oil in a deep fryer or an 8-inch saucepan fitted with a basket insert to 375°F.

3. Shape the mixture into croquettes about 2 inches long using a teaspoon. It's okay if they are rounder. Fry them several at a time (don't crowd them) in the hot oil until golden, 2 to 3 minutes. Remove with a slotted spoon, drain on paper towels, and serve hot. Let the frying oil cool completely, strain through a porous paper filter, if necessary, and save the oil for a future use.

Makes 16 croquettes; 8 servings

Frittatas and
Other Eggy Delights

One of the great curiosities about the cuisines of the Mediterranean is that eggs are popular everywhere, but only in four Mediterranean countries are frittatas eaten. A frittata is not merely an omelette. These dishes are a kind of thick omelette eaten as an antipasto, *tapa*, or meze or as a light lunch. The four countries where this particular kind of dish is made are Italy (after all, the word *frittata* is Italian), Spain, where the frittata is known as a *tortilla*, and Algeria and Tunisia, where they are known by various names but usually as *maꞌqūda* or tagine. There are three Italian frittata recipes and six Spanish *tortilla* recipes, which probably represent about one percent of all the possible frittata recipes. There are also ten North African frittata recipes here, which I believe is the greatest collection in one place of these fabulous dishes from the Maghrib ever published in English. The chapter is rounded out with four really fun recipes. First is a never-before-seen Venetian recipe of pureed fava beans with scrambled eggs, second, a Turkish recipe for poached eggs in garlic yogurt sauce that you may just start eating for breakfast every day, it's so good. Last are two stuffed eggs dishes, one from Italy and one from Egypt.

Two-Cheese Frittata

If you use fresh cheeses in this frittata, you might find the final product too watery, so keep that in mind when you make it. You can avoid this by either cutting up and draining the fresh cheeses for some hours in a strainer or by pouring off the water after it is cooked. If you don't have a skillet that can go under a broiler, use whatever skillet you have and let the handle stick out with the oven or broiler door open.

2 tablespoons extra-virgin olive oil

1 garlic clove, crushed

3 large eggs, beaten well

Salt and freshly ground black pepper to taste

1 ounce fresh mozzarella cheese, cut into 4 slices

⅓ cup fresh ricotta cheese, preferably homemade (page 88), well drained and crumbled or formed into 4 pieces and patted down slightly

1 ounce fontina Val d'Aosta cheese, cut into 4 slices

1 tablespoon finely chopped fresh parsley leaves

1. Preheat the broiler.

2. In a 10-inch ovenproof nonstick skillet, heat the olive oil over medium heat with the garlic; once the garlic begins to turn light brown, remove and discard. Pour in the eggs and season with salt and pepper. Layer the cheeses on top, then place under the broiler until the edges are light brown and the cheeses have melted, about 3 minutes. Serve immediately, cut into wedges.

Makes 4 servings

• ❁ •

The First Frittata

Maestro Martino da Como's *Libro de arte coquinaria* from about 1450 has a recipe for frittata called *frictata*, made with eggs beaten with a little water and milk and grated cheese. He recommends cooking it with herbs such as parsley, borage, mint, marjoram, or sage.

Piovano Arlotto (1396–1484), author of a popular book of humor, practical jokes, dirty stories, and tales of justice, charity, and wisdom, wrote in the popular literary tradition of the facetiae during the Renaissance. His glossary describes a frittata as a large round of beaten eggs cooked in a pan with butter or oil.

Pizza-Style Frittata

This Italian frittata is called frittata alla pizzaiola, *which means something like "a la pizza style," because it is meant to resemble a pizza. The frittata is finished under the broiler and when the sides puff up, it will look like a pizza with an inviting golden crust. If you don't have a skillet that can go under a broiler, use whatever skillet you have and let the handle stick out with the oven or broiler door open.*

1½ tablespoons unsalted butter

1 tablespoon extra-virgin olive oil

4 large eggs, beaten

½ teaspoon salt

4 large, thin slices ripe tomato

6 imported black olives, pitted and chopped

6 thin slices fontina Val d'Aosta or provolone
cheese

1 tablespoon finely chopped fresh parsley leaves

1. Preheat the broiler.

2. In a 10-inch ovenproof nonstick skillet, melt the butter with the olive oil over medium heat until the butter begins to turn light brown. Pour the eggs into the skillet, season with the salt, and quickly arrange the tomato slices on top, along with the olives sprinkled around. Cover with the cheese and sprinkle on the parsley.

3. Place the skillet under the broiler and broil until the top sets, is lightly speckled with brown spots, and the edges have puffed up. Serve immediately, cut into wedges.

Makes 4 to 6 servings

Of Frittatas and Omelettes

A frittata is different from an omelette in that it is made like a pancake. The beaten eggs are poured into a pan and cooked on one side, then the frittata is covered, placed in an oven, or flipped to be finished. The frittata is then eaten cold or hot, usually as a light lunch dish or as an antipasto. An omelette, on the other hand, is cooked in a pan and folded over onto itself, stuffed or not, to form a puffy, soft cylinder. It is always eaten hot.

Artichoke Omelette

One doesn't hear much of artichokes in Italy before the sixteenth century. The artichoke appears to have been introduced first to Sicily by the Arabs, for there is a document from Norman Sicily that distinguishes the artichoke from the cardoon for the first time. The artichoke next appears in Naples and is taken from there to Tuscany in 1466, according to the sixteenth-century botanist Pierandrea Mattioli. But their availability is limited, says Ermolao Barbaro in his In Dioscoridem corollariorum libri quinque, *finally published on 1530, and when it is found it is only found in the foreign gardens in the Moorish quarter of Venice. There is a quite similar dish in Syria called* ardī shawkī bi'l-bayḍ *that is made with eggs, white cheese, and butter. This omelette is particularly nice when you use fresh artichokes.*

3 large eggs

2 tablespoons finely chopped fresh parsley leaves

Salt and freshly ground black pepper to taste

3 medium-size canned artichoke bottoms, finely chopped, or fresh artichokes, trimmed to their bottoms (page 205), cooked until tender, and finely chopped

1 garlic clove, finely chopped

1 tablespoon freshly grated Parmigiano-Reggiano cheese

1 tablespoon extra-virgin olive oil

1. In a medium-size bowl, beat the eggs and parsley together and season with salt and pepper. Add the artichokes, garlic, and cheese and beat well.

2. In an 8-inch nonstick skillet or omelette pan, heat the olive oil over medium heat, then pour in the egg mixture and shake the pan while it sets, about 1 minute. Fold the omelette over with a metal spatula and cook another 30 seconds. Transfer to a plate and serve immediately.

Makes 4 servings

The Frittata in Proverbs

The Italian frittata is not only an old dish but one that lends itself to proverbial Italian sayings. *Fare una frittata* (make a frittata) means to have a bad, disastrous thing happen figuratively or literally, referring to the breaking of the eggs. *Frittata* is also a slang word for a multi-car chain collision. *Voltare o rigirare la frittata* ("turn the frittata") means to twist an argument to mean the contrary. *Non si può far la frittata senza rompere le uova* ("you can't make a frittata without breaking the eggs") means that, for good results, one pays a price.

Eggplant Frittata from Andalusia

In Andalusia, tortillas *are often served as tapas. This* tortilla de berenjenas, *or eggplant frittata, not only is popular and common in Seville but also has a long history, having appeared in the thirteenth-century Arab-Andalusi cookbook of Ibn Razīn al-Tujībī, the* Kitāb faḍālat al-khiwān fī ṭayyibāt al-ṭˁam waʾl-alwān.

This tortilla *is best cut into wedges, drizzled with the sauce, and eaten relatively soon after it has reached room temperature.*

2 pounds eggplant, peeled and thinly sliced
Salt
2 cups fresh bread crumbs
4 large eggs
1 teaspoon freshly ground coriander seeds
⅛ teaspoon ground cinnamon
½ cup extra-virgin olive oil
Freshly ground black pepper to taste
1 garlic clove, peeled
1 tablespoon all-purpose flour
2 teaspoons honey
1 tablespoon white wine vinegar

1. Lay the eggplant slices on some paper towels and sprinkle with salt. Leave them to drain of their bitter juices for 30 minutes, then pat dry with paper towels.

2. Place the eggplant in a large pot of salted water, turn the heat to high, bring to a boil, and let boil for 30 minutes. Drain well, then puree in a food processor. Remove the eggplant to a strainer and let drain some more, pressing out the water with the back of a wooden spoon. It's important that not too much water remains in the eggplant puree. Combine the eggplant puree in a large bowl with the bread crumbs, eggs, coriander, cinnamon, and 1 tablespoon of the olive oil, season with salt and pepper, and mix well.

3. Prepare the sauce by pounding the garlic in a mortar. Incorporate the flour, honey, and ⅛ teaspoon salt to form a paste. Slowly pour in 1

tablespoon of the olive oil and continue pounding. Transfer to a medium-size bowl and slowly whisk in 5 tablespoons of the olive oil into the sauce, as you would for making mayonnaise. Whisk in the vinegar.

4. In a 10-inch nonstick skillet or omelette pan, heat the remaining 1 tablespoon olive oil over medium heat and pour in the egg-and-eggplant puree. Cook until the bottom sets, then flip it over or place under a broiler for a few minutes to set the eggs.

5. Slide onto a round serving platter. When the *tortilla* has reached room temperature or is slightly warm, cut into wedges, spoon some sauce over, and serve.

Makes 4 to 6 servings

Fava Bean Frittata from Andalusia

The tortilla that most Americans are familiar with is the Mexican flatbread used for everything from enchiladas to tacos. But in Spain, a tortilla *is what the Italians call a frittata, a kind of omelette served as a* tapa. *This recipe, called* tortilla de fave, *is inspired both by the variety of wonderful young fava bean recipes I've had in the Mediterranean as well as the multitude of* tortillas *I've had, especially in Andalusia, usually as a* tapa.

2 cups (¾ pound) dried fava beans, rinsed and picked over
2 tablespoons extra-virgin olive oil
3 tablespoons chopped salt pork
1 small onion, finely chopped
1 large garlic clove, finely chopped
1 teaspoon finely chopped fresh mint leaves
3 large eggs
½ teaspoon hot Spanish paprika

1. Soak the fava beans in cold water overnight. Remove the peels and boil in lightly salted water until tender, about 10 minutes. Drain.

2. In a medium-size earthenware casserole, heat the olive oil over medium-high heat, then cook the salt pork, onion, garlic, and mint until the onion is translucent, about 6 minutes, stirring frequently.

3. Preheat the oven to 350°F.

4. Beat the eggs vigorously with the paprika, then pour into the center of the casserole, shaking it so the eggs spread. Place in the oven and bake until a skewer stuck in the center of the eggs comes out clean, about 10 minutes.

5. Remove from the oven and let cool. Cut into wedges or trapezoids and serve at room temperature.

Makes 6 servings

Green Bell Pepper and Manchego Cheese Frittata from Murcia

This tortilla, *called* tortilla di pimiento verde dulce, *is made with lots of the sweet bell peppers that grow so abundantly in the province of Murcia and is served as a* tapa. *If you don't have a skillet that can go under a broiler, use whatever skillet you have and let the handle stick out with the oven or broiler door open.*

The Spanish Tortilla

The Spanish *tortilla*, as I've said elsewhere, is not the same as the Mexican tortilla. Rather, it is identical to the Italian frittata and it's likely that the Spanish learned about frittata making from the Italians and both may have known about it since Roman times. The first-century Roman cookbook author Apicius has a recipe called *ova spongia ex lacte*, which is a kind of frittata (*ova spongea* means "egg sponge") made with milk and served with honey poured over it. In any case, the first mention of *tortilla* that I'm familiar with is by Francisco de Quevedo (1580–1645) the author of *El Buscón* (The Swindler), an early Spanish picaresque novel. At the time, the Genoese had almost all of Spain in a financial stranglehold, leading a character in the story to say about the Genoese businessman: Hardly anyone in business has a conscience because they've heard it's likely to get in your way, so they leave it behind with their umbilical cords when they're born.

4 green bell peppers
3 tablespoons extra-virgin olive oil
3 garlic cloves, 2 finely chopped and 1 crushed
1 tablespoon finely chopped fresh basil leaves
Salt and freshly ground black pepper to taste
1 tablespoon finely chopped pork fatback
3 pequín chiles or any small dried red chiles
6 large eggs
½ cup shredded Manchego cheese or finely diced mozzarella cheese
Paprika for dusting

1. Preheat the oven to 425°F.
2. Place the bell peppers in a roasting pan with a little water and roast until the skins blister black all over, 40 to 45 minutes. Let cool, then peel, seed, and cut into strips.
3. Place the pepper strips in a medium-size skillet with 2 tablespoons of the olive oil, the chopped garlic, and basil and season with salt and pepper. Turn the heat to medium and cook until softened, about 20 minutes, stirring occasionally.
4. In a 10-inch ovenproof nonstick skillet or omelette pan, heat the remaining 1 tablespoon olive oil with the fatback, pequín chiles, and crushed garlic over medium heat until the fatback is crispy, about 12 minutes, stirring and removing the garlic when it begins to turn light brown. Remove and discard the pequín chiles.
5. Preheat the broiler.
6. Beat the eggs until frothy and pour into the pan, shaking to distribute them. Sprinkle the cheese around and cook for 2 minutes. Place under the broiler until the top sets. Remove from the oven and slide the frittata onto a serving platter. Dust lightly with paprika and serve cut into wedges.

Makes 4 servings

Lettuce Frittata from Córdoba

Lettuce was considered a common, poor people's food in sixteenth-century Spain. Even in the anonymous picaresque story "Lazarillo de Tormes," Lazarillo tells of his service to his fifth master, one who sold papal indulgences and whom he thought the most shameless person he had ever seen. He would first, when selling the indulgences, give the priests and other clergy a few little presents. "They weren't worth much, some Murcian lettuce, if they were in season, couple of limes and oranges, peaches, and a big pear."

This very simple frittata called tortilla de lechuga *is made only with lettuce and eggs and is lightly seasoned. Because of the simplicity of this* tapa, *you will want to pair it with richer dishes.*

1 head Boston lettuce
6 large eggs, beaten
1 teaspoon sweet Spanish paprika
Salt and freshly ground black pepper to taste
2 tablespoons unsalted butter, at room
    temperature

1. Bring a large saucepan of lightly salted water to a boil, then plunge the whole head of lettuce in and cook until wilted, about 2 minutes. Drain well, squeezing the water out, and chop, leaves, stems, and all.

2. Preheat the oven to 350°F.

3. In a large bowl, beat the eggs and paprika together and season with salt and pepper. Stir in the chopped lettuce. Spread the softened butter over the bottom and sides of an 8-inch round

preferably earthenware casserole, then pour the egg mixture in and bake until the top is set and a skewer pushed into the center comes out clean, about 25 minutes. Cut into squares and serve hot or warm.

Makes 4 to 6 servings

Zucchini and Bell Pepper Frittata from Murcia

Murcia, a region of Spain, has long been known for its huertas—*large farms given over to vegetable production. Its rich vegetable bounty is certainly evident in this* tortilla Murciana. *In Spain, a* tortilla *is usually served cut into wedges as a* tapa.

¼ pound eggplant, peeled and diced
Salt
6 tablespoons extra-virgin olive oil
1 small onion, finely chopped
1 green bell pepper, seeded and finely chopped
1 small zucchini, peeled, seeded, and diced
1 large ripe tomato, peeled, seeded, and chopped
¼ pound cooked ham, diced
Freshly ground black pepper to taste
8 large eggs, lightly beaten

1. Spread the diced eggplant over some paper towels and sprinkle with salt. Leave it to drain of its bitter juices for 30 minutes or longer, then pat dry with paper towels.

2. In a 10-inch nonreactive skillet or omelette pan, heat the olive oil over high heat, then cook the onion and green pepper until they turn color, about 3 minutes, stirring. Add the egg-

The Bell Peppers of Murcia

According to Christopher Columbus's diary, the capsicum was discovered by Europeans on New Year's Day in January 1493. When the capsicum entered the Mediterranean, it made its first landfall in Spain via the Spanish or in Morocco via the Portuguese. About that time, in the early sixteenth century, the plains of Murcia, Valencia, Lerida, Barcelona, Saragossa, and Andalusia were being irrigated as part of urban investment in the countryside to resurrect the *tierras de riego* (irrigated lands) that had fallen into disuse after having been established by the Arabs centuries earlier. The Arabs' greatest contribution to Spanish agriculture was the improvement and extension of the irrigation system, which had its origins in the Roman period. By the twelfth century the Arabs knew how to drain rivers with precision and to distribute water economically, as they had irrigated an estimated 25,000 acres around Saragossa. Other important systems antedating the Reconquest were found in the Genil valley in Andalusia, in the Segura basin in Murcia, and in the valley of the Segre in Catalonia. One of the great prizes of the victorious Christians under James the Conqueror (1208–1276), king of Aragon, who brought Murcia under Castilian control, was the magnificently irrigated *vega* (fertile plain) of Valencia. The sweet bell peppers of Murcia became famous, and in the sixteenth century it was said that the servant girls of Murcia were content with salad, fruit, melons, and especially red bell peppers for their sustenance.

plant and zucchini and cook until they soften and turn color, about another 5 minutes, stirring a few times. Reduce the heat to medium, add the tomato and ham, season with salt and pepper, and cook until the sauce is denser, about 4 minutes, stirring a few times.

3. Lightly salt and pepper the eggs and pour over the vegetables, shaking the pan to distribute them. Cook until they set and brown ever so slightly, about 4 minutes, then carefully flip the frittata, using a wide spatula and tilting the pan as you do. Cook for a minute, and transfer to a round platter. Serve, cut into wedges, warm or at room temperature.

Note: You can also cook the first side over the burner and the top under the broiler if you feel you are not adept at flipping omelettes.

Makes 4 to 6 servings

Carrot Frittata from Tunisia

This frittata is called maᶜqūda bi'l-jazar; *a* maᶜqūda *is a dish of beaten eggs that sets in the oven, the word derived from the Arabic meaning "to congeal," to set like a pudding. It is a version of what the Italians call frittata and the Spanish call a* tortilla. *It is usually made in a frying pan, while another kind of Tunisian frittata, the tagine, is usually made in an earthenware pan of the same name in the oven, although the names seem to be interchangeable. The Tunisian preparation called a tagine should not be confused with the Moroccan tagine, which is an entirely different dish—namely, a kind of dry stew that the French call* etouffée. *A* ma᷾qūda *(pronounced* ma-KOOD-a*) can be eaten hot, but it is most popular at room temperature, when the flavors have had a chance to permeate the spongy texture of the cooked eggs. You can hard-boil the eggs needed in this recipe at the same time you cook the carrots.*

1 pound carrots, sliced

2 tablespoons freshly ground caraway seeds

1 tablespoon Harīsa (page 468)

¼ cup finely chopped fresh parsley leaves

6 large garlic cloves, finely chopped

1½ teaspoons salt

½ teaspoon freshly ground black pepper

2 large hard-boiled eggs, shelled and finely chopped

8 large eggs, beaten

3 tablespoons extra-virgin olive oil

1. Boil the carrots until tender in large saucepan of salted water, about 25 minutes. Drain and mash the carrots with a fork with the caraway, *harīsa*, parsley, garlic, salt, and pepper. Stir in the chopped eggs and beaten eggs.

2. In an 8- to 9½-inch nonstick skillet, heat the olive oil over high heat. When the oil begins to smoke, add the carrot-and-egg mixture, cover, and cook until the oil is bubbling up around the sides and the edges are browned, about 2 minutes. Reduce the heat to low and cook, covered, until the center is cooked through, 18 to 20 minutes.

3. Gently loosen the sides with a metal spatula and invert the *ma᷾qūda* onto a round serving platter. Serve cut into wedges warm or at room temperature.

Makes 6 servings

Cauliflower and Parsley Frittata from Tunisia

This cauliflower tājīn bi'l-brūklū *is a kind of Tunisian frittata and is eaten the same way an Italian frittata or Spanish* tortilla *would be eaten. (Remember that a Spanish* tortilla *is a frittata, not a flatbread, as it is in Mexico.) I usually hard-boil the eggs in this recipe in the same saucepan I use to cook the cauliflower. Most Tunisians would eat this dish at room temperature as part of a meze or light dinner.*

One 2-pound cauliflower head, cut into florets and stems discarded

1 small onion, finely chopped

6 tablespoons very finely chopped fresh parsley leaves

2 tablespoons freshly grated Parmigiano-Reggiano cheese

4 large hard-boiled eggs, shelled and chopped

4 large eggs, beaten

6½ tablespoons extra-virgin olive oil

2½ tablespoons unsalted butter

½ teaspoon Harīsa (page 468), dissolved in 1 teaspoon water

Salt and freshly ground black pepper

More on Tagines

Let me confuse you some more about tagines. In Morocco, *tagine* is the name of the earthenware pan that an eponymous dish is cooked in, a dish like a dry stew. But in Tunisia, a tagine is not only a stew but more commonly an egg dish that resembles a frittata. But the word *tagine*, which isn't originally an Arabic word but derives from the Greek word *tegame*, meaning "frying pan," has more senses in Tunisia. A tagine in the country is different from one in the city. The rural tagine is a large, round earthenware platter always made by hand without being turned on a spindle. It has sloping sides that end in four or three incised points. It functions as a pan set upon an open fire for griddle-roasting grains, such as wheat or barley. It is also known as a *ghanāᶜā*, which can mean "singer," alluding to the sizzle and jumping sounds of the grains in the pan as they are heated. In the city, a tagine is an earthenware casserole and a prepared dish of stew or eggs.

1. Place the cauliflower in a pot of cold water to cover and bring to a boil. Cook until very soft in the center when pierced with a skewer, about 30 minutes. Drain, then crush with a fork and let cool while you continue the preparation.

2. Preheat the oven to 350°F.

3. Transfer the mashed cauliflower to a medium-size bowl and stir in the onion, parsley, cheese, eggs, 6 tablespoons of the olive oil, 2 tablespoons of the butter, and the diluted *harīsa*. Season with salt and pepper and mix well. Transfer to an 8-inch-diameter earthenware casserole greased with the remaining ½ tablespoon each olive oil and butter and bake until the eggs set, when the tip of a knife inserted into the center of the casserole comes out clean, 25 to 30 minutes.

4. Gently loosen the sides with a metal spatula and invert the tagine onto a round serving platter. Serve, cut into wedges, warm or at room temperature.

Makes 4 to 6 servings

 ## Potato, Onion, and Parsley Frittata from Tunisia

This Tunisian preparation is called maᶜqūda bi'l-baṭāṭa *and although it looks like a huge amount of parsley goes into this frittata, it is actually just perfect. This is a delightful preparation and very satisfying and hot, too, since it contains a healthy amount of cayenne. Some cooks make this dish with the addition of cheese and bread crumbs.*

1 pound boiling potatoes
7 tablespoons extra-virgin olive oil
1 medium-size onion, finely chopped

Leaves from 1 bunch fresh parsley, finely
  chopped
6 large eggs, beaten
1½ teaspoons cayenne pepper
1 teaspoon salt
½ teaspoon freshly ground black pepper
2 tablespoons unsalted butter

1. Put the potatoes in a medium-size saucepan and cover with water by several inches. Turn the heat to medium and, once it reaches a gentle boil in about 20 minutes, cook until the potatoes can be pierced to their centers with a skewer without any resistance, another 20 to 25 minutes. Drain, then peel and pass through a strainer or food mill.

2. In a medium-size skillet, heat the olive oil over medium-high heat, then cook the onion and parsley until the onion is translucent, 5 to 6 minutes, stirring. Let cool. In a large bowl, mix the riced potatoes, onion and parsley, eggs, cayenne, salt, and black pepper.

3. Preheat the oven to 350°F.

4. Use the butter to grease an 8-inch-diameter earthenware casserole on the bottom and sides,

A Tunisian Jewish Frittata

In Tunisia, there is a kind of tagine called *ṭājīn fraylla* that is made like the frittata on page 112, but with fresh bread crumbs and cut-up French fries. *Fraylla* is a Jewish woman's name.

then pour the egg mixture in and flatten with the back of a spoon. Bake until the top is a golden yellow, set firm, and a knife stuck in the middle comes out clean, about 30 minutes.

5. Unmold the *maʿqūda* carefully if you like, divide into portions, and serve warm or at room temperature.

Makes 6 servings

Potato and Bell Pepper Frittata in the Style of the Tunisian Jews

This recipe called makbūba *is said to be typical of the kind of dishes prepared by the Jews of Tunisia, who are and have historically been fond of garlic. It is a kind of* shakhshūka *(page 336), a mélange of saucy vegetables in a casserole cooked with eggs. The eggs are stirred in at the end of the cooking until they set.*

½ pound boiling potatoes, peeled and quartered
½ pound green bell peppers, seeded and cut
  into rings
½ pound small ripe tomatoes, peeled, cut in half,
  and seeded
6 garlic cloves, crushed in a mortar with
  ½ teaspoon salt until mushy
½ teaspoon freshly ground caraway seeds
½ teaspoon freshly ground coriander seeds
1½ teaspoons cayenne pepper
3 tablespoons extra-virgin olive oil
3 tablespoons water
Salt to taste
4 large eggs, beaten

Eggs in North Africa

Eggs are enormously popular in North Africa and are prepared in a variety of ways, some quite similar to the Italian frittata or Spanish *tortilla*. In Algeria, cooks make a *ṭāḥbūlt al-marqa*, a frittata with lamb and chickpeas in semolina sauce, and *maqīna*, a chopped meat frittata. Tunisian Jews make a kind of frittata called *minīna*, which is a *maᶜqūda* (see page 110) made with chicken, veal brains, and many eggs. In the Middle Ages eggs were widely eaten. Doctors repeated the old precepts of the Salerno School in Italy, a health regimen founded upon Arabic learning (the most advanced medical knowledge of the time) that eggs be eaten fresh and not overcooked: *si sumas ovum, molle sit atque novum.* Eggs were so important in the daily economy that a modern statistician can reconstruct changes in the cost of living in the sixteenth-century Mediterranean from a few eggs sold in Florence. Their price alone is a valid measure of the standard of living or the value of money in any given town in any given country. At one time in seventeenth-century Egypt, one "had the choice of thirty eggs, two pigeons or one fowl for a sou."

1. In a large bowl, mix the potatoes, peppers, tomatoes, garlic paste, caraway, coriander, and cayenne.

2. In a 10-inch nonstick skillet, heat the olive oil over very low heat, then add the vegetable mixture and the water. Cook, covered, until the potatoes are soft, about 1½ hours, pushing and turning the food occasionally and seasoning with salt at some point. If there is more than ¼ cup of liquid in the pan at the end of this time, remove some with a spoon.

3. Pour the beaten eggs in, shake the skillet to distribute them, cover, and continue to cook until they have set, about 15 minutes. Cut into wedges in the skillet and serve immediately.

Makes 4 servings

Tuna and Potato Frittata from Tunisia

This preparation is called maᶜqūda bi'l-tunn *and is eaten as a small lunch or an* ādū, *a colloquial Tunisian word for meze. Here the flavors are complementary, and although it contains chile paste, it is not at all spicy hot.*

½ pound potatoes

6 large eggs

3 tablespoons extra-virgin olive oil

One 6-ounce can imported tuna in olive oil, drained

¼ cup finely chopped fresh parsley leaves

1 small onion, chopped

2 tablespoons shredded Gruyère cheese

2 teaspoons Harīsa (page 468), dissolved in 2 tablespoons water

Salt and freshly ground black pepper
   to taste

1. Place the potatoes in a medium-size saucepan and cover with cold water. Bring to a boil, then reduce the heat to medium and cook until a skewer pushed into the center meets with only slight resistance, about 20 minutes more. Drain, peel, and dice.

2. Preheat the oven to 350°F.

3. In a large bowl, mix the potatoes, eggs, olive oil, tuna, parsley, onion, cheese, and diluted *harīsa*, season with salt and pepper, and pour into a lightly oiled 8-inch-diameter earthenware casserole. Spread the mixture in the casserole and flatten with the back of a spoon. Bake until the top is a golden yellow, set firm, and a knife stuck in the middle comes out clean, about 20 minutes.

4. Unmold the *maʿqūda* carefully if you like, divide into portions, and serve warm or at room temperature.

Makes 6 servings

Tunisian Frittata with Grouper and Onions

Mannānī *is grouper, a popular and common fish in the Tunisian kitchen. When I was writing this recipe, called* maʿqūda bi'l-mannānī, *I relied on my notes written a decade ago, which were frustratingly banal: I wrote, "this was really* delicious." *Well, when I tested the recipe, sure enough, it was really delicious. Grouper is a warm-water fish common around Florida, although it can be found farther north in the* Atlantic because of the Gulf Stream. Elsewhere, try using sea bass, striped bass, red snapper, halibut, or yellowtail. This dish contains a goodly amount of chile pepper, so be prepared.

2 boiling potatoes (about 1 pound)
¼ cup extra-virgin olive oil
1 small onion, finely chopped
¼ cup finely chopped fresh parsley leaves
1 pound grouper or other fish fillets (see headnote), coarsely chopped
6 large eggs
2 teaspoons ground red chile or cayenne pepper
Salt and freshly ground black pepper to taste
1½ tablespoons unsalted butter

1. Place the potatoes in a medium-size saucepan and cover with 2 inches of water. Turn the heat to high and, when the water comes to a boil, reduce the heat to medium-high and cook until a skewer glides easily to the center of the potato, about 20 minutes. Drain, peel, and pass through a food mill or strainer. Set aside.

2. In a 10-inch nonstick skillet or omelette pan, heat the olive oil over high heat until nearly smoking, then add the onion, parsley, and fish and cook until the onion turns translucent and the fish white, about 4 minutes. Set aside.

3. In a large bowl, combine the fish mixture, riced potatoes, eggs, and red pepper. Season with salt and pepper.

4. Preheat the oven to 350°F.

5. Use the butter to grease the bottom and sides of an 8-inch-diameter earthenware casserole liberally. Spread the mixture in the casserole and flatten with the back of a spoon. Bake until

The Grouper

The grouper is a large fish that can grow to three feet long and inhabits tropical and semi-tropical waters. It's a very popular fish in Andalusia, along the coast of North Africa, especially from Bizerte in Tunisia all the way to Egypt. The scientific name of the Mediterranean grouper is *Epinephelus guaza*, which means "with clouds upon it," a reference to the dark patches on its skin. The grouper is common in Florida waters, but not much farther north than South Carolina. There are a number of varieties of grouper. It is hard to describe groupers because their coloration and markings change with the stage of life they are in, with the depth and clarity of the water they live in, and if they are in a feeding frenzy or not. If grouper cannot be found, try looking for sea bass, striped bass, wreckfish, or pomano. The popularity of grouper in the Mediterranean is evident in the Spanish proverb "among meats, mutton, among the fish, grouper," an expression that goes back to the words in 1420 of the writer Juan de Avinon, who said that mutton was the most noble of meats. In Tunisia grouper is called *faruj* or *mannāni aḥmar*, while in Egypt they call it *waᶜār*.

the top is a golden yellow, set firm, and a knife stuck in the middle comes out clean, about 20 minutes.

6. Unmold the *maᶜqūda* carefully if you like, divide into portions, and serve warm or at room temperature.

Makes 6 servings

Smoked Herring, Potato, and Parsley Frittata from Tunisia

Although this frittata is a popular maᶜqūda *in Tunisia, where it is called* maᶜqūda bi'l-rinqa, *it is not for everyone, since smoked herring is a very strong, oily fish. If that sounds appealing to you, then by all means make this, you'll enjoy it. Herring (Clupea harengus L.) may not seem like a Mediterranean fish and it is not. Like the nonnative but familiar* baccalà *(salt cod) of the Italians, herring comes from the Baltic or North Atlantic and has been salted, smoked, or pickled in the Mediterranean at least since the fourteenth century. Other little Mediterranean fish are used in place of herring, fish whose names are probably local dialect names and cannot with certainty be linked with specific fish, for example* rīm, shāliḥ, *or* lāj, *used in North Africa.*

1 smoked herring

1 pound boiling potatoes

10 large eggs

2 teaspoons Harīsa (page 468)

1 small onion, finely chopped

Leaves from 1 bunch fresh parsley, finely chopped

1 teaspoon salt, or more to taste
Freshly ground black pepper to taste
6 tablespoons extra-virgin olive oil

1. Remove the smoked herring from its package, then, holding the tail and head with tongs or a fork, hold over the stove burner until the skin blisters off. Once the skin can be removed, remove the head and tail, pull the flesh off the bones, and chop. You should have 2 to 3 ounces of flesh.

2. Place the potatoes in a medium-size saucepan and cover with cold water. Bring to a boil, then reduce the heat to medium and cook until a skewer pushed into the center meets with only slight resistance, about 20 minutes more. Remove the potatoes with a slotted spoon and, when cool enough to handle, peel and dice.

3. Keep the water boiling, gently place 2 eggs in the boiling water, and cook for exactly 9 minutes. Remove the eggs, cool, shell, chop coarsely, and set aside.

4. Preheat the oven to 350°F.

5. In a large bowl, beat the remaining 8 eggs with the *harīsa*, then mix in the smoked herring, potatoes, hard-boiled eggs, onion, parsley, and salt and season with pepper. Coat an 8- to 10-inch-diameter earthenware casserole with the olive oil and pour the egg mixture into it, spreading it around. Bake until the top is a golden yellow, set firm, and a knife stuck in the middle comes out clean, 25 to 30 minutes.

6. Let cool in the casserole, then run a knife around the edge and carefully loosen the bottom of the frittata with a metal spatula, then invert onto a round serving plate and

serve warm or at room temperature, cut into wedges.

Makes 6 servings

Veal Roast and Sweet Pea Frittata in the Style of Granada

In Spain, a frittata is known as a tortilla *and, unlike the Mexican tortilla, which is a flatbread, the Spanish* tortilla *is a kind of omelette that is usually served cut up into wedges as a* tapa. *This dish involves some preparation since the veal must be roasted first, and that is why it makes sense to use leftovers. Serve at room temperature.*

One ¾-pound boneless veal roast in one piece, rolled and tied
¼ cup pork lard or rendered pork fat
½ cup shelled fresh or frozen peas
3 green bell peppers, seeded and very finely chopped
1 teaspoon salt
6 large eggs
2 tablespoons extra-virgin olive oil

1. Preheat the oven to 350°F.

2. Coat the veal with 2 tablespoons of the lard or pork fat, place in a roasting pan, and roast until done (a small piece cut off will taste tender), about 1¼ hours, adding a few tablespoons of water to the pan now and then. Let the roast rest for 20 minutes before chopping it. Mix the chopped veal with the peas and bell peppers along with 2 tablespoons of the juice from the roasting pan.

3. In a 10-inch nonstick skillet or omelette pan, melt the remaining 2 tablespoons pork fat or lard over medium-low heat and lightly cook the chopped veal mixture, seasoning it with the salt, until the peppers are soft, about 30 minutes, stirring occasionally.

4. Beat the eggs and olive oil together and pour into the pan. Cook until the mixture sets, about 3 minutes. Flip and continue to cook for another 3 minutes, or place under a broiler until the top sets. It may seem impossible to flip a 6-egg omelette, but remember that it will be thick, not wide. When you are ready to flip, slide a metal spatula under the omelette until it is directly under the center, making sure all of it is loosened from the pan. Lift it gently and flip in one quick motion.

5. Transfer to a serving platter. Let cool for a few minutes, then cut into squares and serve.

Makes 6 servings

Lamb, Bean, and Parsley Frittata from Tunisia

Called tājīn al-maᶜadnūs *or parsley tagine, this dish gets its name from the earthenware frying pan it is is cooked in. It's called a frying pan because of the sloping sides, but I use a general-purpose earthenware casserole. There are a lot of eggs in this dish, as well as parsley, and it is quite substantial with the addition of the lamb and beans.*

¼ cup extra-virgin olive oil
½ pound boneless lamb shoulder, trimmed of any fat and cut into small pieces
1 small onion, finely chopped
Salt and freshly ground black pepper to taste
2 tablespoons tomato paste mixed with 1 cup water
2 ounces (about ½ cup) dried white beans, rinsed and picked over
1½ teaspoons ground red chile
10 large eggs
Leaves from ½ pound fresh parsley (about 3 bunches), finely chopped
1 ounce Parmigiano-Reggiano cheese, grated
¼ pound Gruyère cheese, shredded
1½ cups fresh bread crumbs
¼ cup (½ stick) unsalted butter or clarified butter
1½ teaspoons Bahārāt (page 470; see also Note)

1. In a large skillet, heat the olive oil over medium-high heat, then brown the lamb with the onion, about 6 minutes, seasoning with salt and pepper and stirring. Add the diluted tomato paste, beans, and ground chile, bring to a boil. Reduce the heat to low, cover, and simmer until the beans are tender, about 1¼ hours, stirring from time to time and adding water if the sauce gets too thick. Remove from the heat and let cool.

2. Preheat the oven to 350°F.

3. In a large bowl, beat the eggs, then stir in the parsley, cheeses, bread crumbs, 2 tablespoons of the butter, and the *bahārāt*. Taste and correct the seasonings. Butter a 9- to- 10-inch round preferably earthenware casserole or mold with the remaining 2 tablespoons butter and pour the mixture in, leveling it off. Bake until golden on top and a skewer stuck into the middle comes out clean, about 35 minutes.

4. Unmold by lifting gently with a metal spatula, then inverting the tagine onto a round platter. Cut into serving squares and serve hot or warm.

Note: To make the spice mix, stir together ½ teaspoon each ground untreated rose petals, cinnamon, and black pepper.

Makes 8 servings

Tunisian Lamb, Brain, and Fried Potato Frittata with Cheeses

This luscious meze is called, simply enough, ṭājīn al-mukh *(brain frittata). It is cooked in a deep earthenware casserole called a tagine and the finished frittata is about 1½ inches deep. It has a wonderful taste and is always well received. Although it contains brains, a milk, creamy meat, you are more likely to notice the European cheeses used, common ingredients in Tunisian cooking.*

½ pound veal or lamb brain (page 333)
2 tablespoons white wine vinegar
¼ cup (½ stick) unsalted butter
½ pound boneless leg of lamb, trimmed of any fat and cut into small dice
Salt and freshly ground black pepper to taste
¼ cup extra-virgin olive oil
One ½-pound baking potato, peeled and cut into small dice
2 large hard-boiled eggs, shelled and chopped
2 ounces Gruyère cheese, shredded
2 ounces Dutch Edam cheese, shredded
6 large eggs
2 teaspoons all-purpose flour
2 tablespoons freshly grated Parmigiano-Reggiano cheese

1. Soak the brain in lightly acidulated (add either lemon juice or vinegar) cold water to cover for 1 to 2 hours, then drain. Bring a medium-size saucepan of lightly salted water and the vinegar to a very gentle boil, with the water only shimmering, and poach the brain until white and firm, about 20 minutes. Drain and dice the brain.

2. In a large skillet, melt 3 tablespoons of the butter over medium-high heat, then brown the lamb about 5 minutes, add the brain, and cook both, seasoning with salt and pepper, until sizzling vigorously, about 5 minutes. Remove from the heat and let cool. Wipe out the skillet, which you will want to use in step 3 because it is now "seasoned" for cooking potatoes.

3. In the same skillet, heat the olive oil over high heat, then cook the potato until golden brown and crispy, about 8 minutes, stirring often. Remove with a slotted spoon and set aside.

4. In a small bowl, mix the chopped eggs, Gruyère, and Edam. In a large bowl, beat the uncooked eggs, flour, and Parmigiano. Add the contents of the small bowl and mix well. Stir in the browned lamb and brain.

5. Preheat the oven to 350°F.

6. In a 10-inch-diameter preferably earthenware casserole, butter the bottom and sides well with the remaining 1 tablespoon butter. Pour the egg mixture into the casserole and bake until a skewer stuck in the middle comes out clean and the eggs are set, about 30 minutes.

7. Remove from the oven, let cool until it is warm. Unmold carefully with a metal spatula, then invert onto a round platter. Cut into wedges and serve.

Makes 8 servings

Lamb, Onion, and Parsley Frittata from Algeria

Called maᶜqūda bi'l-laḥm, *this frittata is flavored with a copious amount of parsley and onions. As in Spain, it is eaten not only as a lunch dish but also as a meze, in which case you will want to cut it into cubes that can be picked up with the fingers. As a more substantial appetizer, cut it into 8 wedges.*

¾ pound boneless leg of mutton or lamb,
  trimmed of any fat and diced
¼ cup clarified butter or unsalted butter, melted
3 medium-size onions, finely chopped
Leaves from ½ pound fresh parsley (about 3
  bunches), finely chopped
½ teaspoon ground cinnamon
Salt to taste
3½ cups water
6 large eggs
½ teaspoon freshly ground black pepper

1. Put the lamb, 2 tablespoons of the clarified butter, one-third of the chopped onions, one-third of the chopped parsley, ¼ teaspoon of the cinnamon, and the salt in a medium-size casserole and cook over medium heat until browned, about 10 minutes, stirring. Add 1 cup of the water and continue to cook, stirring occasional-

ly, until it evaporates. Continue adding the remaining water in 1- or ½-cup intervals until the lamb is tender and there is just a nice gravy left in the casserole and not much liquid, 1 to 1¼ hours. Remove the meat from the casserole with a slotted spoon and let cool, then chop more finely. Save the gravy.

2. Preheat the oven to 350°F.

3. Generously butter an 8- or 9-inch cake pan or earthenware casserole with high sides. In a large bowl, beat the eggs and stir in the remaining onions, remaining parsley, lamb, pepper, remaining ¼ teaspoon cinnamon, and the gravy. Pour this mixture into the cake pan and place in the oven until golden on top and a knife or skewer poked into the middle comes out clean, about 30 minutes. Remove from the oven and pour the remaining 2 tablespoons melted clarified butter over the cracks that have appeared.

4. Let the frittata cool, unmold, and cut into serving portions.

Makes 8 appetizer servings or
12 hors d'oeuvre servings

"Bull's Eye" Fava Bean Puree

This interestingly named recipe called puree di fava "l'ocio de bò" is an adaptation of a well-known Venetian asparagus dish called spàresi al butiro frito (asparagus fried in butter), made with the renowned white asparagus of Bassano, a town in the Veneto outside Venice, along with either crumbled hard-boiled or scrambled egg. Instead of asparagus, I make a fava bean puree using fresh fava beans blended with milk-soaked fresh country bread, extra-virgin olive oil, a little garlic, and a subtle touch of cinnamon. When one places a sunny-side-up egg in the middle of the asparagus (or fava bean puree, in this case) it is known as vovi l'ocio de bò, *or "bull's eye asparagus," in the dialect of Venice. I particularly like it with scrambled eggs. The key to this dish is fantastically fresh every-thing, including the eggs. Typically, this dish would be served as an antipasto.*

4 pounds fresh fava beans in their pods
One 2-inch-thick slice good-quality French
   or Italian country bread (not sourdough),
   crust removed
½ cup milk
1 small garlic clove, crushed in a mortar with
   1 teaspoon salt until mushy
Salt and freshly ground black pepper to taste
Pinch of ground cinnamon
Extra-virgin olive oil
6 large fresh eggs
¼ cup (½ stick) unsalted butter

1. Remove the fava beans from their pods. Bring a medium-size saucepan of water to a boil and plunge the beans in for 4 minutes to loosen their skins. Drain, pinch off and discard the skins, and put the fava beans in a food proces-sor. Soak the bread in the milk for 10 minutes, then squeeze the milk out. Put the bread and garlic paste in the food processor and pulse a few times. Season with salt and pepper, and add the cinnamon. With the machine running, slowly drizzle in enough olive oil so the puree is creamy, like a hummus. Place a few tablespoons

of fava bean puree each on 8 small appetizer plates, spreading it around the plates with the back of a spoon.

2. It is best to make the scrambled eggs in 2 batches. In a medium-size nonstick skillet, melt 2 tablespoons of the butter over medium heat. In a medium-size bowl, whisk the eggs with a little salt until very frothy. Pour in half the eggs and cook until they set but are still slightly wet, push-ing and scraping them around constantly but not by stirring. Spoon portions of the egg in the center of the fava bean puree on 4 plates. Cook the remaining eggs and serve in the same way.

Makes 8 servings

Stuffed Eggs in Medieval Venice

A great favorite on the table of an aristocrat's dinner party in fourteenth-century Venice was stuffed eggs, *ove plene*. Many eggs were hard-boiled, then shelled, cut in half, and the yolks removed and mashed with a sweet herb pesto and some spices, then stuffed back into the whites.

Poached Eggs in Garlicky Yogurt

This dish of poached eggs set in a garlicky and peppery sauce of thick yogurt called çilbir *in Turkish seems so likely to be served for breakfast, but it is, I am told, also served as a meze. See page 66 for information about the Turkish red pepper called for here.*

2 large garlic cloves, peeled

½ teaspoon salt, plus more to taste

2 cups full-fat plain yogurt

3 tablespoons unsalted butter

½ teaspoon Turkish red pepper or a mixture of 2
parts sweet paprika and 1 part cayenne pepper

4 large eggs

Crusty French or Italian bread

1. In a mortar, pound the garlic with the salt until mushy. In a medium-size bowl, beat the yogurt with a fork until smooth, then beat in the garlic paste.

2. In a butter warmer or small saucepan, melt the butter and stir in the red pepper.

3. Bring a few inches of water to a boil in a large saucepan, add some salt, and stir in one direction to start a gentle whirlpool. Break the eggs rapidly in succession into the swirling boiling water. Do this carefully and close to the water by spilling the egg out of its shell. Cook until the white is set but the yolk is runny, about 2 minutes. Remove the eggs with a slotted ladle, arrange them in shallow individual serving bowls, and spoon ½ cup of the yogurt over the whites of each egg. Drizzle the butter-and-paprika mixture over the eggs and serve immediately with fresh crusty bread.

Makes 4 servings

Stuffed Eggs with Spinach and Cream Cheese

In northern Italy this was called uova sode agli spinaci, *a popular party-style antipasto in the 1950s and 1960s, not usually served in restaurants.*

1 pound fresh spinach, heavy stems removed and washed well

1 ounce Parmigiano-Reggiano cheese, grated (about 1 cup)

½ cup (3 ounces) whipped cream cheese

8 large hard-boiled eggs, shelled, cut in half lengthwise, and yolks removed and saved

Salt and freshly ground black pepper to taste

Freshly grated nutmeg to taste

1. Put the spinach in a large pot with only the water adhering to the leaves from their last rinsing, then cook, covered, over high heat until it begins to wilt, about 4 minutes, stirring occasionally. Drain well, squeezing as much liquid out as possible. Pat dry with paper towels, then chop finely. In a medium-size bowl, mash the spinach together with the Parmigiano, cream cheese, and the yolks of 6 of the eggs (reserve the remaining yolks for another purpose). Season with salt, pepper, and nutmeg.

2. Stuff the egg whites with the stuffing mixture, stuffing only the well where the yolk was. Arrange on a serving platter and chill before serving

Makes 16 stuffed egg halves

Stuffed Eggs with Thick Yogurt from Egypt

This meze is called bayḍ maḥshī, *which simply means "stuffed eggs." It is a mild tasting dish and can be eaten with some lettuce, if desired. Labna, sometimes called "lubny" or "yogurt cheese," is strained yogurt. You can make it yourself if your market doesn't carry it, by placing good-quality plain whole cow's milk yogurt in a cheesecloth and hanging it over a sink or bowl to drain overnight. Two cups of yogurt should yield about 1 cup of* labna.

6 large hard-boiled eggs, shelled and cut in half lengthwise
2 tablespoons finely chopped onion
2 gherkins, very finely chopped
½ cup *labna* (strained yogurt; page 56)
Salt and freshly ground black pepper to taste
6 pitted black olives, cut in half

Remove the yolks of the eggs, place in a medium-size bowl with the onion, gherkins, and *labna*; and season with salt and pepper. Mash well until blended. Fill the egg whites with this mixture, then place a black olive half on top of each and serve.

Makes 12 stuffed egg halves

· ❧ ·

Saucy Little Dishes, Part I
(Chicken, Meat, and Seafood)

From Spain to Tuscany to Turkey, Mediterranean cooks love to serve appetizing dishes in small plates that are savory, saucy, and succulent. These dishes are little foods meant to open the appetite or satisfy the soul, or both. In this chapter is a very wide-ranging collection of tastes. The first set of recipes contain poultry or variety meats, and I think once you taste Circassian Chicken (page 126), you may be hard pressed to make anything else that's as good. But press on because in the next set of recipes are meatball and sausage recipes that are forever popular and well received. Three of my favorites are Pork and Pine Nut Meatballs in Romesco Sauce (page 133), Pork and Spinach Sausage from Provence (page 134), and Kibbe with Yogurt (page 137). The second half of the chapter is filled with saucy seafood dishes, with shrimp being well represented. Sorry, I can't pick a favorite because I keep writing one down and then scratching it out, finally realizing I've chosen all of them.

Circassian Chicken

This is a dish attributed to the Circassians, a Turkic people originally from the area of Russia to the east of the Black Sea, who had or have communities in a couple of Russian republics as well as in Turkey, Jordan, Palestine, and Syria. They converted wholesale to Islam in the seventeenth century. This rich and elegant preparation is made by the Turks and the Armenians and is called çerkez tavuğu *(Circassian chicken) in Turkish.*

One 4-pound chicken

Broth

1 medium-size onion, cut up

1 leek (white and green parts), washed well and chopped

1 large carrot, sliced into rounds

6 cloves

6 allspice berries

10 black peppercorns

5 bay leaves

1 teaspoon coriander seeds

Walnut Sauce

1½ cups (6 ounces) walnuts, chopped

6 large garlic cloves, peeled

Two 1½-inch-thick slices French or Italian bread, crusts removed

½ cup milk

Leaves from 1 small bunch fresh coriander (cilantro), finely chopped

1 tablespoon walnut oil

Salt and freshly ground black pepper to taste

Garnishes

1 tablespoon walnut oil

2 teaspoons paprika

1 teaspoon cayenne pepper

¼ cup chopped walnuts

About 20 fresh coriander (cilantro) leaves

1. Make the broth. Put the chicken in a large stockpot with the broth ingredients and enough water to almost cover the chicken. Bring the water to a very gentle boil, reduce the heat so the water is only shimmering, cover partially, and poach until the chicken legs and wings look like they could fall off, about 1 hour. It is important that the broth never come to a hard boil, otherwise the chicken meat will become tough. Remove the chicken from the pot and, when it is cool enough to handle, pull off all the meat, discarding all the skin, fat, and bones. Shred the meat into thin strips by pulling it apart with a fork.

2. Meanwhile, increase the heat to high under the broth and reduce for 20 minutes. Check the seasoning of the broth and strain.

3. Make the sauce. In a food processor or blender, grind the walnuts and garlic together into a paste. Soak the bread in the milk, then squeeze the liquid out in your hands as if you were making a snowball. Add the bread to the food processor and process until homogenous, scraping down the sides when necessary. Transfer the walnut mixture to a large bowl and dilute it with spoonfuls of broth until it has a mayonnaise consistency, using about 1½ cups of broth in all. Add the chicken and coriander leaves, mix well, and bind together with a few more tablespoons

of the broth and as many teaspoons of walnut oil as necessary until the entire mixture has a creamy consistency. Season with salt and pepper.

4. Make the garnishes. Combine the walnut oil, paprika, and cayenne and stir. Transfer the chicken to an oval serving platter and decorate the top with the chopped walnuts and the perimeter of the platter with coriander leaves; drizzle the top with the flavored walnut oil. Serve at room temperature with warm French bread or Arab flatbread.

Makes 8 to 10 servings

Chicken, Beef, and Ham Meatballs in Gravy

Called albóndigas a la Andaluza, *this* tapa *is a delicious combination of ground beef, chicken, and ham, which has an uncanny resemblance to veal in flavor. The recipe comes from the Sierra Parapanda region in Granada, and is spiced with saffron and pimiento and covered with a rich broth.*

1¼ to 1½ pounds bone-in chicken breast
One ¾-pound slice boiled ham, with center bone
2 cups water
2 tablespoons extra-virgin olive oil
½ pound ground beef
1 cup fresh or dry bread crumbs
2 garlic cloves, very finely chopped
2 tablespoons finely chopped fresh parsley leaves
¼ cup finely chopped roasted red bell peppers (page 415)
Pinch of saffron threads, crumbled
2 large eggs, lightly beaten
¾ teaspoon salt
Juice from ½ lemon
6 cups olive oil, olive pomace oil, or vegetable oil for frying
All-purpose flour for dredging
1 large egg yolk

1. Bone the chicken breasts and set the bones aside. Discard any fat or skin. In a food processor, chop the chicken breasts with several short pulses. Remove to a medium-size bowl. There should be about ½ pound of breast meat.

2. Cut the ham slice in half. One half should have the bone. Grind the half without the bone in a food processor. Remove to the bowl with the chicken. There should be about ½ pound of ham meat.

3. Place the chicken bones and ham slice with bone in a medium-size casserole or saucepan with the water and extra-virgin olive oil. Bring to a boil, then reduce the heat to low and simmer for 45 minutes to extract the flavor.

4. Combine the ground beef, bread crumbs, garlic, parsley, roasted peppers, saffron, beaten eggs, salt, and lemon juice with the chicken and ham. Knead the mixture well and form into meatballs with your hands, kept wet with cold water so the mixture doesn't stick. Make 18 meatballs, or, if you have the patience, as many hazelnut-size ones as you can.

5. Preheat the frying oil in a deep fryer or an 8-inch saucepan fitted with a basket insert to 375°F. Dredge the meatballs in the flour, patting off any excess, and deep-fry in the hot oil until golden, about 2½ minutes (much less if hazelnut-size). Remove from the oil with a

slotted spoon, drain on paper towels, and keep warm.

6. Remove and discard the chicken and ham bones from the broth, strain, and return the broth to the pan. Place the meatballs in the broth and poach over low heat until cooked through, about 45 minutes.

7. Remove the meatballs from the casserole and transfer to a serving platter. Whisk the egg yolk into the broth vigorously and heat for 1 to 2 minutes, then pour over the meatballs and serve. Guests can spear meatballs from the platter with cocktail toothpicks or serve themselves on small *tapa* plates. Let the frying oil cool completely, strain through a porous paper filter, if necessary, and save for a future use.

Makes 6 to 8 servings

Veal Nuggets, Sweetbreads, and Squid in Tomato and Almond Sauce

This Catalonian preparation is a rich dish served as a tapa *in sauce. The mixing of land food and seafood in Catalonian cuisine is common and they call these dishes* mar y montunya, *"sea and mountain." You do not need to give large portions; small ones will do, perhaps with a lightly oiled sliced of French bread rubbed with garlic.*

¼ cup extra-virgin olive oil
¼ cup blanched whole almonds
1 ounce French baguette, sliced (about 5 slices)
½ pound veal stew meat, such as shoulder, trimmed of any fat and cut into ¾-inch cubes

1 small onion, finely chopped
2 large garlic cloves, finely chopped
2 tablespoons finely chopped fresh parsley leaves
¼ cup brandy
Salt and freshly ground black pepper to taste
1 pound fresh tomatoes, cut in half, seeds squeezed out, grated against the largest holes of a grater, and skins discarded
½ cup water, or more as needed
Pinch of saffron threads
½ pound squid, cleaned (page 404) and bodies cut into ½-inch-thick rings with their tentacles
¼ cup distilled white vinegar
One ½-pound veal sweetbread, any membranes removed

1. In a large skillet or casserole, preferably earthenware, heat 3 tablespoons of the olive oil over medium-high heat, then brown the almonds, 3 to 4 minutes. Transfer immediately to a food processor. Brown the slices of bread on both sides in the same oil, 1 to 2 minutes, then transfer to the food processor. Process until the bread and nuts are ground.

2. Add the veal, onion, garlic, and parsley to the casserole and brown for 2 to 3 minutes over medium-high heat. Add the brandy and ignite it with a long match (watch for dangling sleeves and long hair while doing this). Once the flames burn out, stir, season with salt and pepper, and add the tomatoes, water, and saffron. Reduce the heat to low, cover, and cook until tender, about 1 hour, moistening with up to another ½ cup of water so the sauce is not too thick, but not too liquidy, either.

3. Meanwhile, heat the remaining 1 tablespoon olive oil in a medium-size skillet over high heat and cook the squid until light golden and stiff, about 4 minutes. Remove from the pan and set aside.

4. Bring a medium-size saucepan of water to a boil with the vinegar, reduce the heat so the water is barely bubbling, and poach the sweetbreads until white and firm, about 20 minutes. Drain and cut into ¾-inch pieces once cool enough to handle. Add the sweetbreads, squid, and bread-and-nut mixture to the casserole and add water, if needed, to make it saucier. Cook, uncovered, until hot, 5 to 10 minutes, stirring, and serve on a large platter or in small, deep plates for tapas.

Makes 6 servings

What is Catalonia?

This is what Colman Andrews, author of *Catalan Cuisine*, has to say: The usual formula for defining the *països catalans*, the Catalan country, is "from Salses to Guardamar and from Fraga to l'Alguer." Salses is about 10 miles north of Perpignan (in France). Guardamar is south of Valenica, south even of Alicante. Fraga is Aragon, just across the border from Lleida. L'Alguer (Alghero) is in Sardinia.

Braised Veal Tongue with Spicy Capers from Tunis

This extraordinary dish called lisān al-kabar *(tongue with capers) will surprise you. It is* extremely flavorful and delicious. When I was growing up in New York City and on Long Island, tongue was a popular meat. Let a New Yorker reminisce about tongue sandwiches with mustard from the local deli and you will see what I mean. In this recipe the veal tongue is boiled until tender, then braised in a light tomato and caper sauce with onion and Tunisian spices. This recipe is adapted from Chef Jaouida Farah, head chef in some of the most renowned restaurants in Tunis, including the Restaurant Essaraya.

1 veal tongue (about 1¼ pounds)
3 tablespoons extra-virgin olive oil
1 medium-large onion, finely chopped
2 teaspoons Harīsa (page 468)
1 cup water
3 ripe plum tomatoes, peeled, seeded, and finely chopped
2 tablespoons salted or brined capers, rinsed or drained and chopped if large
½ teaspoon freshly ground caraway seeds
½ teaspoon freshly ground cumin seeds
½ teaspoon Tābil (page 471)
Salt and freshly ground black pepper to taste

1. Place the tongue in a pot of lightly salted cold water to cover and turn the heat to medium-high. Boil the veal tongue until tender, about 1 hour. Drain and let cool. Make a small incision in the skin of the tongue with a paring knife and peel all the skin off. Cut into ⅜-inch-thick slices. Dry the tongue slices with absorbent paper towels and set aside in a strainer.

2. In a large skillet, heat the olive oil over medium-high heat, then cook the onion until translucent, about 5 minutes, stirring. Add the *harīsa* dissolved in 2 tablespoons of the water and cook for 1 minute, stirring. Add the tomatoes, ½ cup of the water, the capers, caraway, cumin, and *tābil*, season with salt and pepper, reduce the heat to medium-low, and cook until denser, about 15 minutes. Reduce the heat to low, add the tongue slices, the remaining water, and cook until the sauce is even denser and the tongue is very tender, about 30 minutes, turning the tongue slices occasionally. Serve hot on a large platter or on individual meze plates.

Makes 6 servings

Individual Meze Plates

In restaurants, meze are usually served on small oval plates that come out of the kitchen in random order, with only enough to give four people tiny bites. That's why, if they like some meze very much, diners will place more than one order. At home, meze are served on larger platters set on a buffet table for guests to help themselves.

A Little Turkish Dish Called "Albanian Liver"

The name of this meze, Arnavut ciğeri, *literally translates to "Albanian liver." We don't know why this dish is called Albanian, but it is a style that can be found widely dispersed, from Vienna to central Anatolia. This recipe is identical to a dish I had in Istanbul, but some Turkish cooks bake the livers, while others use a heck of a lot more olive oil than I do. Serve with toothpicks.*

1 medium-size onion, sliced paper-thin
¾ cup finely chopped fresh parsley leaves
1½ pounds veal or lamb liver, trimmed of
   arteries and cut into ½-inch cubes
2 teaspoons salt
2 tablespoons hot Hungarian paprika
¾ cup all-purpose flour
1¼ cups extra-virgin olive oil

1. In a medium-size bowl, toss the onion and parsley together and set aside. In another bowl, toss the liver with the salt and 1 tablespoon of the paprika. Place the flour in another large bowl and toss the seasoned liver in the flour. Transfer to a strainer and vigorously shake off excess flour.

2. In a large skillet, heat the olive oil over medium-high heat until it is smoking, then cook the liver in 3 batches until golden, 2 to 3 minutes. Remove the pieces of meat with a skimmer or slotted spoon to drain on paper towels, then remove ½ cup of the oil to a small bowl. Season that oil with the remaining 1 tablespoon paprika and pour over the liver.

3. Arrange on a serving platter and garnish the top of the veal liver with the sliced onion tossed with parsley. You may not need to use all of the onion; it should cover the liver but not smother it.

Makes 8 servings

A Tapa of Stewed Tripe and Sausage in the Style of Seville

This is a tapa *I had in a tapas bar near the cathedral in Seville that I was wild about. They called it* callos, *which can mean "stew" or "tripe." It was served warm and was just perfect with a glass of sherry, although a beer is nice, too. Veal tripe is best, although beef tripe will be more commonly found. Tripe comes already cleaned, but not cooked, so you will have to boil it at least five hours first; keep that in mind when you prepare this. The vinegar is used as an odor purgative, which is important when cooking tripe, although you can use mastic grains, which can be found in Middle Eastern markets. Also, keep your exhaust fan running at full blast. The Spanish chorizo and* morcilla *sausages are available through www.donajuana.com, or you could use a hot salami to replace the chorizo and a cooked blood sausage to replace the* morcilla. *Remember not to use Mexican chorizo, which is entirely different. Don't ignore the marrow bones and foot; without them, you might as well not bother making this.*

2 pounds veal or beef tripe, fat and gristle
   removed, if necessary

1½ pounds veal or beef marrow bones

2½ pounds veal or beef knuckle
   (shank soup bones)

1 calf or cow's foot (about 1¾ pounds)

½ cup distilled white vinegar

6 tablespoons extra-virgin olive oil

1 medium-size onion, chopped

1 carrot, chopped

3½ ounces smoked bacon or Canadian bacon,
   chopped

4 garlic cloves, finely chopped

1 tablespoon hot Spanish paprika

1 teaspoon ground red chile or cayenne pepper

¼ teaspoon freshly ground cumin seeds

One 6-ounce can tomato paste mixed with water
   to make 1 cup

¼ teaspoon freshly ground cloves

1 bay leaf

1 teaspoon dried thyme

Salt and freshly ground black pepper to taste

5 ounces cooked Spanish chorizo, chopped

½ pound smoked or cooked *morcilla* sausage
   (page 375), thinly sliced

1. Place the tripe, marrow bones, knuckle, and foot in a large stockpot, cover by 5 inches with cold water, and add the vinegar. Bring to a boil and cook at a boil until the tripe is tender and the other meat is falling off the bones, about 5 hours. Replenish the water from time to time so that the tripe is always covered. Once it is cooked, remove and reserve ¾ cup of the cooking broth. Drain, then cut the tripe into bite-size pieces and place in an earthenware casserole along with whatever meat can be salvaged from the other bones, including the marrow of the marrow bones. Discard the foot and all the bones. Place the casserole over a burner, using a heat diffuser if necessary.

2. In a large skillet, heat the olive oil over medium-high heat, then cook the onion, carrot, bacon, and garlic until the onion is soft, about 8 minutes, stirring. Add the paprika, red pepper, cumin, diluted tomato paste, and the reserved broth. Stir, then add the ground cloves, bay leaf, and thyme and season with salt and black

The Taste for the Guignol

A famous ditty from Barcelona casts light on tripe in *callos* in a slightly different manner, for they have their own version of Sweeney Todd, the fiendish Fleet Street innkeeper who notoriously ran a cannibal's delicatessen. In Catalan it goes:

Dels que hi venien, alli bevien	From those who came to drink there
alguns mataven; com capolaven	they killed some then they cut them up
feien pastells e dels budells	they made pies and tripe
feien salsisses o longanisses	they made sausages and salami
del mon pus fines	the best in the world

The taste for this kind of *guignol* was so widespread that etiquette books warned against it, such as in 1384 when the Geronan priest Francesc Eiximenis advised the nouveau riche merchants of Barcelona in his opus *Lo Crestià* how to act at the table so that one does not provoke another person to horror or to vomit.

---

pepper. Pour this mixture over the tripe, add the pieces of chorizo and *morcilla*, turn the heat to high under the earthenware casserole, and, once the liquid begins to bubble, cover, reduce the heat to low and simmer until dense and tender, about 1 hour. Serve warm in small bowls or deep plates.

Makes 12 servings

Tuscan Tripe and Parsley Salad

I am hopelessly in love with tripe and love it prepared in all kinds of ways, especially with spaghetti and tomato sauce. It's too bad not many other people are tripe lovers. So when I ran across this antipasto from Tuscany called trippa in salata, *it looked like something I wanted to try and indeed I was in heaven.*

1¾ pounds beef honeycomb tripe, trimmed of
    fat and gristle
½ cup distilled white vinegar
4 large garlic cloves, very finely chopped
¼ cup finely chopped fresh parsley leaves
2 tablespoons extra-virgin olive oil
Salt and freshly ground black pepper to taste
1 tablespoon fresh lemon juice

1. Place the tripe into salted boiling water with the vinegar and cook at a boil until tender, replenishing the water when necessary, 5 to 7

hours. Drain and, when cool enough to handle, slice into very thin strips.

2. In a large bowl, toss the tripe with the garlic, parsley, olive oil, and salt. Sprinkle some pepper over the tripe, then the lemon juice, and serve.

Makes 8 servings

Pork and Pine Nut Meatballs in Romesco Sauce

This meatball tapa, *called* pilota, *is also known in the French Catalonian province of Roussillon by the same name or as* bols-de-picoulat *(literally, balls of ground meat). There are many different recipes, sometimes using pork, sometimes beef, sometimes sausage, and sometimes with the addition of chicken livers. But almost all recipes find the meatballs containing pine nuts and cinnamon. These meatballs are sometimes found in the famous Spanish stew known as* cocido, *made with ground meat, chicken livers, bread crumbs, egg, garlic, parsley, lemon peel, cinnamon, and pine nuts. As a* tapa, *they are most delicious with Romesco sauce, but if you want to keep it simple, at the end of the cooking of the meatballs, add about ½ cup water to deglaze the pan and serve with the resulting sauce.*

1 pound ground pork
2 chicken livers, trimmed of any membranes and ground or finely chopped
1 cup fresh bread crumbs
1 large egg, beaten
¼ cup finely chopped fresh parsley leaves
3 large garlic cloves, very finely chopped
Grated zest from ½ lemon
¼ cup pine nuts
1 teaspoon salt
Freshly ground black pepper to taste
⅛ teaspoon ground cinnamon
2 tablespoons extra-virgin olive oil
1 recipe Romesco Sauce (page 467)

1. In a medium-size bowl, combine the pork, chicken livers, bread crumbs, egg, parsley, garlic, lemon zest, pine nuts, salt, pepper, and cinnamon. Form the mixture into 1-inch balls, keeping your hands wet so the mixture won't stick. Place them on a plate or tray, cover with plastic wrap, and refrigerate for 30 minutes.

Wine with Tapas

Spanish wine is some of the most fantastic wine you will ever drink, and when drunk in situ with some heavenly tapas such as *albóndigas a la Andaluza*, it's positively unforgettable. Remember that not everything is Rioja, the best known and some would say the best of the Spanish wines. Every region of Spain produces wine, but a lot of it is for ordinary table wine. The best wines are from Rioja, where bold reds are found; Catalonia, where the champagne-like cava comes from; and Galicia, where great whites originate. For sherry, Andalusia is the queen. In Catalonia, Penedès is an exciting wine region where many new wines are developed. Two other wine-growing regions are in Catalonia: Alella and Priorato, north of Barcelona.

2. In a large skillet, heat the olive oil over medium heat, then cook the meatballs until firm, about 15 to 20 minutes, turning with a metal spatula. Remove from the skillet with a slotted spoon to a platter covered with the sauce, heated or at room temperature, and lay the meatballs on top. Serve with toothpicks on the side or in small, deep tapas plates.

Makes 8 servings

The Origin of Spanish Meatballs

After centuries of Islamic rule, it is not surprising to find the Muslim influence everywhere in Spain, right down to the meatballs. The Spanish *albóndigas* derives from the Arabic article *al-* and the Arabic word for hazelnut, *bunduq*, describing the shape and size they are expected to be made.

Pork and Spinach Sausage from Provence

These skinless sausages are known as caillettes. *The word has several meanings. It is the name of the fourth stomach of ruminants, cud-chewing animals. The lining of this tripe is used for rennet in cheese making.* Caillette *is also the name of a sausage of ground meat and spinach or Swiss chard that is wrapped in this lining or caul fat and grilled or baked. In Provence,* caillette *can also mean pâté. The caul fat not only acts as a wrapper for the food but also as a self-baster. Caul fat can be ordered from a butcher. This recipe is an amalgam of versions that can be found in the Basses-Alpes of Provence or in Nîmes in Languedoc. In the Var region of Provence, they replace the spinach with Swiss chard. These* caillettes aux épinards *are also known as* crepinettes *elsewhere in France and they are not unknown in Italy. For example, in the Piedmont, cooks enjoy* griva della langa, *made with ground beef and pork liver seasoned with juniper berries, nutmeg, and Parmesan cheese and also wrapped in caul fat.*

¼ cup pork lard
1 medium-large onion, chopped
2 large garlic cloves, finely chopped
¾ pound spinach or Swiss chard leaves, washed well and chopped
¼ pound smoked bacon, cut into several pieces
½ pound pork or veal liver, trimmed of arteries
½ pound ground pork
½ pound ground veal
3 juniper berries, crushed
¼ teaspoon dried thyme
1 small bay leaf, crumbled
Salt and freshly ground black pepper to taste
1 pound caul fat

1. In a large skillet, melt the lard over medium-low heat, then cook the onion and garlic until soft and translucent, about 10 minutes, stirring. Add the spinach and cook until it wilts, about 6 minutes, stirring.

2. Preheat the oven to 375°F.

3. Process the bacon and liver together in a food processor until mushy, then transfer to a large bowl. Add the contents of the skillet to the

Caul Fat

Caul fat is the large fatty and transparent serous membrane or fold of peritoneum that covers the intestines of cows, sheep, and pigs and is also called the omentum, mesentery, or epiplöon, the latter a word from the Greek (these are names you will never hear a butcher use, who know it as caul fat). Caul fat is sold at any supermarket that makes its own sausages or that has a more ethnic clientele. It is very thin and fragile and is also used to wrap food for grilling, a particularly wonderful taste if you have never tried it. In ancient Greece, Athenaeus describes a dish of fried liver wrapped in *epiplus*, or caul fat. And today in Italy *torcinelli* is a rustic caul fat–wrapped dish with roots in shepherding made by rolling lamb or kid liver and lungs in caul fat, tying them, and roasting them. In Abruzzo and Molise, it is flavored with parsley, garlic, and dried chiles. It can also be called *alenoto*, *marro*, *gnumerieddi*, or *mazzacorde*.

bowl along with the ground pork, veal, juniper, thyme, and bay leaf and season with salt and pepper. Carefully unravel the caul fat because it is fragile, and cut out about fifteen 6-inch square pieces. Place a heaping tablespoon or more of stuffing on each square of caul fat and wrap them up as if you were wrapping a present.

4. Arrange them in a baking dish in a single layer and bake until all are crispy looking and golden brown on top, about 35 minutes. Remove from the oven, transfer, using a slotted spoon, to a serving platter, and serve hot or at room temperature.

Makes 15 caillettes; 6 to 8 servings

Chickpeas with Chorizo Sausage from Andalusia

Called garbanzos con chorizo, *this* tapa *is a fragrant and dense ragout of chickpeas flavored with saffron and paprika and cooked with Spanish chorizo sausages, which are quite different from the hot Mexican ones many Americans are familiar with, especially in the Southwest. This is a* tapa *most appropriate in the winter. The chorizo sausage can be ordered on the Internet at* www.donajuana.com. *Alternatively, if you have a Portuguese community nearby, you may be able to find Portuguese* chouriço, *which is closer to the Spanish sausage. Other possibilities are a cooked Italian sweet sausage, chicken sausage, or Polish kielbasa.*

½ cup extra-virgin olive oil

1 medium-size onion, chopped

2 green bell peppers, seeded and cut into strips

2 ripe tomatoes (about 1 pound), peeled, seeded, and chopped

Pinch of saffron threads, crumbled

1 tablespoon paprika

10 ounces cooked Spanish chorizo sausage, thinly sliced

4 cups cooked chickpeas, drained

1 cup chicken broth

1. In a large nonreactive casserole, heat the olive oil over medium heat, then cook the onion until translucent, 8 to 10 minutes, stirring. Add the bell peppers and tomatoes and cook for another 20 minutes, stirring often.

2. Stir in the saffron and paprika and cook, stirring, for 2 minutes. Stir in the chorizo and cook until heated through, about 5 minutes, then add the chickpeas. Stir in the chicken broth and cook until the sausage is tender, about 15 minutes. Serve from the casserole.

Makes 8 servings

Chorizo

The Spanish chorizo is quite unlike the Mexican chorizo. It is much less spicy from chile pepper and has a more pronounced paprika flavor. I usually buy Spanish chorizo off the Internet, www.donajuana.com being a particularly good source. Chorizo seems to have its origins in the Catalan *xoriço* sausage. There are seventeen officially recognized varieties of chorizo in Catalonia. It is usually made from lean pork, garlic, paprika, red bell peppers, and a little red pepper flakes.

Baby Meatballs in Spicy Tomato and Onion Ragout

These small meatballs the size of a large olive, known as kufta daūd bāshā, *are first browned in oil or clarified butter with fried onions, then simmered in a very flavorful tomato sauce made with lots of thinly sliced onions, garlic, lemon juice, and pepper. Although this is thought of as a Lebanese dish because Daūd Bāshā was the first governor of Mount Lebanon, appointed by the Ottomans with the approval of the Western powers after a bloody war that opposed the Druzes and Christian Maronites in 1860, and is said to be his favorite dish, it is also popular in Syria and Egypt. In northern Syria cooks bake the meatballs, rather than frying them in clarified butter, making for a lighter dish. I've had this dish in Egypt, too, at the Paprika Restaurant on the Nile and also at the famous Filfila restaurant, both in Cairo. In each case, the chef added very thinly sliced grill-charred green peppers to the sauce.*

Meatballs

2 pounds lean ground lamb or beef

¾ teaspoon ground cinnamon

½ teaspoon freshly ground allspice berries

Salt and freshly ground black pepper

Sauce

½ cup clarified butter

½ cup pine nuts

1½ pounds onions, very thinly sliced

3 large garlic cloves, finely chopped

One 6-ounce can tomato paste

1¼ cups water

½ teaspoon ground cinnamon

¼ teaspoon freshly ground allspice berries

Salt and freshly ground black pepper to taste

½ cup fresh lemon juice

1 green bell pepper, grilled or roasted (page 415) until very blackened, peeled, seeded, and cut into thin strips

1. Make the meatballs. Mix the meat in a large bowl with the cinnamon, allspice, salt, and pepper. Transfer to a food processor, in two batches, and process until the meat is pasty, about 1 minute. Transfer back to the original bowl while you process the next batch. Form the mixture into about 100 olive-size meatballs.

2. Make the sauce. In a large skillet, melt or heat the clarified butter over medium-high heat, then cook the meatballs until they are all brown on all sides, about 8 minutes. Remove with a slotted spoon and set aside. In the remaining butter, cook the pine nuts until golden, about 2 minutes, then remove with a slotted ladle and set aside with the meatballs. Add the onions and garlic and cook until soft and translucent, about 8 minutes, stirring frequently so the garlic doesn't burn. Add the tomato paste dissolved in the water, stir in the cinnamon and allspice, season with salt and pepper to taste, bring to a boil, then reduce the heat to low and cook for 5

minutes, stirring. Return the meatballs and pine nuts to the skillet and cook, covered, until thickened and flavorful, about 35 minutes.

3. Stir in the lemon juice and green bell pepper, if using, cook for 5 more minutes, correct the seasonings, transfer to a platter, and serve hot.

Makes 12 servings

Kibbe with Yogurt

This is a good recipe for leftover kibbe, the stuffed bulgur-and-meat ovals that is a famous Lebanese meze. Kubba bi'l-laban, *which means kibbe with yogurt, is one of many preparations one can make with kibbe. Here the kibbe are stirred into yogurt for a very satisfying dish served with rice when not serving it as a meze.*

½ recipe uncooked kibbe (12 kibbe; page 364)

1 recipe stabilized yogurt (page 138)

3 garlic cloves, peeled

1½ teaspoons salt

2 teaspoons dried mint

¼ cup clarified butter

Salt to taste

1. Make and shape the kibbe.

2. Bring the yogurt to a boil in a large, heavy saucepan. Reduce the heat to low and simmer for 5 minutes. Add the kibbe and continue to simmer, uncovered.

3. Meanwhile, in a mortar, pound the garlic, salt, and mint together until well mashed. In a small skillet, heat the clarified butter over medium-high heat, then cook the garlic mixture

Stabilized Yogurt

Cow's milk yogurt will separate if brought to a boil, so cooks in the Middle East either use goat's milk yogurt or they stabilize cow's milk yogurt by cooking it with cornstarch and egg whites, as in this recipe.

1 quart full-fat plain cow's milk yogurt

1 large egg white, beaten

1 tablespoon cornstarch

1 teaspoon salt

1. Beat the yogurt in a large, heavy saucepan with a fork until smooth. Beat in the egg white, cornstarch, and salt.

2. Put the saucepan over high heat and start stirring in one direction with a wooden spoon. As soon as the mixture starts to bubble, about 6 minutes, turn the heat to medium and boil gently until it is thick, about 5 minutes. The yogurt is ready to use, or it will keep for a week if refrigerated.

Makes 1 quart

for 30 seconds to 1 minute, stirring. Stir into the yogurt and taste; salt as necessary. Simmer for 15 minutes without stirring; the yogurt should be thick. If it is not, simmer 5 more minutes and serve in individual small, deep plates or in a deep platter on a buffet table.

Makes 4 to 6 servings

Greek Cocktail Meatballs in Sauce

Although keftedes *are often served as a main course, when they are made very small, the size of a large marble, as they are in this recipe for* keftedakia marinata, *they can be served as a meze. There are many recipes for these meat-* *balls: they can be served without the sauce as finger food, or they can be seasoned with oregano rather than parsley and mint, or you could add some allspice, cloves, and Worcestershire sauce to the meatballs, or you could make them with veal and season them with dill, or you could make them in the style I once had them at the Matoyla restaurant in Monemvasia, in the southeastern Peloponnesus, which tasted almost Turkish: the meatballs were soft and very flavorful, seasoned with dill and spiced with cinnamon, coriander, and cumin.*

2 cups cubed Italian or French bread, white part only

¾ cup water

1¼ pounds lean ground lamb

½ cup finely chopped fresh parsley leaves

2 tablespoons finely chopped fresh mint leaves

1 teaspoon freshly ground coriander seeds

2 small onions, 1 grated and 1 chopped

4 large garlic cloves, 2 mashed and 2 finely chopped

Salt and freshly ground black pepper to taste

6 cups pure or virgin olive oil, olive pomace oil, or vegetable oil for frying

All-purpose flour for dredging

2 tablespoons extra-virgin olive oil

2 pounds ripe plum tomatoes, peeled, seeded, and chopped

1 cup dry red wine

1 cinnamon stick

2 tablespoons chopped fresh savory leaves or 1 teaspoon dried savory

1. In a large bowl, soak the bread cubes in the water until sodden. Squeeze the water out between your palms as if you were making a snowball. Drain the water from the bowl and knead together the bread, lamb, 6 tablespoons of parsley, the mint, coriander, grated onion, and mashed garlic and season with salt and pepper. Cover with plastic wrap and refrigerate overnight.

2. Preheat the frying oil in a deep fryer or an 8-inch saucepan fitted with a basket insert to 375°F.

3. Remove the meat mixture from the refrigerator and form meatballs half the size of a walnut, keeping your hands wet with cold water so the meat doesn't stick to them. Dredge the meatballs in flour, tapping off any excess. Deep-

fry the meatballs in batches (do not crowd them) in the hot oil until light brown, about 3 minutes. Drain on paper towels and set aside. Let the frying oil cool completely, strain through a porous paper filter, if necessary, and save for a future use.

4. In a large earthenware or enameled cast-iron casserole, heat the 2 tablespoons extra-virgin olive oil over medium heat, then cook the chopped onion until translucent, about 8 minutes, stirring occasionally. Add the chopped garlic, tomatoes, wine, cinnamon stick, remaining 2 tablespoons parsley, and the savory and season with salt and pepper. Stir well to blend and simmer for 45 minutes.

5. Remove the cinnamon stick and discard. Add the meatballs to the sauce, stir, reduce the heat to low, and cook until thickened a bit, another 15 to 30 minutes. Serve warm, not hot, in a deep platter with cocktail toothpicks.

Makes 12 servings

Beans, Bulgur, and Lamb Salad from Lebanon

This dish called maklūṭa *is a typical preparation found in the Lebanese mountains. In Lebanon, a* maklūṭa *is a potpourri, a mixture of meat, legumes, and other popular vegetables. It can also be made with a variety of ingredients, perhaps a mixture of lentils, rice or bulgur, and chickpeas. Some cooks stir in* qawrama, *a preserved flavored lamb fat used in Lebanese and Syrian cooking. In Algeria, this dish, made a bit differently, is known as* kahlūṭa. *You can serve it hot or at room temperature, perhaps with an extra little drizzle of olive oil.*

2 tablespoons extra-virgin olive oil

½ pound boneless lean leg of lamb, trimmed of any fat and finely diced or ground

Salt and freshly ground black pepper to taste

¼ pound (⅔ cup) dried red kidney beans, picked over and rinsed

¼ pound (⅔ cup) dried large white beans, picked over and rinsed

5 cups water

1 cup cooked chickpeas, drained

¼ pound (⅔ cup) dried brown lentils, picked over and rinsed

1 large onion, finely chopped

¼ pound (⅔ cup) coarse bulgur (no. 4), rinsed and drained

2 teaspoons freshly ground cumin seeds

1. In a medium-size skillet, heat 1 tablespoon of the olive oil over medium-high heat, then brown the lamb seasoned with salt and pepper, about 4 minutes. Remove from the heat and set aside, pouring off any accumulated fat.

2. In a large saucepan, place the kidney and white beans and cover with the water. Bring to a boil, cover, and cook for 5 minutes. Reduce the heat to low, and cook for 45 minutes, then add the chickpeas. When the beans are tender, about 1¼ hours in all, add the lentils, onion, and the remaining 1 tablespoon olive oil, bring to a boil, cover, reduce the heat to low, and simmer until soft, about 15 minutes. Add the lamb, bulgur, and cumin, season with salt and pepper, cover, and cook until the liquid is

absorbed, another 15 minutes. Taste and correct the seasonings.

3. Transfer to a serving platter and let it come to room temperature, although it's also tasty hot.

Makes 10 servings

Lamb Brain with Lemon and Dill Sauce

Brain is a rich meat and very mild tasting. Although veal brain is easier to find, you should try looking for lamb brain from a specialty butcher. This Greek meze, called myala me lemoni, *is very simple. First, the brain must be soaked in acidulated water for one to two hours. It must be poached very gently in water that is merely shimmering. It is cooled and finally tossed with a lemon dressing and left to marinate in the refrigerator for another two hours.*

1 pound lamb or veal brain (page 333)

¼ cup distilled white vinegar

¼ cup extra-virgin olive oil

4 teaspoons white wine vinegar

2 tablespoons fresh lemon juice

2 tablespoons finely chopped fresh dill

Salt and freshly ground black pepper to taste

1. Soak the brain in cold water for 1 to 2 hours, changing the water once, then drain. Place the brain in a medium-size saucepan of lightly salted and gently bubbling water to which the distilled vinegar has been added and poach until white and firm, about 20 minutes. Drain and, when cool enough to handle, cut

Preserved Lamb Fat

In the cooking of Lebanon and Syria and among the Palestinians too, *qawrama* is both the name of a preserved lamb fat, *duhnīyāt*, a kind of flavored fat used for cooking, and the name of a dish of mutton or beef cut into small pieces and braised with lots of onions and tomatoes. The preserved lamb is made by cooking fatty mutton or lamb tail (usually), but also shoulder meat with abundant salt, then pouring the browned meat and its fat into preserving jars. The sheep favored by Arab cooks are the fat-tailed species (*Ovis aries* L. *platura*), with tails that are very wide and up to two feet long, mostly all fat; the sheep were introduced to the Levant by the Turks. After the preparation is made, a layer of fat solidifies on top. The cook scoops out spoonfuls to use in various preparations, including in vegetable cookery. To make *qawrama*, grind together equal amounts of lamb fat and lamb shoulder and neck meat. Place in a stew pot and simmer over medium-low heat while adding abundant salt (1½ teaspoons per 1 pound of meat mixture) and a mixture of black pepper and *bahārāt* (page 470), about 1 tablespoon spice mix per pound of mixed meat). Simmer for 6 hours, then pour off the fat into a container with some of the meat. Freeze and use for a cooking fat in meat or vegetable recipes.

into ½-inch cubes. Set aside in a strainer to drain and cool further.

2. Pour the olive oil into a medium-size bowl and whisk into it the white wine vinegar, lemon juice, dill, salt, and pepper. Add the brain and toss. Let the brain marinate for 2 hours in the refrigerator. Serve cold on small individual plates.

Makes 8 servings

Lamb Liver, Scallions, and Dill

Called sikotaki *in Greek, this meze is really quite simple, but in order to make it appetizing, you need to pay very close attention to the liver,* since overcooked liver is, as far as I'm concerned, garbage. American supermarkets traditionally slice liver too thin, making it very easy for the cook to overcook it. Ideally, the liver should be cut about ½ inch thick so that you can make nice, smaller-than-bite-size cubes. Lamb liver will have to be specially ordered from a butcher, but veal liver is perfectly fine, even if it is too mild and not as distinctive as lamb liver.

1 pound calf or lamb's liver, trimmed of arteries and cut into smaller than bite-size pieces
¼ cup extra-virgin olive oil
1 bunch scallions, thinly sliced
¼ cup finely chopped fresh dill
Juice of 1 lemon

1. Bring a large saucepan of lightly salted water to a boil, then plunge the liver bits in and remove them immediately by draining in a strainer. Set aside.

2. In a medium-size skillet, heat the olive oil over medium-high heat, then cook the liver until still a little pink on the inside, 2 to 3 minutes. Remove with a slotted spoon to a serving platter. Add the scallions and all but 1 tablespoon of the dill to the skillet and cook until the scallions are soft, 2 to 3 minutes, stirring. Pour the scallions over the liver, toss a bit, then sprinkle the lemon juice and the remaining dill over the liver, and serve immediately.

Makes 4 to 6 servings

"Rocky Mountain Oysters" in an Algerian Spicy Sauce

Lamb testicles, which at first blush may sound like something you would never want to eat, is actually a delicious, very mild, finely textured meat that is somewhat bland and therefore this piquant recipe is perfect for it. This dish called ṣawālah bayḍ qasinṭīniya, *"white testicles from Constantine," a major city in eastern Algeria, is made with the testicles of an older sheep, namely mutton. The sauce is called a* dirsa *sauce and is also very popular to use with grilled foods. When I first tested this recipe, for an American crowd, I knew that I should make myself unavailable when people started asking me what it was. Everyone was plowing right into it, gobbling it up and enjoying the dish, but the truth had to come out and there were some shocked wide eyes. I hope you don't have to trick people to eat this, but if you*

do, wait until they're raving about it before you spill the beans. You could also use some unfamiliar euphemisms (see box). And the jokes told at the table—well, you can just imagine.

2 pounds lamb testicles

3 tablespoons extra-virgin olive oil

4 ripe tomatoes (about 1½ pounds), cut in half, seeds squeezed out, grated against the largest holes of a grater, and skins discarded

1 teaspoon sweet paprika

½ teaspoon ground red chile or cayenne pepper

¾ teaspoon freshly ground cumin seeds

4 large garlic cloves, finely chopped

½ to 1 teaspoon salt, or to taste

¼ cup water (optional)

4 large eggs

1. Bring a large saucepan of water to a boil and plunge the testicles in for 2 minutes. Remove, let cool, and make an incision in the skin of the testicles. Remove the cuticule (albuginea), which covers the testicles, peeling it away from the meat.

2. Refill the saucepan with water, salt it, bring to a boil, and boil the testicles for another 5 minutes. Drain, let cool, and cut into small pieces.

3. Meanwhile, prepare the *dirsa* sauce. In a medium-size skillet, heat the olive oil over medium heat, then cook the tomatoes, paprika, ground chile, ½ teaspoon of the cumin, the garlic, and salt until you have a dense sauce, about 10 minutes, stirring occasionally. Moisten with the water if the tomatoes weren't juicy, then add the testicles and cook for 20 minutes, stirring.

4. Preheat the oven to 350°F. Transfer the meat and sauce to a baking dish and spread them around evenly with the bottom of a spoon, making sure the meat and sauce are higher around the edges than in the middle. Make 4 shallow indentations and crack an egg into each one. Bake until the eggs set, about 25 minutes. Sprinkle the remaining ¼ teaspoon cumin on top and serve hot.

Makes 8 servings

Testicles

In the Mediterranean people think nothing when served testicles. They are delicious, as anyone who's tried them will attest. We squeamish Americans have come up with some great euphemisms for testicles and, if I were you, I would use any of these if you decide to make the excellent testicle meze on the opposite page. Try calling them Rocky Mountain oysters, prairie oysters, Montana tendergroin, fries, swinging beef, barnyard family jewels, or ranch fries.

Shrimp in Butter and Garlic Sauce as Made in Turkey

The name of this preparation, sarımsaklı karides, *means garlicky shrimp. It's a wonderful preparation with fresh shrimp and always a favorite as a starter.*

4 pounds fresh large or extra jumbo shrimp with their heads or 2 pounds previously frozen headless shrimp, shells and/or heads removed and saved for making broth, deveined if desired

1 quart water

3 bay leaves

2 tablespoons plus 1 teaspoon salt

1 cup white wine vinegar

½ cup (1 stick) unsalted butter

16 large garlic cloves, finely chopped

1 teaspoon red pepper flakes

10 slices French bread

Chopped fresh dill for garnish (optional)

1. If using extra jumbo shrimp (16 to 20 count per pound), then make a 1¼-inch-long diagonal slit along the top of the shrimp with a sharp paring knife and they will splay open attractively when cooked. If using large shrimp (31 to 40 count), leave them as they are without their shells. Bring the water to a boil in a medium-size saucepan with the bay leaves, 2 tablespoons of the salt, and the vinegar. Add the shrimp a handful at a time, very quickly, then cook until they all turn color, to a pink or orange-red, 1 to 2 minutes. Do not leave any shrimp in the hot water for more than 2 minutes. Remove immediately or drain immediately, but save ¾ cup of the cooking water and set the shrimp aside.

2. In a large skillet, melt the butter with the garlic and 1 teaspoon of the salt over high heat. Drain any liquid that has collected while the shrimp were resting. Add the shrimp to the skillet and stir, then pour in the reserved cooking water and cook until firm, about 5 minutes or less. Sprinkle with the red pepper flakes, stir to

mix well, then transfer by ladlefuls to individual small soup bowls, each of which should have a slice of French bread in it. Spoon the remaining garlic-and-butter sauce over the shrimp and serve sprinkled with the dill if desired.

Makes 8 servings

Pan-Fried Shrimp with Dill

In Greece, there are a variety of meze that go by the name garides tighanites, *"fried shrimp." This particular recipe is best made with fresh shrimp and served warm, although room temperature is very nice, too. I usually serve this with some crusty Greek or Italian bread and a glass of ouzo. Quite perfect, I think.*

3 tablespoons unsalted butter

¼ cup extra-virgin olive oil

2 pounds large fresh shrimp with their heads or 1 pound previously frozen headless shrimp, shells and/or heads removed and saved for making shrimp stock, if desired

Salt to taste

Juice of 1 lemon

1 to 2 tablespoons finely chopped fresh dill, to your taste

1. In a large skillet, melt the butter with 2 tablespoons of the olive oil over medium heat, then cook the shrimp seasoned with salt until red-orange and firm, 2 to 3 minutes, tossing and stirring. Remove and set aside in a serving bowl.

2. In a small bowl, whisk together the remaining 2 tablespoons olive oil, the lemon juice, and

dill to make a creamy yellow vinaigrette and pour over the shrimp. Toss well and serve warm with the sauce on individual small meze plates or on a platter.

Makes 8 servings

Canocchie

Canocchie, also called *canocie, canoce,* or *schile*, is a famous crustacean of the Venetian lagoon known as mantis shrimp (*Squilla mantis*). They are about 6 inches long and taste like a cross between lobster and shrimp. They are usually eaten as a boiled antipasto in Venice, with only a simple dressing of olive oil, lemon juice, salt, and pepper.

Fresh Shrimp in Garlic and Olive Oil

This Italian preparation has come to be known as shrimp scampi in America, which means "shrimp shrimp," since scampi *is the Italian word for "shrimp." In any case, what is meant is that the shrimp are cooked like the Italians make shrimp—namely, in garlic and olive oil. This is a great little appetizer since it's very quick to do.*

4 pounds fresh shrimp with their heads or 2 pounds previously frozen headless shrimp, shells and/or heads removed and saved for making shrimp stock, if desired

½ cup extra-virgin olive oil

3 large garlic cloves, finely chopped

½ cup finely chopped fresh parsley leaves
(optional)
Salt and freshly ground black pepper to taste

1. In a large bowl, toss together the shrimp, olive oil, garlic, and parsley, if using. Season with salt and pepper.

2. Place the shrimp in a large skillet, turn the heat to high, and cook, shaking and turning the shrimp often, until bright red or orange and fragrant, about 7 minutes. Taste for salt. Serve immediately on a large, slightly deep platter.

Makes 8 servings

Pantelleria-Style Shrimp and Tomatoes with Pine Nuts and Capers

This exquisite preparation called gamberetti al pomodoro *(shrimp with tomatoes) is typical of the dishes made around Marsala in Sicily and on the island of Pantelleria, which is famous for its capers. Although this dish is fine when served hot, I like it much better at room temperature after it sits for a day and the luscious flavors of tomatoes, olive oil, pine nuts, celery, capers, and raisins have a chance to mellow.*

4 quarts water
¼ cup sea salt
2 pounds fresh medium-size shrimp with their heads or 1 pound previously frozen headless shrimp, shells and/or heads removed and saved for making shrimp stock, if desired
½ cup extra-virgin olive oil
1 medium-size onion, chopped

1 stalk celery, chopped
1 pound ripe tomatoes, peeled, seeded, and chopped
1 tablespoon pine nuts
1 tablespoon golden raisins, soaked in tepid water for 15 minutes and drained
1 tablespoon salted or brined capers, rinsed or drained and chopped if large
Salt and freshly ground black pepper to taste
2 bay leaves

1. Bring the water to a rolling boil and add the salt. Boil the shrimp until they turn orange, 1 to 2 minutes. Drain immediately and cut the shrimp into thirds.

2. Preheat the oven to 375°F.

3. In a stove-top and ovenproof casserole, heat the olive oil over medium heat, then cook the onion and celery until the onion is translucent, about 10 minutes, stirring frequently. Add the tomatoes, pine nuts, raisins, and capers; season with salt and pepper, and cook 10 minutes more, stirring. Add the shrimp and bay leaves, cook for 1 minute, then remove the casserole from the heat.

4. Put the casserole in the oven and bake 10 minutes. Remove from the oven, let the shrimp come to room temperature in the casserole, remove the bay leaves, and serve on a large platter.

Makes 4 to 6 servings

Spot Prawns in Tomato and Chile Sauce

This extraordinary preparation must be made with fresh spot prawns with their heads on, even though I give you the choice of frozen shrimp. But it would even be better, should you not be able to get fresh prawns or shrimp, to use two small 1-pound lobster rather than frozen shrimp. In any case, this Sicilian recipe called gammareddu a ghiotta spizzusa, *or simply* gamberetti in salsa piccante *in Italian, is adapted from Pino Correnti, a leading Sicilian culinary authority who was of assistance when I was researching my first cookbook on the food of Sicily in the 1980s. (By the way, you notice the use of the word* ghiotta? *Well, look at page 189 for more on that.) The water in which you cook the prawns in step 1 should be abundantly salted, meaning it should taste like seawater— I'd try adding about ¼ cup salt to the water.*

2 pounds fresh jumbo spot prawns or shrimp with their heads (about 10) or 1 pound previously frozen headless shrimp

½ cup extra-virgin olive oil

1 small onion, thinly sliced

3 large garlic cloves, finely chopped

3 pounds very ripe tomatoes, cut in half, seeds squeezed out, grated against the largest holes of a grater, and skins discarded

1 fresh red chile, seeded and finely chopped

Handful of fresh parsley leaves, finely chopped

1 medium-size ripe tomato, peeled, seeded, and chopped

½ teaspoon ground red chile or cayenne pepper

Salt and freshly ground black pepper to taste

1. Bring a pot of abundantly salted water to a boil and cook the prawns or shrimp until they turn color, about 2 minutes. Remove from the water before the water returns to a boil, saving 1 cup of the broth. Remove the shells if you are using previously frozen shrimp. If you are using fresh spot prawns, leave on their heads, shells, and any caviar (eggs) attached to them.

3. In an earthenware casserole, heat the olive oil with the onion and garlic over medium-high heat using a heat diffuser, then cook until translucent, about 10 minutes, stirring frequently so the garlic doesn't burn. If you are using a regular casserole, the onion will be done in half the time. Add the grated tomatoes, reserved broth, and chopped chile and continue to cook until the liquid is much evaporated and the sauce is dense but not a paste, about 30 minutes.

4. Add the parsley, chopped tomato, prawns, and ground chile and bring to a boil. Season with salt and black pepper and cook until the shrimp are firm, about 8 minutes. Serve immediately on a large platter or 2 prawns per individual plate.

Makes 8 servings

Shrimp and Garlic from Granada

One of the most charming restaurants in Granada is the Sevilla Restaurant by the cathedral. When I was there last, I sat outside and had a lovely shaded view of a portal of the cathedral. I ordered gambas al ajillo, *the famous Andalusian tapa shrimp and garlic, and was very disappointed when I saw it. The earthenware casserole it came in was pathetically small and I had just paid $16 for this tapa. But after one taste, I closed my eyes in ecstasy and slowed down.*

The bowl was a bit deeper than I expected, so there were about twenty delicately cooked hidden shrimp that were so fresh they literally melted in your mouth. They were submerged in a liquid that was a very garlicky hot sauce colored with paprika and washed in olive oil. I used my bread to dunk in this powerful garlic sauce, noticing that there were sliced garlic and little black pine nut-sized hot chiles, which had some kind of almost oriental taste to them.

4 pounds fresh large shrimp with their heads or
    2 pounds previously frozen headless shrimp,
    shells and/or heads removed and saved for
    shrimp stock, if desired
2 tablespoons coarse sea salt
2 cups extra-virgin olive oil
8 to 10 large garlic cloves, sliced
20 very small Thai chiles (also called chilipiquin
    or piquín)
2 teaspoons hot Spanish paprika

1. Dry the shrimp with paper towels. Place them in a bowl, sprinkle with the salt, and leave for 10 minutes.

2. In an 8- to 10-inch earthenware casserole (preferably), heat the olive oil over medium-high heat. Once the oil is smoking, add the garlic and chiles and cook until the garlic starts to turn color, 30 to 60 seconds, then add the shrimp and paprika and cook until orange-red, 3 to 4 minutes. Serve immediately from the casserole with lots of crusty Italian or French bread.

Makes 8 servings

Shrimp in Garlic, Bell Pepper, and Hazelnut Sauce

Although Catalans have not traditionally eaten tapas, today tapas are found all over Spain. This dish is garlicky, but given the amount called for, not overly so, and is often served in individual terra-cotta casseroles at tapas bars. The small shrimp called for are 70 to 90 count per pound of headless shrimp.

¼ cup extra-virgin olive oil
1 head garlic (about 12 cloves), cloves separated,
    peeled, and finely chopped
1½ pounds red bell peppers, roasted (page 415),
    peeled, seeded, and cut into thin strips
1 large ripe tomato, cut in half, seeds squeezed
    out, grated against the largest holes of a grater,
    and skins discarded
½ cup hazelnuts, roasted, skins rubbed off (page
    465), and coarsely ground in a food processor
Pinch of saffron threads, crumbled
½ teaspoon red pepper flakes
Salt and freshly ground black pepper to taste
4 pounds fresh small shrimp with their heads or
    2 pounds previously frozen headless shrimp,
    shells and/or heads removed and saved for
    making shrimp stock, if desired
¼ cup dry white wine
2 tablespoons finely chopped fresh parsley leaves

1. In a large skillet, heat the olive oil over high heat, then add the garlic, bell peppers, tomato, hazelnuts, saffron, and red pepper flakes; reduce the heat to low and cook until the liquid has evaporated, about 1 hour, stirring occasionally. Season with salt and black pepper.

2. Increase the heat to high and, once the sauce is bubbling, add the shrimp and cook until beginning to turn orange, about 1 minute. Taste one shrimp and add salt if necessary. Stir in the wine and cook until the shrimp are firm and orange, 1 to 2 minutes more. Transfer to a serving platter, sprinkle with the parsley, and serve immediately.

Makes 8 to 10 servings

Spinach Timbale with Shrimp Cream Sauce

This Italian antipasto called sformatini di spinaci *is best made for a more formal occasion since it is elegant and a bit involved. It is a spinach mold that is baked in the oven, then surrounded with a white wine-reduced cream sauce. This recipe is adapted from the Italian food magazine* La cucina italiana.

Spinach mold
¼ cup (½ stick) unsalted butter
2 shallots, finely chopped
1½ pounds spinach, heavy stems removed, washed well, and dried well
½ cup plus 2 tablespoons heavy cream
2 large egg whites
1 teaspoon salt
Freshly ground black pepper to taste

Sauce
¼ cup extra-virgin olive oil
2 shallots, finely chopped

2 pounds fresh medium-size shrimp with their heads or 1 pound previously frozen headless shrimp, shells and/or heads removed and saved for making shrimp stock, if desired
½ cup dry white wine
⅔ cup heavy cream
⅛ teaspoon cayenne pepper
Salt to taste

1. Preheat the oven to 400°F.
2. Make the spinach mold. In a large skillet, melt the butter with the shallots over medium heat and cook until soft, about 5 minutes, stirring. Add the spinach and cook until it wilts, 3 to 5 minutes, stirring. Remove from the heat and let cool. Transfer the spinach mixture to a food processor, add the cream, egg whites, salt, and pepper and process until smooth, about 2 minutes.
3. Butter eight 2-inch ovenproof ramekins and fill them with the spinach mixture. Place the ramekins in a large baking pan and fill halfway up their sides with warm water. Bake until a skewer inserted in the center comes out relatively clean, 30 to 40 minutes.
4. Meanwhile, make the sauce. In a skillet, heat the olive oil with the shallots over medium-high heat, then cook until soft, about 2 minutes. Add the shrimp and cook until orange-pink, about 2 minutes. Remove the shrimp with a slotted ladle and set aside. Pour in the wine to deglaze and, after it has almost evaporated, add the cream, cayenne, and salt. Reduce the heat to low and cook until the liquid reduces and is syrupy, 10 to 15 minutes. Return the shrimp when there is about 2 minutes left to cook.

5. Unmold the hot *sformatini* into the center of individual serving plates, surround with the sauce, and serve immediately.

Makes 8 servings

Sformato

This Italian expression literally means "to form something," in this case, a timbale, a word we get from the French for the kettle-drum—namely, a mold in the shape of a drum in which ingredients, usually vegetables, are mixed with beaten eggs to produce a light and fluffy soufflé-like dish. *Sformati* are usually made in large molds such as conical molds, savarin, or charlotte molds and are always served as an antipasto with an accompanying sauce. Some popular *sformatini* are made with spinach, or eggplant, or zucchini, or artichokes.

Mussels with Feta Cheese from Rhodes

In the early 1990s, on a research trip to Rhodes while working on my tome A Mediterranean Feast, *I spent a little longer time on the famous island than intended because my friend and I were stranded there by severe weather. But it was a fortunate experience because we met Theo Tsakkis, owner with his wife, Constance, of Nireas, a restaurant serving traditional food from Rhodes, which is a rarity on this tourist-infested island. The old town of Rhodes is a walled city that will make you feel you're about to encounter one of the Knights Templar at any moment. I lost touch with Theo and when I returned to Rhodes nearly six years later, I tried to find him, which I did, and we had a wonderful reunion. He was so excited to see his name and recipes in print in my big book, which I brought as a gift, that he ran into the kitchen and prepared this wonderful dish of mussels and feta cheese he called* midye saganaki.

4 pounds mussels, scrubbed and debearded (page 368)

¼ cup water

6 tablespoons extra-virgin olive oil

2 medium-size onions, chopped

2 green bell peppers, seeded and chopped

¾ pound ripe tomatoes, cut in half, seeds squeezed out, grated against the largest holes of a grater, and skins discarded

¼ pound imported Greek or Bulgarian feta cheese, cut into small cubes

1. Place the cleaned mussels in a pot with the water, cover, and turn the heat to high. Remove the mussels as soon as they open, 6 to 9 minutes. Discard any mussels that remain firmly shut. Remove the mussels from their shells and set aside.

2. In a medium-size skillet, heat the olive oil over medium-high heat, then cook the onions and peppers until the onions are translucent, about 8 minutes, stirring occasionally. Add the tomatoes and cook until the most of the liquid has evaporated, about 5 minutes.

3. Add the mussels and scatter the cubes of cheese around the skillet evenly. Cook until the

Diane Kochilas on the Cuisine of Rhodes

"The priest . . . brought us out plate after plate of delicious country food. Simple stuff—moist, plump, cumin-scented chickpea patties, greens fritters, my sought-after stewed purslane, fish cakes made with small fry, chicken with tomato and sage sauce, his wife's own cheese, and, finally, to wash it all down, a carafe of his own wine, made from one of Rhodes' indigenous grape varietals, Amorghiano. That, in a nutshell, is what the cooking of Rhodes and of the greater Dodecanese is all about."

—FROM *THE GLORIOUS FOODS OF GREECE: TRADITIONAL RECIPES FROM THE ISLANDS, CITIES, AND VILLAGES* (WILLIAM MORROW, 2001)

cheese melts a bit and the food is hot, about 8 minutes, then serve hot right from the skillet with crusty bread.

Makes 8 servings

Valencia-Style Clams

The clams favored in Valencian cooking are not actually called clams, but are another variety of bivalve, such as cockles (berberechos), *carpet shells* (almejas), *and wedge shells* (coquinas). *This style of cooking clams, called* almejas a la Valenciana, *is popularly served as a* tapa *in Valencia. A mildly hot chile to use here would be a poblano.*

16 littleneck clams (about 2 pounds)
1 tablespoon baking soda
½ cup extra-virgin olive oil
2 large, ripe tomatoes (about ¾ pound), peeled, seeded, and finely chopped
1 fresh mildly hot green chile, seeded and finely chopped
2 garlic cloves, finely chopped
1 tablespoon finely chopped fresh parsley leaves
Salt and freshly ground black pepper to taste

1. Wash the clams under cold running water, place in a bowl with cold water to cover, sprinkle with the baking soda, and let set for 1 hour. Drain and rinse the clams, discarding any that won't close.

2. In a large casserole, heat the olive oil over medium-high heat, then cook the tomatoes and chile until softer, about 4 minutes, stirring often. Add the clams and cook until they all open, about 12 minutes. Discard any clams that remain tightly shut. Once the clams are open, stir in the garlic and parsley and season with salt and black pepper.

3. Serve immediately in bowls with bread to dip in the broth.

Makes 4 to 6 servings

Baby Clams in Piquant Tomato Sauce with Sardinian Carta di Música

After many hours of swimming in aqua waves off Capo Spartivento in Sardinia at a gorgeous white sand beach populated by busty German women in thong bikinis, a friend and I took a soothing freshwater shower and walked down the road, stopping after a series of twisting turns at Porto Vecchio-Teulada, a three-house town with a few boats and the Trattoria Da Giani, where we ate a delightful meal under the grape arbor. Our antipasto was called fajolari in zuppeta. Fajolari *is a Sardinian name for a very small kind of clam. These clams are not available in this country, although some Italian markets sell them brined in jars. If you do use these jarred clams, you'll need about three 12-ounce jars. I use the littlest littlenecks I can find, as well as some small Manila clams. The Sardinian flatbread called* carta di música *is so-called because it is as thin as a sheet of music. Actually, the Sardinians don't call it that (Italians do)—they call it* pani carasàu. *Again, Italian markets are beginning to sell imported* carta di música, *or you can take half of a pita bread, toast it a little, and use that. The Vernaccia wine called for in the ingredient list is a dry white Sardinian wine that tastes a little like a cross between dry white wine and a very dry fine sherry. Use whatever Vernaccia wine you can find or a mixture of half dry white wine and half sherry.*

¼ cup extra-virgin olive oil

1 small onion, very finely chopped

1 large garlic clove, very finely chopped

2 tablespoons finely chopped fresh parsley leaves

¾ cup Vernaccia wine or any dry Sardinian white wine

2½ pounds ripe tomatoes, cut in half, seeds squeezed out, grated against the largest holes of a grater, and skins discarded

4 dried chiles

1 cup water

Salt and freshly ground black pepper to taste

24 small littleneck and/or Manila clams (about 2½ pounds), scrubbed well, soaked in cold water to cover with 1 teaspoon baking soda for 1 hour, drained, and rinsed

4 *pani carasàu* or 4 loaves arabic bread, split and toasted, or 4 thick slices Italian country bread, toasted

1. In a medium-size saucepan, heat the olive oil over medium-high heat, then cook the onion, garlic, and 1 tablespoon of the parsley until soft, about 3 minutes, stirring. Pour in ¼ cup of the wine and cook for 2 minutes. Add the tomatoes and chiles, bring to a boil, then pour in the water and remaining ½ cup wine. Reduce the heat to low, season with salt and black pepper, and simmer for 20 minutes. Pass the soup through a food mill, discarding the chile peppers.

2. Return the soup to the saucepan, bring to a boil, add the clams, cover, and cook until they open, 3 to 6 minutes. Discard any clams that remain firmly closed. (If you are using jarred clams, do not cook them more than 1 minute.) Correct the seasoning.

3. Place a piece of bread in each bowl and portion out the soup and clams over the bread. Sprinkle with the remaining 1 tablespoon parsley and serve.

Makes 4 servings

Baked Galician-Style Scallops on the Half Shell

This impressive tapa *comes from the region of Galicia in northwestern Spain. Galicia is a mountainous region, but with important fishing ports on the Atlantic. The dialect of Galicia is akin to Portuguese, and the region's culinary culture shares elements with Portugal to the south and with the Basques. Scallops are famous in Galicia because of the shrine of St. James at Santiago de la Compostela. The "shell of St. James" was the emblem of the pilgrims who journeyed there. His name has given the French their word for scallop,* coquille Saint Jacques. *The Spanish word for scallop,* vieira, *on the other hand, derives from the goddess Venus, who supposedly was born as a young woman from a shell. Ideally, this* tapa *should be served on individual scallop shells, putting three or four scallops on each shell, but lacking that, cook them all together and portion them out as appetizers, either with frilly cocktail toothpicks or as canapés.*

1 pound bay scallops

5 tablespoons extra-virgin olive oil

1 large onion, finely chopped

1½ ounces (about 2 strips) bacon, chopped

2 tablespoons white wine

2 teaspoons hot Spanish paprika

⅛ teaspoon cayenne pepper

1 tablespoon finely chopped fresh parsley leaves

Salt and freshly ground black pepper to taste

Juice from ¼ lemon

2 tablespoons fine dry bread crumbs

1. Preheat the oven to 375°F. Arrange the scallops in a baking dish in one layer.

2. In a medium-size skillet, heat the olive oil over medium heat, then cook the onion and bacon until soft, about 15 minutes, stirring. Add the wine and cook until reduced, about 1 minute. Stir in the paprika, cayenne, and parsley; season with salt and black pepper, cook for 1 minute, and remove from the heat. Spoon this mixture evenly over the scallops. Sprinkle with the lemon juice. Sprinkle the bread crumbs over the surface and bake until golden brown and crispy, about 20 minutes. Serve hot.

Makes 6 to 8 servings

Scallops au Gratin in the Venetian Style

In the Veneto, scallops are often collected by dragging nets along the sea bottom. Although fancied by the natives, scallops are almost always eaten as an antipasto rather than a main dish. This antipasto from Venice is called cape sante gratinate *and is, as one says in Venetian,* da lecarsi i dei, *"finger-lickin' good."*

½ cup fine dry bread crumbs

¼ cup finely grated Parmigiano-Reggiano cheese

3 tablespoons finely chopped fresh parsley leaves

Salt and freshly ground black pepper to taste

1 pound bay or sea scallops

1 tablespoon tomato paste

2 to 3 tablespoons extra-virgin olive oil

1. In a medium-size bowl, mix the bread crumbs, cheese, parsley, salt, and pepper. Toss the scallops in this mixture until well coated.

2. Preheat the oven to 425°F.

3. Arrange the scallops in a lightly oiled baking dish in a single layer. In a small bowl or measuring cup, stir together the tomato paste and olive oil. Brush all the scallops with this mixture and bake until crisp looking, about 20 minutes. Serve hot from the dish with frilly cocktail toothpicks.

Makes 8 servings

Scallops on Carp Roe Caviar

This meze of fried bay scallops on top of taramasalata, *a smooth cream of carp roe eggs blended with olive oil and bread, is called* tarak ve taramasalata. Taramasalata *of very good quality can be purchased in Greek or Armenian markets and many Middle Eastern markets, and sometimes supermarkets carry it, too.*

2 tablespoons extra-virgin olive oil
1 pound bay scallops
Salt and freshly ground white pepper to taste
Hot Hungarian paprika to taste
4 ounces *taramasalata*
10 imported pitted black olives

1. In a medium-size skillet, heat the olive oil over medium-high heat, then cook the scallops until firm, about 4 minutes, stirring. Sprinkle the scallops with salt, white pepper, and paprika as you cook them.

2. Spread the *taramasalata* on a round serving platter and arrange the scallops on top. Garnish the platter with black olives and serve immediately with frilly cocktail toothpicks or with small plates and forks on the side.

Makes 6 servings

Fried Soft-Shell Crabs with Light Tomato Dressing

This recipe comes from an old friend of mine, Wanda Rheindorf, who whipped it up so quickly and effortlessly that whenever the soft-shells are in season, I make this. You clean the crabs by turning them on their backs so their bellies are facing you. With the heads on top, you will notice a little flap on the bottom. Remove the flap and slice open the belly to remove the viscera, then pat dry with paper towels. Simple preparations of olive oil, shellfish, and tomatoes are common from Catalonia to Greece.

1 cup olive oil
4 soft-shell crabs, cleaned (see headnote)
All-purpose flour for dredging
2 tablespoons extra-virgin olive oil
½ pound very ripe tomatoes, peeled and chopped
Salt to taste

1. In a large skillet, heat the olive oil over high heat until it is smoking. Dredge the crabs in flour, shaking or patting off any excess. Fry the crabs in the hot oil until golden on both sides.

2. In a small saucepan, heat the extra-virgin olive oil over medium-high heat and add the tomatoes and salt. Cook for 5 minutes, then pour over the crabs and serve immediately.

Makes 4 servings

Cyprus in the Mediterranean

Although Cyprus had been in the path of the trade routes since ancient times, it was after the tenth century, when sugar was introduced from Egypt, that the island became economically important to Venice. The feudal arrangement benefited the Venetian Cornaro family; the success of their extensive sugar plantations at Episkopi in Cyprus is evidenced in their palazzo in Venice, one of the oldest on the Grand Canal, the Palazzo Cornaro-Piscopia. Cotton was cultivated by serfs and sold at enormous profits, so valuable that they called it "the plant of gold." There were other products from Cyprus desired in the West, including ortolan, a bird of the vineyard, which abounded in Cyprus and from where in the sixteenth century it was exported to Venice preserved in vinegar. But the ortolan was a rare dish and minor overall. Another bird, the figpecker (page 449) or *beccafico*, also called pickled black-caps, was imported from Cyprus and sold by the thousands in the Rialto market in Venice. Another economically important product was wine and strong Cypriot wine became popular in Venice, where 3 million gallons were bought in one year.

The Turks and the Venetians warred over sugar and when Venice occupied Cyprus in 1479, it won the sugar war. After the discovery and introduction of sugar production to Brazil and the Madeira islands, the Venetian economy was hit hard, not only because Portuguese sugar was driving the price down but also because the Turks took Cyprus, the main Levantine source of supply for the Venetians. In 1570, Sultan Selim II sent a powerful fleet to take the island. The Greeks of the island were so oppressed by the Venetians that they welcomed the Turks. The Venetians did little to encourage indigenous industry on Cyprus—there were no schools and hardly any doctors. The mixed population of Levantine peoples in Cyprus when the Turks were threatening attack were considered so unreliable by the defending Venetians that plans called for the internment of all Jews, Copts, Maronites, Syrians, and Armenians.

Wine-Braised Squid from Cyprus

This meze is called kalamarakia krasata, *or squid in wine. The whole squid cooks in the wine and onions until all the liquid evaporates and the sauce remaining is just a thin, syrupy coating. This is delicious at room temperature with a glass of wine or an ouzo and some crusty bread.*

¼ cup extra-virgin olive oil

2 medium-size onions, cut into thin slices and separated into rings

1 pound small squid, cleaned (page 404)

¼ cup white wine vinegar

½ cup dry red wine

2 sticks cinnamon

4 cloves

1 bay leaf

Salt and freshly ground black pepper to taste

¾ cup water

1. In a large skillet, heat the olive oil over medium heat, then add the onions and squid and cook until the onions are soft, about 8 minutes, stirring occasionally. Add the vinegar, wine, cinnamon, cloves, and bay leaf; season with salt and pepper, stir, and add enough water to barely cover the squid, pushing the squid down into the liquid. Cook, uncovered, over medium heat until the squid is tender and all the wine has evaporated, about 45 minutes.

2. Remove and discard the cinnamon sticks, bay leaf, and cloves, if you can find them. Serve at room temperature.

Makes 4 to 6 servings

Baby Octopus in Piquant Sauce

Sardinians and Sicilians are fond of the baby octopus that they serve as an antipasto. The preparation of baby octopus is commonly found in Venice and Genoa, too. This dish is called moscardini in salsa piccante, *and it is cooked the night before and served the next day as an antipasto.* Moscardini *is the word for these baby octopuses in Italian and it appears, so-named, in J. Florio's* A Worlde of Wordes, *published in London in 1598. The word intimates that there*

is a particular musky smell to the cooking octopuses. Baby octopuses sold in this country are almost always sold frozen and already cleaned. The freezing and unfreezing of the octopuses is not a bad thing—it helps tenderize them. You will notice in the method that I call for a trito. *A* trito *is a mixture of very finely chopped vegetables that are the beginning to a sauce.*

2 pounds baby octopuses

6 ounces oil-packed sun-dried tomatoes, drained

6 large garlic cloves, finely chopped

6 tablespoons finely chopped fresh parsley leaves

¼ cup salted capers, rinsed

¼ cup extra-virgin olive oil

¼ cup white wine vinegar

Salt to taste

1. Bring a pot of salted water to a boil and cook the baby octopus until stiff but tender, about 30 minutes. Drain and set aside.

2. Meanwhile, make a *trito* by chopping the sun-dried tomatoes, garlic, parsley, and 3 tablespoons of the capers together very finely. In a medium-size skillet, heat the olive oil over medium heat, then add the *trito* and cook, stirring for 1 minute. Add the vinegar and continue to cook for 3 more minutes, stirring. Add the drained octopus and remaining 1 tablespoon whole capers, stir, season with salt, and transfer to a bowl to cool. Refrigerate overnight before serving at room temperature on a platter with crusty bread.

Makes 8 servings

Musseddu

Musseddu is the name in the town of Trapani on Sicily's west coast for a salted and sun-dried fillet of mahimahi (dolphinfish). Salting and sun-drying mahimahi is also known in northern Italy, where it is called *mosciamme* in Liguria. Although the word originally referred to dried tuna fillet, it is today made with mahimahi. The word comes from the Arabic *mushamma^c*, meaning the drying of fish. This dried mahimahi is used in place of salted anchovies in salads and other *antipasti*. A piece of fish is cut off and soaked in olive oil for 30 minutes before using.

Swordfish or Shark in Tomato and Saffron Sauce

This is a tapa *called* pescado en amarillo, *served at the Bar Bahía in Cádiz in Andalusia, which was collected by Penelope Casas and published in her wonderful book* Tapas: The Little Dishes of Spain, *and which I have adapted.*

¼ cup extra-virgin olive oil

1 medium-size red onion, finely chopped

3 large garlic cloves, finely chopped

1 ripe tomato (½ pound), cut in half, seeds squeezed out, grated against the largest holes of a grater, and skin discarded

1 bay leaf

½ cup brandy or cognac

6 tablespoons chicken broth

Salt and freshly ground black pepper to taste

Pinch of freshly grated nutmeg

Pinch of saffron threads, crumbled

1¼ pounds swordfish or shark steaks, cut into 1½-inch cubes

1. In an earthenware casserole (preferably), heat the olive oil over medium-high heat, using a heat diffuser if necessary, then cook the onion and garlic until the onion is soft, 5 to 6 minutes, stirring frequently so the garlic doesn't burn. Add the tomato and bay leaf and cook for a minute. Stir in the brandy and chicken broth, season with salt, pepper, the nutmeg, and saffron, and cook until reduced by half, about 8 minutes. Turn the heat off. The preparation can be prepared ahead of time up to this point.

2. When you are ready to finish the dish, bring the sauce to a boil, add the fish, cover, and cook until firm, about 10 minutes. Transfer to individual tapas plates or one large, deep platter and serve hot with *crostini* (page 37), if desired.

Makes 8 servings

Carp Croquettes in Walnut Sauce in the Style of the Greek Jews

The majority of Greek Jews are descended from the Sephardim who emigrated from Spain after 1492. A large community grew in Thessaloniki in Thrace. This recipe called peshe en saltsa *(fish in sauce) is adapted from Nikos Stavroulakis's* Cookbook of the Jews of Greece. *It is prepared with freshwater fish such as carp. He tells us that it was once the daily fare of the Jews of Thessaloniki during Passover. Although they are often a dinner in themselves, these croquettes in walnut sauce make a nice meze. You could serve them without the sauce, but it is an intriguing sauce you should try. The matzo meal called for in this recipe is sold in supermarkets. Freshwater carp is caught in the lakes of Greek Macedonia and Halkidiki in northern Greece. You can replace carp with Lake Superior whitefish or walleye pike.*

2 pounds carp or other white-fleshed freshwater fish fillets

Salt to taste

½ cup finely ground matzo meal, plus more for dredging

1 large egg, beaten

2 cups olive oil for frying

1½ to 2 cups water, as needed

½ cup white wine vinegar

½ cup finely chopped walnuts, plus extra for garnish

Freshly ground black pepper to taste

1. Place the fish in a food processor, season with salt, and process until chopped and mashed looking. Form 24 balls from the ground fish with wet hands so that it doesn't stick. Roll the balls in the matzo meal to coat evenly, then dip in the beaten egg.

2. In a large skillet, heat the olive oil over medium-high heat until almost smoking, then cook the fish balls until golden brown on all sides, 3 to 4 minutes. Remove from the oil with a slotted spoon and drain on paper towels.

3. In a skillet large enough to hold all the croquettes in a single layer, bring 1 cup of the water, the vinegar, the ½ cup matzo meal, the walnuts, and salt and pepper to a boil. Reduce the heat to low and simmer for 5 minutes, stirring and adding the remaining ½ to 1 cup water if it is too thick and pasty. Add the fish balls to the sauce and simmer until the sauce is dense and the fish balls springy to the touch, about 15 minutes, stirring and turning the fish balls occasionally.

4. Remove the fish balls to a large serving platter, cover with the sauce, and garnish liberally with chopped walnuts. Serve warm or cold.

Makes 24 croquettes; 8 to 10 servings

La Sartagnado

Sartagnade *is a Provençal word that means, roughly, "pan-fries"—that is, things fried in a pan. The word derives from the old Occitan (spoken in the Languedoc) and Provençal* sartan, *meaning "frying pan," a word that was commonly used in fourteenth-century Provence. A mass of little fish are floured and cooked in a hot pan so the fish form a kind of pancake. Another name for this preparation is* crespeou, *which comes from* crêpe, *reflecting the fact that the finished dish looks like a pancake. The fish used may be of one species or a mixture, such as anchovies, sardines, sand smelts or silversides, or small picarel. The trick for making this is to have a very hot and seasoned pan so the fish don't stick and can be turned easily. It's also best to make two separate pancakes of fish.*

Vegetable oil for seasoning the pan

1 pound small fresh anchovies, cleaned, gutted
with heads and tails left on, and washed

½ cup all-purpose flour

Salt and freshly ground black pepper to taste

½ cup olive oil

¼ cup white wine vinegar

1. Prepare a 10-inch skillet for cooking by washing and thoroughly drying it. Pour a small amount of vegetable oil in the skillet and heat over medium heat for 5 minutes. Turn the heat off and let the skillet cool completely, then wipe dry with paper towels and repeat the process. This seasoning process is necessary to keep the fish from sticking.

2. In a medium-size bowl, toss the fish in the flour to coat and season with salt and pepper until the fish cling together in a mass.

3. In the prepared skillet, heat ¼ cup of the olive oil over high heat. Once the oil is smoking, add half the fish, pushing and pressing it down to form a pancake. Reduce the heat to medium and cook the fish, without stirring or poking, until the bottom is golden, about 3½ minutes. Turn the fish with a metal spatula and cook the other side until golden, about 3½ minutes. Slide the fish onto a round serving platter, deglaze the skillet with 2 tablespoons of the vinegar, pour the juices over the fish cake, and serve.

4. Meanwhile, make the second fish cake, heating up the remaining ¼ cup olive oil, frying the remaining fish, and deglazing the pan with the remaining 2 tablespoons vinegar.

Makes 4 to 6 servings

Fresh Anchovy in Orange Sauce

This is an old Sicilian recipe called alici all'arancia, *"anchovies in orange," which supposedly comes from the Benedictine convents of Catania. Another related preparation,* cicirelli all'arancia, *is also made with oranges and is quite popular as an antipasto. Cicirelli are tiny fish of mixed species that are grilled, fried, or prepared in a similar manner with oranges. Sometimes small sand eels are available in ethnic fish stores in this country, although twice a year my local fish store carries fresh anchovies. For this recipe, fresh anchovies are best, but you will have to use smelts in their place if necessary. The best Sicilian anchovies grow to about six inches at the largest and are caught mostly in the Straits of Messina, where fishermen will skewer the tiny fish with reed splinters made from bamboo or sugar cane and grill them over a fire.*

The seasoning of food with oranges has a long heritage in Sicily. In the twelfth century, Hugo Falcondis, the chronicler of the Norman kings of Sicily, wrote in his Epistola ad Retrum panormitane Ecclesie thesaurarium *of oranges,* arengias, *flavoring foods. It is known that oranges were regularly sold in Palermo in 1287 according to documents in the Archivio di Stato di Palermo, one of the earliest records of their appearance in Italy. This is a nice dish to have with a good, crisp Sicilian white wine.*

¼ cup extra-virgin olive oil

1 cup coarsely crumbled fresh bread crumbs

2 pounds fresh anchovies, cleaned, gutted, and heads removed

1 Meyer or other thin-skinned lemon, ends removed and very thinly sliced

¼ pound imported green olives, drained, pitted, and chopped

3 tablespoons pine nuts

3 tablespoons finely chopped fresh parsley leaves

½ teaspoon red pepper flakes

Salt to taste

½ cup dry white wine

¾ cup fresh orange juice

1. In a small skillet, heat 2 tablespoons of the olive oil over medium heat, then cook the bread crumbs until golden, about 5 minutes, tossing. Set aside.

2. Preheat the oven to 350°F. Arrange the anchovies in a greased earthenware casserole interspersed with the lemon slices. Sprinkle the olives, pine nuts, parsley, and red pepper flakes over the fish and lemon. Salt lightly and pour the remaining 2 tablespoons olive oil and the wine over them. Sprinkle evenly with the bread crumbs. Place the casserole in the oven and bake until crispy on top, about 10 minutes.

3. Pour in the orange juice and continue to bake until cooked through (taste a piece of anchovy), about 10 minutes. Serve immediately from the casserole.

Makes 6 servings

Variation: Coat the bottom of a heavy enameled cast-iron or earthenware casserole with 3 tablespoons olive oil. Layer the bottom with 1½ pounds cleaned little fish and sprinkle with ¼ cup chopped fresh parsley leaves, 2 finely chopped garlic cloves, grated zest from 2 oranges, 5 fresh bay leaves, salt and pepper to taste, and ¼ cup fresh bread crumbs. Layer another 1½ pounds of fish and season again as before. Sprinkle olive oil on the final layer of bread crumbs. Turn the heat to medium, using a heat diffuser if necessary with an earthenware casserole, shaking the casserole so the fish don't stick, and cook for 10 minutes, then pour in 3 tablespoons white wine vinegar, cover, and cook until it is nearly evaporated, about 10 minutes. Let cool in the casserole and serve at room temperature.

Stockfish, Fava Bean, and Potato Stew from Liguria

This is an antique recipe that I'm not familiar with anybody making anymore. It was traditionally served in Liguria as an antipasto and called stocche e bacilli *in dialect or* stoccafisso e favette *in Italian—that is, stockfish and fava beans. This dish was popular in the nineteenth century when the small dried fava beans called* greche *or* bacilli *in Genoese dialect came to be replaced by potatoes. In this recipe, both are combined. In Italy, stockfish is an air-dried cod imported from Norway. It needs to be soaked just like salt cod, but not as long since it is not preserved in salt. In addition to Italian markets, dried stockfish can be purchased in Japanese markets, where it is sold in vacuum-packed bags.*

½ pound dried fava beans, soaked overnight in
water to cover

½ pound boiling potatoes

6 ounces stockfish, soaked in water to cover for
24 hours

5 teaspoons salt, or to taste

¾ cup fresh tomato puree

¼ cup extra-virgin olive oil

1 small onion, finely chopped, soaked in water
for 30 minutes, and drained

1 large garlic clove, finely chopped

2 tablespoons finely chopped fresh parsley leaves

1. Place the fava beans in a medium-size saucepan and cover by several inches with cold water. Turn the heat to high, bring to a boil, and let continue to boil until tender, about 40 minutes. Drain, cool under cold running water, and pop off the skins. Set aside in a large bowl.

2. Place the potatoes in another medium-size saucepan and cover by several inches with cold water. Turn the heat to medium and, once it comes to a boil in about 20 minutes, cook until the potatoes are tender when pierced in the center, about another 20 minutes. Drain and, when cool enough to handle, peel the potatoes and break them up with the fava beans.

3. Place the stockfish in a large saucepan and cover with cold water. Turn the heat to high and cook for 20 minutes, without ever letting the water boil rapidly. Drain the stockfish, remove the bones, and cut into slices. Toss with the fava beans and potatoes. Season with the salt, toss, and add the tomato puree, olive oil, onion, garlic, and parsley. Toss well and serve warm.

Makes 10 servings

· ❀ ·

Saucy Little Dishes, Part II (Vegetables)

A s in the previous chapter, this chapter has saucy little dishes, this time made with vegetables, which you are likely to find served as tapas in Spain or offered on a Near Eastern or North African meze table. The first recipes in the chapter are delectable preparations for legumes, beans, and peas. Then come some recipes that utilize leafy vegetables and root vegetables. Rounding out the chapter are recipes for those famous and favorite Mediterranean vegetables—peppers, tomatoes, artichokes, and eggplants—with a handful of celeriac, carrot, pumpkin, cauliflower, and beet recipes thrown in for good measure.

Moroccan Chickpeas with Preserved Lemons

Called ḥummuṣ bi'l-ḥamaḍ muraqqaḍ, this Moroccan dish is served as a meze. Preserved lemon is a typical condiment in Moroccan cuisine and a delightful one, too, which is very easy to prepare. Rās al-ḥanūt is a famous Moroccan spice mix that can contain up to twenty-seven different spices, but my recipe is more manageable.

½ teaspoon cumin seeds

1 large garlic clove, peeled

½ teaspoon salt

Pinch of saffron threads

2 tablespoons extra-virgin olive oil

¼ teaspoon Rās al-Ḥanūt (page 470)

¼ teaspoon hot Hungarian paprika

Freshly ground black pepper to taste

One 28-ounce can chickpeas, drained, ½ cup of the liquid reserved

¼ cup cut-up Preserved Lemons (page 469)

2 tablespoons finely chopped fresh coriander (cilantro) leaves

1. In a mortar, crush the cumin seeds, then add the garlic, salt, and saffron and pound until mushy.

2. In a medium-size saucepan, heat the olive oil over medium heat, then scrape the garlic paste in and cook until sizzling, 1 to 2 minutes. Add the *rās al-ḥanūt*, paprika, and black pepper and stir. Add the chickpeas and the reserved liquid, reduce the heat to low, cover, and cook until tender and the water is nearly evaporated, 50 to 60 minutes, adding a few tablespoons water to the pot if it seems to be drying out

before that amount of time has passed. Taste and correct the seasonings.

3. Remove from the heat and stir in the preserved lemons and 1 tablespoon of the chopped coriander. Let sit for 2 minutes, then sprinkle the remaining 1 tablespoon coriander on top and serve hot as a meze accompanied by a salad.

Makes 4 to 6 servings

Chickpeas and Hazelnuts with Three Peppers

This is a tapa *inspired by the cooking of Madrid, where tapas bars serve a huge range of foods for their ever-hungry and thirsty guests. The chiles called for in this recipe are not typical Spanish ingredients, but they work well as a substitute for the long red chiles that would be used.*

3 tablespoons extra-virgin olive oil

2 tablespoons finely chopped onion

2 tablespoons finely chopped shallot

1 green bell pepper, seeded and chopped

5 Thai chiles or 1 serrano chile, seeded and chopped

2 red Anaheim chiles, seeded and chopped

1 large garlic clove, finely chopped

2 tablespoons finely chopped fresh parsley leaves

¾ cup cooked chickpeas, drained

¼ cup blanched roasted hazelnuts (page 465)

½ teaspoon dried thyme

¼ cup water

In a medium-size skillet, heat the olive oil over medium-high heat, then cook the onion, shallot, bell pepper, chiles, garlic, and parsley until soft, about 7 minutes, stirring frequently. Add the chickpeas, hazelnuts, thyme, and water and continue to cook until the water is almost evaporated, about 10 minutes. Serve at room temperature.

Makes 4 to 6 servings

Braised Lemony Chickpeas

In Greece, revithia yahni *is a lemony preparation for chickpea ragout and is ideally served at room temperature as part of a meze. If you use dried chickpeas, which will give the dish an earthier taste, soak 1½ cups overnight in water to cover, then drain and boil in fresh water to cover anywhere from 1 to 3 hours, until tender.*

¼ cup extra-virgin olive oil
½ cup chopped onion
3 cups cooked chickpeas (two 15-ounce cans, drained and rinsed)
1 cup water
Salt and freshly ground black pepper to taste
Juice of 1 lemon
1 tablespoon all-purpose flour

1. In a large skillet, heat the olive oil over high heat, then cook the onion until some pieces are turning brown, 4 to 5 minutes, stirring a few times. Add the drained chickpeas and water and season with salt and pepper, then cook for 5 minutes.

2. Meanwhile, in a small bowl, whisk together the lemon juice and flour until well blended and smooth. Whisk several tablespoons of the hot liquid from the chickpeas into the lemon-flour mixture until well blended. Pour into the chickpeas, reduce the heat to low, and simmer until the water is nearly evaporated and the sauce is thickened, 1 to 1¼ hours. Turn the heat off and let the chickpeas cool in the skillet. Serve at room temperature or warm.

Makes 4 servings

White Chickpeas with Lime Juice from Egypt

White chickpeas that have been roasted and dried are popular in Turkey as well as Egypt. In Turkish, they are known as leblebi. *Roasted and dried white chickpeas are best found in Middle Eastern markets; the label will read "Beyaz Leblebi." In Egypt, many different salads are served as meze and this chickpea salad is delightful tossed with lime juice instead of the more common lemon juice one finds in the Levant. You can use canned chickpeas in this recipe, but you will miss out on the nutty taste of roasted white chickpeas.*

3 cups dried white chickpeas, picked over, soaked in cold water to cover overnight, and drained
1 cup finely chopped fresh parsley leaves (from 1 to 2 bunches)
½ cup finely chopped scallions
6 tablespoons extra-virgin olive oil
3 tablespoons fresh lime juice
Salt to taste

1. Place the chickpeas in a large saucepan and cover with several inches of cold water. Bring to

a boil and let continue to boil until tender, 2 to 3 hours. Taste the chickpeas to see whether they are done. Drain well and, when cool enough to handle, rub off as much of the white skin of the chickpea as you can.

2. Place the chickpeas in a large bowl and toss with the parsley and scallions. In a small bowl, whisk together the olive oil, lime juice, and salt until it thickens. Pour over the chickpeas and toss gently to coat, then serve.

Makes 8 servings

Red Bean and Onion Salad with Dill

This Turkish meze called zeytinyağlı barbunya *is from Anatolia but is found everywhere in Turkey. The name refers to a style of cooking in Turkey where the food is cooked in and pre-served in a copious amount of olive oil. The word* barbunya *refers not only to the little red fish called red mullet but also to any dried red shell bean. In this preparation, Turkish cooks favor borlotti beans. Serve at room temperature.*

2 cups dried red borlotti, red speckled (cranberry), or red kidney beans (about 1 pound), rinsed and picked over
Salt
¾ cup extra-virgin olive oil
1 very large sweet onion, cut in half and thinly sliced into half-moons
10 large garlic cloves, sliced or coarsely chopped
1 teaspoon sugar
3 large ripe tomatoes, cut in half, seeds squeezed out, grated against the largest holes of a grater, and skins discarded
Leaves from 1 bunch fresh dill
Leaves from 1 bunch fresh Italian parsley, finely chopped
¼ cup water
Freshly ground black pepper to taste
2 lemons, cut into wedges
Chopped scallions for garnish (optional)

Borlotti Beans

These fancy-sounding Mediterranean beans are a cultivar of the common bean (*Phaseolus vulgaris*) and characterized by their color—white or beige-colored beans splashed with maroon. They are known in the United States as cranberry beans, and much of the borlotti beans used in Turkish or Italian cooking are in fact imported from the United States.

1. Place the beans in a large saucepan and cover by at least 4 inches of cold water. Salt a little, bring to a boil, and cook at a boil until the beans are tender but still maintain their shape, 1¼ to 1½ hours. Drain and transfer to a bowl.

2. In a large skillet or casserole, heat the olive oil over medium-high heat, then cook the onion and garlic until soft and yellow, about 12 minutes, stirring frequently. Stir in the sugar, half the tomatoes, and half the herbs, reduce the heat to low, and cook until thicker, about 15 minutes, stirring occasionally. Add the beans

and water and continue to cook for 15 minutes, stirring occasionally. Stir in the remaining tomatoes and herbs, season with salt and pepper, and simmer another 25 minutes, stirring. Turn the heat off and let the beans cool.

3. Transfer to a serving platter and serve with wedges of lemons and scallions.

Makes 12 servings

Speckled Beans with Carrot and Potato in Olive Oil

This recipe is also called zeytinyağlı kuru fasulya *and is only slightly different from the previous one. This is an "olive oil food" (see page 221). Here, I call for very specific beans, but typically a Turkish cook would use dried white beans. The spring onions I call for here are onions that have developed a bigger bulb than a scallion but are not yet mature onions.*

1 cup dried speckled heirloom beans (½ pound), such as Appaloosa beans or other speckled beans, rinsed and picked over

1 cup extra-virgin olive oil

1 medium-size onion, chopped

1 small potato, peeled and diced

1 large carrot, diced

3 garlic cloves, finely chopped

4 spring onions, chopped

1½ stalks celery, chopped

½ teaspoon sugar

½ cup water

Salt and freshly ground black pepper to taste

3 tablespoons fresh lemon juice

3 tablespoons finely chopped fresh parsley leaves

1. Place the beans in a large saucepan with cold water to cover by several inches and bring to a boil. Let continue to boil until *al dente*, 30 minutes. Drain.

2. In a large skillet, heat ½ cup of the olive oil over medium-high heat, then cook the onion until golden, about 6 minutes, stirring. Add the potato, carrot, garlic, spring onions, celery, drained beans, and sugar; reduce the heat to low, cover, and cook over low heat until the beans are tender, about 10 minutes, stirring occasionally. Add the remaining ½ cup olive oil and the water, season with salt and pepper, and cook until the potato is tender, another 15 minutes. Add the lemon juice, stir, and remove from the heat.

3. Let everything cool in the skillet, transfer to a serving platter, sprinkle with the parsley, and serve.

Makes 6 servings

White Bean and Red Onion Salad from Anatolia

This meze is popular throughout Turkey and is usually served with a garnish of olives, hard-boiled eggs, or tomatoes. The preparation is called fasulye piyası. *A* piyası *dish is one flavored with onions, so this is "beans flavored with onions." The chile should be pretty hot, so if you don't find what I call for, use two or three serranos or one or two jalapeños. Always serve it at room temperature. To hard-boil the eggs so they come out with a bright yellow center, place room-temperature eggs in a saucepan of boiling water and remove them nine minutes later. Place in a bowl of cold water and, once you can handle them, shell them.*

2 cups dried white cannellini beans or other white beans that are not too small (about 1 pound), rinsed and picked over

Salt

5 large garlic cloves, very finely chopped

1 very large red onion, chopped

1 long green chile, seeded and chopped

Leaves from 1 small bunch fresh parsley, finely chopped

½ to ¾ cup extra-virgin olive oil, to your taste

¼ cup fresh lemon juice

Freshly ground black pepper to taste

3 large hard-boiled eggs, shelled and quartered

Handful of imported black olives

1. Place the beans in a large saucepan and cover by at least 4 inches of cold water. Salt a little, bring to a boil, and cook at a boil until tender but still maintaining their body, 1¼ to 1½ hours. Drain and transfer to a bowl. Stir in the garlic and let cool.

2. Stir in the onion, chile, parsley, olive oil, and lemon juice. Season with salt and pepper and transfer to a serving platter, spreading the beans out and garnishing the edges with the olives and eggs.

Makes 12 servings

White Beans and Green Onions in Olive Oil

The amount of olive oil in this preparation called zeytinyağlı kuru fasulya *is quite authentic, as this kind of dish is one of a class of Turkish* foods called "olive oil foods" (see page 221). The tastes are really very heavenly and I would not reduce the amount. This is a dish that is always eaten at room temperature and is served at nearly every restaurant in Turkey, but differently every time. One of the best I've had was at the Ahtapot Restaurant on the little ancient harbor of Antalya, where they made it with a liquidy tomato sauce drizzled with olive oil. Green onions, scallions, and spring onions can all refer to Allium fistulosum, *with their differences being one of cultivar and/or age. They are also known as bunching onions and are grown for their stalks. They are hardy plants that can survive cold winters and are best in the springtime, when this recipe would mostly likely be made. The green onions used in this recipe have small purple-streaked bulbs that are a little larger than scallion bulbs. They are slightly sweeter, as well as a little more pungent.*

1 cup extra-virgin olive oil

1 large onion, chopped

2½ cups water

1½ cups (about ¾ pound) dried small white beans, like navy beans, rinsed and picked over

1 medium-size potato, peeled and diced

2 carrots, diced

2 stalks celery, chopped

3 large garlic cloves, finely chopped

3 large green onions or 6 scallions, chopped

1 teaspoon sugar

Salt and freshly ground black pepper to taste

Juice from 1 lemon

¼ cup finely chopped fresh parsley leaves

1. In a skillet or casserole, heat ½ cup of the olive oil over medium heat, then cook the onion until light brown, about 10 minutes, stirring occasionally. Pour in the water, bring to a boil, and add the beans, potato, carrots, celery, garlic, green onions, and sugar. Cover, reduce the heat to low, and cook until the beans are tender, 1¼ to 1½ hours.

2. Pour in the remaining ½ cup olive oil, season with salt and pepper, and cook until the water and olive oil look emulsified, about 10 minutes. Add the lemon juice, stir, and turn the heat off. Leave the beans in the casserole until they come to room temperature.

3. Transfer to a serving platter, sprinkle with the parsley, and serve with toasted French bread.

Makes 4 to 6 servings

Baked Lima Beans in the Greek Style

On the surface Greek food seems the same as Turkish food, but there are significant differences. I sometimes find it hard to put my finger on it, but in some ways I'd say, and I know this sounds like a platitude given Greece's geography and history, that Greek food is a cross between Italian and Turkish food. In any case, it is satisfying food, as demonstrated by this meze called gigandes plaki.

2 cups (about ¾ pound) dried large white lima beans, rinsed and picked over
2 celery stalks, cut into thirds
1 carrot, quartered lengthwise
8 black peppercorns
¾ cup extra-virgin olive oil, plus more for drizzling
1 medium-size onion, grated
6 large garlic cloves, slivered
1¾ pounds ripe tomatoes, seeds squeezed out, grated on the largest holes of a box grater, and skins discarded
1 teaspoon sugar
6 tablespoons finely chopped fresh parsley leaves
Salt and freshly ground black pepper to taste
½ teaspoon dried oregano

1. Put the lima beans in a large saucepan and cover by several inches of cold water. Add the celery, carrot, and peppercorns and bring to a boil. Reduce the heat to low and simmer until tender, about 1 hour. Drain and discard the celery, carrot, and peppercorns and put the beans in a baking pan, preferably earthenware.

2. Preheat the oven to 350°F.

3. In a medium-size skillet, heat the olive oil over medium-high heat, then cook the onion and garlic until translucent, about 4 minutes. Add the tomatoes and cook for a minute, then add the sugar and parsley, season with salt and pepper, and cook until dense, about 10 minutes. Pour the sauce over the lima beans and season with more salt and pepper, the oregano, and a little olive oil.

4. Bake until all the liquid has evaporated, about 1 hour, adding more water if the beans aren't completely soft. Serve hot or at room temperature.

Makes 6 to 8 servings

Black-Eyed Pea and Cilantro Salad in Olive Oil

Called lūbya musalāṭ bi'l-zayt *(black-eyed peas with olive oil) and served as part of a meze table, this Lebanese dish is beautiful—with the little black eyes of the peas glistening with olive oil, speckled green with coriander, and perfumed with garlic. The black-eyed pea was first cultivated in Ethiopia about 4000* B.C. *The Arabs also call this legume* ḥummuṣ shamī *(Syrian chickpea) or* lūbya balādī *(country bean). Fresh black-eyed peas, which are very popular in the Middle East, are often available at farmer's markets and in many supermarkets, usually sold in plastic containers on one of the shelves in the produce section. In a pinch, you can use frozen ones.*

2 cups fresh black-eyed peas (about ¾ pound)

3 tablespoons extra-virgin olive oil

1 small onion, finely chopped

2 large garlic cloves, mashed in a mortar with
  1 teaspoon salt until mushy

¼ teaspoon freshly ground allspice berries

¼ cup finely chopped fresh coriander (cilantro)
  leaves

Freshly ground black pepper to taste

Fresh lemon juice for drizzling

1. Place the peas in a medium-size saucepan and cover by a couple of inches with water. Bring to a boil and continue to boil until tender but not falling apart, 15 to 20 minutes. Drain, reserving several tablespoons of the cooking liquid.

2. In a small skillet, heat the olive oil over medium heat, then cook the onion until translucent, 2 to 3 minutes, stirring. Add the garlic paste, allspice, and coriander and season with pepper; then continue to cook until the coriander and garlic are completely blended, about 2 minutes, stirring in the reserved cooking liquid so the garlic doesn't burn.

3. Transfer the cooked peas to a medium-size bowl and toss gently with the onion mixture, being careful not to crush the peas. Sprinkle some lemon juice over and serve at room temperature.

Makes 4 to 6 servings

Serving Meze

In a Lebanese restaurant, the meze plates can come out of the kitchen fast and furious, or the cook can take his or her own damn time. You just never know. It is truly chaotic, but you don't have to replicate that situation at home. Remember that when you're in a Lebanese restaurant, you want to be strategically placed at the table so that you can reach all your favorite meze. It seems that no one passes meze—they're all too busy eating—so jump quickly on those little boat-shaped plates. You'll find, once you eat enough meze, that you have your favorites and others you're not wild about.

Lentils with Pomegranate Molasses, Garlic, and Cilantro in the Syrian Style

Lentil preparations are very good in the Middle East, perhaps because they are the earliest pulses to have been domesticated and cooked. The combination of pomegranate, garlic, and fresh coriander is a Syrian favorite, and in this recipe called ʿadas bi'l-ḥāmiḍ the lentils are gently flavored with these ingredients and served warm. The garlic should be mashed in a mortar with a pestle—the food processor will not work. Some people find this to be a very garlicky recipe, but it is authentic and I happen to like it this way, though you can feel free to cut the garlic in half if you must. The name of the dish in Arabic is interesting. It's literally called "lentils with lemon juice," yet the amount of lemon juice is very little, certainly overshadowed by the garlic or coriander. Perhaps this is because the lemon juice indicated that the pulses were acidulated and preserved to be longer lasting at a time before refrigeration. Pomegranate molasses, a thick syrup made from pomegranate seeds, can be found in Middle Eastern markets. Serve the lentils with warm Arabic bread.

1½ cups dried green or brown lentils, rinsed and picked over

¼ cup extra-virgin olive oil, plus more for drizzling

5 large Swiss chard leaves, washed well, dried, stems removed, and sliced into thin strips crosswise

2 tablespoons mashed garlic (about 8 large cloves)

¾ cup finely chopped fresh coriander (cilantro) leaves (from 1 to 2 bunches)

1 cup water

1 tablespoon fresh lemon juice

2 tablespoons pomegranate molasses

1. Bring a pot of lightly salted water to a boil and put the lentils in the pot, continue to boil until tender, 15 to 45 minutes; check often because the cooking time varies depending on the age of the lentils. Drain and set aside.

2. In a medium-size nonreactive skillet, heat 1 tablespoon of the olive oil over medium-high heat, then cook the Swiss chard until it wilts, stirring a few times, 1 to 2 minutes. Drain off any liquid and set aside.

3. In the same skillet, heat the remaining 3 tablespoons olive oil over medium-high heat. Add the garlic and coriander and cook until sizzling, 1 to 2 minutes, stirring constantly. Reduce the heat to medium, add the wilted Swiss chard, drained lentils, and water, and cook for 10 minutes, stirring frequently. Add the lemon juice and pomegranate molasses and continue to cook until the lentils look mushy, about another 10 minutes.

4. Transfer to a serving bowl and drizzle a small amount of olive oil over it before serving it warm with bread.

Makes 6 servings

Lentil Salad in Olive Oil with Egyptian Spices

Edward William Lane tells us in his classic book The Manners & Customs of the Modern

Egyptians, *published in 1908, that many dishes prepared by the Egyptians consist wholly or for the most part of vegetables: "cabbage, purslane, spinach, bamiyeh [okra], beans, lupin, chick-pea, gourds, cut into small pieces, colocasia, lentils etc." Called* salāta ʿadas *(lentil salad) and made with tiny lentils slightly cooked with olive oil, garlic, and spices, this meze was served to me at the Tikka Grill, a restaurant on the Corniche of Alexandria in Egypt.*

¼ cup extra-virgin olive oil

2 large garlic cloves, finely chopped

½ teaspoon freshly ground cumin seeds

½ teaspoon freshly ground coriander seeds

¼ teaspoon freshly ground cardamom seeds

½ teaspoon ground fenugreek seeds

1 cup dried brown lentils, rinsed and
  picked over

Salt and freshly ground black pepper to taste

1. In a small saucepan, heat 3 tablespoons of the olive oil over medium heat with the garlic and, as soon as the garlic begins to sizzle, remove from the burner, add the cumin, coriander, cardamom, and fenugreek, and set aside.

2. Place the lentils in a medium-size saucepan of lightly salted cold water and bring to a boil. Cook until *al dente*, about 25 minutes from the time you turned the fire on. Drain and toss with the garlic, olive oil, and spices while still hot. Season with salt and pepper, toss, and arrange on a serving platter, drizzling the remaining 1 tablespoon olive oil over the top. Serve at room temperature.

Makes 6 servings

Where Do Lentils Come From?

Lentils have been a part of human agriculture since the earliest times. Archeological dating of lentils goes back to the Paleolithic and Mesolithic eras in Greece some 9,000 to 13,000 years ago. The name *lentil* comes from the lens shape of the seeds. In the Middle Ages, lentils and other beans, and peas, were really supplementary "cereals" and also a cheap source of protein. Venetian documents called them *menudi* or *minuti* (minor foods). There are thousands of documents that put these minor foodstuffs on a par with wheat, proving that they were considered cereals. When a boat from Venice was loading in Alexandria, Egypt, in 1550 it could be commissioned to carry either wheat or beans.

Olive Oil–Bathed Green Beans and Tomatoes as Made in Nablus

This delectable dish, which makes copious use of olive oil is popular around Nablus in the West Bank. Olive oil was the most important product of the hinterland of Nablus in the nineteenth century, and the Nabulsi have played a leading role in resisting foreign armies ever since the 1834 revolt against the Egyptians. Palestinian olive production was notable even in the nineteenth century, as we know from J. Thomas's Travels in Egypt and Palestine, *published in 1853, which pointed out that "the immediate vicinity of Nabloos is remarkable for the number of its trees, and its luxuriant vegetation; it is, indeed, one of the most beautiful and fertile spots in all Palestine" and that the land "although finely diversified with hills . . . is almost everywhere cultivable, and in fact highly cultivated."*

Called lūbya bi'l-zayt *(green beans with olive oil), this preparation is found throughout the Middle East. Many vegetable meze dishes are adaptable as side dishes, too, but typically they are served well cooked and at room temperature. In this recipe the green beans should be cooked until there is no crunch left, but not so much that they discolor and become insipid, a situation that can be avoided by blanching them first. In Turkey, a similar dish is prepared and also served at room temperature.*

¾ cup extra-virgin olive oil, plus more for
  drizzling, if you like
2 large onions, chopped
3 garlic cloves, finely chopped
2 pounds fresh green beans, ends trimmed and
  cut into 2-lengths
3 medium-size ripe tomatoes (about 1¼
  pounds), peeled, seeded, and chopped
½ cup water
2½ teaspoons salt
¾ teaspoon freshly ground black pepper

1. In a large skillet or casserole, heat the olive oil over medium-high heat, then cook the onions until light brown, about 15 minutes, stirring often. Add the garlic and cook 1 minute longer, stirring.

2. Reduce the heat to medium. Add the green beans, tomatoes, water, salt, and pepper; cover and cook until the green beans are soft, about 1 hour, but keep checking since young green beans will take less time and some older beans can take longer. Add more water if it is evaporating and salt and pepper if that is your taste. When the beans are done, there should be very little water left.

3. Remove from the heat and transfer to a serving platter, allowing the beans to come to room temperature. Drizzle with more olive oil if you wish.

Makes 6 servings

Green Beans in Arab Cooking

Arab cooks like their green beans very fresh, preferably freshly picked from their own gardens. But unlike some Western cooks who prepare green beans nearly raw or very crunchy, Arab cooks like theirs very tender and soft. Therefore, you will notice the green beans get cooked a long time, up to an hour or more.

Fresh Favas, Young Artichokes, and Spring Peas in the Sicilian Style

This preparation was born in western Sicily, where it is served as a grape 'u pitittu, *an expression that means something like "openers of the mouth," although that should not be thought of as an appetizer, for a* frittedda *is more philosophically related to the Middle Eastern meze.*

This is a dish found nowhere else but Sicily. The Sicilian food authority Pino Correnti believes that the name comes from the Latin frigere *because it is prepared in a large frying pan. Since this dish is affected by the age and size of the vegetables, you will have to judge for yourself the right cooking time and how much salt, pepper, and nutmeg you want to use—so keep tasting. This beautiful green preparation is glorious in the late spring, and your guests will appreciate the work and love you put into it.*

1 pound shelled green peas (from about 2½ pounds of pods)
2 pounds fresh fava beans, skinned (removed from about 5 pounds of pods)
6 young artichokes (if you use older artichokes, with fully developed bracts, cook them longer)
Juice of 1 lemon
½ cup extra-virgin olive oil
½ pound scallions (white part only), finely chopped
1 cup hot water
Salt and freshly ground black pepper to taste
Freshly grated nutmeg to taste
4 fresh mint leaves, finely chopped
1 teaspoon red wine vinegar
4 teaspoons sugar

1. Rinse the peas and fava beans and set aside. Trim the artichokes, quarter, and leave them in cold water acidulated with the lemon juice until they are all prepared.

2. In a large skillet, heat the olive oil over medium heat, then cook the scallions until soft, about 3 minutes. Add the artichokes and cook for 5 minutes, or 15 minutes if they are fully developed globe artichokes, then add ⅔ cup of the hot water. Bring to a boil and simmer for 5 minutes. Add the peas and fava beans. Season to taste with salt, pepper, and nutmeg. Cover, reduce the heat to medium-low, and simmer for 20 minutes.

3. Moisten the vegetables with the remaining ⅓ cup hot water if they look like they are drying out and cook until everything is tender, about 40 minutes.

4. Stir in the mint, vinegar, and sugar while the vegetables are still hot, but serve at room temperature.

Makes 8 servings

Game Plan for Serving the Sicilian Frittedda

The Sicilian vegetable preparation on this page is a perfect springtime dish. Fava beans and spring peas are abundant and delicious in May and June. Mixed with scallions, mint, and olive oil and served at room temperature, this is as perfect a preparation as you can find. It is also one that guests will appreciate because it is special and labor-intensive. I would serve it as an antipasto before a plate of spaghetti. To lessen the amount of work, stretch it out over two days. Remove the beans and peas from their pods and skin the fava beans the day before and refrigerate overnight.

Olive Oil–Bathed Fava Beans with Tomato and Lemon Juice in the Palestinian Style

One cannot underestimate the importance of olive oil in Mediterranean cooking, and this is doubly true in Syria, where the olive has been a very important element of the food of Syrians. Al-Muqqadasī, the Muslim geographer who was born in Jerusalem A.D. in 947, relates how in tenth-century Syria fava beans were fried in olive oil and sold mixed with olives, and that the Christians of Syria prepared foods for the young with great quantities of olive oil and called them "olive oil foods." This is quite true even today, where this Syrian-Lebanese-Palestinian preparation called fūl ākhḍar bi'l-zayt *can also be made with runner beans or green beans. The fava beans used in this recipe should be quite young—young enough so that you can eat the otherwise indigestible skin surrounding the bean, which one normally pinches off. The pods of these young fava beans will be 4 or 5 inches long at the most. Although it can be served hot, I prefer this meze at room temperature.*

½ cup extra-virgin olive oil

1¼ pounds onions, coarsely chopped

1¼ pounds fresh young fava bean pods, ends trimmed, stringed, and cut into 1½-inch pieces

1 large ripe tomato (¾ pound), peeled, seeded, and chopped

2 teaspoons salt

Freshly ground black pepper to taste

½ cup water

3 tablespoons fresh lemon juice

In a large skillet, heat the olive oil over medium-high heat, then cook the onions until golden, about 12 minutes, stirring occasionally. Add the beans and tomato and cook for 10 minutes, stirring. Add the salt, pepper, water, and lemon juice, reduce the heat to low, and simmer until the beans are tender, about 1 hour, stirring occasionally. Serve hot or at room temperature.

Makes 6 servings

Fava Bean Pods in Olive Oil with Dill

This Turkish recipe called zeytinyağlı iç balka *is made with whole fava bean pods. This not-too-frequently-seen meze needs to be made with young fava bean pods that are no more than 5 inches long and preferably younger (smaller) than that. As the name indicates—*zeytinyağlı *means something like "olive-oiled food"—this preparation is cooked in a copious amount of olive oil, then allowed to cool in the olive oil before being eaten as a room-temperature meze.*

2 pounds young fava bean pods (not more than 5 inches long), ends trimmed and stringed

1 quart water

⅔ cup extra-virgin olive oil

3 medium-size onions, very coarsely chopped

2 teaspoons salt

5 teaspoons sugar

Juice from 1 lemon

3 sprigs fresh dill, leaves removed and chopped and stems saved

Place the fava beans in a large saucepan and cover with the water, olive oil, onions, salt, sugar, lemon juice, and dill stems and bring to a boil. Reduce the heat to low, cover, and simmer until tender, about 1 hour. Let cool in the saucepan, covered.

2. Drain, transfer to a serving platter, and garnish with the chopped dill.

Makes 8 servings

Young Fava Beans

Eating fava beans, so young that their thin skins do not need to be peeled off, is popular in many regions of the Mediterranean. An old custom in Provence is to offer a bowl of these young favas piled high and served as *feves à la croque-au-sel* (uncooked fava with salt) for an appetizer. In Syria, too, *fūl mūaᶜlla* are very young fresh fava beans that can be eaten with their skins on and are often had as a snack or meze.

Pearl Onions in Sweet-and-Sour Sauce in the Style of Monaco

This relatively simple hors d'oeuvre called oignons à la Monégasque *is the way the dish is cooked in the Principality of Monaco, or so the name implies. There is evidence here of the old Italian tastes of the Duchy of Savoy with its raisins and vinegar, and it well may have an old history. It is served cold or at room temperature and is very nice with a drink and some crusty bread. This recipe is adapted from Anne Willan's* French Regional Cooking.

20 ounces white pearl onions (see Note on how to peel)
1½ cups cold water
½ cup white wine vinegar
½ cup golden raisins
3 tablespoons extra-virgin olive oil
3 tablespoons tomato paste
¼ teaspoon dried thyme
1 bay leaf
1 sprig fresh parsley
Salt and freshly ground black pepper to taste

1. Put all the ingredients in a medium-size saucepan, bring to a boil, reduce the heat to low, cover, and simmer 30 minutes.

2. Uncover and continue to simmer until the liquid in the pan is much reduced and syrupy, about another 1 hour.

3. Arrange the onions and raisins in a serving platter and spoon over them any sauce left. Let cool, then refrigerate for 1 hour before serving.

Note: To peel the pearl onions, bring a medium-size saucepan of water to a rolling boil, then plunge the onions in, leaving them there for 3 or 4 minutes. Drain and, when cool enough to handle, and cut the root tip off each one and pinch the onion out of its peel.

Makes 6 servings

Spinach with Garlic Yogurt on Fried Arabic Bread

This dish is a meze variation of a famous Lebanese-Syrian-Palestinian casserole called fattat al-sabānikh, *which is not usually served as a meze. It is a very convenient dish because all the components can be made ahead of time, then assembled as a hot dish at the last moment.*

7 teaspoons extra-virgin olive oil

1 medium-size onion, sliced ¼ inch thick and separated into rings

1½ pounds spinach, heavy stems removed and washed well

Salt and freshly ground black pepper to taste

1 large garlic clove, peeled

1 cup full-fat plain cow or goat's milk yogurt, at room temperature

1 teaspoon dried mint

3 tablespoons pine nuts

1 small Arabic flatbread, pan-fried until crispy golden in olive oil

1. In a large skillet, heat 5 teaspoons of the olive oil over medium-high heat, then cook the onion until light brown on the edges and soft, 6 to 7 minutes, without stirring too much. Add the spinach, cover, and cook until it wilts, 2 to 3 minutes. Remove the cover, season with the salt and pepper, and turn the heat off until needed.

2. In a mortar, pound the garlic with ½ teaspoon salt until mushy, then stir into the yogurt. Add the mint and whip with a fork to blend.

3. In a small skillet, heat the remaining 2 teaspoons olive oil over medium-high heat, then cook the pine nuts until golden, 1 to 2 minutes. Set aside.

4. Line a medium-size casserole with the fried bread. When it is time to serve, briefly reheat the spinach, then cover the bread with the spinach and onion and spread the yogurt on top. Sprinkle the pine nuts on top and serve.

Makes 6 servings

Chicory Leaves in Olive Oil

Chicory (Cichorium intybus L.) *is related to endive (escarole) and is a wild herbaceous plant found growing all over the Mediterranean. The Arabs (and Italians too) are particularly fond of chicory and have many names for it such as* shikūriyā *(or* shikūriyya), hindab, hindibā, sarīs, ṭihlīdaj, murra, qishnīza, *and* luᶜāᶜ. *Chicory is a bitter-tasting green popular in the Middle East, with a large head rosette of runcinate leaves, which is typically used in salads. But this ingenious recipe from Lebanon, called* hindab bi'l-zayt, *takes advantage of the bitterness of the chicory, counterbalancing it with the use of a fruity olive oil. The finished dish is garnished with crispy brown slices of onion, a pleasing contrast to the soft green leaves.*

1½ pounds chicory, washed, patted dry, and very finely shredded

1 cup olive oil

1 large onion, sliced into ¹/₁₆-inch-thick rings

3 large garlic cloves, finely chopped

1 tablespoon salt

3 tablespoons fresh lemon juice

The Dish Known as Fatta

I wrote extensively about *fattīt*, a class of Syro-Palestinian crumbled flatbread preparations, in my book *A Mediterranean Feast* (William Morrow, 1999), but I feel it is worthy of repeating, partly because I find it so fascinating and partly because I could live on this stuff. Traditionally, *fatta* dishes are not served as meze, but sometimes a scaled-down version is, and that is what is presented on the opposite page. In Syria, Lebanon, and Palestine, *fatta* (singular, *fattīt* is plural) is a dish made of stale, toasted, or fresh flatbread that is crumbled or ripped and laid down as a foundation for other ingredients to go on top, with the bread acting as an absorbent. The reason these dishes developed is that flatbreads become stale within hours when exposed to air, and rather than throw precious bread away, it is utilized in a wonderful way.

There are many *fatta* dishes, some made with eggplant, others with hummus, or the fabulous *fattāt maqādim al-ghanam* made with lamb shanks, chickpeas, and spices and with yogurt spread over the bread. The Bedouins make *fattīta*, a kind of sausage made with bread, sour milk, and lots of butter, and *taftīt*, a food made of crumbled bread and milk. The famous bread salad called Fattūsh (page 240)—made with toasted pieces of pita bread, cucumbers, tomatoes, scallions, parsley, chickweed, and lettuce—is also a member of this class of dishes, as is the equally beloved *musakhkhan*, probably the national dish of Palestine. So is *fatta*, an Egyptian feast meal, and *fattāt*, a kind of bread soup popular among workers in Damascus for breakfast.

1. In a large pot of boiling water, boil the chicory for 2 minutes. Drain, squeeze dry, and set aside.

2. In a large skillet, heat the olive oil over medium-high heat. Add the onion rings and coat with the oil. Continue turning the onion rings as they turn from white to yellow to brown. Once they turn brown, 10 to 20 minutes, continue to cook until some turn dark brown, another 2 minutes. Remove the skillet from the burner and quickly transfer the onions to a paper towel-lined platter to cool and drain.

Once they are cool, they will have become crispy.

3. Heat the same oil again over medium heat, add the chicory and garlic, sprinkle with salt, and cook until flavorful, about 15 minutes. Pour the lemon juice over the chicory, stir, and let cool.

4. Transfer the chicory, garlic, and oil to a serving bowl, garnish with the onion rings, and serve at room temperature.

Makes 4 servings

Four Young Greens Sauté

This very fresh, exciting dish is made with the young, tender leaves of four greens, young spinach, broccoli leaves, mustard greens, and Swiss chard. I first had this horta *in a little village in Crete, south of Chania. There are lots of* horta *preparations, the key being wild greens, although many* horta *are made with cultivated greens. These are best found in a farmer's market, where they are likely to be a little more tender than the kind found at the supermarket, on top of which, you will not find broccoli leaves at a supermarket. If you have a garden and are growing these plants, one way to assure that the leaves of your greens are delicate and tender is to fertilize the earth with liquid seaweed. This is a dish that should be eaten with at least two other meze and a little warmed pita bread.*

3 tablespoons extra-virgin olive oil
1 large garlic clove, finely chopped
½ pound young spinach leaves, washed well and dried
½ pound young mustard greens, washed well and dried
½ pound young Swiss chard leaves, washed well and dried
¼ pound broccoli leaves, washed well and dried
Salt and freshly ground black pepper to taste

In a large skillet, heat the olive oil over medium-high heat with the garlic. Add the greens and, once they wilt, season with salt and pepper, and serve immediately.

Makes 4 servings

Fried Baby Potatoes in Allioli

This Spanish tapa *from the Levantine coast of Alicante called* patatitas fritas con allioli *was a wonderful morsel I once had at a bar in Benidorm, of all places. I say of all places because it's a bustling Spanish tourist beach town with nothing to recommend unless you're a sociologist of urban Spanish yuppie culture. But that's why I went: because one guidebook said "don't go," and to see lots of teenagers from Madrid having a summer blast. There's nothing notable about the food there; in fact, you'll find more wienerschnitzel and bangers and mash than you will tapas, but I was just crazy about these potatoes. To do them properly, you'll have to make an* allioli.

1 cup Allioli (page 466)
1 pound baby Yukon Gold potatoes, 1 inch in diameter or less, left unpeeled
6 cups olive oil for frying
Salt to taste

1. Prepare the *allioli.*
2. Bring a medium-size saucepan of water to a boil and cook the potatoes until ever so slightly tender, about 5 minutes. Drain and dry thoroughly with paper towels.
3. Preheat the frying oil in a deep fryer or an 8-inch saucepan fitted with a basket insert to 375°F. Cook the whole potatoes in the hot oil until crisp, tender, and brown, about 8 minutes. Remove with a slotted spoon, drain on paper towels, season with salt, and serve with toothpicks with the *allioli* on the side.

Makes 8 servings

Ricotta, Potato, and Salami Cake

This Sicilian antipasto is called gattò di ricotta, *a name that derives from the French word for cake,* gâteau. *This name probably derives from the nineteenth-century* monzù, *the French-trained Sicilian chefs of the aristocracy. Although more unlikely, the name could be much older, from the period when Charles of Anjou ruled Sicily, 1266 to the Sicilian Vespers in 1282 (see my* Mediterranean Feast, *page 495). One could also make this tart in small tartlet molds; it's up to you.*

2 pounds boiling potatoes (such as Yukon Gold)

¾ pound fresh ricotta cheese, preferably homemade (page 88)

3 large eggs, beaten

Salt and freshly ground black pepper to taste

Pinch of freshly grated nutmeg

2 tablespoons extra-virgin olive oil, plus extra for drizzling

Dry bread crumbs for sprinkling

½ pound fresh mozzarella cheese, sliced

½ cup peas, cooked and drained

6 ounces thinly sliced Neapolitan salami, cut into strips

2 large hard-boiled eggs, shelled and thinly sliced

1. Place the potatoes in a large saucepan with water to cover and bring to a boil, about 20 minutes, then boil until a skewer glides easily to the center, about 20 minutes. Drain and, when cool enough to handle, peel and mash the potatoes. In a large bowl, mix the mashed potatoes, ricotta, beaten eggs, salt, pepper, and nutmeg until relatively smooth. Stir in the 2 tablespoons of the olive oil.

2. Grease a 2-quart mold or terrine with butter and sprinkle with enough bread crumbs so that when you shake and tilt the terrine they will coat the bottom and sides with a thin film of bread crumbs. Put in two thirds of the potato mixture, making a well in the center and having the sides of the walls about ½ inch thick. In the cavity that remains, arrange the mozzarella, peas, salami, and sliced eggs, then cover with the remaining potato mixture. Seal the edges carefully so the stuffing remains closed off.

3. Preheat the oven to 350°F. Drizzle some olive oil over the top of the terrine, then sprinkle with some bread crumbs. Bake until golden on top, about 45 minutes.

4. Remove from the oven and let cool for 15 minutes. Unmold if desired and serve by slicing into small serving portions. Serve hot or warm.

Makes 8 servings

Vegetable, Cheese, Bread, and Hazelnut Cake

For years now I've subscribed to an Italian food magazine called La cucina italiana *and later to its English language version,* The Magazine of La Cucina Italiana. *I read the magazine only for the recipes, and it's a nice look into the modern Italian culinary culture that seems to reflect an Italian spin on* Bon Appétit *conceptions. This recipe, called* torta di pane e verdure, *is adapted from one in volume 6, issue 1, from January–February 2001.*

4 large cooked artichoke bottoms (canned or
   fresh), sliced
Juice of 1 lemon
3 tablespoons extra-virgin olive oil
2 shallots, chopped
2 carrots, cut into thin sticks
2 leeks (white and light green parts only), split
   lengthwise, washed well, and sliced
½ red bell pepper, seeded and cut into thin strips
½ pound Swiss chard leaves, chopped
¼ pound spinach, washed well, heavy stems
   removed, and chopped
4 small zucchini, peeled and diced
1¼ cups heavy cream
Salt and freshly ground black pepper to taste
½ cup hazelnuts, roasted (page 465), skins
   rubbed off, and finely ground
14 to 16 slices white bread, crusts removed
½ pound Emmentaler cheese

1. Put the artichoke hearts in water acidulated
with the lemon juice as you prepare the foundations, if you are using fresh artichokes. (This
step is not necessary if you are using canned
artichoke hearts.)

2. In a large skillet, heat 2 tablespoons of
the olive oil over medium heat, then cook the
shallots until softened, 3 minutes, stirring. Add
the carrots and leeks and cook until softened,
about 5 minutes. Add the bell pepper and artichokes and cook another 3 minutes, stirring.
Add the Swiss chard and spinach and cook until
they wilt, 2 to 3 minutes, stirring gently.

3. In a medium-size skillet, heat the remaining 1 tablespoon olive oil over medium heat and
cook the zucchini until lightly browned, about

5 minutes. Fold the zucchini into the other
vegetables.

4. Pour the cream into the skillet and season
with salt and pepper. Bring to a gentle boil
and cook until the cream reduces by half and
thickens, about 3 minutes. Remove from the
heat and let cool. Pour the cream over the vegetables and stir gently.

5. Meanwhile, preheat the oven to 450°F.
Generously butter a round 8- or 9-inch spring-
form mold and sprinkle the bottom and sides
with hazelnuts to cover, pressing them with
your hands to help them adhere. Line the
bottom and sides of the mold with the slices
of bread, cutting the bread so that it fits snugly
and does not hang over the sides of the mold.
The bread slices will hold each other up once
you jam them in the mold.

6. Cut two thirds of the Emmentaler cheese
into thin slices and coarsely grate the remainder.
Place half of the sliced cheese on top of the
bottom layer of bread. Spread half of the vegetable mixture on top of the cheese. Layer the
remaining sliced cheese over the vegetable
mixture, then cover that with the remaining
vegetable mixture. Sprinkle with the grated
Emmentaler and bake until the top is golden
and the *torta* is set, about 30 minutes.

7. Remove the *torta* from the mold, place it
on a serving dish, and serve immediately, slicing
into serving portions.

Makes 8 servings

Mushrooms in Garlic from Spain

This Spanish tapa *is called* championes al ajillo, *which means "mushrooms cooked in abundant garlic and sometimes red pepper." Traditionally, the mushrooms are thinly sliced and cooked in young garlic– and chile-flavored olive oil with a little lemon. The mushrooms should be cooked until all their liquid has evaporated; the flavor is intense. They can be served with toast points, if desired, although that is not traditional.*

½ cup extra-virgin olive oil

6 large garlic cloves, finely chopped

1 large dried red chile

3 pounds button mushrooms, brushed clean, thinly sliced, and tossed with juice from ½ lemon

Salt and freshly ground black pepper to taste

3 tablespoons finely chopped fresh parsley leaves

1. In a nonreactive casserole or skillet, heat the olive oil, garlic, and chile together over medium heat. Once they are sizzling, add the mushrooms, season with salt and pepper, increase the heat to high, and cook until the liquid has evaporated and the mushrooms are golden and beginning to stick to the skillet, 10 to 12 minutes, stirring frequently. Remove and discard the chile.

2. Remove from the heat, toss with the parsley, transfer to a platter or small individual tapas plates, and serve hot or at room temperature with some crusty bread or *crostini*.

Makes 6 to 8 servings

Polenta with Porcini Mushrooms

The flavor, expense, and rarity of porcini mushrooms are incentives to look for a recipe where the mushrooms can shine and, more important, flavor the food it accompanies because you couldn't make a meal out of the mushrooms alone unless you were rich. This preparation from the Veneto region of northern Italy, where polenta is cooked in so many ways, is called polentina mantecata ai funghi porcini, *and is perfect in fulfilling these requirements. This dish is extraordinarily satisfying and suited to cold-weather cooking in September and October, which is also porcini season. Remember not to wash the mushrooms—simply wipe them with a dry paper towel and use the stems, too.*

2 cups coarse-ground cornmeal for polenta

2 quarts beef broth

2½ teaspoons salt

¼ cup (½ stick) unsalted butter

3 tablespoons grated *grano padano* or Parmigiano-Reggiano cheese

1½ pounds fresh porcini mushrooms, sliced

1. Preheat the oven to 350°F.

2. Stir the cornmeal, beef broth, salt, 2 tablespoons of the butter, and the *grano padano* cheese together in a baking dish. Place in the oven and bake for 1 hour and 20 minutes. Stir and bake until thick and dense, another 10 minutes.

3. When the polenta is almost done, melt the remaining 2 tablespoons butter in a large skillet over medium heat and cook the porcini mush-

rooms with a sprinkle of salt until soft and brown, about 25 minutes, stirring occasionally.

4. Pour out the polenta into a 1- or 2-inch-deep 9 x 12-inch baking casserole, top with the mushrooms, and serve immediately.

Makes 8 servings

Variation: In a skillet, melt 3 tablespoons butter with 2 tablespoons extra-virgin olive oil over medium-high heat with 1 crushed garlic clove until nearly smoking. Add the porcini mushrooms and cover for 5 minutes. Pour in

---

Porcini Mushrooms

Porcini are precious mushrooms for both the gourmet and the pocketbook. They can be found in America, but as in Italy and France, where they are also appreciated, they are expensive. There are several kinds of *Boletus*, including *B. edulis*, or common porcini, black porcini (*B. aereus*), reticulated porcini (*B. reticulatus*), and pink-stemmed porcini (*B. pinicola*). The ancient Romans preserved the porcini mushroom and so did the popes in the medieval era. In Sardinia, Morocco, Algeria, and Tunisia, porcini mushrooms grow in the sand and are prized. In September, especially in Italy, it is porcini season and when you attempt to order anything but dishes made with porcini, you will encounter your waiter telling you no, for you are to order porcini only.

½ cup Marsala wine and 1 tablespoon finely chopped fresh basil leaves, reduce the heat to medium, cover again, and cook until the wine is nearly evaporated, about 10 minutes. Pour over the polenta squares and serve.

Okra with Olive Oil in the Style of Homs

Okra is an odd vegetable, with a mucilaginous texture that oozes sticky and slimy once the flesh is cut, but nevertheless is quite popular in West Africa, the Sudan, Ethiopia, Egypt, the Levant, and in the U.S. South, where it often is found in gumbos. Okra originated in either West Africa or Ethiopia and at some point moved into the Mediterranean. One of the first mentions of okra is in the description by a Spanish Arab in 1216, Abul-Abbas al-Nabati, a native of Seville, who on a voyage to Egypt describes okra and says it is eaten when young and tender. It is still eaten young and tender in the Middle East, unlike in America, where it is often eaten large.

It is interesting that this complex recipe, with all kinds of enticing flavors resulting from the tart interplay of garlic and lemon juice with the pomegranate molasses, is so simply named in Arabic. It's called bāmyā bi'l-zayt *(okra with olive oil) and was given to me by George Salloum, who is originally from Homs, Syria. My former mother-in-law, who is Palestinian, would make the same dish without the pomegranate molasses. The kind of okra that Lebanese cooks use is very small, much smaller than you can find in the market here. They should be, ideally, about the size of the last joint of your pinky finger. Pomegranate molasses can be found in Middle Eastern markets.*

1 cup olive oil

2 pounds fresh small okra, bottoms trimmed, washed, and dried well with paper towels

1 large onion, cut in half and very thinly sliced into half-moons

2 heads garlic (about 40 cloves in all), peeled

2 pounds ripe tomatoes, peeled, seeded, and chopped

2 tablespoons pomegranate molasses

½ cup fresh lemon juice

Salt

1 cup loosely packed finely chopped fresh coriander (cilantro) leaves (from about 1 bunch)

½ cup water

1. In a large casserole or wide saucepan, heat the olive oil over high heat until smoking, about 10 minutes. Cook the okra until golden crispy, 3 to 4 minutes. Do not crowd the pan; fry in batches if necessary. Remove the okra as they finish cooking with a slotted spoon, drain on paper towels, and set aside. Reduce the heat to medium.

2. Cook the onion and about 30 cloves of garlic in the same oil until they are soft and a little browned, 8 to 10 minutes, stirring. Return the okra to the pan, add the tomatoes, pomegranate molasses, lemon juice, and a little salt to taste, stir to mix, and continue to cook, covered, until bubbling hard, 8 to 10 minutes.

3. Meanwhile, in a mortar, pound the remaining 10 garlic cloves with the coriander and 4 teaspoons salt until a smooth paste forms, then stir this into the okra. Pour in the water, reduce the heat to low, and simmer until thick, without stirring, about 30 minutes. Turn the heat off and let cool in the casserole to room temperature. Serve from the casserole or transfer to a platter.

Makes 8 servings

Serving Meze at Home

Traditionally, meze are served in Arab restaurants in small boat- or oval-shaped dishes. Although it is elegant and fun to do it this way at home, generally when serving a selection of meze to your family, you don't usually go through the bother, keeping the meze instead in a large platter that gets passed. But if you are serving more than eight people, then the little plates seem appropriate for these little foods.

Peperonata

This Sardinian version of peperonata, *a kind of stew dish popular in southern Italy, too, is made only with yellow bell peppers, which are grilled, then braised slightly in a light tomato sauce with a rich extra-virgin olive oil. This recipe is based on a delightful* peperonata *I enjoyed at the Ristorante La Lepanto in Alghero on the western coast of Sardinia some years ago. It can be served as an antipasto or, if you make enough, as a vegetable stew.*

5 large yellow bell peppers
1½ cups Tomato Sauce (page 465)
Freshly ground black pepper to taste
2 tablespoons extra-virgin olive oil

1. Preheat a gas grill on high for 20 minutes or prepare a hot charcoal fire. Place the peppers on the grill until the skins blister black, 35 to 45 minutes. Alternatively, preheat the oven to 450°F. Place the peppers in a baking sheet and bake until the skins blister black all over, about 30 minutes. Remove from the heat and, once the peppers are cool enough to handle, remove the skin, seeds, and core and discard. Slice the peppers into lengths. Set aside.

2. Prepare the tomato sauce. Once the tomato sauce is ready, add the peppers, black pepper, and olive oil and simmer over medium-low heat until dense and soft, 20 to 30 minutes. Serve hot, warm, or at room temperature.

Makes 6 servings

Red Bell Peppers with Black Olives and Capers from Naples

The capsicums, including the bell pepper and the chile, were among the first of the New World plants to come to those parts of Europe controlled by the Spanish crown. They had an amazing popularity and helped destroy the trade in old spices. The Spanish crown ruled lands from Cadiz to Budapest, including Lombardy and the Kingdom of Naples, which facilitated the spread of peppers. The first Neapolitan recipe we have utilizing the pepper is in Vincenzo

Corrado's Cibo pitagorico, published in 1781 in Naples. He has a number of recipes for peppers, called peparoli, including one stuffed with anchovies, parsley, garlic, and oregano.

This delicious preparation from Naples called peperoni in padella con capperi e olive (peppers in a pan with capers and olives) can be eaten at room temperature, but I like it served quite warm. You cook the bell peppers in a copious amount of olive oil, but you can then save the flavored olive oil to cook other foods. I like to serve this platter of peppers on a buffet table and let people help themselves.

½ cup extra-virgin olive oil
1¾ pounds red bell peppers, seeded and cut into strips
1 large garlic clove, finely chopped
1 tablespoons salted capers, rinsed and chopped
½ cup pitted and coarsely chopped imported black olives
Salt and freshly ground black pepper to taste
3 tablespoons finely chopped fresh parsley leaves

1. In a large skillet, heat the olive oil over medium-high heat, then cook the peppers until slightly blackened on the edges and semi-soft, about 15 minutes, stirring frequently. Remove from the skillet and set aside. Remove all but 2 tablespoons of oil from the skillet, saving the oil for another use. (At this point, I usually pull out as many pieces of red pepper skin as I can find from the oil. It's easy because they curl and stick up so you can just pull them out.)

2. Add the garlic, capers, olives, and a few tablespoons of water to deglaze the skillet,

stirring, over medium-high heat. Cook for 1 minute, return the peppers to the skillet, and cook until they're sticking, 2 to 3 minutes. Season with salt and black pepper, add the parsley, and toss so everything is well mixed. Transfer to a serving platter and let rest 5 minutes before serving.

Makes 6 servings

Peppers from Naples in 1781

Vincenzo Corrado's cookbook from 1781, called *Cibo pitagorico*, has several recipes for peppers, which he calls *peparoli*. *Peparoli all purè di ceci* has the peppers grilled to remove the skin, then fried in olive oil and garlic with parsley and covered with a chickpea puree. *Peparoli alla pignoccata* are boiled peppers with a pesto sauce made of pine nuts, *bottarga* (dried salted tuna roe, page 249), olive oil, and lemon juice.

Bell Peppers and Zucchini with Garlic

This fragrant and colorful Catalan preparation called pebrots i carbaçons a l'all *can be served as a* tapa *or as an accompaniment to roast meat. This recipe is adapted from Marimar Torres's* Catalan Country Kitchen.

6 tablespoons extra-virgin olive oil
7 to 8 large garlic cloves, to your taste, finely chopped

1 large red bell pepper, seeded and cut into strips
1 large yellow bell pepper, seeded and cut into strips
1 large green bell pepper, seeded and cut into strips
Salt and freshly ground black pepper to taste
2 medium-size zucchini (about 1 pound), ends trimmed and cut into ¼-inch-thick rounds
2 tablespoons good-quality sherry vinegar
1 tablespoon finely chopped fresh parsley leaves

1. In a large skillet, heat 2 tablespoons of the olive oil over medium heat, then cook two-thirds of the garlic until very light golden, stirring to make sure you don't burn it. Add the bell peppers, season with salt and pepper, and reduce the heat to medium-low. Cook until the peppers are soft, about 30 minutes, stirring occasionally.

2. Meanwhile, heat 2 additional tablespoons olive oil in another large skillet and cook the remaining garlic until it starts to sizzle. Add the zucchini in one layer, sprinkling the slices with salt and pepper. Cook over medium heat until golden on the bottom, about 5 minutes. Turn them with tongs and cook until the other side is golden. Drain on paper towels.

3. Arrange the zucchini on a serving platter, surround with the peppers, drizzle with the remaining 2 tablespoons olive oil and the vinegar, sprinkle with the parsley, and serve at room temperature.

Makes 4 servings

Peppers and Tomatoes from Granada

This preparation from Granada called plato árabe de pimientos, *whose Spanish name means "Arab dish of peppers," is known as a kind of* hortalizas, *a vegetable preparation made with vegetables grown in the* huertas—*the local truck farms originally established in the Islamic period in Spain (746–1492) by Arab agronomists who revived many of the dormant Roman gardens and established new ones based on new agricultural technology. There are a great many dishes prepared with vegetables grown in the* huertas, *and they are served as stews, as accompaniments to meat, and as tapas. I like to serve this dish as a room-temperature* tapa *with toasted slices of French bread rubbed with garlic.*

8 green bell peppers (about 2¾ pounds)

4 fresh long red chiles (about ¼ pound)

8 ripe tomatoes (about 3¼ pounds), peeled, seeded, and quartered

6 tablespoons extra-virgin olive oil

2 bay leaves

Salt and freshly ground black pepper to taste

1 teaspoon freshly ground cumin seeds

1. Preheat the oven to 425°F and roast the bell peppers and chiles on a baking sheet, turning them to reach all parts of their surfaces, until the skins are black, about 40 minutes. Alternatively, if you are grilling, char them on the grill. Remove the stems and seeds and quarter the peppers and chiles.

2. Place the peppers, chiles, tomatoes, olive oil, bay leaves, salt, and pepper in an earthenware skillet or casserole, turn the heat to medium, and cover. Turn the heat off after 30 minutes, when there is quite a bit of liquid in the pan. Mix in the cumin and leave, covered, for 30 minutes.

3. Remove the peppers, chiles, and tomatoes with a ladle to a serving bowl. Serve with the bread.

Makes 8 servings

Baked Tomatoes and Peppers Provençal Style

The old cookbooks and chronicles are not necessarily good sources for understanding the historic food of Provence. For example, there are only two cabbage recipes in J.-B. Reboul's classic La cuisinière Provençale, *yet cabbage was the most important food of this region in the Middle Ages. By the sixteenth century, new land was coming under cultivation in Provence, in Mandelieu, Biot, Auribeau, Vallauris, Pégomas, Valbonne, Grasse, Barjols, Saint-Paul-de Fogossières, and Manosque, where market gardens were supplying the demand for tomatoes and other New World vegetables within a century of their introduction.*

This dish from Provence, called, simply enough, tomates au four, *"baked tomatoes," is usually eaten at room temperature as an hors d'oeuvre. I've adapted this recipe from Jacques Médecin's* Cuisine niçoise, *published in 1983.*

¼ cup extra-virgin olive oil

6 large ripe tomatoes (about 3 pounds), sliced ¼ inch thick

Salt and freshly ground black pepper to taste

1 teaspoon dried *herbes de Provence*

2 tablespoons finely chopped fresh basil leaves

2 tablespoons finely chopped fresh parsley leaves

4 green bell peppers, roasted (page 415), peeled, seeded, and cut into strips

2 tablespoons dry bread crumbs

1 tablespoon salted or brined capers, rinsed or drained and chopped

1. Preheat the oven to 475°F.

2. Coat the bottom of a small earthenware (preferably) baking dish with 1 tablespoon of the olive oil and arrange a layer of the tomatoes over the bottom. Season with salt, pepper, the *herbes de Provence*, basil, and parsley. Arrange a layer of the peppers on top of the tomatoes and season again. Continue to layer and season the tomatoes and peppers, ending with a layer of tomatoes. Drizzle the remaining 3 tablespoons olive oil over everything and sprinkle evenly with the bread crumbs and capers.

3. Bake until crispy on top, about 20 minutes. Remove from the oven and let cool. Pour off as much liquid as you can and serve at room temperature.

Makes 8 servings

Mashed Zucchini and Yogurt Salad

This Turkish meze called kabak salatası *is a cooked and mashed zucchini salad. Its preparation is very simple, yet very flavorful when you use naturally sweet small fresh zucchini and a good-quality yogurt.*

2 pounds small zucchini, peeled and diced

1 tablespoon extra-virgin olive oil

6 tablespoons full-fat plain yogurt

2 garlic cloves, very finely chopped

Juice of ½ lemon

Salt to taste

Imported black olives for garnish (optional)

Sliced hard-boiled egg for garnish (optional)

2 scallions, chopped, and 2 tablespoons chopped fresh dill

Tomato slices for garnish (optional)

1. Place the zucchini in a large saucepan of boiling water and let continue to boil until very soft and easily squashed with a fork, about 20 minutes. Drain in a strainer and press down lightly with the back of a wooden spoon to squeeze out any liquid.

2. Transfer to a medium-size bowl and mash with a fork, then stir in the olive oil, yogurt, garlic, and lemon juice and season with salt. Arrange on a platter and refrigerate for 1 hour before serving cool or at room temperature.

3. Garnish with black olives, egg slices, scallions and dill, and/or tomato slices.

Makes 8 servings

Golden-Crusted Oven-Baked Zucchini, Tomato, and Fontina Cheese

This preparation, a simple zucchine al forno *(baked zucchini), is a recipe from Emilia-Romagna that can be served as an antipasto or as a side dish. It can be enjoyed at room temperature but I prefer it hot right out of the oven.*

The finished dish will be topped by an attractive golden crust and redolent with oregano.

3 tablespoons unsalted butter

Two ½-inch-thick slices Italian bread, cut into 3-inch-long x ¼-inch-wide strips

Extra-virgin olive oil for drizzling

1 large, ripe but firm tomato (about ¾ pound), peeled, seeded, and cut into strips

3 medium-size zucchini, cut in half, then each half cut into ¼-inch-wide strips

2 ounces fontina Val d'Aosta cheese, cut into 3-inch-long x ¼-inch-wide strips

Salt and freshly ground black pepper to taste

1 to 2 teaspoons dried oregano, to your taste

3 tablespoons dry bread crumbs

1. In a medium-size skillet, melt 2 tablespoons of the butter over medium heat, then cook the bread strips until golden, about 5 minutes.

2. Preheat the oven to 375°F.

3. Spread a little olive oil over the bottom of the baking dish, then arrange the pieces of tomato, zucchini, and bread in alternating strips. Top everything with the fontina cheese, pushing it down into the other ingredients. Season with salt and pepper and the oregano. Drizzle some olive oil on top, then sprinkle with the bread crumbs and dot the top with thin slivers of the remaining 1 tablespoon butter. Cover with aluminum foil and bake for 25 minutes. Remove the foil and continue to bake until the top is golden and crusty, about 15 minutes. Serve hot, warm, or at room temperature from the baking dish.

Makes 6 servings

Poor People's Summer Squash

This simple recipe called zucchette alla poverella, *from the region of Apulia in southern Italy, is excellent in the summer when you don't want to serve steaming hot food and when delicious baby zucchini are being harvested. In Apulia, they serve the dish as part of a* tavola calda, *a buffet table with many different dishes served at room temperature. This recipe can be made with any kind of summer squash.*

1½ pounds zucchini or other summer squash, ends trimmed and cut into ¼-inch-thick rounds

Salt

6 tablespoons extra-virgin olive oil

3 tablespoons white wine vinegar

1. Sprinkle the squash with salt, arrange on a paper towel–covered wooden board, and leave in direct sunlight until they dry, blotting occasionally with paper towels.

2. In a large skillet, heat the olive oil over medium-high heat until it begins to smoke. Cook the squash in one layer, if possible, until golden on at least one side, 8 to 10 minutes, tossing a few times. Remove the squash from the skillet with a slotted spoon, letting the excess oil drip back into the skillet, and transfer to a serving platter or bowl.

3. Add the vinegar to the skillet with the oil and boil until reduced by half, 1 to 2 minutes. Pour 1½ to 2 tablespoons of it over the squash and leave, covered with plastic wrap, at room

temperature for 24 hours before serving. Discard the remaining liquid.

Makes 4 small servings

Pumpkin and Beans in the Calabrian Style

There is a word used in the cooking of Calabria, and Sicily too, meant to capture an earthy, aromatic richness in certain dishes. The dishes will be described as agghiotta *or* ghiotta *in dialect. The word derives from the Arabic* ghatta, *meaning "gravy" or the Latin word for "throat." These dishes usually contain abundant olive oil, garlic, tomatoes, onion, and, in Sicily especially, raisins, olives, and capers.* Ghiotta *is a word that is often used to express that a dish is rich, luscious, and delicious. This rustic dish is a luscious* ghiotta *as well, served at the* tavola calda *of many* trattorie *in Calabria, although suited to be accompanied by even richer food, if you like. I like to serve it in the fall, as cool weather begins to arrive, as an appetizer to a roast beef or lamb.*

¼ pound (½ cup) dried white beans, rinsed and picked over
Salt to taste
¼ cup extra-virgin olive oil
2 large garlic cloves, crushed
½ teaspoon red pepper flakes
1 pound peeled and seeded pumpkin flesh, cut into matchsticks
½ cup water
2 bay leaves
1 teaspoon freshly ground fennel seeds

1. Place the beans in a medium-size saucepan and cover with water by several inches. Bring to a boil and cook at a boil until tender, about 1¼ hours. Drain and salt lightly.

2. In a casserole, heat 3 tablespoons of the olive oil with the garlic over medium-high heat; once the garlic turns light brown, remove and discard. Reduce the heat to low, add the red pepper flakes, pumpkin, water, and bay leaves and cook until the pumpkin is so soft it could be crushed with a fork, about 25 minutes. Add the beans, stir to mix well, and cook for a few more minutes. Sprinkle in the fennel, toss, and transfer to a serving platter.

3. Drizzle with the remaining 1 tablespoon olive oil and serve hot or at room temperature.

Makes 6 servings

Whole Cauliflower with Pine Nut Tarator Sauce

This meze called taratorlu karnıbahar *is impressive served on a grand platter, the whole cauliflower looking rather majestic surrounded by black olives and coated with a rich* tarator *sauce, made from fresh bread, pine nuts, and vinegar. In Egypt, Palestine, Lebanon, and Syria, this* tarator *sauce is made with tahini, parsley, lemon juice, garlic, and pine nuts. Guests dig in, breaking off pieces they want.*

Cauliflower
6 cups water
Juice from ½ lemon
Salt to taste
1 large head cauliflower (about 1¾ pounds)

Tarator Sauce

½ cup pine nuts

1 large garlic clove, chopped

½ cup extra-virgin olive oil

4 slices French or Italian bread, crusts removed, soaked in water, and squeezed dry

½ teaspoon salt

¼ cup white wine vinegar

Garnish

10 imported black olives

1. Cook the cauliflower. Bring the water, lemon juice, and salt to a boil in a large saucepan, then cook the cauliflower, partially covered, until tender, when a skewer glides easily into its core, about 20 minutes. Drain and let cool.

2. Meanwhile, prepare the tarator sauce. Place ¼ cup of the pine nuts in a blender with the garlic, ¼ cup of the olive oil, and half of the bread and pulse it a few times. Add the remaining ¼ cup each olive oil and pine nuts and bread and blend until smooth, scraping down the sides if necessary. Add the salt and vinegar and process in bursts. Transfer to a bowl and refrigerate for 1 hour.

3. When you are ready to serve, spread the sauce on top of the cauliflower and garnish with the olives.

Makes 6 servings

Red Beets with Yogurt

When I first encountered this Lebanese preparation, called shawandar bi'l-laban, *I was quite taken with the appetizing color. But upon tasting it I couldn't believe how good it was— how natural beets, yogurt, and mint seemed even though I'm not sure it would have occurred to me. This dish can also be made with* shawandar—*that is, "white beets," more commonly known as Swiss chard or chard.*

2 pounds fresh red beets, with their leaves

Salt and freshly ground black pepper to taste

2 large garlic cloves, pounded in a mortar with ½ teaspoon salt until mushy

2 heaping tablespoons *labna* (strained yogurt; page 56)

1½ cups full-fat plain yogurt

2 tablespoons finely chopped fresh mint leaves

1. Steam or boil the beet leaves over high heat until wilted, about 10 minutes. Remove and drain. Steam the beets until easily pierced by a skewer, about 30 minutes. Drain and let cool. Cut the leaves into strips and arrange by spreading them on a serving plate. Peel the beets and cut into ¼-inch-thick slices. Arrange the beet slices on top of the leaves. Season with salt and pepper.

2. Stir the garlic paste and *labna* into the yogurt and beat for 1 minute with a fork. Spread the yogurt over the beets and garnish the top with the mint.

Makes 6 servings

Beets with Orange Blossom Water and Moroccan Spices

Morocco is abundant with orange trees and orange juice vendors can be found everywhere.

Orange flower water is distilled using an alembic, a device for distillation brought to Morocco by the Arabs. Paula Wolfert tells us that they call this syrup made from orange blossom water knelba *in Morocco. One usually finds orange blossom water, along with rosewater, sold in Middle Eastern markets, although some supermarkets may have it in their international or baking sections.*

This refreshing meze also goes great with grilled spiced lamb rib chops. This recipe is adapted from Paola Scaravelli and Jon Cohen's A Mediterranean Harvest *published in 1986, where they call it* salata remolacha, *which is the Spanish phrase for "beet salad."*

1 pound beets, leaves removed and saved for
    another purpose
4 cups water
½ teaspoon sweet paprika
1 tablespoon sugar
1 teaspoon orange blossom water
½ teaspoon freshly ground cumin seeds
Pinch of ground cinnamon
Juice of 1 lemon
3 scallions, chopped
Salt to taste

1. Place the beets and water in a large saucepan, bring to a boil, covered, and continue to boil until tender, about 1 hour. Drain, reserving ½ cup of the cooking water, and peel when they are cool enough to handle. Let the reserved cooking water cool, too.

2. In a small bowl, combine the reserved cooking liquid, paprika, sugar, orange blossom water, cumin, cinnamon, lemon juice, scallions, and salt. Slice the beets thinly and arrange in a serving bowl. Pour the dressing evenly over the beets and refrigerate for 1 hour before serving.

Makes 6 servings

Food for the Beautiful Young Ladies

In eighteenth- and nineteenth-century Damascus, street vendors would sell a snack of minced wheat bread upon which they would put pomegranate seeds or butter and sesame seeds. They would sell the morsels to passersby with the cry *"ākl al-sunūnū,"* an expression that literally means "food of the swallows" but which was also a euphemism for "food for the beautiful young ladies," because their exquisitely shaped mouths were like the little swallows of Syria, and small mouths were admired on women.

Fried Eggplant and Chiles with Yogurt and Garlic Sauce

In Turkey, there is a class of dishes known as yoğurtlu, *which means "dishes prepared with yogurt." This simple meze called* yoğurtlu patlıcan biber kızartması, *made with fried eggplant and peppers, is one of my favorites, and nearly every restaurant in Turkey will have it on their menu. As the name indicates (*kızartması *means "to roast"), one usually roasts rather than fries the eggplant and peppers.*

2 eggplants (about 3 pounds), peeled and sliced
into ⅜-inch-thick rounds
Salt
3 large garlic cloves, peeled
6 cups olive oil or olive pomace oil for frying
6 poblano chiles (about ¾ pound)
2 cups full-fat plain yogurt

1. Lay the eggplant slices on some paper towels and sprinkle with salt. Leave them to drain of their bitter juices for 30 minutes, then pat dry with paper towels. Mash the garlic with 1 teaspoon salt in a mortar until completely mushy.

2. Preheat the frying oil in a deep fryer or a deep 8-inch saucepan with a basket insert to 375°F. Deep-fry the eggplant slices in batches, taking care not to crowd them, until golden brown, 7 to 8 minutes, turning once. Drain and transfer to a platter covered with paper towels to drain further. Arrange on a serving platter.

3. Deep-fry the chiles in the hot oil until the skins are crispy and peeling, about 3½ minutes, turning once. Arrange over the eggplant slices. Let the frying oil cool completely, strain, and save for a future use.

4. Mix the yogurt and mashed garlic, stirring well, spoon over the eggplant and peppers, and serve.

Makes 4 to 6 servings

Fried Eggplant with Yogurt and Cilantro in the Lebanese Style

In this preparation called bādhinjān maqlī ma laban, *often served as part of a meze, the egg-plant slices are fried, then arranged on a platter and covered with a pungent garlic-flavored yogurt sauce with lots of fresh coriander. Both Turks and Arabs delight in dishes that are hot and cool at the same time. This eggplant dish is also excellent with grilled lamb.*

2 eggplants (about 2½ pounds), halved lengthwise and cut into ¼-inch-thick rounds
Salt
6 cups olive oil or olive pomace oil for frying
6 large garlic cloves, pounded in a mortar with 1 teaspoon salt until mushy
4 cups full-fat plain yogurt
Leaves from 1 bunch fresh coriander (cilantro), finely chopped

1. Lay the eggplant pieces on some paper towels and sprinkle with salt. Leave them to drain of their bitter juices for 30 minutes, then pat dry with paper towels.

2. Preheat the frying oil to 375°F. Fry the eggplant in batches, taking care not to crowd them, until golden brown, 3 to 4 minutes a side. Remove and drain on a tray lined with paper towels until cooled. Let the frying oil cool completely then strain and save for a future use.

3. Stir the garlic paste into the yogurt along with the coriander. Transfer the eggplant slices to a serving platter and cover with the yogurt. Serve at room temperature.

Makes 6 servings

Fried Eggplant, Pepper, and Tomato Salad from Turkey

This simple meze from the area around Marmaris in Turkey is called çuska. *Although simple, it's packed with flavor, especially if you choose the freshest, fleshiest eggplant, peppers, and tomatoes. Serve with crusty French-style bread.*

2 thin eggplants (about 1¼ pounds), peeled in
    alternate strips like zebra stripes and sliced into
    ½-inch-thick rounds
Salt
1 cup extra-virgin olive oil
2 large green bell peppers, seeded and cut into
    1-inch-wide strips
½ pound ripe but firm tomatoes, peeled, seeded,
    and chopped
3 large garlic cloves, thinly sliced
2 teaspoon white wine vinegar

1. Lay the eggplant rounds on paper towels and sprinkle with salt. Leave them to drain of their bitter juices for 30 minutes, then pat dry with paper towels.

2. In a large skillet, heat the olive oil over medium-high heat until it is smoking, then fry the eggplant rounds until golden, about 6 minutes, turning once. Remove with a ladle or tongs and set aside on a paper towel–lined platter to drain.

3. Cook the pepper slices in the remaining oil until browned and crispy, about 8 minutes, stirring. Remove and set aside with the eggplant (when needed, move both to a platter).

4. Cook the tomatoes and garlic in the remaining oil for 4 minutes, then add the vinegar, season with salt, stir, and pour over the eggplant and peppers. Let the dish come to room temperature before serving.

Makes 4 servings

Eggplant and Tomato Marmalade from Istanbul

This meze, called soslu patlıcan *(or* patlıcan soslu*), is one I ordered at the Hippodrome Restaurant on Papa Yokuğlu Street, across from the obelisk in front of the Blue Mosque in Istanbul, and I liked it very much. In fact, I had this room temperature dish of chopped eggplant stewed with tomatoes and olive oil many times in Turkey, and it became for me a kind of weary-tourist comfort food. Serve with pieces of warmed flatbread.*

1¼ pounds eggplant, peeled and cut into
    small dice
3½ pounds ripe tomatoes, cut in half, seeds
    squeezed out, grated against the largest holes
    of a grater, and skins discarded
1 red bell pepper, seeded and chopped
1 long green chile, seeded and finely chopped
4 large garlic cloves, finely chopped
1 cup extra-virgin olive oil
Salt and freshly ground black pepper to taste

1. Put all the ingredients except the salt and pepper in a large casserole and bring to a boil. Reduce the heat to low and simmer until all the liquid has evaporated, about 4 hours, stirring occasionally. Toward the end of the cooking, season with salt and pepper.

2. Let it come to room temperature, then refrigerate for a day before serving. Serve at room temperature.

Makes 8 servings

Pureed Eggplant, Tomato, and Bell Pepper Salad from Turkey

Patlıcan salatası, *or eggplant salad, has the same name as a number of other eggplant salads in Turkey. It's a popular salad throughout the Middle East and in Lebanon* bādhinjān al-rahab, *Monk's Salad (page 60), is very similar. You can garnish this dish in its serving platter with wedges of tomatoes, dill, parsley, and black olives.*

2 pounds eggplant

1 green bell pepper

2 tablespoons fresh lemon juice

¼ cup extra-virgin olive oil

1 teaspoon salt

4 large garlic cloves, finely chopped

1 large ripe tomato, peeled, seeded, and chopped

Warm Arabic flatbreads, cut into wedges

1. Preheat the oven to 425°F. On a baking sheet, bake the eggplant and green pepper until the skins are blackened, 40 to 45 minutes. Remove from the oven, and when they are cool enough to handle, remove the skins from both. Core, seed, and chop the bell pepper. Place the eggplant in a strainer and chop with a knife by swishing it back and forth. Let the eggplant rest in the strainer to drain of liquid for 15 minutes.

2. Place the eggplant in a large bowl with the lemon juice, olive oil, and salt; mix well and leave for 15 minutes in the refrigerator.

3. Stir the garlic, tomato, and bell pepper into the eggplant, check the seasonings, then refrigerate for another 30 minutes.

4. Arrange attractively on a platter and serve at room temperature with the warm bread.

Makes 6 servings

Eggplant in Olive Oil in the Arab Style

This eggplant preparation called bādhinjān bi'l-zayt *is served as part of a meze table throughout the Levantine Arab world. There is a great variety of eggplant preparations and this one, with its mixture of eggplant, onions, and ripe tomatoes, is one of the most delectable. In parts of the Arab world, a saying has it that a girl should know a hundred ways to prepare eggplant.*

¾ cup olive oil

8 small, long eggplants (about 2 pounds), partially peeled in lengthwise strips (you want a stripe effect) and cut in half

1 large onion (about ¾ pound), thinly sliced

4 ripe tomatoes (about 1½ pounds), sliced

4 large garlic cloves, crushed in a mortar with 1 teaspoon salt until mushy

Freshly ground black pepper to taste

½ cup water

1. In a large skillet, heat the olive oil over high heat, and once it begins to smoke slightly,

about 10 minutes, cook the eggplants, flesh side down, in 2 batches until golden brown on just one side, 3 to 4 minutes. Remove from the skillet and set aside.

2. In the same skillet, cook the onion until half the pieces are light brown, 5 to 6 minutes, stirring. Turn the heat off. Transfer the cooked onion to an earthenware (preferably) casserole, using a heat diffuser to protect the casserole from the heat if using earthenware. Arrange the tomatoes and fried eggplant, flesh side down, on top of the onion.

3. Put the crushed garlic in the same skillet as you cooked the eggplant and onion and cook until very light brown, about 1 minute, stirring. Sprinkle the garlic over the vegetables and sprinkle with a little pepper. Pour the water over the vegetables, then cook over medium heat until the liquid begins to bubble, about 10 minutes. Reduce the heat to low, cover, and cook until the vegetables are very tender, about 2 hours.

4. Remove the eggplant to a serving platter with a slotted spatula, inverting them so the flesh side of the eggplant is facing up, covered with the tomatoes and onion. Season with salt and let come to room temperature before serving.

Makes 4 to 6 servings

Eggplant, Red Bell Pepper, and Tomato Salad from Egypt

Alexandria, with a population of nearly 6 million, is the second largest city in Egypt and has long been a summer holiday escape for heat- and dust-beaten Cairenes, many who have summer condos and homes on the beach to the west of the city. Along the coastal road, or corniche, are many, what I call, restaurant-palaces—huge establishments ready to feed big families and parties and offering many different meze.

This caponata-like salāṭa bādhinjān, *or eggplant salad made with eggplant, tomato, red bell peppers, and olive oil, was served as part of a meze table at the huge seaside Tikka Grill on the corniche when I ate there some years ago. It was delightful, along with a host of other meze, all of which we followed with batter-fried sea bream.*

3 pounds eggplant, sliced ½ inch thick
Salt
¾ to 1 cup extra-virgin olive oil, as needed
1 large ripe tomato, peeled if desired, seeded, and chopped
1 large red bell pepper, seeded and chopped
2 tablespoons finely chopped fresh mint leaves
Freshly ground black pepper to taste

1. Lay the eggplant pieces on some paper towels and sprinkle with salt. Leave them to drain of their bitter juices for 30 minutes, then pat dry with paper towels.

2. Preheat a ridged cast-iron grill over high heat, prepare a hot charcoal fire, or preheat a gas grill on high for 15 minutes. Brush the eggplant slices with olive oil on both sides and cook until streaked with black grid marks and beginning to turn light golden, about 8 minutes in all. You might use up to ¾ cup of olive oil doing this. Remove from the griddle or grill, let cool, and dice a little smaller than bite size.

3. In a large serving bowl, toss the eggplant together with the tomato, bell pepper, mint, and remaining olive oil. Season with salt and pepper, toss again, and serve.

Makes 8 servings

Eggplant Ragout with Hazelnuts, Chocolate, and Raisins

This unusual dish from the hill town of Catanzaro in Calabria, a few miles from the Ionian Sea, is called melanzane alla Catanzarese *and is typically served as an antipasto. Catanzaro was probably founded by the Byzantines after they ousted the then recent Arab interlopers with the help of the Longobards. There is a definite Greco-Byzantine cultural imprint, but the source of this peculiar, yet delicious dish appears to me to be Spanish or Catalan. The city was once the center of a silk and velvet trade, and it's possible that buyers, who came from far and wide, arrived in Catanzaro with culinary ideas as well.*

2 pounds eggplant, peeled and cut into
 ¾-inch cubes
Salt
⅔ cup extra-virgin olive oil
3 tablespoons sugar
¼ cup white wine vinegar
1 ounce unsweetened chocolate, broken up
¼ cup blanched whole hazelnuts (1 ounce),
 crushed
3 tablespoons pine nuts (1 ounce)
¼ teaspoon ground cinnamon

½ cup golden raisins
Grated zest from 1 lemon

1. Lay the eggplant cubes on some paper towels and sprinkle with salt. Leave them to drain of their bitter juices for 30 minutes, then pat dry with paper towels.

2. In a medium-size casserole, heat ⅓ cup of the olive oil over medium heat, then cook the eggplant until softer but still firm, about 12 minutes, stirring occasionally. Add the remaining ⅓ cup olive oil, the sugar, vinegar, chocolate, hazelnuts, pine nuts, cinnamon, raisins, and lemon zest. Season with salt and reduce the heat to low. Cook at a simmer until soft, about 1 hour, stirring occasionally. Transfer to a platter and serve hot, warm, or at room temperature on a buffet table with some crusty Italian bread.

Makes 6 servings

Olive Oil–Bathed Artichokes from Syria

Arab horticulturists experimenting with the cardoon sometime before the thirteenth century developed the artichoke, which was a unique thistle with edible flesh on the inside of its bracts and, most important for this preparation to be born, a fully edible bottom of the flower head, which was not only edible but stuffable once the choke was removed. Called arḍī shawkī bi'l-zayt, *this dish is known throughout the Levant. It can be served as a meze, but is also common as a side dish to some stewed or grilled lamb. When artichokes are in season, Arab cooks make countless artichoke recipes. I like to serve this preparation while the artichokes still retain a hint of their warmth or at room temperature. If you serve this dish as a passed appetizer, it may be easier to use sixteen small artichoke bottoms.*

8 medium-size to large artichokes
   (4 to 6 ounces each)
½ lemon
3 tablespoons fresh lemon juice
¼ cup extra-virgin olive oil
½ cup chopped onion
2 garlic cloves, sliced
2 cups water
Salt to taste

1. Trim the artichokes, removing the outer bracts, inner chokes, and fuzzy centers of the bottoms. Rub the bottoms with the cut half of the lemon to keep them from discoloring. Slice the bottoms and place in a bowl of water acidulated with 1 tablespoon of the lemon juice so they don't discolor.

2. In a nonreactive skillet large enough to hold all the sliced artichoke bottoms flat, heat the olive oil, then cook the onion and garlic over medium-high heat until the onion is softened, stirring frequently so the garlic doesn't burn, 3 to 4 minutes.

3. Add the drained artichokes, the remaining 2 tablespoons lemon juice, the water, and salt to taste. Reduce the heat to low and simmer, uncovered, until the artichokes are tender and the water has evaporated, about 1¼ hours. Serve warm or at room temperature.

Makes 8 servings

Fried Artichoke Bottoms with Tarator Sauce

These delectable deep-fried artichoke hearts known as ardī shawkī maqlī bi'l-taratūr *are served with a tahini, garlic, and parsley sauce as part of a meze table. Tarator sauce exists in Turkey, too, but it can be made with walnuts and vinegar; there is also a North African version, prepared with pine nuts, garlic, and vinegar. Tahini, a sesame seed paste once only found in Middle Eastern markets, is carried today by many supermarkets.*

Tarator Sauce
8 garlic cloves, peeled
1 tablespoon salt
½ cup tahini, stirred if oil has separated out
½ cup fresh lemon juice
¼ cup finely chopped fresh parsley leaves

Artichokes
8 large artichokes (about 3 pounds)
6 cups olive oil or olive pomace oil for frying
½ cup all-purpose flour for dredging
Salt

1. Make the sauce. In a mortar, pound the garlic with the salt until it is a creamy mush. In a small bowl or measuring cup, beat the tahini paste and lemon juice together slowly. Stir the tahini and lemon juice mixture into the garlic and beat well. Stir 3 tablespoons of the parsley into this mixture. Taste to check the consistency and correct the seasoning. If it is too thick, add water, *never* more lemon juice. If you do need to adjust the taste, the process must be repeated, in

other words, mash some more garlic with salt or mix 1 tablespoon tahini with 1 tablespoon lemon juice, otherwise the balance of flavors will be off.

2. Cook the artichokes. In a large saucepan, steam or boil the artichokes until there is a little resistance when pierced by a skewer at its base, 40 to 45 minutes. Trim the artichokes, scrape the inside of the bracts for the flesh and save that for another use, and cut the bottoms in half or quarters.

3. Preheat the frying oil in a deep fryer or an 8-inch saucepan fitted with a basket insert to 375°F. Dredge the artichoke hearts in the flour, tapping off any excess in a strainer, and deep-fry, in batches if necessary so you don't crowd the fryer, until golden, about 2 minutes. Drain on paper towels and season lightly with salt. Let the frying oil cool completely, strain through a porous paper filter, if necessary, and save the oil for a future use.

4. Arrange the hot or warm fried artichokes on a platter, sprinkle with the remaining 1 tablespoon parsley, and serve with the sauce in a small bowl on the side for dipping.

Makes 4 to 6 servings

Artichokes, Carrots, and Rice in Olive Oil

This Turkish meze is yet another version of the popular and common zeytinyağlı enginar, *"olive-oiled artichokes," in this dish made with rice and carrots. The preparation is typically served cold and seasoned with abundant fresh dill. For an intense flavor, the vegetables are allowed to cool in the skillet, then the dill is stirred in and the dish is refrigerated for several hours. Some Turkish cooks call this dish* yer elması, *which means something like a vegetable "jelly." Serve with warm flatbread.*

1 cup extra-virgin olive oil

2 medium-size onions, chopped

1 medium-size ripe tomato, cut in half, seeds squeezed out, grated against the largest holes of a grater, and skin discarded

2 large artichokes, trimmed down to their bottoms (page 205) and bottoms and stems thinly sliced

2½ cups hot water

3 small carrots, cut into small dice

3 large garlic cloves, finely chopped

Salt to taste

¼ cup raw long-grain rice, soaked in water for 30 minutes, drained, and rinsed well

Juice from 1 lemon

Leaves from 1 small bunch fresh dill, finely chopped

1. In a large skillet, heat the olive oil over medium-high heat, then cook the onions until translucent, about 4 minutes, stirring. Add the tomato and cook another 4 minutes. Add the artichokes and ½ cup of the hot water, cover, and cook for 15 minutes, stirring occasionally. Reduce the heat if they are sticking. Add the carrots, garlic, and remaining 2 cups hot water, season with salt, and cook until the artichokes and carrots are beginning to become tender, about 10 minutes. Add the rice, cover, reduce the heat to low, and cook until the rice is tender,

about 10 minutes. Stir in the lemon juice and cook, uncovered, for a minute, then turn the heat off.

2. Allow the vegetable to cool in the skillet, then stir in the dill and transfer to a serving platter or bowl. Refrigerate for at least 2 hours before serving and serve cold.

Makes 6 servings

Spicy Carrot Salad from Morocco

This carrot salad from Morocco called salātat al-jazar *is usually served as a meze and can be made in a number of ways, either "hot" or "sweet." To make it sweet, the cooked or grated carrots are tossed with lemon juice, rosewater, sugar, and cinnamon. To make it "hot," cook the carrots in a little water with garlic, paprika, cayenne pepper, and argan oil (see opposite), then toss the drained cooked carrots with white wine vinegar, ground cumin, and chopped fresh coriander (cilantro) leaves. Some cooks like to toss the cooked carrots with a paste made of pounded garlic, parsley, red chiles, red bell pepper, and cumin, and then finish the dressing with a little lemon juice.*

2 quarts water

2 large garlic cloves, crushed into a paste

1 pound small thin carrots, peeled

2 teaspoons extra-virgin olive oil

2 tablespoons fresh lemon juice

½ teaspoon sweet paprika

⅛ teaspoon cayenne pepper

¾ teaspoon freshly ground cumin seeds

1 tablespoon finely chopped fresh coriander
   (cilantro) leaves, plus more for garnish

1. Bring the water to a boil in a saucepan with the garlic, add the carrots, and cook the carrots until very tender, about 20 minutes. Drain and let cool.

2. Cut the carrots in half lengthwise, place in a bowl, and toss with the garlic, olive oil, lemon juice, paprika, cayenne, cumin, and fresh coriander until well coated. Refrigerate until needed but serve at room temperature, sprinkled with more coriander.

Makes 4 servings

Argan Oil

The famous Arab explorer Hasan al-Wazan, who was known as Leo Africanus (c. 1465–1550) in the West and journeyed into Africa, gives a recipe: Boil water in a large pot, add the barley flour, stirring with a stick. Pour the gruel into a plate and in the center make a small shallow where one puts the argan seed oil. The argan seed oil he mentions is extracted from the argan tree (*Argania sideroxylon* Roem. et Schult.), a kind of evergreen, the word coming from the Arabic *ārjān*, where an oil is extracted from the seed. It is still used today in Moroccan cooking, and is also known as the "almond of Barbary."

Celeriac in Olive Oil

There are two basic ways this Turkish winter dish called zeytinyağlı kereviz *can be presented. In both cases, the dish is served as a meze. In the first, the cooked celery root is hollowed out and the other cooked vegetables are stuffed into the hollow. In the second version, the one I prefer and give you here, the celery root is cut up along with the other vegetables.*

Salt to taste
Juice from 1 lemon
1 celeriac (about 1¼ pounds), peeled and cut in half
½ cup extra-virgin olive oil
1 medium-size onion, chopped
2 carrots, quartered lengthwise and cut into 2-inch pieces
1 medium-size potato, peeled and cut into the same size shapes as the carrots
4 cups plus 2 tablespoons water
½ cup peas
1 teaspoon sugar
2 tablespoons chopped fresh dill, plus more for garnish
Freshly ground black pepper to taste
1 tablespoon all-purpose flour

1. Bring a large saucepan of water to a boil with some salt and half the lemon juice, then cook the celeriac until almost tender, about 15 minutes. Drain and slice into ⅜-inch-thick rounds.

2. In a casserole or skillet, heat the olive oil over medium heat, then cook the onion until soft, about 4 minutes, stirring. Add the carrots, potato, and 2 cups of the water and bring to a boil. Reduce the heat to low, cover, and simmer for 10 minutes. Add the celeriac, peas, sugar, remaining lemon juice, and the dill, stir, and season with salt and pepper. Blend the flour with the remaining 2 tablespoons water and stir into the vegetable mixture. Bring to a boil, then cook at a gentle boil until all the vegetables are very tender and the liquid has thickened, 18 to 20 minutes, stirring. Let the vegetables cool in the pan.

3. When you are ready to serve, arrange the vegetables on a serving platter, pour the remaining liquid from the skillet over the vegetables, and refrigerate for 1 hour, but serve at room temperature with a sprinkle of dill.

Makes 4 to 6 servings

Stuffed Vegetables

How ingenious these Mediterranean cooks are! I can't prove it, but it seems likely that stuffing vegetables was first invented in the Mediterranean. This chapter of stuffed vegetable appetizers and little foods starts off with the queen of vegetables, the artichoke, which, when trimmed of its bracts, choke, and woody parts, offers the eater a beautiful hand-held morsel begging to be stuffed. Recipes for stuffed zucchini follow, including recipes for stuffing their flowers, then on to tomatoes, mushrooms, olives, avocados, eggplant, and bell peppers. There are also a couple of recipes for potatoes and onions, which you may never have thought of stuffing. Next come several recipes that use leaves, including grape leaves, escarole, endive, and Swiss chard. Finally, the chapter concludes with recipes for cold stuffed vegetables using cucumbers, celery stalks, and bell pepper quarters.

Artichokes

Artichokes must rank as one of the most Italian of vegetables. You will see *carciofi* on every menu—grilled, boiled, stuffed, and every other which way. In southern Italy you will see fields called *carciofaie* filled with artichoke plants. There are about fifty varieties of artichokes around the world, but the ones you are most likely to see in Italy are the globe artichoke and the Tuscany Violet, which tapers at the top. Most artichokes, but not all, have thorns at the ends of their bracts (they are not leaves). Those without thorns are called *mammole* in Italian, which means violet. There are very small artichokes cut before they form a choke and preserved under olive oil. Artichoke bottoms, called *fondi di carciofi* in Italian, are the bases, hearts, or foundations of the flower heads. Once the bracts and hairy choke are cut away, this portion is edible and considered a delicacy. One can find artichoke bottoms sold in cans of water or you can prepare them fresh (page 205).

Artichoke Bottoms Stuffed with Tuna

The bottom, heart, or foundation of an artichoke is a natural receptacle for foods and makes it an ideal antipasto, like this one, called carciofi farciti di tonno. *If using fresh artichokes, see page 205 on preparing them and the Note below on cooking them for this recipe.*

One 3-ounce can imported tuna in olive oil, drained
2 tablespoons salted or brined capers, rinsed or drained
10 salted anchovy fillets, rinsed
1 large garlic clove, peeled
2 tablespoons finely chopped fresh parsley leaves
Freshly ground black pepper
14 cooked artichoke bottoms (fresh or canned)
¼ cup fresh bread crumbs, or more
2 tablespoons extra-virgin olive oil

1. Preheat the oven to 375°F.

2. Place the tuna, capers, anchovies, garlic, parsley, and black pepper in a food processor and pulse several times until pasty. Divide and spoon a little more than 1 teaspoon into each artichoke bottom. Arrange them in a lightly oiled baking dish. Sprinkle the bread crumbs over the top of each and drizzle with the olive oil. Bake until crisp on top, about 15 minutes. Serve hot or at room temperature.

Note: If using fresh artichokes, place some stuffing in each artichoke after you have trimmed them, then place them in a large nonreactive skillet with a little water in the bottom. Drizzle some olive oil over the top of each one. Turn the heat to medium and, once the water starts to shimmer, reduce the heat to low and simmer, uncovered, until tender, 40 to 50 minutes, adding water to the skillet if necessary, but never so much that it covers the artichoke bottoms. Transfer to a baking dish, sprinkle on the bread crumbs, drizzle some olive oil over each one, and bake at 375°F until crispy on top, about 15 minutes.

Makes 8 servings

Artichoke Bottoms Stuffed with a Macédoine of Vegetables

A macédoine *is a mixture of different fruits or vegetables chopped into very tiny dice and usually used as a garnish in French and Italian cuisine. The word derives from Macedonia, the country formed by Alexander the Great in the fourth century* B.C. *from the multitude of tiny states in what was recently southern Yugoslavia. But the word did not come to be used in a culinary sense until the late eighteenth century, at the earliest, in France. In this preparation, a mixture of flavorful vegetables is chopped fine and stuffed into cooked artichoke foundations. If using fresh artichokes, see page 205 on preparing them.*

1 small carrot, peeled
1 small turnip, peeled
3 ounces fresh green beans, ends trimmed
12 asparagus tips (about ¼ inch in diameter)
½ cup peas

¼ cup mayonnaise
Salt and freshly ground black pepper to taste
12 cooked artichoke bottoms (fresh or canned)

1. Cook the carrot, turnip, green beans, asparagus tips, and peas separately in water to cover until all are tender. Drain, let cool, and dice all the vegetables very finely, including the peas.

2. In a medium-size bowl, mix the vegetables with the mayonnaise. Season with salt and pepper. Stuff the artichoke bottoms with the mixture and serve at room temperature.

Makes 12 servings

Artichoke Bottoms Stuffed with Sausage and Ham from the Languedoc

This hors d'oeuvre from the Languedoc is called fonds d'artichauts farcis. *There, the cook would use prosciutto or some other locally cured ham in the stuffing. The finished artichoke foundations should be sitting on a bed of tomato sauce, not swimming in it. Because of the labor and expense involved with preparing twenty-eight artichokes, I usually used canned artichoke hearts. But if you do use fresh artichokes, then you can save all the bracts and use them for a number of appetizers (page 206). If using fresh artichokes, see opposite page on preparing them.*

¼ pound prosciutto, chopped
¼ pound garlic sausage or sweet Italian sausage, casings removed and meat crumbled

Preparing Artichoke Bottoms

The flesh at the bottom of the inside of the bracts (they are not properly called leaves) is edible, as is the bottom, or foundation or heart, of the artichoke. When you pare an artichoke, the hairy choke is removed to reach the bottom. Choose artichokes that feel heavy and whose bracts are not widely splayed open. Brown splotches are only frost damage and do not harm the artichoke. The type of artichoke you are most likely to find in the market is the globe artichoke, an Italian cultivar, in various sizes, which is the one used for recipes calling for artichoke bottoms.

Preparing a raw artichoke bottom is labor intensive, but a number of recipes call for just that. Wash the artichoke and cut off the top half of the artichoke with a large chef's knife. Remove the little bracts at the stem. Cut the stem off at the point near the bottom so the artichoke can stand up. Many people throw away the stem, but the flesh inside is edible, so slice off the skin and reserve the stem flesh. As you peel, slice, or break off the little pale green bracts near the choke, discard them, and with a paring knife, cut off the woody parts surrounding the bottom, slicing in a circular motion as you hold the artichoke with one hand. Now, from the top and in a circular motion, cut out the hairy choke. Once the raw artichoke is cut, it will blacken, so you must always keep a cut half of a lemon nearby to immediately rub the artichoke heart when you reach it. As you finish each artichoke, put the heart in a bowl of water acidulated with lemon juice or vinegar to keep them from blackening and continue.

4 slices stale French or Italian bread, soaked in milk, then squeezed out and crumbled

2 large eggs

1 shallot, very finely chopped

1 large garlic, finely chopped

2 tablespoons finely chopped fresh basil or parsley leaves

Salt and freshly ground black pepper to taste

2 tablespoons extra-virgin olive oil

2 cups Tomato Sauce (page 465) made with 3 sprigs fresh thyme

28 cooked medium-size artichoke bottoms (fresh or canned)

1. Preheat the oven to 400°F.

2. In a medium-size bowl, mix the prosciutto, sausage, bread, eggs, shallot, garlic, and basil. Season with salt and pepper, toss again, then stuff the artichoke bottoms with it. Place the stuffed bottoms in a well-oiled baking dish and bake until the bottoms are soft and the stuffing is crispy looking on top, about 25 minutes.

What to Do with All the Artichokes?

Some recipes in this book use a good number of artichoke bottoms. If you are using fresh artichokes, you will be left with a lot of bracts (they are improperly called leaves). Don't throw them away because they can be used as an appetizer or for making a sauce. If you want to serve them as an appetizer, put them all in a large pot of lightly salted boiling water and cook until soft, about 40 minutes. Drain and serve with olive oil and vinegar, or an *avgolemono* (a lemon-and-egg) sauce, or a mignonette, or some kind of vinaigrette. You could also use them as dippers for any of the dips in the chapter "Dips, Spreads, and Pâtés." Alternatively, should you decide to make a sauce from the flesh on the inside of the bracts, you'll have more work on your hands. Boil them until soft, then scrape off all the flesh with a spoon. In a skillet, heat a little olive oil with a crushed garlic clove, remove and discard the garlic, then sauté a little onion before putting in the collected artichoke flesh. Dilute with broth, heavy cream, or a little wine and cook over low heat until smooth. Pour over boiled meats or toss with pasta.

3. Meanwhile, heat the tomato sauce and, once it is bubbling, transfer to a deep serving platter. Transfer the artichoke bottoms to the platter, resting them on top of the sauce. Serve hot or warm.

Makes 28 foundations; 14 servings

Artichokes, Celeriac, and Potatoes in Olive Oil

There are many variations of this Turkish meze whose name, zeytinyağlı enginar, *means something like "olive-oiled artichokes." Some cooks don't use the celeriac and potatoes, but I like them. In the spring, scallions would be included, while shallots would be typical at other times of the year. As you follow the instructions on trim-*

ming the artichokes down to their foundations, keep a little of the trimmed stem on them too if you like, but always make sure that all the woody inedible parts are cut away.

2 tablespoons all-purpose flour

4 cups water

Juice of 1 lemon

6 large artichokes (about 4 pounds), trimmed down to their bottoms (page 205)

12 scallions, chopped

2 medium-size potatoes (about ¾ pound), peeled and cut into small dice

1 medium-size celeriac (about ¾ pound), peeled and cut into small dice

1 large carrot, cut into small dice

1 cup extra-virgin olive oil

½ cup shelled fresh or frozen peas

Leaves from 1 small bunch fresh dill, ¼ chopped and the remainder left whole

1 teaspoon sugar

Salt to taste

1 lemon, cut into 6 wedges

1. In a large bowl, mix the flour with a little of the water until it is runny, then add the remaining water and the lemon juice. Place the artichokes, scallions, potatoes, celeriac, and carrot into this bowl as you prepare them.

2. Remove the vegetables from the water once they are prepared and arrange in a large skillet or casserole. Add the olive oil, peas, chopped dill, sugar, salt, and the soaking water. Cover the vegetables with a piece of waxed paper, pressing down, then cover with the lid and turn the heat to high. Once the water is boiling, reduce the heat to low and cook, covered, until all the vegetables are tender, about 40 minutes.

3. Leave the vegetables to cool in the skillet, then remove and discard the waxed paper, transfer to a serving platter, using the artichoke bottoms as containers for the other vegetables, and refrigerate.

4. When you are ready to serve, garnish with the remaining dill, chopped, and serve cold with the lemon wedges.

Makes 6 servings

• ❀ •

Baked Zucchini Stuffed with Beef, Olives, and Capers in the Sicilian Style

These stuffed zucchini from Sicily, called simply zucchini ripieni, *are best eaten hot right out of the oven, although many Sicilians like to eat them at room temperature. The so-called white zucchini is a cultivar that is squat and has pale green skin with some white stripes or splotches; it's also known as Lebanese-style zucchini at some farmer's markets. These are the zucchini that the Lebanese use to stuff.*

4 Lebanese-style white zucchini or any other zucchini (about 2 pounds)

¾ pound ground sirloin (7% fat)

1 medium-size onion, finely chopped

2 tablespoons salted capers, rinsed and chopped if large

⅓ cup pitted and chopped imported green olives

2 tablespoons finely chopped fresh basil leaves

Salt and freshly ground black pepper to taste

1 tablespoon tomato paste dissolved in 2 tablespoons water

Extra-virgin olive oil for drizzling

1. Bring a large saucepan of lightly salted water to a boil and blanch the zucchini for 10 minutes. Drain, let cool, and cut lengthwise into halves. Using a sharp 3-inch parer, cut the flesh to separate it from the skin, being careful you don't break through, scoop it out with a spoon, and set it aside in a bowl. Cut each zucchini half in half crosswise and let rest skin side up on some paper towels for 30 minutes. Arrange the zucchini in a single layer an oiled baking dish, skin side down.

2. Preheat the oven to 400°F.

3. Add the beef to the bowl with the zucchini pulp along with the onion, capers, olives, and basil. Season with salt and pepper. Stir in the tomato mixture and mix well. Salt and pepper the zucchini, then stuff them with the meat mixture. Drizzle the tops with a little olive oil and bake until the tops look a little crusty and everything is sizzling, about 35 minutes. Serve hot, warm, or at room temperature on a large platter on a buffet table or on individual plates.

Makes 8 servings

Baked Zucchini Stuffed with Shrimp in the Provençal Style

This hot hors d'oeuvre is typical of what one would find in small restaurants in Provence. It's delicious as it is, but I find the tarragon adds just the right element to make it a memorable taste.

4 medium-size zucchini (about 2 pounds)
1 pound fresh large shrimp with their heads or
  ½ pound previously frozen headless large
  shrimp, shells and/or heads removed and saved
  for shrimp stock, if desired
4 to 5 tablespoons unsalted butter
4 teaspoons extra-virgin olive oil
3 shallots, finely chopped
3 small garlic cloves, finely chopped
3 cups coarse fresh bread crumbs made from
  white part of French bread
3 tablespoons pine nuts
1 tablespoon finely chopped fresh tarragon leaves
Salt and freshly ground black pepper to taste

1. Bring a large pot of water to a boil, add the zucchini, and cook until slightly tender, about 8 minutes. Remove the zucchini, but leave the water boiling. Cut the zucchini into 1½-inch-thick slices. Once they are cool, remove the center portion with a melon baller, making sure you don't break through the bottom. Salt the boiling water abundantly and cook the shrimp until they turn orange, about 2 minutes. Drain, remove their heads and/or shells, and chop. You can save this water for making a stock if you like.

2. In a medium-size skillet, melt 3 table-spoons of the butter with the olive oil over medium-high heat, then cook the shallots and garlic until soft, about 4 minutes, stirring. Add all but 6 tablespoons of the bread crumbs and cook until browned, 4 to 5 minutes, stirring. Add the shrimp, pine nuts, and tarragon, season with salt and pepper, and cook for another 2 minutes, then remove from the heat.

3. Preheat the oven to 450°F.

4. Lightly salt the hollows of the zucchini. Stuff the zucchini slices with the shrimp stuffing. Sprinkle a small amount of the remaining bread crumbs on top, dot with the remaining 1 to 2 tablespoons butter, arrange in a baking dish, and bake until golden brown on top, 10 to 12 minutes. Serve hot, warm, or at room temperature from the dish.

Makes 24 slices;12 servings

Stuffed Fried Zucchini Blossoms

I have always admired the Italian or French markets for offering bright yellow zucchini blossoms. I had never seen them in an American market until the mid-1990s. Your local market may not carry them, but that gives you all the more reason to grow at least one zucchini plant, even if it's only in a pot on your balcony. The beautiful yellow flowers, which spread wide open in the daytime, are wonderful to behold. Stuffing the flowers and deep-frying them is extraordinary. It's very hard for me to actually get this to dinner guests—I usually eat them all as they finish cooking. To grow your own, see opposite. This recipe is inspired by a dish I had many years ago in a trattoria in Tuscany.

10 zucchini blossoms

10 fresh mozzarella cheese cubes cut to the size of dice

5 salted anchovy fillets, rinsed and cut in half lengthwise

6 cups sunflower seed or vegetable oil for frying

½ cup all-purpose flour

1 teaspoon extra-virgin olive oil

1 large egg white

Salt to taste

Scant cup water

1. Open the flowers and remove the pistil, then very carefully wash the insides by dunking the flowers in a bowl of cold water. Dry the flowers by dabbing with paper towels.

2. Stuff each blossom with a cube of mozzarella wrapped in an anchovy piece. The flowers can be refrigerated for up to 24 hours at this point.

3. Preheat the frying oil in a deep fryer or an 8-inch saucepan fitted with a basket insert to 360°F.

4. In a small bowl, mix the flour, olive oil, egg white, salt, and enough of the water to make a slightly thick batter. Dip the blossoms in the batter, letting the excess drip off, then deep-fry several at a time until golden, turning once, about 30 seconds. Remove with a slotted spoon and drain on paper towels for a minute before serving hot either as a passed appetizer or on a serving platter on a buffet table.

Makes 4 to 5 servings

Growing Zucchini

These big plants are favorites with cook-gardeners, not only because you can pluck baby zucchini and save yourself the fortune you pay at the market, but also because you can pick those beautiful yellow flowers and stuff them. Buy a small zucchini plant in early June and place it in the garden at least four feet from any other plant in well-fertilized soil, then water regularly through the summer and you can begin to harvest by late summer. In warmer parts of the country, you can plant and grow zucchini year-round.

Les Fleurs de Courgettes Farcies à la Brandade de Morue de Nîmes avec Sauce Romarin

This very elegant and delicate preparation was created by Michel Kayser, chef and owner of Restaurant Alexandre in Garons-Nîmes, demonstrating the connection between local cooking and contemporary haute cuisine, at his Michelin-starred restaurant outside Nîmes in southern France. I've kept the French name as it appears on the menu because it is so special. It means zucchini flowers stuffed with brandade of salt cod with rosemary sauce. Large fresh zucchini flowers are stuffed with a mousse of whipped salt cod and coated with a rosemary cream sauce. Chef Kayser's signature preparation is a fantastic dish and amazingly delicious.

Although one can enjoy stalls piled with tiny zucchini with their yellow blossoms still attached in les Halles de Nîmes, the central food market, I have found zucchini blossoms sold in the United States only at a select few farmer's markets, mostly in California. Therefore, you will need to take the flowers from your garden zucchini plant. You need about four plants to produce ten flowers a day. Once the flowers are picked, they will wilt rapidly, so pick the baby zucchini they are attached to also. Wash the flowers carefully by soaking them in a bowl of cold water, especially the inside of the flower, where bugs might like to hide. Keep refrigerated until needed.

Simply put, brandade, called baccalà mantecato by the Venetians and brandada by the Catalans, is hard to make because the salt cod must not be waterlogged nor stringy when finally processed into the brandade. I think, though, that if you follow my instructions closely, you should be able to pull it off.

½ pound salt cod, soaked in cold water for 2 to 3 days, changing the water 2 to 3 times a day

3 garlic cloves, finely chopped

2 cups milk

½ cup extra-virgin olive oil

1 cup crème fraîche

Salt and freshly ground black pepper to taste

8 to 10 large freshly picked zucchini flowers (see headnote)

½ cup white wine (Cabernet Blanc)

½ cup white wine vinegar

4 sprigs fresh rosemary

6 tablespoons whipped unsalted butter

½ cup heavy cream (preferably not ultra-pasteurized), beaten until soft peaks form

1. Drain the salt cod, arrange in a medium-size saucepan, and cover with the garlic and milk. Turn the heat to medium. When the milk begins to shimmer, 12 to 14 minutes, reduce the heat to low and cook until the cod flakes very easily. The time will vary, so keep checking. Make sure the milk never reaches even a gentle boil or it will curdle. Drain well, break the cod into flakes, and remove and discard any skin or bones. Pat dry with absorbent paper towels, if necessary. Place a metal bowl in the freezer. Discard the milk.

2. Wash and dry the saucepan, combine the salt cod and olive oil in the pan, and cook over low heat, mashing with a spatula, potato masher, or fork, until well mashed but not entirely smooth, about 8 minutes. Remove from the heat and refrigerate for 1 hour.

3. Remove the metal bowl from the freezer, place the salt cod in it, and vigorously beat in the crème fraîche, salt, and pepper or process until smooth in a food processor. Check the

Salt Cod in the Mediterranean

Fishermen from Norway, England, Iceland, Holland, and Brittany were going as far as the Newfoundland banks by the 1500s to haul in their huge loads of abundant cod. The cod was eviscerated and salted on board ship, and the greater part of the catch was sold to the people of the Mediterranean. Northern salt cod made its entrance at Marseilles, a major transshipment port and reseller of the cod, and from there it was sold to Venice, where *baccalà mantecato* (see headnote, page 75) was prepared, or perhaps to Nîmes, where the equally famous Brandade de Morue (page 75) was made. Other regions were prodigious eaters of salt cod, especially Italy, Greece, and Spain, where on the island of Minorca it might find its way into an empanada (page 324). There are two dried cod products found in the Mediterranean, what the Italians call *baccalà*, dried and salted cod, and *stoccafisso* (or *stoccofisso*), cod air-dried without the use of salt. Both these products came from northern Europe and both Italian words probably derive from Old Dutch.

Salt cod was an important staple aboard ships that plied the Mediterranean as well as the new convoys beginning to head for the Americas. Cod was eaten aboard ships two to four times a week. A typical diet for sailors aboard a Spanish galley in 1560 was $1\frac{1}{2}$ pounds of bread, a quart of 15 percent alcohol wine, a half pound of salt beef, salt cod, or cheese, depending on the day, a little less than a quarter pound of dried beans or chickpeas, half an ounce of olive oil, and a little vinegar. The daily caloric value of this diet was about 3,750, meaning that sixteenth-century sailors were among the best-fed people in the Mediterranean region.

seasonings. Place everything in a food processor and pulse in bursts until very well blended with no evidence of stringiness.

4. Transfer the salt cod mixture (*brandade*) to a pastry bag with a small nozzle. Remove the zucchini flowers from the water and remove their pistils. Don't worry if the flowers rip a little. Stuff each flower with the *brandade*.

5. In a saucepan, combine the wine, vinegar, and rosemary and reduce to ¼ cup over medium-high heat. Whisk the butter in a little at a time, then add the cream. Season with salt and pepper. Remove and discard the rosemary.

6. Arrange one or two stuffed zucchini flowers on each plate, surround with the sauce, and serve immediately.

Makes 6 servings

Stuffed Cherry Tomatoes with Mascarpone and Pancetta

This is a very sweet-looking platter of cherry tomatoes stuffed with mascarpone cheese and sprinkled with parsley. When serving this appetizer, place some mixed herbs in the center of the serving platter as a garnish. If you make this a few hours beforehand, leave it to rest at room temperature; don't refrigerate it at any time.

Salt to taste
60 cherry tomatoes, stem part cut off and
   hollowed out using a demitasse or baby spoon
Freshly ground black pepper to taste
½ pound mascarpone cheese
1 ounce *pancetta,* sliced, microwaved until
   crispy between 2 sheets of paper towels,
   and chopped; or pan-fried until crispy in a
   nonstick skillet and finely crumbled
Finely chopped fresh parsley leaves

1. Salt the inside of the cherry tomatoes if time allows and let drain hollow side down for 30 minutes.

2. Season the cut side of the tomatoes with salt and pepper. Stuff with mascarpone and top with some pancetta bits. Arrange on a platter and sprinkle with the parsley. Serve at room temperature.

Makes 8 servings

Stuffed Tomatoes with Tuna, Eggs, and Mayonnaise in the Style of Monaco

In French they call this dish, attributed to the cooks of the Principality of Monaco, tomates à la Monégasque. It is a familiar preparation and as pomodori ripieni it is served as an antipasto in northern Italy with just about the same stuffing. Look for tomatoes about the size of a golf ball.

2 large hard-boiled eggs (see opposite page),
   shelled and chopped
Two 3-ounce cans imported tuna in olive oil,
   drained and mashed
Salt and freshly ground black pepper to taste
1 tablespoon salted or brined capers, rinsed or
   drained and chopped if large
1 tablespoon finely chopped fresh parsley leaves
¼ cup mayonnaise, preferably homemade
   (page 466)
1 teaspoon finely chopped fresh parsley leaves
1 teaspoon finely chopped fresh tarragon leaves
1 teaspoon finely chopped fresh chervil leaves
14 small ripe but firm tomatoes, cut in half and
   hollowed out

In a medium-size bowl, mix all the ingredients except the tomatoes, then stuff into the tomatoes and serve. Do not refrigerate at any time.

Makes 10 servings

The Perfect Hard-Boiled Egg

To hard-boil an egg to perfection, bring water to a boil and carefully place the room-temperature egg in the water and cook exactly 9 minutes. Remove immediately, cool under cold running water, and shell when cool enough to handle comfortably.

Stuffed Tomatoes with Tuna and Potatoes

This antipasto from Liguria in northwestern Italy is called simply pomidori farciti, *"stuffed tomatoes." What makes it unique is that it is stuffed with a fine mixture of potatoes mashed with tuna.*

4 small boiling potatoes (about 1 pound)
8 pearl onions
4 large ripe but firm tomatoes
One 3-ounce can imported tuna in olive oil, drained
¼ cup extra-virgin olive oil, plus more for drizzling
1 tablespoon very finely chopped fresh basil leaves
Salt and freshly ground black pepper to taste
8 small fresh basil leaves

1. Place the potatoes in a medium-size saucepan of cold water to cover by several inches and turn the heat to medium. Once the water starts to bubble, in about 20 minutes, cook at a gentle boil until a skewer glides easily to the center of the potato, another 20 minutes. Add the pearl onions for the last 10 minutes of cooking. Drain, and when they are cool enough to handle, peel the potatoes. When the onions are cool enough to handle, remove their skins and set aside.

2. Preheat the oven to 400°F.

3. Cut the tomatoes in half and remove the seeds.

4. In a medium-size bowl, mash the tuna and boiled potatoes together very well. Stir in the olive oil and chopped basil and season with salt and pepper. Stuff the tomatoes with the mixture and arrange in a single layer in a baking dish. Garnish each tomato with an onion, pushing it down slightly into the mashed potatoes, drizzle with a little olive oil, and bake until the tomatoes are soft, 25 to 30 minutes.

5. Remove from the oven, garnish each tomato with a basil leaf, and serve hot.

Makes 8 servings

Stuffed Tomatoes in Olive Oil

This Turkish preparation is a famous one in the category of foods known as zeytinyağlılar, *"olive oil foods." This particular dish is called* zeytinyağlı domates dolması, *which means something like "olive oiled–stuffed tomatoes." This category of foods is characterized by vegetables, stuffed or not, cooked in a copious amount of olive oil and served at room temperature, the olive oil both providing flavor and a preservative effect for the dish.*

24 small to medium-small Roma plum or
   Carmelo tomatoes (about 4 pounds)

1 cup extra-virgin olive oil

½ cup sunflower oil

2 tablespoons pine nuts

2 medium-large onions, finely chopped

1 cup raw medium-grain rice, rinsed well
   in a strainer under cold running water or
   soaked in tepid water to cover for 30 minutes
   and drained

2 tablespoons dried currants, soaked in tepid
   water for 15 minutes and drained

1 teaspoon ground cinnamon

1 teaspoon freshly ground allspice berries

1 teaspoon freshly ground white pepper

1 teaspoon salt

1 teaspoon sugar

1 cup boiling water

Leaves from ½ bunch fresh mint, finely chopped

Leaves from 1 bunch fresh dill, finely chopped

½ cup water

1. Slice the tops off the tomatoes, saving
them. Slice off a tiny portion of the opposite
end of the tomato, just enough so the tomato
can stand up on its own without falling over but
not enough to make a hole. Scoop out the
insides of the tomatoes using a small spoon to
make it hollow, making sure you don't puncture
the cavity you will stuff.

2. In a large skillet, heat ½ cup of the olive oil
with all of the sunflower oil over medium heat,
then lightly brown the pine nuts. Add the
onions and cook until they turn translucent, 6
to 7 minutes, stirring. Add the rice and cook for
5 minutes. Add the currants, cinnamon, all-

spice, white pepper, salt, and sugar, and stir.
Add the hot water, bring to a boil, reduce the
heat to low, cover, and cook until most of the
liquid is absorbed, about 15 minutes. Turn the
rice into a large platter to cool and, once cool,
toss with the mint and dill.

3. Preheat the oven to 475°F.

4. Stuff the tomatoes tightly with the rice
mixture and place the lid back on top. Arrange
the tomatoes in a baking pan and pour the
remaining ½ cup olive oil over them. Add the
½ cup water to the pan and bake until the
tomatoes are tender and the tops look a little
crusty, about 25 minutes. Remove from the
oven and let cool in the baking pan. Transfer to
a serving platter and let cool further but do not
refrigerate. Serve at room temperature.

Makes 12 servings

 ## Portobello Mushrooms
Stuffed with Herbs and Eggs
à la Provençale

This interesting recipe called oeufs aux sanguins
à la manosquine *is adapted from the book*
Recettes des provinces de France, *published in
1961, by the famous nineteenth-century French
gastronome Curnonsky. Sanguin is a kind of
local wild mushroom with a pinkish hue found
in the Lubéron region of Provence. Apparently,
this is a dish in the style of the cooks of Manosque,
a town in the Lubéron, the mountainous region
of the Durance Valley. In the sixteenth century,
Manosque was brought under cultivation and
vegetables found their way to the towns along*

*the Rhône, and Aix-en-Provence and Marseilles.
Note that you use the smallest eggs you can find.*

5 tablespoons extra-virgin olive oil

1 small onion, finely chopped

3 garlic cloves, finely chopped

¼ cup dry white wine

1 pound ripe tomatoes, cut in half, seeds
   squeezed out, grated against the largest holes
   of a grater, and skins discarded

2 tablespoons finely chopped fresh tarragon leaves

1 teaspoon dried *herbes de Provence*

Salt and freshly ground black pepper to taste

6 large portobello mushrooms (4 to 5 inches in
   diameter)

1 tablespoon finely chopped fresh parsley leaves

1 tablespoon finely chopped fresh chives

1 large hard-boiled egg, shelled

¾ cup coarse fresh bread crumbs (about 1 ounce)

¼ cup chopped bacon (about 1 ounce)

2 teaspoons sweet Hungarian paprika

6 teaspoons anchovy butter (page 23)

6 small or medium-size eggs

3 tablespoons freshly grated Parmigiano-
   Reggiano cheese

1. In a medium-size saucepan, heat 2 table-spoons of the olive oil over medium-high heat, then cook half the onion and one third of the garlic until soft, about 3 minutes, stirring frequently so the garlic doesn't burn. Add the wine, tomatoes, 1 tablespoon of the tarragon, and the *herbes de Provence*; season with salt and pepper, reduce the heat to medium, and cook until dense, about 20 minutes, stirring frequently. Set aside and keep warm.

2. Remove and finely chop the stems from the mushrooms. In a medium-size bowl, toss the stems with one third of the garlic, the remaining onion, the parsley, chives, and the remaining 1 tablespoon tarragon. In a small bowl, mash the egg until a paste with the remaining garlic clove, then turn into the bowl with the chopped mushroom stems. Add the bread crumbs and bacon, and season with salt and pepper. Toss well to mix.

3. Preheat the oven to 350°F.

4. Season the insides of the mushroom caps with salt, pepper, and the paprika and a little drizzle of 1 tablespoon of olive oil. Stuff the caps with the stuffing, leaving a well or indentation in the center, and place the caps in a single layer in a baking dish coated with the remaining 2 tablespoons olive oil. Place 1 teaspoon of anchovy butter in the center of each cap and bake until the mushrooms look soft and the tops are bubbling slightly, about 30 minutes.

5. Remove from the oven. Carefully crack an egg into each cap without breaking the yolk. Season with salt and paprika. Sprinkle on the Parmesan and return to the oven until the egg whites are hard but the yolk remains soft, about 8 minutes.

6. Spread a film of the tomato sauce on the outside edge of 6 individual small plates and place the mushroom in the center. Serve immediately.

Makes 6 servings

Olives Stuffed with Ground Beef in Piquant Tomato Ragout

This Tunisian ragout called maraqat al-zaytūn *is served as a main course, but because of the convenience of the olives and their size, I think the dish lends itself well to a meze table. This recipe requires large pitted olives preserved in a mild brine, not a strongly flavored one. You'll notice that this recipe calls for a huge amount of parsley—three to four bunches, and you must trust me that that is not excessive.*

½ pound ground beef
2 cups finely chopped fresh parsley leaves (3 to 4 bunches)
1 medium-size onion, finely chopped
1 large egg
1 teaspoon Tābil (page 471)
Salt and freshly ground black pepper to taste
2 pounds pitted large green olives, drained
½ cup extra-virgin olive oil
2 tablespoons tomato paste mixed with ¼ cup water
1 teaspoon red pepper flakes
1 tablespoon Harīsa (page 468)
1¼ cups water

1. In a large bowl, knead together the beef, parsley, onion, egg, *tābil*, salt, and black pepper. Stuff the olives with this stuffing, using a small, narrow baby spoon or the handle end of a teaspoon.

2. In a casserole, preferably earthenware, heat the olive oil over medium-high heat, then add the diluted tomato paste, red pepper flakes,

harīsa, 1 teaspoon salt, and the water. Bring to a boil and add the olives. Reduce the heat to low, cover, and cook until the meat is done (you'll need to taste one), about 1 hour.

3. Serve the olives with the sauce if serving this dish as an appetizer at the table or serve with cocktail toothpicks if serving as a passed appetizer.

Makes 8 servings as a plated appetizer and 12 servings as a passed appetizer

Avocado Stuffed with Shrimp and Spicy Mayonnaise

This might not strike you as typically Mediterranean, and I'm not sure if it is, but I first had this as an appetizer in Italy so that's why I include it. To make this manageable as an appetizer, given how rich avocado is, you will need to use the smallest, ripest avocados you can find. Ideally, your shrimp will be fresh too, and then you will have a perfect dish. Remember that shrimp is unforgiving, so be careful not to overcook them.

1 pound fresh large shrimp with their heads or ½ pound previously frozen headless shrimp, shells and/or heads removed and saved for making shrimp stock, if desired
¼ cup mayonnaise
1 teaspoon fresh lemon juice
Salt to taste
½ teaspoon Tabasco sauce
3 small, ripe avocados (about ¾ pound), peeled, halved, and stones removed

1. Bring a pot of abundantly salted water to a boil, then cook the shrimp until they turn orange-red and are firm, about 2 minutes. Drain and let cool.

2. In a small bowl, stir together the mayonnaise, lemon juice, salt, and Tabasco. Fill the wells of the avocado halves with the mayonnaise and push the shrimp into it, arranged attractively. Serve chilled.

Makes 6 servings

Oven-Baked Stuffed Eggplant

This melanzane al forno *from the southern Italian region of Apulia is powerfully aromatic. The eggplant is hollowed out and stuffed with the diced flesh of eggplant fried in olive oil mixed with bread crumbs, anchovies, capers, olives, and oregano. The cook typically serves this dish at room temperature as part of a* tavola calda, *a buffet table lined with mostly vegetable antipasto dishes in majolicaware platters.*

2 large eggplants (about 2¼ pounds)

Salt

3 cups extra-virgin olive oil

¼ cup fresh bread crumbs

8 salted anchovy fillets, rinsed and chopped

¼ cup salted or brined capers, rinsed or drained and chopped if large

½ cup imported black olives, drained and pitted

2 garlic cloves, finely chopped

1 tablespoon finely chopped fresh parsley leaves

1 teaspoon dried oregano

2 ripe tomatoes, sliced

1. Trim the eggplants of their stems and slice in half lengthwise. Hollow out the flesh from the inside, leaving about a ¼-inch-thick wall. Salt and dice the removed eggplant flesh. Salt the hollowed-out eggplants and lay on some paper towels, hollow side down, along with the diced pieces so they can drain of their bitter juices for 1 hour, then pat dry with paper towels.

2. Preheat the oven to 325°F.

3. Meanwhile, heat 2 cups of the olive oil in a medium-size skillet over high heat for 8 minutes, then cook the diced eggplant until golden brown, about 8 minutes. Remove with a slotted spoon, set aside on paper towels to absorb excess oil, and salt. Toss the fried eggplant, bread crumbs, anchovies, capers, olives, garlic, parsley, and oregano together in a medium-size bowl.

Majolica

I don't care what you say, I think all Italian antipasto served on a *tavola calda* (buffet table), whether in a restaurant or in your house, should be served on attractive polychromatic majolicaware platters, such as the ones made by the famous Deruta in Italy. They aren't always expensive, either. Deruta, in fact, has licensed a Chinese firm to make Deruta-designed plates as in the home country, and they are just fine and add another level of desire to the whole culinary experience.

4. Lightly oil a baking pan and arrange the hollowed-out eggplants in it. Salt and divide the stuffing equally in among the hollowed-out halves. Cover with the slices of tomato. Season with salt and pour over the remaining 1 cup olive oil. Bake until bubbling and sizzling on top, 1 to 1¼ hours. Serve hot or at room temperature, sliced into serving portions.

Makes 6 servings

The Imam Fainted

The Imam Fainted, ımam bayıldı, *is the most famous of Turkish eggplant meze.* İmam bayıldı *is an eggplant slashed down the middle and stuffed with onions, garlic, and tomatoes, then simmered in olive oil to cover. There are several apocryphal stories about the origins of the dish. The imam (Muslim prayer leader) fainted or swooned when he tasted how good it was; that the imam fainted when he saw how much expensive olive oil was used; that the imam was delighted when a shopkeeper's wife was required to quickly prepare a dish for the imam's unexpected visit.*

4 small eggplants (about 1½ pounds)
Salt to taste
10 tablespoons extra-virgin olive oil
2 medium-size onions, cut in half and thinly
  sliced into half-moons
6 large garlic cloves, chopped
½ pound ripe tomatoes, peeled, seeded, and
  chopped
¼ cup finely chopped fresh parsley leaves
2 tablespoons chopped fresh dill

1 teaspoon sugar
2 tablespoons fresh lemon juice
¼ cup water

1. Peel off strips of the eggplant skin at 1-inch intervals to make a striped affect. Cut off the stem portion, then cut each eggplant in half lengthwise. Make a deep lengthwise slit along the flesh side of the eggplant, making sure you don't puncture the skin. Cut off a very small portion of the skin side of the eggplant to make a flat section so the eggplant can sit flat in the skillet later. Salt the flesh and set aside, flesh side down, on some paper towels for 30 minutes to leach the eggplant of its bitter juices. Dry with paper towels.

2. In a large skillet, heat ¼ cup of the olive oil over high heat; once it's smoking, fry the eggplant, flesh side down, until golden brown, about 4 minutes. Remove from the skillet to drain on some paper towels.

3. In the same skillet you cooked the eggplant, add the remaining 6 tablespoons oil and heat over medium-high heat, then cook the onions and garlic until soft and yellow, about 5 minutes, stirring frequently so the garlic doesn't burn. Transfer the onions to a medium-size bowl and mix well with the tomatoes, parsley, dill, sugar, salt to taste, and a few tablespoons of the cooking oil.

4. Arrange the eggplant halves in a large skillet or casserole with the slit side up. Gently open the slit so that it can accommodate as much of the stuffing as possible. Season the eggplant with salt, then stuff each one so that the stuffing fills the slits and is spread to cover all the flesh.

Sprinkle the lemon juice over the eggplant. Pour any remaining sauce or juices, along with the water, into the skillet, cover, and cook over low heat until the eggplant are soft, about 50 minutes, adding water to the skillet if it is getting too dry. Let the eggplant cool in the skillet and serve whole at room temperature.

Makes 8 servings

Stuffed Eggplant with Rice, Currants, and Dill in Olive Oil

These delicious stuffed eggplants called zeytinağlı patlıcan dolması *in Turkey are served at room temperature, either as a vegetable side dish or as a meze. Spicing with allspice and the use of currants and pine nuts in prepared dishes is typical of Turkish cuisine. In Turkey, a whole class of foods is called* zeytinağlılar, *meaning "olive oil foods." Olive oil foods are foods that are braised in copious amounts of olive oil, then allowed to cool in the oil, which acts as a preservative. The Turks are crazy about olives and olive oil is the prestigious cooking oil, even in this age when sunflower oil is gaining in popularity in Turkey. The best way to serve the stuffed eggplant is sliced, with a sprig of mint or parsley.*

3 large eggplants (about 3½ pounds)
¾ cup extra-virgin olive oil
2 medium-size onions, coarsely chopped
1 teaspoon salt
½ cup raw medium-grain rice, soaked in tepid water 30 minutes and drained or rinsed well
1 tablespoon pine nuts

1¾ cups water
½ cup peeled, seeded, and finely chopped fresh tomato or canned crushed tomatoes
1 tablespoon dried currants
½ teaspoon freshly ground black pepper
½ teaspoon freshly ground allspice berries
1 tablespoon finely chopped fresh mint leaves
¼ cup chopped fresh dill
½ teaspoon sugar

1. Cut off the stem ends of the eggplants and save these "lids." Hollow out the seeds and flesh of the eggplants, leaving a ¼-inch-thick wall, being careful you do not puncture the skin. Reserve the eggplant pulp to make eggplant fritters, if you like. Place the eggplants in a large bowl or stew pot filled with salted water and leave to leech of bitter juices for 30 minutes. Drain and pat dry with paper towels.

2. In a skillet, heat ¼ cup of the olive oil over medium heat with the onions and ½ teaspoon of the salt and cook until the onions turn translucent, about 8 minutes, stirring. Add the drained rice and pine nuts, and cook until the rice is well coated with oil, about 2 minutes, stirring frequently. Add ¾ cup of the water, the tomato, currants, black pepper, allspice, mint, and dill; stir, reduce the heat to low, cover, and cook until the rice has absorbed the liquid but is still a little hard, about 15 minutes. Sprinkle with the sugar.

3. Stuff the eggplants with the rice mixture, not too tightly, not too loosely, then replace the tops of the eggplants and arrange in a deep casserole, side by side. Add the remaining 1 cup water, ½ cup olive oil, and ½ teaspoon salt;

cover and cook over low heat until the eggplants are soft but still maintaining their shapes, about 1¼ hours.

4. Let the eggplants cool in the casserole. Cut in half lengthwise and serve at room temperature.

Makes 6 servings

Stuffed Eggplant with Lamb and Pine Nuts in the Style of a Sheik

An Arab sheik (properly pronounced "shake") is a prominent chief of a community or tribe. This Lebanese meze is called shaykh al-maḥshī bādhinjān, *"sheik-style stuffed eggplant," so-called in recognition of its magnificence, of the fact that it is bigger and grander than other eggplant preparations, and that it contains lamb, meat being for special occasions or people. In fact, the word for meat and lamb is the same in Arabic,* laḥm.

12 long eggplants (about 4 pounds), stalk ends trimmed

7 tablespoons extra-virgin olive oil

¼ cup pine nuts

1 pound ground lamb

1 large onion, finely chopped

1 garlic clove, finely chopped

¼ teaspoon ground cinnamon

¼ teaspoon freshly ground allspice berries

1 teaspoon Bāhārāt (page 470)

¼ cup finely chopped fresh parsley leaves

Salt and freshly ground black pepper to taste

One 6-ounce can tomato paste mixed with 2 cups water

1 tablespoon fresh lemon juice

1 mild green chile, such as an Anaheim, seeded and chopped

1. Peel the eggplants lengthwise in zebra-like stripes. In a large skillet, heat 5 tablespoons of the olive oil over medium-high heat, then brown the pine nuts, watching carefully because they can turn brown suddenly, 2 to 3 minutes. Remove with a slotted spoon and set aside. Cook the eggplant in the same oil until the peeled parts are lightly browned and feel a little soft to the touch, 8 to 12 minutes, cooking in 2 batches if necessary to keep them from crowding. Remove from the skillet and set aside.

2. Preheat the oven to 375°F.

3. In the same skillet, heat the 2 remaining tablespoons olive oil with the meat, onion, and garlic and cook over medium-high heat until the liquid has evaporated, 4 to 5 minutes, stirring frequently. Add the toasted pine nuts, cinnamon, allspice, *bāhārāt*, and parsley; season with salt and black pepper, then cook until the meat loses its color, breaking it up as it cooks and mixing it with the other ingredients, about 2 minutes. Remove from the heat.

4. Cut the eggplants open lengthwise in one long, deep slit, making sure you don't cut all the way through. Stuff them with the meat mixture, opening the slit enough to accommodate the stuffing. Arrange in a baking pan and pour the tomato mixture and lemon juice on top. Season with salt and black pepper, sprinkle with the chile, and bake until bubbling, about 30 minutes, basting occasionally.

Olive Oil Foods

The Ottoman court cuisine began to use an uncommon amount of olive oil in the seventeenth century. A class of dishes arose called "olive oil foods," *zeytinyağlılar*. These were usually vegetables cooked in copious amounts of olive oil and served at room temperature as a meze. One of the most famous of the "olive oil foods" is The Imam Fainted (page 218). Some regions in the Levant used more olive oil than others. The Syrians in particular used lots of it. Al-Muqqadasī (writing circa 985–90) relates how fava beans were fried in olive oil and sold mixed with olives. The Christians of Syria prepared foods for their children with great quantities of olive oil, thought to be healthful, and also called them "olive oil foods."

The concept of "olive oil foods" has roots in the ancient Greek dietetic theory of humors, which had currency throughout the Middle Ages. *Zeytinyağlı* dishes, which are usually eaten cold, fit the prescriptions of this theory. It was customary to eat cold and moist foods in the summer during medieval times because that counteracted the hot, dry humor of summer that, it was thought, caused an increase in bile.

5. Serve warm or at room temperature, whole, or cut into slices on a large platter on a buffet table.

Makes 12 servings

Stuffed Eggplant from Sicily

No matter what home, no matter what trattoria one steps into, Sicilian cooks will offer up melanzane ripiene, *"stuffed eggplant." This recipe was given to me years ago and every time I make it, I alter it a little, for there are hundreds of stuffed eggplant recipes in Sicily. Typically, these stuffed eggplant are served as an antipasto, either small ones whole, or cut up into bite-size portions. They can be served hot, warm, or at room temperature.*

6 small eggplants (about 2½ pounds in all, 6 x 3 inches), split in half lengthwise
¾ cup grated pecorino cheese
½ cup shredded provolone cheese
⅓ cup chopped salami
6 tablespoons finely chopped fresh parsley leaves
2 large eggs, beaten
Salt and freshly ground black pepper to taste
2 to 3 tablespoons extra-virgin olive oil, to your taste

1. Bring a large pot of lightly salted water to a boil, add the eggplants, and cook for 12 minutes. Drain in a colander, flesh side down, for 1 hour. Remove some of the pulp of the eggplants with a small spoon or paring knife, making sure there is enough left over to prevent the egg-

plants from collapsing too much. Mash the pulp with ½ cup of the pecorino cheese, 6 tablespoons of the provolone, and the salami, parsley, and eggs, then season with salt and pepper.

2. Preheat the oven to 375°F.

3. Grease a baking dish with olive oil and arrange the eggplants so they fit tightly in a single layer, cut side up. Fill the eggplants with the stuffing. Sprinkle the top of each with the remaining ¼ cup pecorino and 2 tablespoons provolone and the olive oil. Bake until dappled golden brown on top, about 45 minutes. Serve hot, warm, or at room temperature on a large platter on a buffet table.

Makes 12 servings

Stuffed Bell Peppers with Rice and Currants

The Turks are big fanciers of stuffed vegetables, and there is no vegetable that begs more to be stuffed than the bell pepper. This meze is called zeytinyağlı biber dolması *and is one of the foods in Turkish cuisine known as "olive oil foods."*

Stuffing

¼ cup extra-virgin olive oil

1¾ pounds onions, finely chopped

1½ teaspoons salt

½ cup raw long-grain rice, rinsed well or soaked in tepid water to cover for 30 minutes and drained

1 cup water

One ¾-pound ripe tomato, cut in half, seeds squeezed out, grated against the largest holes of a grater, and skin discarded

2 tablespoons dried currants

1 tablespoon pine nuts

½ teaspoon freshly ground black pepper

½ teaspoon freshly ground allspice berries

¼ teaspoon ground cinnamon

1 teaspoon sugar

Leaves from ½ bunch fresh mint, finely chopped

Leaves from 1 bunch fresh dill, finely chopped

Bell peppers

8 medium-size green bell peppers (about 2¼ pounds)

1 cup water

¼ cup extra-virgin olive oil

Salt

1. Make the stuffing. In a large skillet, heat the olive oil over medium-high heat, then cook the onions with 1 teaspoon of the salt until yellow, about 15 minutes, stirring. Add the rice and cook until the mixture starts to stick to the bottom of the skillet and is browning, 7 to 8 minutes, stirring. Add the water, tomato, currants, pine nuts, black pepper, allspice, cinnamon, sugar, the remaining ½ teaspoon salt, the mint, and dill; reduce the heat to low and cook until the liquid has evaporated, about 15 minutes. Turn the heat off and leave the stuffing in the skillet.

2. Preheat the oven to 400°F.

3. Prepare the peppers. Cut the tops off the peppers and remove the seeds. Save the tops for lids. Stuff the peppers with the rice mixture with a spoon, but not too tightly. Replace the tops, but setting them on upside down with the stems stuck in the stuffing, and set the peppers in a baking pan. Add the water to the pan and

drizzle the olive oil over the peppers. Season with salt and bake until the peels wrinkle and the tops are blackened, 50 to 55 minutes.

4. Remove from the oven and let them come to room temperature before serving.

Makes 12 to 16 servings

Stuffed Yellow Peppers in the Style of Bari

The rustic flavor of the cooking of Apulia is a style that very much appeals to me. Take this recipe from the city of Bari. I dare say that it is probably my favorite stuffed pepper recipe, which the locals called peperoni imbottiti alla barese. *It's very flavorful and aromatic yet light, and perfect for hot summer days, when I usually serve it warm rather than hot. The color, too, is very appetizing, as you will see.*

3 tablespoons extra-virgin olive oil

1½ cups fresh bread crumbs

8 salted anchovy fillets, rinsed

¼ cup salted capers, drained and rinsed

½ pound imported black olives, drained, pitted, and cut in half

¼ cup golden raisins, soaked in tepid water 15 minutes and drained

¼ cup pine nuts

2 tablespoons finely chopped fresh parsley leaves

2 tablespoons finely chopped fresh basil leaves

Salt and freshly ground black pepper to taste

Pinch of freshly grated nutmeg

6 yellow bell peppers (about 3½ pounds), seeded and cut in half lengthwise

2 cups tomato puree (preferably fresh)

1. In a medium-size skillet, heat 5 teaspoons of the olive oil over high heat and, once it is smoking, brown the bread crumbs, tossing or stirring constantly, 1 to 2 minutes.

2. In a medium-size bowl, mix the bread crumbs, anchovies, capers, olives, raisins, pine nuts, parsley, basil, and 1 teaspoon of the olive oil. Season with salt, pepper, and the nutmeg.

3. Preheat the oven to 350°F.

4. Stuff the peppers with the bread crumb mixture and arrange in a baking pan with the remaining tablespoon of olive oil on top of the peppers and on the bottom of the pan. Pour the tomato puree in the pan and bake until the peppers are soft but firm, 50 to 60 minutes. Add water to the tomato puree if it is getting too thick. Serve hot or at room temperature.

Makes 8 servings

Baby Potatoes Stuffed with Ground Lamb, Pine Nuts, and Pomegranate Molasses

This rich, complex meze called baṭāṭa mahshī, *"stuffed potatoes," is a preparation from the city of Homs in Syria. If you were to use larger potatoes than I call for here, you would serve the dish as a main course. It might not seem a lot of food, especially once it's in the baking pan, but this quantity serves at least eight. This recipe comes from George Salloum, an Arab-American originally from Homs, whose mother, Ovilia, showed him how to make it. One would find stuffed potatoes like this in Palestine, too, but made in a simpler peasant style, usually just lamb seasoned with cumin and maybe cooked in chopped tomatoes. The sumac and pomegranate molasses called for can usually be found in a Middle Eastern market.*

24 Red Bliss or other red potatoes
  (about 3 pounds)
6 cups vegetable oil, olive oil, or olive pomace oil
  for frying
2 tablespoons clarified butter or unsalted butter
½ pound onions, finely chopped
1 pound ground lamb
8 large garlic cloves, finely chopped
2 tablespoons pomegranate molasses
2 teaspoons Bāhārāt (page 470)
¼ teaspoon sumac (page 427)
½ teaspoon dried mint
3 tablespoons pine nuts
1 teaspoon salt
Freshly ground black pepper to taste
2 cups Béchamel Sauce (page 468)

1. Peel and core the potatoes with a melon baller, being careful not to puncture or break them. Save the peels and cored section for another purpose. Keep the potatoes in a bowl of cold water after you peel and core them so they don't turn color.

2. Preheat the frying oil in a deep fryer or an 8-inch saucepan fitted with a basket insert to 375°F. Fry the whole cored potatoes in the hot oil until barely tan, about 4 minutes. Carefully remove with tongs and set aside to drain, hollow side down, on a paper towel–lined plate.

3. Preheat the oven to 375°F.

4. In a large skillet, melt the butter over medium heat, then cook the onions until soft, about

8 minutes, stirring occasionally. Increase the heat to medium-high, add the ground lamb, garlic, pomegranate syrup, *bāhārāt*, sumac, and mint, and cook until the meat turns color, about 5 minutes, stirring frequently. Add the pine nuts and continue to cook for 2 minutes. Season with salt and pepper. Taste and correct the other seasonings.

4. Stuff the cored potatoes with the meat stuffing. Butter a large baking pan and arrange the stuffed potatoes in the pan in a single layer. Cover the potatoes with the béchamel sauce.

5. Bake the potatoes for 30 minutes. Increase the oven temperature to 450°F and bake until the tops are speckled brown, about another 5 minutes. Serve hot from the casserole.

Makes 8 servings

 ## Cottage Fries Stuffed with Sour Cream and Salmon Caviar

This preparation is an elegant restaurant dish typical in northeastern Italy. The secret to these delicious fried potatoes is to cook them twice. Also, be careful that you don't spread the sour cream too early or it will melt too much and the whole thing will be unappetizing, yet you do want to serve it warm.

6 cups olive oil, olive pomace oil, or vegetable oil
  for frying
1 large baking potato, peeled, cut into about
  twelve ⅛-inch-thick slices, and dried with
  paper towels
Salt to taste

¼ cup sour cream
1 tablespoon salmon caviar

1. Preheat the frying oil in a deep fryer or an 8-inch saucepan fitted with a basket insert to 375°F. Fry the potato slices in the hot oil until half-cooked, about 3 minutes. Remove with tongs or a slotted spoon and let cool on paper towels. They can be kept like this, wrapped in plastic, until you are ready to serve them.

2. When it is time to serve, reheat the frying oil to 375°F and fry the potato slices again until golden, 3 to 4 minutes. Remove from the oil, spread on a paper towel–lined platter or tray to drain, salt lightly, and keep them warm. Let the frying oil cool completely, strain through a porous paper filter if it is dirty, and save for a future use.

3. Once the potatoes are warm and no longer hot, spread 1 teaspoon of sour cream over each slice, then place a ¼ teaspoon of salmon caviar on top of that and fold the potato in half. Arrange on a platter and serve.

Makes 12 slices; 6 to 8 servings

Tiny Stuffed Onions with Ground Veal, Mushrooms, and Olives

This antipasto is very nice to pass around at a party, even if it is a bit of work stuffing the onions. Another thing: you must be careful not to overcook the onions when you boil them and, when you hollow them out, don't remove too few or too many of their inner layers.

¼ cup dry bread crumbs
2 tablespoons finely chopped fresh parsley leaves
24 small white onions (about 1 pound)
2 tablespoons extra-virgin olive oil
1 large garlic clove, finely chopped
½ pound ground veal
Salt and freshly ground black pepper to taste
1 tablespoon finely chopped fresh basil leaves
3 tablespoons chopped black olives
¼ cup chopped mushrooms
Butter for dotting the tops of onions

1. In a small bowl, mix the bread crumbs and parsley and set aside.

2. Bring a large saucepan of water to a boil and cook the onions until their peels can come off easily and they are only partially tender, 8 to 10 minutes. Drain and let cool. Cut the top fifth of the nontapered end off each onion and pinch the peel off. Make a small well to accommodate the stuffing by using the tip of a small paring knife to pick out some of the inner layers of the onion, which pull out easily. Finely chop the onion you have removed and set aside ¼ cup of it; discard the rest.

3. In a medium-size skillet, heat the olive oil over medium heat, then cook the chopped onion and garlic until translucent, about 3 minutes, stirring frequently so the garlic doesn't burn. Add the veal and cook until it turns color, seasoning with the salt, pepper, and the basil and breaking it up with a wooden spoon as it cooks. Add the olives and mushrooms, and cook until all the liquid has evaporated, about 5 minutes, stirring. Remove from the heat and let cool.

4. Preheat the oven to 400°F.

5. Stuff the onions with the veal mixture. It is probably easiest to do this with your fingers. Place a little bit of stuffing on top of the hole and push down gently, then place some more over the hole and push down some more. Arrange the stuffed onions in a single layer in a lightly oiled baking dish. Sprinkle the bread crumb mixture evenly over the top and dot them with butter.

6. Bake until tender and the tops are turning golden brown, 20 to 25 minutes. Serve hot or warm from the dish. If you serve them warm, you can also serve them as a passed appetizer.

Makes 24 stuffed onions; 8 to 12 servings

Stuffed Grape Leaves in Olive Oil

A properly made stuffed grape leaf should appear as a thoroughly inviting morsel, shiny with olive oil and plump with a rice filling. Throughout the Middle East, waraq ïnab bi'l-zayt, "stuffed grape leaves with olive oil," are a popular meze—small foods served on small plates as a kind of smorgasbord. They are usually served at room temperature when they are served as a meze and are served hot when served for a more substantial dinner. The flavor of this recipe is ever so slightly tart, and you will notice that it is a very simple recipe, relying on fresh herbs and vegetables rather than elaborate spicing. This recipe is the way rural Palestinians do it.

¼ cup extra-virgin olive oil

1 small onion, finely chopped

4 scallions, chopped

1 cup raw medium-grain rice, washed well or soaked in tepid water to cover for 30 minutes and drained

½ cup finely chopped fresh parsley leaves

½ cup finely chopped fresh mint leaves

2 teaspoons salt

Freshly ground pepper to taste

2¼ cups water

½ pound ripe tomatoes, peeled, seeded, and finely chopped

Peeling Onions

Peeling small onions, white onions that are about 24 count per pound and a wee bit larger than pearl onions, is a real trick. First, you must plunge them in boiling water, which will make it easier to pop their outer skin off. But here's where it is tricky. If you've plunged them into the boiling water for too long, then more than the skin will come off—some of the outer layers of the onion will, too, and it will not retain its shape for stuffing. When you plunge the onions into boiling water, err on the safe side, timewise, in deciding when to take them out.

Rolling Grape Leaves

Rolling a grape leaf is not as hard as it sounds. And rolling 100 grape leaves is not as tedious as it sounds. The key to both is as follows: Remove the grape leaves from the jar and spread the packed bunch out in front of you. Then take one at a time, lay the stem end toward you, dull side up (shiny side down), and cut off the stem. Place the stuffing horizontally on the length of leaf directly above the stem. Roll up once away from you, then fold the two ends of the leaf inward to cover the rolled-up section. Then continue rolling until you have a little cylinder and set aside. Now, to do this without tedium, you are probably imagining little old Arab, Greek, or Turkish ladies in black doing this interminably with sisters and daughters by their side. Well, that happens, too. But I usually do it with one of my buddies, after popping open a couple of brewskies and chatting hopefully about our "portfolios."

60 brined grape leaves, drained, or fresh grape
    leaves, blanched in boiling water for 5 minutes
    and drained
¼ cup fresh lemon juice

1. In a heavy stove-top casserole or saucepan, heat 2 tablespoons of the olive oil over medium-high heat, then cook the onion and scallions until translucent, about 4 minutes, stirring. Add the drained rice, stir, and cook for 1 minute. Add ¼ cup each of the parsley and mint, the salt, pepper, and 2 cups of the water; stir, and bring to a boil. Reduce the heat to low, cover with a paper towel, place the lid of the casserole or saucepan over the paper towel, then cook until all the liquid is absorbed and the rice is tender, 18 to 20 minutes.

2. Transfer the rice to a platter, let cool completely, then stir in the tomatoes. Taste and correct the seasonings if necessary. Cover the bottom of a medium-size saucepan with grape leaves in a single layer.

3. Lay a grape leaf in front of you, stem side up and nearest to you. Cut off the little portion of the stem and place about 1 tablespoon of rice stuffing just above the stem. Roll up once away from you, tuck in the 2 side portions of the leaf, and continue rolling. Repeat with the remaining leaves and filling. Place the now tightly rolled-up grape leaves snugly in the skillet or saucepan. Pour the remaining 2 tablespoons olive oil, the lemon juice, the remaining ¼ cup each mint, parsley, and water over the grape leaves. (If there is more than one layer of stuffed leaves, drizzle each layer with the olive oil, lemon juice, mint, and parsley.)

4. Place an inverted plate or the lid to a smaller saucepan on top of the grape leaves and

turn the heat to medium. Cook until you see bubbling on the sides, about 30 minutes. Remove from the heat, let cool completely in the saucepan, transfer to a serving platter, and serve at room temperature.

Makes 50 to 60 grape leaves (some may rip)

Stuffed Grape Leaves with Rice, Currants, and Pine Nuts

Stuffed grape leaves are as popular in Turkey and Greece as they are in the Middle East. In Turkey they are called zeytinyağlı yaprak dolması *and they have some similarity to the Arab-style stuffed grape leaves, but they are intriguingly different.*

¼ cup extra-virgin olive oil

1 medium-size onion, finely chopped

1 cup raw medium-grain rice, soaked in water to cover for 30 minutes and drained or rinsed well

¼ teaspoon freshly ground allspice berries

⅛ teaspoon ground cinnamon

1 teaspoon sugar

2 teaspoons salt

Freshly ground black pepper to taste

¼ cup finely chopped fresh parsley leaves

3 tablespoons finely chopped fresh dill

2 tablespoons dried currants, soaked in warm water for 15 minutes and drained

2 tablespoons pine nuts

2¼ cups water

60 brined grape leaves, drained, or fresh grape leaves, blanched for 5 minutes in boiling water and drained

Juice of 1 lemon

1. In a heavy stove-top casserole or saucepan, heat 2 tablespoon of the olive oil over medium-high heat, then cook the onion until translucent, about 4 minutes, stirring. Add the rice, stir, and cook for 1 minute. Add the allspice, cinnamon, sugar, salt, pepper, parsley, dill, currants, pine nuts, and 2 cups of the water; stir and bring to a boil. Reduce the heat to low, cover with a paper towel and the lid of the casserole or saucepan, then cook until all the liquid is absorbed and the rice is tender, about 20 minutes. Transfer to a platter to cool completely.

2. Cover the bottom of a skillet or saucepan with grape leaves in a single layer.

3. Lay a grape leaf in front of you, stem side up and nearest to you. Cut off the little portion of the stem and place about 1 tablespoon of rice stuffing just above the stem. Roll up once, tuck in the two side portions of the leaf, and continue rolling. Repeat with the remaining leaves and filling. Place the rolled-up grape leaves snugly in the skillet or saucepan. Pour the remaining 2 tablespoons olive oil, the lemon juice, and the remaining ¼ cup water over the grape leaves. (If there is more than one layer of stuffed leaves, drizzle each layer with the olive oil and lemon juice.) Place an inverted plate or the lid to a smaller saucepan on top of the grape leaves and turn the heat to medium. Cook until you see bubbling on the sides, about 30 minutes. Remove from the saucepan, let cool completely, and serve at room temperature.

Makes 50 to 60 grape leaves (some may rip)

Belgian Endive Leaves Stuffed with Grilled Swordfish, Vegetable Mayonnaise, and Diced Beets

This Italian antipasto called insalata di pesce spada con indivia e barbietole *consists of slivers of grilled swordfish cut so they fit into Belgian endive leaves. The leaves are then topped with a mixture of finely chopped parsley, lettuce, and basil that has been mixed with mayonnaise, seasoned with paprika and mustard, and garnished with small diced cooked beets.*

One ¾-pound swordfish steak

2 Belgian endive, leaves separated

6 tablespoons finely chopped fresh parsley leaves

½ cup finely chopped fresh lettuce

½ cup finely chopped fresh basil leaves

¾ cup mayonnaise, preferably homemade (page 466)

½ teaspoon paprika

1 teaspoon Dijon mustard

1 small cooked beet, cut into tiny dice

Salt and freshly ground black pepper to taste

1. Prepare a hot charcoal fire or preheat a gas grill on high for 15 minutes or preheat a stove-top cast-iron ridged griddle. Oil the fish and grill until firm to the touch, about 4 minutes per side. Let cool, then cut into small batons that will fit in the endive leaves.

2. In a medium-size bowl, mix the parsley, lettuce, basil, mayonnaise, paprika, and mustard. Lay a baton of swordfish in an endive leaf, then top with a little mayonnaise mixture, spreading it over the length of the baton. Dot

with several pieces of diced beets and arrange on a round serving platter in spoke fashion, with the heavier part of the leaf in the center. Repeat with the remaining ingredients. Season everything with salt and pepper and refrigerate until served. Serve cool as a passed antipasto at a cocktail party.

Makes 24 to 26 stuffed leaves; 10 to 12 servings

Stuffed Escarole with Ground Beef, Pine Nuts, Raisins, and Olives as made in Sicily

The stuffing of vegetables is as popular in Sicily as it is, more ubiquitously, in the Near East. Some culinary historians believe that the popularity of stuffed vegetables in Sicily is due to an Arab influence. This recipe called scarola imbottita *is unique in that the individual leaves of the vegetable are not used for stuffing, as you might expect, but the whole head of escarole is flattened and stuffed, then closed up, tied up, and cooked whole. It will not appear at first glance that this is possible to do, but it is, although you do need a bit of dexterity to pull the splayed leaves all together to encase the stuffing. Remember that the kind of escarole used here is also called curly endive. The stuffing of ground meat, pine nuts, olives, raisins, and anchovy is typically Sicilian in inspiration. This dish is usually served as an antipasto or sometimes as a first or main course, but hardly ever as a side dish.*

½ cup extra-virgin olive oil

½ pound ground sirloin (7% fat)

Salt and freshly ground black pepper to taste

1 tablespoon pine nuts

1 tablespoon raisins

5 imported black olives, pitted and chopped

½ cup fresh bread crumbs

4 salted anchovy fillets, rinsed and chopped

1 tablespoon finely chopped fresh parsley leaves

1 garlic clove, finely chopped

2 medium-size to large heads escarole
(curly endive)

1. In a medium-size skillet, heat 2 tablespoons of the olive oil over medium-high heat, then brown the ground beef, about 4 minutes, breaking up the clumps of meat and seasoning with salt and pepper as it cooks. Remove the skillet from the burner and stir in the pine nuts, raisins, olives, bread crumbs, anchovies, parsley, and garlic, mixing well.

2. Remove the outer leaves of the escarole if damaged or broken. Gently set the whole escarole on its stem and flatten it out. Place half the mixture in the center of the escarole, then pull up all the leaves so they enclose the stuffing and tie off with twine in one or two places so it can't escape. Stuff the second head of escarole with the remaining meat stuffing.

3. Place both heads of escarole in a large, preferably earthenware, casserole and pour the remaining 6 tablespoons olive oil over them. Cover tightly and cook over low heat, using a heat diffuser if necessary, until the escarole is tender and fragrant, about 40 minutes, turning the escarole once or twice.

4. Remove the escarole from the casserole and split each lengthwise in two. Of the 4 halves, split the largest 2 in half again lengthwise, place on individual plates, and serve.

Makes 6 servings

Stuffed Swiss Chard Leaves with Ground Lamb, Rice, and Parsley in Cool Yogurt

In Turkey, stuffed grape leaves are a very popular meze, but cooks also like to stuff other vegetables, including peppers, zucchini, cabbage leaves, and, in this incredibly delicious dish called kıymalı pazı dolması, *Swiss chard leaves, which remain a beautiful dark green after cooking.*

1 bunch red Swiss chard (about 2 pounds),
trimmed of heavy stalks and washed well

¼ cup extra-virgin olive oil

1 large onion, finely chopped

½ cup plus 2 tablespoons water

½ cup raw medium-grain rice, soaked in water
for 30 minutes and drained or rinsed well

10 ounces ground lamb

½ teaspoon freshly ground allspice berries

Leaves from 1 bunch fresh parsley, finely
chopped

Salt and freshly ground black pepper to taste

1 cup full-fat plain yogurt

1. Place the Swiss chard in a large stew pot with only the water adhering to it from its last rinse. Turn the heat to high and wilt completely, about 5 minutes. Plunge into cold water and leave it there while you continue.

2. In a large skillet, heat 2 tablespoons of the olive oil over medium-high heat, then cook the onion until translucent, 4 to 5 minutes, stirring. Add ½ cup of the water, the drained rice, meat, allspice, and parsley; season with salt and pepper, reduce the heat to low, and cook until the rice is *al dente*, 12 to 15 minutes. Stir and fluff the rice mixture.

3. Arrange the Swiss chard leaves in front of you on a plate. Take one of the leaves and lay it down with the stalk end toward you and the inside of the leaf facing up. Place a walnut-size piece of stuffing on the end of each leaf and press into a cylindrical shape. Carefully fold the stalk over and away from you over the stuffing, being careful that you don't rip the leaf. The stalk should be a little stiff but soft enough to bend. Fold the sides in and roll up like a cigar. Stack the rolled Swiss chard leaves in a saucepan tightly in as many layers as it takes, and cover with the remaining 2 tablespoons each olive oil and water. Cover with an inverted plate, then place the lid on and cook over medium heat until the water is bubbling and they are cooked through, 35 to 40 minutes. Check doneness by tasting.

4. Transfer the chard roll-ups to a platter and serve hot with the cool yogurt.

Makes 4 to 6 servings

Cucumber Cups with Lobster Salad

This is a cucumber version of the croûtes *made with bread. This Provençal preparation is quite nice because the rich taste of lobster is suited to the light, watery cucumber.*

One 1⅓-pound live lobster
¼ cup mayonnaise, preferably homemade (page 466)
Salt and freshly ground white pepper to taste
⅛ to ¼ teaspoon hot Hungarian paprika, to your taste
2 large cucumbers, tiny portion of the ends trimmed, peeled, and cut into 1-inch-thick rounds (18 or so rounds total)
18 small fresh parsley leaves

1. Bring a large pot filled with an inch of water to the boil and cook the lobster until bright red, about 15 minutes. Drain, let cool, crack all the shells, and remove the meat and any tomalley and coral. Once the lobster is cool, chop and mix it with the mayonnaise, salt, pepper, and paprika.

2. With a melon baller, scoop out the center of the cucumber slices to create a small well, making sure you don't cut through the bottom or sides. Stuff the lobster mixture into the cucumbers, garnish the top with a parsley leaf, and refrigerate until needed.

Makes 18 cups; 10 servings

Cucumber Cups with Cream Cheese and Feta Cheese

This Greek take on a vegetable croûte *is very nice as a passed meze at a cocktail party.*

One 8-ounce container whipped cream cheese

5 ounces imported Greek or Bulgarian feta cheese, soaked in water for 2 hours, drained, and crumbled

2 large cucumbers, peeled, tiny portion of the ends trimmed, and cut into 1-inch-thick rounds

1. Place the cream cheese and feta cheese in a food processor and run for a few minutes, until creamy smooth.

2. With a melon baller, scoop out a section of the cucumber slices, being careful you don't break through the bottom or sides. Stuff the cucumbers with the cheese stuffing, refrigerate for 1 hour, and serve.

Makes about 20 cups; 10 servings

Cucumber Cups with Eggs and Radishes

This Italian antipasto is called cetrioli alla duse, *and traditionally one would serve it as a passed appetizer at a cocktail party.*

2 large eggs

1 teaspoon dry mustard

1 small onion, finely chopped

8 salted anchovy fillets, rinsed and mashed

3 radishes, grated or finely chopped

1 teaspoon extra-virgin olive oil

2 large cucumbers, peeled, tiny portion of the ends trimmed, and cut into 1-inch-thick rounds

1 slice ripe tomato, slivered into wedges, for garnish

1 slice lemon, slivered into wedges, for garnish

1. Bring a medium-size saucepan of water to a boil, add the eggs, and cook for 9 minutes. Remove from the water and cool immediately under cold running water. Shell and chop finely once they are cool.

2. In a small bowl, mix the eggs with the mustard, onion, anchovies, and radishes. Bind this with the olive oil.

3. With a melon baller, scoop out a little well in the cucumber pieces, being careful you don't break through the bottom or sides, and stuff with the egg mixture. Refrigerate for 1 hour before serving. Garnish with a small sliver of tomato and lemon and serve.

Makes 20 cups; 10 servings

Celery Sticks Stuffed with Taramasalata

Taramasalata *is a Greek preparation of creamed carp roe. It's rich and delicious and you don't need to use much. It's available in Middle Eastern, Greek, and Italian markets.*

1 bunch celery, stalks separated and ends trimmed

½ cup taramasalata

Fill all the celery stalks with *taramasalata*, spreading with a knife, then cut into 2-inch lengths and arrange on a serving platter.

Makes 10 servings

Sweet Bell Pepper Squares with Lebanese "Crushed" Cheese

The kind of cheese used in this Lebanese meze called filfil rūmī bi'l-jubn *is called* jubna harīsh, *which means "crushed cheese." It is a kind of cottage cheese, but not as creamy. The best replacement is crumbled farmer cheese or Mexican* queso fresco, *both of which can easily be found in the supermarket. Garnished with bits of tomato, scallions, and black olives, this is a pretty starter.*

½ pound farmer cheese
3 tablespoons finely chopped sweet onion
1 small garlic clove, finely chopped
2 teaspoons fresh lemon juice
2 tablespoons extra-virgin olive oil
Salt and freshly ground black pepper to taste
4 large green bell peppers, seeded, cut in half lengthwise, then quartered lengthwise and each quarter cut in half crosswise
2 scallions, chopped
12 miniature teardrop tomatoes, cut in half
12 imported black Kalamata olives, pitted and cut in half

1. In a medium-size bowl, mix the cheese, onion, garlic, lemon juice, and olive oil, then season with salt and pepper.

2. Spread 1 tablespoon or so of this mixture over each bell pepper square and garnish with a piece of scallion, a tomato half, and an olive half. Serve at room temperature.

Makes 32 pieces; 12 servings

· ❀ ·

Salads and Other Cold Vegetable Dishes

My favorite vegetable salads come from the Middle East, where the repertoire for preparing refreshing salads for the meze table seems endless. Nearly half the recipes in this chapter come from there, and I encourage you to try Carrot Slaw in Yogurt Sauce (page 247) or Palestinian Shepherd's Salad (page 240) or Fattūsh (page 240), the salad that should be as well known as Tabbouleh (page 238) in this country because it's so easy and good. Salads make wonderful starters because they are not heavy and they stimulate the appetite.

Cabbage Salad with Lemon and Garlic in the Syrian Style

Salāṭat malfūf *can be served both as a meze and as a straightforward salad. The salting and dunking in water reduce the bitter taste resulting from the glucosinolates in the cabbage, which are broken down once the leaves are cut. There are some 200 cultivars of cabbage, but Savoy is considered the best.*

1 small head Savoy cabbage (about 1 pound), damaged outer leaves removed, cored, and shredded
¼ cup sea salt, or more to taste
6 garlic cloves, very finely chopped
2 tablespoons fresh lemon juice
6 tablespoons extra-virgin olive oil
¾ teaspoon dried mint

1. Toss the shredded cabbage in a large bowl with the salt and let sit for 1 hour.

2. Thoroughly wash the salt from the cabbage by dunking it in water. Taste a piece of the raw cabbage to make sure the salt is washed off. Let drain in a colander. Return to the cleaned bowl. Toss well with the garlic, lemon juice, olive oil, and mint. Check the seasonings, although it should not need any more salt, and serve at room temperature within the hour.

Makes 4 to 6 servings

Cucumber, Bell Pepper, and Olive Salad from Algeria

Usually served as part of a qimiyya *table, an Algerian Arabic word meaning a meze table,* salāṭat al-khiyār *is also quite nice with fiery hot foods. Medieval Muslim doctors recommended eating cucumbers. In Turkey, milk products were almost the sole food of the poor, especially in the form of yogurt and cucumbers. Make the salad at the last minute so the water is retained in the cucumber and not the bowl.*

2 large cucumbers, peeled, halved lengthwise, seeded, and thinly sliced into half-moons
1 green bell pepper, cut in half lengthwise, seeded, and cut into strips
⅔ cup pitted and coarsely chopped imported green olives
8 large fresh mint leaves, finely chopped
¼ cup finely chopped fresh coriander (cilantro) leaves
1 teaspoon hot paprika
6 tablespoons extra-virgin olive oil
2 tablespoons white wine vinegar
Salt and freshly ground black pepper to taste

Toss the cucumbers in a salad bowl with the green pepper, olives, and mint. Add the coriander, paprika, olive oil, and vinegar; season with salt and pepper, toss again, and serve.

Makes 5 to 6 servings

Artichoke Salad with Lemon and Mint

Although the Roman writer Pliny bad-mouthed the thistle and it was thought of as the food of the poor—or donkeys—by the time of the Renaissance the artichoke had developed and one flower head cost more than 300 grams of meat. Although this Lebanese preparation, called salāṭat al-ardī shawkī, *is served as a meze, it is very nice as a side dish with grilled lamb.*

16 large fresh (page 205) or canned artichoke
  bottoms
2 large garlic cloves, peeled
2 teaspoons salt
6 tablespoons fresh lemon juice
6 tablespoons extra-virgin olive oil
¼ cup finely chopped fresh mint leaves

1. Slice the artichoke bottoms into 4 pieces and place in a bowl.

2. In a mortar, pound the garlic cloves with the salt until mushy with a pestle. Add the lemon juice gradually until it is incorporated into the mashed garlic. Whisk in the olive oil. Toss the artichokes with the mint. Pour in the dressing, toss again, and serve.

Makes 8 servings

Seviche of Artichoke Bottoms

We know that the artichoke was introduced to Italy in the fifteenth century. The etymology of the Spanish, Provençal, and French indicates a Spanish introduction from the word alcachofas. *But the Spanish word derives from the Arabic* al-kharshūf, *indicating that the Arabs were likely responsible for its introduction or development in the Mediterranean.* Alcachofas en escabeche *is a* tapa *from the Spanish province of Valencia. The artichokes become a golden brown and are*

delectable little morsels that beg to be eaten. It's an elegant preparation for a noble vegetable, and I allow two artichokes per person, although you could easily eat the whole dish yourself. You will have enough marinated garlic sauce leftover for another recipe.

8 artichokes (about 3 pounds)
1 lemon, cut in half
1 cup extra-virgin olive oil, plus more
  for drizzling
1 bay leaf
3 large garlic cloves, peeled
½ teaspoon salt
1 tablespoon sherry vinegar, plus more
  for drizzling
Freshly ground black pepper to taste (optional)

1. Wash the artichokes and steam until a skewer can be pushed easily into the center of each artichoke, 45 to 50 minutes. Remove their bracts (leaves), and when you reach the bottom, cut out the hairy choke, rubbing the entire bottom with half a lemon to prevent it from discoloring. Place in a bowl of water acidulated with the juice from the other half of the lemon so the artichokes don't discolor while you continue working.

2. In a skillet, heat the olive oil over medium to medium-high heat until nearly smoking, about 10 minutes, then cook the artichokes with the bay leaf until golden brown on the outside and a skewer glides to the center of the artichoke bottom without too much resistance, 5 to 6 minutes. Remove from the oil with a slotted ladle and transfer to a shallow serving platter or bowl.

3. Pound the garlic with the salt in a mortar until mushy. Stir 3 tablespoons of the oil you cooked the artichokes in into the garlic, ½ teaspoon at the time. Now, stir in the vinegar, ½ teaspoon at a time, until the garlic is a creamy-looking sauce. Spoon small amounts of this mixture over the artichokes. Drizzle the artichokes with a little olive oil and a splash of vinegar and set aside for 1 hour before serving. Correct the seasoning with salt and pepper if desired.

Makes 4 to 6 servings

Artichoke Bottoms Salad with Harīsa, Olives, and Capers

In this Tunisian meze called salāṭat al-qan-nāriyya, *the artichokes are boiled first, then the bottoms are removed and sliced and served with a flavorful dressing made with* harīsa, *a hot chile paste used ubiquitously in Tunisian cooking, and the water the artichokes were cooked in.*

2½ pounds artichokes (4 or 5 medium-size)
1 lemon, cut in half
½ teaspoon Harīsa (page 468)
12 imported pitted black olives
1 tablespoon salted or brined capers, rinsed or drained
2 large hard-boiled eggs, shelled and sliced
Salt to taste
Extra-virgin olive oil

1. In a large saucepan of water, boil the artichokes with the lemon until easily pierced by a skewer, 50 to 60 minutes. Drain, saving 3 table-spoons of the water you cooked the artichokes in. Arrange in a salad bowl or platter and let cool. Remove the bracts (leaves) and, when you reach the bottom, cut out the hairy choke, rubbing the entire bottom with half a lemon to prevent it from discoloring. Scrape off the flesh at the base of the bracts and add it to the salad bowl or platter or save for another use. Slice the bottoms.

2. Dissolve the *harīsa* in the reserved artichoke water. Arrange the olives on the platter. Sprinkle with the capers and then with the *harīsa*. Arrange the slices of egg around the platter. Salt to taste, drizzle with olive oil, and serve at room temperature.

Makes 4 servings

Tabbouleh

I worry that although everyone has heard of tabbouleh, no one has actually tasted a proper one. Tabbouleh is a Lebanese herb salad with bulgur, not a bulgur salad with herbs, as it often seems to be made. It's served as a meze in the Middle East and has migrated to America, where it is now regularly sold prepackaged in supermarkets. The taste of a true tabbouleh should not be of wheat but of herbs. The longer the bulgur sits and absorbs the olive oil, lemon juice, tomato, and onion juices, the more it will swell and dominate the salad, so keep that in mind when you prepare this salad. Remember that the proper ratio of parsley to bulgur is about 7 to 1. Many cooks make tabbouleh with a food processor by pulsing in short bursts, although I still prefer the texture of the labor-intensive method of hand-chopping all the ingredients with a large chef's knife. Tabbouleh is properly eaten by scooping up small amounts of it with pieces of romaine lettuce, not with a fork and knife, nor with pita bread.

½ cup medium or coarse bulgur (no. 3 or no. 4)

Juice of 4 lemons

6 cups finely chopped fresh parsley leaves
   (6 to 7 bunches)

1 cup finely chopped fresh mint leaves

1 pound ripe tomatoes, very finely chopped

2 large onions, very finely chopped

Salt and freshly ground black pepper to taste

1¼ to 1¾ cups extra-virgin olive oil, as needed

1 bunch romaine lettuce, leaves separated,
   washed, and dried

8 scallions, cut into 1-inch lengths

1. Cover a strainer with cheesecloth and place the bulgur on top. Place the strainer in a pot filled with cold water and soak the bulgur for 10 minutes. Pull up the sides of the cheesecloth, encasing the bulgur, and squeeze out all the water. Transfer to a large bowl.

2. Toss the bulgur with the lemon juice. Toss again with the parsley, mint, tomatoes, and onions and season with salt and pepper. Stir in 1¼ cups of the olive oil and leave to rest at room temperature until the bulgur has absorbed enough liquid to be tender, 4 to 6 hours. Correct the seasonings and olive oil; there should be enough that it looks shiny and moist but not gooey and oily.

3. Serve garnished with romaine lettuce leaves and scallions. Place a few slices of scallion in a leaf of romaine lettuce, then scoop up the tabbouleh with the lettuce leaf.

Makes 6 servings

Turkish Shepherd's Salad

Called çoban salatası, *this is considered the most popular of the Turkish salads and is found throughout the country. Its secret is very fresh vegetables. You should spare no expense or time to get the best, and for that reason you turn to your local farmer's market or your garden. Typically this salad is served both as a meze and with other food. The recipe is based on the salad I enjoyed at the Villa Restaurant on the road to Ephesus, just past the rotary in Seljuk.*

2 large ripe tomatoes (about 1¼ pounds), peeled,
   seeded, and coarsely chopped

1 large cucumber, peeled, seeded, and coarsely
   chopped

1 long green Italian frying pepper, seeded and
   coarsely chopped

½ small hot green chile, seeded and chopped

½ small red onion, diced

¼ cup loosely packed coarsely chopped fresh
   Italian parsley leaves

3 radishes, thinly sliced

1 tablespoon finely chopped fresh dill

1 tablespoon finely chopped fresh mint leaves

1 teaspoon sumac (page 427)

1 teaspoon Turkish red pepper (page 66)

Salt to taste

3 tablespoons extra-virgin olive oil

2 tablespoons fresh lemon juice

Romaine lettuce leaves for garnish

Black and green imported olives for garnish

Toasted pita bread for accompaniment

1. Place the first 11 ingredients in a bowl, season with salt, then toss with the olive oil

and lemon juice. Cover and refrigerate for 30 minutes.

2. Remove from the refrigerator 1 hour before serving.

3. Arrange some lettuce leaves on a serving platter and mound the salad attractively on top. Garnish the sides with the olives and toasted bread and serve.

Makes 4 servings

Palestinian Shepherd's Salad

This salad, called salāṭat al-khuḍr, *meaning simply "vegetable salad," is a name found throughout the Middle East in a variety of forms, but for some reason it's thought of as a shepherd's salad. In this preparation, romaine lettuce is the central vegetable, but it is tossed with a variety of other vegetables that, when allowed to rest for a while, will turn the salad soupy, which is not how some people like it. This particular salad is derived from a salad my ex-wife makes, which we used to call Najwa's salad. The white Syrian cheese called for is called* jubna bayḍāʾ *and is readily available in Middle Eastern markets. A variety of mass-produced Mexican cheeses works too, such as* queso ranchero *or* queso fresco, *both sold in supermarkets. In California, they are sometimes sold as "California cheese." If you are not going to eat the salad right away and intend on refrigerating it, don't toss with the tomatoes, dressing, or salt.*

1 large head romaine lettuce, leaves separated, washed, dried, and chopped

2 large ripe tomatoes, seeded and chopped

2 large green bell peppers, seeded and chopped

1 large cucumber, peeled, seeded, and sliced, or 6 small Persian cucumbers, peeled and sliced

½ fresh long red or green chile, seeded and finely chopped

2 cups chopped scallions

¼ cup finely chopped fresh parsley leaves

¼ cup fresh lemon juice

¼ cup extra-virgin olive oil

Salt to taste

Pinch of sumac (optional, page 427)

Handful of imported black olives, pitted

½ pound white Syrian cheese, crumbled

1. In a large bowl, toss together the lettuce, tomatoes, green peppers, cucumber, chile, scallions, and parsley.

2. Stir together the lemon juice, olive oil, salt, and sumac, if using, then toss with the salad. Arrange the salad on a serving platter, garnish with the olives, and sprinkle the cheese on top. Serve immediately.

Makes 8 servings

Fattūsh

This is a Lebanese and Palestinian salad of pita bread and greens. Arab cooks use stale bread for making fattāt *(plural) or* fatta *(singular). Fatta refers to a family of Arab culinary preparations in the Levant in which pieces of stale, toasted, or fresh flatbread (also known as* fatta) *are crumbled and used as the foundation of a prepared dish. These preparations developed quite naturally in the Arab world because much of the bread that is consumed there is flatbread, a bread that dries out quickly. The famous bread salad called* fattūsh *(and deriving from the word* fatta*), made with toasted pieces of* khubz ʿarabī *(Arabic flatbread or pita bread), cucumbers, tomatoes, scallions, parsley,* baqlī *(a word meaning any wild green—for example, chickweed), and lettuce, is also a member of this class of dishes. I'm surprised that this salad is not as well known as tabbouleh in this country. It's less time-consuming and easier to make and quite nice. In Lebanon, it is made with a variety of greens, but especially romaine, cucumbers, parsley, purslane or watercress, scallions, mint, tomatoes, and, most important, fried ripped-up pieces of Arabic flatbread.*

2 large garlic cloves, finely chopped

1 teaspoon salt

¼ cup fresh lemon juice

¼ cup extra-virgin olive oil

¾ pound ripe tomatoes, very coarsely chopped

5 scallions, sliced ½ inch thick

6 large radishes or 10 French breakfast radishes, cut in half

1 cucumber, peeled, cut in half lengthwise, seeded, and sliced into half-moons

1 bunch arugula, washed, dried, and shredded

8 large leaves romaine lettuce, shredded

1 handful fresh mint leaves, chopped if large

Leaves from ½ bunch fresh parsley, coarsely chopped

1 bunch watercress or chickweed, washed, dried, and sliced

1 tablespoon sumac (page 427)

3 small Arabic pita bread loaves, quartered, separated, and toasted or fried (see Note) until crispy

1. In a small bowl, stir together the garlic, salt, lemon juice, and olive oil.

2. In a large bowl, toss all the vegetables and greens and herbs together. Sprinkle on the sumac and the toasted or fried pita bread, and pour in the dressing. Toss well and serve immediately. Do not prepare this salad before you intend on eating it.

Note: Preheat 6 cups olive oil or olive pomace oil in a deep fryer or an 8-inch saucepan fitted with a basket insert to 375°F. Fry the bread several pieces at a time, without crowding, until golden, about 1 minute. Drain on paper towels.

Makes 10 servings

· ❧ ·

Tunisian Salad

This salad is actually called "Tunisian salad" in Arabic, salāṭat al-Tūnisiyya. *It is found everywhere in Tunisia, as common there as a Greek salad is in Greece, and is always a welcome sight because it is refreshing, light, and accompanies everything well. As with many salads in North Africa and the Middle East, it is often served as a meze. You will need to make this salad if you intend on making Casse-Croûtes (page 48). For the white cheese, use either the cheese called Syrian cheese in Middle Eastern markets, or Mexican* queso fresco, *found in many supermarkets, or farmer cheese.*

¾ pound ripe tomatoes, peeled, seeded, and cut into small dice

½ pound green bell peppers, peeled, seeded, and cut into small dice

2 long green or red chiles, seeded and cut into small dice

1 small onion, chopped

¼ pound white cheese (see headnote), crumbled

One 3-ounce can imported tuna in olive oil

1 ounce imported black olives (6 or 7), drained and pitted

1 tablespoon white wine vinegar

3 tablespoons extra-virgin olive oil

1 teaspoon dried mint

Salt and freshly ground black pepper to taste

2 large hard-boiled eggs, shelled and quartered

1 lemon, quartered

1. In a large bowl, toss the first 7 ingredients.

2. In a shallow bowl, whisk together the vinegar, olive oil, and mint. Pour the vinaigrette over the salad and toss well. Season with salt and pepper and toss again.

3. Arrange the salad on a serving platter and garnish with the egg and lemon quarters.

Makes 6 servings

Diced Vegetable Salad from Turkey

This preparation is called ezme salatası *and is excellent as an accompaniment to grilled food, although I was first introduced to it as a meze. In this recipe, "very finely chopped" means about the size of this "O." I've tried this in a food processor, but even pulsing doesn't work; it just*

makes it too liquidy and mushy. You've got to do this by hand for a perfect result.

½ pound ripe tomatoes, peeled, seeded, and very finely chopped

1 green bell pepper, peeled (optional), seeded, and very finely chopped

½ small cucumber, peeled, seeded, and very finely chopped

2 spring onions (see headnote, page 167), wilted leaves removed and very finely chopped

¼ teaspoon dried mint

½ teaspoon hot paprika

½ teaspoon freshly ground black pepper

Salt to taste

2 teaspoons white wine vinegar

1 tablespoon extra-virgin olive oil

In a medium-size bowl, toss all the ingredients together and serve at room temperature.

Makes 4 servings

Purslane and Yogurt Salad

Called yoğurtlu semizotlu salatası, *this recipe may have a long history. The medieval Muslim doctor and philosopher Avicenna, who lived from 980 to 1037 and who tried to reconcile Aristotelian thought with Islam, recommended the medicinal benefits of eating purslane and yogurt. This salad is very refreshing, and I like to make it in the summer or with grilled foods.*

3 garlic cloves, pounded in a mortar with 2 teaspoons salt until mushy

1½ cups full-fat plain yogurt

1 tablespoon extra-virgin olive oil

1½ pounds purslane, heavy stems removed, washed well, and dried

Stir the garlic paste into the yogurt along with the olive oil until well blended. Toss with the purslane. Refrigerate for 1 hour before serving and serve cold.

Makes 6 servings

Purslane

Purslane is an annual succulent with thick leaves that are edible. It is mostly used in salads in Turkey and other Middle Eastern countries and is especially popular in North Africa. Purslane is most likely to be found in a farmer's market. It is not difficult to grow and because it's an invasive plant, most gardeners grow it in pots. Because it retains water so well, it can be grown in dry soil. If you plant seeds in the spring, you can harvest the leaves and stems, which are also edible, throughout the summer.

Diced Chile and Tomato Salad

This is my translation for a meze served at almost every restaurant in Turkey called antep ezme *(which means, very roughly, "crushed salad from Gaziantep"), a dish that I believe is originally from the eastern Turkish city of Gaziantep.*

The Ahtapot Restaurant on the harbor in Antalya makes it with hot chiles, tomatoes, and parsley all very finely chopped, drained of liquid, dressed with olive oil and lemon juice, and seasoned with garlic, salt, and pepper. But at the very pretty Çam Restaurant on the harbor at Kuşadası, I believe they stirred a little sugar into the finished dish because it had a hint of sweetness beyond that naturally found in the tomatoes.

4 large long red chiles (¼ pound), seeded and finely diced

1¼ pounds ripe tomatoes, peeled, seeded, finely diced, and left in a colander for 2 hours to drain

2 large garlic cloves, finely chopped

3 tablespoons finely chopped fresh parsley leaves

½ teaspoon sugar

Salt and freshly ground black pepper to taste

2 tablespoons extra-virgin olive oil

1 tablespoon fresh lemon juice

Flatbread as an accompaniment

In a medium-size bowl, stir all the salad ingredients together about 30 minutes before serving and serve at room temperature with flatbread.

Makes 6 servings

Fresh Green Pepper Salad with Caraway and Olives from Tunisia

This salad of fresh bell peppers called hrūs *is perfect alongside typically hot Tunisian food. You eat the salad with pieces of flatbread, not*

with utensils. I first had this in Tunisia as a meze and have been fond of it ever since.

4 green bell peppers (about 1¼ pounds), seeded
1 small fresh long green chile, seeded
7 tablespoons extra-virgin olive oil
½ teaspoon freshly ground caraway seeds
3 garlic cloves, finely chopped
Salt to taste
10 imported black olives, pitted
1 tablespoon salted or brined capers, rinsed or drained and chopped if large
One 3½-ounce can imported Moroccan sardines with chiles or tuna in olive oil (optional)

1. Place the green peppers and chile in a food processor and pulse until mushy. Transfer to a strainer and leave to drain for 30 minutes.

2. In a medium-size bowl, mix the pepper puree, olive oil, caraway, garlic, and salt. Arrange on a serving platter and garnish with the olives, capers, and sardines or tuna, if using. Serve at room temperature with flatbread.

Makes 6 servings

Radish Salad from Tunisia

Radishes have a long history in the Mediterranean, which is remarkable because it is a cool weather annual. This salāṭat al-fijil, *or radish salad, would be served in Tunisia as part of an* ādū *table, the smorgasbord that is called meze elsewhere in the Mediterranean. Don't cut the radishes too far in advance because they will then release too much water and dilute the dress-*

ing. The small amount of hot chile paste, harīsa, *provides just the right amount of zing.*

6 bunches radish (about 2¼ pounds), trimmed and sliced into paper-thin rounds using a food processor or other slicer
¼ cup finely chopped fresh parsley leaves
¼ cup extra-virgin olive oil
1 tablespoon white wine vinegar
1 teaspoon Harīsa (page 468)
Salt and freshly ground black pepper to taste

Toss the radishes with the parsley. Stir the olive oil, vinegar, and *harīsa* together and toss with the radishes. Taste and correct the seasoning with salt and pepper. Serve.

Makes 6 to 8 servings

Sicilian Red Radishes with Fresh Peppered Pecorino

This antipasto called ravanelli con pecorino pepato fresco *is really quite nice alone. Sicilians have not traditionally eaten* antipasti; *it is a modern introduction from northern Italy. In this dish, because everything is so simple, the quality of your ingredients becomes all important. The pecorino required is called* pecorino pepato *in Italian and it is not too hard to find in this country. It is a semi-soft six-month-old pecorino made with whole peppercorns thrown into the curd. Almost all Italian delis carry it as well as gourmet supermarkets. It is called "table" or "eating" pecorino and may also be called Crotonese. When a pecorino is older, it becomes harder and drier and is used for grating onto* pasta, for instance. The best radishes to use are the young so-called French breakfast radishes, with a good portion of their root being white. Also use the best quality estate-bottled olive oil and don't cut the radishes and let them sit around, otherwise they will emit too much water and make the whole thing unappetizing.

¼ pound *pecorino pepato* cheese, cut into thin slices, at room temperature
½ pound French breakfast radishes, trimmed and sliced, at room temperature
Extra-virgin olive oil to taste

Arrange the cheese and radishes on a serving platter or plate, drizzle with olive oil, and serve immediately, letting guests pop a slice of radish and a slice of cheese in their mouths. Alternatively, serve it as an antipasto for a sit-down dinner.

Makes 4 servings

Provençal Celeriac Rémoulade

This is a classic French hors d'oeuvre or salad. It is still frequently made in the home and you will see why once you taste it. It's perfectly simple, perfectly tasty.

1 large celeriac (about 1½ pounds), peeled and cut into chunks
½ cup mayonnaise, preferably homemade (page 466)
2 tablespoons finely chopped gherkins
2 tablespoons salted or brined capers, rinsed or drained and finely chopped

1½ tablespoons finely chopped fresh tarragon leaves
1½ tablespoons finely chopped fresh chives
1½ tablespoons finely chopped fresh parsley leaves
1½ tablespoons finely chopped fresh chervil leaves
2 teaspoons Dijon mustard

Grate the celeriac using a food processor grating attachment. Stir together all the remaining ingredients and toss very well with the celeriac. Refrigerate at least 3 hours before serving.

Makes 6 servings

Eighteenth-Century French Hors d'Oeuvre

In the eighteenth century, French hors d'oeuvre were delicate little dishes set out to accompany more substantial dishes. Some of these hors d'oeuvre could be quite complex in modern terms—for example, little mutton chops with chicory, glazed eels in Italian sauce, chicken breasts, veal sweetbreads, artichokes, duck tongues, and eggs with meat sauce.

Turkish Celeriac Slaw

Celeriac or celery root is such an ideal vegetable for making grated salads or slaws. This recipe, called kereviz kökü salatası, *is adapted from Özcan Ozan's* The Sultan's Kitchen. *The easiest way to prepare this meze is by using the grating attachment of your food processor.*

1 large celeriac (about 1½ pounds), peeled
1 lemon, cut in half
1 medium-size carrot, peeled
¼ cup finely chopped fresh parsley leaves
2 teaspoons freshly ground cumin seeds
6 tablespoons mayonnaise, preferably homemade
   (page 466)
2 tablespoons fresh lemon juice
Salt and freshly ground black pepper to taste
Mixed salad greens
2 medium-size ripe tomatoes, quartered

1. Set up the grating attachment of your food processor. Cut the celeriac into portions that can fit through the feed tube of the processor, rubbing the cut portion with lemon as you slice them so they don't discolor. Run the carrot through the feed tube. You can also chop the parsley with the food processor instead of chopping it by hand.

2. Transfer the vegetables to a medium-size bowl. Add the cumin, mayonnaise, and lemon juice and toss to coat evenly. Season with salt and pepper and mix very well. Refrigerate for 30 minutes before serving.

3. Serve on a bed of mixed salad greens garnished with the tomatoes.

Makes 8 servings

Celeriac and Carrot Salad with Tuna-Flavored Mayonnaise

Celeriac (celery root) and carrot are favorite ingredients in Provence, northern Italy, and Croatia for making a variety of salads or slaws. I've adapted this recipe from one by Paola Boni, in Paola Scaravelli and Jon Cohen's A Mediterranean Harvest *published in 1986. It is said to be an antipasto popular in Verona in northern Italy.*

¾ pound carrots, shredded
1 pound celeriac, peeled and shredded
Juice of 1 lemon
One 3-ounce can imported tuna in olive oil,
   drained
1 cup mayonnaise, preferably homemade
   (page 466)
3 salted anchovy fillets, rinsed
1 tablespoon salted or brined capers, rinsed or
   drained
1 small head curly endive

1. In a large bowl, mix the carrots and celeriac. Stir in the lemon juice and toss well.

2. In a food processor, process the tuna and mayonnaise together until smooth, then add the anchovies and capers and continue to blend.

3. Combine the vegetables and mayonnaise, tossing well. Refrigerate for 2 hours before serving. Serve cold or cool on top of curly endive leaves.

Makes 6 servings

Carrot Slaw in Yogurt Sauce

This Turkish carrot slaw, yoğurtlu havuç, *was very popular with my kids, although they had to be coaxed because they were unable to imagine its tasting good, which it does. The dish is traditionally served at room temperature, and it can also be served as part of a meze table or as a side dish.*

¼ cup extra-virgin olive oil
1 pound carrots, shredded
½ teaspoon salt
4 garlic cloves, peeled
2 cups full-fat plain yogurt

1. In a large skillet, heat the olive oil with the carrots and ¼ teaspoon of the salt over medium-high heat and cook until the carrots are soft, 5 to 6 minutes, stirring occasionally. Transfer the carrots to a serving bowl.

2. In a mortar, pound the garlic with the remaining ¼ teaspoon salt until mushy. Stir the garlic into the yogurt and whisk vigorously. Once the carrots are cool, stir in the yogurt and serve at room temperature.

Makes 6 servings

Tomato and Avocado Salad from Andalusia

As most people know, Andalusia is the home of gazpacho, but it is also the home of other tomato dishes that are just as satisfying, such as this pretty salad called ensalada de tomates, *which can be served as a* tapa, *too. If you can find a variety of different tomatoes, such as orange* cherry tomatoes and teardrop tomatoes, to throw in, it makes the salad all that more attractive. Do not refrigerate, and make the salad about 30 minutes before serving at the earliest.

1½ pounds ripe tomatoes of different varieties and colors
1 ripe avocado, peeled, pitted, and diced or sliced
1 small garlic clove, finely chopped
1 tablespoon finely chopped fresh basil leaves
Salt and freshly ground black pepper to taste
½ teaspoon sugar
Extra-virgin olive oil
Very good quality Spanish sherry vinegar

Trim the tomatoes and cut the larger ones and cherry tomatoes in half. Squeeze out the seeds. Toss the tomatoes with the avocado and garlic in a serving bowl. Sprinkle on the basil, salt, pepper, and sugar. Drizzle with olive oil and vinegar to taste and toss gently again. Serve.

Makes 4 servings

Sliced Tomatoes with a Mirepoix "Mask"

The name of the dish reflects that the tomatoes are hidden behind the mask of the very finely minced vegetables, what the French call a mirepoix *and the Italians call a* trito, *just like the mask worn by the Neapolitan character Pulcinella from the* commedia del arte *and for that reason, this Neapolitan antipasto is called* pomodori alla Pulcinella. *Don't even bother to make this until the end of summer, when only the best, juiciest, and sweetest tomatoes are coming from the garden. Your tomatoes should be big, ripe Big Boys or something similar. This is an antipasto that must be followed by a thick grilled beefsteak, I think, and a drizzle of olive oil over the tomatoes.*

4 large, round, ripe tomatoes, cut into ½-inch-thick slices

1 celery stalk

4 small green bell peppers, seeded

1 carrot

1 garlic clove, peeled

¼ cup extra-virgin olive oil

Salt to taste

½ teaspoon dried oregano

3 large fresh basil leaves, sliced into ribbons

Neapolitan Tomatoes

The tomato arrived in Naples in the mid-sixteenth century, but it took some time before it was accepted in the cuisine, having started life in Neapolitan gardens as an ornamental. By the time Vincenzo Corrado published his *Il cuoco galante* in Naples in 1786, it was in kitchen use, although not in a major way. His recipe *pomidoro alla corradina* could be made today. The tomatoes are hollowed out and stuffed with roasted veal kidneys that have been chopped and seasoned with egg yolks, Parmigiano, and spices. They're sprinkled with bread crumbs and Parmigiano on top, then fried in lard and served with *crostini*.

1. Arrange the tomato slices on a serving platter.

2. Put the celery, bell peppers, carrot, and garlic in a food processor and pulse until chopped. In a bowl, whisk the olive oil, salt, and oregano together, then slowly pour into the food processor as you continue to pulse, making sure the vegetables are very finely chopped and not mushy.

3. Spread the sauce over the tomatoes, garnish with the basil, and serve.

Makes 6 servings

 Miniature Tomatoes and Chickpeas with Bottarga

This simple little Sardinian-style antipasto requires the dried tuna roe known as bottarga. *It is increasingly available in this country, usually in Italian markets.*

One 15-ounce can chickpeas, drained

½ pound miniature tomatoes

2 tablespoons extra-virgin olive oil

1 tablespoon grated *bottarga*

Salt and freshly ground black pepper to taste

Toss all the ingredients together in a large bowl, then transfer to a serving platter and serve with fancy toothpicks to skewer the chickpeas and tomatoes.

Makes 6 servings

Bottarga

Bottarga is a preparation made of fish eggs; the ovarian membrane containing the eggs of either tuna or gray mullet is salted and dried, and sometimes pressed into a sausage shape. The final product is dry enough to grate, although crumbling, less dry *bottarga* is common. *Bottarga* is made commercially and sold in specialty shops in Italy. In Sardinia, home preparation is common and one can find *bottarga* in local *alimentari* (groceries). The Sicilians and Egyptians also make it, and so do the fishermen along the Adriatic coast of Dalmatia, where the fishermen of Trappano (Trpanj) and Makarska are expert in making *bottarga* from gray mullet roe. Bottarga is also made in Provence, where it is called *poutargue*. Both words derive from the Arabic *baṭārikh*, "salted fish," this word itself coming from the Coptic *pitaoichion* and resembling the Greek word *tarichios*, "dried meat or fish." *Bottarga* is known as *butaraca* in Sicily; it was during the Arab era (827–1091) that the Arabs taught the Sicilians how to extract salt from the sea and preserve anchovies, sardines, mackerel, tuna, and tuna by-products like the roe, heart, liver, and lungs. To salt fish is called *saraca* in Sicilian, from the Arabic *shalih*. Originally, *bottarga* was made from mullet roe and its production has been known since Pharonic Egypt.

Green Bean Salad with Lemon and Dill in the Greek Style

This bean salad, or fasolakia salata, *is seasoned with fresh dill and served at room temperature as a meze. Do not be tempted to add too much feta cheese; it should be minimal.*

1 pound green beans, ends trimmed
2 tablespoons extra-virgin olive oil
2 tablespoons fresh lemon juice
1 garlic clove, very finely chopped
1 tablespoon chopped fresh dill

Salt and freshly ground black pepper to taste
Imported Greek or Bulgarian feta cheese
  (optional), crumbled

1. Bring a large saucepan of water to a boil and blanch the green beans for 5 minutes. Drain and cool under cold running water to stop their cooking (this will preserve their color). Bring another large saucepan of water to a boil again and cook the green beans until tender, not crunchy, 12 to 15 minutes. Drain well.

2. Whisk the olive oil, lemon juice, garlic, dill, salt, and pepper together. Arrange the green

beans on a platter and pour the dressing over it. Garnish the platter with feta cheese if desired.

Makes 4 servings

Corsican Chickpea Salad

Corsica is a traditionally poor and isolated island, but as a part of France, French culture is embedded in the life of Corsica. Nevertheless, having had an historical relationship with Italy, Italian culture is also evident in aspects of Corsican culture such as foods, as demonstrated in the Italian name of this dish of chickpeas, insalata di ceci. *Chickpeas are a popular food in the islands of the Mediterranean since they are a rugged plant grown in sandy soil in warm climates.*

3 tablespoons extra-virgin olive oil

1 tablespoon white wine vinegar

1 tablespoon Dijon mustard

2 tablespoons finely chopped freshly parsley leaves

2 cups cooked chickpeas, drained

1 small onion, finely chopped

2 garlic cloves, finely chopped

Salt and freshly ground black pepper to taste

In a medium-size bowl, stir together the olive oil, vinegar, mustard, and parsley. Add the remaining ingredients, toss well, and serve at room temperature.

Makes 4 servings

Antipasto of Asparagus with Freshly Grated Parmigiano Cheese

Asparagus has been served like this in Italy for centuries. In Platina's De honesta voluptate et valetudine *from 1468, in his* de asparago condito *(on seasoned asparagus) he suggests that the asparagus be boiled, then dressed with salt, oil, and vinegar and eaten as a first course. In Italy, one will often find this very pretty dish,* insalata d'aspargi alla parmigiana, *served as part of a* tavola calda, *a buffet table filled with a variety of* antipasti. *When composing the platter of vegetables, keep in mind that you want to present it artfully so that it looks as appetizing as possible. And make sure you use freshly grated Parmigiano-Reggiano cheese and not something out of a can or pre-grated.*

1½ pounds asparagus with stems about ½ inch thick, bottoms trimmed and stems peeled

4 cups ripped red leaf lettuce

1 cup yellow cherry tomatoes

3 tablespoons freshly grated Parmigiano-Reggiano cheese

3 tablespoons extra-virgin olive oil

Salt to taste

1. Place the asparagus in a nonreactive wide skillet, cover with water, and bring to a boil. Cook until tender, 8 to 10 minutes. Drain and set aside.

2. Arrange the lettuce on an oval platter, and when the asparagus are cool, arrange them on top in the center with all the spears pointing in one direction. Scatter the tomatoes about

and sprinkle with the cheese, olive oil, and salt. Serve.

Makes 4 servings

Boiled Asparagus with Maltese Mayonnaise

An emulsion sauce made with oranges or orange zest is known as Maltese sauce. There are two basic kinds, one is based on a Hollandaise sauce with the addition of orange and the other is mayonnaise with orange. The name Maltese came about because of the fame of oranges from Malta, especially blood oranges as used in this recipe, which could be as at home in Venice as Palermo.

2 pounds asparagus
Salt to taste
1 recipe homemade mayonnaise (page 466), made substituting 1 tablespoon blood orange juice and 1 tablespoon grated blood orange zest for the vinegar or lemon juice; or 1½ cups store-bought mayonnaise with 1 tablespoon blood orange juice and 1 tablespoon grated blood orange zest stirred in

1. Place the asparagus in a large, wide non-reactive skillet, cover with water, and bring to a boil. Cook the asparagus until tender, about 10 minutes. Drain, pat dry, and let cool.

2. Arrange the asparagus attractively on a serving platter, season with salt, and serve with the mayonnaise on side.

Makes 8 servings

Genovese-Style Antipasto of Lemon-Flavored Rice

This is an impressive looking Genoese preparation called, logically enough, antipasto di riso, *which is not very well known and usually made as an emergency antipasto when unexpected guests arrive. It is rice molded into a dome and flavored with a variety of ingredients.*

3¾ cups water
2 teaspoons salt
2 tablespoons unsalted butter
2 cups short-grain Arborio rice, soaked in water for 30 minutes and drained or rinsed well
¼ cup extra-virgin olive oil
Juice from 1 lemon, with 1 thin slice taken from the middle and reserved, plus extra juice for sprinkling if desired
Freshly ground black pepper to taste
8 salted anchovy fillets, rinsed
12 to 14 imported black olives, pitted
1 tablespoon salted or brined capers, rinsed or drained
2 large hard-boiled eggs, shelled and sliced

1. In a large heavy saucepan, bring the water to a boil with the salt and butter. Pour in the rice and bring back to a boil. Reduce the heat to low, cover, and cook until the liquid is absorbed, about 15 minutes. Remove the saucepan from the heat, cover the surface of the rice with paper towels, replace the lid, and let sit for 5 minutes. Spread the rice on a platter to cool.

2. In a small bowl, mix the olive oil, lemon juice, a little salt, and some pepper. Once the rice is cool, toss it with the dressing in a large

The Blood Orange

The blood orange is a sweet orange cultivar with juicy, rich orange tastes and overtones of raspberries. Its flesh is bloody red. Blood oranges are popular in Italy, where the best known cultivars are the Tarocco, Sanguinello, and Moro. Malta is famous for its blood oranges and, in fact, the first blood orange to be planted in California is known as the Maltaise Sanguine (Bloody Maltese). Blood orange are often used in salads and for juicing.

bowl. Form the rice into a dome on a round serving platter and garnish it with the anchovy fillets, arranging the fillets with one end at the top of the dome and having then drape down the sides in spoke fashion. Place the slice of lemon on the top and make a crown of olives at the base of the dome. Sprinkle some more olive oil, lemon, juice, salt, and pepper over everything if desired, then arrange the capers just below the lemon slice on top and the egg slices in between the anchovy fillets. Use only egg slices that have some yolk showing. Refrigerate until needed, but serve at room temperature.

Makes 8 servings

Summer Antipasto of Vegetables, Beans, and Rice from Genoa

This is a rice antipasto popular during the summer in Genoa. Although there was rice produc-tion in Lombardy's Po Valley in the fifteenth century, Genoa's rice was imported directly from Sicily at that time and so, too, their pasta. Italian riziculture had its beginnings in tenth century Arab Sicily, but the most famous prepa-ration for rice, coming from fifteenth century Lombardy, was the precursor to risotto. Risotto is more typical of the regions to the east of Liguria, while in Genoa and other Ligurian towns rice salads are more prevalent. I find that this platter makes an ideal late summer antipasto served before grilled beef, veal, or even fish.

⅔ cup (about ¼ pound) dried white beans, like cannellini, rinsed and picked over

¼ pound eggplant, peeled and diced

2 tablespoons unsalted butter

1⅔ cups short-grain Arborio rice (about ¾ pound), soaked in water for 30 minutes and drained or rinsed well

1¾ teaspoons salt

3⅓ cups water

One ¼-pound zucchini

1 yellow bell pepper

¾ cup extra-virgin olive oil

2 to 3 tablespoons fresh lemon juice, to your taste

1 garlic clove, finely chopped

½ teaspoon fresh thyme leaves

1 teaspoon finely chopped fresh oregano leaves

One ¼-pound cucumber, peeled, seeded, and sliced

1 ripe but firm tomato, chopped

2 tablespoons chopped fresh basil leaves

Freshly ground black pepper

1. Place the beans in a medium-size saucepan with cold water to cover, bring to a boil, add a little salt, and cook until tender, about 1¼ hours. Drain and set aside.

2. Preheat the oven to 425°F. Lay the eggplant pieces on some paper towels and sprinkle with salt. Leave them to drain of their bitter juices for 30 minutes, then pat dry with paper towels.

3. In a large heavy saucepan, melt the butter over medium-high heat, then add the rice and stir for 1 minute to coat the grains. Add the salt and water, bring to a boil, reduce the heat to low, cover, and cook until the water is absorbed and the rice tender, about 12 minutes. Spread the rice on a baking tray to cool.

4. Boil the zucchini in water to cover in a medium-size saucepan until tender but still showing a little resistance when you pierce it with a skewer, about 10 minutes. Drain, let cool, and cut in half lengthwise, then cut again into thin half-moons.

5. Meanwhile, place the yellow pepper in a baking dish and bake until the skin is black, about 35 minutes. Once it is cool enough to handle, peel, seed, and cut into strips.

6. In a large skillet, heat ½ cup of the olive oil over medium-high heat, then cook the eggplant with a little salt until golden brown, about 8 minutes, turning them once. Remove with a slotted spoon and drain on paper towels.

7. In a small bowl, whisk together the remaining ¼ cup olive oil, the lemon juice, garlic, thyme, and oregano. Combine all the rest of the ingredients in a large bowl and toss well with the vinaigrette, then arrange on a platter or in a shallow bowl, mold with your hands, and serve at room temperature.

Makes 12 servings

Filled Pastries, Puffs, and Pies and Baked Turnovers

My favorite appetizers are found in this chapter because I love anything made of baked dough stuffed with a variety of ingredients. I tend to overeat these kinds of starters because they're so delicious. Some of them are extravagant, as I think of Barquettes with Lobster from the Languedoc (page 256) with its lobster, cream, and cognac. Others are spicy and so unusual, such as Spicy Octopus Pie in a Red Wine Crust from the Port of Sète (page 262), that you should really give them a try. I could keep popping beignets (pages 260–262) into my mouth until I explode. The Spanakopita (page 268) you've probably seen a million times, but try this recipe because I doubt you've eaten one this good.

Puff pastry is one of the most delicious doughs to use for hors d'oeuvre, and I've tried to give you a good sampling of its use in the Mediterranean. I can't tell you my favorite use because I keep crossing one suggestion off and filling it in with another, and then I repeat the process. But a fascinating place to begin is with the Puff Pastry Crescents with Saffron Chicken and Almonds from Spain (page 285). It's not the easiest recipe, but it is one that will open your eyes. I'm also a fan of rustic preparations like Puff Pastry of Swiss Chard and Onion from Corsica (page 288), which you will not want to pass by. The Greeks use puff pastry, too, and you will enjoy Lamb Pies in Phyllo Pastry (page 290), fragrant with fresh mint and parsley. As passed appetizers at cocktail parties, nothing beats the recipes in this chapter. The hardest thing about them is choosing because you can't eat them all.

Barquettes with Lobster from the Languedoc

A barquette *is a kind of* croustade *(page 51), using either short dough or flaky puff pastry dough, fashioned in the shape of a little boat (a bark) and usually filled with a puree, fish mousse, cooked shellfish, or* salpicon—*a mixture of diced meat, fish, or vegetables bound with a cream sauce. Although there is a lot of minute work involved in making these, in addition to having to purchase the* barquette *molds (they're available at good cookware and baking supply stores such as Sur la Table and Williams-Sonoma), it is a task well rewarded with delicious little boats and happy guests. For some reason, I like the idea of these boats filled with shellfish, and although lobster is the most elegant choice, another nice preparation is called* petites barquettes de moules à la mayonnaise, *made with short dough and filled with wine-steamed cold mussels topped with a dollop of mayonnaise.*

3 tablespoons unsalted butter

¼ cup fresh bread crumbs

One 1¼-pound live lobster

½ pound Basic Puff Pastry Short Dough for Empanadas (page 475) or frozen puff pastry, defrosted if necessary

1 tablespoon finely chopped onion

1 tablespoon finely chopped fresh parsley leaves

2 large egg yolks

½ cup heavy cream

¼ cup cognac

3 tablespoons freshly grated Parmigiano-Reggiano cheese

1. In a medium-size skillet, melt 1 tablespoon of the butter over medium heat, then brown the bread crumbs, 4 to 5 minutes, stirring. Set aside.

2. Bring about 1 inch of water to a boil in a stockpot, then steam the lobster until bright red, 17 to 18 minutes. Remove from the pot, let cool, then crack all the shells and remove the meat. Chop the meat and set aside.

3. Preheat the oven to 375°F.

4. On a lightly floured work surface, roll the dough out until about ⅛ inch thick. Line up the *barquette* molds and drape the dough over them, pushing down the dough into the molds. Press firmly to cut out the shapes. Prick the dough all over with a toothpick or fork. Cover with waxed paper and fill with dried beans to hold down the puff pastry. Place all the molds on a baking sheet and bake until light golden, about 20 minutes. Remove from the oven, let cool, then remove the beans and the *barquettes* from their mold and set aside. Turn the oven onto the broiler setting.

5. In a medium-size skillet, melt the remaining 2 tablespoons butter with the onion and parsley over medium-high heat, then cook until sizzling, 1 to 2 minutes. Add the lobster meat and cook for 1 minute, stirring. Beat the egg yolks into the cream and add to the skillet along with the cognac. After a few seconds, reduce the heat to low and stir constantly until the sauce is thick like a custard, making sure that the eggs don't curdle from too high a heat, 5 to 10 minutes.

6. Fill the *barquettes* with the lobster mixture with a small spoon. Sprinkle each with Parmigiano and buttered crumbs, arrange on a baking sheet, and broil until dappled golden

brown, almost black in places, on top, about 2 minutes. Serve hot or very warm.

Makes 18 barquettes; 8 servings

Barquettes with Crab and Mayonnaise

This barquette *from Provence is made with the common edible crab of the Riviera called* crabe *or* tourteau *(Cancer pagurus L.). There are many varieties of crabs in the Mediterranean, but not all are large enough to make it worthwhile to extract their meat for other preparations. In this country it is easy enough to buy crab meat at fish stores, saving a lot of work. The great French chef Auguste Escoffier called this variety of hors d'oeuvre* frivolités. *These barquettes are quite delectable as there is a natural affinity between the garlic-based mayonnaise called* aïoli *and crustaceans.*

1 cup backfin or lump crab meat, picked over for shells and cartilage
1 tablespoon very finely chopped onion
Pinch of dried thyme
½ cup mayonnaise, preferably homemade (page 466), or Allioli (page 466)
Salt and freshly ground black pepper to taste
¼ cup dry bread crumbs
2 tablespoons freshly grated Parmigiano-Reggiano cheese
1 tablespoon finely chopped fresh parsley leaves
½ pound Basic Puff Pastry Short Dough for Empanadas (page 475) or frozen puff pastry, defrosted if necessary
Unsalted butter for dotting

1. In a medium-size bowl, mix the crab meat, onion, thyme, and mayonnaise and season with salt and pepper. In another small bowl, mix the bread crumbs, Parmigiano, and parsley.

2. Preheat the oven to 375°F.

3. On a lightly floured work surface, roll the puff pastry out until about ⅛ inch thick. Line up the *barquette* molds and drape the dough over them, pushing down the dough into the wells of the molds. Press firmly to cut out the shapes. Prick the dough all over with a toothpick or fork. Cover with waxed paper and fill with dried beans to hold down the puff pastry. Place the molds on a baking sheet and bake until light golden, about 20 minutes. Remove from the oven, let cool, then remove the beans and *barquettes* from their molds and set aside. Turn the oven onto the broiler setting.

4. Fill the *barquettes* with the crab mixture using a small spoon. Sprinkle each with the bread crumb mixture, arrange on a baking

Freezing Pastries

Pastries generally freeze quite well as long as they are properly wrapped in freezer wrap. Once the pastries are cool, wrap them well and arrange in a flat container or tray and freeze. Once they are frozen, you can rearrange them to make more room in your freezer. To reheat, place the frozen pastry on a baking sheet and bake in a preheated 350°F oven until very warm or hot.

French Hors d'Oeuvre Pastries

French cuisine has a world of wonderful little hors d'oeuvre that can entice everyone at a party. There are *barquettes*, *croûtes*, *croustades*, and *vols-au-vent* (see this chapter) and much, much more. A classically trained French chef would make *carolines*, small eclairs stuffed with mousses and purees made of shrimps, langoustines, lobsters, crab, foie gras, salmon, chicken, duck, and other ingredients; and *allumettes*, little rectangular strips of puff pastry stuffed with forcemeats or mousses. *Fanchonnettes* are very small patties of puff pastry garnished as you would a canapé. Blinis, originally Russian, are petite crêpes stuffed with caviar, or carrots, or eggs, and many other ingredients. *Columbines*, small semolina tartlets, are stuffed with purees; and *dartois*, basically enclosed *allumettes* cut after they are cooked, can be stuffed with mousses, concentrated sauces, foie gras, anchovies, spinach Florentine, poultry, truffles, and/or mushrooms. *Pannequets* are tiny crêpes stuffed with cheese or vegetables mixed with sauces, while *pomponnettes*, rissoles made into the shape of a very small pouch with tart pastry, are filled with puree and deep-fried.

sheet, and broil until dappled golden brown, almost black in places, on top, about 2 minutes. Serve hot or very warm.

Makes 18 barquettes; 8 servings

Vols-au-Vent Stuffed with Veal Sweetbreads and Black Truffles

This antipasto called vols-au-vent con animelle e tartufo nero *is the kind of dish served in the* alta cucina *(haute cuisine), particularly in the Piedmont, Lombardy, or in Emilia-Romagna.* Vols-au-vent *probably arrived in northern Italy along with the great internationally trained chefs, such as Luigi Carnacina, in the early twentieth century. It is an elegant dish that can*

be made much simpler by buying frozen vols-au-vent in the frozen food section of your supermarket. In place of the black truffle you can use a half pound of porcini mushrooms. If using frozen vols-au-vent puff pastry, defrost according to the package instructions.

¼ pound veal sweetbreads, sinews or vessels removed
2 quarts water
1 tablespoon salt
12 vols-au-vent (opposite page)
2 tablespoons unsalted butter
¼ cup brandy
1 black truffle (about ¾ ounce), finely chopped, or
  ½ pound fresh porcini mushrooms (see Note)
Freshly ground black pepper

Vols-au-Vent

Vols-au-vent are puff pastry shells made by placing two puff pastry disks on top of each other and cutting a smaller circle out of the top pastry disk so that when it bakes and rises a well is formed by the rising dough. The shells are then filled with various stuffings and usually eaten as an hors d'oeuvre. The expression *vols-au-vent* means "flying in the wind" to reflect the lightness of the pastry. Vols-au-vent appear to have seen the light of day in early nineteenth-century France. We know that the great French chef Antoine Carême (1783–1833) was partial to them. Although vols-au-vent are sold frozen, you may not readily find them and therefore will need to make your own. Vols-au-vent are usually made in one of two sizes. When they are 4 to 5 inches in diameter, they are usually served as an appetizer at the table. When they are 2 to 3 inches in diameter, they are served as finger food at a cocktail party.

Take a sheet of puff pastry and roll it out until $1/4$ inch thick, unless it is already that thickness. With a cookie cutter, cut into smaller disks, either 2 to $3^1/_2$ inches in diameter (for finger food) or 4 to 6 inches in diameter (for an appetizer). Gather the pastry scraps, form into a ball, and roll out again to cut more disks. Place half the disks on a baking sheet. Make a small circular depression in the center of the remaining half of the disks, being careful not to cut all the way through the dough. Brush the edges of the disks on the baking sheet with egg white. Make sure you don't get too much egg elsewhere because the dough will not puff properly. Using the tines of a fork, make ridges around the edges of all the disks, then place the disks with the smaller circles pushed into them on top of the disks on the baking sheet. Bake according to the recipe instructions and carefully remove the center "lid" in order to fill the vols-au-vent.

1 tablespoon all-purpose flour

⅔ cup milk

5 ounces aged Montasio or fontina Val d'Aosta cheese, diced

1. Soak the sweetbreads in cold water for 2 hours. Drain and rinse. Bring the water to a boil in a medium-size saucepan and add the salt. Reduce the heat of the water until just below a boil. Add the sweetbreads and poach until firm and white, about 15 minutes. Drain and dice.

2. Preheat the oven to 400°F. Arrange the vols-au-vent on an ungreased baking sheet and bake according to the package instructions— that is, until golden, about 25 minutes. Remove from the oven, let cool, and remove the top lid with a fork, saving it to the side.

3. In a medium-size skillet, melt the butter over medium-high heat. Once it stops sizzling, cook the sweetbreads in the hot butter until they begin to stick to the pan, 4 to 5 minutes. Add the cooked mushrooms, if using, deglaze the skillet with the brandy, and flambé by lighting the contents of the skillet carefully with a long match, taking care with possibly dangling hair or long sleeves. Reduce the heat to medium, and when the flame extinguishes itself, season with salt and pepper, add the truffle, if using, and cook for 2 minutes, stirring. Remove the sweetbreads and truffle or mushrooms from the skillet and set aside, keeping warm.

4. In a small saucepan, dissolve the flour in the cold milk, beating it with a wire whisk over medium-high heat. Once the liquid starts to bubble gently, reduce the heat to medium and add the cheese, stirring constantly until the cheese has completely melted. Fill the vols-au-vent shells with the sweetbread mixture and spoon the sauce over the top. Cover with the lids and serve immediately.

Note: If using porcini mushrooms instead of the truffle, melt 3 tablespoons unsalted butter in a skillet over medium heat and cook the porcini mushrooms until soft, about 5 minutes. Set aside until needed.

Makes 12 servings

Nantua-Style Shrimp Beignets

Known as beignets de crevette à la Nantua, *it may be a stretch to think of these as Medi-* terranean food, being that Nantua is in the Jura, but if we follow the concept of the infinite Mediterranean of French historian Fernand Braudel, then we can. Dishes described as à la Nantua *refer to many things in France, but the name always means a dish that contains crayfish, shrimp, shrimp puree, or shrimp coulis.*

½ recipe Basic Beignet Dough for Baking (page 476)
1 pound fresh shrimp with their heads or ½ pound previously frozen headless shrimp, shells and/or heads removed and saved for making shrimp stock, if desired
5 tablespoons unsalted butter
2 tablespoons all-purpose flour
1½ cups hot whole milk
½ cup hot heavy cream
1 teaspoon fresh lemon juice
Salt and freshly ground white pepper to taste
2 tablespoons grated fresh black truffle (optional)
¼ teaspoon cayenne pepper

1. Prepare the beignet dough and bake them according to the instructions on page 476. When they are done, set the oven temperature to 350°F.

2. Meanwhile, bring a medium-size saucepan of abundantly salted water to a boil, then cook the shrimp until orange, about 2 minutes. Drain, let cool, and transfer to a food processor. Run the processor until the shrimp are finely crumbled. Remove all but ¼ cup of the shrimp from the food processor and set aside. You should have about 1 cup of crumbled shrimp. Add 3 tablespoons of the butter to the shrimp

Sweetbreads

Veal sweetbreads are considered by gourmets to be one of the greatest delicacies in meats. The sweetbread is the thymus of the calf, an organ at the top of the chest. The delicacy of this soft white meat comes from the fact that it is richer in albumen and gelatin than beef. Sweetbreads sold today, and almost exclusively at butcher shops and not supermarkets, are already cleaned and prepared for cooking. The calf's thymus is in two parts, the round "heart" section and the long "throat" section. The first section, what the French called *noix de ris*, is the choice part and that is the part the butcher will sell you. The home cook must prepare the sweetbreads for cooking by removing any bloodstains, then soaking them in cold water for an hour or washing them under running water. Some cooks cook the sweetbreads as is, but many cooks, myself included, prefer to then blanch the sweetbreads in very gently bubbling water until they are firm, about 20 minutes, before proceeding.

remaining in the processor and process until very well blended. Remove from the food processor and set this shrimp butter aside.

3. In a medium-size heavy saucepan, prepare a béchamel sauce by melting the remaining 2 tablespoons butter over medium-high heat, then add the flour and cook, stirring constantly, until a very light brown roux forms, then cook for about another minute. Remove the saucepan from the heat and pour the milk and cream in slowly, whisking all the time. Once the liquid is incorporated, return to the burner and simmer over medium-low heat until it is thick and dense, about 15 minutes. Season with the lemon juice, salt, white pepper, and cayenne. Add the cooked shrimp, truffle if using, shrimp butter, and cayenne to the béchamel sauce. Stir

to blend, cook for 2 minutes, and correct the seasoning.

4. Cut open the beignets and fill them with the shrimp sauce, but not so they are overflowing. Place in the oven for a few minutes if they need reheating and serve hot. Freeze any remaining unstuffed beignets for another recipe.

Makes 20 to 25 beignets

Beignets with Smoked Salmon Mousse

This French hors d'oeuvre called beignets de mousse de saumon fumé *is rich and elegant and will please any guest. It sounds difficult to make, but it is not at all. It is unlikely you will need to salt anything because the smoked salmon will be salty enough, but taste the final mousse mixture to be sure before stuffing them into the beignets.*

1 recipe Basic Beignet Dough for Baking (page 476)

3 ounces smoked salmon

1 tablespoon unsalted butter

⅛ teaspoon cayenne pepper

Pinch of freshly grated nutmeg

¾ teaspoon unflavored gelatin

¼ cup shrimp stock (see below)

1 tablespoon fresh lemon juice

2 tablespoons cognac

¼ cup heavy cream, whipped to firm peaks

Salt to taste (optional)

1. Prepare the beignet dough and bake them according to the instructions on page 476.

2. In a food processor, puree the salmon, butter, cayenne, and nutmeg together until very crumbly. Transfer to a medium-size bowl and set aside.

Shrimp Stock

Making shrimp stock is very easy and you should be making some anytime a recipe calls for shrimp to be shelled. Place the shells in a saucepan, cover with water, and bring to a boil. Reduce the heat to low and simmer 30 minutes. Drain, discarding the shells, let the stock cool, and then freeze for future use.

3. In a small saucepan, soften the gelatin in the shrimp stock and dissolve over low heat. Let cool. Add to the salmon mixture, along with the lemon juice and cognac.

4. Fold the whipped cream into the salmon mixture until well blended, check for salt, then stuff into the beignets and serve or hold in the refrigerator up to 4 hours until ready to serve. Serve at room temperature or a little cooler.

Makes 50 to 60 beignets; 16 servings

Spicy Octopus Pie in a Red Wine Crust from the Port of Sète

This small pie filled with a octopus ragout called tielle de poulpe Sètoise *is a traditional preparation from the small port of Sète near Cap d'Agde in the Hérault department of the Languedoc. The pie is made in a* tielle, *an earthenware pan about 5 inches in diameter of the same name, and is covered with pastry dough flavored with sweet wine. The wine-colored crust glistens with a golden aura because of an egg yolk–and–tomato paste glaze. Down the road from Sète, in Bouzigues, a similar preparation is made with mussels and called* chausson de moule.

2 to 2¼ cups all-purpose unbleached flour

3½ ounces pork lard

¼ cup sugar

¼ teaspoon salt

¾ cup sweet red wine

1½ pounds octopus, cleaned (see opposite page)

2 tablespoons red or white wine vinegar

2 tablespoons extra-virgin olive oil, plus extra
  as needed
1 medium-size onion, finely chopped
4 garlic cloves, finely chopped
2 pounds ripe or canned plum tomatoes, peeled,
  seeded, and crushed
Salt and freshly ground black pepper to taste
¾ teaspoon cayenne pepper
1 teaspoon dried thyme
1 bay leaf
1 large egg yolk
1 teaspoon tomato paste

1. In a cold, large metal bowl, work 2 cups of the flour, the lard, sugar, and salt together with your fingers or a pastry cutter until the mixture is pebbly and well blended. Alternatively, pulse in a food processor, then transfer to a cold metal bowl. Add the wine and knead until you have a supple dough, adding more flour if the dough is sticking. Form the dough into a ball, wrap in waxed paper, and leave in the refrigerator for 2 hours.

2. Put the octopus in a large pot of boiling salted water with the vinegar and boil until tender, about 45 minutes. Drain, rinse under cold running water, and peel as much of the skin off as you can while it is still hot. Chop the octopus into smaller than bite-size pieces.

3. In a large skillet, heat the olive oil over medium heat, then cook the onion, garlic, and octopus until the onion is soft, about 8 minutes, stirring frequently. Add the tomatoes and season with salt, black pepper, cayenne, thyme, and bay leaf. Reduce the heat to medium-low and let simmer until the water is evaporated, 1¼ to 1½ hours, stirring occasionally.

4. Preheat the oven to 350°F.

5. Remove the dough from the refrigerator and roll out thin on a lightly floured work surface. Cut out sixteen 5-inch disks. Lightly grease eight 4-inch tart pans with lard or butter and cover each with a disk of dough, fitting it in snugly. Prick the dough all over with a toothpick. Spread several tablespoons of the tomato-and-octopus stuffing over it. Cover with the remaining dough disks and pinch down the edges so they meet the bottom disk. Pinch off any excess dough. Prick the top with a toothpick. Whisk together 2 or 3 drops of olive oil with the egg yolk and tomato paste and brush on the top crust.

6. Bake until a glistening golden color, about 30 minutes. Once they have cooled a bit,

Cleaning Octopus

Cleaning octopus if you've caught one yourself is a big deal; if you've bought a frozen one in the market, it's not. In the first instance, you need to tenderize the octopus, which requires a lot of beating and results in a tired arm. In the second instance, the tenderizing has already been done and the freezing and unfreezing actually contribute to the tenderizing effect. All you need to do is turn the octopus over and see if the little beak inside the mouth has been removed. If it has, then you're set to go; if it hasn't, just reach inside with a paring knife or even your fingers and pull it out.

remove the tarts from their pans, arrange on a serving platter, and serve hot.

Makes 8 servings

Fontina Val d'Aosta Cheese Pie

This simple antipasto from the Piedmont in northern Italy is called crostata di fontina delle Valle d'Aosta *and is made with the famous cheese of that region. It would be best to try getting geniune fontina Val d'Aosta, as it is far superior to the Swedish fontina commonly sold in supermarkets. If you don't have a local cheese store (I've never seen it in a supermarket), you can try ordering it through Internet sources (page 496).*

2 cups all-purpose unbleached flour

7 tablespoons unsalted butter, melted

½ teaspoon salt

7 tablespoons dry white wine

2 large eggs, beaten

2 tablespoons freshly grated Parmigiano-
 Reggiano cheese

Salt to taste

Pinch of freshly grated nutmeg

¼ pound fontina Val d'Aosta cheese, thinly sliced

1. Place the flour in a large bowl and make a well. Pour in the melted butter and salt. Working gently with your fingers, incorporate 6 tablespoons of the wine and form the dough into a smooth ball. Wrap in waxed paper and leave in the refrigerator for 1 hour.

2. Cut the dough in half and roll each ball out on a lightly floured work surface into a thin sheet large enough to cover the bottom and sides of an 8-inch pie pan. Butter the pie pan and cover with one sheet of dough.

3. Preheat the oven to 350°F.

4. In a small bowl, beat 1 egg, the Parmigiano, salt, and nutmeg together and dilute with the remaining 1 tablespoon wine. Pour three-quarters of the egg mixture into the crust and layer the fontina cheese on top of the egg mixture. Coat the cheese with the remaining beaten egg. Cover the pie with the top crust and crimp the edges together, cutting off any excess dough with kitchen scissors. Bake until light golden on top, 35 to 40 minutes.

5. Let rest a few minutes and serve warm, cut into small serving portions.

Makes one 8-inch pie; 8 servings

The Guards Who Came to Petralia

*This curiously named Sicilian pie (*Guarda-cuvèni di Petralia*) is also called* focaccia della Madonie. *I got the recipe when I visited Fiametta di Napoli Oliver in Mondello, near Palermo, many years ago. Fiametta had written a Sicilian cookbook and other works on Sicilian history, but she couldn't explain the name. This pastry is not a focaccia as we usually think of it, as a kind of thick seasoned bread or pizza. Rather, it is a short dough pie with a crumbly crust filled with eggs and vegetables. It actually is more similar to the Tunisian* ṭājīn al-malsūka, *a pie of eggs wrapped in phyllo pastry. It is un-*

clear what the reference is in the name. Petralia is the name of two towns in the Madonie mountains in Sicily, Petralia Soprana and Petralia Sottana, both at about 3,000 feet above sea level. During the Norman invasion of Sicily from 1060 to 1090, Petralia Sottana was probably not much more than a castle, although it was populated by both Christians and Muslims. Although it is romantic to think that this pie received its name from the Norman guards who arrived in 1066 from Messina, the "guards who came to Petralia" probably date from a much later time during the Spanish Bourbon period.

1 recipe Basic Short Dough (page 475), adding 1 teaspoon sugar

1 cup shelled fresh or frozen peas

4 canned artichoke bottoms or fresh artichokes, trimmed down to bottoms (page 205)

10 thick asparagus spears, bottoms trimmed

10 large eggs

2 tablespoons grated pecorino cheese

6 ounces thinly sliced Genoa salami or sweet *soppressata*, chopped

2 ounces fresh mozzarella cheese, chopped

Salt and freshly ground black pepper to taste

1. Prepare the short dough and chill in the refrigerator.

2. Meanwhile, separately cook the peas, artichokes, and asparagus until tender in boiling water. If the peas are fresh, boil for 10 minutes, 5 minutes if frozen. The asparagus should take about 10 minutes. Boil the artichokes for 50 minutes, whole, then trim them to their bottoms if using fresh; canned artichoke hearts do not need to be cooked. Chop the artichokes and asparagus.

3. In a large bowl, beat the eggs with the pecorino. Stir in the artichokes, asparagus, salami, mozzarella, and then the peas. Season with salt and pepper.

4. Preheat the oven to 350°F. Grease a 9-inch deep-dish pie pan with olive oil. Remove the dough from the refrigerator and divide in half, with one half being a little larger than the other. Roll the larger piece of dough out on a flat surface, making sure you flour it liberally to keep it from sticking. This is crumbly dough, so you may have to be more careful than usual when you roll it. Lay this larger sheet of dough in the pie pan so it covers the bottom and side of the pan. Pour the stuffing ingredients into the crust. Roll out the second sheet of dough, using plenty of flour. Lay the top sheet over the pie and crimp the edges together. With scissors or a knife, cut off the excess dough. Gather and roll out the remaining trimmed dough. Using a short paring knife, cut out 4 small disks and place them evenly around the edges of the pie. Cut out a *fleur-de-lys* and place it in the middle. Score the pie in 4 places and bake until golden, about 1 hour. Remove from the oven and let cool. Serve at room temperature.

Makes one 9-inch pie; 10 servings

Provençal Pine Nut and Bacon Quiche

Although the quiche has its origins in Lorraine, this dish, called quiche aux pignons, *traces its roots to the garrigue (moors) of the Camargue of Provence. It's a simple quiche, but the taste is not: it is luscious. To make this properly, you will need to focus on the bacon lardons. Make sure you only use a smoked bacon slab cut into batons about ¼ inch thick and 1½ inches long. Don't use your typical supermarket bacon because it is sliced and too fatty. If you must, blanch it first in boiling water for about 10 minutes.*

1 tablespoon unsalted butter

½ pound smoked slab bacon, cut into lardons

1 tablespoon dried savory

¼ pound Gruyère cheese, coarsely shredded

½ cup light cream

2 tablespoons crème fraîche

5 large eggs, 2 left whole and 3 separated

Salt and freshly ground black pepper to taste

⅛ teaspoon freshly grated nutmeg

1 garlic clove, lightly crushed

½ pound store-bought puff pastry, defrosted if necessary and rolled out thinner to cover the bottom and side of the tart pan

½ cup pine nuts

1 tablespoon finely chopped fresh parsley leaves

1. In a medium-size skillet, melt the butter with the bacon lardons over medium-high heat, then cook until the bacon is emitting some fat, 4 to 5 minutes, stirring. Add the savory and stir, then cook until the bacon is sticking, adding 2 tablespoons of water to scrape up the bits, about 3 minutes, stirring. Remove the bacon and transfer to a bowl to cool. Add the Gruyère to the bowl and toss.

2. Preheat the oven to 400°F.

3. In another bowl, mix the light cream, crème fraîche, 2 whole eggs, and 3 of the egg yolks. Season with salt, pepper, and nutmeg and leave to rest for a moment. Rub the sides and bottom of a 10-inch tart pan with the crushed garlic clove. Cover with the puff pastry, fitting it in snugly. Puncture the puff pastry with a fork and crimp the border attractively. Arrange the bacon and cheese mixture and pine nuts evenly over the puff pastry.

4. In a small bowl, beat the egg whites until frothy, then brush the edges of the puff pastry with it. Beat the cream-and-egg mixture vigorously for 1 minute with an electric mixer. Add the remaining egg white to the mixture and stir in gently. Pour into the tart pan. Sprinkle the parsley on top of the quiche and bake until golden brown on top, 25 to 30 minutes.

5. Remove from the oven, let rest for 20 minutes, then cut into wedges and serve.

Makes one 10-inch quiche; 10 servings

Tartlet Pans

If you like, you can make the quiche on this page in 2-inch-diameter tartlet pans for elegant hors d'oeuvre to be passed at a cocktail party. Tartlet pans are sold in sizes ranging from 1 inch in diameter to about 5 inches and are found in fine kitchenware stores such as Sur la Table or Williams-Sonoma and baking supply stores.

Lamb and Feta Pie from Cephalonia

Cephalonia (Kefallinía) is an Ionian island off the western coast of Greece. During the Middle Ages, it belonged to the Norman kings of Sicily before becoming a Frankish fief. Italian overlords ruled the island from 1155 to 1478, first under the Arsenio family and then the Tocchi family. The Turks captured the island and held it for twenty years, until the Venetians supplanted them in 1500, ruling until 1797. As a result, the influence of Italian cookery is still felt today in the island's cuisine. Typically, this preparation, called kreatopitta Kefalonitiki, *is served on the Feast Day of Analipseos (Ascension Day) and on the day of Apokreos, before the beginning of Lent. This recipe comes from a Greek neighbor in Arlington, Massachusetts, where I once lived. There are very many versions of this pie; other cooks might mix meats, or use* kefalotyri *instead of feta cheese, or they may include potatoes.*

¼ cup extra-virgin olive oil

3 tablespoons unsalted butter

1 cup hot water

1¾ pounds boneless leg of lamb, trimmed of all fat and cut into bite-size pieces

3 garlic cloves, crushed

¼ cup finely chopped fresh parsley leaves

Salt and freshly ground black pepper to taste

½ cup dry white wine

⅓ cup raw long-grain rice, soaked in cold water for 30 minutes and drained

¾ pound feta cheese, crumbled

¾ pound phyllo pastry, defrosted if necessary

3 medium-size ripe tomatoes, peeled and sliced

3 large hard-boiled eggs, shelled and sliced

1 tablespoon unsalted butter, melted

2 to 4 tablespoons milk, as needed

1. In a large skillet, heat 2 tablespoons of the olive oil with 1 tablespoon of the butter and the hot water over medium heat. Add the lamb, garlic, and parsley; season with salt and pepper, cover, and cook until the lamb is tender, about 1 hour and 15 minutes, adding more water to keep the skillet from drying out completely.

2. Add the wine and cook, uncovered, until reduced somewhat, 12 to 15 minutes. Remove from the heat and toss with the rice and feta cheese until well combined. Set aside.

3. Preheat the oven to 350°F.

4. Using 1 tablespoon of the butter for each, grease two 9-inch cake pans very well. Divide the phyllo sheets in half. Layer 4 sheets on the bottom of each pan, brushing each sheet with the remaining 2 tablespoons olive oil. Divide the meat

Feta Cheese on Cephalonia

Diane Kochilas, in her magnificent book *The Glorious Foods of Greece: Traditional Recipes from the Islands, Cities, and Villages*, published in 2001, tells us that the feta cheese of Cephalonia is famous throughout Greece and that at most feta factories, including in America, the cheese master will be a scion of the cheese makers from one of Cephalonia's mountain villages.

mixture between the 2 pans and spread over the phyllo sheets. Layer the tomatoes and eggs evenly over the meat in each pan. Cover with 4 more phyllo sheets, brushing each with olive oil. Brush the top and final layer with the melted butter. Moisten the edges of the phyllo with water and crimp them together with your fingers. Prick the top of the pie with a fork and make a small hole in the center to vent the steam. Bake until golden brown, about 1 hour, pouring a few tablespoons of milk in the center hole of each while it bakes to keep the stuffing moist. Serve hot.

Makes two 9-inch pies; 16 servings total

Variation: You can make about 50 individual meat pies by cutting the phyllo into 3 x 14-inch strips. Place a heaping teaspoon of the meat mixture at one end and fold one corner over to the opposite edge of the phyllo to form a triangle. Continue in this way up the strip until you end up with a triangular pie. Continue the preparation. These individual triangles freeze well and make very appetizing *mezedes* for surprise guests. Just heat them up on a baking sheet if still frozen.

Spanakopita

The Greek spinach pie made with phyllo pastry known as spanakopita *(meaning, sensibly, "spinach pie") is now to be found throughout America. This famous Greek meze consists of a stuffing made of spinach, cheese, eggs, and white sauce, which is wrapped in phyllo pastry and baked until golden brown, either as individual triangle pies or in one large baking tray.*

Spanakopita and the two recipes that follow are often made in Greece during Apokreos, the week preceding Lent, where tradition calls for eating only eggs, butter, and milk products.

3 pounds spinach, washed well and heavy stems removed

¾ cup (1½ sticks) plus 1 tablespoon unsalted butter

3 large eggs, beaten

1 cup grated *kefalotyri* cheese (page 361)

1 tablespoon finely chopped fresh parsley leaves

¾ cup Béchamel Sauce (page 468)

1 teaspoon salt

Freshly ground black pepper to taste

¼ cup extra-virgin olive oil

¾ pound phyllo pastry, defrosted if necessary

1. Put the spinach in a large pot with only the water clinging to it from the last washing, cover, and cook over medium heat, turning occasionally with a long wooden spoon or a fork, until it has wilted, 15 to 20 minutes. Drain very well, pressing the water out with the back of a wooden spoon, and chop.

2. In the pot you cooked the spinach, melt 6 tablespoons (¾ stick) of the butter, then cook the spinach over medium heat for 10 minutes, stirring. Turn into a large bowl. Add the beaten eggs, *kefalotyri* cheese, parsley, béchamel, and salt; season with pepper and mix well.

3. Preheat the oven to 350°F. Melt the remaining 7 tablespoons butter with the olive oil in a small saucepan. Using a brush, grease a 9 x 12-inch baking pan with some of this mixture. Unravel the phyllo pastry following the

Working with Phyllo Pastry

Phyllo (also spelled *filo*) is a pastry as thin as a leaf (which is what "phyllo" means in Greek) and is a time-consuming and artful pastry-making skill in Greece. Phyllo and phyllo-like pastries are used commonly throughout the Near and Middle East, but are most often associated with Greek cooking. Today, excellent commercially made phyllo is available in many supermarket frozen foods sections and certainly in Greek and Middle Eastern markets. Because phyllo is so thin and fragile, you must work with more care than with other doughs.

Commercial phyllo is usually sold in 1-pound packages wrapped in plastic. It freezes well, so defrost it slowly in the box, which is best accomplished by putting it in the refrigerator the night before you need it. Most sheets of dough are 14 x 18 inches and each recipe will instruct you on how to cut these sheets.

Once you have opened the package, the phyllo sheets can dry out so quickly as to become brittle and useless. Remove the number of sheets you will need and set them to the side, covered with a slightly damp kitchen towel to provide moisture. Rewrap tightly and refrigerate or refreeze the phyllo you are not using. The rule of thumb with phyllo pastry is to work more quickly than you usually do with pastry.

Brush each sheet with melted butter or olive oil as you work with it, folding it according to the directions in the recipe. You might find it efficient to dedicate a 2-inch-wide brush for buttering phyllo pastry. Make sure all parts of the phyllo pastry in the baking pan or tray that are exposed to air are brushed with butter or oil so they do not become brittle while baking.

directions on the package. Lay in 6 sheets of the phyllo pasty sheets, brushing each with the melted butter and oil, brushing the first layer liberally. Keep the phyllo pastry sheets humidified with a slightly damp kitchen towel draped over them as you work so they don't dry out. The pastry should go up the sides of the pan. Spread the spinach mixture evenly over the top of the pastry sheets. Cover the spinach with 6 more sheets of pastry, brushing each with the butter and oil. Fold the edges of any phyllo pastry sheets over and liberally brush the top with the remaining butter and oil.

4. Bake until the top is golden, about 40 minutes. Let cool for 20 minutes, cut into squares, and serve at room temperature.

Note: You may add some chopped scallions or fresh dill to the spinach.

Makes 8 servings

Zucchini and Cheese Pie from Greece

This meze is called kolokythotyropitta, *which means, straightforwardly, "zucchini and cheese pie." There are a number of squash pies in Greece, some use summer squashes while others use winter squashes such as pumpkin. This recipe can be made in a large rectangular baking pan and then cut up later, but I think folding them into individual triangle pies is much nicer, although a little more time-consuming. These individual cheese triangles freeze well unbaked and make very appetizing mezedes for surprise guests. All the cheeses called for are found in Middle Eastern or Greek markets. Alternatively, you could replace the cheese with Muenster and feta cheese in equal amounts. The use of Muenster cheese is typical among Greek Americans.*

3 pounds small zucchini, peeled

1 cup (2 sticks) unsalted butter

Salt and freshly ground black pepper to taste

2 large eggs

6 ounces *kefalotyri* cheese, grated (page 361)

6 ounces *kasseri* cheese, shredded (opposite page)

½ pound *halloumi* cheese, shredded (opposite page)

3 tablespoons finely chopped fresh parsley leaves

3 tablespoons finely chopped fresh dill

3 tablespoons milk

1 pound phyllo pastry, defrosted if necessary

1. Finely shred the zucchini into a colander and let stand over the sink for 1 hour to drain.

2. In a large skillet, melt ½ cup (1 stick) of the butter over medium-high heat, then cook the zucchini until most of the liquid has evaporated, but not until they are browning, about 10 minutes, stirring frequently. Season with salt and pepper. Remove from the heat. Melt the remaining ½ cup (1 stick) butter in a small saucepan and keep warm on the side.

3. In a large bowl, beat the eggs, then stir in the cheeses, parsley, dill, and milk and season with salt and pepper. Pour the zucchini into this mixture and stir until smooth.

4. Unravel the phyllo pastry following the directions on the package. Cut the unwrapped leaves of phyllo in three, making strips about 3 inches wide. Keep the phyllo pastry sheets humidified with a slightly damp kitchen towel draped over them as you work. Arrange a 3 x 14-inch strip in front of you and brush with the melted butter. Place a heaping teaspoon of the zucchini-and-cheese mixture at one end and fold one corner over to the opposite edge of the phyllo to form a triangle. Continue in this way up the strip until you end up with a triangular pie. Brush both sides with butter and arrange on a large, buttered baking sheet in a single layer. Continue with the remaining phyllo and filling.

4. Preheat the oven to 350°F. Bake until golden brown, about 15 minutes. Set aside until they cool down a bit and serve warm.

Makes 35 phyllo pies

Variation: With a pastry brush, butter the bottom of a 9 x 12-inch baking pan and layer in 7 or 8 sheets of phyllo pastry, brushing melted butter on each layer. Let the phyllo edges droop over the sides of the pan. Pour in the zucchini-and-cheese mixture, making sure it is spread

Some Greek Cheeses

The cheeses used in the *kolokythotyropitta* (Zucchini and Cheese Pie from Greece) on the opposite page are typical Greek cheeses that can be found in a Greek or Middle Eastern market. In addition, an imitation *kasseri* cheese made of cow's milk by the huge American cheese company Athenos can increasingly be found in a supermarket. On page 361 I describe *kefalotyri*. *Kasseri* cheese, a sheep's milk or combination of sheep and goat's milk cheese, is similar to *kashkaval* cheese (page 92). *Kasseri* is a mass-produced *pasta filata* cheese, made in the same style as mozzarella, although it is yellower and harder. After the cheese comes out of its warm water bath, just like mozzarella, it is shaped into 22-pound pieces, then drained in molds and aged for three months before being sold. One of the first mentions of the famous Cypriot cheese *halloumi* is in an account by the tenth-century Arab writer al-Muqqadasī, who says that *halūm* cheese, a salted cheese, was being used in Egyptian cuisine. *Hallūm* or *halloumi* cheese is very popular in Greece, Turkey, Syria, and Lebanon, although most of today's production is in Cyprus. *Halloumi* is a semi-soft cheese made from raw sheep's milk sometimes mixed with goat's milk. The cheese is formed into blocks 6 x 4 x 1 inch. These blocks are then cooked in the hot whey, after which they are salted, folded over on themselves, and submerged in brine. The cheese is now very hard and once the *halloumi* is brought home, it is soaked in several changes of fresh cold water for 24 hours, then sliced lengthwise and fried in clarified butter.

evenly over the pastry. Fold the edges of the phyllo over into the pan and butter them, too. With the remaining 5 to 6 phyllo sheets, cover the pan, buttering each sheet and tucking the edges over and into the pan. Bake until the top is golden brown, 35 to 40 minutes. Remove, let it rest for 15 minutes, then cut into squares. Serve warm.

Cheese Pie in Phyllo Pastry

Tyropitakia (tyropitta) are small cheese pastries made during Apokreos, the period before Lent when dairy products are eaten. Tyri means "cheese" in Greek, and this cheese pie is typical of a wide range of dishes that cover cheese with pastry. There are many recipes for this dish, the ingredients depending on the region or even the island. For instance, in Thessaly, a short dough of flour, water, and vinegar is used. Sometimes a puff pastry is used or shortbread, as in a cheese-and-egg pie called kouroumbougatses. In the region of Rumelia in northern Greece, they make a tyropitakia that includes nearly a dozen eggs. Another name for this pie is kalitsounia, as it is known on Crete. In Greece they are all generally called pittes or pies.

These pastries contain a mixture of feta cheese and mezithra (also transliterated mizithra and myzithra), a kind of Greek ricotta salata, or kefalotyri, a hard grating cheese usually made of sheep's milk, though sometimes goat's milk. Another traditional cheese mixture would use manouri, a soft, unsalted white cream cheese made of whey of sheep and goat's milk, and grated kefalotyri. It is made as one large baked pie, although pastry triangles are typical, too.

Many Greek Americans replace the Greek cheeses with an Italian pecorino Romano and with cream cheese, cottage cheese, or Muenster cheese. Because I have never had difficulty finding Greek cheeses in this country, I prefer the traditional way of making tyropitakia (also spelled tyropittes) and provide this recipe from Návplion (Nauplia).

6 tablespoons (¾ stick) unsalted butter
3 large eggs
6 ounces mizithra or kefalotyri cheese, crumbled or grated
14 ounces imported Greek or Bulgarian feta cheese, crumbled
1 tablespoon very finely chopped parsley leaves
Pinch of freshly grated nutmeg

¾ pound phyllo pastry, defrosted if necessary

1. Melt the butter in a small saucepan and keep warm. In a large mixing bowl, beat the eggs, then stir in the mizithra cheese, feta, parsley, and nutmeg.

2. Unravel the phyllo pastry following the directions on the package. Keep the phyllo pastry sheets humidified with a wet kitchen towel draped over them as you work. With a pastry brush, butter the bottom of a 9 x 12-inch baking pan and layer in 7 or 8 sheets of phyllo pastry, brushing butter on each layer. Let the phyllo edges droop over the sides of the pan. Pour in the cheese mixture, making sure it is spread evenly over the pastry. Fold the edges of the phyllo over into the pan and butter them, too.

3. Preheat the oven to 350°F. With the remaining 5 to 6 phyllo sheets, cover the pan, buttering each sheet and tucking the edges over and into the pan. Bake until the top is golden brown, about 40 minutes. Remove from the oven, let it rest for 15 minutes, then cut into squares. Serve warm.

Makes 8 servings

Variation: You can make about 50 individual cheese pies by cutting the phyllo into 3 x 14-inch strips. Place a heaping teaspoon of the cheese mixture at one end and fold one corner over to the opposite edge of the phyllo to form a triangle. Continue in this way up the strip until you end up with a triangular pie. Continue with the remaining filling and phyllo. Bake them in a single layer on a buttered baking

Touts, Waiters, Moms, and Pops

It amazes me how thoroughly the Greek economy is tied to tourism. When I first went to Greece in 1971, it was poor and backward. It's all Euro-Greece now and often feels like a GreekWorld theme park. For anyone looking for more than sea and sun, it takes some patience and good investigating skills because the first casualty of the tourist hordes is the perversion of real Greek food. So how do you find a place that serves real Greek food? One way is to seek the mom-and-pop restaurants and not the places with a slick tout and waiter luring you into the establishment with its menu in three languages. Mom and pop will invite you back to the kitchen for you to see what's cooking. They usually have about six to eight dishes to offer plus a few made to order, items like fish and salads like *skordalia* or a Greek salad. There will be a tablecloth and bread will arrive in a basket with napkins and cutlery. They will have no menu, or a menu only in Greek, or maybe Greek and poorly spelled English. The tourist restaurants will offer omelettes, toast, pizza, lazania, spaghetti bolognese, hamburger, schnitzel, and tzatziki (which is an authentic Greek dish but usually transformed into pathetic tourist food). In both kinds of places the food comes fast and with lots of French fries too. One little place that I loved was the Chrisse Taverna in Corfu. We had a meze of an out-of-this-world *tyropitta* (page 271), a dish of fava beans with tomato sauce spiced with cinnamon; *pastithatha*, yearling calf stewed with tomato, olive oil, and spiced with onions; and *briam*, a dish of zucchini, eggplant, potatoes, and tomatoes cooked very soft and slowly in olive oil. The gyro was made of pork and dipped in an excellent Tzatziki (page 56).

sheet until golden, about 25 minutes at 350°F. These individual cheese triangles freeze well unbaked and make very appetizing *mezedes* for surprise guests.

Fougasse

This fougasse *is a flat puff pastry stuffed with anchovies and olives or walnuts. The shapes and even the dough of a* fougasse *can vary according to the mood and artistic talent of the* baker, *as well as the region. Their shapes can range from "N's," flower petals, and rectangles to intricate intertwinings of dough that looks like lacework.*

A fougasse *can be made with frozen store-bought* pâte feuilletée *(puff pastry) and baked until light and fluffy in any shape you wish. In Aigues-Mortes, an old medieval town that once had quick access to the Mediterranean Sea, one can find* fougasse noël, *a large flat rectangle of dough, yellow from a glaze of yolks, spongy, light, and frosted with sugar that is made at Christmas time. In Bouzigues, farther down the coast, one can find the* fougasse *(or sometimes* faugasse *or* fougassette*) stuffed with ground walnuts. This recipe uses chopped imported black olives and salted anchovies, and is my favorite. If using frozen puff pastry, defrost according to package instructions.*

1 pound store-bought puff pastry
⅔ cup pitted and chopped imported black olives
12 salted anchovy fillets, rinsed and chopped
1 large egg, beaten

1. Preheat the oven to 350°F.

2. Roll out each sheet of puff pastry to an 11 x 14-inch rectangle on a lightly floured work surface, following the directions on the package for handling. Cut each sheet in half crosswise. Fold each of the 4 pieces in half and cut out 2 triangles on the top and bottom to form an "N."

3. Mix the olives and anchovies, spread this stuffing on one side of each sheet of pastry, and fold the other side over, crimping the edges together with the tines of a fork. Place on a baking sheet and brush with some beaten egg. (It is not necessary to grease the baking sheet as the pastry has plenty of butter worked into it.)

4. Bake until golden brown, about 20 minutes. Let cool slightly on a wire rack and serve.

Makes 8 servings

Four-Cheese Puff Pastry Roll in the Greek Style

This preparation inspired by the little Greek cheese pies is a mixture of four cheeses layered on a sheet of puff pastry, is rolled up into a log and baked until golden brown. The log is then cut into meze portions and served. If using frozen puff pastry, defrost according to package instructions.

½ cup finely crumbled or shredded white cheese (such as farmer cheese or Mexican *queso fresco*)
½ cup finely crumbled feta cheese
½ cup finely shredded Dutch Edam cheese
½ cup finely shredded *kashkaval* cheese
¼ pound store-bought puff pastry

1. Preheat the oven to 400°F.

2. In a medium-size bowl, mix the cheeses.

3. Roll the puff pastry out on a lightly floured work surface until about ¹⁄₁₆ inch thick and a rectangle about 14 x 9 inches and arrange with a short end nearest you. Sprinkle a quarter of the cheese on the bottom border of the short end and roll up once. Sprinkle the next quarter of the cheese and roll again. Continue with the remaining cheese until the pastry is rolled up like a log. Crimp the edges closed and score the long edge closed with the tines of a fork. Place on a baking sheet and bake until golden brown, about 25 minutes.

4. Remove from the oven, let sit for 5 minutes, then cut in half lengthwise and then cut each half crosswise into eighths.

Makes 16 pastries; 6 servings

The Origins of Puff Pastry

One of the earliest descriptions of the making of puff pastry is found in the thirteenth-century (some place it in the late eleventh century) cookery book by Ibn Razīn al-Tujībī called *Kitāb faḍālat al-khiwān fi ṭayyibāt al-ṭaᶜm wa'l-alwān*, one of the earliest works on cookery from the Hispano-Islamic era in Spain. It seems likely that the Arabs in Spain were responsible for inventing puff pastry—that is, pastry layered with butter or other fat that is folded upon itself many times to create a multitude of leaves of pastry when it puffs up during baking. The Arabic word for puff pastry both today and ten centuries ago is *muwarraqa*, which derives from the word *waraq*, meaning "leaf."

Phyllo-Wrapped Cheese Rolls

This Greek meze called bourekakia apo tyri (bourekia) *consists of feta and* graviera *cheese, a Greek version of Gruyère cheese, mixed with a white sauce, eggs, and parsley, which are rolled in phyllo pastry and baked. The word* bourekakia *comes from the Turkish word* börek, *meaning "a pastry." This phyllo pastry roll can be filled with any combination of crab, shrimp, chicken, chicken liver, ground lamb, spinach and cheese, mushrooms, and artichokes, or it can be made as a sweet.*

½ pound feta cheese
½ pound *graviera* or Gruyère cheese, shredded
10 tablespoons (1¼ sticks) unsalted butter
¼ cup all-purpose flour
1 cup milk
2 large eggs, beaten
1 tablespoon finely chopped fresh parsley leaves
Pinch of freshly grated nutmeg
¾ pound phyllo pastry, defrosted if necessary

1. Crumble the feta into a medium-size bowl and mix with the *graviera*. In a medium-size saucepan, melt ¼ cup (½ stick) of the butter over medium heat, then blend in the flour to make a roux and cook for 1 minute. Remove the saucepan from the burner and whisk in the milk a little at a time. Return to the burner and cook over medium heat until it is a thick white sauce, 3 to 4 minutes, stirring constantly. Remove the white sauce from the heat and let cool slightly. Add the cheeses, eggs, parsley, and nutmeg and stir well to combine. In a small saucepan, melt the remaining 6 tablespoons (¾ stick) butter.

3. Preheat the oven to 350°F.

4. Cut the phyllo sheets in half lengthwise. Keep the phyllo pastry sheets humid with a wet kitchen towel draped over them as you work. Lay one sheet down and brush with the melted butter. Lay another sheet on top and brush with butter. Spoon 2 tablespoons of the cheese stuffing on one end of the sheet and fold the top over lengthwise. Fold 1 inch of each side over, brush with butter, and roll up. Arrange the pastry cylinders in a single layer in a large buttered baking dish, seam side down. Bake until golden, about 30 minutes. Remove, let

cool a bit, and serve warm or freeze (you can pop them in the oven still frozen) for later use.

Makes 18 to 20 rolls; 8 servings

 ## Anchovy in Puff Pastry

Feuilletée aux anchois *is a delicate little hors d'oeuvre from Provence and the Languedoc that consists of salted anchovies surrounded by puff pastry. The difference between salted anchovies and the little cans of oil-packed anchovies you may be familiar with is significant enough for me to highly recommend that you use salted anchovies. They are usually sold in 14-ounce cans or loose at Italian markets. If using frozen puff pastry, defrost according to package instructions.*

10 ounces salted anchovy fillets (about 40 fillets), rinsed

2 tablespoons unsalted butter, softened

Pinch of cayenne pepper

1 pound puff pastry

1 small egg, beaten

1 tablespoon finely chopped fresh parsley leaves (optional)

1. Preheat the oven to 450°F.

2. Take 8 of the anchovy fillets and cut each into 3 pieces. Set aside. Mash the remaining anchovies together with the butter and cayenne.

3. Roll the puff pastry out until it is about ⅓ inch thick or less. Cut as many 2 x 3½-inch rectangles as you are able. Place half the rectangles on a baking sheet and brush with the beaten egg. Bake until light golden, 7 to 8 minutes.

4. Spread the anchovy butter on the remaining rectangles and top with a small piece of anchovy. Place on another baking sheet and bake until golden, 7 to 8 minutes. Remove from the oven and let cool on a wire rack. Reduce the oven temperature to 350°F (or you can reserve the baked rectangles at this point and refrigerate for later use if desired).

5. Cover each anchovy-slathered rectangle with a plain rectangle and place in the oven until deep golden, about 10 minutes. Sprinkle with parsley if desired before serving hot.

Makes 10 servings

· 🐚 ·

The Pope and the Poor

After Pope Clement V (1305–1314) moved the papal court to Avignon in southern France to escape the anarchy of Italy, an extravagant court cuisine developed. In the Middle Ages, Avignon was an important trading city situated on the routes of great commerce. It was the capital of Latin Christianity and a fortified city of 40,000. The pope's table saw its exquisite fish coming from the fishermen of the Martigue, but the millions of anchovies caught did not go to the pope. They were layered in barrels with salt and this is what the poor ate.

Puff Pastry Squares with Za᷎tar and Feta Cheese in the Style of Damascus

This appetizer is based very loosely on a pastry I had once in Damascus. The za᷎tar (pronounced (ZAA-ter) called for can be bought in Middle Eastern markets or you can mix up your own, combining ½ cup dried thyme, 2 tablespoons sesame seeds, 2 teaspoons ground sumac, and a little salt. If using frozen puff pastry, defrost according to package instructions.

½ pound puff pastry, rolled out thinner and cut into twelve 2½-inch squares
2 tablespoons *za᷎tar*
3 ounces feta cheese, crumbled
Extra-virgin olive oil for drizzling

1. Preheat the oven to 385°F.
2. Arrange the squares on a baking sheet, sprinkle with a little *za᷎tar*, then push some feta cheese down into the center of the pastry. Drizzle with very little olive oil and place in the oven. Bake until golden brown, about 20 minutes. Remove and serve hot.

Makes 12 servings

Puff Pastry Fingers with Sesame Seeds and Feta Cheese

Although feta cheese is thought of as a Greek cheese, and it is, it is also found in the Levant, as much production is imported from nearby Cyprus. This pastry is similar to the previous one, but goes lighter on the spices. If using frozen

puff pastry, defrost according to package instructions.

½ pound store-bought puff pastry
2 to 3 ounces imported feta cheese, washed of salt and crumbled
1 small egg mixed with 1 tablespoon water
1 tablespoon sesame seeds

1. Preheat the oven to 425°F.
2. Roll out the puff pastry on a lightly floured work surface until a little thinner. Cut into rectangles about 2½ x 1¼ inches and place on a baking sheet. Divide the feta among the rectangles and brush with the egg wash. Sprinkle the tops with the sesame seeds. Bake until golden, about 15 minutes. Serve immediately.

Makes 48 pastries; 16 servings

Puff Pastry Squares with Sobressada Majorcana

This is a very quick tapa that you can make on some moments' notice if need be, although you will need to already have the cold cut in your pantry. Sobressada Majorcana is a dried sausage popular in Majorca that is available via www. donajuana.com. In its place, use a soft salami. If using frozen puff pastry, defrost according to package instructions.

½ pound store-bought puff pastry, cut into twelve 2½-inch squares
Twelve ¹⁄₁₆-inch-thick slices *sobressada Majorcana*

1. Preheat the oven to 385°F.

2. Arrange the pastry squares on a baking sheet and place a slice of *sobressada* on top. Bake until golden brown, about 20 minutes. Serve hot.

Makes 12 servings

Puff Pastry Squares with Botifarra Sausage and Mushrooms

This is an extraordinary tapa *that utilizes a famous sausage from Catalonia called* botifarra *(in Catalan) or* butifarra *(in Spanish). It is the most common of Catalan pork sausages and is spiced with cinnamon, fennel seeds, and black pepper. It is sometimes made with veal, and* botifarra negra *is made with pig's blood. One can replace this sausage with kielbasa or chicken sausage or order the Catalan sausage from www.donajuna.com. If using frozen puff pastry, defrost according to package instructions.*

3 tablespoons extra-virgin olive oil

1 large shallot, chopped

3 garlic cloves, finely chopped

¼ cup finely chopped fresh parsley leaves

10 ounces mixed white button and portobello mushrooms, chopped

½ pound cooked *botifarra* sausage, kielbasa, or Italian veal or chicken sausage, cut into small dice

¼ cup cognac

2½ ounces (about ½ cup) blanched whole almonds, roasted in a 350°F oven until lightly browned, cooled, and crushed very small in a food processor

1 large slice Italian bread (about 2 ounces), crusts removed, fried in a little olive oil until brown on both sides, and crumbled small in a food processor

½ teaspoon salt

½ teaspoon freshly ground black pepper

Pinch of saffron threads, toasted in a dry skillet over medium heat 3 minutes and crumbled

⅛ teaspoon ground cinnamon

1 large hard-boiled egg, shelled and chopped

¾ pound store-bought puff pastry

1. In a large skillet, heat the olive oil over medium-high heat, then cook the shallot, garlic, and parsley until the shallot is translucent, about 3 minutes, stirring so the garlic doesn't burn. Add the mushrooms and sausage, and continue to cook until the mushrooms are dark and sticking to the bottom of the pan and there is little liquid left, 7 to 8 minutes. Add the cognac and, once it evaporates, about 2 minutes, reduce the heat to low and add the almonds, fried bread, salt, pepper, saffron, cinnamon, and chopped egg. Stir and cook for 5 more minutes.

2. Preheat the oven to 425°F.

3. Roll the puff pastry out on a lightly floured work surface so it is thin, about ¹⁄₁₆ inch, then cut into 3½-inch squares. Place the squares on a baking sheet and fill each with a heaped tablespoon of the filling. Place in the oven and cook until the pastry is golden, about 10 minutes. Serve hot or warm.

Makes 28 squares; 14 servings

Puff Pastry Squares with Italian Sausage and Homemade Goat's Milk Ricotta

These nice little appetizers require goat's milk ricotta cheese, which you can make yourself following the recipe on page 88 and using all goat's milk. Alternatively, fresh cow's milk ricotta cheese will work perfectly fine. Goat's milk ricotta, ricotta caprina, *is found in the Fruili-Venezia Giulia region north of Venice. If using frozen puff pastry, defrost according to package instructions.*

1 tablespoon unsalted butter

6 ounces mild or hot Italian sausage (2 links)

½ pound store-bought puff pastry

¼ pound fresh goat's milk ricotta cheese, preferably homemade (page 88)

3 very thin slices lemon, cut into 16 small triangles

8 black olives, pitted and cut in half

1 tablespoon finely chopped fresh parsley leaves

1. In a small skillet, melt the butter over medium-high heat and fry the sausage until golden all over and firm, about 25 minutes, turning occasionally. Let cool, then slice thinly.

2. Preheat the oven to 400°F.

3. Roll the puff pastry out on a lightly floured work surface to a sheet 12 inches square. Cut out 16 squares and lay them on a large baking sheet. Put 1 to 2 teaspoons of ricotta cheese on each square and squish it down a bit. Put 3 thin slices of sausage on each square and place in the oven. Bake until golden brown, about 20 minutes.

4. Remove from the oven and let cool on a wire rack until warm, not hot. Garnish each square with a triangle of lemon, half an olive, and a sprinkle of parsley. Serve.

Makes 16 pastries; 16 servings

Arab Spinach Pie Triangles

This very popular Lebanese version of spinach pie is known as faṭayr bi'l-sabānikh, *or just* faṭayr *for short. They appear on nearly every meze table. These pies are also called* sabānikh bi'l-ᶜajīn, *the vegetable version of* laḥm bi'l-ᶜajīn *or colloquially,* laḥm bī ajīn, *and in Palestine as* āqrās bi'l-sabānikh, *an expression more generic in meaning. Although they are eaten by all segments of the population, they are particularly common on Christian tables during the Lenten period. They have something similar in Egypt, called a* faṭīr *(page 341), which is nevertheless quite different.*

*When making the spinach stuffing, it's important that the spinach be completely dry, so it's best to wash it in the morning and let it dry on some kitchen towels during the day or use a salad spinner, then blot with paper towels. The dried berries of the sumac bush (*Rhus coriaria*), with their tart taste, are used in Lebanese cooking with enthusiasm. The maroon-colored ground berries are sold in Middle Eastern markets.*

279

1 Basic Bread and Pizza Dough recipe
(page 473), adding ½ teaspoon sugar

3 tablespoons extra-virgin olive oil

1 medium-size onion, finely chopped

4 scallions, chopped

1½ pounds spinach, heavy stems removed,
washed well, and dried thoroughly

¼ cup pine nuts

1½ tablespoons sumac

Salt and freshly ground black pepper to taste

¼ teaspoon freshly grated nutmeg

3 tablespoons fresh lemon juice

1. Prepare the pizza dough with the addition of the sugar.

2. In a large nonreactive skillet, heat the olive oil over medium-high heat, then cook the onion and scallions until soft, about 5 minutes, stirring. Add the spinach in handfuls and cook until wilted, adding more spinach as it wilts, about 5 minutes, tossing occasionally. Add the pine nuts, sumac, salt, pepper, nutmeg, and lemon juice and cook until most of the moisture has evaporated, about 5 more minutes, stirring occasionally. Leave in the pan until cool, then chop coarsely.

3. On a lightly floured work surface, roll out the dough ¼ inch thick and cut out as many 4-inch rounds as you can, rerolling the scraps of dough when necessary. Place the rounds on several kitchen towels, cover with more towels, and leave to rest as you continue cutting out disks.

4. Place 1 tablespoon of spinach filling in the center of a round and bring up the sides at 3 points to form a triangle. Press the edges together firmly to seal. Make sure none of the spinach juices get onto the edges.

5. Preheat the oven to 400°F. Arrange the pies on a greased baking sheet and bake until light golden, about 25 minutes. Serve hot or warm. These pies also freeze very well.

Makes 24 pies; 12 servings

Puff Pastry Triangles with Smoked Salmon, Olives, and Anchovy

This hors d'oeuvre from Provence, called an allumette *in French, is usually served passed on a tray, still hot from the oven. Although I normally recommend the opposite, if you leave the anchovies out of these puff pastries, it will not adversely affect the taste. I like the taste, though, and usually make it with more anchovies than I recommend here. You can also make 10 squares and cut them in half after they are baked. If using frozen puff pastry, defrost according to package instructions.*

¾ pound store-bought puff pastry, rolled thinner
and cut into 20 squares

¼ pound smoked salmon

¼ pound imported black olives, drained, pitted,
and chopped

15 salted anchovy fillets, rinsed and cut in half

1. Preheat the oven to 425°F.

2. Lay a square of puff pastry in front of you and in the middle place a small slice of smoked salmon. On top of the salmon, place an olive and half an anchovy fillet (or more if you like). Fold the pastry over to form a triangle and pinch the edges closed, crimping with a fork.

3. Place the pastries on a baking sheet so they don't touch each other and bake until golden brown, about 15 minutes. Serve hot.

Makes 20 pastries; 10 servings

Puff Pastry with Roquefort and Walnuts

The town of Roquefort in the Haut Languedoc sits on a limestone plateau that is highly permeable. Water disappears into the ground to carve caverns and grottos. Here at the foot of the causses, *air moves through vertical passageways, allowing for a constant humidity and temperature ideal for the growth of a certain bacteria that turns ordinary white ewe's cheese into blue cheese. One such system of grottos is at Roquefort, and it gave birth to that famous cheese. Cheese is a great, cheap source of protein, and French peasants made fortunes in about 1698 by carrying cheeses to the armies fighting in Italy and Germany. Nevertheless, cookery books of the time barely mention cheese, rarely giving their names or describing their qualities. As late as 1702, the medical writer Louis Lemery recognized only three great cheeses: Roquefort, Parmesan, and those from Sassenage in Dauphiné. But Roquefort was a cheese that local cooks used in their cooking, especially pastries—for example,* gatis, *a brioche made with Roquefort cheese, or this typical hors d'oeuvre, called* allumettes au Roquefort, *which is incredibly rich. These* allumettes *end up being short and squat, but you can make them about 3 inches long and 1½ inches wide. If using frozen puff pastry, defrost according to package instructions.*

1 cup mashed Roquefort cheese
¼ cup coarsely crushed walnuts
1 tablespoon finely chopped fresh parsley leaves
Freshly ground black pepper to taste
2 tablespoons heavy cream
½ pound store-bought puff pastry
1 large egg, beaten

1. Preheat the oven to 400°F.

2. In a medium-size bowl, mix the Roquefort cheese, walnuts, parsley, pepper, and cream until smooth. If desired, fill a small pastry bag fitted with a ¼-inch nozzle with the stuffing.

3. Prepare the puff pastry by rolling it out into 2 rectangles about ⅛ inch thick and not wider than 9 inches and about 12 inches long.

4. Pipe ½-inch-long lines of stuffing on the bottom 4 inches of each sheet of the puff pastry, leaving a space at the edges and in between each of 6 columns of stuffing. (If you are not using a pastry bag, spoon the stuffing in neat columns.) Fold the top portion over the bottom portion of the puff pastry with its columns of stuffing and seal the edges. Cut into 6 *batons* and crimp the edges closed with the tines of a fork. Make sure that the pastries are well sealed so no stuffing oozes out. Arrange the pastries on an ungreased baking sheet. Brush the tops with the egg wash. Bake until golden, about 20 minutes. Serve warm.

Makes 12 pastries; 6 servings

Snails

One of the greatest little foods around is the snail. They are popular everywhere in the Mediterranean, but in America snails are not eaten. When they are, and that is pretty rare, they are offered in some French restaurants as *escargots*. I don't have any snail recipes in this book, not because I don't like them or because Americans don't eat them, but because it's virtually impossible to find live snails. In thirty years, I've seen them only twice sold live, once in an Italian grocery in Boston's North End and once in a market in New York's Chinatown. I've used canned snails, but there just isn't any comparison. In any case, let me describe a nice dish called *cacalauso a la Prouvençalo* in Provençal, which means *escargots à la Provençale*. The dish is known simply as *caragou*. Live snails are first purged for several days, then boiled in a court bouillon of fennel stalks with their leaves, orange peel, a bouquet garni, and 1 tablespoon of vinegar. After they are boiled, the snails are drained, chopped very fine, and sautéed in olive oil with bread soaked in milk, very finely chopped shallots, garlic, parsley, and mushrooms seasoned with salt and pepper. A good amount of white wine is added and reduced until the mixture has the consistency of a stuffing. The snails can be stuffed into a tomato half or puff pastry and baked au gratin.

Puff Pastry Squares with Olive Oil–Cured Tuna

The salting or marinating of tuna fish in olive oil was an old industry in Provence. We know that in 1424, a good amount of tuna, caught off Andalusia, was exported to Marseilles and resold. Salted tuna was also a staple on galleys. Every part of the tuna was used. In 1515, the master Provençal sugarer Berthomeu Blanch received 236 kilos of confectioners' sugar (sugar for preserving) for Christmas and prepared a very refined confit *of tuna tongue preserved in sugar and stored in earthenware pots. An eighteenth-century gastronomic specialty was fresh tuna pâté from Toulon, while today we can enjoy these petits pâtés au thon mariné. It's essential you use a good-quality tuna packed in olive oil and not white meat albacore tuna in water. If using frozen puff pastry, defrost according to package instructions.*

Two 1½-inch-thick (4-inch-diameter) slices
  French bread, crusts removed
1 cup milk
One 6-ounce can imported tuna in olive oil
2 tablespoons unsalted butter
3 tablespoons heavy cream
Salt and freshly ground black pepper to taste

1 pound store-bought puff pastry, rolled out
   thinner and cut into 24 squares
1 large egg, beaten

1. Soak the bread in the milk in a small bowl,
then squeeze out the liquid. Place the bread in a
food processor with the tuna and its oil and
pulse a few times to blend. Add the butter and
cream and season with salt and pepper. Process
until creamy and thick.

2. Preheat the oven to 400°F.

3. Arrange half the puff pastry squares on a
baking sheet. Place about 1 tablespoon of stuffing on top of each and cover with the remaining
squares. Crimp the edges with a fork to seal
them. Brush the tops with the beaten egg and
bake until golden, 20 to 25 minutes. Serve hot
or warm.

Makes 12 pastries; 12 servings

A French Apéritif

A place one might encounter some of
Provence's delightful *petits pâtés* are in
cocktail or wine bars. An apértif is enjoyed
before the meal, accompanied by small hors
d'oeuvre. Usually something sweet or slightly
bitter would be in the offing. A sweet *vin
jaune* from the Jura or a glass of Champagne,
a port or sherry, a vermouth on the rocks, or
the famous kir royale—a glass of Champagne
mixed with black currant liqueur—might be
drunk with little morsels to eat.

Puff Pastry Squares with Veal, Ham, and Marrow from Provence

*This puff pastry hors d'oeuvre from Provence,
called* petits pâtés à la Provençal, *can be made
into four-inch square pastries or twenty-four
smaller ones with some stuffing left over. I like to
save the stuffing and keep it for an emergency
appetizer when I need it. If using frozen puff
pastry, defrost according to package instructions.*

6 ounces boneless veal leg, trimmed of any fat
   and finely chopped (not ground)
6 ounces cooked ham, finely chopped
2 ounces beef marrow (from ¾ pound beef
   bones)
1 large egg yolk
1 teaspoon salt
1 tablespoon eau-de-vie or grappa
4 salted anchovy fillets, rinsed and chopped
1 shallot, finely chopped
1 large garlic clove, finely chopped
2 tablespoons finely chopped fresh parsley leaves
1 scallion, finely chopped
1 tablespoon extra-virgin olive oil
1 pound store-bought puff pastry, rolled out
   thinner and cut into 24 squares
1 large egg, beaten

1. Preheat the oven to 400°F.

2. In a large bowl, mix the veal, ham, marrow,
egg yolk, salt, and eau-de-vie. Stir in the
anchovies, shallot, garlic, parsley, and scallion.
Add the olive oil and toss again.

3. Place a heaping tablespoon of stuffing in
the center of a puff pastry square and cover with

another square. Crimp the edges together with the tines of a fork to seal the two halves. Arrange the pastries on a baking sheet, brush each pastry with a little of the beaten egg, and bake until golden, about 25 minutes. Serve hot.

Makes 12 pastries; 12 servings

Marrow Bones

The rich marrow inside bones is an essential ingredient in many preparations because of its delicious and unique taste and its melting-ly soft texture. Marrow bones of either veal or beef are sold in supermarkets, but pay attention to what you are buying because some bones are soup bones and it is impossible to get at the marrow. Look for cross cuts of beef or veal shank bones. The marrow can be spooned out with a narrow spoon or cut out with a paring knife.

Puff Pastry Squares with Quail from Catalonia

Called pastissets fullats amb colomins *in Catalan, this tapa or snack is traditionally made with squab (pigeon), but I find it quite delicious prepared with quail. Since both those birds are a bit hard to find, and sometimes quite expensive, a turkey thigh would work very nicely. These can easily be cut in half as a triangle for serving because they are quite substantial, and this recipe can easily feed eighteen people as a passed tapa.*

What to Do with Leftover Stuffing

There will be enough stuffing left over from Puff Pastry Squares with Veal, Ham, and Marrow from Provence (page 283) to make some nice *pizzette*. Prepare the pizza dough on page 473 and roll it out thin to form 24 disks 2½ inches in diameter. Put a heaping teaspoonful of leftover stuffing on top of each disk and cover with a thin slice of cheese, such as a goat cheese, and bake according to the instructions on page 283.

If using frozen puff pastry, defrost according to package instructions.

1 tablespoon pork lard
4 quail, cut in half lengthwise; or 1 large turkey thigh, 2 squabs, or 1 pheasant, cut into 4 pieces (1 to 1½ pounds)
2 large eggs
One 1½-inch-thick (about 4-inch-diameter) slice French bread, crust removed, toasted, and crumbled
¼ pound ground veal
1 ounce Manchego or pecorino cheese, grated (½ cup)
2 tablespoons finely chopped fresh parsley leaves
2 teaspoons finely chopped fresh tarragon leaves
½ teaspoon dried thyme
½ teaspoon dried oregano
Salt and freshly ground black pepper to taste
¼ teaspoon ground cinnamon
Pinch of freshly grated nutmeg

1 small black truffle (optional), grated
1 pound store-bought puff pastry

1. In a skillet, melt the lard over medium-high heat, then brown the quail, turkey, squabs, or pheasant on both sides. This will take 6 to 8 minutes for the quail and squabs. For the other meats, it will depend on how thick they are. The meat doesn't have to be cooked through since it will cook some more in the pastry. Cook the meat until it is nearly firm when poked with your finger. Remove the meat from the bone and set aside, discarding the bones, or saving them to make stock.

2. In a medium-size bowl, beat 1 of the eggs, then add the bread and let it soak for a few seconds. Add the veal, cheese, parsley, tarragon, thyme, oregano, salt, pepper, cinnamon, nutmeg, and truffle, if using.

Medieval Quail

Catalans have been fond of quail for centuries. They eat it grilled, in paella, and as a tapas (see headnote, opposite page). Hunters abound in Catalonia. King Jaime II, when he was not engaged in overseeing the complicated foreign policy of the Aragonese-Catalan Empire in 1307, was kept busy strengthening the administrative network and checking the efficiency of the judicial system. He was meticulous and even worried about establishing a hunting season for quail and partridge.

3. Preheat the oven to 400°F.

4. Without rolling out the puff pastry, cut it into 18 squares. Arrange 9 squares on a large baking sheet and place a piece of fowl and 1 tablespoon of stuffing in the center of each square, pushing it down slightly into the dough. Drizzle with a little cold water. Place the other 9 squares on top and crimp the edges closed. With the tip of a small paring knife, make small incisions on the tops of the square. Beat the remaining egg in a small bowl, then brush the pastries with it. Bake until golden, 20 to 25 minutes. Serve immediately.

Makes 9 pastries; 9 servings

Puff Pastry Crescents with Saffron Chicken and Almonds from Spain

The Spanish love of chickens, almonds, and saffron as a culinary combination is old enough to be reflected in the inventory of Spanish galleons from 1560, where we find a complete supply of condiments including saffron. Just before the fleets left Seville or put to sea at San Lucar de Barrameda, live chickens and other livestock would be loaded for the voyage. The officers also had raisins, almonds, eggs, sugar, and fresh meat such as mutton, beef, and pork, but these foods were not all available to the sailors. This luscious tapa *has a delightful mix of chicken, almonds, and saffron that will remind you of a purely Iberian experience every time you sink your teeth into it. Unfortunately, in two bites it's done. But you can always make more.*

3 tablespoons extra-virgin olive oil

1 medium-size onion, finely chopped

½ red bell pepper, seeded and finely chopped

3 large garlic cloves, finely chopped

½ pound boneless skinless chicken breast, cut into small dice

¼ cup brandy

1 large ripe tomato, cut in half, seeds squeezed out, grated against the largest holes of a grater, and skin discarded

½ cup sliced (shaved) almonds

1 teaspoon hot Spanish paprika

Pinch of saffron threads, crumbled

Salt and freshly ground black pepper to taste

1 pound store-bought puff pastry, defrosted if necessary

1 medium-size egg, beaten with 1 tablespoon water

1. In a large skillet, heat the olive oil over medium-high heat, then cook the onion, bell pepper, and garlic until sizzling, stirring. Add the chicken and cook, stirring, until browned, about 2 minutes, then pour in the brandy. Once it has evaporated, add the tomato, ¼ cup of the almonds, the paprika, and saffron. Cook until dense, 4 to 5 minutes, stirring. Season with salt and pepper and let cool in the skillet.

2. Preheat the oven to 425°F.

3. Roll out the puff pastry on a lightly floured work surface until a little thinner. Cut out twenty-four 4-inch-diameter rounds. Place about 1 teaspoon of stuffing in the center of each round and fold over to form a crescent, crimping the edges closed with the tines of a fork. Brush the surface of each pastry with the egg wash. Place on a baking sheet, arrange a pinch of the remaining slivered almonds on top, and bake until golden, 10 to 12 minutes. Serve warm.

Makes 24 pastries; 12 servings

Spanish Paprika

I sometimes call for Spanish paprika, which has a different aroma from Hungarian paprika, the typical paprika found in supermarkets. Although Spanish paprika is a bit harder to find, you can order it from Web sites such as www.donajuana.com. This paprika, called *pimentón* in Spanish and on the container itself, is sold as either hot (*picante*) or sweet (*dolce*). Its unique aroma comes from the fact that the peppers are smoked before they are dried and ground.

Puff Pastry Triangles with Ham and Fontina Cheese

Cooked ham (prosciutto cotto) *is almost unknown in southern Italy and found only in northern Italy, such as the Alto Adige, whence this antipasto. Cured ham* (prosciutto crudo), *on the other hand, is very popular and far more common. For this recipe you will use cooked ham and the kind you use should be something flavorful such as Black Forest ham. The cheese, too, should be very flavorful, such as fontina Val d'Aosta (rather than a Swedish fontina) or Montasio cheese, usually found in a cheese store*

Fontina Val d'Aosta Cheese

Fontina cheese from the northern Italy region of Val d'Aosta is considered one of the finest cow's milk cheeses in the world. Fontina is made from whole cow's milk from a single milking from local Valdostana cows, whose diet consists of foragings from the local meadows. The cheese is seasoned (aged) for three to eight months in wheels about 4 inches high that weigh on average 18 pounds. Fontina Val d'Aosta has a thin, pale golden crust, a soft consistency with very few holes, melts very well, and contains a minimum of 45 percent fat. It is produced throughout the year, notably in the villages of Valtournanche, Champoluc, and Aosta. Fontina has a very long history, the name being first recognized in 1270. It was described in the one of the first works on cheese in Italy, the *Summa lacticiniorum*, published in 1477. Fontina is a much reproduced cheese, but only the fontina Val d'Aosta achieves the goal of a supreme cheese.

or Italian market. If using frozen puff pastry, defrost according to package instructions.

6 ounces cooked ham, chopped

6 ounces fontina Val d'Aosta cheese, cut into small dice

¾ pound store-bought puff pastry

1. In a medium-size bowl, toss the ham and cheese together.

2. Preheat the oven to 425°F.

3. Roll the puff pastry out slightly so it is a 14-inch square, then cut into 12 squares. Divide the stuffing evenly among the squares, placing some in the center of each. Fold the puff pastry over to form a triangle, crimp the edges closed with the tines of a fork, and arrange on a baking sheet. Bake until golden brown, about 20 minutes. Let cool slightly and serve warm or hot.

Makes 12 pastries; 12 servings

Pastizzi—A Maltese Ricotta and Parsley Puff Pastry

Although Malta is strategically located for any navy wishing to control the Mediterranean, it is today rather inconvenient to get to as a tourist. But there is no grander entry to any port in the Mediterranean than the entry into Valletta by ship at dusk. Once you do arrive at Vulletta, the capital, you will not find any Maltese food, only Italian. But should you be invited into a home or go to outlying villages or to the other major island of Gozo, you will encounter Maltese cuisine, a fascinating fusion of Sicilian and Arab cooking liberally spiced with the culinary sprinklings of many more. In this pastry, ideally the ricotta cheese you use should be rather dense, and this is why homemade ricotta will work better, because commercial ricotta cheese is not drained long enough. This recipe is adapted from Anne and Helen Caruana Galizia's The Food & Cookery

Maltese Appetizers

If ever there was a fusion cuisine, it would be the cuisine found on Malta. This "aircraft carrier" of an island, as the British, who owned Malta at the time, called it during World War II, has a fusion of Arabic and Italian cuisine that reveals itself most obviously in the language. For example, the Maltese *hobż biż-żejt* (bread and oil) is related to the Arabic *khubz bi'l-zayt*, while the rolled beef slices called *braġoli* in Maltese are the Italian *braciole*. Some dishes show the combination of both the Arabic and Italian names—for example, *timpana tarross bil-qaqoċċ*, "timbale of rice with artichokes." The Maltese serve *antipasti* rather than meze, but they call them by the English word *appetizers*, demonstrating that the long English rule also left vestiges. *Pastizzi* are often served as a snack, and in Valletta until recently waiters from local bars would sell trays of hot *pastizzi* and tumblers of hot tea or coffee to local office workers.

of Malta *(Pax, 1999). If using frozen puff pastry, defrost according to package instructions.*

2 large eggs
½ cup finely chopped fresh parsley leaves
15 ounces fresh ricotta cheese, preferably
   homemade (page 88)
Salt and freshly ground black pepper to taste
1¼ pounds store-bought puff pastry

1. In a medium-size bowl, beat the eggs with the parsley. Add the ricotta, season with salt and pepper, and mash it all together until homogenous. Taste and check the seasoning.

2. Preheat the oven to 400°F.

3. Roll the puff pastry out a little thinner on a lightly floured work surface and cut into forty 4-inch squares. Place a spoonful of the ricotta mixture in the center of each and fold over,

enclosing the stuffing and forming a triangle, and crimp the edges together with a fork. Arrange the pastries on 2 large baking sheets and bake until golden brown, 20 to 25 minutes. Let cool slightly and serve warm or hot.

Makes 40 pastries; 20 servings

Puff Pastry of Swiss Chard and Onion from Corsica

This recipe from Ajaccio on the island of Corsica is called bastella. *It is exceedingly simple, and on the face of it doesn't look like it would be tasty, but it is—very much so. The Swiss chard is cooked in olive oil with sliced onions, then stuffed inside rectangles of puff pastry before being baked. Some Corsican cooks also add ground beef or veal to the stuffing. There may be a long and twisted history to the Corsican* bastella *and you can read about it by looking at pages 294–95 in my* A Mediterranean Feast *or by visiting my Web site at www.cliffordawright. com/history/pigeon_pie.html. If using frozen puff pastry, defrost according to package instructions.*

3 tablespoons extra-virgin olive oil
1 medium-size onion, very thinly sliced
1½ pounds Swiss chard, white stems removed, leaves washed well, dried well, and chopped
Salt and freshly ground black pepper to taste
¾ pound store-bought puff pastry

1. In a large skillet, heat the olive oil over medium-high heat, then cook the onion until soft, about 4 minutes, stirring. Add the Swiss chard and cook until it wilts, about 5 minutes, stirring. Season with salt and pepper.

2. Preheat the oven to 400°F.

3. Roll the puff pastry out slightly on a lightly floured work surface so it is a 14-inch square. Cut into 12 squares and evenly divide the stuffing among the squares, placing some in the center of each. Fold the puff pastry over to form a rectangle, crimp the edges together with the tines of a fork, and arrange on a baking sheet. Bake until golden, about 25 minutes. Serve warm or hot.

Makes 12 pastries; 12 servings

Puff Pastry of Spinach and Egg

This recipe, a spinach pastry made with puff pastry, eggs, and cheese, is mentioned in the first Turkish cookbook translated into English, by

Effendi Turabi in 1862, and is called màr-màrina, *which, in a curious culinary reversal, is derived from the Greek. (Many Greek dishes have Turkish names.) The Turks are likely to have learned how to make puff pastry from the Arabs. If using frozen puff pastry, defrost according to package instructions.*

2 tablespoons extra-virgin olive oil
½ cup finely chopped onion
2 large garlic cloves, finely chopped
1 tablespoon chopped fresh dill
2 tablespoons chopped fresh chives
¾ pound spinach, heavy stems removed if desired, washed well, and dried well
Salt and freshly ground black pepper to taste
3 large eggs
1½ cups shredded *kashkaval* cheese (page 92)
¾ pound store-bought puff pastry

1. In a a medium-size skillet, heat the olive oil over medium-high heat, then cook the onion, garlic, dill, and chives until translucent, 2 to 3 minutes, stirring frequently so the garlic doesn't burn. Add the spinach in batches, constantly turning as each batch wilts, about 4 minutes, then cook another 3 minutes until most of the liquid evaporates, seasoning with salt and pepper. Let it cool slightly.

2. Bring a saucepan of water to a boil and cook the eggs for 7½ minutes exactly. Remove from the water and shell under cold running water.

3. In a medium-size bowl, mix the cheese with the spinach mixture.

4. Preheat the oven to 400°F.

The Why of Corsican Cuisine

Corsica is an integral part of France, a large island south of Provence and north of the Italian island of Sardinia. But Corsica's historic isolation has meant a more insular culture than one finds in France. Not only is Corsica an island but every *pieve* (canton) on this island is an island within an island, having no contact with the next valley over the mountain. The people of Cruzzini, Bocognano, and Bastelica—villages that lie behind Ajaccio—consider each other foreigners. This is reflected in the cuisine, for one finds both pork lard and olive oil as the essential cooking fat, when normally in traditional societies it's one fat or another, not both. These were closed economies in the Middle Ages, although some trade escaped as the Corsican *pievi* exchanged goods with the outside world through their shepherds and might barter pigs and chestnuts for oil, fabric, or money.

5. Roll the puff pastry out on a lightly flour work surface until it's about ¹⁄₁₆ inch thick, then cut into three 8-inch squares and three 6-inch squares. Fill the smaller squares with the stuffing, making a well in the middle. Place an egg in each well. Cover with the larger square and crimp the edges together with a pastry wheel or the tines of a fork. Transfer to a baking sheet and bake until golden, about 20 minutes. Remove from the oven and serve hot or let cool on a rack and reheat and serve later.

Makes 3 pies; 9 servings

Lamb Pies in Phyllo Pastry

This Greek meze is called bourekia apo kima *or* kreatopitakia, *the meat cousin of the cheese* bourekia *(Phyllo-Wrapped Cheese Rolls; page 275). There are many versions of this meat pie throughout Greece from Epirus, the islands, Roumelia, and Macedonia. Instead of the tomato-based sauce I use here, some cooks use a béchamel.* Kefalotyri *cheese is a hard, salty, sheep's milk cheese from Greece that is easily found in Greek and Middle Eastern markets, or you can substitute pecorino cheese.*

¾ cup (1½ sticks) unsalted butter, melted

1 tablespoon extra-virgin olive oil

1 small onion, finely chopped

1 pound ground lamb

½ cup dry white wine

2 tablespoons tomato paste mixed with 6 tablespoons water

3 tablespoons finely chopped fresh basil leaves

1 tablespoon finely chopped fresh mint leaves

Salt and freshly ground black pepper to taste

1 large egg, lightly beaten

½ cup grated *kefalotyri* cheese

½ pound phyllo pastry, defrosted if necessary

1. In a large skillet, heat 2 tablespoons of the butter with the olive oil over medium heat, then cook the onion until translucent, about 4 minutes, stirring. Add the meat and cook until it has turned color, breaking it up with a fork or wooden spoon as you do, about 5 minutes. Add the wine and simmer until evaporated, about 15 minutes, then stir in the diluted tomato paste, basil, and mint and season with salt and pepper. Cook until dense and very little liquid is left, about 10 minutes, stirring occasionally. Let cool in the skillet.

2. Once the stuffing is cool, stir in the egg and cheese. Unroll the phyllo sheets and cut through the roll into 3-inch-wide 14-inch-long strips. Remove one sheet, keeping the remaining sheets covered with a damp kitchen towel, brush the entire strip with some melted butter, and place a little less than 1 tablespoon of stuffing at the bottom of the strip. Fold the lower right corner of the phyllo strip over to the opposite edge to begin making a triangle. Fold a ½ inch of the entire right edge of the phyllo over, then continue folding the phyllo pastry as a triangle, brushing each exposed section of the bottom unbuttered portion of the pastry as you fold. Fold the entire strip until it is a triangle and arrange in a single layer on a large baking sheet buttered with 2 tablespoons of the butter. Continue with the remaining phyllo strips and stuffing.

3. Preheat the oven to 350°F. Bake the pastries until golden, 20 to 25 minutes. Serve hot or very warm.

Makes 36 pastries; 12 servings

Phyllo "Cigars" with Pastourma

These delicious "cigars" of stuffed phyllo pastry called floyeres me pastourma *are typically served as part of a meze. The stuffing consists of what the Greeks call* pastourma, *known to the Turks as* pastırma *and to the Arabs as* basṭurmā. *These words give us our word* pastrami, *although our pastrami is an entirely different product. Pastourma is a cured and dried meat originally from Turkey or Armenia usually made from beef fillet. Sun-dried slices of meat are coated with a paste made of garlic, fenugreek seeds, paprika, and salt and are left to cure. The cheeses used in the stuffing are* graviera, *a Greek version of Gruyère, and* kasseri, *mild and creamy and resembling cheddar or provolone in texture but saltier, and made of whole sheep's or goat's milk. All these ingredients can be found in Greek or Middle Eastern markets. This recipe is adapted from Vefa Alexadriou, author of several Greek cookbooks.*

4 large eggs, beaten
¼ pound thinly sliced *pastourma*
1 cup extra-virgin olive oil
8 scallions, finely chopped
¾ pound phyllo pastry, defrosted if necessary
¼ pound *graviera* or Gruyère cheese, cut into 20 "sticks"
1 cup shredded *kasseri* cheese
¼ cup sesame seeds

1. Beat the eggs and soak the *pastourma* in them for 1 hour.

2. In a small saucepan, heat 3 tablespoons of the olive oil over medium heat and cook the

Basṭurmā

This cured beef filet seasoned with spices and known as *pastourma* in Greece, *pastırma* in Turkey, and *basṭurmā* in Arab countries is found in Middle Eastern markets. Several good brands are made in California in pre-sliced vacuum-packed packages. I like to use *basṭurmā* for breakfast and as a meze. For breakfast, I slit a small pita bread open and heat it, then lay in the pocket a slice of *basṭurmā*, a fried egg, and a smear of strained yogurt. Ohhh, that's delicious. I also make emergency appetizers by smearing a little strained yogurt on a slice of *basṭurmā* and rolling it up. Those are very popular and no can guess what they are.

scallions until soft, 4 to 5 minutes, stirring. Set aside.

3. Arrange a sheet of phyllo in front of you lengthwise. Using a 2-inch brush, oil the left half, then fold the other half of the phyllo over the oiled part. Place a stick of *graviera* cheese in the center of the bottom portion of the phyllo about 1 inch from the bottom edge and a few inches from each side. Put a slice of *pastourma* and some of the egg dripping from it on top of the cheese. Add a little scallion and shredded *kasseri* on top. Roll once away from you, then fold the two sides over on top of the rolled part, brush with oil, and continue rolling until the pastry looks like a cigar. Continue in the same way with the remaining ingredients. Store in an airtight container and freeze at this point or go ahead and cook them.

4. Preheat the oven to 400°F. Arrange the rolls in a single layer on a greased baking sheet and brush them with the remaining oil and some egg. Sprinkle with the sesame seeds. Bake until golden brown, about 15 minutes. Serve immediately.

Makes 20 pastries; 8 to 10 servings

Pizzas, Calzones, and Empanadas

ll the recipes in this chapter are made with bread dough, pizza dough, or short dough, and they are all baked. The chapter starts off with a pizzette, which is nothing but a small pizza. To serve these preparations as *antipasti* or appetizers, you will slice the pizzas into smaller wedges than the typical slice. Then come three recipes for thicker pizzas or focaccia, Corsican-Style Pizza Flamiche (page 305) and Pissaladière (page 307) being two that are really something to taste. One doesn't associate pizza with Egypt, but there are pizzas in Egypt (page 308), an influence of Italian traders and tourists. Then come two Arab entries in the pizza pantheon, Ṣfīḥa (page 309) and Palestinian Thyme and Sesame Seed Pizza (page 310), both standards on the Middle Eastern meze table. The chapter concludes with calzones and empanadas and a couple of other enclosed stuffed baked doughs.

Pizzette di San Gennaro

San Gennaro (St. Januarius) was the Bishop of Benevento in A.D. 304, during the Roman Emperor Diocletian's persecution of the Christians. He was beheaded at Pozzuoli, and the story goes that the Romans had to have him beheaded because when they had thrown him to the lions, the animals refused to attack him. The miracle of San Gennaro, and the reason for the celebratory feast, is said to be the liquefaction of his preserved blood, contained in a vial in the Cathedral of Naples. This liquefaction happens two times a year at the Duomo (Cathedral) of Naples and at the Church of San Gennaro at Solfatara in Pozzuoli, at the spot where he was killed. (Not to be a stick-in-the-mud, but there is a scientific explanation for the liquefaction, which I can't go into here.)

There are many foods associated with the feast of San Gennaro, including these miniature pizzas made without cheese, and his martyrdom is celebrated from Benevento to the streets of Little Italy in New York. You will have some dough left over.

1 recipe Basic Bread and Pizza Dough (page 473)
Coarse cornmeal
6 small ripe tomatoes, each cut into 8 slices
16 salted anchovy fillets, rinsed and cut into thirds
¼ pound imported green olives, drained, pitted, and chopped
Extra-virgin olive oil
Dried oregano

1. Prepare the pizza dough and let rise as instructed.

2. Preheat the oven to 450°F.

3. On a lightly floured work surface, roll the dough out until thin and cut out 48 disks 2½ inches in diameter with a glass or pastry cutter, re-rolling the dough when necessary. Sprinkle a 16-inch-wide pizza baking pan or baking sheet with cornmeal. Arrange the disks on the baking sheet or pizza pan. Place a slice of tomato, an anchovy fillet piece, and a little of the chopped olive on top, then drizzle a bit of olive oil over each. Sprinkle with a little oregano.

4. Bake until the crust is golden on the edges, about 15 minutes. Serve hot.

Makes 48 pizzette; 12 servings

Making Pizzas

There are many different ways you can make pizzas, beyond the topping. They can be cooked at temperatures ranging from 350°F in a home oven to 900°F in a commercial wood-burning brick pizza oven. I tend to make pizzas in three different ways. Sometimes I make pizza on a large 16-inch pizza pan, either solid or perforated, or directly on a baking stone. The dough is about ⅓ thick, and I bake it at either 555°F for just a few minutes or at 450°F for a little longer. Or I make a thinner pizza, about ⅛ inch thick, which I cook for about 10 minutes at 400°F.

Pizza Margherita

The modern-day pizza has its roots in prehistoric times, when dough was thrown on top of hot rocks and cooked. Over time these flatbreads developed into the Roman placenta, *a kind of cake or focaccia that was sold by the* pistores clibanari *(bread brokers) of the markets. Today the pizza is sold by* pizzaiuoli *(or pizzaioli*), *pizza makers. This kind of flatbread, focaccia, or pizza was always food of the poor. Once the tomato arrived from America, a modern pizza could develop. The old* pizza aglio e olio, *with garlic and olive, could now become the* pizza alla marinara, *with tomatoes, garlic, oregano, and olive oil, as well as the famous* pizza Margherita. *It was made for the first time, so they say, in 1889 for Queen Margherita, the wife of Alfonso of Aragon, by a Neapolitan pizza maker, with tomatoes, mozzarella, olive oil, and basil. But this story is in dispute, as there was a second Margherita, Queen Margherita, wife of Italian king Umberto I, who, others maintain, went to the Capodimonte palace in Naples for this pizza. The greatest pizza maker at the time in Naples was Don Raffaele Esposito, owner of the celebrated Pietro il Pizzaiuolo. This pizza is based on the* pizza Margherita verace col sapore della tradizione *("the true pizza Margherita with the flavor of tradition") as it is prepared at Da Ciro Trianon at via Pietro Colletta, 42-44-46 in Naples.*

1 recipe Basic Bread and Pizza Dough (page 473)
Extra-virgin olive oil
3 tablespoons freshly grated Parmigiano-
  Reggiano cheese
1¼ pounds ripe tomatoes, peeled, seeded,
  chopped, and drained in a strainer for 1 hour
¾ pound fresh mozzarella cheese (buffalo's milk,
  if possible), diced
10 fresh basil leaves
Salt and freshly ground black pepper to taste

1. Prepare the pizza dough. Divide the dough into 2 balls and let rise as instructed.

2. Preheat the oven to 555°F with a large baking stone and let it stay at that temperature for 30 minutes.

3. Roll or stretch the dough out until 16 inches in diameter using either a rolling pin on a lightly floured work surface or by rotating the pizza while it's draped over your fist until about ⅓ inch thick. Place each crust on a 16-inch solid pizza pan or the baking stone sprinkled with cornmeal to prevent sticking. Or use a 16-inch perforated pizza pan, making sure the border of the dough is a little high than the center. Make indentations all over the pizza with your fingertips and grease the top, including the borders, with olive oil. Sprinkle the Parmesan evenly over the 2 pizzas, leaving a 1-inch border all around, then evenly distribute the tomatoes and mozzarella. Lay the basil leaves over the top and oil the top again. Season with salt and pepper.

4. Bake until the borders are charred in places and the top is dappled brown in certain places on the cheese, 8 to 9 minutes. Remove from the oven, let cool a minute or two, cut each pizza into 16 slices with a wheeled pizza pie cutter, and serve.

Makes two 16-inch pizzas;
12 servings each

Pizza al Formaggio #1

This pizza is made only with cheese. It would be best to use homemade ricotta cheese since the commercially made ricotta is too soft— that is, not drained enough and not flavorful enough. Also make sure that the mozzarella is drained. If using commercial ricotta, let it drain in a strainer for 2 hours.

1 recipe Basic Bread and Pizza Dough (page 473)
Extra-virgin olive oil
¾ pound fresh mozzarella cheese, shredded
¼ pound fresh ricotta cheese, preferably
  homemade (page 88)
Salt and freshly ground black pepper to taste
20 large fresh basil leaves, thinly sliced

1. Prepare the pizza dough. Divide the dough into 2 balls and let rise as instructed.

2. Preheat the oven to 450°F with a large baking stone for 30 minutes.

3. Roll or stretch each ball of dough out until 16 inches in diameter using either a rolling pin on a lightly floured work surface or by rotating the pizza while it's draped over your fist until about ⅓ inch thick. Place on a 16-inch solid pizza pan or baking stone sprinkled with cornmeal to prevent sticking or, preferably, use a 16-inch perforated pizza pan, making sure the border of the dough is a little higher than the center. Make indentations all over the pizza with your fingertips and grease the top, including the borders, with olive oil.

4. Place the pizzas in the oven until light brown, about 8 minutes. Remove from the oven and lay the mozzarella and ricotta all over the pizzas, leaving a 1-inch border all around. Season with salt and pepper, drizzle with a little more oil, and return to the oven until the borders are charred in places and the top is dappled brown in certain places on the cheese, 12 to 15 minutes.

5. Remove from the oven and sprinkle the basil over the pizza. Cut each pizza into 16 slices with a wheeled pizza pie cutter and serve hot.

Makes two 16-inch pizzas;
12 servings each

Pizza al Formaggio #2

Here's another all-cheese pizza, made with different cheeses from the previous pizza. This pizza is not rolled thin, but kept thicker and baked in a baking pan, not a pizza pan.

1 recipe Basic Bread and Pizza Dough
  (page 473), substituting ¾ cup cool water and
  ¼ cup warm milk for the warm water
2 large eggs
¾ cup freshly grated Parmigiano-Reggiano
  cheese
½ cup grated pecorino cheese
½ cup shredded mild provolone or *caciocavallo*
  cheese
2 tablespoons extra-virgin olive oil and more

1. Prepare the pizza dough and let rise as instructed.

2. Meanwhile, in a medium-size bowl, beat the eggs with the cheeses. After the dough has risen the first time, punch it down and knead in the 2 tablespoons of olive oil, then form the

The Home of Pizza

When I tell people that there are only about ten places in all of the United States that can make pizza, they will immediately tell me about such and such and how good it is. Often I'm familiar with the place they're mentioning and patiently apologize because I've had pizza in its home, in Naples, and that can be the only benchmark as far as I'm concerned. Furthermore, there are only nine individual pizzerias and the Bertucci's chain of pizzerias in New England that are U.S. members of the Italian organization known as Associazione della Vera Pizza Napoletana, an association dedicated to maintaining the integrity of pizza by defining what constitutes a true Neapolitan pizza—namely, that it must be mixed from "oo" flour, yeast, and water exclusively, kneaded by hand, and baked in a wood-burning oven. Is there a secret to perfect pizza? Giuseppe Leone of the Trianon da Ciro in Naples said that there is, when asked some years ago. He didn't say what it was, but I suspect it has to do with the quality of the flour used. There have to be other secrets though.

dough so it has a well in the center and pour in the cheese and eggs. Knead the dough again, making sure the eggs don't run out at first until you have a smooth ball of dough with all the eggs and cheese incorporated. At this point it will be very wet and sticky. Turn the dough out

Serving Pizza as an Antipasto

Remember when serving pizza as an antipasto that an antipasto serving is smaller than a normal slice of pizza. Cut the pizza into 16 slices rather than 8.

onto a well-floured work surface and sprinkle more flour on top. Knead the dough until a soft ball is formed and all the ingredients are incorporated. Cover and let rise for another hour.

3. Preheat the oven to 400°F. Grease a 9 x 12-inch baking pan with olive oil.

4. Roll the dough out on a floured surface until it is the same size as the pan. Transfer it to the pan and bake until light golden on top, about 20 minutes. Cut into portions and serve hot.

Makes one 9 x 12-inch pizza; 16 servings

San Vito's Pizza

This Sicilian specialty pizza known as sfinciuni di San Vitu *is called San Vito because it has been preserved and made for centuries*

by the sisters of the celebrated monastery in Palermo, the Convent of San Vito. Some recipes do not call for a second sheet of dough over the topping, but this recipe is probably closer to the original. In Antonino Traina's Nuovo vocabulario siciliano-italiano published in 1890, sfincia is described as a food made of a soft, swollen dough that is fried. The word derives from the Arabic word isfanj, which comes from the word for "sponge." The Arabic isfanj is described as a soft, yeasted dough fried in oil that one eats with honey. Even today the word means "donut" in North Africa.

1 recipe Basic Bread and Pizza Dough (page 473)

¼ cup extra-virgin olive oil

¼ cup chopped onion

3 tablespoons finely chopped fresh parsley leaves

½ pound boneless pork shoulder, trimmed of fat and cut into very small pieces (reserve ¼ cup of the fat, finely chopped)

One 6-ounce can tomato paste

2 links mild Italian sausage (about ½ pound), casings removed and meat crumbled

¼ cup chopped *soppressata* or other Italian salami

½ cup dry red wine

1 cinnamon stick

Cornmeal

¾ cup diced fresh mozzarella cheese

¼ cup diced young provolone or *caciocavallo* cheese

Salt and freshly ground black pepper to taste

1 tablespoon fennel seeds

1 large egg, beaten with 1 teaspoon water

¼ cup dry bread crumbs

1 teaspoon fresh or dried oregano

1. Prepare the pizza dough. Divide the dough into 2 balls and let rise as instructed.

2. In a large casserole, heat 2 tablespoons of the olive oil over medium heat, then cook the onion, parsley, pork, and tomato paste until sticking to the bottom of the casserole, stirring and scraping the bottom, about 5 minutes. Add the sausage meat and *soppressata* and continue to cook for 5 minutes, stirring and adding a few tablespoons of water if it is sticking too much. Add the red wine and cinnamon stick, reduce the heat to low, and simmer until very dense, 12 to 15 minutes. Remove from the heat and discard the cinnamon stick.

3. Preheat the oven to 400°F.

4. Roll the dough balls out into 2 disks each 16 inches in diameter and about ⅜ inch thick on a lightly floured work surface or by tossing and stretching. Lay the first pizza down on a large baking stone strewn with cornmeal or on a solid or perforated 16-inch pizza pan, making sure the borders are a little thicker than the center. Spread the sauce over the pizza, then sprinkle on the mozzarella, provolone or *caciocavallo*, and reserved pork fat, then season with salt and pepper and the fennel seeds. Cover with the other disk of dough and pinch the borders together to seal. Puncture the top of the pizza with a fork all over. Brush the top of the pizza with the egg wash.

5. Put the pizza in the oven. Meanwhile, heat a small nonstick skillet with the bread crumbs over medium heat, and as they begin to turn golden, moisten with the remaining 2 tablespoons olive oil, then remove from the heat. When the pizza begins to turn golden brown, about 25 minutes,

pull it out of the oven for a moment and spread the bread crumbs and oregano on top and finish baking, about 5 minutes.

Makes one 16-inch stuffed pizza; 12 servings

Where to Eat Pizza in Naples

Here's a few places you shouldn't miss, but check locally before going to make sure of the hours: Trianon da Ciro, via Pietro Coletta 42-46 (553 94 26); Bellini, via Costantinopoli, 79/80 (45 97 74); Brandi, salita S. Anna di Palazzo, 1 (41 69 28) (those in the know say it's past its time, though); Di Matteo, via dei Tribunali 94 (45 52 62); Europcoom, via Marchese Campodisola, 4/8 (552 13 23); Pizza Lombardi, via Benedetto Croce 59 (552 07 80); Da Michele, via C. Serale, 1/3t (553 90 24) (go here to see what a purist's pizza is like); 'O Calamaro, via Campi Flegrei, 30a (570 43 87); Gorizia, via Bernini 29 (578 22 48).

Pizza Ericina

This pizza comes from the little medieval mountain town of Erice overlooking Trapani on Sicily's west coast. It is traditionally made with the first cold-pressed extra-virgin olive oil, called olio d'oliva di prima spremitura, *which is very green.*

Erice was in Arab hands from the ninth century until 1077, when the Norman Count Roger returned it to Christian rule. The great Muslim traveler Ibn Jubayr left us a description of Erice and the surrounding area when he visited in 1184. On his way to Trapani, he passed by many farms that he said were very fertile. "We spent a night in Alcamo which had a souk and mosque. The inhabitants of the town and all the farmers were all Muslims." He said that Trapani had the most beautiful port, that the lands of western Sicily were populated by Muslims and Christians, and that the women of Erice were the most beautiful in Sicily. The Sicilian gastronome Pino Correnti tells us that one of the great examples of cucina arabo-sicula *(Arab-Sicilian cuisine) is found in Erice, a classic couscous made in Signor Alestra's "Il Ciclope" Ristorante, where he jealously guards the recipe.*

1 recipe Basic Bread and Pizza Dough (page 473)
Extra-virgin olive oil
2 to 3 teaspoons dried oregano
2 to 3 teaspoons fresh rosemary, finely chopped
4 large garlic cloves, finely chopped
Salt and freshly ground black pepper to taste

1. Prepare the pizza dough and let rise as instructed.

2. Preheat the oven to 400°F.

3. Roll the dough out on a lightly floured work surface until ⅜ inch thick and place in a 12 x 17-inch baking pan greased with olive oil. Sprinkle the top evenly with the oregano, rosemary, and garlic and make indentations over its entirety with your fingertips, pushing the herbs and garlic down into the soft dough. Season with salt and pepper and drizzle a little more live oil over the top.

4. Bake until puffy and golden in places, about 25 minutes. Cut into small pieces and serve.

Makes one 12 x 17-inch pizza; 16 servings

Pizza Sarde

This is a great Sardinian pizza, which I had at the Ristorante Il Girasole da Pepper in Sana Teresa di Gallura on the very northern tip of Sardinia. It was topped with very thin slices of the earthy local prosciutto di cinghiale, *a cured ham made with wild boar. This is not a product imported into this country, and I don't know anyone who makes it, so you will have to use prosciutto. A search on the Internet might turn up something.*

1 recipe Basic Bread and Pizza Dough (page 473)
½ pound eggplant, peeled and cut into ⅛-inch-thick slices
Extra-virgin olive oil
¼ pound black olives, drained, pitted, and cut in half
½ pound fresh mozzarella cheese, thinly sliced
3 ounces very thinly sliced *prosciutto di Parma*

1. Prepare the pizza dough. Divide the dough into 2 balls and let rise as instructed.

2. Preheat a ridged cast-iron skillet or griddle over high heat for 20 minutes. Brush the eggplant with olive oil and cook until browned with grid marks on both sides, 6 to 8 minutes. Remove from the pan and set aside.

3. Preheat the oven to 450°F with a large baking stone for 30 minutes.

4. Roll or stretch both balls of dough out until 16 inches in diameter, using either a rolling pin on a lightly floured work surface or by rotating the pizza while it's draped over your fist until about ⅛ inch thick. Place on a 16-inch solid pizza pan or baking stone sprinkled with cornmeal to prevent sticking or, preferably, use a 16-inch perforated pizza pan, making sure the border of the dough is a little higher than the center. Make indentations all over the pizza with your fingertips and grease the top, including the borders, with olive oil. Layer the eggplant, olives, and mozzarella over both pizzas.

5. Bake until the cheese is dappled with brown spots and the crust is golden, 13 to 15 minutes. Remove from the oven, layer the prosciutto slices on top, cut into slices, and serve.

Makes two 16-inch pizzas; 16 servings each

Pizza Rustica #1

This is a version of pizza rustica *(there are many) that my children particularly like, which is interesting because they would otherwise never eat arugula. Both the prosciutto and arugula go on after the pizza is cooked. You can bake both pizzas at the same time if you like. This* pizza rustica *is from Naples, but the term applies to several pizzas found in southern Italy.*

1 recipe Basic Bread and Pizza Dough (page 473)

Extra-virgin olive oil

¾ pound fresh mozzarella cheese, thinly sliced or shredded

¾ pound fresh ricotta cheese, preferably homemade (page 88)

Salt to taste

4 to 5 ounces baby arugula

6 ounces thinly sliced *prosciutto di Parma*, pulled apart into smaller pieces

1. Prepare the pizza dough. Divide the dough into 2 balls and let rise as instructed.

2. Preheat the oven to 450°F with a large baking stone for 30 minutes.

3. Roll or stretch the 2 balls of dough out until 16 inches in diameter using either a rolling pin on a lightly floured work surface or by rotating the pizza while it's draped over your fist until about ⅛ inch thick. Place on a 16-inch solid pizza pan or baking stone sprinkled with cornmeal to prevent sticking or, preferably, use a 16-inch perforated pizza pan, making sure the border of the dough is a little higher than the center. Make indentations all over the pizza with your fingertips and grease the top, including the borders, with olive oil. Evenly distribute the mozzarella and ricotta cheese over both crusts. Season with salt.

4. Bake until the cheese is melted and dappled slightly with brown spots, about 15 minutes. Remove from the oven, scatter the arugula and prosciutto over both pizzas, then cut each into 16 slices and serve.

Makes two 16-inch pizzas;
16 servings

Pizza Rustica #2

This Neapolitan pizza pie filled with cheeses and eggs is an enclosed pizza made from short dough or pizza dough, so it is more like a torta *or savory pie than it is a pizza. I prefer it made with pizza dough, and that's the recipe I give you here. This recipe is quite different from the preceding* pizza rustica *and is more substantial, so the portions can be cut up smaller. There are many versions of* pizza rustica *throughout Italy and it's unclear what makes them "rustic."*

1 recipe Basic Bread and Pizza Dough (page 473)

½ pound fresh ricotta cheese, preferably homemade (page 88)

2 or 4 large eggs

½ cup freshly grated Parmigiano-Reggiano cheese

5 ounces *provola*, provolone, or *caciocavallo* cheese, cut into small dice

5 ounces fresh mozzarella cheese, cut into small dice

5 ounces salami, cut into small dice

2 tablespoons finely chopped fresh parsley leaves

Salt and freshly ground black pepper to taste

1 large egg white, beaten until foamy

1. Prepare the pizza dough. Divide the dough into 2 balls and let rise as instructed.

2. Pass the ricotta cheese through a strainer or food mill into a bowl if fresh or homemade, then beat in 4 eggs (if using commercial ricotta, add only 2 eggs), the Parmigiano, *provola*, mozzarella, salami, and parsley and season with salt and pepper.

3. Preheat the oven to 375°F with a baking stone.

4. On a lightly floured work surface, roll out the 2 balls of dough about ⅛ inch thick and place one on a 16-inch pizza pan. Spread the stuffing evenly over the surface, leaving about a 1-inch border along the edge. Cover with the other piece of dough and crimp the edges together to seal in the stuffing. Brush the top with egg white.

5. Place the pizza pan in the oven, and bake until golden, about 30 minutes. Slice into 16 segments, either wedges or squares.

Makes one 16-inch stuffed pizza;

12 to 16 servings

Provola *Cheese*

Provola cheese is a Sicilian and southern Italian cheese of the *pasta filata* type (page 95), as is mozzarella. Similar to *caciocavallo*, it is made from buffalo milk and aged six to tenth months. Its unique pear shape, weighing about 3 pounds, makes it easily identifiable. It can be replaced with *caciocavallo* or *scamorza*.

Pizza con Pancetta

This is my interpretation of a Sardinian focaccia I once had that I found particularly good and well suited as a morsel to pass at a party. The pancetta should be chopped into about ⅜-inch cubes. Pecorino pepato *cheese is a young pecorino cheese with peppercorns thrown into the curd. It can usually be found in Italian markets. See page 321 for sources for* scamorza *cheese if you don't find it locally.*

1 recipe Basic Bread and Pizza Dough (page 473)
Extra-virgin olive oil
1½ cups chopped *pancetta* (about 5 ounces)
1 cup chopped *scamorza* cheese
1 cup chopped *pecorino pepato* cheese
Dried oregano
Salt and freshly ground black pepper to taste

1. Prepare the pizza dough. Divide the dough into 2 balls and let rise as instructed.

2. Preheat the oven to 450°F with a large baking stone for 30 minutes.

3. Roll or stretch the dough out until 16 inches in diameter using either a rolling pin on a lightly floured work surface or by rotating the pizza while it's draped over your fist until about ⅛ inch thick. Place on a 16-inch solid pizza pan or baking stone sprinkled with cornmeal to prevent sticking or, preferably, use a 16-inch perforated pizza pan, making sure the border of the dough is a little higher than the center. Make indentations all over the pizza with your fingertips and grease the top, including the borders, with olive oil. Sprinkle the pancetta, cheeses, and oregano evenly over the surfaces of both pizzas, leaving a 1-inch border. Season with salt and pepper.

4. Bake until the cheese is dappled with brown spots and the crust is golden, 10 to 13 minutes. Cut into slices and serve immediately.

Makes two 16-inch pizzas; 16 servings

Pizza Calabrese

This pizza pie from Calabria can legitimately be called a pie, for it is made in a cake or pie pan, with the topping enclosed in a sheet of dough, as you would a pie. The savory flavors of this pizza pie are a memorable mix of tuna, anchovies, olives, and capers. The crust is slightly flaky and should look rough when you seal the two sheets together.

1 recipe Basic Bread and Pizza Dough (page 473)

2 tablespoons chopped pork lard

Salt and freshly ground black pepper to taste

6 tablespoons extra-virgin olive oil

1¼ pounds ripe tomatoes, peeled, seeded, and very coarsely chopped

One 3-ounce can imported tuna in olive oil, drained and flaked apart

10 salted anchovy fillets, rinsed and chopped

⅓ cup pitted imported black olives, drained and cut in half

1 tablespoon salted capers, rinsed

1. Prepare the pizza dough. After it has risen the first time, work the lard and a little salt and a good amount of pepper into the center of the dough, punch down, knead a little, then cover and let rise for another hour.

2. In a large skillet, heat 4 tablespoons of the olive oil over medium heat, then cook the tomatoes with a little salt until much of the liquid has evaporated, but not until the tomato pieces are mushy, about 15 minutes, stirring occasionally. Set aside.

3. Preheat the oven to 350°F.

4. Grease a 10-inch cake pan with 1 tablespoon of the olive oil. Divide the dough into 2 pieces, one somewhat larger than the other one, then roll both out until ⅛ inch thick on a flour-strewn work surface. Because the dough now has some lard in it, you will want to make sure you use flour to keep the dough from breaking apart. Lay the larger piece down to cover the sides and bottom of the cake pan. Layer in the tomatoes, then the tuna, anchovies, olives, and capers. Cover with the smaller piece of dough, fold the edges over, and pinch to close tightly. Brush the top with the remaining 1 tablespoon olive oil.

5. Bake until golden brown, about 1¼ hours. Remove from the oven and cut into 16 wedges for serving.

Makes one 10-inch stuffed pizza; 16 servings

Stuffed Pork Crackling and Ricotta Pizza

This is as rustic as it gets. This enclosed pizza from Calabria, the region known as the toe of the Italian boot, is called pitta inchiusa, *which means "stuffed pizza" in dialect. It is made with* ciccioli, *also called* frittoli, *which are pork cracklings, the crispy solid bits left over from the rendering of pork fat. This pizza may also be called* alla Pugliese *because it is also popular in Apulia, or simply* pizza di ciccioli, *"crackling pizza." When it is made with ricotta and pork crackling, it is called* sfogliata. *The dough could also be stuffed with cooked greens, red bell peppers, or fresh sardines in thick tomato sauce.*

To prepare the cracklings, unless you buy them packaged, allow 2 hours to render about 5 pounds of pork fat over low heat to produce about ¾ pound cracklings. Personally, I find the cracklings (pork rinds) made by Guerrero called chicharrones *to be the light and fluffy kind that work so well in this pizza. They are available in most supermarkets or by writing to Guerrero, Consumer Affairs, P.O. Box 226706, Los Angeles, CA 90022.*

Pizza

1 recipe Basic Bread and Pizza Dough (page 473)
2 tablespoons pork lard, at room temperature
1 small egg, beaten
Salt and freshly ground black pepper to taste

Topping/Stuffing

Pork lard for greasing
¼ pound pork cracklings (one 4-ounce bag)
½ pound fresh ricotta cheese, preferably
  homemade (page 88)

1. Prepare the pizza dough. After the dough has had its first rise, punch it down and knead the lard into it as well as most of the beaten egg, saving a little of it for brushing the pizza later, and season with salt and pepper. Knead the dough until it is a smooth, elastic ball again, then place back in the bowl, cover with a towel, and let rise until it has doubled in bulk, 1 to 1¼ hours. If at any time the ball of dough becomes too sticky from water or fat, sprinkle with flour.

2. Preheat the oven to 450°F.

3. Divide the dough into 2, one piece slightly larger than the other, and grease a 14-inch pizza pan with lard. On a heavily floured work surface, roll the larger piece of dough out until large enough so that it overlaps the edges of the pan a bit. Layer the crackling over the crackling, then distribute the ricotta evenly over it, and cover

with the other ball of rolled out dough. Crimp the edges closed. Brush the top with the remaining egg.

4. Bake until golden brown, about 25 minutes.

Makes one 14-inch stuffed pizza; 16 servings

Piadina

The poet Giovanni Pascoli called *piadina* the national dish of the Romagnoli, as it used to be the daily bread of the peasants of Romagna. Today, it has become a fashionable accompaniment to local salami as an appetizer. It used to be cooked on a *testa*, an earthenware disk (sort of like a baking stone), but cast iron is used today. This dish is also called *piada* or *piè*, both deriving from the word *piadena*, a wide bowl or flat, low vase. *Piadini* are made into a ball with flour, lard, and baking soda, then flattened and rounded before being grilled until charred in a cast-iron skillet. After they're cooked, some salami, ham, or sausages or a local cheese is laid on top and they are eaten with Sangiovese wine.

Corsican-Style Pizza
Flamiche

A flamiche is usually a kind of leek tart made in northern France, Burgundy, and Picardy, but when I had it in Corsica, it was an incredibly delicious sweet onion and smoked bacon pizza with lots of local cheese, a little red chile, bay leaf, and olive oil. Corsican pizzas are very good. They are a little thicker than Italian pizzas, but not by much. The toppings go right to the edge, so there is hardly a visible crust to speak off. The real difference comes with the richer tastes derived from using a variety of Corsican cheeses, such as brocciu, *which is like ricotta, or* u rustinu, *a soft sheep's milk cheese that is un-pressed and has a red rind. Corsican or Corsican type cheeses are not imported or made in the United States, so I've devised the substitutes below, which work very well. If you can't find some of the cheeses I call for, then use a combi-nation of ricotta, Gruyère, and goat cheese. This recipe is based on the pizza I had at La Chariot in Algajola on the northern coast of Corsica.*

1 recipe Basic Bread and Pizza Dough (page 473)

1 cup extra-virgin olive oil

3¾ pounds sweet onions, such as Maui or Vidalia, thinly sliced

3 ounces plain soft goat's milk cheese, crumbled

3 ounces Tronchon cheese (semi-soft Spanish sheep's milk cheese), thinly sliced

¼ pound fresh mozzarella or *burrata* (see opposite) cheese, thinly sliced or shredded

¼ pound fresh ricotta cheese, preferably homemade (page 88)

¼ pound smoked slab bacon, cut into 1-inch matchsticks

2 dried red chiles, seeded and crumbled

9 small bay leaves

Salt and freshly ground black pepper to taste

1. Prepare the pizza dough. Let rise as instructed.

2. Meanwhile, in a large skillet, heat the olive oil over medium heat, then cook the onions until golden, about 35 minutes, stirring occasionally.

3. Preheat the oven to 400°F.

4. On a lightly floured work surface, roll the dough out so it fits into a 12 x 17-inch baking sheet and is ¼ inch thick, and make indentations over its entirety with your fingertips. Arrange the cheeses so they are intermingled over the top of the pizza. Spread the onions evenly over the top, then sprinkle on the bacon strips evenly. Sprinkle with the chiles, place the bay leaves around, and season with salt and black pepper.

5. Bake until golden and the bacon is a little crispy, 30 to 35 minutes. Cut into serving portions and serve hot.

Makes one 12 x 17-inch pizza; 15 servings

Burrata Cheese

Burrata is a fresh southern Italian cheese made in the same manner as mozzarella with whole cow's milk and cream. The mozzarella-like cheese is formed around a rich, buttery cream, which is extremely soft. It is made in the United States in limited production and most likely found in Italian markets. One excellent *burrata* is made in California by the Gioia Cheese Company; phone 562-942-2663.

Miniature Focaccia with Tomato and Mushroom

These elegant little morsels apparently were served as an hors d'oeuvre at the Ristorante Cava-

letto and Doge Orseolo in Venice, a restaurant popular in the 1950s that no longer exists. They called them pizzette di Sciullo *and, unlike most* pizzette, *or small pizzas, which are usually thin crusted, these have a thick crust, almost like a focaccia. You will have some dough left over.*

1 recipe Basic Bread and Pizza Dough (page 473), prepared substituting milk for ½ cup of the water and 2 tablespoons unsalted butter for the olive oil, and adding 1 large egg

Extra-virgin olive oil for brushing and drizzling

½ pound fresh mozzarella cheese, cut into small dice

1¼ pounds ripe tomatoes, cut in half, seeds squeezed out, grated against the largest holes of a grater, skins discarded, and drained in a strainer for 30 minutes

8 salted anchovy fillets, rinsed and each cut into 4 or 5 pieces

½ pound button mushrooms, stems discarded and caps sliced ¹⁄₁₆ inch thick

Dried oregano

Salt and freshly ground black pepper to taste

1. Prepare the dough and let rise as instructed.

2. Preheat the oven to 400°F.

3. Roll the dough out on a lightly floured work surface into a large disk about ⅓ inch thick. Cut out 36 disks 2 inches in diameter, re-rolling the dough when necessary, and place on a greased baking sheet or a cornmeal-strewn baking stone about 1½ inches apart. Brush each pizza with a little olive oil. Cover the top with a few pieces of mozzarella, 1 teaspoon or so of tomato, a piece of anchovy, 2 or so slices of mushrooms. Sprinkle with oregano, salt, and pepper, then drizzle some more olive oil over the pizzas.

4. Bake until the crust is golden brown and the sauce bubbling, about 20 minutes. Serve hot.

Makes 36 pizzette; *12 servings*

Mistocchine

In the province of Emilia-Romagna in Italy, on the streets of Bologna, vendors once sold a snack called *mistocchine*, which were small *focaccette*, or small pizzas, made of chestnut flour.

Pissaladière

The Provençal pissaladière *is an oven-baked focaccia or* torta *topped with caramelized onions, black Niçoise olives, and anchovies. It is a specialty street food of Nice and often sold by street vendors or at local markets. Even though it is thought of as street food,* pissaladière *is many times served as an appetizer. The word* pissaladière *derives from the fermented anchovy sauce known as* pissala, *which is related to the classical Roman* garum *and is used on the pizza. These words derive from the Provençal dialect word in Nice for salted fish,* pèi salat. *But the essential feature of a true* pissaladière *are the onions. They are cooked down in olive oil until a kind of marmalade and fantastically delicious. Some cooks add eggs or milk to the dough and others layer the onion half as thick as the crust.*

In Provence, home cooks would have bought their dough at a local bakery or made it with short dough. I prefer it with a yeasted dough, closer to a pizza. Pissadella *is the Ligurian version of the* pissaladière *and it usually also contains bits of tomato. It is a typical Ligurian* torta *that is attributed to the sixteenth-century Genoese admiral Andria Doria; in fact, it is also known as* piscialandrea *(*pizza all'Andrea*), as well as* sardenaira.

1 recipe Basic Bread and Pizza Dough (page 473)

¼ cup extra-virgin olive oil

3½ pounds yellow onions, very thinly sliced

3 large garlic cloves, very finely chopped

Salt and freshly ground black pepper to taste

1 teaspoon dried *herbes de Provence*

2 cloves

Cornmeal for sprinkling

1 tablespoon anchovy paste

⅓ cup pitted black Niçoise olives (about 45), drained

20 salted anchovy fillets, rinsed and split lengthwise

1. Prepare the pizza dough and let rise as instructed.

2. Meanwhile, in a large skillet, heat the olive oil over medium heat, add the onions and garlic, season with salt and pepper and the *herbes de Provence* and cloves, and cook covered, until light golden, about 40 minutes, stirring occasionally. Uncover, reduce the heat to medium-low, and cook until all the moisture has evaporated and the onions are cooked down to a marmalade looking substance, about 30 minutes, stirring occasionally and making sure the onions don't burn or stick to the skillet, adding 1 tablespoon of water or so if they do. Remove and discard the cloves if easily found, and set the onions aside.

3. Preheat the oven to 450°F with a baking stone for 30 minutes.

4. Roll the dough out on a lightly floured work surface into a thin rectangle that covers the bottom of a 12 x 17-inch baking sheet dusted with cornmeal. Cover the dough with a damp cloth and let rest 30 minutes.

5. Remove the cloth and spread a thin layer of anchovy paste on top. Spread the onion mixture over that evenly without leaving a crust border on 2 sides. Arrange the olives and the anchovy fillets in a crisscross pattern and season lightly with pepper.

6. Bake until the crust has browned, about 20 minutes. Cut into squares of your choosing and serve hot or warm.

Makes one 12 x 17-inch pie;
8 to 16 servings

Pizza from Egypt

One doesn't associate pizza with Egypt, but there are many foreign culinary influences there, the most prominent being Lebanese, Turkish, Greek, and Italian, but also Syrian, Libyan, and Indian. Years ago my brother-in-law, Omar al-Qattan, had returned from a trip to Egypt and told me that I just had to have the pizza. I was quite skeptical, but he said the best pizza in Egypt was in Alexandria. The Baraka restaurant on the Maydan Orabi in Alexandria is a small pizza and faṭīr *(page 341) joint that serves some very good pizza. I had a pizza with* basṭurmā, sujuk, *cheese, tomatoes, and parsley that was marvelous and original. They also served a variety of other pizzas, including a take-off on the classic Neapolitan Pizza Margherita (page 296) with tomatoes, cheese, and black olives, as well as pizza with shrimp, cheese, a bit of spinach, and tomatoes and pizza with calamari, both of which were great.*

The two important ingredients for this pizza, the basṭurmā, *a spiced and dried beef filet cut into very thin slices, and the* sujuk, *a spicy beef sausage, can be found in most Middle Eastern markets as well as from Ohanyan's Bastirma and Soujouk Company, 3296 W. Sussex Way, Fresno, CA 93722 (phone: 559-243-0800), or you can order it on the Internet from www.shamra.com/index.asp.*

1 recipe Basic Bread and Pizza Dough (page 473)
Cornmeal
Extra-virgin olive oil
4 plum tomatoes, peeled, seeded, and chopped
2 large garlic cloves, finely chopped
1 ounce *basṭurmā*, thinly sliced
2 ounces *sujuk*, thinly sliced
½ pound fresh mozzarella cheese, diced
1 ounce *kashkaval* cheese (page 92), cut into small dice
Salt and freshly ground black pepper to taste
2 tablespoons finely chopped fresh parsley leaves

1. Prepare the pizza dough. Divide the dough into 2 balls and let rise as instructed.

2. Preheat the oven to 555°F. with a large baking stone for 30 minutes.

3. Roll or stretch the dough out until 16 inches in diameter using either a rolling pin on a lightly floured work surface or by rotating the pizza while it's draped over your fist until about ⅓ inch thick. Place on a 16-inch solid pizza pan or baking stone sprinkled with cornmeal to prevent sticking or use a 16-inch perforated pizza pan, making sure the border is a little higher than the center. Make indentations all over the pizzas with your fingertips and brush the pizza with a little olive oil, including the borders. Cover the top of each with the tomatoes and garlic, leaving at least a 1-inch border around the edge. Arrange the *basṭurmā* and *sujuk* evenly around the pizzas, then top with the mozzarella and *kashkaval* cheese. Sprinkle with salt and pepper, then drizzle some more olive oil.

4. Bake until the crust is golden brown and the sauce bubbling, about 9 minutes. Remove from the oven, sprinkle on the parsley, let cool a few minutes, cut into slices, and serve.

Makes two 16-inch pizzas; 16 to 32 servings

Ṣfīha

These Arab open-faced meat pies, a kind of small pizza also called laḥm bī ajīn, *are made with the basic Arabic-style pita bread dough. Some Syrian cooks mix yogurt into the dough. The version I had at the al-Az restaurant in Damascus was a dough called* raqīq *(also* ruqāq), *a kind of buttery puff pastry, but this recipe is based on a Palestinian version. The filling is made with spiced lamb, pine nuts, onions, spices, and sometimes tomatoes, all mashed in a mortar until a paste. It is garnished with yogurt or pomegranate seeds. The name ṣfīḥa comes from the root word meaning "to flatten."*

1 recipe Basic Bread and Pizza Dough (page 473)

3 tablespoons extra-virgin olive oil

⅓ cup pine nuts

1 pound lean lamb sirloin, ground or chopped

1 large onion, chopped

1 medium-size ripe tomato, peeled, seeded, chopped, and drained of liquid for an hour

6 tablespoons finely chopped fresh parsley or coriander (cilantro) leaves

1 tablespoon pomegranate molasses

1 teaspoon freshly ground allspice

¼ teaspoon ground cinnamon

2 teaspoons salt

Freshly ground black pepper to taste

¼ teaspoon cayenne pepper

Plain yogurt or pomegranate seeds for garnish

1. Prepare the bread dough. After the first rise, punch the dough down and divide into 24 balls. Flatten each ball slightly with a rolling pin on a lightly floured work surface until about 2 inches in diameter. Arrange the balls on a lightly floured kitchen counter, cover with a kitchen towel, and let rest for 1 hour.

2. In a small skillet, heat 1 tablespoon of the olive oil over a medium-high heat and cook the pine nuts until golden, about 1 minute.

3. Meanwhile, prepare the topping. In a large bowl, mix the lamb, onion, tomato, parsley, pomegranate molasses, allspice, cinnamon, salt, black pepper, and cayenne. Place the filling in-

gredients in a food processor and run until smooth and pasty.

4. Preheat the oven to 500°F. Grease 2 baking sheets with the remaining 2 tablespoons olive oil.

5. Roll the balls of dough into disks 4 inches in diameter. Place 1 to 2 tablespoons of the meat mixture in the center of each disk and press down gently, spreading it over the surface of the disk, but leaving a border. Arrange on the baking sheets and bake until crispy on the edges and bubbling, 8 to 10 minutes.

6. Sprinkle the pine nuts over the pies and serve hot or at room temperature garnished with a dollop of yogurt or sprinkling of pomegranate seeds.

Makes 24 pies; 12 servings

Palestinian Thyme and Sesame Seed Pizza

In Palestine, a favorite breakfast preparation is manaqish bi'l-zaᶜtar *(pronounced* mana-EESH-bee-ZAA 'tar*). A thin flatbread, a kind of pizza, is spread with* zaᶜtar *mixed with olive oil and baked in a hot oven. Whenever I visited the family of my Palestinian former wife, we would always have them and I just loved them. Some American palates might find them too bitter, but that can be taken care of with the addition one of two typical garnishes, either crumbed fresh feta cheese or a dollop of strained yogurt,* labna. Manaqish *is also served as a snack and as a meze, and is sometimes offered with hot mint tea and feta cheese on the side. Although* zaᶜtar *is the name for thyme, it actually is a spice mix used by Palestinian and Lebanese cooks for this* dish, for mixing with olive oil as a dip, and for sprinkling on plain labna or other cheeses. Za‘tar is easy enough to make or you can buy some at Middle Eastern markets.

1 recipe Basic Bread and Pizza Dough
  (page 473), with 1 teaspoon sugar added
½ cup za‘tar (page 277)
¾ cup extra-virgin olive oil
Labna (strained yogurt; page 56) for garnish
  (optional)
Crumbled feta cheese for garnish (optional)

1. Prepare the bread dough. Once it has risen, divide the dough into 12 balls. Roll each ball out on a lightly floured work surface until ¼ inch thick and about 6 inches in diameter. Place the disks on a baking sheet or leave on the counter surface, cover with a clean kitchen towel, and let rest for 30 minutes in a warm, draft-free place to rise a bit.

2. Preheat the oven to 450°F.

3. In a medium-size bowl, stir the za‘tar and olive oil together. Make indentations on the dough surfaces with your fingertips. If you haven't already, arrange the disks on a baking sheet, in batches if you have to. Spread a heaped tablespoon of the za‘tar over the surface of each, leaving a very narrow border all around.

4. Bake until slightly brown on the edges and bubbling, about 5 minutes. Serve hot or warm with or without one or both garnishes of yogurt and feta cheese.

Makes 12 disks; 12 servings

Prosciutto and Five-Cheese Calzone

This oversized calzone is meant to be cut into strips for serving as an antipasto after it becomes golden brown in a hot oven. Take it easy with the cheese; too many American cooks overcheese their pizzas and calzone, turning what should be a sublime experience into a drippy, gooey unappetizing mess.

½ recipe Basic Bread and Pizza Dough
  (page 473)
¼ pound fresh mozzarella cheese, thinly sliced
  or diced
¼ pound mixed cheeses (equal amounts of thinly
  sliced, diced, or grated soft *pecorino pepato*,
  fontina Val d'Aosta, Parmigiano-Reggiano, and
  caciocavallo or provolone cheese)
¼ pound thinly sliced *prosciutto di Parma*
1 large egg, beaten with 1 teaspoon water

1. Prepare the bread dough.

2. Preheat the oven to 450°F with a large baking stone for 30 minutes.

3. Roll the dough out until it is 14 inches in diameter. Distribute the cheeses and prosciutto over the surface of the disk, leaving a 1½-inch border. Fold the disk over to form a large crescent, crimping the edges together with a fork. When crimping the calzone, make sure you press down firmly and that there are no space, otherwise, cheese will ooze out while baking. Lightly grease a pizza pan and place the calzone on it. Make 3 small slits in the top of the calzone so the steam can escape. Brush the calzone with the egg wash and bake until golden

brown, 17 to 20 minutes. Remove from the oven, let rest on a wire rack for a few minutes, cut into strips, and serve.

Makes 1 calzone; 8 servings

The History of the Calzone

One of the first written recipes for calzone appears in the fifteenth-century cookbook of Maestro Martino, called *Libro de arte coquinaria*. There it is called a *caliscioni* and the dough is made with sugar and rosewater. Carol Field, author of several books on Italian food, suggests that calzone may have existed in medieval Latin as early as 1170, according to a reference in Padua, although the historian Luigi Sada, also the author of several cookbooks on the region of Apulia, suggests a statute from Bisceglie around 1400 as being the first appearance of the word. Chef Carlo Middione, the author of *The Food of Southern Italy*, makes the plausible suggestion of a Muslim introduction in medieval Arab times. If this is true, then the calzone, not to mention the empanada, would be related to the very old fried pastry of the medieval Arab world, Sanbūsak (page 353).

Rustic Mountain-Style Calzone from Sicily

This big calzone, called 'mpanata di muntagna *(mountain empanada) or* pastizzu *(small pie) in* Sicilian, *is a rustic calzone—they actually tend to use the word* empanada *in Sicily—made in the rural mountainous areas of the island, although on the coasts it can be made with fish. Elsewhere in Sicily cooks add anything from eel and vegetables to chopped meat and homemade sausages. It's considered rustic since traditionally it is made with gathered wild greens. Although my recipe calls for pork sausage, which is authentic, that addition is not always found. If you can't find the mix of borage, beet leaves, and broccoli leaves I call for, you can use my suggestions. The idea is that the empanada should be filled with vegetables. All of Sicily's calzone and focaccia like this one, called by a variety of names such as* 'mpanate, scacciate, pastizzi, cuddure, cudduredda, ravazzate, focacce, fuazza, fucaccia, sciaguazze, crispeddi, *and* panini farciti, *probably derive from Spanish cuisine during the time that Spain ruled Sicily in the sixteenth and seventeenth centuries. There may be an even older Arab influence on both the Spanish and Sicilian preparations. Although this calzone is typically eaten as a snack, I serve it as an antipasto by cutting it into ½-inch-thick slices.*

1 recipe Basic Bread and Pizza Dough (page 473) with 1 tablespoon sugar added along with the salt

1 pound mild Italian sausage, casings removed and meat crumbled

¼ cup extra-virgin olive oil

½ pound spinach, heavy stems removed, washed well, and drained well

6 large beet leaves or ¼ pound baby Swiss chard leaves, washed well, dried, and cut into strips

Handful of broccoli leaves or ¼ pound baby
   mustard leaves, washed well, dried, and cut
   into strips

Handful of borage leaves or ¼ pound arugula,
   washed well, dried, and cut into strips

¼ pound cauliflower, broken into florets

4 medium-size fresh artichokes, trimmed to the
   bottoms (page 205) and sliced

½ cup shelled fresh or frozen peas

Salt and freshly ground black pepper to taste

3 tablespoons pine nuts

3 tablespoons golden raisins

3 tablespoons finely chopped fresh parsley leaves

1 tablespoon fresh thyme leaves

2 tablespoons finely chopped fresh mint leaves

2 tablespoons finely chopped fresh basil leaves

1 stalk celery, finely chopped

1 large egg, beaten

1. Prepare the bread dough, allow to rise once,
then divide the dough into 2 and allow to rise a
second time.

2. Place the crumbled sausage in a medium-
size skillet and turn the heat to medium. Cook
the sausage until all the pink is gone, about 30
minutes, breaking up the lumps into smaller
pieces. Remove the sausage with a slotted spoon
to paper towels to drain.

3. In a large skillet, heat the olive oil over
medium-low heat, then cook the spinach and
other greens, cauliflower, artichokes, and peas
until soft, about 30 minutes, stirring and tossing.
Season with salt and pepper. Add the reserved
sausage, pine nuts, raisins, herbs, and celery; stir,
and cook for another 5 minutes, stirring.

4. Preheat the oven to 350°F.

5. Roll out both dough balls on a lightly
floured work surface until 10 inches in diameter.
Place half the stuffing on each disk and fold over
to make a large half-moon, crimping the edges
closed. Brush the calzone with the egg wash and
make a slit in the top in 2 places to let steam
escape. Place the calzone on a greased baking
sheet and bake until golden, about 45 minutes.
Let rest 15 minutes, then slice and serve.

Makes 2 calzone; 12 servings

Variation: Replace the pork sausage with eel.
To prepare the eel, ask the fishmonger to skin it
for you and remove the central bone. Chop the
eel and add it when you would the sausage.

Prosciutto, Olive, and Mushroom Calzone from Venice

Rusteghi *is a typical Venetian focaccia or calzone
about 6 inches in diameter and about 1½ inches
thick. The dough is a sticky yeast dough similar
to the one used in another Venetian bread called*
ciabatta. *The dough is thick with many holes
from a long proofing. The meaning of the Venetian word* rusteghi *is "rustic," and this focaccia
is quite rustic in taste and slightly moist and
springy. This recipe is based on the one that I had
at a little street stall bakery at 1465 Calle de la
Madonete in Venice years ago. Stuffed inside were
sliced marinated wild mushrooms, prosciutto,
and chopped green olives. The instructions here
specify a heavy-duty mixer. If you don't have one
and must make the dough by hand, follow the
kneading instructions on page 473.*

3 ounces prosciutto, thinly sliced or chopped

⅔ cup pitted and chopped green olives

⅔ cup Marinated Mushrooms (page 455 or from a jar)

One ¼-ounce package active dry yeast

1 cup hot water (105 to 115°F)

5 tablespoons hot milk

1 tablespoon olive oil

3¾ cups unbleached all-purpose flour or bread flour

1 tablespoon salt

Cornmeal as needed

1. In a medium-size bowl, mix the prosciutto, olives, and mushrooms.

2. Heat the metal mixing bowl of a stand mixer under hot running water and dry. Place the yeast in it and pour in the water, milk, and olive oil. Let rest, covered with a kitchen towel, for 10 minutes to allow the yeast to activate. Attach the paddle to the mixer and attach the bowl. Mix on the lowest setting for 2 minutes. Remove the paddle and attach the dough hook. Add the flour and salt and mix for 2 minutes on the lowest setting. Turn the setting to the next highest one and mix until the dough is one big ball, about 2 more minutes. Lightly oil a bowl, place the dough in it, and cover with plastic wrap. Leave in a turned-off oven for 1¼ hours. The dough should be full of air bubbles and very elastic and sticky.

3. Cut the dough into 4 pieces on a floured work surface and roll each into a cylinder. Flatten each cylinder and stretch into a 10 x 4-inch rectangle using your hands and dimpling the surface of the dough with your fingertips.

Divide the stuffing into 4 and lay one portion on top of a rectangle of dough, leaving room at the edges so it doesn't spill out, and fold over, pinching and shaping the dough so that the stuffing is enclosed. Repeat with the remaining dough and filling

4. Cover a large baking or cookie sheet with parchment paper or waxed paper and lay the bread rectangles on top. Dimple the tops again by pushing down gently with your fingertips. Cover with a kitchen towel and leave to rise in a turned-off oven for 2 hours.

5. Remove the baking sheet from the oven and preheat to 425°F with a baking stone. Gently sprinkle some coarse cornmeal on the baking stone so the bread won't stick and lay the stuffed breads on top. Spray some water over the bread and over the next 10 minutes, spray 2 more times, then bake another 20 minutes (30 minutes in all), until golden. Remove from the oven and place on a wire rack to cool for a few minutes. Slice into whatever thickness you like and eat hot or at room temperature.

Makes 4 calzones; 8 to 16 servings

Tomato, Olive, and Pecorino Calzone from Apulia

Although calzones are thought of as street food, which they are, they make excellent appetizers, too. This calzone is typical of the southern Italian region of Apulia. Any kind of calzone could be made, but some favorite stuffings are those with sausage and mozzarella cheese; or tomatoes, olives, anchovies, sliced onions, and capers; or with caramelized sweet red onions, anchovies,

Eating Panini in Venice

In the early 1990s, I lived in Venice a while, spending my days wandering, writing, studying, and eating. One day I crossed over the Rio di Noale and the name changed to Via V. Emanuele and then to Via Maddelena. After a walk down this largish, for Venice, street until the Calle de Ancoretta, I stopped at the Bar Central to have a drink and some *tramezzini*, a kind of *panini* made with white bread rather than a roll. They were made with a dense white bread, with the consistency of a mildly hard Wonder bread, but with ten times the taste. The crusts were sliced off and the bread cut into triangles. I ordered two, one with prosciutto, sliced marinated mushrooms, and a light spread of mayonnaise. The other was roasted red pepper, mozzarella, mortadella, and lots of mayonnaise. I ate these standing up and it was the best thing I ate that day.

capers, olives, and perhaps golden raisins. Other calzones might include Parmigiano-Reggiano, caciocavallo, or pecorino cheese or fresh basil and a hard-boiled egg. In the Abruzzi, one finds calzone stuffed with ricotta and mortadella. They also can be found under the names panzerotti, calzengiedde, *or* caviciuncelli *in Foggia in Apulia. Some cooks like to deep-fry rather than bake them.*

1 recipe Basic Bread and Pizza Dough (page 473)
¼ cup extra-virgin olive oil
2 large white onions (about 1 pound), sliced
2 cups peeled, seeded, and chopped ripe tomatoes
⅔ cup pitted and chopped imported black olives
1 tablespoon salted or brined capers, rinsed or drained
6 salted anchovy fillets, rinsed and chopped

2 tablespoons finely chopped fresh parsley leaves
Salt to taste
4 ounces pecorino cheese, cut into ⅛-inch dice (about 1 cup)
1 large egg, lightly beaten with 1 tablespoon water
Semolina (durum wheat flour) or cornmeal for sprinkling (optional)

1. Prepare the pizza dough and let rise once until the dough has doubled in size. Divide the dough into 8 balls, arrange on a tray, cover with a kitchen towel, and let rise a second time, about 1¼ hours.

2. In a large casserole, preferably earthenware (which enhances the flavor), heat the olive oil over medium heat, then cook the onions until soft and turning color, 12 to 15 minutes, stirring occasionally. Add the tomatoes, olives,

capers, anchovies, and parsley, mix well, and season with salt. Cook until thicker, about 10 minutes, stirring occasionally. Increase the heat to high, add the pecorino, and cook 2 to 3 minutes, stirring. Remove from the heat and transfer to a medium-size bowl.

3. Preheat the oven to 400°F with a pizza stone, if desired.

4. Push each ball of dough down with the palm of your hand and roll or stretch into a disk with the thickness of a pizza, about ⅛ inch thick and 8 to 10 inches in diameter. Divide the tomato-and-onion stuffing among them, flip over one-half of the dough to form a half-moon, and pinch the edges together with a fork to seal them. Puncture the tops so that the calzones can breath while baking. Brush each calzone with the egg wash. Place on an oiled or semolina-strewn baking sheet or stone and bake until the tops are golden brown, 15 to 20 minutes. Let cool on a wire rack for a few minutes before serving warm.

Makes 8 calzone; 16 servings

Fish and Tomato Calzone from Bari in Apulia

This calzone Barese is filled with tomato sauce and fried mackerel. It reminds me of the same intense flavors of the fried mackerel sandwiches prepared by the boatmen in Istanbul, near the Galata Bridge. If you can't find mackerel, you will want to use an equally oily fish, such as bluefish, yellowtail, or sardines.

1 recipe Basic Bread and Pizza Dough (page 473)
¼ cup extra-virgin olive oil
2 large white onions (about 1 pound), sliced
2 cups peeled, seeded, and chopped ripe tomatoes
Salt and freshly ground black pepper to taste
6 cups pure, virgin, or pomace olive oil for frying
1 pound mackerel fillets
All-purpose flour for dredging
¼ cup melted pork lard
1 large egg, beaten lightly with 1 tablespoon water
Semolina (durum wheat flour) for sprinkling (optional)

1. Prepare the pizza dough and let rise once until the dough has doubled in size. Divide the dough into 8 balls, arrange on a tray, cover with a kitchen towel, and let rise a second time, about 1¼ hours.

2. In a large casserole, preferably earthenware (which enhances the flavor), heat the olive oil over medium heat, then cook the onions until soft and turning color, 12 to 15 minutes, stirring occasionally. Add the tomatoes and cook until thicker, about 10 minutes, stirring a few times. Season with salt and pepper.

3. Preheat the frying oil to 375°F in a deep fryer or an 8-inch saucepan fitted with a basket insert.

4. Dust the mackerel pieces with flour, tapping off any excess, and deep-fry without crowding them until golden, about 2½ minutes. Drain on paper towels and set aside. Let the frying oil cool completely, strain through a porous paper filter, and save for a future use.

5. Preheat the oven to 400°F.

6. Push each ball of dough down with the palm of your hand and roll or stretch into a disk

with the thickness of a pizza, about ⅛ inch thick and 8 to 10 inches in diameter. Brush the dough with the melted lard. Divide the tomato sauce among them, spreading it on top somewhat thick, then place several pieces of fish on top. Fold the dough over to form a half-moon and pinch the ends together with the tines of a fork. Puncture the tops so that the calzones can breath while baking. Brush each calzone with the remaining melted lard mixed in with the egg and water.

7. Place the calzone on an oiled or semolina-strewn baking sheet or stone and bake until the tops are golden brown, 15 to 20 minutes. Let cool on a wire rack a few minutes before serving warm.

Makes 8 calzone; 16 servings

Mackerel

The mackerel is a sleek, dark blue fish streaked with dark, wavy lines running halfway down its sides; it can grow to a foot and a half. Many people don't care for this very nutritious fish because of its dark skin and high oil content, declaring the flavor to be "fishy." But in southern Italy as well as Turkey, it is a very popular fish grilled or in a calzone. In Bartolomeo Scappi's *Opera (dell'arte del cucinare)*, published in 1570, he recognizes that the mackerel of Venice is better than that found in Rome and recommends grilling the fish.

Spinach, Ricotta, Pine Nut, and Raisin Calzone in the Old Style

This traditional calzone, called calzone antica, *old-style calzone, is found in rural Apulia where the cook is as likely to use Swiss chard, beet greens, spinach, and the particularly delightful escarole. In Italian cooking, a recipe described as* antica, *"antique" or "old," does not necessarily mean it has an ancient history. It can simply mean that it is the traditional way of cooking it or a simple way.*

1 recipe Basic Bread and Pizza Dough (page 473)
⅓ cup raisins
1 cup tepid water
10 ounces fresh spinach, heavy stems removed and washed well
3 tablespoons extra-virgin olive oil
1 garlic clove, crushed
⅓ cup pine nuts
1 pound fresh ricotta cheese, preferably homemade (page 88)
Semolina (durum wheat flour) for sprinkling (optional)

1. Prepare the pizza dough and let rise once until the dough has doubled in size. Divide the dough into 8 balls, arrange on a tray, cover with a kitchen towel, and let rise a second time, about 1¼ hours.

2. Preheat the oven to 400°F. Put the raisins in the water to soak until you need them.

3. Place the spinach with only the water adhering to its leaves from the last rinsing in a large saucepan and steam over medium-high

heat until it wilts, 4 to 5 minutes. Drain well in a colander, pressing the excess liquid out with the back of a wooden spoon, and chop coarsely.

4. In a large casserole, preferably earthenware (which enhances the flavor), heat the olive oil over medium heat, then cook the garlic until it just begins to turn light brown. Discard the garlic. Add the pine nuts and cook until almost golden, about 2 minutes. Be careful not to burn them. Add the spinach, stir, and cook for 3 minutes. Drain the raisins, add them to the casserole, and cook for another 2 minutes. Remove from the heat and set aside.

5. Push each ball of dough down with the palm of your hand and roll or stretch into 8 disks with the thickness of a pizza, about ⅛ inch thick and 8 to 10 inches in diameter. Divide the spinach mixture among them and place a heaping tablespoonful of ricotta cheese on top. Fold the other half of the dough over to form a half-moon and pinch closed with the tines of a fork. When crimping the calzones, make sure you press firmly down and that there are no spaces, otherwise cheese will ooze out when baking. Puncture the tops so that the calzones can breath while baking.

6. Place the calzones on an oiled or semolina-strewn baking sheet or stone and bake until golden on top, 15 to 20 minutes. Let cool on a wire rack for a few minutes before serving.

Makes 8 calzone; 16 servings

Variation: Steam a head of escarole until wilted and the core or heart is softer. Drain well and chop together with several anchovy fillets and some imported pitted black olives. Mix this with the ricotta or omit the cheese, whatever your preference. Stuff the calzones with this mixture.

Beet, Black Olive, and Chile Calzone from Basilicata

This spicy hot calzone, called calzone Lucana, *is typical home fare from Basilicata. In Matera, these calzone, distinguished by being made with beets, are very popular. Sometimes the beets are replaced by spinach or Swiss chard. Although not traditional with spicy food, adding several tablespoons of ricotta is a very nice touch. Lucana is another name for Basilicata, the region that is the so-called instep of the Italian boot.*

1 recipe Basic Bread and Pizza Dough (page 473)
6 tablespoons extra-virgin olive oil
4 medium-size beets (about 1 pound), peeled and very thinly sliced
2 dried red chiles, crumbled
Salt to taste
¾ pound imported black olives (about 40 olives), drained, pitted, and chopped
4 salted anchovy fillets, rinsed and chopped
Semolina (durum hard wheat) for sprinkling (optional)

1. Prepare the pizza dough and let rise once until the dough has doubled in size. Divide the dough into 8 balls, arrange on a tray, cover with a kitchen towel, and let rise a second time, about 1¼ hours.

2. In a large skillet, heat the olive oil with the beets over medium-high heat, then cook until slightly soft, about 20 minutes, stirring fre-

Basilicata

This poor southern region of Italy is almost always forgotten by food and travel writers. For centuries it has been known as a land of bandits. The English traveler Thomas Hoby in 1550 mentions a land of "marvelous plentie of corn and all kindes of fruites." But he also reports, with a sense of foreboding, the Bosco del Pellegrino, a forest which is "verie jeapardous to passe. For there do the banisshed men of the kingdom lie . . . and many a man is robbed and slaine in the yere by them." Hoby comments on the cooks of Basilicata, mentioning the 364 "friers," but not mentioning the 1,000-egg omelette they are supposed to have served to the Holy Roman Emperor Charles V (1500–1558) fifteen years before.

Half of Basilicata is mountainous and the other half is hilly, desolate, and barren. The access to the sea is not easy, and all these factors contribute to the cuisine, which can be thought of as *cucina povera*, "poor people's cuisine." This means it's a cuisine based on vegetables, mushrooms, and wild greens. Among the meats, lamb is the most common and popular, and it finds its way into many stews, such as *agnello ai funghi* (lamb and mushrooms). Offal is very popular, and there are countless recipes for innards stewed, baked, or grilled. Pasta dishes are cheap and therefore found richly flavored in Basilicata, including the famous *strangolapreti*, "priest stranglers."

quently. Add the chiles, season with salt, and cook for 1 minute, then toss in the olives and anchovies and cook another 2 minutes. Set aside.

3. Preheat the oven to 400°F.

4. Push each ball of dough down with the palm of your hand and roll or stretch into a disk with the thickness of a pizza, about ⅛ inch thick and 8 to 10 inches in diameter. Divide the stuffing mixture among the disks. Fold half of the dough over to form a half-moon and pinch closed with the tines of a fork. Puncture the tops so that the calzones can breath while baking.

5. Place the calzones on an oiled or semolina-strewn baking sheet or stone and bake until the tops are golden, 15 to 20 minutes. Let cool on a wire rack for a few minutes and serve.

Makes 8 calzones; 16 servings

Calzone Napoletana

The word calzone *comes from the Italian word meaning "pant leg," and indeed this disk of dough is filled like pants, with delicious cheeses and a variety of meats. There are many varieties of calzone, but this one is typical of Naples. The* salami Napoletana *called for is sometimes called sweet* soppressata, *but it is frequently replaced with prosciutto by many cooks. Often, when calzone are made in the home, the cook will use commercial lard or even* 'nzugna, *a lard that has not been purified through rendering. This one from Naples is similar to the* panzerotti *of Apulia.*

1 recipe Basic Bread and Pizza Dough (page 473)

2 large eggs

½ pound fresh ricotta cheese, preferably homemade (page 88)

Salt to taste

½ cup freshly grated Parmigiano-Reggiano cheese

6 ounces fresh mozzarella cheese, cut into tiny dice

2 ounces *salami Napoletana* (or any salami), sliced ¹⁄₁₆ inch thick and slivered

1. Prepare the pizza dough and let rise once until the dough has doubled in size. Divide the dough into 8 balls, arrange on a tray, cover with a kitchen towel, and let rise a second time, about 1¼ hours.

2. Preheat the oven to 400°F.

3. Lightly beat 1 egg in a medium-size bowl. Push the ricotta through a sieve or food mill into the bowl. Season with salt and stir in the Parmigiano, mozzarella, and salami.

4. Roll each of the disks of dough out on a lightly floured work surface into circles as thin as a pizza and about 7 inches in diameter. Divide the ricotta mixture among the disks. Fold one edge of the disk over onto the other to form a half-moon and pinch the ends together with a fork. When crimping the calzones, make sure you press firmly down and that there are no spaces, otherwise cheese will ooze out when baking. Puncture the tops so that the calzones can breath while baking. Beat the remaining egg and brush each calzone with it. Place on a baking stone or pan in the oven and bake until golden brown on top, about 20 minutes. Let cool on a wire rack for a few minutes before serving.

Makes 8 calzone; 16 servings

Cheese Crescents from Crete

These little half moon–shaped pies called kalitsounia *are found in Crete in many varieties, including a sweet one. This particular variety is made with the Greek version of ricotta cheese called* mizithra *or* myzithra. *When I was last in Crete, in a mountain village near Chania, I ate* kalitsounia *made with* malaka, *a local soft cheese similar to mozzarella but made from sheep's milk. Some Greek cooks use orange juice to make the dough, it's quite nice. Others use olive oil instead of butter to make the short dough, while some cooks deep fry the crescents instead of baking them. The sweet versions usually use cinnamon, too.*

2 cups unbleached all-purpose flour

¼ cup (½ stick) cold unsalted butter

2 teaspoons salt

⅔ cup water

½ pound fresh *mizithra* or ricotta cheese, preferably homemade (page 88)

1 large egg, beaten

2 tablespoons sesame seeds

1. In a medium-size bowl, mix the flour, butter, and 1 teaspoon of the salt and cut the butter into the flour with a pastry cutter until it looks like oatmeal. Add the water to form a ball. Once the ball of dough is smooth, cover it with plastic wrap and leave in the refrigerator for 1 hour.

2. Preheat the oven to 350°F.

3. In a medium-size bowl, mash the *mizithra* with the remaining 1 teaspoon salt.

4. Roll the dough out ⅛ inch thick on a lightly floured work surface. Cut out as many 4-inch rounds as you can, re-rolling the dough scraps when necessary. Put a heaping tablespoon of cheese in the center of each round, fold over to form a crescent, and crimp closed with the tines of a fork. Arrange the pastries on a greased baking sheet. Brush all the pastries with the egg, sprinkle the sesame seeds over them, and bake until golden, about 30 minutes. Serve hot or warm.

Makes 30 crescents; 10 servings

"The origin and the beginning of all good things in life lies in pleasing the stomach."

—EPICURUS (341–270 B.C.)

Baked Scamorza, Ricotta, and Salami Pastry Coins

These southern Italian pastries called pasticetti rustici *are disks of* pasta frolla *(short dough) stuffed with salami, ricotta, and* scamorza *cheese. Scamorza is a soft mozzarella-type cheese originally made in the Abruzzi and Molise provinces of Italy with water buffalo milk. Today it is made with cow's milk. Two fine* scamorza *cheeses are made in the United States by F. Cappiello Dairy Products, Schenectady, New York (www.capiello.com), and the Calabro Cheese Corporation of East Haven, Connecticut (www.calabrocheese.com).*

Double recipe Basic Short Dough (page 475)

¼ pound fresh ricotta cheese, preferably homemade (page 88)

2 large eggs, separated

2 ounces salami, cut into small dice

Salt and freshly ground black pepper to taste

¼ pound *scamorza* cheese, cut into small dice

1. Prepare the short dough.

2. In a medium-size bowl, whisk the ricotta, egg yolks, 1 egg white, and the salami together and season with salt and pepper. Stir in the *scamorza*.

3. Preheat the oven to 400°F.

4. Roll the short dough out until very thin and cut out as many 2½-inch-diameter rounds as you can, collecting the dough and re-rolling the scraps as necessary. Place a heaping teaspoonful of stuffing on top of one round and cover with another, pinching the sides closed with a fork. Arrange the *pasticetti* on a greased

baking sheet, brush with the remaining beaten egg white, and bake until golden, about 25 minutes. Remove from the oven and let rest 10 minutes before serving.

Makes 32 pastries

Red and Green Bell Pepper Empanada from Valencia

When I first had this empanada, stuffed with bell peppers and simmered with some tomatoes and garlic until thick, at the Restaurant "Port" on the Esplanada Bella Vista in Denia on Valencia's coast, I was surprised that they called it tortilla Española. A tortilla usually refers to a frittata, but I didn't care because it was a hot, blue-sky day at this restaurant on the beach, and the empanada was served in slices and just delicious. It is not necessary to peel the peppers if you don't mind the skin, but if you do, then roast them at 425°F until blackened, about 40 minutes, let cool, then peel and seed them. If you do this, you need only cook them half the time stated in step 1 below.

¼ cup extra-virgin olive oil

3 large garlic cloves, finely chopped

1¼ pounds red bell peppers, seeded

1¼ pounds green bell peppers or long green peppers (Italian frying peppers or *peperoncini*), seeded

1¾ pounds ripe tomatoes, cut in half, seeds squeezed out, grated against the largest holes of a grater, and skins discarded

2 teaspoons hot Spanish paprika

2 teaspoons freshly ground cumin seeds

Salt and freshly ground black pepper to taste

Double recipe Basic Short Dough (page 475) or Basic Puff Pastry Short Dough for Empanadas (page 475)

1 large egg, beaten

1. In a medium-size skillet, heat the olive oil with the garlic over medium heat; when the garlic begins to turn very light brown, add the peppers and cook until softened, about 15 minutes, stirring. Add the tomatoes, paprika, and cumin; reduce the heat to low, and cook until the liquid has evaporated and the sauce is thick and dense, about 40 minutes, stirring occasionally. Season with salt and pepper. Remove from the heat and let cool.

2. Prepare the dough according to the directions. After the 2 balls of dough have rested in the refrigerator for an hour and been removed for a few minutes to soften, roll each of them out until ⅛ inch thick, and cut out twenty 4-inch rounds altogether, re-rolling the dough as necessary.

3. Preheat the oven to 400°F.

4. Place about 1 tablespoon of stuffing in the center of each round, fold it over, and crimp closed with the tines of a fork. Arrange the empanadas on a greased baking sheet, brush with the egg wash, and bake until golden, about 25 minutes. Let cool for 10 minutes on a wire rack before serving.

Makes 20 empanadas; 10 servings

Lamb and Salami Empanadas from Majorca

In Mallorquin, the Majorcan dialect of Catalan spoken on the Balearic Island of Majorca, this empanada is called panades d'anyell llises *and is a savory lamb pie usually made around Easter. The recipe is adapted from Elizabeth Carter's* Majorcan Food and Cookery. *The panades, though, are quite different from empanadas made on the Iberian peninsula. They are shaped and stuffed very much the way the Lebanese would make kibbe (page 363); the dough is formed into a ball, then hollowed out with one's finger. The cavity of this empanada, now looking like a small potbellied pot, is filled with the stuffing and a small piece of flattened dough, a lid, is placed on top before you bake it (rather than frying it). The short dough, too, is unique in being made with orange juice and olive oil. When I make these, I don't bother making the little lid. The* sobressada *called for in the recipe is quite different from the Italian salami known as* soppressata; *it is spicier and leaner and can be ordered through www.donajuana.com. For serving purposes, you can cut each empanada in half.*

Dough

3 cups all-purpose unbleached flour, sifted
¾ teaspoon salt
¼ cup diced pork lard
½ cup extra-virgin olive oil
Juice of 1 orange
½ cup water

Stuffing

¾ pound boneless lamb shoulder, trimmed of excess fat and cut into bite-size pieces

Juice of 1 lemon
Salt and freshly ground black pepper to taste
1½ ounces salt pork, rind removed if necessary and cut into small dice
½ pound *sobressada* (Catalan-style salami), thinly sliced and cut into quarters

1. Make the dough. Pour the flour and salt into a large bowl and cut the pork lard in with a pastry cutter until it looks like dry oats. Add the olive oil, orange juice, and water and knead until you can form a round, smooth dough. Cover with plastic wrap and leave to rest in the refrigerator for 1 hour.

2. Make the stuffing. In a glass or ceramic bowl, marinate the lamb in the lemon juice, salt, and pepper for 4 hours in the refrigerator.

3. Preheat the oven to 400°F.

4. Pinch off some dough to make lids if you want. Then take an egg-size piece of dough and hollow it out with your forefinger, shaping it into a small pot with straight sides and thin walls by holding the ball in one hand and forming the hole with the forefinger of the other, turning the ball of dough around your extended finger as if it were a spindle and you were making pottery. Stuff in the salt pork first, then some of the marinated lamb, and finally a few slices of salami. Cover each with a lid, if making one, and pinch and fold over the overlapping edge of the dough. Arrange in a baking dish and bake until golden, 30 to 40 minutes. Serve hot or warm.

Makes 12 to 14 empanadas; 12 to 14 servings

Minorcan Salt Cod, Spinach, and Lettuce Empanadas for Midday

In Catalonian lands, of which Minorca, the second largest of the Balearic Islands off Spain, is part, cooks make a kind of Catalonian pizza called coca. *They can be flat like a pizza or folded over like a calzone. Usually, when they're served in the turnover style, they are cut in half or sliced for smaller tapas-size bites. These particular empanadas or stuffed baked turnovers called* coca noïs per menjar al mitgdia, *or "empanada for midday snack" in Catalan (a dialect of which is spoken on the island) refers to a calzone-like empanada.*

1 recipe Basic Bread and Pizza Dough (page 473)
1 pound fresh spinach, washed well and heavy stems removed
6 ounces salt cod, soaked in water to cover for 3 days, changing the water 2 times a day, and drained
1 tablespoon extra-virgin olive oil
2 tablespoons unsalted butter
1 head Boston lettuce, damaged leaves removed, washed well, dried, and chopped
8 large garlic cloves, finely chopped
½ cup finely chopped fresh parsley leaves
2 tablespoons heavy cream
2 large egg yolks
2 large eggs, beaten
Semolina or cornmeal

1. Prepare the bread dough.
2. Put the spinach in a large pot with only the water adhering to the leaves from their last rinsing, then cook, covered, over high heat until it begins to wilt, about 4 minutes, stirring occasionally. Drain well, squeezing out the excess water by pushing a wooden spoon against it in a strainer. Chop finely.

3. Place the salt cod in medium-size saucepan of water heated to just under a boil, then poach the fish at a gentle simmer until it almost flakes, about 30 minutes. Drain and chop very finely.

4. In a casserole, heat the olive oil with the butter over medium-high heat until the butter melts, then cook the salt cod, spinach, lettuce,

What to Do With Salt Cod

Salted cod is a dried fish product popular in Spain, France, Italy, and Greece, but it is imported to the Mediterranean from northern European countries or Canada. Salt cod is usually found sold by the side in Italian markets. Some supermarkets carry already-cut-up salt cod in small wooden boxes, which are usually from Canada. Salt cod must be soaked in multiple changes of water to be made ready for cooking. Place the salt cod in a basin or pan of cold water and leave it for two to three days in the refrigerator, changing the water twice a day. Any cartilage, bone, or skin can be removed at this point, and it is now ready for use in the recipe. If you find that you're not going to cook it, then wrap it properly and freeze until it is needed. Some salt cod products are presoaked and will be so labeled.

garlic, and parsley together until much of the remaining liquid has evaporated, about 6 minutes, stirring. Set aside in a bowl, allowing it to cool, then stir in the cream, egg yolks, and 1 whole egg.

5. Roll the dough out on a lightly floured work surface until ⅛ inch thick and cut out seven 8-inch-diameter disks. Place 3 to 5 tablespoons of the stuffing in the center of each and fold the disk over to seal, crimping the edges closed with the tines of a fork. Arrange the empanadas on a large semolina- or cornmeal-strewn baking sheet, cover with a kitchen towel, and let rest inside a turned-off oven, covered with a kitchen towel, for 45 minutes.

6. Remove the baking sheet from the oven and preheat to 400°F. Brush the *coques* (plural) with the remaining beaten egg and bake until golden, about 30 minutes. Remove from the oven and let them cool to warm. Slice in half and serve.

Makes 7 empanadas; 14 servings

Catalonian Spinach Empanadas with Raisins and Pine Nuts

These delectable empanadas called panadons amb espinacs *are filled with fresh baby spinach leaves tossed with golden raisins and pine nuts. The combination of spinach, raisins, and pine nuts is well known elsewhere in the Mediterranean, especially Sicily.*

1 recipe Basic Short Dough (page 475)
1 pound baby spinach, stems removed and
    washed well

An Empanada You Would Not Eat

At one time unscrupulous traders would put inferior or unknown ingredients into empanadas and the preparation acquired a bad reputation, as we see in the picaresque tale in Francisco de Quevedo, the seventeenth-century Spanish satirical writer, who told the story of an *empanada de ajusticiuiado,* supposedly made of the flesh of an executed criminal.

⅓ cup golden raisins
¼ cup pine nuts
2 tablespoons extra-virgin olive oil
1 garlic clove, finely chopped
½ teaspoon salt
1 large egg, lightly beaten

1. Prepare the short dough according to the directions. After it has rested in the refrigerator for an hour and been removed for a few minutes to soften, roll the dough out until ⅛ inch thick and cut out ten 4-inch rounds, re-rolling the dough as necessary. Set aside.

2. Put the spinach in a large pot with only the water adhering to the leaves from its last rinsing, then cook, covered, over high heat until it begins to wilt, about 4 minutes, stirring occasionally. Drain very well in a colander, pressing out the excess water with the back of a wooden spoon. Chop the spinach and, in a medium-size bowl, toss it with the raisins and pine nuts.

3. In a medium-size skillet, heat the olive oil with the garlic over medium heat, then cook until the garlic begins to turn very light brown, 1 to 2 minutes, stirring frequently so it doesn't burn. Add the spinach mixture, season with salt, and cook for 2 to 3 minutes. Remove from the heat and let cool.

4. Preheat the oven to 425°F.

5. Place a tablespoon of spinach stuffing in the center of each round of dough, fold over, and pinch the edges shut with a fork. Brush with the beaten egg and bake until golden, about 20 minutes. Let cool a few minutes on a wire rack before servings.

Makes 10 turnovers;
5 to 10 servings

Fried Turnovers

I n this chapter you will be introduced to all those fried turnovers that you
may remember from your travels, or had at a local Mediterranean-style
restaurant, or have seen or heard about and only wished you could get
your hands on a recipe. The first ten recipes in this chapter are from
North Africa, and if you've never had a North African *brīk* (pages 329–333),
then this is the place you want to start. Sinking your teeth into a crisp, golden
brown triangle that explodes in flavor, and with egg yolk, is quite an experience.
Don't forget to lean over slightly so you don't dribble on your shirt.

Following the North African treats are two recipes from Turkey and one from
Greece, made with phyllo pastry; these recipes are for meze that you will find
virtually everywhere in Turkey and Greece, and if you haven't already, you will
fall in love with them and be delighted to make them at home. Following the
phyllo pastry fritters are a round-robin of recipes from Sicily and Italy using
either short dough, bread dough, or pizza dough. These are all delicious, but the
Panzerotti (page 345) and Fried Dough with Fried Shrimp, Crispy Chard, and
Zucchini Flowers (page 346) are just so unique I must encourage you to give
them a try.

Toward the end of the chapter are seven recipes for traditional empanada-style
fritters from the Mediterranean. These are classics that you will encounter in
your travels and even in literature. Starting with the famous calzone (page 348),
you will also find the Arab Sanbūsak (page 353), a simply amazing preparation,
and Empanadillas (page 356), which are associated with Valencia.

Brīk with Eggs

In Tunisia, a brīk (pronounced BREEK) is a deep-fried savory pastry stuffed with a variety of ingredients that is very popular as a street food. This brīk is called brīk bi'l-ᶜaḍam and its main stuffing is a raw egg, which goes into every brīk, no matter what kind. This street food is also known in Algeria, where it is called būrāk, and in Morocco, where it is known as brīwat. All these words apparently derive from the Ottoman Turkish börek, which in turn may derive (perhaps excepting the word brīwat) from the Persian barg, meaning "leaf." The Turkish cookbook writer Ayla Esen Algar mentions one account that attributes the invention of the börek to Bugra Khan (died 994), a ruler of eastern Turkistan, from where it gradually spread westward to Khorasan and finally to the Mediterranean. She says that the börek appeared in Turkey before the Turks.

The dough used for making brīk is called malsūqa in Tunisia. It is a thin phyllo-like sheet made from very fine semolina flour. In Algeria, this thin dough is called diyūl; and warqa, meaning "leaf," in Morocco, where it is made with sifted white flour. In place of phyllo dough, Chinese egg roll wrappers found in any supermarket work perfectly for making brīk. There are several ways to fold the dough if it is circular. Fold two sides in, slightly overlapping them so you have a rectangle with convex edges. Fold the convex edges over, slightly overlapping them to make a square. Place the stuffing in the middle and fold one edge over to make a triangle. Or you can roll the brīk up like a cigar, as they like to do in Algeria. They are then fried in olive oil or vegetable oil until golden. The brīk will come out crispy brown on the outside with the egg yolk and white being runny. The Tunisians love it this way, but if you are not wild about the idea of runny eggs, use only the yolk from a small egg or use a soft-boiled egg.

Tunisians also eat brīk in a particular way. Someone who is truly adept will start right in the middle where the runny egg is, the secret being not to allow any of the egg to fall. Others like to work from the outside in, leaving the egg to last. In any case, brīk are meant to be eaten with the fingers.

6 cups olive oil, olive pomace oil, or vegetable oil for frying
1 small onion, grated
¼ cup finely chopped fresh parsley leaves
Salt and freshly ground black pepper to taste
8 Chinese egg roll wrappers, 6 inches square (about ¼ pound)
8 small to medium-size eggs
1 large egg white, lightly beaten

1. Preheat the frying oil in a deep fryer or an 8-inch saucepan fitted with a basket insert to 375°F.

2. Mix the onion and parsley in a fine-mesh strainer and plunge into boiling salted water for 2 minutes. Drain well, then season with salt and pepper.

3. Place an egg roll wrapper on a plate. Spoon a heaping tablespoon of the onion mixture in the center. Form a small well in the mixture and carefully break an egg into the center. Sprinkle some salt and pepper over the yolk and fold one

corner of the wrapper over to meet another, forming a triangle. Seal the edges by rubbing with the egg white or water. (Make them one at a time.) Pick the brīk up with two hands by the corners, place in the hot oil, and cook until golden brown, 30 seconds to 1 minute. Don't worry if the edges aren't completely sealed or if some of the egg white has run off, because the hot oil will quickly puff the edges together and all will be fine.

4. Remove from the oil with a skimmer or lift the fitted basket insert and drain on paper towels for a minute. Continue making and cooking the remaining brīk. Serve without utensils, mopping up the egg with the fried piece of egg roll wrapper. Let the frying oil cool completely, strain through a porous paper filter, if necessary, and save the oil for a future use.

Note: Notice that you use small or medium eggs for this recipe.

Makes 8 pastries; 8 servings

Brīk with Tuna and Egg

A brīk *is a messy food to eat, but fun and very tasty. They are often sold by street vendors, but can also be found in restaurants as meze. There is a variety of* brīk *to choose from, and a vendor will cook up what you want fresh. Once the pastry triangle slips into the hot oil, you await this crunchy golden morsel expectantly. Out it comes and you sink your teeth in, bending over slightly so nothing drips on your clothes. I first had this pastry in Djerba, a beautiful island off the coast of southern Tunisia. This egg-*

and tuna-stuffed brīk *called* brīk bi'l-tūnn *is very popular in Tunisia and found everywhere in that country. Use the best brand of imported tuna packed in olive oil you can find.*

6 cups olive oil, olive pomace oil, or vegetable oil for frying
1 tablespoon shredded Gruyère cheese
1 small onion, very finely chopped
2 tablespoons very finely chopped fresh parsley leaves
One 3-ounce can imported tuna in olive oil, drained (you may want to save this oil for any of the vegetable salads in "Salads and Other Cold Vegetable Dishes")
1 tablespoon salted or brined capers, rinsed or drained and chopped if large
1 teaspoon freshly ground black pepper
1 tablespoon clarified butter or unsalted butter, softened
8 Chinese egg roll wrappers, 6 inches square (about ¼ pound)
8 small to medium-size eggs
Salt to taste
1 large egg white, lightly beaten

1. Preheat the frying oil in a deep fryer or an 8-inch saucepan fitted with a basket insert to 375°F.

2. In a small bowl, mix the cheese, onion, parsley, tuna, capers, pepper, and butter.

3. Place an egg roll wrapper on a plate. Spoon a heaping tablespoon of the tuna mixture in the center. Form a small well in the mixture and carefully break an egg into the center. Sprinkle some salt over the yolk and fold one corner of the wrapper over to meet another, forming a

triangle. Seal the edges by rubbing with egg white or water. (Make them one at a time.) Pick the *brik* up with 2 hands by the corners, place in the hot oil, and cook until golden brown, 30 seconds to 1 minute. Don't worry if the edges aren't completely sealed or if some of the egg white has run off, because the hot oil will quickly puff the edges together and all will be fine.

4. Remove from the oil with a strainer or the fitted basket insert, drain on paper towels for a minute. Continue making and cooking the remaining *brik*. Serve without utensils, mopping up the egg with the fried piece of egg roll wrapper. Let the frying oil cool completely, strain through a porous paper filter, if necessary, and save the oil for a future use.

Note: Notice that you use small or medium eggs for this recipe.

Makes 8 pastries; 8 servings

Brīk "aux Fruits de Mer"

I went crazy over brīk, *the deep-fried turnovers stuffed with various ingredients (but always a raw egg), when I was in Tunisia, my favorites being the egg and parsley one and the tuna and egg. This* brīk *had shrimp and tuna and it was also very good.*

6 cups olive oil, olive pomace oil, or vegetable oil for frying
1 tablespoon shredded Gruyère cheese
1 small onion, very finely chopped
2 tablespoons very finely chopped fresh parsley leaves

One 3½-ounce can imported tuna in olive oil, drained (you may want to save this oil for any of the vegetable salads in "Salads and Other Cold Vegetable Dishes")
¼ pound medium-size shrimp, cooked in boiling water until pink, drained, shelled, and chopped
1 tablespoon salted or brined capers, rinsed or drained and chopped if large
1 teaspoon freshly ground black pepper
1 tablespoon clarified butter or unsalted butter
8 Chinese egg roll wrappers, 6 inches square (about ¼ pound)
8 small to medium-size eggs
Salt to taste
1 large egg white, lightly beaten

1. Preheat the frying oil in an 8-inch saucepan or deep fryer to 375°F.

2. In a medium-size bowl, mix the cheese, onion, parsley, tuna, shrimp, capers, pepper, and butter.

3. Place an egg roll wrapper on a plate. Spoon a heaping tablespoon of the tuna mixture in the center. Form a small well in the mixture and carefully break an egg into the center. Sprinkle some salt over the yolk and fold one corner of the wrapper over to meet another, forming a triangle. Seal the edges by rubbing with egg white or water. Pick the *brik* up with 2 hands by the corners and place in the hot oil until golden brown, 30 seconds to 1 minute. Don't worry if the edges aren't completely sealed or if some egg leaks out because the hot oil will quickly puff the edges together.

4. Remove from the oil with a strainer or the fitted basket insert, drain on paper towels for a

My Favorite Brīk

The deep-fried pastry turnovers known as *brīk* in Tunisia are some of my favorite foods. They are to be found in restaurants, little hole-in-the-wall cook shops, and sold by street vendors. The first time I went to Tunisia, my port of entry was Djerba, the island off Tunisia's southern coast. A group of us hooked up with two charming guides named Nureddin and Fathi, who took us to our hotel, one of the nicest on the island, the Hotel Ulysse, where we had a late-night dinner. And what a spectacular dinner! Set out on buffet tables were rows of bowls of black pepper, freshly ground cumin, coriander seed, the surprisingly mild Berber *harīsa*, dried ginger, dried whole turmeric, olives that were tangy and bitter, and capers, and all this was simply condiments, which we could sprinkle on more food to come. There were salted preserved lemons to be used with an exquisite squid couscous from the town of Gafsa called *barkūkish*; the kind of couscous that looks like little pasta balls; *shūbiya maḥshī*, stuffed squid; and ᶜ*ujja mirqas*, scrambled eggs with merguez sausage and bell peppers. There was also a *brīk* called by the French name *aux fruits de mer*, which was extraordinary, made with the freshest shrimp and the finest bluefin tuna preserved in Tunisian olive oil.

minute. Serve without utensils, mopping up the egg with the fried piece of egg roll wrapper. Let the frying oil cool completely, strain through a porous paper filter, if necessary, and save the oil for a future use.

Note: Notice that you use small or medium-size eggs for this recipe.

Makes 8 pastries; 8 servings

Brīk with Brains and Egg

This Tunisian brīk bi'l-mukh *is a fried pastry filled with the delicious, creamy soft meat of brains. It is a mild taste, much milder than* that of the tuna in the Brīk *with Tuna and Egg (page 330), which may seem surprising. Brain is a popular food in the Mediterranean because of its rich taste.*

1 lamb or veal brain, soaked in cold water to cover for 1 hour, changing the water 3 times, drained, and membrane removed

Salt

2 tablespoons white wine vinegar or fresh lemon juice

6 cups olive oil, olive pomace oil, or vegetable oil for frying

1 tablespoon freshly grated Parmigiano-Reggiano cheese

1 small onion, very finely chopped

2 tablespoons very finely chopped fresh parsley
leaves

1 tablespoon clarified butter or unsalted butter,
softened

Freshly ground black pepper to taste

8 Chinese egg roll wrappers, 6 inches square
(about ¼ pound)

8 small to medium-size eggs

1 large egg white, lightly beaten

1. Place the brain in a large nonreactive saucepan and cover with lightly salted water acidulated with the vinegar. Bring to a gentle boil for 20 minutes. Drain and chop into small pieces.

2. Preheat the frying oil in a deep fryer or an 8-inch saucepan fitted with a basket insert to 375°F.

3. In a medium-size bowl, mix the chopped brain, Parmigiano, onion, parsley, and butter with a fork until well blended and season with salt and pepper.

4. Place an egg roll wrapper on a plate. Spoon a heaping tablespoon of the brain mixture in the center. Form a small well in the mixture and carefully break an egg into the center. Sprinkle some salt over the yolk and fold one corner of the wrapper over to meet another, forming a triangle. Seal the edges by rubbing with egg white or water. (Make them one at a time.) Pick the *brīk* up with two hands by the corners, place in the hot oil, and cook until golden brown, 30 seconds to 1 minute. Don't worry if the edges aren't completely sealed or if some of the egg white has run off, because the hot oil will quickly puff the edges together and all will be fine.

5. Remove from the oil with a strainer or the fitted basket insert, drain on paper towels for a minute. Continue making and cooking the remaining *brīk*. Serve without utensils, mopping up the egg with the fried piece of egg roll wrapper. Let the frying oil cool completely, strain through a porous paper filter, if necessary, and save the oil for a future use.

Note: Notice that you use small or medium-size eggs for this recipe.

Makes 8 pastries; 8 servings

Brains

The creamy, rich taste of calf and lamb brains makes them a favorite food in the Mediterranean. Prepared most simply, they are poached in a court-bouillon, then rolled in bread crumbs and fried. Brains are rich in vitamins and phosphorus and are quite nutritious. However one prepares brains, they are always purged in acidulated water beforehand. Sometimes there are little bits of fat still connected, which should be pulled off, but generally brains are sold already cleaned and ready to soak. Because Americans are not big eaters of brains, or any offal for that matter, you need to seek out an ethnic butcher or order them because you will see them in your supermarket seldom, if ever.

Cheese and Potato Cigars of the Tunisian Jews

This preparation from Tunisia is said to be popular with Tunisian Jews. It is a cheese and potato stuffed phyllo-like pastry that is rolled up like a cigar, similar to the Turkish börek, *and is called by the Tunisian Arabic name* brīk. *Although this turnover is called a* brīk, *it doesn't contain an egg as is typical because of the way it is rolled up rather than folded, making the addition of an egg an impossibility. The turmeric turns the insides a very appetizing golden yellow, and it's hard not to just keep popping these tidbits into your mouth. Although I call for the roll-ups to be cut in half, you can cut them in quarters for bite-size pieces.*

1 large potato (about ¾ pound)

½ pound Gruyère cheese, shredded

2 large eggs

1 teaspoon salt

1 teaspoon freshly ground black pepper

2 teaspoons freshly grated nutmeg

2 teaspoons turmeric

14 Chinese egg roll wrappers, 6 inches square (7 ounces)

1 egg white, lightly beaten

6 cups olive oil, olive pomace oil, or vegetable oil for frying

1. Place the whole potato in a medium-size saucepan and cover with cold water by several inches. Bring to a gentle boil over medium heat, about 20 minutes, then continue to cook at strong simmer until a skewer glides easily to the center of the potato, about another 25 minutes.

Drain, peel when cool enough to handle, and mash.

2. In a medium-size bowl, mix the potato, cheese, eggs, salt, pepper, nutmeg, and turmeric.

3. Arrange an egg roll wrapper in front of you and place a portion of stuffing, about 2 tablespoons, along the end nearest to you, roll it up one roll, fold the sides in, and continue rolling it up like a cigar. Seal the edges by rubbing them with egg white with your finger. Set aside as you repeat with the remaining wrappers and filling. They can be frozen at this point if you like.

4. Preheat the frying oil in a deep fryer or an 8-inch saucepan fitted with a basket insert to 375°F. Fry a few of the cigars at a time, being careful not to crowd them, until golden, 2 to 3 minutes. Remove with a strainer and let drain on paper towels. Cut in half on the bias, arrange all the cooked cigars on a platter, and serve immediately. Let the frying oil cool completely, strain through a porous paper filter, if necessary, and save the oil for a future use.

Makes 14 cigars; 14 servings

Fried Lamb Cigars from Algeria

This preparation called būrāk ᶜannābī *comes from the large port city of Annaba in Algeria. Annaba was once known as Buna al-Hadida, which the French, when they ruled Algeria, shortened to Bône. Although Annaba is not known as a Mecca of Algerian cuisine, I like this recipe, which I've adapted from one found in Salima Hadjiat's* La cuisine d'Algerie.

The Food of Bône

In the sixteenth century, Muslim supremacy in the southern Mediterranean led to the rise of ports such as Oran, Bougie (Bejaïa), Algiers, and Bône, today known as Annaba. A city of about 500,000 and the fourth largest city in Algeria, Annaba was a populous town even then and known as an important center for the manufacture of earthenware, and a city that consumed a lot of beef and exported wool, butter, and honey. On the plain of Annaba so many farms were planted with jujubes that the city became known as the "city of jujubiers." Although the city is not known as a culinary center, unique dishes (if we could only come up with recipes) are heard about, such as *qraytliyya* (the spelling is unsure), a dish prepared in Annaba with a pasta made of white flour, eggs, saffron, olive oil, and water that is then tossed with beef meatballs in a sauce of ground beef, onions, chickpeas, and cinnamon. Their delicious meze of *būrāk ᶜannābī*, a kind of "firecracker" fritter because the ends may be twisted like a firecracker (page 334), is made with ground lamb or mutton and abundant parsley and cinnamon and is often served as the first food to break the Ramadan fast.

¾ pound ground or finely chopped mutton or lamb

1 medium-size onion, finely chopped

Leaves from 1 bunch fresh parsley, finely chopped

½ teaspoon salt

½ teaspoon ground cinnamon

½ teaspoon freshly ground black pepper

½ cup clarified butter or unsalted butter

6 cups olive oil, olive pomace oil, or vegetable oil for frying

8 Chinese egg roll wrappers, 6 inches square (about ¼ pound)

8 small to medium-size eggs

8 lemon wedges

1. In a medium-size bowl, mix the meat, onion, parsley, salt, cinnamon, and pepper.

2. In a medium-size skillet, melt the butter over medium heat, then cook the meat mixture until it has turned color and is tender, about 15 minutes, stirring occasionally. Let cool in the skillet.

3. Preheat the frying oil in a deep fryer or an 8-inch saucepan fitted with a basket insert to 375°F.

4. Place an egg roll wrapper on a plate in front of you. Spoon a heaping tablespoon of the stuffing in the center. Form a small well in the stuffing and carefully break an egg into the center. Season the yolk with salt and pepper. Don't

worry too much if some of the white spills over. Use the white to spread on the edges of the wrapper with your finger to act as a kind of glue, then fold the wrapper over to form a rectangle, pressing down gently on the edges. Carefully lift the pastry with 2 hands and place in the frying oil to cook until golden brown, about 1 minute. Don't worry if the edges aren't completely sealed or if some of the egg white has run off, because the hot oil will quickly puff the edges together and all will be fine. As they finish cooking, remove them with a strainer to a paper towel–lined platter to drain. Continue with the remaining wrappers and stuffing. Serve without utensils, mopping up the egg with a fried piece of egg roll wrapper. Serve the *būrāk* with the lemon wedges. Let the frying oil cool completely, strain through a porous paper filter, if necessary, and save the oil for a future use.

Makes 8 cigars; 8 servings

Variation: Add to the stuffing 1 medium-size potato, boiled until tender, peeled, and thinly sliced; 2 scallions, finely chopped; and ¼ pound Gruyère cheese, shredded. Roll the wrappers up like cigars, making sure the egg doesn't spill out, and twist the ends closed.

Fried Peppers and Tomatoes with Beef Turnovers from Algeria

This Algerian preparation is called būrāk filfil, *which is made with a mélange of peppers and tomatoes called a* shakshūka. *The very thin, phyllo-like pastry used in Algeria for this prepa-* ration, called diyūl, *resembles a Chinese egg roll wrapper, which is what I use here. It will taste flakier if you use phyllo pastry and form the turnovers into small triangles as you would in the variation on page 268 (follow the instructions for baking there). If you use the smaller egg roll wrappers, you can double the number you make and they will all be bite-size.*

3 tablespoons clarified butter, melted
6 ounces ground beef
1 small onion, finely chopped
1 tablespoon finely chopped fresh parsley leaves
Salt and freshly ground black pepper to taste
3 tablespoons extra-virgin olive oil
3 large red bell peppers, roasted (page 415), peeled, seeded, and finely chopped
1 large green chile, roasted (page 415), peeled, seeded, and finely chopped
1 large ripe tomato, peeled, seeded, and chopped
2 large garlic cloves, finely chopped
12 Chinese egg roll wrappers, 6 inches square (6 ounces)

1. In a medium-size skillet, melt 1 tablespoon of the butter over medium-low heat, then cook the beef, onion, parsley, salt, and pepper until the meat has turned color and the onion is a little soft, about 8 minutes, stirring with a wooden spoon and breaking up the meat. Allow to cool in the pan.

2. Meanwhile, in another large skillet, heat the olive oil over medium-low heat, then cook the peppers, tomato, and garlic until the liquid is much reduced and the sauce is thick, about 30 minutes, stirring occasionally.

3. Lay an egg roll wrapper in front of you and put about a heaping tablespoon of the pepper filling in the center. Push about a tablespoon of the meat filling on top of the peppers. Wet the edges of the wrapper to seal them. Fold over to form a triangle, pushing the stuffing down a bit and sealing the edges by running you finger over it. Finish stuffing and folding the remaining wrappers.

4. Preheat the oven to 375°F. Arrange the turnovers on 2 baking sheets, brush each with the remaining butter and bake until golden, 10 to 12 minutes. Serve hot or at room temperature, cut in half or whole.

Makes 12 turnovers; 12 servings

Moroccan Fish and Fresh Herb Turnovers

In Morocco, a favorite street food or meze is brīwat, *a deep-fried stuffed turnover made with a dough as thin as phyllo pastry called* warqa. *Chinese egg roll wrappers work very well in this recipe, which is related to the Tunisian* brīk *(pages 329–333). This preparation is called* brīwat al-ḥūt *or fried fish turnover.*

6 cups olive oil, olive pomace oil, or vegetable oil for frying

¼ pound ground cooked white-fleshed fish, such as cod, halibut, red snapper, flounder

¼ cup finely chopped fresh coriander (cilantro) leaves

¼ cup finely chopped fresh parsley leaves

½ teaspoon salt

Freshly ground black pepper to taste

1 teaspoon freshly ground cumin seeds

1 teaspoon sweet Spanish paprika

1 tablespoon extra-virgin olive oil

6 Chinese egg roll wrappers, 6 inches square (3 ounces)

1. Preheat the frying oil in a deep fryer or an 8-inch saucepan fitted with a basket insert to 375°F.

2. In a medium-size bowl, mix the fish, coriander, parsley, salt, pepper, cumin, paprika, and olive oil.

3. Place an egg roll wrapper on a plate. Spoon 2 tablespoons of the stuffing in the center. Wet the edges of the wrapper with a little water, then fold one edge over to form a triangle, pressing the edges closed. (Make them one at a time.) Pick the turnover up with 2 hands by the corners, place in the hot oil, and cook until golden brown, 30 seconds per side. Remove from the oil with a skimmer or tongs or lift the basket insert and drain on paper towels for a minute. Continue making the remaining turnovers and serve. Let the frying oil cool completely, strain if necessary, and save for a future use.

Makes 6 turnovers; 6 servings

Algerian Fish and Shrimp Cigars

This Algerian appetizer is a fish börek *called* būrāk al-ḥūt, *which uses a kind of phyllo-like pastry sheet called* diyūl. *In its place a Chinese egg roll wrapper is perfect. The turnover is rolled up to look like a cigar. Any kind of white fish is*

Making Warqa Pastry

Warqa is a very thin pastry leaf (from the word meaning "leaf"). Warqa pastry begins as a spongy dough that is tapped or slapped against a hot convex sheet of pounded metal (called a *ṭubsil*) set over a hot charcoal brazier. The dough is applied in a series of overlapping concentric circles to form a large film of pastry. This collection of leaves, now forming a whole thin sheet, is carefully but quickly peeled off the metal and set side. Warqa pastry is thinner than phyllo. It is called *diyūl* in Algeria and *malsūqa* in Tunisia. Watching women make warqa is fascinating because it requires speed and dexterity. The uncooked dough is a very sticky, unpromising mass when it is picked up in one fistful and then dabbed very quickly on the hot *ṭubsil*, moving around so the overlapping dabs of dough form one very thin translucent sheet. Then the sheet is pulled up off the hot surface and laid aside while the next one gets cooked just as quickly. It looks impossible to do, and even having watched it being done, I doubted I could successfully make a warqa pastry on my first shot.

fine to use here, such as cod, halibut, monkfish, sea bass, sole, flounder, or grouper. This is a mild-tasting fried pastry that is attractively served when cut in half on the bias and offered as an appetizer.

¾ pound white-fleshed fish fillets
1 pound fresh shrimp with their heads or
  ½ pound previously frozen headless shrimp
1 sprig fresh thyme
2 bay leaves
Salt to taste
Three 1½-inch-thick slices Italian bread,
  crusts removed
½ cup milk
¼ cup (½ stick) unsalted butter
1 medium-size onion, finely chopped
½ cup pitted and chopped imported green olives
Freshly ground black pepper to taste
6 cups olive oil, olive pomace oil, or vegetable oil
  for frying
16 Chinese egg roll wrappers, 6 inches square
  (½ pound)
1 large egg white, beaten until frothy

1. Put the fish and shrimp in a saucepan with the thyme and bay leaves, cover with water, and season with salt. Bring to a boil and cook at a simmer until the fish begins to flake, 4 to 8 minutes (depending on the kind of fish you use). Remove the fish and shrimp and save the broth. Break the fish into pieces, remove the shells and/or heads of the shrimp, and cut into 3 pieces.

2. In a small bowl, soak the bread in the milk.

3. In a medium-size skillet, melt the butter over medium-low heat, then cook the onion

until translucent, about 15 minutes, stirring. Moisten with ½ cup of the reserved fish broth. Squeeze the milk out of the bread. Add the olives to the skillet and cook for 10 minutes, then add the bread, adding a little more broth if necessary to make a thick, dense mixture and cook over low heat for 10 minutes, stirring. Remove from the heat and let cool.

4. Preheat the frying oil in a deep fryer or an 8-inch saucepan fitted with a basket insert to 375°F.

5. Lay an egg roll wrapper in front of you and put some fish and shrimp along the border of the edge at the bottom. Place about a tablespoon of the onion mixture on top of the seafood. Season with salt and pepper. Roll up once to cover the stuffing, then fold in ½ inch of the right and left sides of the wrapper, brush the edges of the wrapper with the egg white, and finish rolling so the stuffing is enclosed, the wrapper is the shape of a cigar, and the egg white seals the edges. Finish stuffing and wrapping the remaining sheets of dough.

6. Cook the turnovers a few at a time, taking care not to crowd them, until golden brown, about 2 minutes. Cut each cigar in half on the bias and serve hot or warm with a wedge of lemon. Let the frying oil cool completely, strain through a porous paper filter, if necessary, and save the oil for a future use.

Makes 16 whole cigars;

12 servings

Lamb Pastries in the Style of the Tunisian Jews

This meze of ground lamb flavored with cinnamon and wrapped in a thin phyllo-like pastry is called bastāl bi'l-lahm *in Tunisia and is popular among Tunisian Jews. The word* bastāl *comes from the Spanish word* pastel, *which means "pastry." Given this etymology, it is thought that this dish was probably inherited from the Muslim and Jewish Andalusi, who were expelled from Spain in 1492 and throughout the Christian Reconquest. Many of these Jews and Muslims emigrated to Tunisia in the fifteenth and sixteenth centuries. In this recipe I use Chinese egg roll wrappers, which are somewhat similar to the phyllo-like pastry called* malsūqa *in Tunisia.*

1 pound boneless leg of lamb, trimmed of fat and ground
15 garlic cloves (about 1 head garlic), very finely chopped
1 teaspoon salt
1 teaspoon freshly ground black pepper
1 teaspoon ground cinnamon
½ teaspoon freshly grated nutmeg
¾ cup plus 1 tablespoon extra-virgin olive oil
Juice from 1 lemon
20 to 22 Chinese egg roll wrappers, 6 inches square (10 to 11 ounces)
1 large egg white, lightly beaten

1. In a medium-size bowl, mix the lamb, garlic, salt, pepper, cinnamon, and nutmeg until well blended. In a deep casserole, heat 1 tablespoon of the olive oil over low heat, then cook

the meat until it turns color, about 8 minutes, stirring and breaking it up with a wooden spoon. Add the lemon juice and continue to cook until the meat has completely turned color, about 20 minutes. Check the seasonings and correct if necessary.

2. Cut each egg roll wrapper in half to form 2 rectangles. Arrange an egg roll wrapper half with a short end facing you. Place a tablespoon or so of the meat at the bottom of the wrapper and fold the lower right edge over to the middle of the left edge, sealing the edges by brushing them with egg white. Fold the bottom left corner up to touch the top left corner. You will now have a square again. Fold the bottom left corner to the top right corner to form a little triangle and set aside while you continue making the remaining pastries. As you do this, brush all the edges as you fold them with egg white so they will seal when you cook them.

3. In a large skillet, heat 2 tablespoons of the olive oil over medium-high heat, then cook 7 of the pastries until golden, making sure they don't overlap, turn once, and cook the other side until golden, about 6 minutes in all. Remove from the pan and set aside, keeping them warm while you make the rest. Add another 2 tablespoons olive oil to the skillet and cook the next bunch of pastries. Continue with more oil and pastries until they are all cooked. Serve hot or warm.

Makes 42 pastries; 12 servings

"Cigar" Börek

All over Turkey one can find these deep-fried böreks *called* sigara böreği *because they are rolled up to look like a cigar. Many of them are simply quark (a fresh curd cheese made from skimmed milk) rolled up in cigarette- or cigar-shaped phyllo.* Kashkaval *cheese can be found in Greek or Middle Eastern markets. If you can't find it, use a young pecorino or a mild cheddar cheese. Cooks make large batches of* böreks *and store them in a cool place covered with a damp cloth, then fry them at the last minute.*

½ pound soft white cheese, such as Syrian white cheese, farmer cheese, or mozzarella, finely chopped
¼ pound feta cheese, crumbled
¼ cup shredded *kashkaval* cheese (page 92)
1 large egg, beaten
1 tablespoon finely chopped fresh parsley leaves
¾ pound phyllo pastry, defrosted if necessary
2 cups sunflower seed or vegetable oil

1. In a medium-size bowl, mix the cheeses, egg, and parsley.

2. Cut the phyllo pastry in half so the dimensions are 14 x 9 inches. Take 2 sheets of dough and lay them on top of one another. Place a small amount of cheese filling, about 1 tablespoon, in the center of the short end, spreading it out into the length of a cigarette, and roll the phyllo over the filling several times. Fold about 2 inches of each side over, then continue rolling until you have a cigar shape. Dip your finger in a bowl of water and seal the edges. Repeat with the remaining filling and phyllo.

3. In a medium-size skillet, heat the oil over medium heat to 375°F., then fry the roll-ups, without crowding the pan, until golden brown,

Faṭīr

There is a special kind of restaurant in Egypt called a faṭaran where one finds faṭīr made, a cross between a crêpe and a layered phyllo-type pastry pancake stuffed with either savory or sweet ingredients and made into big rounds or squares. The fillings can be either savory, made from onion, egg, and ground meat, or sweet with raisins, sugar, and spices. My favorite faṭaran in Alexandria, Egypt, was the Baraka restaurant at Orabi Square no. 4. Here we met Essam el din Adly, who introduced us not only to his wonderful faṭīr but also to a great Egyptian-style pizza (page 308).

To make his faṭīr dough, a wad of dough about the size of the palm of a man's hand, made with flour, water, and clarified butter, is flattened until very, very thin and twirled in the air as you would a pizza. It is extraordinarily elastic and pliable. Then it is laid on a marble slab, all flat and thin. Another wad of dough is prepared in the same manner and laid in the middle of the first faṭīr. Into this faṭīr go about 2 cups of shaved coconut, golden raisins, and confectioners' sugar. Melted clarified butter is poured all over, then the bottom faṭīr is folded over into a square to cover the second faṭīr. The end product, a square piece of stuffed dough, is picked up, put on a baking sheet greased with clarified butter, then baked in a gas-fired brick oven about 500°F for 10 minutes. The square of pastry is about a foot square, enough for two people.

When the faṭīr is pulled out of the oven, it is cut crisscross into squares. A small amount of milk is poured on top, as is more clarified butter and confectioners' sugar. It is very tasty and not too sweet. Essam's faṭīr was just as he described it—very good. Because of the complexity of making and wielding the dough, I could also see how awful faṭīr could be in the hands of an uncaring cook.

about 15 seconds, turn with tongs, and cook another 15 seconds. Remove to paper towels to drain and serve hot.

Makes 16 to 18 roll-ups;

16 servings

Spinach and Feta Cheese Börek

This recipe called ıspanaklı peynirli tepsi böreği means "spinach-cheese tray-pie" for it bakes in a rectangular tray and is then cut into portions. The same preparation is made in Greece, with slight differences. The original recipe for this börek *comes from the Sultan's*

Kitchen restaurant in Boston. Although ubiquitous in Turkey, I most enjoyed having this börek
at the Hippodrome Restaurant across from the
obelisk in front of the Blue Mosque in Istanbul.
We watched the lights twinkle on the minarets
of the mosque as we took bites of the börek.

Spinach and Cheese Filling

4 pounds spinach, heavy stems removed and
washed well several times
¼ cup extra-virgin olive oil
¼ cup clarified butter
1 bunch scallions (white and light green parts),
finely chopped
2 large eggs
¾ pound imported feta cheese, crumbled
6 tablespoons finely chopped fresh parsley leaves
6 tablespoons finely chopped fresh dill
Salt and freshly ground black pepper to taste

Pastry

¼ cup clarified butter
⅓ cup milk
¼ cup extra-virgin olive oil
1 large egg
1 pound phyllo pastry, defrosted if necessary

Glaze

2 large egg yolks
¼ cup milk

1. Make the filling. In a large saucepan or
stockpot, place the spinach with only the water
adhering to it from its last rinsing, cover, and
wilt over high heat, about 4 minutes, turning
once or twice. Remove to a strainer and drain

well by pressing the water out with the back of
a wooden spoon. Chop the spinach.

2. In a large skillet, heat the olive oil and clarified butter together over medium heat, then
cook the scallions and spinach, stirring, for 2
minutes. Remove to a bowl and let cool. Mix in
the eggs, feta cheese, parsley, and dill. Season
with salt and pepper. Set aside.

3. Preheat the oven to 375°F.

4. Prepare the pastry. In a medium-size bowl,
mix the butter, milk, olive oil, and egg. Brush
some of this mixture on the bottom of a 9 x 12
dish. Lay 10 sheets of phyllo pastry on the
bottom, brushing each layer with the butter
mixture. Spread the spinach mixture on top.
Layer in another 10 sheets of phyllo, brushing
each layer with the butter mixture.

5. Make the glaze. Stir the egg yolks and milk
together and brush this glaze over the top of the
pie. Bake for 20 minutes, then lower the oven
temperature to 325°F and bake until the top is
light brown and crispy, another 10 to 20 minutes. Remove from the oven and let rest 10
minutes before cutting into 12 sections and
serving hot.

Makes 12 servings

Fried Wontons Stuffed with Pork, Broccoli, Olives, and Walnuts

*This fascinating recipe came about from three
widely disparate influences—the Turkish* mantı,
*a kind of meat-stuffed miniature wonton; the
Tunisian fried turnover known as* brīk; *and the*

stuffing from a southern Italian calzone. When my three kids were young, they were wild about this recipe and I couldn't make them fast enough. Serve this appetizer as a plated dish at a sit-down dinner.

One ½-pound head broccoli

2 tablespoons extra-virgin olive oil

1 small onion, finely chopped

3 large garlic cloves, finely chopped

1 pound pork tenderloin or sirloin, trimmed of any fat or silverskin and chopped

¼ cup pitted and chopped imported black olives

2 tablespoons salted or brined capers, rinsed or drained and chopped

¼ cup chopped walnuts

2 tablespoons finely chopped fresh basil leaves

1 tablespoon finely chopped fresh tarragon leaves

Salt and freshly ground black pepper to taste

6 cups olive oil, olive pomace oil, or vegetable oil for frying

16 to 20 Chinese egg roll wrappers 6-inches square (8 to 10 ounces)

¾ pound fresh mozzarella cheese, cut into finger-size pieces

1. Bring a pot of water to a boil and cook the broccoli until tender, about 8 minutes. Drain and chop.

2. In a large skillet, heat the olive oil over high heat, then cook the onion and garlic until translucent, about 4 minutes, stirring. Add the pork and brown, 4 to 5 minutes. Add the broccoli, olives, capers, walnuts, basil, and tarragon and season with salt and pepper. Cook for 3 minutes, then let cool in the skillet.

3. Preheat the frying oil in a deep fryer or an 8-inch saucepan fitted with a basket insert to 360°F.

4. Arrange an egg roll wrapper in front of you and spoon some of the stuffing in the center with a piece of cheese. Fold one corner over to another to form a triangle and use a little bit of water to seal the 2 edges together by pressing down. Continue filling the egg roll wrappers.

5. Place several wontons at a time (don't crowd them) in the hot oil and fry until light brown, 1 to 2 minutes. Remove with a slotted spoon and drain, then transfer to a paper towel–lined platter to drain further, cut in half, and serve hot. Let the frying oil cool completely, strain through a porous paper filter, if necessary, and save the oil for a future use.

Makes 8 servings

Fried Cheese Pies from Lesbos

From the island of Lesbos in the Ionian, these cheese pies called gyouslemethes *differ from the cheese pies called* tyropitta *(page 271) in that they are fried rather than baked. Typically, they are served as part of a meze and pair very nicely with a glass of ouzo. Although I instruct you to make little half-moon-shaped pies, you can also fold them up wrapped any which way, or in little squares, although the half-moon is the traditional shape. The cheeses called for are typical Greek cheeses that are quite commonly found in this country, especially at Greek, Italian, or Middle Eastern markets.*

3 large eggs

2 cups grated *mizithra* (or ricotta salata) or *kefalotyri* cheese

½ pound phyllo pastry, defrosted if necessary

6 cups vegetable oil or a mixture of vegetable and olive oil for frying

1. In a medium-size bowl, beat the eggs with the cheese.

2. Unfold the phyllo pastry and count out 6 layers. Cut the phyllo pastry into rounds 2½ inches in diameter with a cookie cutter (each disk will be 6 sheets). Place 1 teaspoon of cheese mixture on each disk. Moisten the edges with water and fold the dough over to form a half-moon, then seal the edges well by pressing them together with your fingers. Set them aside as you continue working, draping a damp kitchen towel over them.

3. Preheat the frying oil in a deep fryer or an 8-inch saucepan fitted with a basket insert to 360°F. Deep-fry the small pies several at a time (do not crowd them) until golden brown, about 90 seconds. Remove them with a slotted spoon, drain on paper towels, and keep warm in a low oven while you continue to cook the rest of them. They can be served at this point or refrigerated and reheated later in the oven for 20 minutes at 350°F. Let the frying oil cool completely, strain through a porous paper filter, and save the oil for a future use.

Makes about 2 dozen pies; 12 servings

The Island of Lesbos

Lesbos is the home of the early sixth-century B.C. Greek lyrical poet Sappho, whose love poems were characterized by a vehement expression of passion. Those who have tasted the food of Lesbos may express their enthusiasm in the same meter. Lesbian food (actually one would say Mytilenian, after the name of the major port and the alternative name of the island) is simple and based on fish. A visitor should seek out the *sardeles pastes*, a kind of sardine sashimi, as well as the fava bean dishes cooked in olive oil and oregano. Grilled octopus is a favorite and deep-fried zucchini flowers are special, too.

Fried Sicilian Cheese Coins

These deep-fried disks, called crispeddi 'i furmàggiu *in Sicilian, are usually served as a little snack. They start out looking like coins, then, once they are fried, they turn golden brown and puff up slightly. There are many varieties of fritters in Sicily, some using beignet dough, others a yeasted dough such as the one on page 347, or a short dough as here.* Crispeddi *is an old Sicilian word; it has meant "dough fried in oil" since the mid-fourteenth century.*

2 cups unbleached all-purpose flour

1 large egg, beaten

2 tablespoons unsalted butter, melted

1 teaspoon salt

½ cup water

¼ pound *caciocavallo* or provolone cheese, cut
into 1-inch pieces

12 salted anchovy fillets, rinsed and chopped

6 cups olive oil or olive pomace oil for frying

1. In a medium-size bowl, pour the flour and
make a well. Add the egg, melted butter, salt,
and water to the well; mix thoroughly to form
into a ball, cover with plastic wrap, and let rest
for 30 minutes.

2. Roll the dough out thinly on a lightly
floured work surface and cut out 3-inch-
diameter disks. Re-roll the scraps to cut out
more. Place a piece of cheese on half the disks,
then lay a piece of anchovy on top. Cover with
the remaining the disks and seal the edges by
crimping them together with a fork.

Crispelle

Crispelle is usually translated as "crêpe," but
they are more than that. They can also be
fried disks of dough, as they make them in
Sicily, where they are called *crispeddi*. These
fried doughs or fried breads have an old
history, as we know from the fourteenth-
century Sicilian vocabulary of the lingua
franca, the *Declarus* of Angelo Senisio, which
dates from 1348. In describing a kind of donut
that the Arabs called *sfinj*, Senisio informs us
that the very same *sfingia* is a fried bread that
the common people also call *crispella*.

3. Preheat the frying oil in a deep fryer or an
8-inch saucepan fitted with a basket insert to
375°F. Cook several disks at a time (do not
crowd) in the hot oil until golden, about 2
minutes, turning once. Remove with a slotted
spoon, let drain on paper towels, and serve hot
or warm. Let the frying oil cool completely,
strain through a porous paper filter, if necessary,
and save the oil for a future use.

Makes 24 coins; 12 servings

Panzerotti

The history of panzerotti *is quite old. In
the Neapolitan chef Francesco Leonardi's*
L'Apicio moderno *(The Modern Apicius), published in Rome in 1797, he describes a* rissole
alla napolitana *and tells us that "in Naples
they call this rissole* panzerotti.*" In eighteenth-
century Naples, they were made with* provature
fresche, *a fresh buffalo milk cheese, Parmigiano,
and* caciocavallo *cheese, some cooked ham, parsley, nutmeg, and hard-boiled egg yolks, all of
which were stuffed inside disks as thin as a
big coin made of a flour-and-lard short dough.
They were crimped closed like a ravioli and
deep-fried in lard. The* panzerotti *of today are
not much different. Nancy Harmon Jenkins,
author of* Flavors of Puglia, *tells us that they are
traditionally made on January 17 for the feast of
Sant' Antonio Abate, the day that marks the
beginning of Carnival in Bari in Apulia. They
get their name from the southern Italian word
for "stomach,"* pancia, *because of their swollen
look. My recipe calls for prosciutto and mozzarella cheese, but you could also use salami,*

ricotta, smoked provola, *Parmigiano-Reggiano, hard-boiled egg yolks, and/or parsley.*

3 large eggs

1 tablespoon sugar

½ teaspoon salt

2 cups unbleached all-purpose flour

¼ cup water

Freshly ground black pepper to taste

6 ounces fresh mozzarella cheese, cut into 20 small pieces

One ¼-pound slice prosciutto, cut into 20 small pieces

6 cups olive oil or pork lard for frying

1. In a medium-size bowl, beat the eggs. Add the sugar, salt, and flour and mix until thick. Stir in the water and pepper to make a supple dough and knead to form a smooth ball. It will be sticky. Spread a good amount of flour on a work surface and dump the ball of dough out on it. Roll the dough until it is as thin as a half dollar. Cut out twenty 4-inch-diameter disks, re-rolling the dough scraps when necessary. Place a piece of mozzarella and prosciutto in the center of each, fold over, and seal the edges, crimping them with a fork.

2. Preheat the frying oil or lard in a deep fryer or an 8-inch saucepan fitted with a basket insert to 375°F. Fry the *panzerotti* several at a time in the hot oil (don't crowd them) until golden, about 3½ minutes. Remove with a slotted spoon, drain on paper towels, and serve hot. Let the frying oil cool completely, strain through a porous paper filter, if necessary, and save the oil for a future use.

Makes 20 panzerotti*; 10 servings*

Fried Dough with Fried Shrimp, Crispy Chard, and Zucchini Flowers

This antipasto is known as pasta cresiuta, *which means "risen dough," because it uses yeast. There are a variety of ways the dish can be served: you can flatten the dough so it holds the other ingredients on top once they're cooked, or you can make balls of dough and scatter the ingredients on top of them, or you can stuff the garnish ingredients inside the dough balls and fry them—this is how my kids like it. It's a very pretty dish, too. When you fry the leafy green vegetable, cut the leaf in half and deep-fry until crispy, about 1 minute or less, then crumble over the fried dough. This preparation is best served as an antipasto at a sit-down dinner.*

1 recipe Basic Bread and Pizza Dough (page 473)

6 cups olive oil or olive pomace oil for frying

Choose 1 or 2 seafood toppings from the following for garnish: 6 ounces small pieces firm-fleshed white fish and/or 1 pound very small shrimp with their heads or ½ pound previously frozen very small headless shrimp, shells and/or heads removed

All-purpose flour for dredging

Salt to taste

Choose 2 vegetable toppings from the following for garnish: 3 large Swiss chard or borage leaves; ¼ cup finely chopped dried seaweed; 6 large zucchini flowers

1. Prepare the bread dough.

2. Preheat the frying oil in a deep fryer or an 8-inch saucepan fitted with a basket insert to

375°F. Dredge the fish and/or shrimp in the flour, patting off any excess, and fry in the hot oil until the shrimp are orange-red, 1 to 2 minutes, or the fish pieces are golden, 2 to 3 minutes. Remove with a slotted spoon, drain on paper towels, salt, and set aside.

3. Cook the Swiss chard or borage leaves in the hot oil until crispy, about 1 minute or less, if using. Drain, crumble, and set aside.

4. Pinch off golf ball–size pieces of dough, either leave them as balls or flatten them slightly, and drop them in the hot oil to cook (do not crowd them) until golden, 5 to 6 minutes. Remove with a slotted spoon and drain on paper towels. Season with salt, then sprinkle the fritters with the garnishes you have chosen and serve immediately. Let the frying oil cool completely, strain through a porous paper filter, if necessary, and save the oil for a future use.

Makes 24 fried dough balls; 12 servings

Fried Pizzas with Sweet Tomato Sauce

This is a popular antipasto in Neapolitan homes called pizzelle fritte. *It can be served with Parmesan cheese, ricotta, or leafy green vegetables sautéed with garlic and olive oil, but be careful because they are addictive and you'll find yourself just popping them in your mouth one after the other. These little pizzas are almost always served as a passed cocktail antipasto.*

1 recipe Basic Bread and Pizza Dough (page 473)
6 tablespoons extra-virgin olive oil
8 large garlic cloves, finely chopped

2 dried red chiles
2 pounds ripe tomatoes, cut in half, seeds squeezed out, grated against the largest holes of a grater, and skins discarded
Salt to taste
2 tablespoons sugar
12 fresh basil leaves

1. Prepare the bread dough.

2. In a large skillet, heat the olive oil with the garlic and chiles over medium heat until the garlic starts to sizzle, stirring frequently so it doesn't burn, then add the tomatoes and cook until the liquid has evaporated, 20 to 25 minutes. Season with salt and the sugar. Turn the heat off, stir in the basil, and let rest, covered.

3. Roll the dough out 1 inch thick on a lightly floured work surface and cut slices at 1-inch intervals. Roll each piece of dough out to a ¼-inch-thick disk.

4. Preheat the frying oil in a deep fryer or an 8-inch saucepan fitted with a basket insert to 375°F. Fry several pieces of dough at a time in the hot oil (do not crowd them) until puffy and light golden, 1½ to 2 minutes. Remove with a slotted spoon, drain on paper towels, and serve with a dollop of the tomato sauce on top.

Makes 24 pizzas; 12 servings

Stuffed Fried Sicilian Pizza

In Sicily, there is a whole family of little baked or fried pizzas. One can buy them as street food from vendors whose stalls or carts are called friggitorie. *One kind is called* crispeddi *in Sicilian or* crispelle *in Italian, basically* meaning something like a fried crêpe, and it is popular in Catania, the largest city in eastern Sicily. In Ragusa, they also make crispeddi, where it may likely be called friteddi si Sammartinu, made for the festival of San Martino, with only boiled turnips greens or flowering broccoli. But this particular crispeddi is a kind of pizza stuffed with ricotta salata and anchovies and deep-fried until golden. It is also known as a kind of sfinci (page 298), while another kind is a little pizza called fravioli. The yeasted dough needs to rise for a long time before it is shaped into half-moons, like an empanada. Some cooks work the anchovies into the dough, while others work pork lard into it.

Some other Sicilian pizzas like this are quite fun and delicious to make—for example, a tarongia is a fried pizza, also called a fritelle, that simply has the anchovy fillets laid on top of the fried pizza once it comes out of the oil. The word tarongia derives from the Arabic word turunj, which means "citron" or "orange," which is what it looks like after it's fried. Another delicious topping is fennel and grated provolone cheese. You can make both by following this recipe, but fry the circles of dough once you've rolled them out.

1 recipe Basic Bread and Pizza Dough (page 473)
1 cup crumbled ricotta salata
24 salted anchovy fillets, rinsed
6 cups olive oil or olive pomace oil for frying
Salt to taste (optional)

1. Prepare the pizza dough, but let the dough rise 2 more hours than called for in step 4 on page 473. Divide into 8 balls and roll each out on a floured work surface into an 8-inch disk.

2. On one half of each disk place 2 tablespoons of ricotta salata and 3 anchovy fillets, then fold the other half over so it forms a crescent and crimp the edges together with the tines of a fork.

3. Preheat the frying oil in a deep fryer or an 8-inch saucepan fitted with a basket insert to 375°F. Fry the crispeddi several at a time in the hot oil (do not crowd them) until golden, about 2 minutes per side. Drain well on paper towels and serve hot, salting, if necessary. Let the frying oil cool completely, strain through a porous paper filter and save the oil for a future use.

Makes 8 crispeddi; 8 servings

Fried Escarole Calzone

This simple tidbit is called pizzelle di scarola. It is made with only some sautéed escarole, a slightly bitter salad green, which doesn't sound as if it would have enough flavor, but it does and it's not bitter at all since you neutralize the bitterness with a little sugar. The calzone can be cut in half to make smaller serving portions.

1 recipe Basic Bread and Pizza Dough (page 473)
1½ pounds escarole, washed well
2 tablespoons extra-virgin olive oil
2 large garlic cloves, very finely chopped
Salt to taste
1 teaspoon sugar
6 cups olive oil, olive pomace oil, or vegetable oil for frying

Pizza of the Women's Mouths

This recipe was called *pizza di bocca di dama* in sixteenth-century Naples, according to the cookbook author Bartolomeo Scappi in his book *Opera (dell'arte del cucinare)* published in 1570.

In a large mortar, pound the meat from 3 pigeons, half-spit roasted, without their bones or skin, and the meat from 3 boiled pigeons with 4 ounces of dates, and 8 ounces of marzipan and 4 ounces of beef bone marrow, and if there is no marzipan, then 8 ounces of almonds cooked in water, and 4 ounces of fine sugar and mix with 6 portions of heavy cream and if there is no fresh heavy cream, use 1 pound of fresh sheep's cheese and pass through a sieve then mix with 10 fresh egg yolks and 4 more ounces of fine sugar and one ounce cinnamon, and 1/2 ounce each of cloves and nutmeg. Cover a pie pan with a sheet of dough, made with fine flour, egg yolks, sugar, butter, rose water, and salt, in a spiral shape. Place the stuffing into this pie and cover with latticework strips of pie dough. Cook in an oven. In this pie musk-flavored biscotti *(mostaccioli muschiati)* can be put and a sauce made of malvasia wine, pomegranate sauce and a little sugar can be poured over.

1. Prepare the bread dough.

2. Boil the escarole in lightly salted water until the water returns to a boil and the escarole has been cooking 3 minutes, then drain, pressing the excess water out, and chop coarsely. In a large skillet, heat the olive oil with the garlic over medium heat, and once the garlic starts to sizzle, cook the escarole for 2 minutes, stirring. Season with salt and the sugar, mixing well.

3. Preheat the frying oil in a deep fryer or an 8-inch saucepan fitted with a basket insert to 375°F.

4. Roll the dough out on a lightly floured work surface until about 1/16 inch thick, then cut out 4-inch-diameter disks, re-rolling the dough scraps when necessary. Place some escarole in the middle of each, fold the disk over to form a half-moon, then crimp the edges together with a fork.

5. Fry several *pizzelle* at a time in the hot oil (do not crowd them) until golden, about 6 minutes. Remove with a slotted spoon, drain on paper towels, and serve hot or warm. Let the frying oil cool completely, strain through a porous paper filter, and save the oil for a future use.

Makes 20 calzone; 10 to 12 servings

Escarole, Chicory, and Endive

These are all very confusing and I'll tell you why. The leaves of endive have been used in salads since at least Greek and Roman times. Endive and chicory are two different species of the same genus, endive being an annual and chicory a perennial. There are several theories about the origins of chicory, but it seems most likely that it originated in the eastern Mediterranean. The reason for the confusion in names is because the French and English names get reversed. So the English chicory (*Cichorium intybus*) is called *endive* in French, while what is referred to as endive in English (*Cichorium endivia*) is known as *chicorée frisée* in French, a name used for the cut-leaf variety. Meanwhile, the broad-leaf variety of *Cichorium endivia* is known in English by the word *escarole*, derived from the French, *scarole*, which, fortunately, also refers to the broad-leaf variety. Got that? It's actually so confusing that there is a Web site devoted to "Sorting Cichorium," so don't feel so lost.

Olive Empanadillas

An empanadilla *is a small empanada and is the perfect* tapa *because of its bite-size nature. This preparation is quite simple and made all the easier by using pimiento-stuffed olives from a jar.*

Dough

3 cups unbleached all-purpose flour
6 tablespoons pork lard
1 teaspoon salt
¾ cup milk

Stuffing

1 cup chopped cooked ham (about 6 ounces)
1 large hard-boiled egg, shelled and chopped
60 pimiento-stuffed Spanish olives (about one 7-ounce jar)

6 cups olive oil, olive pomace oil, or vegetable oil for frying

1. Prepare the dough. Pour the flour in a large bowl, then cut in the lard with a pastry cutter until it looks like coarse meal. Season with the salt and pour in the milk. Form the dough into a smooth ball and refrigerate for 30 minutes.

2. Meanwhile, prepare the stuffing. Mix the ham and chopped egg.

3. Remove the dough from the refrigerator and cut in two. Roll half of the dough out on a lightly floured work surface until about ⅛ inch thick. Cut out 2½-inch disks, re-rolling the dough scraps when necessary. Roll out the second half of the dough and repeat. As you prepare to stuff each disk of dough, roll them out just a little thinner, then place 1 teaspoon of

the stuffing and 1 olive in the center of each disk. Fold the disk over to form a half-moon and pinch the edges together securely. Set aside on a baking sheet as you finish making the rest.

4. Preheat the frying oil in a deep fryer or an 8-inch saucepan fitted with a basket insert to 375°F. Cook the *empanadillas*, about 8 at a time (do not crowd them), in the hot oil until golden, about 3 minutes. Remove with a slotted spoon, drain on paper towels, and serve hot or warm.

Makes 60 empanadillas; 15 to 20 servings

Fried Sausage, Provolone, and Tomato Empanada

These empanadas known as ravazzati *are described in an old Sicilian dictionary as a kind of focaccia stuffed with a variety of ingredients. They are traditionally formed with two 5-inch-wide disks of dough encasing the stuffing. In this recipe I make them more like calzone or empanadas and deep-fry them until an appetizing orange color. This recipe calls for a stuffing of sausage, salami, peas, ricotta, and provolone, although the stuffing can vary. Some Sicilian cooks dip the* ravazzati *in eggs, then dredge them in bread crumbs before frying them.*

1 recipe Basic Bread and Pizza Dough (page 473), made with the addition of 2 tablespoons pork lard, melted, and 2 large eggs, beaten, in step 2

¾ cup fresh tomato puree mixed with 1 tablespoon tomato paste

½ pound fresh ricotta cheese, preferably homemade (page 88)

¾ cup shelled fresh or frozen peas, cooked in water to cover until tender and drained

2 sweet Italian sausages (about ½ pound), cooked fully and thinly sliced

1 ounce thinly sliced Neapolitan-style salami

2 large hard-boiled eggs, shelled and each cut into 7 or 8 slices

¼ pound thinly sliced provolone

Salt to taste

6 cups sunflower seed or vegetable oil for frying

1. Prepare the bread dough, incorporating the pork lard and beaten eggs. The dough will be sticky. Form the dough into 8 balls about the size of a large lemon and lay on a floured baking tray, covered with a kitchen towel, to rise for 2 hours in a warm place, such as a turned-off oven.

2. Roll each ball of dough out into an 8-inch-diameter disk on a well-floured work surface. The dough will be sticky, so it's important to make sure the surface and both sides of the disk are floured. Smear 1 tablespoon of tomato puree over each disk, leaving at least a 1-inch border with no sauce. In the center, place a dollop of ricotta, pushing it down slightly, then push about 1 tablespoon of peas into the ricotta. Lay a slice each of sausage and salami, 2 egg slices, and a slice of provolone on top. Season with salt, then fold one side over to the other to form a half-moon and crimp the edges together with a fork.

3. Preheat the frying oil in a deep fryer or an 8-inch saucepan fitted with a basket insert to 375°F. Fry the *ravazzati* several at a time (do not crowd them) in the hot oil until orange, about 5 minutes, turning once. Drain on paper towels,

In the traditional cuisine of Sicily, there is an absence of *antipasti* as they are known elsewhere in Italy. Some Sicilians believe this absence to be an Arab legacy. What the Sicilians call *grape 'u pitittu* are "openers of the mouth," not meant to stimulate the appetite, but rather served as snacks or tidbits, a lot like meze. They may be offered in restaurants as a *tavola calda*, a buffet table filled with a bewildering variety of preparations that one takes samples from. Some examples are Arancini (page 380), a ragout-stuffed deep-fried saffron rice ball, or *ravazzati* (Fried Sausage, Provolone, and Tomato Empanada; page 35), what we would call street food. One Sicilian food writer refused to open his book with an appetizer section because he didn't want to give the impression that Sicilians needed stimulation to relish a meal.

cut in half, or leave whole for a larger-than-appetizer portion. Serve immediately. Let the frying oil cool completely, strain through a porous paper filter, if necessary, and save the oil for a future use.

Makes 8 empanadas; 16 servings

Spicy Fried Meat Empanadillas

This tapa *called* empanadilla de carne *is one that I once had in Andalusia, but Penelope Casas in* Tapas: The Little Dishes of Spain *suggests Arab and Catalan overtones. Certainly the idea of mixing meat such as veal, pork, and beef is Catalan, and the spicing of oregano, cumin, and paprika seems Andalusian, especially when you put that egg in there, too. These empanadillas are very nice as a passed appetizer served with glasses of Rioja or a Catalan wine.*

1 recipe Basic Puff Pastry Short Dough for Empanadas (page 475)
2 tablespoons olive oil
1 medium-size onion, finely chopped
2 large garlic cloves, finely chopped
½ pound ground veal
½ pound ground beef
½ pound ground pork
Salt and freshly ground black pepper to taste
1 large hard-boiled egg, shelled and chopped
2 tablespoons finely chopped fresh parsley leaves
½ teaspoon dried oregano
1 teaspoon hot Spanish paprika
2 teaspoons freshly ground cumin seeds
1 tablespoon tomato paste mixed with ¼ cup dry red wine
6 cups olive oil, olive pomace oil, or vegetable oil for frying

1. Prepare the empanada dough.

2. In a large skillet, heat the olive oil over medium-high heat, then cook the onion and garlic until the onion is softened, about 5 minutes, stirring. Add the veal, beef, and pork and continue to cook until the meat loses its color, about 8 minutes, stirring and breaking up any clumps with a wooden spoon. Season with salt and pepper. Add the egg, parsley, oregano, paprika, cumin, and diluted tomato paste; reduce the heat to medium, cover, and cook for 5 minutes, stirring a few times. Turn the heat off. If there is a lot of liquid in the skillet, drain through a strainer.

3. On a floured work surface, roll the dough until ⅛ inch thick and cut out as many 3-inch disks as you can. Place about 2 teaspoons of filling in the middle of each disk, fold over, and crimp the edges together with the tines of a fork.

4. Preheat the frying oil in a deep fryer or an 8-inch saucepan fitted with a basket insert to 375°F. Fry several turnovers at a time (do not crowd them) in the hot oil until golden brown, about 4 minutes. Remove with a slotted spoon, drain on paper towels, and serve hot. Let the frying oil cool completely, strain through a porous paper filter, if necessary, and save the oil for a future use.

Makes 80 empanadillas; 20 to 25 servings

Making Empanadillas

Making short dough for *empanadillas* can be tricky because the ratio of fat to flour and liquid must be just right. Too much fat makes for a too crumbly dough. Too little liquid and it doesn't bind. It's best to start with all your ingredients cold. Try to handle the dough (with your hands, I mean) as little as possible. Use flour liberally if you believe there is too much fat in the dough when you are rolling it out. Roll the dough carefully and gently and use a dough scraper to lift it from the work surface if necessary.

Sanbūsak

This famous Arab pie called sanbūsak *may be the progenitor of the Spanish empanada and the Italian calzone.* Sanbūsak, *an Arabic word that comes from a Persian word referring to anything triangular, was first described as a stuffed pastry in the early ninth century. The famous tenth-century poet al-Masᶜūdī wrote an ode to* sanbūsak *in his* Meadows of Gold.

Pastry
2½ cups unbleached all-purpose flour, sifted
1 teaspoon salt
½ cup (1 stick) unsalted butter, cut into bits
½ cup cold water

Filling
2 tablespoons clarified butter
½ cup finely chopped onion
¾ pound lean ground lamb
¼ cup pine nuts
¼ teaspoon ground cinnamon
1 teaspoon freshly ground allspice berries
Salt and freshly ground black pepper to taste

6 cups olive oil, olive pomace oil, or vegetable oil

The Spanish and the Arabs

The Arabs ruled Spain or portions of Spain from 711 to 1492. The vestiges of their presence is evident today in everything from toponyms to architecture to cuisine. The Spanish find the idea of their cuisine being indebted to the Arabs exotic and exciting, and they are quite proud of this heritage. So much so that the famous El Caballo Rojo restaurant at Cardenal Herrero 28 in Córdoba near the Mezquita, one of the most popular restaurants in the city, calls its style of Andalusian cuisine *la antigua cocina mozarabe-magribi* ("the old cuisine of the Mozarab-Maghribis"). They have created interesting dishes that could be called Moroccan-Andalusian fusion cuisine, a not far-fetched idea since it has existed for 1,000 years in one sense. They offer dishes such as *rape Mozarabe*, a monkfish with carrots, raisins, and cognac, and *cordero a la miel*, lamb with green bell peppers and saffron in a honey and cognac sauce.

1. Make the pastry. Pour the flour and salt into a medium-size bowl. Work the butter into the flour with your fingertips until the mixture resembles coarse meal. Add the water slowly to make a soft, pliable dough. Form into a ball, then roll out to ⅛ inch thick on a lightly floured work surface and cut into 3-inch disks with a cookie cutter.

2. Prepare the filling. In a medium-size skillet, melt the clarified butter over medium heat, then cook the onion until translucent, 6 to 7 minutes, stirring. Add the lamb, pine nuts, cinnamon, and allspice, season with salt and pepper, and cook until the meat loses all its pinkness, breaking up lumps with a fork or wooden spoon and stirring occasionally to mix the ingredients well. Pour off the excess fat, squeezing the fat out of the meat by placing it in a slotted spoon and pressing with the back of a wooden spoon. Check the seasonings. Put about 1 teaspoon of stuffing on each disk. Fold over and pinch the edges together with the tines of a fork, forming a half-moon.

3. Preheat the frying oil to 375°F in a deep fryer or an 8-inch saucepan fitted with a basket insert. Deep-fry the pastries in batches (do not crowd them) in the hot oil until golden, about 4 minutes. Remove with a slotted spoon and drain on paper towels. Serve hot or at room temperature. Freeze any remaining stuffing for several months. Let the frying oil cool completely, strain through a porous paper filter, if necessary, and save the oil for a future use.

Makes 40 to 45 pies; 15 servings

• ❀ •

Remember to Seal

When making calzones, empanadas, *san-būsak*, or any other pastry or dough that gets stuffed and sealed before frying, remember to make sure that the edges are sealed properly, pinched together with the tines of a fork or a good pastry wheel—otherwise, the stuffing will escape into the frying oil and will be irretrievable.

Anchovy Empanada from Tuscany

It is not known whether there is any Spanish influence in this kind of calzone or empanada called figattole *from Tuscany, but it seems as if there is because you don't find these empanada types of preparations in northern Italy very often. As simple as this is, it is a very pleasant snack and you have a choice of doughs to use if you like.*

1 recipe Basic Bread and Pizza Dough (page 473), Basic Short Dough (page 475), or Basic Puff Pastry Short Dough for Empanadas (page 475)
24 to 48 salted anchovy fillets, rinsed
6 cups pure or virgin olive oil, olive pomace oil, or vegetable oil for frying

1. Prepare the bread dough. Roll out until thin on a lightly floured work surface and cut into thirty to forty 3-inch disks. Freeze any leftover bread dough for another use. Place one or two anchovy fillets on each disk and fold over to form a half-moon, using the tines of a fork to pinch the dough closed.

2. Preheat the frying oil to 375°F in a deep fryer or 8-inch saucepan fitted with a basket insert. Deep-fry several empanadas at a time (do not crowd them) in the hot oil until golden, about 2 minutes per side. Remove with a slotted spoon and drain on paper towels for a few minutes, then serve. Let the frying oil cool completely, strain through a porous paper filter, if necessary, and save the oil for a future use.

Makes 30 to 40 empanadas; 12 servings

More Tapas

When writing this book, I anguished over which tapas I should include. The book could have included 500 tapas alone. There are hundreds I've eaten in Spain that don't appear in this book. All I can do is mention some, and although you can't do a genuine *tapeo*—tapas bar crawl—you can at least imagine a *tasca*, or tapas bar, by eating all these delicious tapas. Be convivial and try to make the following based on the ingredients alone: *anguilas a la vasca*, eels with chiles and lots of garlic; baby octopus in olive oil; *calamares en su tinta*, baby squid in its ink, which isn't bad out of a can; tuna with sautéed green bell peppers; raw clams with sherry; snails cooked in garlic.

Valencia-Style Empanadillas

An empanadilla *is simply a small empanada—stuffed bread or short dough that is formed into a half-moon, like the calzone, to which it is related, and fried or baked and eaten as a* tapa *or sandwich in Spain.*

I am providing two different recipes for you to choose from for the empanadilla *dough. The first is a more rustic short dough typical of these small pies of Valencia and sometimes used for the larger pies of Galicia and Asturia. The second dough recipe is a yeasted bread dough.*

Short Dough

6 tablespoons extra-virgin olive oil

½ cup water

½ teaspoon salt

3 cups unbleached all-purpose flour

½ teaspoon aniseeds

Yeasted Bread Dough

1 cup tepid water

1 tablespoon active dry yeast

1 tablespoon extra-virgin olive oil

1 ounce pork lard, cut into small pieces

1 teaspoon salt

3½ cups unbleached all-purpose flour

Stuffing

3 tablespoons extra-virgin olive oil

1 small onion, finely chopped

1½ cups canned or fresh peeled, seeded, and ground or crushed tomatoes

One 3-ounce can imported tuna in olive oil

Salt to taste

6 cups olive oil or olive pomace oil

1. Make one of the doughs. For the short dough, pour the olive oil, water, and salt in a medium-size bowl, then add the flour and aniseeds. Mix well, then knead until you have a smooth, pliable ball of dough. Cover with plastic wrap and leave for 30 minutes at room temperature.

For the yeasted bread dough, pour the tepid water in a small bowl and stir in the yeast until dissolved. Stir in the olive oil and lard. Let rest for 10 minutes. Sift the salt and flour together in a large bowl. Make a well in the flour and pour in the yeast water. Mix until a ball can be formed, then knead for 5 to 10 minutes. Cover with a kitchen towel and leave the dough to rise for 6 hours in a warm place, punching it down twice.

2. Make the stuffing. In a small skillet, heat the olive oil over medium heat, then cook the onion until translucent, about 8 minutes, stirring. Add the tomatoes and cook until thickened, about 20 minutes. Take the skillet off the heat and stir in the tuna and salt, mixing well. Set aside.

3. When it is time to make the *empanadillas*, roll a portion of the dough out very thin on a lightly floured work surface and cut out 4- to 5-inch circles. Place a heaping teaspoon of stuffing in the center of each circle of dough and fold over to form a half-moon. Pinch together the edges with the tines of a fork, flip to other side, and pinch them together again. Set aside until ready to bake or fry.

4. Preheat the frying oil to 360°F in a deep fryer or an 8-inch saucepan fitted with a basket insert or preheat the oven to 350°F. Deep-fry

several *empanadillas* at a time in the hot oil (do not crowd them) until golden, about 1 minute, turning once, or bake on a lightly greased baking sheet until golden, about 25 minutes. If frying, drain on paper towels. Serve hot or warm. Let the frying oil cool completely, strain through a porous paper filter, if necessary, and save the oil for a future use.

Makes 40 empanadillas; 12 servings

Variation: The *empanadillas* can be stuffed with a mixture of chopped fresh tomato, cooked and flaked hake, seeded and chopped green bell pepper, chopped wilted spinach, and toasted pine nuts.

Fried Tidbits

This is the most hypocritical chapter in the book. Why? Because in this chapter you will find all the recipes that guests will tell you they can't eat and yet these are the preparations they request most often. Let's be honest, people are far more afraid of frying than they are of fried foods. Properly fried foods are delicious and not necessarily fat-laden. Improperly fried foods, on the other hand, can be greasy, unappetizing, and definitely not good for you. In this chapter I explain how to fry properly, and you should pay attention to that advice if you have not fried regularly before.

This chapter has an extraordinarily wide range of fried foods. Some are delicious and challenging, like making a perfect Fried Kibbe (page 363). I also have given you a lot of recipes that I think are easy and delicious, such as Ham Fritters in the Andalusian Style (page 361) and Ham and Almond Beignet Fritters (page 362). I'm also a fan of old-fashioned recipes that one probably never will see in a restaurant, such as Shrimp, Mushroom, and Béchamel Croquettes (page 369) and Fish, Shrimp, and Parmesan Beignet Fritters from Modena (page 371). Two of my favorite recipes are Sicilian Fried Eggplant "Sandwiches" (page 378) and Batter-Fried Spring Onions with Almond and Hazelnut Sauce (page 379). I am also quite fond of straightforward vegetable fritters such as Cauliflower and Cheese Fritters from Algeria (page 384) and Leek Beignet Fritters from Corsica (page 387). They don't sound elegant, but you will be surprised at how popular they are at parties. The last recipe in this chapter is, for me, the most famous fritter of the Mediterranean, falafel. Make it yourself and you can consider yourself a real cook.

Fried Mortadella

This preparation from Emilia-Romagna is a milk-soaked mortadella fried in oil. Mortadella is a quite lean pork sausage with "eyes" of fat, flavored with peppercorns, pistachios, wine, sugar, and olives and stuffed into beef bladder casing, giving the final product a huge shape. Mortadella has an old history in the Mediterranean, being mentioned in the statutes of the Cathedral of Nice from 1233 as food for holidays such as Easter, Pentecost, and Christmas. In the fourteenth century, mortadella is mentioned again in the anonymous Liber de coquina, *apparently written by someone familiar with the Neapolitan court then under the sphere of Charles II of Anjou, and in the* Libro per cuoco *by an anonymous Venetian, where it is made with the addition of pig's liver. Today, this preparation is an unusual* passatempo, *or cocktail tidbit, delicious—but you must soak the mortadella in milk before cooking during the day or overnight to remove any saltiness. I like to serve this as a plated appetizer before people have a first course, accompanied by a glass of Lambrusco.*

One ¾-inch-thick piece mortadella (½ pound)
Milk for soaking
All-purpose flour for dredging
1 large egg, lightly beaten and salted
Dry bread crumbs for dredging
3 tablespoons unsalted butter
3 tablespoons extra-virgin olive oil

1. Cut the mortadella into 3-inch squares. Place in a small bowl, cover with milk, and let soak for 6 to 8 hours in the refrigerator. Drain.

2. Dredge the mortadella pieces in flour, shaking off any excess. Dip in the beaten egg, then dredge well in bread crumbs. Set aside on a plate in the refrigerator for 30 minutes.

3. In a small skillet, melt the butter with the olive oil until very hot, almost smoking, over medium-high heat and cook the breaded mortadella until golden on both sides, 2 to 3 minutes. Drain on paper towels and serve hot.

Makes 4 servings

Mortadella

Mortadella is a pork baloney made in Italy in the region of Emilia. But don't call it baloney; it's much more tasteful than that. Fine pork meats are selected and so finely ground that the semi-finished product is creamy. Cubes of pork fat cut from the throat, the most prized fat on a pig, are added to this pork "cream." These chunks of fat are called *lardelli*. The mixture is put into casing with whole peppercorns and pistachios, cooked in a dry-air stove, and then cooled. When finished, the mortadella is a huge cylinder, up to a foot in diameter. The inside slices are pink and dotted with the attractive white cubes of *lardelli*, the brilliant green of the pistachios, and the black of the peppercorns. The aroma is unmistakable and the flavor slightly sweet, full, and rich. The best place to buy top-quality domestically produced mortadella is at an Italian market.

Meat and Kefalotyri Cheese Croquettes

This meze, called kroketes apo kreas, *or meat croquettes, is usually prepared with leftover cooked pork or veal roast.* Kefalotyri *cheese is a pale yellow sheep or goat's milk cheese that is hard and slightly salted. You can find it in Greek markets and many Middle Eastern markets. I would replace it with a young pecorino cheese, known as pecorino Crotonese or table pecorino in Italian markets. These croquettes are nice to serve as a passed appetizer.*

2 large eggs, separated, whites beaten until frothy
½ cup grated *kefalotyri* cheese
¾ cup plus 2 tablespoons Béchamel Sauce
   (page 468)
1 tablespoon finely chopped onion
1 tablespoon finely chopped fresh parsley leaves
2 cups finely chopped leftover roast pork or veal
   (about 10 ounces)
Salt and freshly ground black pepper to taste
Dry bread crumbs for dredging
6 cups olive oil or olive pomace oil for frying
1 lemon, cut into 8 wedges

1. In a large bowl, beat together the egg yolks, cheese, béchamel sauce, onion, parsley, and meat. Season with salt and pepper, then let stand for 20 minutes.

2. Take a small amount of the mixture and form it into a patty using wet hands so it doesn't stick too much. Dredge the croquettes in bread crumbs, coating them evenly and shaping them more into a cylinder as you do, then dip in the egg whites and dredge again in the bread crumbs. Arrange on a tray and refrigerate for 30 minutes.

3. Preheat the frying oil in a deep fryer or an 8-inch saucepan fitted with a basket insert to 375°F. Fry several at a time (don't crowd them) until golden brown, about 4 minutes. Remove with a slotted spoon, drain on paper towels, and serve hot with a wedge of lemon. Let the frying oil cool completely, strain through a porous paper filter, if necessary, and save the oil for a future use.

Makes 16 croquettes; 8 servings

Kefalotyri Cheese

Kefalotyri is a hard *grana* type of cheese, like this Parmigiano-Reggiano, so-called because when aged they are densely granular, hence *grana*. The cheese is made from sheep's or goat's milk, mostly in Greece, but also in Syria. The wheel of cheese is said to resemble a hat, *kefalo* in Greek, giving the cheese its name.

Ham Fritters in the Andalusian Style

This tapa *from southern Spain is called* buñuelitos de jamón, *and it is usually served in tapas bars as one of the first to come out. It's all very simple, but remember that it doesn't cook for long. Although a traditional* tapa, *these ham fritters are very nice served as a passed appetizer at a cocktail party with a glass of fine sherry.*

6 cups olive oil or olive pomace oil for frying

1 large egg, lightly beaten

Salt and freshly ground black pepper to taste

¼ teaspoon paprika

½ cup beer (lager)

½ cup all-purpose flour, sifted

2 tablespoons extra-virgin olive oil

1 cup chopped boiled ham (about 6 ounces)

1 small onion, very finely chopped

1. Preheat the frying oil in a deep fryer or an 8-inch saucepan fitted with a basket insert to 375°F.

2. In a medium-size bowl, mix the egg, salt, pepper, paprika, and beer. Add the flour and whisk until the batter is smooth and dense.

3. In a medium-size skillet, heat the extra-virgin olive oil over medium-high heat, then cook the ham and onion until the onion is soft, about 3 minutes, stirring. Let cool, then stir into the batter.

4. Drop tablespoonfuls of the batter into the oil (make sure not to crowd them) and fry until golden brown, about 2 minutes. Remove with a slotted spoon, drain on paper towels, and serve hot. Let the frying oil cool completely, strain through a porous paper filter, if necessary, and save the oil for a future use.

Makes 16 fritters; 8 serving

Ham and Almond Beignet Fritters

This northern Italian beignet fritter is made with thinly slivered almonds and is called beignets pignatelli. *You can vary the spicing if you like by adding more salt, black pepper, or cayenne. Serve these with a sparkling white wine.*

1 recipe Basic Italian-Style Beignet Batter for Frying (page 477), adding 1 ounce boiled ham, trimmed of fat and chopped, and a pinch of freshly grated nutmeg (optional) after adding the eggs

1 tablespoon unsalted butter

¼ pound (1 cup) slivered blanched almonds

Salt and freshly ground black pepper to taste

Cayenne pepper to taste (optional)

6 cups olive oil or olive pomace oil for frying

1. Prepare the beignet batter.

2. In a medium-size skillet, melt the butter over medium-high heat, then cook the almonds until golden, 3 to 4 minutes, stirring or shaking the skillet and being careful not to burn them. Drain on some paper towels, then mix into the dough. Correct the seasoning of the batter with salt, black pepper, and cayenne, if you like.

3. Preheat the frying oil in a deep fryer or an 8-inch saucepan fitted with a basket insert to 375°F. Drop tablespoonfuls of the batter into the oil (do not crowd them) and fry until golden and crisp, about 3 minutes. Remove with a slotted spoon, drain on paper towels, salt and pepper them, and serve immediately. Let the frying oil cool completely, strain through a porous paper filter, if necessary, and save the oil for a future use.

Makes 26 to 30 beignets; 10 servings

Fried Kibbe

Kubba maqliyya (maḥshiyya), *a lamb-and-bulgur mixture ground to a paste and formed into a hollow ball for stuffing, is often considered to be the national dish of Lebanon and Syria. The word* kibbe *comes from the Arabic verb "to form into a ball." The perfect kibbe is considered the apex of the culinary art in the Arab world. The hardest thing to achieve is forming the ball of kibbe into a long, hollow, smooth-skinned oval shell. Women with long, graceful fingers are admired by both sexes because it is rightly assumed that they have the ability to make perfect kibbe with their slender fingers.*

I learned this recipe from my former wife, Najwa al-Qattan, who learned it in turn from her grandmother. There are many ways of preparing the basic kibbe mixture. It can be formed into hollow shells, then stuffed and fried, as in this recipe. When kibbe are charcoal-grilled, they are called manqal. *Kibbe Nayya (page 76) is a raw, steak tartare version. In* kubba bi'l-ṣiniyya, *or pan kibbe (see Note), half the kibbe mixture is pressed into the bottom of a baking tray or pan and covered with the meat stuffing and then the remaining kibbe mixture. It is cut on the diagonal into trapezoids or diamonds (see Note).*

All the ingredients should be kept cold while you work. Since forming the kibbe shell is the most important part of preparing kubba maqliyya, *you will need to pay special attention. Take a ball of kibbe, one about the size of a small egg. Roll it between the palms of your hands until it is smooth. Dip your hands occa-*

Ordering Meze

When ordering meze for a group of, let's say, eight people at a Middle Eastern or Greek restaurant, you could easily order sixteen meze. But remember to mix them up so that you have a few cold and a few hot meze, as well as a few that are saucy and a few that are dry. Hummus (page 68) is obligatory on every meze table.

sionally in a pan of cold water so the meat doesn't stick to them; the wetness also helps in smoothing out cracks in the kibbe. Put your forefinger in the center of the ball and begin to make a hole. Use the hand with which you are holding the ball to turn the ball and use your finger as a stationary device that makes the hole, much as if your finger were the spindle on a potter's wheel. The walls of the kibbe shell must be very, very thin. Because the bulgur will expand as it cooks, what you think are thin walls will become thick, so continue flipping the kibbe shell in your palm, pressing your finger against the walls until they are about ⅛ inch thick. This is quite difficult to achieve, so you may want to practice with a ball of kibbe before actually stuffing it. See also Kibbe with Yogurt (page 137) and Grilled Kibbe with Pomegranate Syrup (page 427).

Kibbe

2 cups raw fine bulgur (no. 1)

2 teaspoons black peppercorns

2 teaspoons salt

2 pounds ground lamb, cut from the leg or
shoulder

1 medium-size onion, grated

1 teaspoon Bahārāt (page 470)

Stuffing

½ teaspoon black peppercorns

1 teaspoon salt

6 tablespoons clarified butter

1 medium-size onion, finely chopped

¼ cup pine nuts

1 pound ground lamb, cut from the leg or
shoulder

1 teaspoon Bahārāt (page 470)

6 cups olive oil, olive pomace oil, or vegetable oil
for frying

Fresh parsley leaves for garnish

Plain yogurt (optional)

Chopped scallions (optional)

Arabic bread (optional)

1. Make the kibbe. Cover a strainer with cheesecloth and place the bulgur on top. Place the strainer in a pot filled with lightly salted cold water and soak the bulgur for 10 minutes in the refrigerator. Pull up the sides of the cheesecloth, encasing the bulgur, and squeeze out all the water. Transfer to a large bowl.

2. Grind the peppercorns with the salt in a mortar. Mix the ground lamb, salt and pepper, grated onion, and *bahārāt* in a large bowl. Add the bulgur to the meat mixture. Place the meat mixture in a food processor in batches and process until it is a paste. Remove to a large metal bowl and refrigerate for 1 hour.

3. Meanwhile, make the stuffing. Crush the peppercorns with the salt in a mortar. Heat the clarified butter in a medium-size skillet over medium heat, then cook the onion until yellow, about 5 minutes, stirring a few times. Add the pine nuts and cook for 2 minutes. Add the ground lamb and *bahārāt*, season with the salt and pepper, and brown the meat until it loses its pink color, 8 to 10 minutes, breaking the meat up further and mixing the ingredients as you cook.

4. Form the ball of kibbe as described in the headnote above and hollow it out so the walls are ⅛ inch thick. Stuff it with a heaping tablespoon of the cooked lamb mixture and close the opening with your fingers. Keep your hands wet and gently roll the kibbe between your palms to perfect a teardrop shape, fixing cracks and making the surface very smooth. Continue in this way to make all the kibbe.

5. Preheat the frying oil in a deep fryer or an 8-inch saucepan fitted with a basket insert to 360°F. Deep-fry the kibbe, not crowding them, until brown, 4 to 5 minutes. Remove the first one, cut it open, and check to see if the timing is correct for doneness. Drain on paper towels. Repeat for the remaining kibbe. Let the frying oil cool completely, strain through a porous paper filter, if necessary, and save the oil for a future use.

6. Serve the kibbe on a bed of parsley leaves on a platter. Kibbe are eaten with one's fingers, plain, or served with yogurt and scallions wrapped in soft and warm Arabic bread.

Note: To make pan kibbe, *kubba bi'l-ṣiniyya,* butter a 14-inch round baking pan and preheat the oven to 360°F. Press half the kibbe mixture to cover the bottom of the pan. Cover with the kibbe stuffing. Cover the stuffing with the remaining kibbe mixture, pressing down carefully so that you do not compact the stuffing. Smooth the top with a spatula. Using a sharp knife, score the kibbe into diamond or trapezoid shapes. Pour up to ¾ cup melted clarified butter or olive oil mixed with a little water over the pan. Bake until deep brown, about 30 minutes. Finish cutting the score marks all the way through. Serve with a slotted spoon to leave the fat behind in the pan.

Makes 24 kibbe or one 14-inch baking pan of kibbe; 12 servings

Curried Cucumber and Lamb Tongue Skewers

This party appetizer inspired by some of the meze I've had in Tunisia may be off-putting because of the tongue, but let me assure you that if you're from New York City and loved tongue sandwiches as a kid, you'll love this preparation. And if you've never had tongue before, then this is the place to start. Lamb tongue is likely to be found in a supermarket that caters to an ethnic population or you may need to make a trip to a local ethnic butcher, such as a kosher or halal *butcher.*

2¼ pounds lamb tongues, coarse skin and gristle removed and cut into ¼-inch-thick slices
2 tablespoons vegetable oil
Juice from 1 lemon
2 teaspoons freshly ground cumin seeds
2 teaspoons freshly ground coriander seeds
Salt and freshly ground black pepper to taste
5 teaspoons clarified butter
1 teaspoon mild curry powder
¼ teaspoon garlic powder
¼ teaspoon cayenne pepper
1 cup mayonnaise, preferably homemade (page 466)
6 cups vegetable oil for frying
9 medium-size cucumbers, peeled, seeded, and cubed

1. Toss the lamb tongues with the oil, lemon juice, cumin, and coriander in a ceramic bowl. Season with salt and pepper to taste, cover with plastic wrap, and let marinate for 6 hours in the refrigerator.

2. In a small skillet, heat or melt the clarified butter over medium heat, then stir in the curry powder, garlic powder, and cayenne. Stir until tiny bubbles appear. Remove from the heat and let cool completely. Stir into the mayonnaise.

3. Preheat the frying oil in a deep fryer or an 8-inch saucepan fitted with a basket insert to 375°F. Pat the lamb dry with paper towels and fry in batches until crisp looking, about 3 minutes. Remove with a slotted spoon and let drain on paper towels.

4. Skewer a piece of lamb with a slice of cucumber using a party toothpick. Serve warm with the curry mayonnaise.

Makes 20 skewers; 10 to 12 servings

Batter-Fried Lamb Brains from Lebanon

This preparation, called nukha^cāt maqliyya, *is very popular in Lebanon and usually serves as part of a meze table. In the Middle Ages, though, especially in northwestern Arabia, eating sheep's brains was not advised because it was thought that it caused loss of memory and would make you stupid, since sheep are stupid animals. Today, connoisseurs know that the mild taste of veal brains and their soft texture make a truly heavenly morsel when batter-dipped and fried to an attractive golden color. Also see page 333 for more on brains.*

1 pound veal or lamb brain

1 tablespoon white wine vinegar

Salt to taste

6 cups olive oil, olive pomace oil, or vegetable oil
    for frying

1 large egg

¾ cup milk

¾ cup all-purpose flour

Lettuce leaves for garnish (optional)

Lemon wedges

1. Soak the brain in cold water to cover for 1 hour, changing the water 3 times. Bring a medium-size pot of water acidulated with the vinegar to just below a boil. Poach the brain until firm, about 20 minutes. Drain, cut into bite-size pieces, and season with salt.

2. Preheat the frying oil in a deep fryer or an 8-inch saucepan fitted with a basket insert to 375°F.

3. Make the batter by beating the egg, milk, and flour together in a medium-size bowl. Dip the pieces of brain into the batter, letting excess batter drip off, and deep-fry several at a time (don't crowd them) in the hot oil until golden, about 3½ minutes. Remove from the oil with a slotted spoon, drain on paper towels for a moment, and serve immediately on a bed of lettuce leaves, if desired, with lemon wedges. Let the frying oil cool completely, strain through a porous paper filter, if necessary, and save the oil for a future use.

Makes 4 servings

Chicken Croquettes from Emilia

Known as crocchette di pollo, *this is an old-fashioned recipe, but delicious. The outside of the croquette is cooked until crusty and golden brown, while the inside is succulent and soft. They make this croquette in Sicily, too, usually with cheese instead of mushrooms.*

3 cups Béchamel Sauce (page 468)

2 tablespoons unsalted butter

¼ pound button mushrooms, thinly sliced

3 large egg yolks

1 pound ground chicken, cooked in a skillet over
    medium-high heat with ½ tablespoon unsalted
    butter until all pinkness is gone

Salt and freshly ground black pepper to taste

2 tablespoons finely chopped fresh parsley leaves

All-purpose flour for dredging

2 large eggs, beaten

Dry bread crumbs for dredging

6 cups olive oil or olive pomace oil for frying

1. Place the béchamel sauce in a medium-size saucepan and reduce to 1 cup over medium-low heat, 15 to 20 minutes, stirring frequently.

2. In a medium-size skillet, melt 1 tablespoon of the butter and cook the mushrooms, covered, over medium-low heat until golden, about 6 minutes, stirring a few times. Chop the mushrooms and reserve any liquid left in the pan. Once the mushrooms are cool, stir into the egg yolks and beat well. Slowly add the mushroom mixture to the béchamel and cook, stirring constantly, over low heat for 2 minutes. Remove from the heat. Stir in the remaining 1 tablespoon butter and the chicken and season with salt and pepper. Stir in the parsley. Cover with plastic wrap and refrigerate for 2 hours.

3. Form the mixture into croquettes about the size of a thumb with moistened hands so they don't stick. Dredge in the flour, patting off any excess flour, then dip into the eggs and finally roll in the bread crumbs to coat evenly. Set aside on a plate and refrigerate for 30 minutes.

4. Preheat the frying oil in a deep fryer or an 8-inch saucepan fitted with a basket insert to 375°F.

5. Fry several croquettes at a time (don't crowd them) until golden brown, 3 to 3½ minutes. Remove using a slotted spoon, drain on paper towels, and serve hot. Let the frying oil cool completely, strain through a porous paper filter, if necessary, and save the oil for a future use.

Makes 24 croquettes;

12 servings

Fried Mussels from Antalya in Turkey

The preparation of midye tava *is popular in most of Turkey, but it is a specialty of Antalya on Turkey's Mediterranean coast. The mussels are always shucked at the last minute, then quickly dipped in beer batter, fried in olive oil, and served as a meze, usually with tarator sauce (see Note on page 368). This recipe comes from the Pink Restaurant on Mermerli Sokak in Antalya. My friend David Forbes and I ate these mussels with a cold beer while on a promontory above the tiny harbor of Antalya with its magnificent view of the mountains of ancient Lycia in the distance; we feel that these mussels are as memorable as that view.*

½ cup all-purpose flour

1 tablespoon tomato juice (from a fresh or canned plum tomato, or tomato paste mixed with water)

2 large eggs, separated

¾ cup beer (lager)

Salt to taste

48 mussels, scrubbed and debearded

1½ cups olive oil or extra-virgin olive oil

1. In a large bowl, mix the flour, tomato juice, egg yolks, beer, and salt. In a medium-size bowl, beat the egg whites until stiff peaks form, then fold into the batter.

2. Shuck the mussels with a clam knife. Discard the shells. Drain the mussels.

3. In a large skillet, heat the olive oil until nearly smoking. Dip the mussels in the batter, let any excess drip off, and fry in batches until

golden, 2 to 3 minutes, making sure you don't crowd the skillet. Remove with a skimmer or slotted spoon to a paper towel–lined platter to drain. Salt and serve immediately or keep warm until they are all cooked.

Note: Tarator sauce is made by grinding 1 cup walnuts to a powder in a food processor, then mixing in 4 mashed garlic cloves and 2 to 3 cups diced French bread without its crust, which has been previously soaked in milk and squeezed dry. Beat olive oil and fresh lemon juice into the mixture as one would make mayonnaise until it reaches that consistency.

Makes 6 to 8 servings

Debearding

Nearly all the mussels you will encounter in the market today are cultivated mussels. They will usually be rather well cleaned for you already, but it's a good idea to give them a cleaning in fresh cold water. They will have a little string of what looks like seaweed hanging off their hinge by which they attach themselves to rocks. This "beard," called a byssus, must be pulled off.

Crispy Fried Galician-Style Oysters on the Half Shell

The Spanish province of Galicia borders the Atlantic north of Portugal and has long been a supplier of excellent seafood. In 1536 all the sardines eaten in Toulouse came from Galicia. The Spanish food authority José María Castroviejo described the cuisine of Galicia as una cocina barroca *("baroque cuisine"), partly because it devolves from the sea and the mountains, from peasants, and from a landed feudal aristocracy. This* tapa *is also very nice accompanied with a small dollop of* allioli. *It would be best to shuck your own oysters rather than buying the pre-shucked jarred oysters, which tend to be very big and not as fresh.*

2 cups olive oil or olive pomace oil for frying
24 oysters, washed well, soaked in cold water to cover with 1 tablespoon baking soda for 1 hour to remove sand and grit, rinsed, and shucked (saving the deeper of the shell halves)
Juice from 1 lemon
1 large egg, beaten
Fine corn flour for dredging
½ cup Allioli (page 466)
Salt to taste

1. In a large skillet, heat the olive oil over medium-high heat to 375°F. Meanwhile, dip the oysters in the lemon juice, then in the egg, and finally dredge them in the corn flour, shaking off any excess flour.

2. Fry the oysters, in batches if necessary to avoid crowding, until golden and crispy, turning once carefully with a fork, 2 to 4 minutes, depending on the size of the oysters. Place the cooked oysters on a shell half with a small dollop of *allioli* and a sprinkle of salt, and serve immediately.

Makes 12 servings

Dressed Crab Venetian Style

Granceola, granzeola, granseo'le, *or* grancevola *is a kind of crab from the Venetian lagoon also known as the spider crab* (Maja squinado *Herbst*), *which can grow up to 8 inches in diameter. When I was living in Venice, I discovered that when you saw* granceola *on a menu, it could mean a variety of things because there are a variety of ways to prepare this crab, the most common being dressed simply with olive oil, lemon juice, and parsley. But this recipe comes by way of the Arsenalbar, a little cafe near where I went to school, across from the Arsenale. It is actually a crab claw that has been shelled, rolled in bread crumbs, and fried in olive oil until a very attractive orange-golden color. As you will be unable to find spider crab, I've used Alaskan king crab legs to great success. When you crack the shells, try and keep the meat as intact as possible so they are in pieces about 2 inches long. Serve these as a passed appetizer or for a sit-down dinner.*

2 large eggs

2 teaspoons tomato paste

Salt and freshly ground black pepper to taste

4 large cooked Alaskan king crab legs (about 2 pounds), shelled carefully and the meat extracted as whole as possible

Fine dry bread crumbs for dredging

2 cups olive oil

1. Stir the eggs and tomato paste together and season with salt and pepper. Dip the crab pieces in the eggs, then roll in the bread crumbs. Set on a baking tray and refrigerate for 30 minutes.

2. In a large skillet, heat the oil to 375°F. Fry the crab several pieces at a time (do not crowd them) in the hot oil until golden, about 2 minutes. Remove with a slotted spoon, drain on paper towels, and serve hot.

Makes 6 to 8 servings

Little Foods in Renaissance Venice

In the palace of the doges in Renaissance Venice, most banquets began with eleven ordover, a Venetian word for "hors d'oeuvre." Often there were plates of fresh fruit and small pastries, salted tongue; and Florence salami and the local spider crabs of the Venetian lagoon were common. The main course was mostly meat, such as veal tripe, stuffed meat loaf, chicken, roast or boiled veal, or grilled lamb offal. Then vegetables like asparagus, artichokes, and fennel would arrive cold on plates to clean the palate.

Shrimp, Mushroom, and Béchamel Croquettes

This quite luscious croquette found in northern Italy is called crocchetta di gamberi *and is a little tricky to make, but worth the effort because it is truly sinful. The difficult part is getting the consistency of the béchamel just right, then being able to form the croquettes without their falling apart. The béchamel should be thick enough so that when it cools it is stiff. Nevertheless, there's a limit to how stiff it will be and still be good, so just remember to handle it as little as possible, packing it as you would a snowball when you're making the croquettes. Once they are breaded, the croquettes will hold together fine and they will cook fine, too. If you like, serve these croquettes with Marsala sauce (see box).*

¼ cup (½ stick) unsalted butter

¼ cup all-purpose flour, plus more for dredging

½ cup heavy cream

1¼ cups milk

Salt and freshly ground black pepper to taste

¼ teaspoon freshly grated nutmeg

1 tablespoon extra-virgin olive oil

1 pound fresh shrimp with their heads or
    ½ pound previously frozen headless shrimp,
    shells and/or heads removed

½ pound button mushrooms, chopped

2 large eggs, beaten

Dry bread crumbs for dredging

6 cups olive oil, olive pomace oil, or vegetable oil
    for frying

Chopped fresh parsley leaves for garnish

1. In a large saucepan, melt 2 tablespoons of the butter over medium-high heat, then stir in the flour to form a roux, stirring for about a minute. Remove the saucepan from the heat and slowly whisk in the cream and milk. Season with salt, pepper, and the nutmeg. Return to the burner, reduce the heat to low, and simmer until very thick, about 20 minutes, stirring occasionally.

2. In a medium-size skillet, melt 1 tablespoon of the butter with the olive oil over high heat, then cook the shrimp until firm and orange, about 2 minutes. Remove the shrimp with a slotted spoon and set aside. Add the mushrooms to the skillet and cook, stirring frequently until golden, 8 to 10 minutes. Transfer to the shrimp, then stir both into the béchamel.

3. Spread the béchamel until ½ inch thick in a rectangular rimmed baking sheet. Dot the top with the remaining 1 tablespoon butter and smear it over once it's melted. Place the baking sheet in the refrigerator and allow to cool completely.

4. Divide the chilled béchamel into 1-ounce thumb-size portions, then transfer to a plate with the flour to dredge them in. Handle them carefully and roll in the flour, forming the croquettes in your palms as you do. Dip or roll in the eggs, then roll in the bread crumbs. Place on a baking sheet or tray while you continue to

Marsala Sauce

To make a Marsala sauce for croquettes, first prepare a meat sauce by sautéing a small onion in olive oil until soft. Add ½ pound ground beef, cook until it turns color, then add 3 pounds canned crushed tomatoes, 3 finely chopped garlic cloves, and 1 teaspoon dried oregano, and cook over medium heat for 20 minutes. Transfer the meat sauce to the top of a double boiler so you can heat it while you whisk in 2 tablespoons butter and ½ cup sweet Marsala wine, whisking the whole time you pour.

make the remaining croquettes. Refrigerate for 1 hour before cooking.

5. Preheat the frying oil in a deep fryer or an 8-inch saucepan fitted with a basket insert to 375°F. Cook the croquettes several at a time (do not crowd them) in the hot oil until golden brown, about 3 minutes. Remove with a slotted spoon and drain on paper towels. Serve hot garnished with parsley. Let the frying oil cool completely, strain through a porous paper filter, if necessary, and save the oil for a future use.

Makes 18 croquettes; 6 servings

Shrimp Fritters from Andalusia

In this tapa, *called* buñelos de gambas, *shrimp are dipped in a tempura-like yeasted batter and deep-fried. This is a recipe popular in coastal cities like Cadiz, where the shrimp is really fresh. Although these fritters are good for any occasion, they are preferable to serve it as a passed appetizer with white wine.*

2 pounds fresh shrimp with their heads or
  1 pound previously frozen headless shrimp,
  shells and/or heads removed
One ¼-ounce package active dry yeast
2 cups warm milk
1½ cups unbleached all-purpose flour
1 teaspoon salt, or to taste
6 tablespoons finely chopped fresh parsley leaves
6 cups olive oil or olive pomace oil for frying

1. Bring a large saucepan of abundantly salted water to a boil, then plunge the shrimp in and cook until they turn orange, about 2 minutes. Drain.

2. In a medium-size bowl, dissolve the yeast in 3 tablespoons of the warm milk. Stir in the flour, salt, parsley, and remaining milk and beat until smooth. Cover with a kitchen towel and leave to ferment for 2 hours inside a turned-off oven.

3. Preheat the frying oil in a deep fryer or an 8-inch saucepan fitted with a basket insert to 375°F. Dip the shrimp into the batter, letting any excess drip off, and fry several at a time (do not crowd them) in the hot oil until golden, about 2 minutes. Remove with a slotted spoon, drain on paper towels, and serve hot. Let the frying oil cool completely, strain through a porous paper filter, if necessary, and save the oil for a future use.

Makes 6 servings

Fish, Shrimp, and Parmesan Beignet Fritters from Modena

These beignet fritters, called bignè di pesce alla Modenese, *are said by the great Italian chefs Luigi Carnacina and Luigi Veronelli to be from Modena, an old city-state in Emilia-Romagna that was the archrival of Bologna in the twelfth century. They suggest offering the fritters with tomato sauce on the side if you are serving at the table. If the fritters are to be passed, they make excellent pop-in-your-mouth morsels. If you don't have any leftover cooked white fish, buy some flounder, red snapper, or other white-fleshed flaky fish and cook it in a little olive oil for 5 to 7 minutes over medium-high heat, breaking it apart with a wooden spoon. The shrimp can be cooked with the fish: place them in the pan a couple of minutes before the fish is done and cook until they are orange-red, 2 to 3 minutes.*

1 recipe Basic Italian-Style Beignet Batter for Frying (page 477)

½ pound leftover cooked fish, finely chopped

¼ pound shrimp, shelled, cooked in boiling water until pink, drained, and finely chopped

¼ pound Parmigiano-Reggiano cheese, grated (about 1½ cups)

1¼ teaspoons salt

Freshly ground black pepper to taste

3 large egg yolks

6 cups olive oil or olive pomace oil for frying

1. Prepare the beignet recipe.

2. In a medium-size bowl, mix the fish, shrimp, Parmigiano, salt, pepper, and egg yolks. Refrigerate for 2 hours.

3. Form the mixture into balls the size of a walnut with wet hands so they don't stick.

4. Preheat the frying oil in a deep fryer or an 8-inch saucepan fitted with a basket insert to 375°F. Dip the fish balls in the beignet batter. Drop several beignets at a time (do not crowd them) in the hot oil and cook until golden, about 3 minutes. Remove with a slotted spoon, drain on paper towels, and serve hot. Let the frying oil cool completely, strain through a porous paper filter, if necessary, and save the oil for a future use.

Makes 20 fritters; 10 servings

Sea Anemone Fritters

In Malta, these fritters are called *fritturi tal-artikli. Artikli* are the sea creatures known as sea anemone (*Anemonia sulvcata* Pennant). Children in Malta, but also in Sicily and Provence, love to find sea anemones in the tidal pools along rocky shorelines. They are pried out of their holes with penknives. To prepare them, first rub the anemones under running water to remove their grit. You can then marinate them in vinegar, if desired. In any case, boil them for about 1 minute, then dust with flour, dip into beaten egg flavored with garlic and parsley, fry them in hot olive oil, and serve with lemon wedges.

Mediterranean-Style Fried Small Fish

This is a preparation found everywhere in the Mediterranean. In Andalusia, it would be a frittura de pescado, *while in Lebanon a favorite meze is* sultan Ibrahim maqlī, *fried red mullet. In Sicily they would call these little fried fish* sciabbacheddu, *an Arabic-derived word that refers to the little fish caught in the trawl net. In Greece, you would find* marides tiganita, *fried picarel, and in France coastal restaurants always offer* fritture de poisson. *Serve these on a large platter and let everyone help him or herself.*

6 cups olive oil or olive pomace oil for deep-
frying

2 pounds small whitebait, sardines, anchovies,
smelt, or other small fish, gutted if over 3
inches long and washed well

All-purpose flour for dredging

Salt to taste

Lemon wedges for garnish

1. Preheat the frying oil in a deep fryer or an 8-inch saucepan fitted with a basket insert to 375°F.

2. Dust the fish with the flour in a colander or strainer, vigorously shaking it so excess flour falls off. Fry in batches in the hot oil, without crowding, until golden, about 2 minutes. Taste one of the fish to see if it is done to your liking. If ready, remove with a slotted spoon to paper towels to drain and salt immediately. Serve hot with lemon wedges. Let the frying oil cool completely, strain through a porous paper filter, if necessary, and save the oil for a future use.

Makes 6 to 8 servings

Fried Fish Balls in the Arab Style

Along the coasts of Lebanon and Syria, one is likely to find these deep-fried fish balls served as a meze. Kafta samak, as it is called, can be made with any white-fleshed fish, although in the eastern Mediterranean the Arab cook prefers sea bass or any kind of bream. Before you begin to use the parsley, make sure it is dried very well. Dip the fried fish balls in parsley-and-tahini sauce, which can be called either ṭaraṭūr or baqdūnis bi'l-ṭaḥīna.

2 medium-size onions, cut up

Leaves from ½ bunch fresh Italian parsley

1½ pounds white-fleshed fish fillets

1½ cups fresh bread crumbs

1 large egg

1 teaspoon white wine vinegar

1 tablespoon salt

½ teaspoon freshly ground black pepper

½ teaspoon freshly ground cumin seeds

½ teaspoon freshly ground coriander seeds

6 cups vegetable oil for frying

1 cup dry bread crumbs

½ recipe Parsley in Tahini Sauce (page 469)

Little Fried Fish Everywhere

If there is any little food that can be described as ubiquitous in the Mediterranean, it is the platter of fried little fish. Whether it's the extraordinarily fresh red mullet fried in olive oil that they serve at the Qaddura in Alexandria, Egypt, or the lightly floured and deep-fried *marides* (picarel) that I ate at the Taverna Bonne Petite in the covered market of Chania on Crete, or the *petit fritture d'éperlans*, the tiny silver smelts served at A la Brise de Mer in the coastal town of Les Saintes-Marie de la Mer in the Camargue of Provence, it is iterated throughout the ports of the Mediterranean.

Istanbul's Legendary Fish Sandwiches

Can one say that you haven't lived until you've eaten the fish sandwiches sold by the boatmen near the Galata bridge on the Eminönü side in Istanbul—one of the most memorable foods I ate in Turkey? No, you haven't lived. The Turks say *şimdi İstanbul'da olmak vardı Boğazda balık ekmek yemek*. ("Now I wish I was in Istanbul eating a fish sandwich by the Bosphorus.") Oh, I do, too. By the bridge are little boats fitted with wood-fired griddles where huge metal pans filled with sunflower seed oil fry up schools of *uskumru* (mackerel), which are then slapped into Turkish bread (like French bread). Customers lean over the edge of the dock and pay, asking for one, two, or three fish fillets for their sandwiches. We put some raw sliced onions on top of the golden fillets of mackerel, all very fresh, and sprinkled them with salt. Boy, was it good. The weather was windy and cold, the sea choppy, the skies gray, so they tasted all the better. There were about four or five men on the bobbing boat taking orders and cooking, and lots of men around eating and watching. What a spectacle! But we should remember the words of the French historian Fernand Braudel concerning this sight at Galata: *mais si le spectacle laisse un souvenir aussi vivace, n'est-ce pas parce qu'il est rarissime* ("But if the spectacle leaves a lively memory, isn't that because it is so rare?"). It is rare, but as another historian, Robert Mantran, tells us in his *Istanbul dans la seconde moitié du XVIIe siècle* (Bibliothèque Archéologique et Historique de l'Institut Français d'Archéologie d'Istanbul 12. Paris: Adrien Maisonneuve, 1962) that it was a sight seen in seventeenth-century Istanbul, which was famous with Western travelers for its fish even then. So why don't I give a recipe? Well, because I believe you must eat it on a cold and windy day at the Galata bridge yourself.

1. Place the onions and parsley in a food processor and pulse a few times to break them down, then pulse until chopped, but not mushy. Add the fish and run the processor until well blended with the onions. Add the fresh bread crumbs, egg, vinegar, salt, pepper, cumin, and coriander and blend until mixed well. If the food processor receptacle is not large enough, mix this in a bowl. Form the fish into golf ball–size balls with hands wetted with cold water to prevent sticking. Arrange on a tray and refrigerate for 30 minutes.

2. Preheat the frying oil in a deep fryer or an 8-inch saucepan fitted with a basket insert to 375°F. Dredge the fish balls in the dry bread crumbs, shaking off any excess crumbs. The balls will feel very soft. Deep-fry several at a time (do not crowd them) in the hot oil until

dark brown, about 6 minutes. Remove with a slotted spoon, drain on paper towels, and serve with the tahini sauce. Let the frying oil cool completely, strain through a porous paper filter, if necessary, and save the oil for a future use.

Makes 32 to 35 balls; 10 servings

Hot Meze and Cold Meze

Meze are usually divided into cold meze and hot meze. When preparing a meze party or when ordering at a restaurant, try to have half and half. In Greece, meze are divided further into those you have with drinks and those you enjoy without.

Fried Stuffed Cabbage Bundles from Catalonia

This Catalan tapa *is found elsewhere in Spain in a variety of guises. It's very simple, although the quality and type of sausage you use helps the final flavor enormously. The* morcilla *sausage called for in this recipe is one sold by La Española in Harbor City, California, which can be purchased online by visiting their Web site, www.donajuana.com.*

8 leaves green cabbage
2 tablespoons unsalted butter or olive oil (optional)
½ pound *morcilla* sausage
2 cups olive oil or grapeseed oil, or as needed
1 or 2 large eggs, beaten
All-purpose flour for dredging

1. Bring a large saucepan of lightly salted water to a gentle boil and cook the cabbage leaves at a boil until soft, about 5 minutes. Drain, remove the hard core section with a small paring knife unless you have already done that, and cut the cabbage leaf in half along the stem.

2. If the sausage is uncooked, melt the butter in a small skillet over medium heat, then cook the sausage until firm and cooked through, 20 to 30 minutes. Cut the sausage in half, then in half again lengthwise.

3. In a cast-iron skillet, pour in the oil until ½ inch deep and turn the heat to medium-high.

4. Meanwhile, lay a piece of sausage on a half cabbage leaf and roll up, tucking in the sides. Dip the cabbage in the beaten egg, then dredge in the flour. Give a shake to get rid of excess flour and carefully place in the hot oil, several at

---

Blood Sausage

Blood sausage was once a popular sausage in America, but today it is harder to find and often not very well made. In Catalonia, they make a blood sausage called *morcilla*, which is made with pig's blood mixed with rice, paprika, onions, garlic, and other spices. Rudolf Grewe, an independent scholar of Hispano-Muslim cuisine, believed the contemporary *morcilla* sausage derived from the medieval *mirqas* sausage, which exists today as *merguez* sausage in Morocco and France.

a time, and fry until golden brown, about 1 minute, and no more. Remove with a slotted spoon, drain on paper towels, and serve hot.

Makes 8 servings

Variation: Replace the sausage with 1 pound small cooked and lightly salted shrimp.

 ## Fried Stuffed Olives from Venice

One spring I lived in Venice and regularly ate at the Arsenalbar, a little cafe near the school I went to across from the Arsenale. They served a variety of ciccheti, *a Venetian category of small tapas-like foods to be enjoyed with drinks, one of which I was always quite impressed with, but rarely ordered because they were a dollar each. These were large green olives, called* olive farcite, *which were stuffed with a flavorful chopped meat mixture, coated with very fine bread crumbs, and fried until a golden orange.*

2 tablespoons unsalted butter
¼ pound ground chicken breast
¼ pound ground veal
¼ pound ground ham
2 large eggs, separated and whites beaten until frothy
3 tablespoons freshly grated Parmigiano-Reggiano cheese
½ teaspoon salt
¼ teaspoon cayenne pepper
¼ teaspoon freshly grated nutmeg
100 big pitted green olives

1½ cups dry bread crumbs
6 cups olive oil or olive pomace oil for frying

1. In a medium-size skillet, melt the butter over medium-high heat, then cook the chicken, veal, and ham until they all lose their pinkness, about 4 minutes, stirring and breaking up the meat with a wooden spoon. The meat may not be crumbly enough after cooking, in which case, run it in a food processor for a minute.

2. In a large bowl, mix the cooked meats with the egg yolks, Parmigiano, salt, cayenne, and nutmeg. Stuff the olives with the mixture, then dip in the beaten egg whites and dredge in the bread crumbs. Place on a baking tray and refrigerate for 20 minutes.

3. Preheat the frying oil in a deep fryer or an 8-inch saucepan fitted with a basket insert to 375°F. Fry the olives a handful at a time (do not crowd them) in the hot oil until golden, 1 to 2 minutes. Remove with a slotted spoon, drain on paper towels, and serve hot as a passed antipasto. Let the frying oil cool completely, strain through a porous paper filter, if necessary, and save the oil for a future use.

Makes 100 stuffed olives; 20 servings

French-Fried Pumpkin with Green Sauce from Naples

This Neapolitan antipasto is served hot and uses a kind of flavorful squash they call zucca napoletana *or, more popularly,* cocozza, *a zucchini cultivar. I actually prefer making it with pumpkin, as in this recipe. One will find mint used in Naples and Sicily more often than in the north.*

Andiamo per una Ombra

My friend Francesca Piviotti worked at La Fenice, the opera house in Venice that tragically burned down in the 1990s, and after work for her and school for me, we would go for a "shade" (*andiamo per una ombra*). I'm not sure about the origin of this expression, but it means "let's get a glass of wine or *prosecco* at the local *bacari* (like a tapas bar) and eat *ciccheti*," little nibbly things less elaborate than tapas. *Ciccheti* is said to derive from the French word *chiqueter*, "to dribble" or "crumble," or perhaps from the Provençal word *chiquet*, "little glass." It may also derive from, of all things, the language of the Aztecs who took their chocolate from a vessel called *xicalli*, a word which the Spanish transformed into *jicara* and which entered into Italian as *chicchera*, meaning "cup." My two favorite Venetian *bacari* are Da Mori, on the difficult-to-find (as is everything in Venice) Calle Do Mori (go over the Rialto Bridge to San Polo, straight to Ruga Vecchia San Giovanni, left, and then look for the Calle to the right), and another near the Campo San Maria Nova in Cannareggio.

Two 1½-inch-thick slices French or Italian bread,
   crusts removed
¼ cup water
7 tablespoons white wine vinegar
1 cup loosely packed fresh mint leaves
Leaves from ½ bunch fresh Italian parsley
Pinch of ground cinnamon
3 tablespoons extra-virgin olive oil
6 cups olive oil or olive pomace oil for frying
2 pounds pumpkin or zucchini squash, peeled,
   seeded, and cut into French fries
Salt to taste

1. Soak the bread in the water and 4 tablespoons of the vinegar in a small bowl for 10 minutes. Squeeze the liquid out; put the bread in a blender along with the mint, parsley, cinnamon, extra-virgin olive oil, and the remaining 3 tablespoons vinegar, and process until smooth,

adding more vinegar and oil if the blade doesn't turn or if the sauce is too much like a paste.

Sophia Loren on Appetizers

My favorite Italian movie star, Sophia Loren, wrote a charming cookbook in the early 1970s called *In the Kitchen with Love*. She tells us that her *antipasti* chapter "ought to be called 'fun dishes,' which is a broad way of translating the Neapolitan word *sfizio*, meaning 'the urge to enjoy.' Anything *sfizioso* whets the appetite, makes the mouth water, and rouses the spirit of the *bon vivant* who lives in the heart of all Italians."

2. Preheat the frying oil in a deep fryer or an 8-inch saucepan fitted with a basket insert to 375°F. Cook the pumpkin fries several at a time (do not crowd) in the hot oil until crispy looking and tender, about 3 minutes. Remove with a skimmer, drain on paper towels, arrange on a serving platter, salt immediately, and pour the sauce over them once they're all fried. Serve immediately as an antipasto at a sit-down dinner.

Makes 4 servings

Sicilian Fried Eggplant "Sandwiches"

This preparation is known as sciàtara-e-màtara *in Sicilian, which is an admiring interjection, such as, "Oh, good God!" Linguists trace the expression to the Arabic exclamation* shātiru yā mā tāra, *which means something like, "My God, he did it" or "oh my, the ability you see." It was an expression used to exclaim one's surprise when someone else, from whom you expect very little, actually accomplishes something. Perhaps the Sicilians felt one expected so little from the eggplant, yet this sandwich is so delicious. Michele Pasqualino, the eighteenth-century Sicilian lexicographer, defined the expression in his Sicilian vocabulary published in 1785 as a euphemism for buttocks, but it's unclear what that might have to do with this dish. I usually cut the finished sandwiches in half and serve them on a platter on a buffet table.*

3 medium-size eggplants (about 3 pounds), peeled and sliced ⅝ inch thick, keeping the slices together to make sandwiches later

Salt
2 tablespoons unsalted butter
2 tablespoons all-purpose flour
1 cup hot milk
Salt and freshly ground black pepper to taste
Freshly grated nutmeg
6 cups olive oil or olive pomace oil for frying
6 large eggs, lightly beaten
Dry bread crumbs for dredging
Whole and chopped fresh mint leaves for garnish

1. Lay the eggplant pieces on some paper towels and sprinkle with salt. Leave them to drain of their bitter juices for 30 minutes, then pat dry with paper towels.

2. In a small saucepan, melt the butter over medium heat, then stir in the flour, whisking or stirring until a roux is formed but without letting it color. Remove the saucepan from the heat and slowly pour in the hot milk, whisking constantly until the sauce is thick. Return the saucepan to the heat and cook, stirring until dense, about 15 minutes. Season with salt and pepper.

3. Spread a very thin layer of the sauce on each side of the eggplant, as if you were buttering bread. Don't be tempted to slather it on or the taste will be overpowering and unpleasant. Grate a small amount of nutmeg over the sauce and lay the matching slice of eggplant on top to make a sandwich.

4. Preheat the frying oil in a deep fryer or an 8-inch saucepan fitted with a basket insert to 365°F. Pour the eggs in a bowl and spread the bread crumbs over a piece of waxed paper or in a plate. Dip each eggplant sandwich in the egg,

then dredge in the bread crumbs, making sure all sides, including the edges, are coated with bread crumbs.

5. Fry the sandwiches in the hot oil until golden brown on one side, then carefully turn them over using tongs and cook the other side, 3 to 4 minutes in all. Don't cook too many sandwiches at once; cook in batches. Remove with tongs and drain on a paper towel–lined platter or tray. Salt them while they are still hot and let them cool. Once they are cool, transfer to a serving platter and garnish the border of the platter attractively with mint leaves, sprinkle some chopped mint over the sandwiches, and serve. The sandwiches can all be cut in half if you would like to make smaller portions. Serve at room temperature. Let the frying oil cool completely, strain through a porous paper filter, if necessary, and save the oil for a future use.

Makes 14 to 28 sandwiches (if cut in half);

14 servings

Batter-Fried Spring Onions with Almond and Hazelnut Sauce

In the springtime, the eating of very young onions takes on a quasi-religious rite of passage in a celebration called the calçotada *in Catalonia. Spring onions, baby leeks, and scallions are coated in oil and grilled over an open flame, or they are batter-fried, as in this recipe, called* calçots fregits, *which is always served with a dipping sauce and drinks. If you prepare this*

with the sauce, you'll need to serve it plated for a sit-down dinner.

1 package (7 grams) active dry yeast
⅓ cup warm water (105° to 115°F)
2 large eggs, lightly beaten
⅔ cup all-purpose flour
1 teaspoon salt
Freshly ground black pepper to taste
6 cups olive oil or olive pomace oil for frying
16 spring onions or scallions, trimmed so they are 4 inches long, including all of the white part
1 recipe Almond and Hazelnut Sauce (page 465; optional)

1. In a wide bowl, dissolve the yeast in the water, letting it rest for 5 minutes. Stir in the eggs, flour, salt, and pepper. Cover the bowl and let rest for 1 hour in a warm place such as a turned-off oven.

2. Preheat the frying oil in a deep fryer or an 8-inch saucepan fitted with a basket insert to 375°F. Dip the scallions into the batter, letting the excess batter drip off, and fry in the hot oil, in batches so the fryer never becomes crowded, until golden, 4 to 5 minutes. Remove with a skimmer, drain on paper towels, and serve hot as is or with the sauce. Let the frying oil cool completely, strain through a porous paper filter, if necessary, and save the oil for a future use.

Makes 6 servings

Arancini

Arancini *are a favorite Sicilian antipasto or snack. They are stuffed balls of rice coated in bread crumbs and deep-fried to a golden orange. They look like little blood oranges, hence their Italian name, "little orange." The famous Sicilian gastronome Alberto Denti di Pirajno suggested that* arancini *were created by Arab chefs experimenting with pilaf. In the thirteenth-century Arabic cookbook known as the* Baghdad Cookery Book, *there is a recipe called* naranjiyya *that, although not made of rice, is a ball of meat fried to look like an orange using saffron and eggs for coloring, hence the use of the Arabic word* naranj, *meaning "orange." Sicilian food commentators like to point to* arancini *as a mirror of Sicilian history because they believe that the cheese stuffing was brought by the Greeks, the rice and saffron by the Arabs, the tomato by the Spanish, and the ragout stuffing by the French. In Rome, cooks make a very similar preparation called* supplì al telefono.

2 cup raw arborio rice

2 cups chicken broth

Pinch of saffron threads, crumbled and steeped in ½ cup water for 30 minutes

2¼ teaspoons salt

2 tablespoons unsalted butter

2 large eggs, separated

1½ cups grated *caciocavallo* or pecorino cheese

2 tablespoons extra-virgin olive oil

1 small onion, finely chopped

¼ pound lean ground beef, cooked until no longer pink and drained of fat

1 small ripe tomato, peeled, seeded, and very finely chopped

1 tablespoon finely chopped fresh rosemary leaves

⅛ teaspoon freshly ground black pepper

½ cup shelled fresh or frozen peas, cooked in water to cover until tender and drained

¼ cup dry white wine

All-purpose flour for dredging

Dry bread crumbs for dredging

6 cups olive oil or olive pomace oil for frying

1. Put the rice in a large, heavy saucepan and pour in the chicken broth. Stir in the saffron and water, 2 teaspoons of the salt, and the butter and bring to a boil, stirring a few times. Reduce the heat to low, cover tightly, and cook until all the liquid is absorbed, 15 to 20 minutes, without removing the cover or stirring.

2. Remove the rice to a large platter or baking dish and stir in the egg yolks and cheese. Mix well, then spread the rice out in the platter or dish to cool.

3. In a skillet, heat the olive oil over medium heat, then cook the onion until translucent, about 7 minutes, stirring. Add the ground beef, tomato, rosemary, the remaining ¼ teaspoon salt, and the pepper and cook, covered, for about 8 minutes. Add the peas and wine and cook until the wine has evaporated. This stuffing should look like a thick ragout.

4. Spread some flour on a piece of waxed paper or in a plate. Lightly beat the egg whites in a shallow bowl. Spread the bread crumbs on a piece of waxed paper or in a plate. Set out a bowl with cold water in it to occasionally dip your

hands so the rice doesn't stick to them when you form the balls. Grab a handful of rice about the size of a lemon, and flatten it in your palm. Cup your palm and, with your other thumb, make an indentation in the rice, right at the center of your palm. Place about 1 tablespoon or a little more of the ragout in the center and fold the edges of the rice patty over to completely encase the ragout and form a ball. You may have to use a little more rice to surround it. Shape the ball with both hands until it looks the size of a small lemon, smoothing the surface for cracks. Squeeze just tightly enough to form a ball but not so tightly that it falls apart. Continue making and stuffing balls in the same fashion.

The Secret to Making Arancini

Arancini are stuffed rice balls formed in the palm of one's hand. By all means, you want to avoid making a large, leaden ball of rice that fills you up. Because it's easier to stuff an apple-size ball of rice, too many cooks opt out of making small, lime-size *arancini*. Yes, it requires a little more patience and a bit more finesse, but they are far more pleasant to eat and more appropriately sized for an antipasto. When you are handling the ball of rice, use a light hand. Don't squeeze it tight like a snowball; just give it a light squeeze so the stuffing put in the cavity is covered, then form it like a snowball, but without packing it.

5. Dredge each ball in the flour, patting off any excess flour. Dip in the beaten egg whites, and dredge in the bread crumbs on all sides, coating the ball evenly. Refrigerate for 30 minutes.

6. Preheat the frying oil in a deep fryer or an 8-inch saucepan fitted with a basket insert to 365°F. Deep-fry several rice balls at a time (do not crowd them) in the hot oil until golden, about 4 minutes. Do not fry more than 4 at a time. As the rice balls finish cooking, remove to a paper towel–lined platter to drain and serve warm or at room temperature. Let the frying oil cool completely, strain through a porous paper filter, and save the oil for a future use.

Makes 12 arancini

Ricotta-Stuffed Potato Croquettes

Deep-fried potato croquettes are popular everywhere in the Mediterranean, and their varieties seem endless. These croquettes are stuffed with cheese and in Sicilian they are called crucché di ricótta. *I like to serve them as a passed appetizer as my guests circulate.*

2 pounds boiling potatoes
4 large eggs
¼ pound aged *caciocavallo* or provolone cheese, grated
Salt and freshly ground black pepper to taste
6 cups olive oil or olive pomace oil for frying
½ pound fresh ricotta cheese, preferably homemade (page 88)
1½ cups dry bread crumbs

1. Place the potatoes in a large saucepan and cover by several inches with cold water. Turn the heat to high and, once it comes to a boil in about 20 minutes, reduce the heat to medium-high and boil until a skewer glides easily to the center of the potato, about 20 minutes more. Drain and, when cool enough to handle, peel and pass through a ricer, food mill, or strainer. In a large bowl, beat 2 of the eggs, add the mashed potatoes and cheese, and season with salt and pepper. Mix well. Beat the 2 remaining eggs in a small bowl and set aside.

2. Preheat the frying oil in a deep fryer or an 8-inch saucepan fitted with a basket insert to 375°F. Take a small handful of the potato mixture in the palm of one of your hands, wetted with water to keep it from sticking, then place about a ½ tablespoon of ricotta cheese in the center and form the potato around it, enclosing it entirely and making sure it is sealed by forming the croquette with your hands. The ball should be a little smaller than a golf ball. Dip the balls in the beaten eggs, then dredge in the bread crumbs and fry several at a time (do not crowd them) in the hot oil until golden, 3 to 3½ minutes. Remove with a slotted spoon and drain on paper towels. Serve immediately or reheat later. Let the frying oil cool completely, strain through a porous paper filter and save the oil for a future use.

Makes 32 croquettes; 14 servings

Little Pricks

In Sicilian, these small potato and pecorino cheese croquettes are known as cazzilli, *which means "little pricks" to give you an idea of their shape. They are very popular and usually served as an antipasto or snack. They are very common in* trattorie *as an antipasto. This recipe is based on some excellent ones I had years ago at La Scoiattolo ("The Squirrel") restaurant on the Lungomare in Mazara del Vallo.*

2 pounds boiling potatoes, peeled and quartered
3 large eggs, separated
½ cup grated pecorino cheese
1½ cups dry bread crumbs
1 large garlic clove, very finely chopped
3 tablespoons finely chopped fresh parsley leaves
Salt and freshly ground black pepper to taste
6 cups olive oil or olive pomace oil for frying

1. In a large saucepan, place the potatoes in lightly salted cold water to cover by several inches and turn the heat to medium-high. Once the water comes to a boil in about 20 minutes, let continue to boil until a skewer pushed into the center of the potato glides in easily, about another 20 minutes. Drain, let cool, then push the potatoes through a ricer, food mill, or strainer. In a large bowl, beat 2 egg yolks with the potatoes. Add the cheese and 3 tablespoons of the bread crumbs. Add the garlic and parsley and season with salt and pepper. Mix very well with a fork.

2. Roll a heaping tablespoon of potato mixture on a work surface into a small cylinder and set aside as you make all of them. In a small bowl, beat the egg whites until frothy but not stiff, then stir in the remaining egg yolk. Pour the bread crumbs onto a piece of waxed paper

Vulgar Cuisine

The Sicilians are renowned for their *cucina erotica*, food meant to enhance the sexual experience. Even Plato wrote more than 2,000 years ago, "When I came [to Sicily] I was in no wise pleased at all with 'the blissful life,' as it is there termed, replete as it is with Italian and Syracusean banqueting; for thus one's existence is spent in gorging food twice a day and never sleeping alone at night." In ancient Syracuse, cakes were made in the shape of female genitalia and in medieval times pastries resembling both male and female sex organs were common. Even today *sciarabbaddazzu* is an old Sicilian word for a kind of focaccia made lovingly into the shape of a female pudendum. The Sicilian propensity for using sexual vulgarities to name dishes is famous in Italy. I remember the fun of eating the delicious little potato croquettes called *cazzilli*, "little pricks," or the sweets called *minni di virgini*, "virgins' tits," and *fedde del cancelliere*, "chancellor's buttocks."

or a plate. Dip the *cazzilli* in the (mostly) whites, then dredge them in the bread crumbs and set aside.

3. Preheat the frying oil in a deep fryer or an 8-inch saucepan fitted with a basket insert to 375°F. Fry the *cazzilli*, in batches without crowding them, in the hot oil until golden, about 2 minutes. Remove with a slotted spoon, drain on paper towels, and serve lukewarm. Let the frying oil cool completely, strain through a porous paper filter, and save the oil for a future use.

Makes 36 croquettes; 10 to 12 servings

Potato, Prosciutto, and Scamorza Cheese Patties

When I came across these delectable appetizers in Italy, they were called pizzelle con patate, *"fried potato pizzas." But they're not really* pizzelle, *which are made from bread or pizza dough; they're potato fritters and very good ones at that.* Scamorza *is a cheese-like provolone, and it sounds like it may be impossible to find here. In fact, there are two fine* scamorza *cheeses made in the United States, one by F. Cappiello Dairy Products, Schenectady, New York (www.cappiello.com), and one by the Calabro Cheese Corporation of East Haven, Connecticut (www.calabrocheese.com). Serve these as a passed appetizer or as an antipasto at a sit-down dinner.*

1¾ pounds boiling potatoes

½ pound *scamorza* cheese, shredded or cut into small dice

4 large eggs

One ¼-pound slice prosciutto, diced

6 tablespoons finely chopped fresh parsley leaves

¼ pound Parmigiano-Reggiano cheese, grated

1 teaspoon extra-virgin olive oil

Salt and freshly ground black pepper to taste

Dry bread crumbs for dredging

6 cups olive oil or olive pomace oil for frying

1. Place the potatoes in a large saucepan and cover by several inches with cold water. Turn the heat to high and, once it comes to a boil in about 20 minutes, reduce the heat to medium-high and boil until a skewer glides easily to the center of the potato, about 40 minutes more. Drain and, when cool enough to handle, peel and pass through a food mill or strainer into a large bowl. Add the *scamorza*, 2 beaten eggs, the prosciutto, parsley, Parmigiano, and olive oil and season with salt and pepper. Form this mixture into patties about 2½ inches in diameter, then dip into the 2 remaining beaten eggs and dredge in the bread crumbs, tapping off any excess crumbs. Set on a baking tray.

2. Preheat the frying oil in a deep fryer or an 8-inch saucepan fitted with a basket insert to 375°F. Fry several patties at a time (do not crowd them) in the hot oil until golden, 2½ to 3 minutes. Remove with a slotted spoon, drain on paper towels, and serve hot. Let the frying oil cool completely, strain through a porous paper filter, if necessary, and save the oil for a future use.

Makes 32 patties; 14 servings

Cauliflower and Cheese Fritters from Algeria

This Algerian dish called ᶜajījāt al-flūr bi'l-jubn *in Arabic is found on the* qimiyya *table, the colloquial Algerian Arabic expression for a meze table. Spoonfuls of egg batter incorporating the mashed cauliflower and cheese are dropped into hot oil and fried until golden brown. Deep-fried croquettes are popular meze in Algeria, especially the ones made from sardines. As for cauliflower, it too seems a popular vegetable in Algeria and Tunisia and one finds it in everything from these tidbits to couscous.*

1 head cauliflower (about 1¾ pounds), cut into florets and stems discarded

1 cup distilled white vinegar

6 cups olive oil, olive pomace oil, or vegetable oil for frying

½ cup all-purpose flour

1 ounce Gruyère cheese, shredded

2 large eggs

Salt to taste

1 lemon, cut into 6 wedges

1. Soak the cauliflower in the vinegar and water to cover for 15 minutes. Bring a large pot of water to a boil and cook the cauliflower until tender, about 25 minutes. Drain the cauliflower in a colander and crush with a potato masher.

2. Preheat the frying oil in a deep fryer or an 8-inch saucepan fitted with a basket insert to 375°F.

3. In a medium-size bowl, mix the cauliflower, flour, cheese, eggs, and salt. Carefully slide heaping tablespoonfuls of the mixture into

Chickpeas in the Mediterranean

The lowly chickpea is quite a favorite legume in the Mediterranean, and it finds its way into many appetizers. The *socca* of Nice is a sweet or savory pancake made with chickpea flour that is cooked by street vendors. *Panisse* is a thick fried pancake made of chickpea flour found in other parts of Provence. In northern Italy, the chickpea was popular for centuries and often the food of the poor. The anonymous Tuscan cookbook published in Florence in 1927 called *Cucina Toscana* claims that *torta di ceci*, a chickpea dish, was an old speciality of Genoa and was mentioned by the name *scribilita* in a document from the local communal government dated to 1383. Chickpea flour is dissolved in water, then baked with olive oil at about 350°F. for one hour. It is eaten hot with a sprinkle of salt and pepper. It is also known as *farinata*, and called *fainâ* in Ligurian dialect. Some cooks add some sliced cooked Italian sausages on top before placing it in the oven. Sicilian chickpea flour fritters, called *panelle*, may also be known in northern Italy as *frittelle di farina di ceci* and are made as a yeasted dough that is kneaded with salt and marjoram. In northern Tunisia and the Kabylie region of Algeria, *assidat ḥummuṣ* is a preparation used as a weaning food for babies made of two parts roasted wheat and one part roasted chickpeas.

the hot oil (do not crowd them) and fry until golden brown, about 3½ minutes. Remove with a slotted spoon and drain on paper towels. Serve hot immediately with the lemon wedges. Let the frying oil cool completely, strain through a porous paper filter, if necessary, and save the oil for a future use.

Makes 6 servings

Panisse or Panelle

The Sicilian chickpea flour fritters called panelle *are popular in Palermo, where some people like to put them between two slices of bread with a squirt of lemon and a sprinkle of salt for a sandwich. They are known in Provence, too, where they are called* panissa *or* panisse *(which gave its name to Alice Waters' famous restaurant Chez Panisse). Chickpea flour can be found in Italian markets or whole food stores. Keep it in the freezer if you don't use it all within six months.*

1⅓ cups chickpea flour (about ½ pound)
1 quart cold water
1½ teaspoons salt
2 tablespoons finely chopped fresh parsley leaves
6 cups sunflower seed oil (preferably) or vegetable oil for frying

1. In a 2- or 3-quart saucepan, dissolve the chickpea flour in the water. Add the salt and parsley, turn the heat to medium, and cook, stirring almost continuously, until the mush becomes fairly thick, about 20 minutes. It will be rather dense, like Cream of Wheat. You won't think it is done, but it is. Remove immediately from the heat.

2. Spread the mush over a large rimmed baking sheet to cool slightly, spreading until it is about ⅛ inch thick. After it has cooled and dried a bit but is still warm, cut the dough into rectangular shapes about 2 x 3 inches.

3. Preheat the frying oil in a deep fryer or an 8-inch saucepan fitted with a basket insert to 365°F. Cook the pieces several at a time (do not crowd them) in the hot oil until golden, about 1 minute. Remove with a slotted spoon, drain on paper towels, and serve warm or reheat later. Let the frying oil cool completely, strain through a porous paper filter, if necessary, and save the oil for a future use.

Makes 8 servings

Radicchio de Treviso Fritters

The small maroon ball of radicchio found in your market with its tightly packed leaves is known as radicchio di Verona, while the kind with the same color and long leaves is known as radicchio di Treviso. Quartering the radicchio di Treviso lengthwise and batter-frying it is a popular antipasto preparation in the Veneto. The frying oil should be a light oil, ideally grapeseed, sunflower seed, canola, or corn oil. Olive oil is good too, but make sure it is a light-tasting one. When you quarter the radicchio, do it carefully so the leaves stay attached to the stem end.

1 package (7 grams) active dry yeast
⅓ cup warm water (105° to 115°F)
2 large eggs, lightly beaten
⅔ cup all-purpose flour
1 teaspoon salt
Freshly ground black pepper to taste
6 cups sunflower seed oil, grapeseed oil, or
    vegetable oil for frying
4 radicchio di Treviso, quartered lengthwise
Salt to taste
1 lemon, quartered

1. In a wide bowl, dissolve the yeast in the water, letting it rest for 5 minutes. Stir in the eggs, flour, salt, and pepper, cover the bowl, and let the batter rest for 1 hour in a warm place such as inside a turned-off oven.

2. Preheat the frying oil in a deep fryer or an 8-inch saucepan fitted with a basket insert to 375°F. Dip the radicchio quarters in the batter, flipping them on both sides to make sure the batter clings to the leaves. Let the excess batter drip off, then fry several at a time (do not crowd them) in the hot oil until light golden and crispy, 3 to 4 minutes, turning once. Remove with a slotted spoon, drain on paper towels, and salt immediately. Keep warm while you cook the remaining radicchio quarters. Serve with lemon wedges at a sit-down dinner party. Let the frying oil cool completely, strain through a porous paper filter, if necessary, and save the oil for a future use.

Makes 16 fritters; 16 servings

Leek Beignet Fritters from Corsica

Fried beignets are quite popular in Corsica, where one will find nearly anything going into the batter, although leeks, onions, herbs, squid, and snails are popular ingredients. Beignets au brocciu à la farine de châtaigne *is a ricotta beignet made with chestnut flour, which the Corsicans have been using for centuries after the ruling Genoese appropriated all the grain. These* beignets de poireaux *are delightful when passed and served with a sparkling wine.*

1 recipe Basic French-Style Beignet Batter for Frying (page 476)

2 tablespoons extra-virgin olive oil

4 leeks (white part only), split lengthwise, washed well, dried, and chopped

¼ cup finely chopped fresh mint leaves

½ cup water

Salt and freshly ground black pepper to taste

6 cups olive oil or olive pomace oil for frying

1. Prepare the beignet batter.

2. In a medium-size skillet, heat the olive oil over medium heat, then cook the leeks and mint for 2 minutes, stirring. Add the water and season with salt and pepper. There should be only enough water to cook the leeks. Cook until the leeks are soft and the water evaporated, about 6 minutes.

3. Preheat the frying oil in a deep fryer or an 8-inch saucepan fitted with a basket insert to 375°F. Stir the leek mixture into the batter, then drop walnut-size pieces of batter into the oil (don't crowd them) and fry until golden, about 3 minutes. Remove with a slotted spoon, drain on paper towels, and serve hot. Let the frying oil cool completely, strain through a porous paper filter, if necessary, and save the oil for a future use.

Makes about 28 fritters; 10 servings

Herb Fritters from Corsica

These beignets are made throughout Corsica, where they are usually served in convivial settings. Called fritelle d'herbes, *they are usually made in the spring when wild herbs are young and tasty, using water, not milk, to better preserve the aroma of the herbs. Ideally you would use wild herbs and greens, but that might not be possible, so try some of the suggestions below, a few of which are more likely to be found in a farmer's market than your supermarket.*

¾ cup all-purpose flour

1 tablespoon extra-virgin olive oil

1 teaspoon salt

1 large egg, separated, white beaten until stiff peaks form

¾ cup water

½ cup each coarsely chopped fresh herbs and greens (choose 3): wild mint, marjoram, baby Swiss chard, borage, cress, purple orach

6 cups peanut oil or vegetable oil for frying

1. In a large bowl, mound the flour and make a well in the middle. Pour the olive oil, salt, and egg yolk in the well and begin to incorporate the water to form a very thick batter that is still able to flow. Cover with a kitchen towel and leave for 2 hours.

2. Mix the egg white and herbs and greens into the dough.

3. Preheat the frying oil in a deep fryer or an 8-inch saucepan fitted with a basket insert to 370°F. Drop large spoonfuls of the dough into the hot oil (do not crowd them) and fry until golden, about 5 minutes. Remove with a slotted spoon, drain on paper towels, add salt, then serve hot. Let the frying oil cool completely, strain through a porous paper filter, if necessary, and save the oil for a future use.

Makes 16 fritters; 8 servings

Zucchini Flower Fritters

This is an hors d'oeuvre that one will see often in Provence, where zucchini flowers are quite popular and prominently sold in local open air markets. It's called a beignet de fleur de courgette, *"zucchini flower beignet," and the only thing it really needs after it's cooked is a sprinkle of salt.*

½ recipe Basic French-Style Beignet Batter for Frying (page 476)
6 cups olive oil or olive pomace oil for frying

André Castelot on Hors d'Oeuvre

"It should never be forgotten that the object of the hors d'oeuvre is to excite and not cut short the appetite."

—L'HISTOIRE A TABLE

10 zucchini flowers with attached baby zucchini, washed and dried carefully if necessary
Salt to taste

1. Prepare the beignet batter and leave in the refrigerator 1 more hour than specified in the basic recipe.

2. Preheat the frying oil in a deep fryer or an 8-inch saucepan fitted with a basket insert to 375°F. Dip the zucchini flowers in the batter, let the excess drip off, and fry several at a time (do not crowd them) in the hot oil until golden brown, 3 to 4 minutes. Remove with a slotted spoon, drain on paper towels, salt, and serve hot as a passed appetizer.

Makes 10 fritters; serves 10

Falafel and Ṭaᶜmiyya

Falafel are little hockey puck–shaped spiced bean rissoles fried in oil and typically are served as street food or as a meze in the Levantine Middle East. They are made with crushed dried fava beans called fūl madshūsh *or crushed chickpeas or a mixture of both. Claudia Roden, the author of a number of books on Middle Eastern cooking, says that falafel are made with* fūl nabid, *which are fava bean sprouts, but I've never seen them made with sprouts. In Palestine and Israel, they make falafel with chickpeas. But it is the Christian Copts of Egypt who claim falafel as their own, and theirs is a more delicate, spicier version of the Levantine falafel, made into the shape of a lozenge about 1½ inches in diameter and called* ṭaᶜmiyya. *It's basically the same thing as a fala-*

fel, usually made from fava beans and sometimes stuffed with a little spiced ground meat, and flavored with much more coriander and parsley.

Falafel should be served hot with Arabic bread, Cucumber, Bell Pepper, and Olive Salad (page 236), and Parsley in Tahini Sauce (page 469) or a tarator sauce made with ⅓ cup tahini, ⅓ cup fresh lemon juice, a little water for thinning, 2 tablespoons plain yogurt, and 2 garlic cloves crushed with salt. Other relishes to put on the falafel, which then get wrapped in thin Arabic bread, are chopped onions, chopped scallions, chopped garlic, chopped fresh coriander leaves, and chopped fresh parsley leaves. A relish made of chopped tomato, cucumber, green bell pepper, chile, parsley, fresh coriander, and lemon juice can be made.

When making falafel, it's important that everything be rather dry, otherwise the rissoles will not hold together when you fry them. After the beans soak, drain them and dry them by leaving them out on some kitchen or paper towels. Let the onions and garlic sit in a strainer for 2 hours to drain. The dried beans can be found in Middle Eastern markets. You may be tempted to use a falafel mix for making these, but this personal rendition is so much more memorable.

1 cup dried split yellow fava beans, picked over and soaked overnight in water to cover
½ cup dried chickpeas, picked over and soaked overnight in water to cover
½ cup medium coarse bulgur (no. 3), soaked in water for 1 hour and drained
2 heads garlic, cloves separated, finely chopped, and placed in a strainer for 2 hours to drain
5 medium-size onions, finely chopped and placed in a strainer for 2 hours to drain
½ cup finely chopped fresh coriander leaves
½ cup finely chopped fresh parsley leaves
2 tablespoons salt
2 tablespoons all-purpose flour
1 teaspoon freshly ground black pepper
1 teaspoon freshly ground coriander seeds
½ teaspoon ground red chile
½ teaspoon freshly ground cumin seeds
½ teaspoon ground cinnamon
½ teaspoon baking soda
1 tablespoon baking powder
6 cups vegetable oil

1. In a large bowl, mix all the ingredients except the vegetable oil. Place in a food processor, in batches if necessary, and pulse until everything is very well ground and smooth. Return to the bowl and stir several times with a wooden spoon. Transfer to a strainer and let drain for 1 hour.

2. Form the dough in tablespoon increments into hockey puck–size rissoles about 1¾ inches in diameter. Arrange on a tray and let rest in the refrigerator for 30 minutes.

3. Preheat the frying oil in a deep fryer or an 8-inch saucepan fitted with a basket insert to 375°F. Fry the rissoles in batches of 5 or 6 in the hot oil until golden brown, about 3 minutes. Remove with a slotted spoon and drain on a paper towel–lined tray. Serve with a wrapping of Arabic bread and any of the garnishes mentioned in the headnote.

Makes 70 falafel; about 20 servings if served plain, with no bread or accompaniments

Ṭaᶜmiyya

This Egyptian version of the falafel is so much a staple food in Egypt that the word *ṭaᶜmiyya* derives, in fact, from the Arabic word for nourishment. The best *ṭaᶜmiyya* I ever had was in Marsa Matruh in Egypt's Western Desert. We had a newspaper cone full (that's what street vendors wrap them up in) of freshly cooked *ṭaᶜmiyya*, which were spicy with onions, garlic, cayenne pepper, chopped coriander leaves, and parsley and had a little pocket of ground beef in the center. The outside was fried to a deep brown in olive oil and the inside was light green. *Rīhàn*, a sweet basil that tastes like mint, was sprinkled on top. *Turshy*, pickled turnips in this case (elsewhere we've had carrots and cucumber) laid on a bed of arugula-like leaves known as *gargīr* in Egypt, were also served. In Egypt, the hyacinth bean (*Lablab purpureus* (L.) Sweet.), also called the Egyptian bean, is also used for making *ṭaᶜmiyya*, as a substitute for the fava beans.

Roll-ups and Wraps

Nothing is easier than wrapping some food in another food for an appetizer. In this chapter, Italian cold cuts are the star, wrapping fruit, pâté, or cheese. But there are some other wonderful preparations that I couldn't even touch upon in this book using all manner of cold cuts, Italian or otherwise. Nearly anything can be used to wrap foods with, although two favorites are Potato Crispelle with Salmon Caviar and Mascarpone (page 397) and Lentil and Bulgur Rissoles in Romaine Leaves (page 398). Besides using cold cuts and very flat bread, such as the Middle Eastern flatbreads, you can also employ lettuce leaves or crêpes, and you can make them as small and as elegant as your energy allows.

Broiled Bacon-Wrapped Dates from Madrid

I once ate this Spanish tapa in a bar in Madrid, where it was served with sherry, and I was quite enamored of its taste and simplicity. It is called escolanets, *meaning "altar boys," because the dates are wrapped like the black-and-white robes of the boys. Some cooks stuff almonds in the dates.*

24 fresh, ripe Medjool or Honey dates, pitted
12 strips lean bacon, cut in half crosswise

1. Preheat the broiler.
2. Wrap the dates in the bacon, secure with a toothpick, and arrange on a broiler tray. Place under the broiler until the bacon is crisp, about 8 minutes, turning once. Serve hot.

Makes 24 roll-ups; 10 to 12 servings

Basṭurmā Roll-ups with Strained Yogurt

I describe basṭurmā *and* labna *(strained yogurt) elsewhere, but this is such a simple little meze that I nearly forgot to include it in this book. It's a slice of* basṭurmā *rolled into a cone around a teaspoon or a little more of thick yogurt. Refrigerate until needed and serve as a passed appetizer at a cocktail party. Both* basṭurmā *and strained yogurt (*labna*) are sold at Middle Eastern markets.*

½ pound *basṭurmā* (page 292), thinly sliced
1 cup *labna* (strained yogurt; page 56)

Lay a slice of *basṭurmā* before you, place a teaspoon or a little more of *labna* on top, and roll into a cone. Set aside on a platter and continue rolling.

Makes 32 roll-ups; about 10 servings

Prosciutto Roll-ups Stuffed with Chicken, Pork, and Pistachio Pâté

This Neapolitan invention of the monzù (page 37) is a very rich and "intense" preparation, so you will find that each prepared slice of the roll-up will go far and feed a lot of people. Make sure that the prosciutto you buy is cut properly, namely thinly and layered separately so the slices don't stick together.

1 cup (2 sticks) unsalted butter, at room temperature
1 small onion, chopped
1 stalk celery, chopped
1 carrot, chopped
1 tablespoon salt
½ teaspoon freshly ground allspice berries
2 large boneless, skinless chicken breast halves (about ¾ pound)
One ½-pound pork tenderloin, trimmed of any fat or silverskin
½ cup cognac or brandy
3 tablespoons raw unsalted pistachios
Salt and freshly ground black pepper to taste
1 pound thinly sliced *prosciutto di Parma*

1. In a casserole, mix ½ cup (1 stick) of the butter, the onion, celery, carrot, salt, allspice,

the whole chicken breasts, and the whole piece of pork. Cover, turn the heat to medium, cook until about to bubble vigorously, then reduce the heat to low and cook until the chicken and pork are tender, 25 to 30 minutes, stirring and turning occasionally. Remove the chicken and pork from the pan and let cool. Let the sauce in the casserole cool, too.

2. Place the chicken and pork in a food processor and pulse until the meats are finely chopped. Add the butter and 2 or 3 ladlefuls of the vegetables from the casserole to the food processor, enough liquid so the meat gets blended and process until the mixture is smooth. Add the remaining ½ cup (1 stick) butter in small amounts through the feed tube while the machine is running, then pour the cognac in a small stream. Transfer this mixture to a bowl and fold in the pistachios. Correct the seasonings.

3. Place four 12-inch squares of waxed paper on a work surface in front of you, spoon a fourth of the mixture onto one end of the waxed paper, and roll it up into a log about 1 inch in diameter, making sure that the roll is smooth and evenly cylindrical. Repeat with the remaining sheets and mixture. Refrigerate for at least 2 hours.

4. Arrange the slices of prosciutto over four 10-inch squares of waxed paper, covering the whole sheet of waxed paper by overlapping the slices of prosciutto. Remove the waxed paper from the refrigerated stuffing, place this log of stuffing on at end of a square and roll it up in the prosciutto. Remove the waxed paper from the now rolled-up log. Repeat with the remaining prosciutto and stuffing. Wrap the prosciutto logs in plastic and refrigerate for several hours.

5. When ready to serve, cut each roll-up into ½-inch-thick slices, arrange on a serving platter, and serve as a passed appetizer at a cocktail party.

Makes 40 slices; 20 servings

Prosciutto and Mozzarella Roll-ups

There are times when I'm having a dinner party and discover that I've put so much effort into dinner that I have no energy left to make a complicated appetizer. This is where little wrapped foods work so well. They are effortless to make and are enjoyed by everyone. Make them small so they just pop into your mouth and you don't need to take bites. A simple antipasto like this requires the best prosciutto di Parma *and fresh mozzarella.*

24 thin slices *prosciutto di Parma*, cut in half
1 pound fresh mozzarella cheese, cut into 48 small "fingers"
Dried oregano
Salt and freshly ground black pepper to taste

Arrange a slice of prosciutto in front of you and lay a mozzarella finger at the edge. Sprinkle with oregano, salt, and pepper and roll up. Repeat with the remaining prosciutto and cheese. Serve.

Makes 48 roll-ups; about 16 servings

Prosciutto and Peaches

The antipasto of prosciutto and canta-loupe is a familiar one to Americans who fre-

quent Italian restaurants, but wrapping peaches in prosciutto, prosciutto e pesca, is how my grandfather, who was from a little village near Benevento, used to eat it. The success of this preparation rests on your obtaining prosciutto di Parma, the best cured ham, and the sweetest, ripest peaches, and, probably most importantly, that you wrap the peaches just before serving them. If you peel the peaches by plunging them in boiling water, it will affect their taste, so try to plunge them in for just seconds and not minutes.

3 pounds ripe peaches, peeled if desired and pitted
½ pound thinly sliced *prosciutto di Parma*

Cut the peaches into wedges and wrap each one in a slice of prosciutto. Serve at room temperature.

Makes 30 wrapped pieces; about 12 servings

Prosciutto and Cantaloupe

We can't be sure of when the classic Neapolitan prosciutto and cantaloupe antipasto first came about, but we do know something about the cantaloupe. The French king Charles VIII (1470–1498) began the Italian Wars with the short-lived conquest of Naples in 1495. Shortly before this time, newer vegetables and fruits that were eaten as vegetables were becoming more common, the products of European and especially Italian gardens that gradually varied the Western diet. Some of the popular foods on the table were asparagus, spinach, lettuce, artichokes, peas, cauliflower, and melons. Charles

VIII is known to have brought the melon from Naples back to France. The cantaloupe, popular in Naples, had come from Armenia.

Salt to taste
1 ripe cantaloupe, cut in half, seeded, rind cut away, and cut into thin wedges
½ pound thinly sliced *prosciutto di Parma*

Salt the cantaloupe lightly and wrap each wedge in a slice of prosciutto not too long before serving.

Makes 30 wrapped pieces;
about 12 servings

Smoked Ham of Cyprus

One of the most famous of Cypriot meze is *chiromeri*, a kind of prosciutto from Cyprus. It is usually served by itself as a meze, or with slices of melon, or fried in an omelette. It is made from the hind quarter of a pig and marinated in dry red wine and a thick layer of salt for about a month, then it goes into a smoker, traditionally a fireplace. It is smoked for a long time, and is removed every couple of days to be pressed under very heavy stones, which squeeze out the liquid; this pressing goes on for two weeks. The butt is salted, too. It is a man's responsibility to make this smoked ham and the tradition is passed down from father to son.

Prosciutto and Figs

Another classic combination is prosciutto with figs. Some people peel figs, but it's not necessary. The key, though, is that they are fully ripe, so they can melt in your mouth in one bite.

15 ripe green figs
½ pound thinly sliced *prosciutto di Parma*

Cut the figs in half, then wrap each half in a slice of prosciutto and serve within an hour or so.

Makes 30 wrapped pieces; about 12 servings

Prosciutto and Strawberries

This preparation is not seen as often as the other prosciutto wraps, but it is quite pleasing, assuming the strawberries are ripe, well washed, hulled, and dried.

30 ripe large strawberries, hulled
½ pound thinly sliced *prosciutto di Parma*

Wrap each strawberry in a slice of prosciutto and serve within an hour or so.

Makes 30 wrapped pieces; about 12 servings

Mortadella Roll-ups

This antipasto, or better, passatempo, *is called* involtini di mortadella *and can be stuffed with just about anything, although these are my favorite ingredients. Mortadella is a pork baloney made in Italy in the region of Emilia (page 360). But baloney is probably not a good way to describe it since it is worlds away from* American sandwich baloney. *It is made with good-quality pork that is ground so fine it is creamy. Then it is mixed with chunks of fat called* lardelli, *whole peppercorns, and pistachios. The best place to buy top quality domestically produced mortadella is at an Italian market. Stay away from its American cousin baloney.*

Cream cheese
Mascarpone cheese
Fresh mozzarella cheese, cut into sticks
24 thin slices mortadella (about ¾ pound),
    cut in half, or quarters if greater than 8 inches
    in diameter

Spread or lay the cheese, either alone or any combination, on one end of the mortadella and role up. Refrigerate until needed, but try to serve cool, almost at room temperature.

Makes about 48 roll-ups; 12 servings

Horns of Ham Stuffed with Walnuts and Cream Cheese

This party antipasto, called cornetti di prosciutto alle noci *in northern Italy, is simple to make and can be refrigerated until needed, although it's best to serve at near room temperature.*

¼ pound walnuts, crushed, plus 20 walnut
    halves for garnish
One 8-ounce container whipped cream cheese
2 tablespoons finely chopped fresh parsley leaves,
    plus 20 small fresh parsley leaves for garnish
½ pound sliced cooked ham, each slice cut into
    smaller 4 x 3-inch slices

1. In a medium-size bowl, mix the crushed nuts, cream cheese, and parsley.

2. Place a small amount of the cheese mixture on a ham slice and roll it up to form a cone or horn. Repeat with the remaining ham and cheese mixture.

3. Garnish with a piece of walnut and arrange on a platter, garnished with parsley.

Makes 20 roll-ups; 10 servings

Smoked Salmon and Crab Rolls

One will find smoked salmon served at elegant French and Italian restaurants as an hors d'oeuvre. This Italian recipe, though, is from an American food magazine from the late 1970s or early 1980s. It's quite rich and I can't imagine guests would eat more than one or two. Then again, they're delicious and the taste encourages excess.

1½ cups fresh crab meat, liquid squeezed out and picked over for shells and cartilage
½ cup whipped cream cheese, at room temperature
2 tablespoons mayonnaise
½ teaspoon cayenne pepper (optional)
Salt and freshly ground white pepper to taste
1 teaspoon unflavored gelatin
1 tablespoon cognac
½ pound smoked salmon, in 8 thin slices

1. In a medium-size bowl, mix the crab meat, cream cheese, mayonnaise, and cayenne, if using, and season with salt and black pepper.

2. In a small bowl, sprinkle the gelatin over the cognac and let sit for 5 minutes. Set the bowl in a bowl of hot water, stir until the gelatin is dissolved, then stir into the crab-meat mixture.

3. Arrange the smoked salmon slices on a flat surface, then spread the crab mixture lengthwise over the slices, leaving a ¼-inch border along the long sides. Starting with the short end, roll the salmon up. Chill, loosely covered, for 4 hours in the refrigerator.

4. Slice the rolls crosswise into ½-inch-thick slices, arrange cut side up on a serving platter, and serve.

Makes about 30 hors d'oeuvre; 12 to 15 servings

Potato Crispelle with Salmon Caviar and Mascarpone

This elegant antipasto is the kind of preparation one would find in a fancy restaurant in Lombardy or Emilia-Romagna. It is a favorite starter to pass around while people are still milling at a party. The inspiration is purely haute cuisine, but surprisingly easy to prepare.

2 tablespoons extra-virgin olive oil
1½ pounds boiling potatoes, peeled and shredded
3 tablespoons finely chopped onion
2 garlic cloves, finely chopped
Salt and freshly ground black pepper to taste
2 tablespoons whipped unsalted butter
3 ounces salmon caviar
2 ounces mascarpone cheese

1. Preheat a flat cast-iron griddle that will fit over 2 burners with a light film of oil over

medium-high heat until the oil begins to smoke.

2. Meanwhile, in a large bowl, mix the potatoes, onion, and garlic and season with salt and pepper. Divide the potato mixture in half and place each half over the portion of the griddle that rests over a burner. Flatten them into *crispelle*—that is, crêpes—with a metal spatula until they are about ⅛ inch thick. Cook until golden brown, 7 to 8 minutes, turn, and cook until that side is also golden brown, another 7 to 8 minutes.

3. Transfer the *crispelle* to a serving platter, spread with the whipped butter, then place half the salmon caviar and mascarpone over each of them. Fold in half, cut them in quarters, and serve immediately.

Makes 4 to 8 servings

Lentil and Bulgur Rissoles in Romaine Leaves

This recipe called mercimekli köfte *was prepared for me by Ms. Neriman Dal, the cook of Ildiz Carpet Farm in Milas, Turkey. I spent an afternoon with her and Tunjer Oklu, one of the managers, talking about and eating various Turkish dishes and this was quite delightful in the shade of a tree on a very hot October day. Tunjer says that a good cook must form the lentils with his hands so that everything from your soul flows into the food you've prepared. These are indeed soulful* köfte. *There are several things you need to be careful about when you make this. First, red lentils, which are usually used for soups in the Near East, can disintegrate rapidly if you are not*

careful, so it's important to keep your eye on them while they cook. Second, when you stir the bulgur in, do it carefully so you don't break the lentils. Finally, remember to use plenty of lemon juice squeezed on at the end—it really gives it a great taste. The Turkish red pepper can be found at many Middle Eastern markets or via the Internet at www.zingermans.com, www.turkishdeli.com/index2.html, or www.kalustyan.com.

½ pound (about 1¼ cups) red lentils, rinsed and picked over
1½ teaspoons salt
¼ cup raw fine bulgur (no. 4)
1 tablespoon sunflower seed oil
1 tablespoon extra-virgin olive oil
1 small onion, finely chopped
2 tablespoons tomato paste
½ teaspoon ground red chile or Turkish red pepper (*kirmiz biber*, page 66)
2 tablespoons finely chopped fresh parsley leaves
1½ scallions, finely chopped
Leaves of 1 small head of romaine lettuce, separated
2 lemons, quartered

1. Place the lentils in a medium-size saucepan with the salt and cover by half an inch of water. Bring to a boil and cook until the water is absorbed, about 10 minutes, without stirring. Pour the raw bulgur in the center of the lentils while still in the pot, stir very gently, turn the heat off, and set aside while you continue the preparation.

2. Meanwhile, heat the oils together in a small skillet over medium-high heat, then cook the

onion, tomato paste, and ground red pepper until blended and the onion is soft, about 4 minutes, stirring frequently. Add the parsley and scallions and cook a few more minutes until soft. Stir this mixture into the lentil mixture, stirring carefully.

3. When the lentil mixture is cool enough to handle, but still quite warm, form into thumb-size croquettes with your hands and arrange on a serving platter. Serve immediately with the romaine lettuce leaves while still warm (not later, and never refrigerated), wrapping a lentil *köfte* in a leaf and giving it a squirt of lemon juice before eating.

Makes 20 rissoles; 8 servings

Seafood Salads and Platters

One of the great delights of eating in a trattoria, *osteria*, or *ristorante* in Italy is seeing the large buffet table spread with *antipasti* of countless varieties from which you choose a selection of foods for your appetizer. They are usually sitting in gaily colored polychromatic platters and sometimes you help yourself, although more commonly the waiter will concoct an antipasto platter for you. You can replicate this experience in your home by choosing any number of Italian *antipasti* to make from this book. But this chapter offers a selection of antipasto platters that stand well above the usual red-clothed Italian-American restaurants' antipasto of years ago, with its iceberg lettuce, rolled provolone cheese, pickled chiles, and slices of salami. Here you will find an intriguing offering of seafood *antipasti* and salads, as well as seafood dishes from Tunisia, Spain, and Turkey. The chapter concludes with six recipes for shellfish that make great small bites as they come with their own little built-in plates—the shell.

Venetian Seafood Antipasto

The classic Venetian antipasto di pesce *is varied, depending on the whims of the chef and the realities of the Rialto fish market, but it usually includes fish, mollusks, and shellfish, such as red and pink shrimp with bewildering names like* mazzancole, *which are your basic shrimp as far as I can tell, but with a bit stronger taste, so said the fishmonger. There are also* vivi, *"little shrimp," and* gamberetti, *a larger shrimp. Seasoned with olive oil and lemon juice, they make a light and flavorful appetizer. Sometimes local snails called* bòvoli, s'ciosi, *or* chiocciole, *which are as popular in Venice as they are in Provence, are included. This recipe is based on whatever is locally available, so what I call for here is just a suggestion, but I think you get the idea. It is best to stay away from anything frozen except for the octopus. Soak the mussels, cockles, clams, and oysters in cold water to cover with 1 tablespoon baking soda for 1 hour first to purge them of any sand.*

12 medium-size fresh shrimp with their heads
   (about ¾ pound) or, if you must, about 6
   ounces previously frozen headless shrimp
8 mussels (about ½ pound), scrubbed and
   debearded (page 368), if necessary
12 cockles (about 1 pound), scrubbed
8 littleneck clams (about ½ pound), scrubbed
4 oysters (about 1 pound), scrubbed
8 baby octopus, cleaned (page 263), cooked in a
   large pot of boiling salted water for about 30
   minutes until stiff but tender, and drained
¼ pound tuna steak, cut into 4 pieces
¼ pound cod or halibut fillet, cut into 4 pieces

All-purpose flour for dredging
2 tablespoons extra-virgin olive oil, plus extra for
   drizzling
Fresh lemon juice to taste
Salt and freshly ground black pepper to taste

1. Place all the shellfish in a steamer and steam until the shrimp are pink (then shell them) and the shellfish have all opened, 4 to 12 minutes in all. Keep checking and removing them as they finish cooking or opening. Remove them from their shells and set aside in a bowl. Add the octopus. Dredge the fish pieces in flour and shake off any excess.

2. In a small skillet, heat the olive oil over high heat and cook the fish on both sides until light golden and cooked through, 3 to 4 minutes in all. Remove and arrange the fish on a serving platter.

3. Toss the shellfish and octopus with olive oil and lemon juice, season with salt and pepper, scatter around the fish, and serve.

Makes 4 to 6 servings

Roman Lobster and Squid Salad with Artichokes, Lupine Beans, and Grilled Eggplant in Olive Oil

This wonderful antipasto was called fagioli, carciofi, melanzane e insalata di mare *on the menu of Trattoria Pizzeria Severo 2000, at via Vincenza 10 in Rome when I ate there. It was a four-part salad consisting of a finely chopped mixture of cooked artichoke hearts that were marinated in olive oil, along with boiled lupine*

Cappon Magro

One of the most famous, most unusual, and most unseen preparations (because not many chefs make it) is an antipasto dish of fish and vegetables from Genoa called *cappon magro alla Genovese*. Simply seeing a picture of the finished dish is enough to discourage everyone but the culinarily mad from attempting it. Not only do all the different items get cooked separately, but the entire ensemble is constructed in such a way that it seems a shame to eat it. It is usually assembled in a rather magnificent way, vegetables piled high into the sky, and served with an anchovy sauce. The name means "fast-day capon" and it is thought to have originated as some kind of mariner's food, which became elaborate once landlubber chefs got their hands on the concept. It also doesn't contain capon. It begins with a very large shallow bowl, which is rubbed with garlic and laid with garlic- and olive oil–rubbed hardtack (ships' biscuit). Then the cooking and layering begin, the structure being built with the express purpose of looking complex, extraordinary, and pyramidal. Boiled potatoes, white beans, cauliflower, asparagus, fennel, scorzonera (a plant with a thin, long, and slimy black-skinned root that is edible), artichokes, celery, and carrots are arranged and garnished with pine nuts, olives, eggs, capers, gherkins, tomatoes, and lettuce hearts. Then the cooked seafood is arranged, using hake or any kind of bream such as sea bream or gilt-head bream, two dozen jumbo shrimp, lobster, oysters, fresh anchovies, and *bottarga* (dried, pressed, and salted tuna roe). A sauce is prepared and poured over the structure, either an anchovy sauce or a vinaigrette of olive oil, vinegar, lemon juice, and salt.

beans with green bell pepper and celery, and a little salad composed of lobster, squid, celery, and olive oil, and finally slices of grilled eggplant with olive oil.

One 1½-pound live lobster

1 small eggplant (about 1 pound), sliced ¼ inch thick

Salt and freshly ground black pepper to taste

6 tablespoons extra-virgin olive oil, plus more for brushing

2 tablespoons white wine vinegar

6 squid (about ½ pound), cleaned (page 404)

1 large garlic clove, finely chopped

½ stalk celery, finely chopped

2 teaspoons fresh lemon juice

8 fresh medium-size artichoke bottoms (page 205), boiled in water to cover until tender and drained, or one 15-ounce can cooked artichoke bottoms, cut into small dice

1 cup cooked lupine beans from a jar, skinned, soaked in water for 1 hour, and drained

1 green bell pepper, roasted (page 415), peeled, seeded, and chopped

Cleaning Squid

Three important things must be done to clean squid. First, their skin must be pulled off, then the internal viscera pulled out and the bodies and tentacles washed, and finally you need to separate the head from the tentacles. To do this, grasp the body in one hand and pull out the head and tentacles with as much attached viscera as you can get. Cut the tentacles off just below the eyes, making sure they remain whole and attached to each other. Discard the head. Reach into the body cavity with a forefinger and pull out any remaining viscera and the hard quill-like cartilage called the chiton, discarding both. Included in this viscera is the ink sack, which you can discard if the squid bodies are less than 6 inches long. If they are larger, you can try saving the ink sacks to squeeze the ink out for black pasta or rice. Pinch the blackish skin of the body to separate it from the white flesh and peel it away; it will come off easily. Wash both the body and tentacles and proceed with the recipe's instruction.

1. Bring a large pot with about 2 inches of water to a boil and cook the lobster until bright orange-red, 17 to 18 minutes. Remove from the pot, let cool, crack the shells, and remove the meat. Slice the meat and set aside.

2. Lay the eggplant pieces on some paper towels and sprinkle with salt. Leave them to drain of their bitter juices for 30 minutes, then pat dry with paper towels. Brush both sides of the eggplant slices with 2 tablespoons of the olive oil or more as needed. Heat a ridged cast-iron griddle over medium-high heat, then cook the eggplant until brown grid marks appear, about 4 minutes per side. Remove and arrange the eggplant slices around the edge of the platter.

3. Bring a small saucepan of salted water to a boil with the vinegar, then cook the squid until they are stiffened, about 4 minutes. Drain and let cool. Toss the squid bodies and their tentacles with the lobster, one-third of the chopped garlic, 1 tablespoon of the olive oil, half the celery, and 1 teaspoon of the lemon juice and season with salt and pepper. Arrange the lobster and squid in the center of a large oval or round serving platter.

4. In a bowl, toss the artichokes with the remaining garlic, 2 tablespoons of the olive oil, the remaining 1 teaspoon of lemon juice, and a little salt and pepper. Arrange the artichokes to one side of the lobster salad.

5. In a bowl, toss together the lupine beans, green pepper, the remaining 1 tablespoon olive oil, and the remaining celery and season with salt and pepper. Arrange the lupine beans to the other side of the lobster salad and serve.

Makes 6 servings

Lupine Beans

Lupine beans (*Lupinus sativus*) are usually served as a snack or tidbit in the Mediterranean and rarely in cooked dishes. The plants are short, hairy annuals that grow about four feet high, with edible seeds. The seeds are brined, salted, or toasted and served as one would nuts, toasted pumpkins seeds, or olives. Traditionally, they have been thought of as the food of the poor. When you do find lupine beans cooked, they are almost always in soups.

Lobster Salad with White Beans and Red Potatoes

Lobster was almost always served in restaurants and rarely in the home in the 1950s, and restaurant chefs would concoct elegant presentations like this to wow their guests. This magnificent northern Italian lobster salad, called insalata di aragosta, *has lost some of its popularity among Italian chefs; its only crime is that it's old-fashioned, a pretty silly reason not to make something so delicious.*

One 1¾-pound live lobster
¼ cup dried white haricot beans, picked over
2 medium-size red potatoes (¾ pound)
2 carrots, peeled
1 cup shelled fresh or frozen peas
1 stalk celery, chopped
3 tablespoons chopped gherkins
¼ cup mayonnaise, preferably homemade (page 466)
Salt and freshly ground black pepper to taste
2 large hard-boiled eggs, shelled and sliced
15 imported black olives, pitted

1. In a large stockpot or lobster pot, steam the lobster until bright orange or red, about 20 minutes. Remove from the pot, let cool, and remove all the meat. Chop the meat smaller than bite size and refrigerate until needed.

2. Place the dried beans in a small saucepan and cover with cold water by several inches. Bring to boil, then reduce the heat to medium and cook until tender, about 1¼ hours. Drain and set aside. Meanwhile, place the potatoes in a medium-size saucepan and cover with cold water. Bring to a boil, then cook at a brisk simmer until a skewer glides easily to the center of the potato, about 20 minutes. Drain, peel when cool enough to handle, cut into small dice, and set aside. Place the carrots in same saucepan, add water to cover, bring to a boil, and cook at a brisk simmer until tender, about 15 minutes. Drain, cut into small dice when cool enough to handle, and set aside with the potatoes. Place the peas in the same saucepan, cover with water, bring to a boil, and cook at a brisk simmer until tender, about 4 minutes for frozen peas and a little longer for fresh peas, then drain and set aside with the potatoes. Let all the vegetables cool.

3. In a serving bowl, carefully toss together the lobster meat, potatoes, carrots, peas, white beans, celery, gherkins, and mayonnaise, seasoning with salt and pepper at the same time.

Transfer the lobster salad to a round serving platter, mold it with your hands into a dome, and garnish the sides with the sliced eggs, forming a border, and the top with the olives. Cover with plastic wrap, chill for 1 hour, and serve.

Makes 8 servings

Mediterranean Lobsters

Although the large-clawed *Homarus americanus* that we call the Maine lobster doesn't exist in the Mediterranean, its slightly smaller large-clawed cousin *Homarus vulgaris* does. Even so, they are not plentiful and the lobster one is more likely to encounter on a restaurant menu is the spiny lobster (*Palinurus vulgaris*), lacking the distinctive claws of the Maine lobster. This is the lobster the Italians call *aragosta*. The so-called flat lobster (*Scyllarides latus*), better known by its French name *cigale*, is another lobster that one is likely to find in fish soups in Italy.

Octopus Salad from the Island of Djerba

This octopus salad called salāṭa ākhṭabūt *from the island of Djerba off the coast of southern Tunisia is a recipe from Chef Abdel Haouari Abderrazak, one of Tunisia's best known chefs both in and outside the country. Octopuses are plentiful and popular in Djerba, and this recipe is quite simple and delightful as a refreshing summer meze.*

1½ pounds octopuses, cleaned (page 263)
¼ cup distilled white vinegar
2½ tablespoons extra-virgin olive oil
2 teaspoons white wine vinegar
2 teaspoons Harīsa (page 468)
3 ripe tomatoes, 2 peeled, seeded, and chopped, and 1 cut into eighths
1 green bell pepper, seeded and chopped
½ fresh red chile, finely chopped
Salt and freshly ground black pepper to taste
1 head Boston head lettuce
2 large hard-boiled eggs, shelled and quartered

1. Put the octopuses in a large pot of boiling salted water with the vinegar and boil until tender, about 45 minutes. Drain, rinse with cold water, and peel as much of the skin off the octopuses as you can while it is still hot. Chop into smaller than bite-size pieces.

2. Pour the olive oil in a shallow bowl and whisk the vinegar and *harīsa* into it until you have a smooth vinaigrette. In a medium-size mixing bowl, toss the octopus with the chopped tomatoes, bell pepper, chile, and vinaigrette. Season with salt and pepper.

3. Arrange on a platter covered with lettuce and garnish with the tomato wedges and quartered eggs. Serve at room temperature.

Makes 6 to 8 servings

Octopus and Radicchio Salad from Sardinia

I first tasted this really delightful salad called polpo al radicchio *at the little Trattoria Da Giani in Porto Vecchio-Teulada on Sardinia's southwestern coast. The boiled octopus was sliced thin and served with shredded radicchio, parsley, garlic, and olive oil. This preparation uses the leafier radicchio known as radicchio di Treviso, while the more commonly found, compact-headed radicchio is known as radicchio di Verona. Soak the radicchio in ice water for several hours to reduce its bitterness slightly.*

¼ cup extra-virgin olive oil

2 large garlic cloves, very finely chopped

1 small onion, quartered

1 bay leaf

½ cup white wine vinegar

Salt to taste

1 small octopus (about 1¼ pounds), cleaned (page 263)

1 small radicchio di Treviso (about 6 ounces), soaked in ice water

¼ cup finely chopped fresh parsley leaves

Freshly ground black pepper to taste

1. In a small bowl, mix the olive oil and garlic and set aside while you continue the preparation.

2. Bring a large saucepan of water to a boil with the onion, bay leaf, vinegar, and salt; add the octopus and cook until tender, about 1¼ hours. Test the octopus for doneness by removing it and slicing one of the arms off. Taste and, if it is not to your liking, cook it another 10 to 20 minutes. Remove the octopus, wash under cold water or leave to cool, then slice the body and head thin, leaving the arms whole.

3. Drain the soaking radicchio, spin dry, then dry with paper towels if there is any remaining moisture. Slice the radicchio into thin strips and arrange on individual salad plates. Arrange the octopus slices on top of the radicchio, spoon some of the olive oil over each serving, and season with salt and pepper. Serve.

Makes 4 to 6 servings

Antipasti di Mare

While traveling in Italy, you will see on many menus *antipasto di mare*, a seafood antipasto that will always be different, showcasing either the talents and ingenuity of the chef or the local foods or both. An antipasto that was a delicious little surprise was one I ate at the Ristorante da Marino, outside Lucca. It included cold mussels marinara in their shells served with grilled baby squid, soft white haricot beans, small steamed clams, rice with teeny clams, octopus, fresh anchovy seviche, and olives. Each of the seafood ingredients was cooked separately in white wine seasoned with thyme, marjoram, and parsley. It was especially good eating outdoors with crusty, spongy bread to soak up the olive oil and juices.

Antipasto of Shrimp and Artichoke in Lemon and Herbs

This dish of scampi e carciofi is typically served chilled or at room temperature as an antipasto. If you are using fresh shrimp and fresh artichokes, it will be much better, but it is still a favorite of mine even when made with previously frozen shrimp and canned artichoke bottoms.

2 pounds fresh shrimp with their heads or 1 pound previously frozen headless shrimp

7 to 8 large fresh artichokes, trimmed to their bottoms (page 205), or one 15-ounce can artichoke bottoms

Juice of 1 lemon

¼ cup extra-virgin olive oil

2 tablespoons finely chopped fresh mint leaves

2 tablespoons finely chopped fresh parsley leaves

Salt and freshly ground black pepper to taste

1. Bring a pot of abundantly salted water to a boil and cook the shrimp until orange, about 2 minutes. Remove with a slotted spoon and set aside to cool. Remove the shells and/or heads and save for making shrimp stock, if desired. Cut each cooked shrimp into 4 or 5 pieces and set aside.

2. In the same water, cook the fresh artichoke bottoms until tender, about 40 minutes. Drain, let cool, and chop small. If using canned artichokes, drain and chop them, too.

3. Mix the shrimp, artichokes, and the remaining ingredients in a large mixing bowl. Refrigerate for 1 hour and serve, attractively presented, on a platter.

Makes 8 servings

White Beans and Shrimp Antipasto

This Tuscan antipasto is made in many different ways, depending on the cook. However you

make it, rest assured it will always be well received. The leftovers can be made into canapés.

¾ pound small fresh shrimp with their heads or 6 ounces previously frozen headless small shrimp

1 cup dried white beans, rinsed and picked over

¼ cup finely chopped red onion

2 ripe plum tomatoes, peeled, seeded, and chopped

1 large garlic clove, finely chopped

½ cup imported black olives, drained, pitted, and cut in half

¼ cup extra-virgin olive oil

1 tablespoon finely chopped fresh basil leaves

Salt and freshly ground black pepper to taste

12 small fresh basil leaves

1. Bring a 4-quart saucepan of lightly salted water to a rolling boil. Add the shrimp and cook until they turn orange, about 2 minutes. Drain, let cool, then remove the shells and/or heads (save for making shrimp stock, if desired), and chop. Set aside.

2. In the same saucepan, place the beans and water to cover. Bring to a boil, reduce the heat to medium, and simmer until tender, 45 minutes to 1½ hours, so keep checking, then drain and let cool.

3. Toss the beans, shrimp, onion, tomatoes, garlic, olives, oil, and basil together in a large mixing bowl. Season with salt and pepper, toss again, and transfer to a serving platter. Let everything come to room temperature, garnish with the basil leaves, and serve.

Makes 4 to 6 servings

White Beans and Lentils with Shrimp

This recipe is inspired by a number of different family-style meals I have had in the Veneto and Tuscany regions of Italy. I was really turned on by the idea of beans with seafood and think you will see why in this recipe when you feel the delicate crunch of each individual bean. I make this preparation a lot in the summer and my family likes to eat it alone or sometimes with a grilled fish.

1 cup dried white beans, rinsed and picked over
¼ cup dried black lentils, rinsed and picked over
2 teaspoons extra-virgin olive oil
3 ounces cooked shrimp, chopped
4 scallions (white and light green parts only), finely chopped
1 large garlic clove, finely chopped
1 tablespoon finely chopped fresh basil leaves, or more to taste
Salt and freshly ground black pepper to taste
Celery sticks or *crostini* (page 37)

1. Bring a medium-size saucepan of lightly salted water to a boil, add the white beans, and cook until tender, 45 minutes to 1 hour. Drain well and place in a mixing bowl to cool.

2. Bring a small saucepan of lightly salted water to a boil and add the lentils. Cook until *al dente*, 20 to 45 minutes. Drain well and place in the mixing bowl with the white beans to cool.

3. Toss the white beans and lentils with the olive oil, shrimp, scallions, garlic, and basil and season with salt and pepper. Taste and correct the seasonings. Serve with celery sticks or *crostini*.

Makes 8 servings

Roasted Peppers with Fresh Sardines from Valencia

Although this preparation is known simply as roasted peppers, peberadas torrades, *there is more to it than that. First, it is a flavorful* tapa *with fresh sardines; but it can also be eaten, and traditionally is, after a famous and somewhat heavy Valencian preparation known as* arròs i fesols i naps, *or rice with white beans and turnips (see my* A Mediterranean Feast, *page 288).*

1½ pounds red bell peppers, roasted (page 415), peeled, cored, and cut into strips
Salt to taste
1 cup extra-virgin olive oil
1 pound fresh sardines (about 8), cleaned, heads and tails removed, and gutted
8 slices crusty French or Italian bread

1. Place the peppers in a deep platter and sprinkle with salt.

2. In a large skillet, heat the olive oil over medium-high heat, then cook the fish in batches, never crowding the skillet, until crisp on both sides, about 2 minutes.

3. Place the fish over the peppers, drizzle with several spoonfuls of the oil it was fried in, season with salt, and serve with crusty bread.

Makes 8 servings

Latticework of Salted Fat Anchovies and Roasted Bell Peppers

I first encountered this hors d'oeuvre as anxoves de Cotlliure amb pebrots vermells *at Le Café*

Catalan, in Perpignan in the Roussillon, the area of historic Catalonia that is part of France. The chef used the local anchovies of Colliure, a small fishing port where they are salted quickly after being caught so that they are delicious and fat. From the nearby terraced hills of the Côte Vermeille, farmers grow bell peppers in abundance and they find their way into many local dishes. This was attractively presented as a latticework of anchovy fillets over strips of roasted red bell peppers, sprinkled with parsley and olive oil. This dish can only be made with the whole salted anchovies that are sold in large cans or in bulk in Italian markets, or that you have preserved yourself. You will then peel the fillets off the backbone and rinse them. Do not attempt to make this with anchovy fillets in the little cans of oil—it's just not the same thing. Although pebrots vermells means "green peppers," most cooks use red or yellow bell peppers.

3 large red bell peppers (about 2 pounds)
24 salted anchovy fillets, rinsed
Fresh parsley leaves and finely chopped fresh
    parsley leaves for garnish
Extra-virgin olive oil for drizzling

1. Prepare a hot charcoal fire or preheat a gas grill on high for 15 minutes. Grill the peppers until the skins are charred and blackened, about 40 minutes, or preheat the oven to 425°F and roast until blackened, 35 to 40 minutes. Once the peppers are cool enough to handle, remove the skins, stem, and seeds.

2. Slice the peppers into long, thin strips and arrange them in a crisscross pattern on a serving platter. Arrange the anchovy fillets over the red peppers diagonally. Garnish the edges of the platter with parsley leaves and sprinkle the chopped parsley over the peppers. Drizzle some olive oil over the top and serve.

Makes 6 to 8 servings

Variation: Use roasted yellow peppers.

Red Cabbage Salad with Anchovies

This Catalan recipe, called amanida de col llombarda amb seitons, *literally means "salad of Lombardy cabbage with anchovies." Lombardy cabbage refers to red cabbage. I've adapted this recipe from Marimar Torres's* The Catalan Country Kitchen, *published in 1992. It is best served at room temperature.*

1 pound red cabbage, cored and finely shredded
3 tablespoons fine sherry wine vinegar
1 teaspoon salt
2 cups water
6 salted anchovy fillets, rinsed
¼ cup extra-virgin olive oil
3 tablespoons finely chopped fresh parsley leaves
Freshly ground black pepper to taste

1. In a large saucepan, combine the cabbage, vinegar, salt, and water. Bring to a boil, reduce the heat to medium-low, and cook, covered, until a lavender color, about 15 minutes. Let stand, covered, at room temperature for 24 hours.

(continued on page 412)

The Traditional Hors d'Oeuvre of Provence

Most important are the anchovies, but herring, too, is served as rollmops or in other ways. Rollmops are highly seasoned herring fillets wrapped around gherkins. Artichokes are cooked in salads with vinaigrette. Celery is cut into sticks and served with mayonnaise. Red cabbage salads are popular. A great variety of shellfish is available, which you will see advertised as *coquillages* on restaurant menus. There are the *clovisses* or carpet shells, a type of Venus clam, as well as *palourdes*, a kind of littleneck clam. Also found are *preires* or *praires*, the dog cockle shellfish also called "sea almond," *amande de mer*. Oysters are usually eaten raw with a squirt of lemon juice or maybe a mignonette made with shallots, pepper, and vinegar. Mussels are also eaten raw. Periwinkles, *bigorneau*, are eaten raw or after a quick plunge in boiling broth or water, their flesh extracted with a special pin. Scallops prepared au gratin are popular and sea urchins are eaten raw, cut in half and the meat scooped out. Crabs and shrimp are available, as are spiny lobster, crayfish, and *langoustines*, called "scampi" by Italians and known as Dublin Bay prawns in English, creatures that look like a cross between a lobster and a shrimp. The tiny species of fish called *nonats* or *poutina*, popular in many Mediterranean ports, is usually lightly coated with flour and deep-fried or cooked in an omelette-like dish. Smoked salmon, although very popular, is not traditional. One of the most unusual of the *coquillages* is the *violet*, or sea egg, a strange creature with flesh that looks like scrambled eggs and a distinctive iodine taste, one that not everyone finds pleasing. Snails are fantastically popular, and I imagine a whole cookbook could be devoted to escargots in France. In the springtime, fresh fava beans, called *favetta* when very young, are eaten raw or with some smoked ham. Chiles and bell peppers are grilled and served with marinades as simple as olive oil or with other vegetables and seasonings. Radishes are served with sardines in oil. Several fruit are eaten as appetizers too. The famous melons of Cavaillon are served not only as dessert but also as an hors d'oeuvre, just as figs, mulberries, and blackberries are. A variety of smoked, cured, and cooked hams are available, as are various pâtés, usually served with sliced baguettes and fine butter. Sausages, too, are traditional, usually cooked and served cold, the ones from Lyon and Arles being particularly well known. Eggs are made into a variety of appetizers such as hard-boiled egg slices with mayonnaise or blinis with eggs. Olives, of course, are the quintessential Mediterranean appetizers, and they are equally popular in Provence.

(continued from page 410)

2. Place the anchovies and olive oil in a small food processor or blender and process until smooth. Drain the cabbage and squeeze out the excess moisture. In a large mixing bowl, toss the cabbage with the anchovy mixture and parsley. Correct the seasonings and toss again with black pepper. Serve at room temperature.

Makes 6 servings

Tuscan Beans and Tuna

This Tuscan antipasto called fagioli e tonno, *"beans and tuna," has a long history. In Boccaccio's* Decameron, *a group of men sit down in Florence for a breakfast of* fagioli e tonno *and a* fritto misto *of fish. The fourteenth-century beans of Boccaccio were chickpeas because the cannellini bean and the tomato used in this recipe had not yet arrived from the New World.*

I like to use the plump medium-size can-nellini beans, but any dried white bean will do as long as they are not too small.

1½ cups dried cannellini beans, rinsed and
  picked over
1 cup loosely packed fresh sage leaves
½ cup extra-virgin olive oil
Salt to taste
2 garlic cloves, crushed
2½ pounds ripe tomatoes, peeled, seeded,
  and chopped
¼ cup loosely packed finely chopped fresh
  basil leaves

Freshly ground black pepper to taste
Two 6-ounce cans imported tuna in olive oil

1. Place the beans in a large pot, cover with 3 inches of cold water, and add the sage, 1 tablespoon of the olive oil, and some salt. Bring to a gentle boil, then cook gently over medium-low heat until tender, 1 to 1½ hours, uncovered. Drain.

2. In a large nonreactive skillet, heat the remaining 7 tablespoons olive oil over medium-high heat and cook the garlic cloves, stirring, until they begin to turn light brown, about 1 minute. Remove the garlic from the pan and discard. Add the tomatoes and season with salt. Raise the heat to high and cook until slightly thicker, about 8 minutes, stirring frequently to prevent sticking and lowering the heat if it splatters too much. Reduce the heat to low, add the drained beans and the basil, season with pepper, and simmer, covered, until the beans are hot, about 10 minutes, stirring occasionally.

3. Turn the heat off, add the tuna and its oil, and stir. Let the mixture rest for 15 minutes. Serve hot or at room temperature.

Makes 16 servings

Antipasto Magro #1

Boiled vegetable platters dressed with mayonnaise or a vinaigrette are typical of Italian antipasti, which diverge dramatically from the Italian-American antipasto platter of iceberg lettuce and some rolled-up salami and provolone cheese that was popular forty years ago. This is a Lenten antipasto platter from

Eels as Appetizers

In nineteenth-century New England, eel was a popular food, served as an appetizer after having been hung in the chimney for a day to smoke it. Today, eel is no longer eaten by Americans, except for Italian Americans on the East Coast around Christmastime and among Japanese Americans on the West Coast, usually as sushi, and a few other ethnic groups. But in the Mediterranean, especially in Italy and Spain, eel is still very popular. A famous Spanish *tapa* is *angulas en cazuelita*, baby eels known as elvers fried in olive oil with garlic and chiles. In Italy, they love to eat marinated eels seasoned with basil or oregano as an antipasto. And in Sardinia, an unusual eel antipasto is *panada di anguille*. A recipe from Assemini for this dish can be traced to the fourteenth century, when it was known as *panadas*. Eel is stuffed into a calzone made from durum wheat and pork lard, then fried in oil and served with a sauce made from sun-dried tomatoes, garlic, and parsley.

Umbria, and it's all the more attractive if you spend a bit of time thinking about how to decorate it in a pretty way. I've made a suggestion here, but you can do something different as long as you remember to keep the colors interspersed. Umbrian cooks like their vegetables well cooked, so there should be no crunchiness; everything should be very tender.

8 small beets, trimmed
1 pound boiling potatoes
½ cup shelled fresh or frozen peas
¼ cup extra-virgin olive oil
1 tablespoon white wine vinegar
Salt and freshly ground black pepper to taste
Two 6-ounce cans imported tuna in olive oil, drained a little
2 tablespoons salted capers, rinsed and left whole

6 large hard-boiled eggs, shelled and sliced
40 imported black Gaeta or Kalamata olives, pitted
1 cup mayonnaise from a tube or transferred to a squirt bottle

1. Place the beets and potatoes in the top portion of a steamer and steam until a skewer glides easily to their centers, about 30 minutes for both, but keep checking. Remove from the steamer, let cool, peel, and slice both about ¼ inch thick. If you like, you could also dice both vegetables. Set aside.

2. Bring a small saucepan of lightly salted water to a boil and cook the peas until tender but still bright green. Drain and set aside.

3. In a small bowl, whisk together the olive oil and vinegar and season with salt and pepper.

Making an Antipasto Platter

When I was a teenager on Long Island in the 1960s, my family regularly went to Italian restaurants, which we loved, with their red sauce, red-and-white checkered tablecloths, candle in a wicker-encased Chianti bottle, and all the other kitsch of Italian-American dining. An antipasto in those days was always a platter of iceberg lettuce, with a thin wedge of provolone cheese, a rolled-up slice of salami, a few hot peppers, some tomato wedges, and black olives; and it was the same thing no matter where you went. It took me many trips to Italy to see the glories of a true antipasto platter like *il gran fritto vegetale con filetto di baccalà*, the grand platter of fried vegetables and salt cod fillet that I was served at the delightful trattoria Ristorante Paris on the Piazza San Calito, in the Trastevere area of Rome. This Roman-style tempura was all the more enjoyable as we sat at outdoor tables covered by a yellow awning, where we found the atmosphere very relaxing. The platter we were served consisted of a salt cod fillet that was lightly coated with batter and fried in olive oil, accompanied by eight potato croquettes, a bunch of green beans boiled until tender (not crunchy, as is so typical in America), eight little mozzarella balls called *bocconcini*, batter-fried zucchini flowers stuffed with anchovies, and a boiled artichoke that was trimmed and flattened with a mallet and deep-fried just like that.

Layer the potatoes, interspersed with the beets and peas, on a large platter and pour the vinaigrette over them or, if they are diced, toss both with the dressing along with the peas and scatter over the platter. Arrange the tuna on top of the potatoes and beets. Scatter the capers on top of the tuna. Decorate the perimeter of the platter with the egg slices. Surround the potatoes and tuna on top with the olives. Using the mayonnaise tube or squirt bottle, form a curlicue pattern over the eggs all around the platter, squirting some over the top in a decorative fashion also. Serve warm.

Makes 8 servings

Antipasto Magro #2

These vegetable-based antipasti *are common throughout Italy and the mix of vegetables is really up to the cook, although this recipe is typical. Notice that there is no cheese or salami; it's a fish-oriented vegetable antipasto. A "new" potato is a newly dug up potato, whatever the type, also called a baby potato.*

1 pound new Yukon Gold potatoes
2 large eggs
2 large yellow bell peppers
2 large red bell peppers
2 large green bell peppers

1 bunch radishes, trimmed and cut in half

½ fennel bulb, trimmed of stalks and thinly
   sliced

1 large cucumber, peeled, seeded, and sliced

One 6-ounce can imported tuna in olive oil,
   drained slightly

4 salted anchovy fillets, rinsed and cut into thirds

1 heaping tablespoon salted or brined capers,
   rinsed or drained and chopped if large

1 small onion, cut in half and thinly sliced into
   half-moons

3 tablespoons extra-virgin olive oil

2 teaspoons white wine vinegar

Salt and freshly ground black pepper to taste

1. Place the potatoes in a medium-size casserole or saucepan and cover with cold water by 1
inch or so. Turn the heat to medium and, when
the potatoes come to a boil, after about 20 minutes, cook another 20 minutes. The potatoes are
done when a skewer glides easily to the center of
the potato. Drain, peel if desired, and slice ¼
inch thick. Arrange the potatoes around the
perimeter of a large serving platter. You can boil
the eggs at the same time if you like. Place them
in the boiling water and cook exactly 9 minutes.
Remove, let cool, shell, and cut into quarters.

2. Preheat the oven to 425°F. Place the
peppers in a large baking dish and roast until
the skins blister black, about 35 minutes, turning them once or twice. Remove and, when they
are cool enough to handle, peel and seed the
peppers and cut them into strips. Arrange the
peppers, all mixed up, next to the potatoes.

3. Arrange the radishes, fennel, and cucumber
attractively around the platter. Place the tuna

directly in the center. Scatter the anchovies and
capers around the vegetables and arrange the
onion slices over the potatoes. In a small bowl,
whisk the olive oil and vinegar together until
thickened, then drizzle over all the vegetables,
season lightly with salt and pepper and serve.

Makes 6 to 8 servings

Choosing and Roasting Bell Peppers

Bell peppers usually come in three colors—
green, red, and yellow—although there are
orange and deep violet ones, too. But there
are only two kinds of bell peppers really—less
ripe ones, which are green, and ripe ones,
which are red, yellow, or orange. When buying peppers, look for heavy ones with firm,
unblemished flesh and their stems attached.
If the recipe calls for roasting and peeling the
peppers, place them whole in a baking dish in
a 425°F oven until blistered black all over, 35
to 40 minutes, turning once or twice. Remove
them from the oven and place in a paper bag
to help loosen their peel before removing it
with your fingers. Then seed them and continue with your recipe.

Turkish-Style Stuffed Mussels

Ancient Ephesus, near Izmir, was noted in classical times by the writer Diphilus of Siphnos as having excellent mussels. Midye dolması, *mussels stuffed with rice, are a popular restaurant meze in Istanbul and Izmir, where mussels are abundant. The stuffing can also be used for grape leaves, tomatoes, peppers, and cabbage.*

48 large mussels, scrubbed and debearded
  (page 368)

¾ cup extra-virgin olive oil, plus more
  for drizzling

1 large onion, finely chopped

2 tablespoons pine nuts

1 cup raw long-grain rice, soaked in tepid water
  for 30 minutes and drained or rinsed under
  cold running water

½ cup canned crushed tomatoes

2 tablespoons dried currants, soaked in tepid
  water for 15 minutes and drained

1 teaspoon sugar

¼ teaspoon freshly ground allspice berries

¼ teaspoon ground cinnamon

¼ teaspoon freshly grated nutmeg

Salt and freshly ground white pepper to taste

1 teaspoon finely chopped fresh thyme leaves

1 teaspoon chopped fresh dill

1. Over a bowl, open the mussels with a clam or oyster knife, collecting the liquid and making sure the two shell halves don't come completely apart. Do this gently because the mussel shells are fragile and can crack easily. You should have about ½ cup of mussel liquid.

Cultivated mussels will not have this much liquid, so add enough water to whatever is collected to bring it up to ½ cup. Strain the mussel liquid, if necessary, to remove sand and set aside in the refrigerator until needed. Set aside the mussels while you make the stuffing.

2. In a large skillet, heat the olive oil over medium heat, then cook the onion and pine nuts until the onion is translucent, about 8 minutes, stirring. Add the rice and cook until glazed and translucent, about 6 minutes, stirring occasionally. Reduce the heat to low and stir in the tomatoes, reserved mussel liquid, drained currants, sugar, allspice, cinnamon, nutmeg, salt, and white pepper. Stir, cover, and simmer until the liquid is absorbed, about 10 minutes, without stirring or removing the cover. Add the thyme and dill, stir, turn off the heat, cover, and leave for 10 minutes.

3. Stuff each mussel with the rice mixture, using your fingers. Close the mussel shells with your hands as best you can and arrange them in a steamer so they press against one another tightly, which will force them a little bit closed. Place a weight on top of the mussels, such as a cast-iron lid smaller than the steamer or a heavy plate. Bring a very small amount of water to a boil in the bottom portion of the steamer, place the steamer with the mussels on top, cover, and steam over simmering water until the mussels are cooked, about 35 minutes, adding small amounts of water to the pot if necessary.

4. Remove the steamer with the mussels from the heat and let them cool in the steamer. Arrange attractively on a platter and chill in the refrigerator. Brush or drizzle each mussel with

some olive oil before serving cold. Set the platter out and let guests help themselves.

Makes 12 servings

Mussels with Spicy Mayonnaise

This wonderful little tapa *called* mejillones con allioli picante *is from Spain, although I'm not sure which region. Probably it is from Galicia on the Atlantic since this is where most of Spain's mussels come from.*

48 mussels, scrubbed and debearded (page 368)
6 tablespoons Allioli (page 466)
5 teaspoons dry mustard
2 teaspoons dry sherry
1 teaspoon fresh lemon juice
One 4-ounce jar chopped pimientos, drained
Pinch of cayenne pepper

1. Place the mussels in a large saucepan, turn the heat to high, and cover. Once all the mussels have opened, 5 to 8 minutes, cool, remove the mussels from their shells, and set aside. Discard all the shells and any mussels that remain firmly closed. Arrange the mussels in a small platter.

2. In a small bowl, mix the *allioli*, mustard, sherry, lemon juice, and pimientos. Spoon the mayonnaise over the mussels, sprinkle with the cayenne, and serve.

Makes 8 to 10 servings

Baked Oysters in the Style of Taranto

Although my favorite way of eating oysters is raw, this preparation for ostriche alla Tarantina *from Apulia in southern Italy, is a close second. They are quite heavenly, especially if your oysters are briny and salty.*

There are few places one finds oystering in today's Mediterranean outside of the Gulf of Taranto. However, in the eleventh century the coast of Palestine was attractive enough for the maḥārī, *the catchers of shellfish, based in Alexandria, Egypt, to make the long journey to dredge for the precious "purple" shellfish—that is, oysters. These oystermen belonged to the lowest strata of society and some of their Muslim compatriots were horrified that these Alexandrian oystermen would end the day by cruising into the taverns operated by the Crusaders in Acre, Palestine, and drink beer. Across the bay is Haifa, whose Greek name in the eleventh century was Porphyrion, the town of the purple shell.*

¾ cup fresh bread crumbs
2 large garlic cloves, very finely chopped
3 tablespoons finely chopped fresh parsley leaves
Salt and freshly ground black pepper to taste
24 oysters, opened, adductor muscle cut, and oyster left in the bottom, deeper, shell half
Extra-virgin olive oil for drizzling
Lemon wedges

1. Preheat the oven to 325°F.
2. In a small bowl, mix the bread crumbs, garlic, and parsley and season with salt and pepper. Place between ½ and 1 teaspoon of the

crumb topping on each oyster. Drizzle a few drops of olive oil on each one and bake in their half-shells until the edges of the oysters have curled and the tops are a light golden, about 25 minutes. Serve hot with lemon wedges.

Makes 8 servings

Baked Oysters

When I was a teenager on Long Island, my family would go Friday nights to Brancato's, an Italian-American restaurant in Huntington. The place was fantastic with the smells of garlic and salami and the sights of people eating baked manicotti, fried calamari, lasagne, a variety of macaroni dishes, and the ubiquitous veal piccata. For an antipasto, one would see clams and oysters gratinate *coming out of the kitchen, as well as raw ones. I don't remember ordering them because I don't remember loving oysters until I was about seventeen. But once I discovered the taste, there was no turning back. An oyster is a beautiful thing, and one can wax quite poetic over the smooth sliding of an oyster down the gullet. Next to raw, this is my favorite way of preparing them, the way they made them in countless Italian-American restaurants in Manhattan, Queens, and Long Island in the 1960s. On Long Island, we would use Blue Point oysters.*

40 oysters
½ cup dry bread crumbs
¼ cup freshly grated Parmigiano-Reggiano
   cheese
½ cup finely chopped fresh parsley leaves
1 teaspoon dried oregano
1 large garlic clove, very finely chopped
½ cup very finely chopped onion
¼ cup extra-virgin olive oil
½ cup (1 stick) unsalted butter, at room
   temperature
Salt and freshly ground black pepper
   to taste
¼ teaspoon red pepper flakes

1. Shuck the oysters, making sure they rest loose on the deeper shell half. Arrange the oyster shells in one or two baking dishes in a single layer.

2. Preheat the oven to 350°F.

3. In a medium-size bowl, mix the bread crumbs and cheese. In another small bowl, mix the parsley, oregano, garlic, and onion. Combine the contents of the 2 bowls and add the olive oil and butter, mixing well. Season with salt, black pepper, and the red pepper flakes until very well blended. Place 1 or 2 teaspoons of stuffing on top of each oyster, spreading it with the back of a small spoon or your finger so it covers the entire oyster.

4. Cover the pan(s) with a sheet of aluminum foil and bake for 10 minutes. Turn the oven to broil, remove the foil, and broil until the tops are golden brown and crispy looking, about 5 minutes. Serve hot from the oven

Makes 10 servings

Antipasti Misti

Every restaurant in Italy serves an *antipasti misti*, a mixed antipasto platter, with endless varieties of prepared food. When I was last in Genoa I had a fabulous one at the Ristorante Da Genio on the Salita San Leonardo, 61, off the via Fieschi. It consisted of a croquette of finely sliced anchovy with bread soaked in milk, mixed with eggs, Parmesan cheese, salt, and pepper. It was then rolled in flour or bread crumbs and deep-fried in olive oil. We also had fresh anchovies marinated in olive oil and lemon juice, and placed on top of a fresh tomato with a sprinkle of salt. The *misti* continued with a dish of poached salmon with boiled potatoes and carrots, which were all cooked in butter with a drizzle of olive oil and a sprinkle of parsley. The antipasto was not yet done because we were also offered hake braised with fennel, tomato, parsley, garlic, olive oil, and onions.

Clams Oreganata

This antipasto of vongole ripiene *seems more common among Italians in America than in Italy, but nevertheless it's magnificent as far as I'm concerned. In many restaurants it is too bready and pasty, with no taste of clams. This recipe is the way they should do it.*

24 littleneck clams (about 3½ pounds), opened, top shell discarded, and clam loosened from the shell, leaving it in the bottom shell and saving the liquid

½ cup fresh bread crumbs made from French or Italian bread

1 teaspoon dried oregano

1 tablespoon finely chopped fresh parsley leaves

3 tablespoons freshly grated Parmigiano-Reggiano cheese

Salt and freshly ground black pepper to taste

Extra-virgin olive oil for drizzling

1. Preheat the oven to broil. Place the clams on the half shell on a baking sheet.

2. In a small bowl, toss the bread crumbs, oregano, parsley, and cheese together until well blended and season with salt and pepper. Place about 1 teaspoon on each clam and drizzle the tops with olive oil.

3. Broil until golden brown on top, 2 to 3 minutes, but watch carefully. Serve hot.

Makes 6 to 8 servings

Clams Gratinate

This Italian antipasto is a little different from the preceding recipe. The clams are cooked in the same way, but the flavoring is an aromatic blend of tomatoes, parsley, capers, and anchovies.

2 tablespoons extra-virgin olive oil, plus more for
   drizzling
¼ cup finely chopped fresh parsley leaves
1 large garlic, finely chopped
1 tablespoon salted or brined capers, rinsed or
   drained and chopped
3 tablespoons finely chopped shallots
1 salted anchovy fillet, chopped
Salt and freshly ground black pepper to taste
2 tablespoons tomato puree, or 1 tablespoon
   tomato paste mixed with 1 tablespoon water
24 littleneck clams (about 3½ pounds),
   scrubbed well
½ cup fresh bread crumbs

1. In a small skillet, heat the olive oil over medium heat. In a small bowl, mix the parsley, garlic, capers, shallots, and anchovy, then cook for 1 minute, seasoning with a little salt and pepper and stirring. Add the tomato puree and cook another 2 minutes.

2. Preheat the oven to 425°F.

3. Shuck the clams and place the half shells on a baking sheet. Put a little more than 1 teaspoon of the sauce on top of each of the clams, then cover with 1 teaspoon of bread crumbs and drizzle with some olive oil. Bake until golden and sizzling, 12 to 15 minutes. Serve hot.

Makes 6 to 8 servings

Kebabs, Skewers, and Other Grilled Foods

Whether it's the smoky smells of the Grilled Moroccan-Style Skewers of Spicy Ground Beef (page 424) molded around their little swords grilling over hardwood charcoal in the public square of Marrakech, or the miniature morsels of Chop Shish (page 432)—lamb and lamb fat seasoned with cumin—which you can watch being grilled at truck stops in Turkey, kebabs and grilled foods sometimes seem to be what the Mediterranean is all about. How wonderful that all of it can be reproduced on your own home grill. In this chapter, you start by getting a fire going or preheating your gas grill. When I've done that, then I often grill a number of things. After all, it has taken a bit of effort to start everything, and it's wonderful to keep a fire in use, and last, it's a great way to continuously feed party guests. Some of the recipes here require skewers, and others just get slapped onto the grill, while others still are grilled and eaten later at room temperature.

Grilled Chicken Kebabs

The popular grilled chicken kebabs of Lebanon and Syria, called shīsh tawūq *in Arabic, are probably of Turkish origin, from the Turkish word for chicken,* tavuk. *As with so many grilled foods in the Arab world, this preparation is traditionally served at special grill restaurants in Lebanon. Every cook uses, it seems, a different spice blend, so I give you some options to play with. Serve these hot as a passed appetizer or at a sit-down dinner or meze party. If you are serving it as a passed appetizer, use 6- or 8-inch wooden skewers with fewer pieces of meat on them. You may have to cut the skewers down to size.*

2 pounds skinless, boneless chicken breasts, trimmed of any fat and cut into cubes
½ cup extra-virgin olive oil
3 tablespoons fresh lemon juice
1 small onion, grated
½ teaspoon ground cinnamon
½ teaspoon freshly ground cardamom seeds (from about 20 pods)
1 teaspoon dried or fresh thyme
Salt and freshly ground black pepper to taste
1 teaspoon freshly ground cumin seeds (optional)
1 teaspoon Bahārāt (page 470; optional)
½ teaspoon paprika (optional)
Ten 10-inch wooden or metal skewers

1. Marinate the chicken cubes in a glass or ceramic bowl or pan with the olive oil, lemon juice, onion, cinnamon, cardamom, thyme, salt, pepper, cumin, *bahārāt*, and paprika, if using, for 6 hours, covered, in the refrigerator, turning the cubes occasionally.

2. Preheat a gas grill for 15 minutes on high or prepare a hot charcoal fire. Skewer the chicken cubes so they touch each other but do not press against each other. If possible, use a skewer rack so the chicken grills without touching the grilling grate. Grill until golden brown, 20 to 30 minutes, turning frequently. Serve hot.

Makes 10 servings

Grilled Spiced Chicken Hearts

This little appetizer is inspired by a dish I once had in Marsa Matruh, in Egypt's Western Desert, called muḥammar, *which was made with lamb's liver. In this preparation, the tiny hearts are tossed with the spice mixture and either fried quickly in a pan or drizzled with olive oil and grilled and eaten before you begin grilling the main meat for dinner.*

½ pound chicken hearts
1 large garlic clove, finely chopped
½ teaspoon freshly ground cumin seeds
¼ teaspoon ground red chile
Salt and freshly ground black pepper to taste
Extra-virgin olive oil for drizzling
Six 8-inch wooden skewers

1. In a medium-size bowl, toss the chicken hearts, garlic, cumin, red pepper, salt, and pepper together and refrigerate for 2 hours.

2. Skewer the chicken hearts and drizzle with olive oil.

3. Prepare a hot charcoal fire or preheat a gas grill on high for 15 minutes. Place the skewers on the grill and cook until crispy brown, 8 to 10

minutes, turning. Serve immediately on the skewer as a passed appetizer.

Makes 6 servings

Variation: If you are going to fry the chicken hearts, heat 1½ tablespoons olive oil in a pan over medium heat and cook the hearts until firm and brown, 7 to 8 minutes.

Grilled Pork Kebabs from Andalusia

Both the spicing and the name of these kebabs, pinchon moruno *("Moorish skewers"), if not the meat used (pork), indicate a perceived Muslim heritage. These skewers of spiced pork are marinated and grilled slowly until the meat is succulent and falls apart with each bite. They are a typical* tapa *in Andalusia. If you serve it as a seated, rather than passed,* tapa *dish, garnish the platter with tomato slices and lettuce leaves.*

½ cup extra-virgin olive oil

1½ teaspoons freshly ground cumin seeds

2 teaspoons paprika

2 teaspoons salt

Freshly ground black pepper to taste

¼ teaspoon cayenne pepper

2 teaspoons dried thyme

2 bay leaves, finely crumbled

2 pounds boneless pork country ribs, trimmed of fat and cubed

Ten 10-inch wooden skewers

1. In a medium-size glass or ceramic baking dish, mix the olive oil, cumin, paprika, salt, black pepper, cayenne, thyme, and bay leaves.

Toss the pork with this mixture and let marinate for 24 hours, covered, in the refrigerator, turning the cubes occasionally. This long marinade breaks down the meat, making it very tender and succulent.

2. Prepare a charcoal fire and let it die down considerably or preheat a gas grill for 15 minutes on very low. Skewer the pork and place on the grill until golden and crispy looking, about 50 minutes to 1 hour, turning frequently and making sure the meat is not too close to the fire. Serve hot.

Makes 10 servings

Grilled Moroccan-Style Skewers of Spicy Ground Beef

These kafta, *ground meat molded by hand around a sword-like skewer and grilled, are typical street food in Morocco. Sometimes they are served as a meze. These particular skewers are called* qutbānis diyal kafta *and are more boldly spiced than the following recipe. This particular spice mix is just one you could use; cooks often will concoct their own. The meat should be well mixed or kneaded; the best way to do this is in a food processor. Serve with warm flatbread, if desired.*

2 pounds ground beef chuck (15% fat)

1 pound onions, finely chopped

4 large garlic cloves, finely chopped

2 tablespoons finely chopped fresh coriander leaves (cilantro)

2 tablespoons finely chopped fresh parsley leaves

2 tablespoons finely chopped fresh mint leaves

1 tablespoon sweet paprika

2 teaspoons hot paprika

1½ teaspoons ground red chile

1½ teaspoons freshly ground cumin seeds

1 tablespoon salt

1 teaspoon freshly ground black pepper

1 teaspoon ground cinnamon

1 teaspoon ground ginger

8 flat metal sword skewers or sixteen 10-inch
wooden skewers

Olive oil for drizzling

Arabic bread for wrapping or serving

Ground cumin for garnish

1. Mix all the ingredients except the olive oil, bread, and garnish in a large bowl with your hands. Place the mixture in batches in a food processor and process until it looks pasty. Refrigerate for 1 hour.

2. Prepare a hot charcoal fire or preheat a gas grill on high for 15 minutes.

3. Form handfuls of the meat mixture around a metal skewer or hold 2 wooden skewers parallel about ¼ to ⅓ inch apart, putting 3 balls per single or double skewer and flattening them slightly, and mold the meat around them so it doesn't fall off when you grill them. Drizzle some olive oil over the meat and grill directly over the hottest part of the fire until firm and dark brown, 5 to 10 minutes, moving the skewers around to avoid scorching or flare-ups, if necessary. Serve hot wrapped in warm Arabic bread with a sprinkle of cumin.

Makes 8 servings

Grilled Moroccan-Style Skewers of Beef and Lamb

In Marrakech, the background ratatatat of sibilants and glottal stops is, I suppose, part of the allure of buying a skewered kafta *(also heard as* kufta *or* kifta*) sizzling over glowing hardwood from the vendors in the Jama al fina Square. This is one of the easiest do-at-home recipes from North Africa, and it is a standard* chez moi *during the spring and summer. You can actually make the whole thing with a food processor, and that is how this recipe is written.*

1 small onion, quartered

Leaves from 3 leafy sprigs fresh parsley

Leaves from 1 small bunch fresh coriander
(cilantro), finely chopped

Leaves from 2 leafy sprigs fresh mint

Leaves from 4 leafy sprigs fresh marjoram or
¼ teaspoon dried marjoram

½ pound ground beef

½ pound ground lamb

¼ teaspoon ground red chile

1 teaspoon Rās al-Ḥanūt (page 470)

1 teaspoon freshly ground cumin seeds

1 teaspoon salt

½ teaspoon freshly ground black pepper

4 flat-bladed metal skewers or eight 10-inch
wooden skewers

Arabic bread for wrapping or serving

¼ cup Harīsa (page 468) made with only chile,
garlic, salt, and olive oil

Ground cumin for garnish

1. Place the onion, parsley, coriander, mint, and fresh marjoram, if using, in a food processor

and pulse until finely chopped. Transfer to a medium-size bowl. Add the beef and lamb to the food processor and process until pasty. Transfer the meat to a bowl along with the dried marjoram, if using, red pepper, *rās al-ḥanūt*, cumin, salt, and black pepper. Blend this mixture very well with your hands, then form into 12 egg-size balls. Skewer the balls of meat with a flat-bladed metal skewer or 2 wooden skewers held parallel to each other about ½ inch apart. Skewer 3 balls per single or double skewer and flatten them. Refrigerate for 2 hours.

2. Prepare a hot charcoal fire or preheat a gas grill on high for 15 minutes. Let the coals die down a bit, or push them to one side, or turn the gas heat down to low.

3. Grill the skewers slowly, turning occasionally, until golden brown and firm, about 30 minutes. Serve immediately as a passed appetizer if you like, wrapped in some Arabic bread with a little Moroccan-style *harīsa* and a sprinkle of salt and cumin.

Makes 8 servings

Spicy Veal and Lamb Kebabs from Turkey

This Turkish dish is known as Adana kebabı, *named after the city of Adana in southeastern Turkey in the middle of the fertile Cilician (Çukurova) Plain. The cooking of this region is spicier than in the rest of Turkey and that fact is reflected in this preparation.*

¾ pound boneless leg of lamb, trimmed of fat and cut into ½-inch cubes

¾ pound boneless veal shoulder or leg, trimmed of fat and cut into ½-inch cubes
2 teaspoons cayenne pepper, or more to taste
2 teaspoons freshly ground coriander seeds
2 teaspoons freshly ground cumin seeds
2 teaspoons freshly ground black pepper
Salt to taste
5 flat-bladed metal or 10 wooded skewers
2 *pide* breads (page 432)
Extra-virgin olive oil, melted unsalted butter, or vegetable oil for brushing
2 medium-size onions, thinly sliced
1 tablespoon sumac (page 427)
Finely chopped fresh parsley leaves for garnish

1. In a large bowl, toss the lamb and veal with the cayenne, coriander, cumin, black pepper, and salt; cover with plastic wrap and refrigerate for 1 hour.

2. Prepare a charcoal fire or preheat a gas grill on medium-low for 15 minutes.

3. Skewer the lamb and veal cubes, making sure they are not pressed against each other too tightly. Grill until the kebabs are springy to the touch, about 20 minutes, turning often.

4. Meanwhile, brush the *pide* bread with olive oil, melted butter, or vegetable oil and grill or griddle for a few minutes until hot but not brittle.

5. Arrange the kebabs on a serving platter or individual plates and serve with the *pide* bread, sliced onions, a sprinkle of sumac, and chopped parsley as a garnish.

Makes 4 servings

<table>
<tr><td>

Sumac

Sumac is a sour, lemony spice made from the dried red berries of the sumac bush (*Rhus coriaria*), which grows wild throughout the Middle East. It is a deep maroon color and is sold in ground form in Middle Eastern markets.

</td></tr>
</table>

Veal and Lamb Finger Kebabs from Anatolia

These Turkish Bergama köfte, *or grilled ground meat from Bergama, the ancient Pergamon, in northwestern Anatolia, are mildly spiced and grilled over a hardwood fire. The town is today an agricultural market surrounded by a well-irrigated plain.*

Technically, when pieces of meat are grilled they're called kebabs and when the meat is ground first and formed into balls or patties before being grilled they're called köfte.

½ pound ground veal

½ pound ground lamb

3 tablespoons very finely chopped onion

1 teaspoon freshly ground cumin seeds

1 teaspoon freshly ground coriander seeds

Salt and freshly ground black pepper to taste

Extra-virgin olive oil

Lettuce leaves for garnish

1 large red onion, thinly sliced

Pide bread (page 432) for garnish

1. In a large bowl, knead together the veal, lamb, chopped onion, cumin, coriander, salt, and pepper very well with wet hands to keep the meat from sticking. Cover and let rest in the refrigerator for 1 hour.

2. Prepare a charcoal fire or preheat a gas grill for 15 minutes.

3. Form the meat into thumb-sized pieces. Brush with olive oil and place on the grill. Grill on medium-low heat, turning often, until the *köfte* are golden brown and succulent without being mushy to the touch, about 20 minutes.

4. Serve on a platter lined with lettuce leaves with sliced red onion and *pide* bread.

Makes 6 servings

Grilled Kibbe with Pomegranate Syrup

The variety of kibbe preparations is enormous; Paula Wolfert lists over fifty in one of her books. In this recipe for grilled kibbe, kubba mishwiyya, *from the Syrian city of Homs, the kibbe are formed by layering two little pancakes of kibbe about 3 inches in diameter together with a stuffing in between of ground lamb cooked with* shaᶜmī, *a flavorful lamb fat, and seasoned with the spice mix* bahārāt *and pomegranate syrup. The kibbe are brushed with olive oil, grilled, and eaten hot stuffed inside some warm fresh pita bread. Serve with the Turkish yogurt-and-garlic dip known as* Cacık (page 56) *or* Parsley in Tahini Sauce (page 469).

Kibbe

1 cup raw fine bulgur (no. 1)

1½ pounds ground lamb, cut from the leg or
shoulder

Salt and freshly ground black pepper to taste

1 medium-size onion, grated

1 teaspoon Bahārāt (page 470)

Stuffing

½ pound ground lamb, cut from the leg or
shoulder

2 ounces lamb fat, finely chopped

½ teaspoon Bahārāt (page 470)

Salt and freshly ground black pepper to taste

1 tablespoon pomegranate molasses

Extra-virgin olive oil

1. Make the kibbe. Cover a strainer with
cheesecloth and place the bulgur on top. Place
the strainer in a pot filled with lightly salted
cold water and soak the bulgur for 10 minutes.
Pull up the sides of the cheesecloth, encasing the
bulgur, and squeeze out all the water. Transfer to
a large bowl.

2. Add the remaining kibbe ingredients and
knead everything together until homogenous.
Transfer in batches to a food processor and
process into a paste. Remove to a large metal
bowl, cover with plastic wrap, and refrigerate for
1 hour.

3. Meanwhile, prepare the stuffing. Place the
ground lamb and lamb fat in a small skillet and
turn the heat to medium-high. Add the *bahārāt*,
season with salt and pepper, and cook, stirring
frequently, until the lamb is browned and the

lamb fat pretty much rendered, about 10 minutes. Add the pomegranate syrup and cook
another minute, stirring.

4. Remove the meat mixture from the refrigerator and form 28 patties about 3 inches in
diameter. Place a heaping teaspoon or more of
the stuffing on one patty and cover with
another, sealing the edges until you have 14
hamburger-like patties.

5. Prepare a hot charcoal fire or preheat a gas
grill for 15 minutes on high. Brush the kibbe

On Grilling Skewers

In the Middle East, special grill restaurants
grill kebabs on long metal skewers that look
like swords. They are placed in holders so
that no part of the skewer or the skewered
meat touches the grilling grate. For meze
made in your home, you may find it more
convenient to cut down your typical 10-inch
wooden skewers to about 6 inches, put fewer
pieces of meat on each one, and grill the
short skewers for little appetizing bites. Soak
the wooden skewers in water before skewer-
ing and placing on the grill to avoid scorching. It is sometimes easier to use two skewers
held parallel to each other to skewer meats
so the pieces don't twirl when you turn them
on the grill. Make sure the pieces of meat
are squished up against each other when
you skewer them and turn them often on
the grill.

with olive oil and grill until golden brown with black grid marks, about 20 minutes, turning once. If desired, cut the kibbe in half, and stuff them inside a small pita bread, also cut in half, drizzle either of the sauces suggested above into the sandwich, and serve.

Makes 14 servings without bread;
28 smaller servings with bread

Levantine Grilled Lamb Kafta

Kafta mishwiyya is very finely ground and well-blended spiced lamb molded by hand around a metal skewer that is then set over a grill. Traditionally, it is a typical offering of Lebanese grill restaurants, which use flat metal skewers that look like swords. The skewers are fitted on a skewer holder, a rectangular metal frame with notches to fit the skewers, so that the meat is suspended and never actually touches any part of the grill; then they are grilled over a charcoal fire. It always looks very appetizing, smells terrific, and is best eaten in a wrap of very thin Arabic bread known as marqūq bread, which can be found in this country sold by the Armenian name "lavash" or "mountain bread." Although it is most popular as a street or take-away food throughout Lebanon, Syria, Palestine, and Jordan, it can be found served as a meze in grill restaurants, although that is not typical.

3 pounds ground lamb, cut from the neck or shoulder
3 medium-size to large onions, grated
1 cup very finely chopped fresh parsley leaves
1 tablespoon Bahārāt (page 470)
2 teaspoons freshly ground allspice berries
1 teaspoon freshly ground cumin seeds
1 teaspoon freshly ground coriander seeds
½ teaspoon ground cinnamon
Salt and freshly ground black pepper to taste
10 flat metal sword skewers or twenty 10-inch wooden skewers
Extra-virgin olive oil for drizzling

Garnishes
½ cup coarsely chopped fresh parsley leaves
5 ripe plum tomatoes, chopped
1 large red onion, chopped
¼ teaspoon ground cinnamon
1 tablespoon sumac (page 427)
¼ cup finely chopped fresh mint leaves
6 to 8 large pita breads

1. In a large bowl, knead together the lamb, grated onions, parsley, *bahārāt*, allspice, cumin, coriander, cinnamon, salt, and pepper until well blended, using wet hands to keep the meat from sticking to them. Transfer to a food processor in batches and process until smooth and pasty. Transfer back to the bowl, cover with plastic wrap, and refrigerate for 2 to 6 hours.

2. Preheat a gas grill for 20 minutes on low or prepare a charcoal fire and let it die down a bit.

3. Take a handful of meat and press it around a skewer, forming the meat so it surrounds the skewer. If using wooden skewers, use 2, holding them parallel to each other about ¼ to ½ inch apart so the molded meat doesn't fall off when you turn them. Moisten the meat with some

olive oil, place the skewers on a skewer holder, and grill until golden brown and springy to the touch, 30 to 40 minutes. If you don't have a holder, just lay the skewers on the grill. Keep the skewers turning, as if on a rotisserie (or use a roto-kebab if you have one).

4. Toss all the garnish ingredients together. Slice an Arabic bread in half and open up the pocket. Place the meat on the bread and sprinkle on some garnish. Roll up and eat.

Makes 10 servings

Grilled Spiced Lamb Meatballs from Turkey

These little grilled Turkish-style meatballs called cıbız köfte *are excellent served on a bed of parsley, with diced red onions and some grilled hot chiles for a meze.*

1 large onion, coarsely chopped

2 pounds ground lamb

3 cups cubed day-old white French or Italian bread

1 large egg

1 garlic clove, very finely chopped

½ cup finely chopped fresh parsley leaves

½ teaspoon freshly ground cumin seeds

¼ teaspoon ground cinnamon

¼ teaspoon cayenne pepper

2 teaspoons salt

1 teaspoon freshly ground black pepper

Extra-virgin olive oil for basting

1 red onion, diced, for garnish

3 chiles, grilled until blackened, for garnish

Warmed *Pide* (page 432) or pita bread for accompaniment

2 cups plain yogurt whipped with 2 mashed garlic cloves

1. Place the onion in a food processor and process until mushy. Transfer to a large bowl. Place the meat in batches in the food processor and process until pasty. Transfer to the bowl. Soak the bread in water for a minute, then drain and squeeze the excess water out of the bread. Transfer to the bowl. Add the egg, garlic, 3 tablespoons of parsley, the cumin, cinnamon, cayenne, salt, and black pepper to the meat mixture and knead well with your hands to distribute the ingredients evenly. Return the meat mixture to the food processor, in batches, and process until pastier. Form the mixture into balls ½ inch in diameter and place them on a baking tray covered with a film of olive oil. Place the meatballs in the refrigerator for 30 minutes while you prepare the fire.

2. Preheat a gas grill on high or prepare a hot charcoal fire.

3. Drizzle the meatballs with more olive oil and place on the grill close to the fire. Grill until golden brown, about 20 minutes, basting with olive oil and turning frequently.

4. Transfer the finished meatballs to a serving platter covered with the remaining 5 tablespoons of parsley and garnish the edges with diced red onion and the grilled chiles. Serve with warm pita bread and the garlic-flavored yogurt.

Makes 8 to 10 servings

Kebabs in Turkey

The kebabs and *köfte* (ground meat molded around a skewer and grilled) of Turkey are endless—endless in variety and endlessly sold. No matter where you go or where you are, you will find them, their wafting smells beckoning you to eat more even if you've just had some. They are so ubiquitous and wonderful smelling, it's hard to remember to eat other things. I've always enjoyed saddling up to a *kebabçı* or *köfteçi* with the working-men of whatever town we happen to be in and ordering some. It's fun and people are friendly. I remember once being helped by a couple of gruff-looking men, who showed me that the real secret to a Chop Shish (page 432) was to sprinkle on the freshly ground cumin that was in a small bowl for customers on the serving counter.

Shish Kebab

In Turkey today, şiş kebabı *(shish kebab) and many other grilled preparations are usually served as a main course in restaurants or grill restaurants and not as a meze. But sometimes a restaurant will serve smaller portions as a meze with some alcoholic drink. In the home, they are rarely served as meze, although it might be common among some Turkish yuppies to serve them at a party with drinks. Shish kebab are simply pieces of meat stuck on a skewer and grilled over a fire. In the Arab world, the same preparation is called* shīsh kabāb *or* laḥm mishwī *(grilled meat). Serve the skewers with* pide *bread and* cacık.

1 cup full-fat plain yogurt
3 tablespoons extra-virgin olive oil
3 tablespoons onion juice (grated from 1 medium-size onion)
Salt and freshly ground black pepper to taste
2 pounds boneless lamb, cut from the leg with its fat into ½-inch cubes
Ten 10-inch metal or wooden skewers
4 *pide* bread (page 432) or pita bread (optional)
1 cup Cacık (optional; page 56)

1. Stir together the yogurt, olive oil, and onion juice in a medium-size glass or ceramic pan or bowl and season with salt and pepper. Add the lamb cubes, coat with the marinade, and refrigerate, covered, for 4 hours.

2. Prepare a charcoal fire and let it die down a bit or preheat a gas grill for 15 minutes on low. Skewer the lamb cubes. Set the skewers in a skewer holder over the fire and grill until golden brown and succulent, turning often, about 20 minutes. Or, lacking a skewer holder, place them on the grill and grill to perfection. Serve with or on a piece of griddled or grill-warmed *pide* bread and the *cacık* on the side.

Makes 10 servings

Variation: An Arab recipe for shish kebabs calls for marinating 1¾ pounds boneless leg of lamb, cut into ½-inch cubes, in 3 tablespoons chopped onion, ¼ cup extra-virgin olive oil, 1 teaspoon fresh lemon juice, 1 teaspoon Bahārāt

Pita Bread or Pide Bread

These two breads sound like they are the same, but they're not. Pita bread is the name for the ubiquitous flatbread of the Arab world that has a pocket. But in Arabic it is known as *khubz ͨArabī*, not as pita bread, and sold in this country as Arabic bread, pita bread, pocket bread, or Syrian bread. *Pide* bread, on the other hand, is a Turkish and Greek flatbread without a pocket. In Greece, this is the bread used for making a gyro sandwich. Pocket breads are made everywhere in this country and are easy to find, although I think the best ones are still sold in Middle Eastern markets because they are fresher. These flatbreads dry out easily, so they must be consumed the day they are purchased or frozen that day. *Pide* bread is much more difficult to find and even Middle Eastern markets don't always carry them. Greek markets do though, usually sold in their frozen foods section. I have also found them, curiously, in my local Indo-Pakistani market in Los Angeles. Always warm flatbread before using it.

(page 470), and black pepper to taste for 2 hours in the refrigerator, covered. A hot fire is started and the lamb is skewered with pieces of onion, green bell peppers, and cherry tomatoes, then cooked for about 20 minutes. It is served with warmed Arabic bread and chopped fresh mint leaves.

Chop Shish

Chop shish are tiny morsels of lamb, properly çöp şiş *in Turkish, grilled over a wood fire and served with tomatoes, peppers, onions, and* pide *bread on the side with freshly ground cumin. They are more a street food or snack food than a meze, but I like to serve them as a meze.*

Çöp şiş are found everywhere in Turkey and they never fail to please. Because of their simplicity, it is important to following the directions explicitly. The secret to a successful preparation is the little pieces of lamb fat necessary for the tenderizing effect and a pinch of ground cumin sprinkled over the skewers after they're grilled. And you need to watch them constantly as they cook to be careful you don't overcook them, otherwise the lamb fat will just melt away. Because the pieces of meat are so little, it is important to use thin wooden skewers, which are easily found in supermarkets or barbeque grill stores. Lamb tail fat can be found by asking your butcher. In its place, the fat found on the upper portion of a leg of lamb is excellent.

1 pound boneless lamb, cut from the leg with its fat into ⅜-inch cubes

¼ pound lamb tail fat (preferably), cut into ⅜-inch cubes

Salt and freshly ground black pepper to taste

2 tablespoons extra-virgin olive oil

Twelve 8-inch thin wooden skewers

1 tablespoon freshly ground cumin seeds

Chopped onions for garnish (optional)

Chopped fresh tomatoes for garnish (optional)

Seeded and chopped green bell peppers for garnish (optional)

Turkish/Greek-style *pide* bread for garnish (page 432; optional)

1. Prepare a medium-hot charcoal fire or preheat a gas grill for 20 minutes on medium.

2. Skewer the lamb and lamb fat, a piece of fat for every 4 pieces of meat. Season with salt and pepper and drizzle with the olive oil.

3. Set the skewers on a rack over the grilling grate, or directly on the grilling grate, and cook until the lamb is golden brown and the edges of the fat are crispy, about 30 minutes, turning occasionally.

4. Remove to a serving platter and sprinkle with the cumin. Serve with chopped onions, tomatoes, green peppers, and *pide* bread, if desired.

Makes 6 servings

Lamb Flank Kebabs in Yogurt and Tomato Sauce

This Turkish preparation called yoğurtlu kebab *is always grilled and sometimes served as a meze.*

1 large onion, peeled

¼ cup extra-virgin olive oil

2 tablespoons white wine vinegar

½ teaspoon dried thyme

2 pounds lamb flank steak or boneless leg of lamb, cut into ½-inch cubes and flattened with a meat mallet

Salt and freshly ground black pepper to taste

½ cup (1 stick) unsalted butter

2 pounds ripe tomatoes, cut in half, seeds squeezed out, grated against the largest holes of a grater, and skins discarded

¼ cup tomato paste

½ cup water

4 large garlic cloves, mashed

1 teaspoon hot paprika

½ teaspoon cayenne pepper

2 cups good-quality full-fat plain yogurt

4 Turkish/Greek-style *pide* flatbreads (page 432) or Indian naan bread (6 to 8 inches in diameter), cut in half

Tomato wedges

2 green chiles, thinly sliced

1. Grate the onion into a large bowl, then add the olive oil, 1 tablespoon of the vinegar, the thyme, lamb, salt, and pepper. Toss well, cover with plastic wrap, and refrigerate for 6 hours.

2. In a medium-size saucepan, melt 1 tablespoon butter over medium heat, then cook the tomatoes for 5 minutes. Add the tomato paste and water, stir, cook for 2 minutes, then add the garlic and cook 2 more minutes, stirring. Add the remaining 1 tablespoon vinegar, stir, remove the pan from the heat, cover, and set aside.

Kebabs

If you've been to Turkey, you know that a kebab is not just a piece of skewered grill meat. It's any gobbet of meat cut and cooked any which way. There are many, many ways of cooking kebabs, the favorite being *izgara*, grilled, on a *şiş*, or skewer. In Istanbul, don't fail to order a *döner kebab*, the Turkish version of what is commonly known as a Greek gyro in this country. Available as a meze, kebabs are usually found sold at hole-in-the-wall cheap eateries called *kebabçı*, which offer grilled kebabs, salads, and something to drink with no frills.

3. In a small saucepan, melt 4 tablespoons of the butter, then stir in the paprika and cayenne. In another small saucepan, melt the remaining 3 tablespoons butter and keep warm. Beat the yogurt until smooth.

4. Prepare a hot charcoal fire or preheat a gas grill on high for 15 minutes. Grill the lamb close to the fire, turning frequently, until crispy brown, about 3 minutes per side. It should not be dry, but rather pink and tender and juicy.

5. Heat the bread in a cast-iron skillet without any grease until nearly crisp or do the same over the grill. Arrange the pieces of bread on a large serving platter. Pour equal amounts of the unseasoned melted butter over each of the cut pieces of flatbread, then pour the tomato sauce

evenly over the buttered bread, then place a good-size dollop of yogurt, reserving one quarter of the yogurt. Place the grilled lamb on top of the yogurt and finally a small dollop of yogurt on top of the lamb. Pour the paprika butter over the top and serve immediately with tomato wedges and chiles, letting people help themselves.

Makes 10 servings

 ## Lamb and Cherry Kebabs from Aleppo

This famous preparation, called kabāb bi'l-karaz, *is made with a special kind of cherry found around Aleppo, St. Lucie's cherry (*Prunus mahaleb L.), *which is a small, bitter, crimson-colored black cherry. This is a recipe you'll want to make when cherries hit your farmer's market. You can use either a sweet or a sour cherry.*

1½ pounds boneless leg of lamb, trimmed of fat and cut into ½-inch cubes
2 teaspoons Bahārāt (page 470)
½ teaspoon freshly ground cumin seeds
½ teaspoon freshly ground coriander seeds
¼ teaspoon ground cinnamon
Salt and freshly ground black pepper to taste
Ten 8- to 10-inch wooden skewers
50 pitted fresh black or Bing cherries
Arabic bread
Tomato wedges
Pitted black olives

1. In a medium-size bowl, toss the lamb, *bahārāt*, cumin, coriander, cinnamon, salt, and

pepper together. Cover with plastic wrap and refrigerate for 2 hours.

2. Meanwhile, prepare a hot charcoal fire or preheat a gas grill for 15 minutes on high.

3. Skewer the lamb, interspersed with cherries, using 5 pieces of meat and 4 or 5 cherries per skewer. Place the skewers on the grill and cook, turning occasionally, until the meat is browned and springy to the touch, about 15 minutes. Serve immediately on a platter with pita bread, tomato wedges, and black olives.

Makes 8 servings

Grilled Lamb's Tongue Marinated in Garlic and Lemon

Don't let the idea of tongue put you off—this is delicious. Keep the grill going and you can make a variety of grilled appetizers. In this country, lamb tongue is sometimes seen in the supermarket. Don't use beef tongue—it won't work. In Lebanon, Syria, and Palestine, this is not an uncommon meze—it is much liked.

10 lamb's tongues (about 2¼ pounds)
1 large garlic clove, finely chopped
Juice from ½ lemon
3 to 4 tablespoons extra-virgin olive oil
Salt to taste
½ teaspoon freshly ground black pepper
1 tablespoon coarsely chopped fresh parsley
 leaves

1. Prepare a hot charcoal fire or preheat a gas grill on high for 15 minutes.

2. Plunge the tongues into boiling water and cook for 5 minutes. Drain and plunge into cold water. Remove the skin with a paring knife, as well as any fat the gristle at the base of the tongue.

3. Lightly oil the tongues and grill until firm and brown, about 12 minutes per side. Slice the tongues into ⅛-inch-thick slices. Arrange the slices in a spiral fashion on a large round ceramic serving platter. Sprinkle with the garlic, lemon juice, olive oil, salt, and pepper, then sprinkle with the parsley and serve after letting it rest for 5 minutes. Lamb tongue can also be garnished with onions, tomatoes, and tahini (page 59).

Makes 12 servings

Variation: Alternatively, let the tongues cool before you slice them, then combine with the garlic, lemon juice, olive oil, salt, pepper, and parsley, cover, and let marinate in the refrigerator for a day. Remove from the refrigerator 30 minutes before serving.

Turkish-Style Grilled Marinated Swordfish

In Turkey, kılıç şiş, swordfish kebabs (literally "swordfish skewers"), are a very popular fish dish usually served in restaurants, but not typically as a meze. Grilling times may change, depending on how far the food is from the fire, so check occasionally for doneness; the swordfish should feel slightly springy to the touch, not hard and not mushy.

2 tablespoons extra-virgin olive oil

¼ cup fresh lemon juice

1 small onion, sliced

1 teaspoon paprika

1 teaspoon salt

Freshly ground black pepper to taste

2 bay leaves, crumbled

2 pounds swordfish steaks, skin removed and cut into 1½-inch cubes

Twelve 10-inch wooden skewers

1 to 2 lemons, sliced and quartered

1 to 2 ripe tomatoes, cut into wedges

1. Prepare the marinade by whisking together the olive oil, lemon juice, onion, paprika, salt, pepper, and bay leaves. Arrange the swordfish in a ceramic or glass baking dish and cover with the marinade. Marinate the swordfish cubes for 3 hours, covered in the refrigerator, turning occasionally.

2. Preheat a gas grill on high for 15 minutes or prepare a hot charcoal fire.

3. Thread the swordfish onto the skewers intermingled with slices of lemon and tomato. Coat the swordfish with some of the marinade and grill until springy to the touch with attractive grid marks, 5 to 6 minutes per side, basting with the marinade a few times. Serve hot arranged on a platter or let people help themselves to the skewers.

Makes 10 to 12 servings

Turkish Seafood

The Turks are not huge eaters of fish even though they are surrounded by the Black Sea, the Sea of Marmara, the Aegean, and the Mediterranean. The most popular fish and shellfish are found in the coastal ports, seafood such as *hamsi* (anchovy), the very popular *lüfer* (a kind of bluefish) and *kılıç* (swordfish), the wonderful mackerel *uskumru*, which goes into the sandwich the boatmen sell by the Galata bridge in Istanbul, and *lakerda*, a rich, oily salted bonito that one eats as a meze.

Sea Bass Kebabs from Alexandria

These kabāb samak, *fish kebabs, are typically served at fish restaurants on Egypt's Mediterranean coast, and they display a Turkish heritage in the use of cumin and bay leaves, which are native to the Mediterranean. As in Lebanon, grilled foods are often restaurant and street foods, and one is likely to find such a preparation in one of the delightful seaside grill restaurants in Alexandria, Abu Qir, Damietta, or Port Said on the Mediterranean coast, where sea bass,* ᶜārūs *(pronounced* QA-roos*), or a kind of grouper,* waᶜār, *is typically used. Although not often served as a meze, they do in fact make great ones.*

Juice of ½ lemon

¼ cup extra-virgin olive oil

3 medium-size onions, 1 very finely chopped and
  2 quartered and layers separated
2 teaspoons freshly ground cumin seeds
Salt and freshly ground black pepper to taste
2 pounds firm, white-fleshed fish steaks or thick
  fillets, such as sea bass, grouper, swordfish,
  marlin, or shark, skin removed and cut into
  1-inch cubes
Eight 10-inch wooden skewers
1 large green bell pepper, seeded and cut into 20
  to 24 square pieces
18 bay leaves, soaked in tepid water to cover
  30 minutes (no need to soak if using fresh)
  and drained
Lemon wedges for garnish
Chopped fresh parsley leaves for garnish

1. Whisk together the lemon juice, olive oil, chopped onion, cumin, salt, and pepper in a large ceramic or glass baking dish; add the fish cubes, cover with plastic wrap, and let marinate 4 to 6 hours in the refrigerator, turning occasionally.

2. Prepare a charcoal fire or preheat a gas grill on high for 20 minutes.

3. Skewer the fish, putting a piece of quartered onion and a piece of green pepper between the pieces of fish and using 2 to 3 bay leaves per skewer. Continue in this manner until all the ingredients but the garnishes are skewered. Grill the skewered fish for 10 to 12 minutes, brushing with the marinade and turning once.

4. Serve on a platter garnished with lemon wedges and parsley and let people help themselves.

Makes 8 servings

Grilled Sardines in Grape Leaves

In the Mediterranean there are several culinary cultures that claim this dish. The Greeks make grape leaf–wrapped grilled sardines, stuffing them with mint; and so, too, do the Turks and Arabs. In Provence, an old dish of grape leaf–wrapped sardines is called sardines grillées aux feuilles de vigne, *and even the great Escoffier has a recipe. Both Escoffier and Arab cooks like to use small red mullet for this dish, too. When choosing a grape leaf, make sure it is very large so that the fish can be wrapped at least twice around to secure the leaf well. Stuff the sardines, wrap them up, and grill until the leaves begin to turn black, then serve.*

3 tablespoons extra-virgin olive oil
5 teaspoons fresh lemon juice
Salt and freshly ground black pepper to taste
8 sprigs fresh mint or rosemary
8 fresh sardines (about 1½ pounds), cleaned,
  washed well, and dried with paper towels
8 very large grape leaves from a jar
Extra-virgin olive oil for drizzling
1 lemon, cut into 8 wedges

1. In a shallow bowl, stir together the olive oil, lemon juice, salt, and pepper. Stuff a sprig of the mint in the belly cavity of each sardine, then dip the fish in the olive oil mixture, coating it completely. Lay the fish at the stem end of the grape leaf, roll it up tightly, and set aside while you continue stuffing and wrapping the remaining fish.

2. Prepare a hot charcoal fire, preheat a gas grill on medium for 15 minutes, or preheat a

LITTLE FOODS OF THE MEDITERRANEAN

Poor People's Fish

In the Middle Ages, popular fish were those caught in nets in large quantities as they swam in schools, such as mackerel, anchovies, and sardines. These fish were not appreciated by the wealthy, who preferred big, white-fleshed fish like bream or sea bass, and were considered poor people's fish. As the Italian historian Giovanni Rebora commented, the prejudice concerning different species of so-called pauper's fish lasted until recent decades, when anchovies began to rise in price until they became more expensive than white-fleshed fish. Now the rich bourgeois adore them and cook anchovies in the worst possible manner, the way they think fishermen would cook them. The Greeks would call this the revenge of fat, or Nemesis. Voltaire observed in his *Philosophical Dictionary* that if a pauper gnawed on a mutton bone on Friday, he would go straight to hell, whereas those who buy and eat expensive sea bream on Friday find the gates of paradise open for them. Rebora observed that the number of people able to appreciate the irony of Voltaire's irreverent remark was and remains limited, very limited.

ridged cast-iron skillet on medium for 15 minutes.

3. Drizzle the wrapped sardines with olive oil and place on the grill, away from direct flames if using a grill, and cook until the leaves begin to blacken, about 7 minutes per side. Serve hot with lemon wedges.

Makes 8 servings

Grilled Baby Squid on Skewers in the Sicilian Style

Here's a beautiful way to start a grill party by the water, whether you're at the ocean, docked in an inlet, or watching the sun set. This grilled baby squid preparation, known as spitini di calamari, *is often served while everyone awaits the first course of spaghetti. Since it's unlikely you will actually encounter baby squid in the market, simply buy the smallest squid available.*

6 tablespoons extra-virgin olive oil

1 cup dry bread crumbs

¼ cup finely chopped fresh parsley leaves

1 garlic clove, very finely chopped

¾ teaspoon salt

¼ teaspoon freshly ground black pepper

1½ tablespoons white wine

2 pounds small squid, cleaned (page 404) and cut in half or quarters, depending on their size

Eight 10-inch wooden skewers

1 lemon, sliced

1½ teaspoons dried oregano

1. Prepare a hot charcoal fire and let it die down a little or preheat a gas grill on medium for 20 minutes.

2. In a small skillet, heat 1 tablespoon of the olive oil over medium heat, then cook the bread crumbs until golden, about 4 minutes, tossing almost constantly. Transfer to a medium-size bowl and add the parsley, garlic, ½ teaspoon of the salt, ⅛ teaspoon of the pepper, 1½ teaspoons of the olive oil, and 1 teaspoon of the wine. Add the squid and toss well so they are coated with bread crumbs. Skewer the squid, threading a slice of lemon every few pieces of squid and using their tentacles, too.

3. Place the skewers on the grilling grate. In a small bowl, mix the oregano, the remaining 4½ tablespoons olive oil, 1 tablespoon plus ½ teaspoon wine, ¼ teaspoon salt, and ⅛ teaspoon pepper. Baste the skewers with this mixture, turning occasionally and basting each time, grilling until they look crisp, 30 to 40 minutes. Serve immediately on a platter passed around while people await other food.

Makes 8 servings

Grilled Stuffed Squid in the Sardinian Style

This Sardinian preparation simply called cala-maris imbuttíus *(stuffed squid) is typical in households and* trattorie *alike, where they are likely to be served as* antipasti. *This recipe is one that I collected in Carloforte, on the coast in southwestern Sardinia. Some housewives prefer grilling the stuffed squid, and that is a particularly nice way of doing them, especially in the summer. There is some difficulty in this preparation, as you will need to hold these tiny and slippery squid and stuff an impossibly small opening. There is no easy way to do this; it's simply time-consuming. But to make everything a little simpler, hold the squid by the opening with your forefinger and thumb, then fill a very small baby spoon with the stuffing and try to slide the stuffing down into the opening, using your middle finger to push it off the spoon while holding the squid open. The reason you use such small squid is that they make perfect little appetizers that are nearly bite size and can be eaten off a toothpick.*

3 pounds squid (about 32), cleaned (page 404)
1 lemon, cut in half
3 large garlic cloves, peeled
6 tablespoons finely chopped fresh parsley leaves
10 salted anchovy fillets, rinsed
2 large eggs, beaten
Freshly ground black pepper to taste
3 cups finely ground fresh bread crumbs
½ cup extra-virgin olive oil
Salt to taste

1. Trim the tentacles of the squid just below the eyes. Boil the tentacles in water with the squeezed lemon halves until firm, 7 to 8 minutes. Drain, discard the lemon, and chop the tentacles with the garlic, parsley, and anchovies. Mix with the eggs in a medium-size bowl, season with pepper, add the bread crumbs, and mix again. Stuff the squid bodies with the mixture and interlace a toothpick through the opening so the stuffing doesn't escape.

Really Big Squid

The squid we eat or use as a bait are small creatures. When I was growing up, we never called them squid—they were always called calamari. But there is a species of squid called giant squid. The largest ever found was one weighing 550 pounds with tentacles 50 feet long that washed up on a beach in Tasmania in Australia. Their high ammonia content makes these squid inedible.

2. Preheat the oven to 350°F or preheat a gas grill on medium heat for 15 minutes or prepare a charcoal fire to one side of the firebox of a charcoal grill.

3. If baking, place the stuffed squid in a baking casserole with the olive oil, toss gently so the stuffed squid are coated with oil, season with salt and pepper, and bake until some of the squid look like they might split and they are firm, 30 to 35 minutes. If grilling, coat with the olive oil, and don't grill over direct heat. They are done when firm and golden. If you are serving them while people are standing, leave the toothpick in to hold it when picked up, otherwise, remove the toothpicks.

Makes 12 servings

Grilled Marinated Octopus

This is a meze I first encountered in Greece, where it was called oktapodi sta karvouna. *In Greece, grilled octopus is typically made during Lent because of the abstinence from eating meat. Most octopus sold in this country is imported frozen, already cleaned and tenderized so all you need do is defrost it, which actually helps in the tenderizing process, and rinse it clean.*

One 2- to 3-pound octopus, defrosted, cleaned (page 263), tenderized if necessary, and washed
1 cup white wine vinegar

Marinade
½ cup extra-virgin olive oil
1 cup dry white wine
1 teaspoon dried oregano
2 bay leaves
10 black peppercorns
Salt to taste

Garnishes
Extra-virgin olive oil
Dried oregano
1 lemon, cut into wedges

1. Put the octopus in a medium-size nonreactive pot, cover with water, and add the vinegar. Bring to a boil, reduce the heat to medium-low, and simmer, covered, until tender, about 1½ hours. Drain and wash well in cold water, peeling off the skin. Place the octopus in a large, deep bowl.

2. Make the marinade. Mix the ingredients and pour over the octopus. Cover with plastic wrap and let marinate in the refrigerator for 24 hours, turning occasionally.

3. Prepare a charcoal fire or preheat a gas grill on medium for 20 minutes.

4. Remove octopus from the marinade, place on the hot grill, and cook for 8 to 10 minutes per side, basting all the time with the marinade. It will look golden brown, black in spots, with curled tentacles when it's done.

5. Remove to a serving platter, drizzle some olive oil over, sprinkle with oregano, and garnish with lemon wedges. Serve immediately or at room temperature.

Makes 8 servings

Grilled Eggplant from Sicily

In every Sicilian trattoria, on a tavola calda—*a large buffet table spread with various prepared dishes displayed on polychromatic serving platters—you will find grilled eggplant and many other delectable prepared* antipasti. *This* melanzane in graticola *is quite simple to prepare.*

6 small eggplants (about 3 pounds)
Salt
½ cup extra-virgin olive oil
2 large garlic cloves, finely chopped
¼ cup finely chopped fresh parsley leaves
Freshly ground black pepper to taste
A brush made from fresh oregano twigs

1. Slice the eggplants into ½-inch-thick pieces lengthwise. Lay them on some paper towels and sprinkle with salt. Leave to drain of their bitter juices for 30 minutes, then pat dry with paper towels.

2. Preheat a gas grill on high for 20 minutes or prepare a hot charcoal fire.

3. Stir the olive oil, garlic, parsley, and salt and pepper together. Brush the eggplant slices on both sides with the mixture using the oregano twig brush, then place on the grill. When they begin to brown, about 10 minutes, turn and grill for another 10 minutes, basting if necessary with the marinade.

4. Remove to a platter, pour the remaining marinade over the eggplants, and serve hot or at room temperature.

Note: You can also grill tomatoes, peppers, zucchini, and pumpkin with the same basting mixture.

Makes 6 servings

Grilled Eggplant with Fresh Herb and Garlic Dressing from Apulia

This recipe from Italy's heel is called melanzane alla campagnola, *or eggplant country style. Typically, one would find it served in restaurants as part of a* tavola calda, *a buffet table filled with a variety of* antipasti. *In Sicily, a similar preparation is called* melanzane all'Usticese, *Ustica being a small island off Italy's shores; it might be fried cubes of eggplant seasoned afterwards with vinegar, sugar, mint, and garlic or it may go under the name* melanzane arrostite *(roast eggplant) or* melanzane ad insalata *(eggplant salad).*

2½ pounds eggplant, peeled and sliced
  ½ inch thick
Salt
Olive oil for brushing
1 tablespoon finely chopped fresh mint leaves
1 tablespoon finely chopped fresh parsley leaves
1 tablespoon finely chopped fresh basil leaves
1 large garlic clove, finely chopped
¼ cup extra-virgin olive oil
Freshly ground black pepper to taste

1. Lay the eggplant slices on some paper towels and sprinkle with salt. Leave to drain of their bitter juices for 30 minutes, then pat dry with paper towels.

2. Prepare a hot charcoal fire or preheat a gas grill on high for 15 minutes.

3. Brush the eggplant on both sides with olive oil, then grill until black grid marks are made on both sides, about 4 minutes per side.

The Eggplant in Sicily

It is well known that the Arabs introduced the eggplant to the Mediterranean. The eggplant's point of contact with Christian Europe was in Spain and Sicily. It was first thought to be a poisonous plant, and only slowly it came to be accepted into the local cuisine. One of the first mentions of a culinary use for eggplant is in an anonymous fourteenth-century Valencian cookbook.

---

4. Arrange the eggplant on a serving platter. In a small bowl, whisk together the mint, parsley, basil, garlic, and olive oil. Spoon the dressing over the eggplant and season with salt and pepper. Serve on a platter at room temperature.

Makes 6 to 8 servings

Spicy Grilled Eggplant "Sandwiches"

This spicy grilled eggplant "sandwich," called melanzane piccanti sulla graticola, *is a popular antipasto in Apulia in southern Italy and is a wonderful thing to make when you have a grill going for other foods. It will keep the hungry hordes at bay. Once the little sandwiches are cooked, arrange them nicely on a platter so they look even more inviting. If you don't happen to have a grill blazing away, you could also make these on a very hot ridged cast-iron skillet or griddle.*

2 pounds eggplant, cut into ¼-inch-thick rounds
Salt
2 large garlic cloves, finely chopped
½ teaspoon freshly ground black pepper
1 fresh red chile, seeded and finely chopped
1 tablespoon dried oregano
¾ cup grated pecorino cheese
¼ cup extra-virgin olive oil
3 tablespoons pork lard, melted

1. Keep the slices of eggplant in order so you can match them later to make "sandwiches." Lay them on some paper towels and sprinkle with salt. Leave to drain of their bitter juices for 30 minutes, then pat dry with paper towels.

2. In a small bowl, mix the garlic, black pepper, chile, oregano, and pecorino cheese.

3. Prepare a hot charcoal fire or preheat a gas grill for 15 minutes on high.

4. Arrange half the eggplant slices on your work surface, keeping their top halves on the side. Sprinkle each slice with the cheese mixture, then drizzle with a little oil. Place the top slice over and gently squeeze down. Brush with the melted lard and place the eggplant sandwich on the grill, lard side down. Brush the top of the sandwich with melted lard and grill until golden brown on both sides, about 8 minutes, basting with more melted lard, if desired. Turn with tongs or a metal spatula. Serve immediately.

Makes 4 to 6 servings

Leaching Eggplants

It's necessary to leach eggplant because the fruit of the plant, the edible part, contains a high degree of bitter-tasting water. Not all cultivars are bitter in this way, but the elongated deep purple variety found in a typical supermarket certainly is and it needs to be leached. Lay the eggplant pieces on some paper towels without overlapping, sprinkle salt on them, which will draw out the bitter water, and then pat them dry with paper towels 30 minutes later. They are now ready to use for cooking.

Grilled Peperoncini

Peperoncino is a sweet capsicum cultivar also known as the Italian long pepper, whose name derives from the Italian word for pepper. These peppers are often found pickled in Italian-style giardiniera *preparations. They are pale green when unripe, about 4 inches long, and make an excellent and simple appetizer when grilled as in this recipe.*

Extra-virgin olive oil
16 *peperoncini* (Italian long peppers)
Salt and freshly ground black pepper to taste

1. Prepare a hot charcoal fire or preheat a gas grill on high for 15 minutes.

2. Spread a thin film of olive oil over the peppers, then place the peppers close to the fire and grill until 2 sides are blackened and flaking. Remove from the fire and let them cool for a few minutes.

3. Peel the skin off. Make a small slit on one side of each pepper and pull out the seeds, leaving the stem intact. Lay the peppers on a serving plate and serve with a drizzle of olive oil and salt and pepper. They don't really need more than that.

Makes 8 to 10 servings

Grilled Chiles with Yogurt

When my friend David Forbes and I traveled throughout Turkey, we were always quite taken by a very simple meze called yoğurtlu biber kızartması *served nearly everywhere: grilled chiles in yogurt. The Turks do the*

Tavola Calda

It was originally in cheap *trattorie* that one would find the *tavola calda*, a large buffet table spread with appetizing little foods to be selected for an antipasto. Now it is so popular that fancy restaurants have them, too. Typically, and traditionally, a small trattoria would set up their *tavola calda*, which literally means "hot table," and spread on it the day's offering of hot and room temperature dishes. Today, this buffet table will be filled with polychromatic majolicaware platters filled with grilled marinated vegetables, vegetable salads, and other kinds of wonderful foods. Usually, when you order from the antipasto table a waiter will accompany you and you can choose any selection you want to try or you can ask the waiter to choose for you.

same thing with eggplant. This recipe is how we had it at the Villa Restaurant on the road to Ephesus, just past the rotary in Seljuk.

1 large garlic clove, peeled
½ teaspoon salt
1 cup full-fat plain yogurt
8 mildly hot green chiles, such as poblano (also called ancho chiles)
Extra-virgin olive oil

1. In a mortar, mash the garlic with the salt until mushy, then stir into the yogurt and beat until smooth and creamy.

2. Prepare a hot charcoal fire or preheat a gas grill on high for 15 minutes or preheat a ridged cast-iron griddle.

3. Coat the chiles with some olive oil and grill until their skins are black and peeling, about 30 minutes, turning them as necessary.

4. Peel the peppers, although Turks leave the peel on for diners to remove themselves, and arrange on a serving platter, coat with some dollops of the yogurt, and serve.

Makes 8 servings

Grilled Polenta with Artichoke Mascarpone Sauce

This is a delicious starter and quite ideal to make when you have leftover polenta. You can also pass the squares topped with a little sauce while people are still standing about.

2 cups coarse-ground cornmeal for polenta
2 quarts water
2 teaspoons salt
2 tablespoons unsalted butter
6 large cooked fresh (page 205) or canned artichoke bottoms
1½ cups mascarpone cheese
1 large garlic clove, peeled
1 tablespoon extra-virgin olive oil
2 tablespoons white wine
Salt and freshly ground black pepper to taste
Pinch of freshly grated nutmeg
2 tablespoons finely chopped fresh parsley leaves

1. Preheat the oven to 350°F.

2. Stir the polenta, water, salt, and butter together in a baking dish. Place in the oven and bake for 1 hour and 20 minutes. Stir and bake until thick and dense, another 10 minutes. Transfer the polenta to a large greased baking sheet with low sides and spread the polenta out evenly ½ inch thick to cool. Once the polenta is cool, cut into 2 x 3-inch rectangles.

3. Put the artichoke bottoms, mascarpone, garlic, olive oil, and wine in a blender and blend until smooth, scraping down the sides when necessary. Transfer to a medium-size saucepan, season with salt, pepper, and the nutmeg, and heat until bubbling over medium heat. Turn the heat off, cover, and keep warm.

4. Prepare a hot charcoal fire or preheat a gas grill on high for 15 minutes.

5. Grease the polenta with oil and grill until black grid marks appear and they are very hot, about 6 minutes a side. Transfer the polenta to a serving platter, top with the sauce, and sprinkle with the parsley. Serve immediately.

Makes 8 servings

• 🌸 •

Pickled, Marinated, and Preserved Little Dishes

A pickle is a very simple thing. And many things can be pickled, as we see when we visit the culinary world of the Mediterranean. This chapter could have hundreds more recipes, but the ones here are some of my favorites. All the recipes utilize vinegar, lemon juice, or olive oil for pickling or preserving. They are all served at room temperature. My favorite recipe in this chapter is the Sicilian Eggplant Seviche (page 451), which you will wish to have with you if you are ever stranded on an island with only one thing to eat.

Pickled Stuffed Eggplant

In Turkey and the Middle East, a wide variety of vegetables are pickled. Some of my favorite preparations are stuffed vegetables that are then pickled, like this patlıcan turşusu *from Turkey.*

2 pounds small eggplants (14 to 16)
Juice of ½ lemon
1 large red bell pepper, seeded and chopped
3 carrots, 2 chopped and 1 thinly sliced on the diagonal
1 small head green cabbage (about 1 pound), cored and chopped
1 quart white wine vinegar
1 tablespoon salt
7 to 8 scallions (green part only), split lengthwise
½ lemon, thinly sliced
4 heads of garlic, as much skin rubbed off as possible

1. Wash the eggplants, then make a slit down the middle of each. Bring a large saucepan of water to which the lemon juice has been added to a boil and cook the eggplants until tender, about 20 minutes. Drain and let cool.

2. Put the red bell pepper, chopped carrots, and cabbage in a large bowl and cover with the vinegar with the salt dissolved in it. Press the vegetables down into the vinegar and leave for 1 hour.

3. Fill the eggplants with the vegetable mixture. Tie each eggplant shut with a length of scallion green. Pack the eggplants into two 2-quart jars, placing slices of carrot, slices of lemon, and a small handful of chopped vegetables between each layer. Place 2 of the whole garlic at the appropriate intervals in both jars. Pour the vinegar-and-salt mixture in to cover, then place a weight on top and tightly close the jars. Leave in the refrigerator for 30 days before using and use within 1 year.

Makes 1 gallon eggplant pickles

Pickled Walnut-Stuffed Baby Eggplants from Lebanon

This preparation, called makdūs al-bādhinjān, *is found on the meze table in many homes. Arab cooks are quite fond of nuts in cooking, and one will encounter numerous dishes made with pine nuts, almonds, hazelnuts, and walnuts—those being the most popular.*

1 pound baby eggplants (about 8), about 2½ inches long
1 quart water
4½ ounces walnuts, crushed (about ¾ cup)
4 garlic cloves, crushed with 1½ teaspoons sea salt in a mortar until mushy
3 fresh red chiles, 2 seeded and finely crushed and 1 left whole
Extra-virgin olive oil

1. In a medium-size saucepan, place the eggplants and water, bring to a boil, and let continue to boil until half-cooked, about 6 minutes. Drain. Make a slit lengthwise in the eggplants, place them in a 1-quart jar, turn the jar upside down on a plate, and let drain of their bitter juices for 36 hours.

2. In a small bowl, combine the walnuts, garlic paste, and crushed chiles. Push about 1 teaspoon of this stuffing into the slit of each eggplant. Return the stuffed eggplants to the sterilized jar. Lay the remaining whole chile in the middle of the container. Pour in enough olive oil in the jar to completely cover the eggplants; you may need several cups. Seal, refrigerate, and wait for 48 hours before using. Will keep up to 2 weeks.

Makes 8 servings

Figpeckers

Ambelopoulia are little birds known as figpeckers, which populate the island of Cyprus. They are known as *beccafica* in Italian and they are also popular in Italy. In Cyprus, they are preserved in vinegar and eaten whole, bones and all. They are prepared by removing the feet and head, then the birds are boiled, without being gutted, in salted water for 5 minutes and drained and cooled. The birds are placed in a glass or earthenware container, covered with salted vinegar, and stored for up to a year before eating. In the Middle Ages, Cyprus—then a Venetian possession—packed stuffed pickled buntings and shipped them to Venice as a delicacy.

Caponata

The Sicilian antipasto relish known as caponata is said to be of Spanish origin. The Sicilian food authority Pino Correnti believes that the name and dish derive from the Catalan caponada, *a similar kind of relish, and says it first appears in a Sicilian etymology of 1709. This Catalan word, which literally means "something tied together like vines," can also refer to an enclosure where animals are fattened for slaughter. But the root word* capón *figures in the expression* capón de galera, *which is a gazpacho or a caponata-like dish usually served shipboard. According to Juan de la Mata in his* Arte de reposteria, *published in 1747, the most common gazpacho was known as* capón de galera, *consisting of a pound of bread crust soaked in water and put in a sauce of anchovy bones, garlic, vinegar, sugar, salt, and olive oil to soften it. Then one adds "some of the ingredients and vegetables of the Royal Salad [a salad composed of various fruits and vegetables]."*

Alberto Denti di Pirajno, the learned Sicilian scholar, medical doctor, and gastronome, suggested that the dish was born shipboard as a mariner's breakfast because of the large amount of vinegar used, which would have acted as a preservative. Giuseppe Coria, author of an authoritative tome on Sicilian cooking, offers another suggestion: that the word derives from the Latin word caupo (tavern), *where* cauponae *was served—that is, tavern food for travelers. Even if this interpretation is correct,* cauponae *certainly wasn't the* caponata *we know today because both the eggplant and the tomato were unknown to the Romans.*

The earliest recipe I am familiar with of a dish that is a kind of caponata is the cappone di galera alla siciliana *in Francesco Leonardi's*

L'Apicio moderno *(The modern Apicius)* published in 1790.

> Dip a few fresh new beans [freselle maiorchine, an esteemed bean from Majorca] in Malaga wine, then arrange them on a serving platter, and put over them a garnish of anchovy fillets and thin slices of tuna salami, rinsed of its salt, capers, pieces of citron zest, stoned olives, fried shrimp and squid, oysters poached slightly in their own liquid and several fillets of fried linguattola [Citharus linguatula, *a kind of flatfish*] until the platter is well garnished and full. At the moment of serving pour over it a sauce made as follows: in a mortar pound two ounces of peeled green pistachios soaked in olive oil, vinegar, and tarragon or vinegar, salt, and ground pepper.

Given how similar this dish sounds to a modern-day Sicilian caponata, coupled with the fact that Leonardi calls it "Sicilian style," leads me to believe that the capón de galera, *this ship's "chicken," is indeed a kind of mariner's preparation that was preservable on board the galleons.*

Cooking the ingredients separately in the same pan, then mixing them afterwards, improves the quality of the dish. Your frying oil should be clean and new. Versions of this famous preparation call variously for fried pine nuts, almonds, sliced eggs, basil, or ground chocolate. Sicilian restaurants add lobster, shrimp, or bottarga *(dried tuna roe). Other additions found are artichokes, wild asparagus, and baby octopus. The following recipe is the basic one.*

2 medium-size eggplant (about 3 pounds), left unpeeled and cut into ¾-inch cubes

Salt

6 cups olive oil or olive pomace oil for frying

1 bunch celery, leafy tops discarded and cut into 1-inch pieces

½ cup extra-virgin olive oil

1 large onion, thinly sliced

One 6-ounce can tomato paste, or 3 ripe plum tomatoes, peeled, seeded, and finely chopped

4 teaspoons sugar

1 cup red wine vinegar

2 tablespoons salted or brined capers, rinsed or drained and chopped if very large

½ cup imported green olives, drained and pitted

Freshly ground black pepper to taste

½ teaspoon unsweetened cocoa powder (optional)

1. Lay the eggplant cubes on some paper towels and sprinkle with salt. Leave them to drain of their bitter juices for 30 minutes, then pat dry with more paper towels.

2. Preheat the frying oil in a deep fryer or an 8-inch saucepan fitted with a basket insert to 375°F. Deep-fry the eggplant cubes in batches without crowding them until brown and crispy, 7 to 8 minutes, turning once. Remove with a slotted spoon, drain on paper towels, and set aside.

3. Clean the celery and wipe dry with paper towels. Deep-fry the celery pieces in batches without crowding them until the edges are golden, about 2 minutes. Remove with a slotted spoon, drain on paper towels, and set aside. Let the frying oil cool completely, strain through a porous paper filter, if necessary, and save for a future use.

4. Take ½ cup of the oil you used to deep-fry the eggplant and celery, mix it with the extra-virgin olive oil in a large casserole, and heat it over medium-high heat, then cook the onion until translucent, about 6 minutes, stirring. Reduce the heat to medium, add the tomato paste mixed with a little water or the tomatoes, stir, and cook for 15 minutes, stirring occasionally. Gently stir in the sugar, vinegar, capers, olives, eggplant cubes, and celery. Sprinkle with salt, if necessary, and pepper and add the cocoa, if using. Cook until the mixture is heated through, about 10 minutes, folding carefully several times instead of stirring. Leave to cool in the pan and serve at room temperature with crusty bread or *crostini* (page 37).

Note: Caponata can be served hot, but does not have a chance to mellow that way, and is preferable at room temperature as an antipasto.

Makes 8 servings

Sicilian Eggplant Seviche

This antipasto, called in dialect mulinciana a schibecci, *is truly extraordinary. Schibecci means "seviche" and the dish gets this name because of the use of vinegar and its preserving effect. Every time I make this eggplant relish, my guests are very much wowed and I know yours will be, too. I would not cut the recipe in half because you will find yourself dipping into this dish as long as you have it. A tomato sauce, needed in this recipe, can be made quickly by heating some olive oil with chopped garlic and a little onion and cooking it for a few minutes, then adding crushed tomatoes and some whole fresh basil leaves and cooking for another 30 minutes.*

2 large eggplants (about 4 pounds), cut into ¼-inch-thick rounds, then each slice cut in half
Salt
6 cups olive oil or olive pomace oil for frying
2 tablespoons extra-virgin olive oil
1 large onion, thinly sliced
1 tablespoon sugar
½ cup white wine vinegar
2 cups tomato sauce (see headnote)
2 teaspoons finely chopped fresh mint leaves
1 teaspoon freshly ground black pepper
½ cup finely diced *caciocavallo* or mild imported provolone cheese

1. Lay the eggplant slices on some paper towels and sprinkle with salt. Leave them to drain of their bitter juices for 30 minutes, then pat dry with paper towels.

2. Preheat the frying oil in a deep fryer or an 8-inch saucepan fitted with a basket insert to 375°F. Fry the eggplant a handful of slices at a time until golden on both sides, about 8 minutes in all. Don't crowd the fryer; fry in batches. Remove with a slotted spoon and let drain on paper towels.

3. In a large skillet or casserole, heat the extra-virgin olive oil over medium-high heat, then cook the onion until yellow, about 10 minutes, stirring frequently. Add the eggplant and mix very gently, lifting and folding rather than stirring. Dissolve the sugar in the vinegar and pour into the casserole. Cook for 5 minutes, then

add the tomato sauce. Simmer over low to medium heat for 15 minutes. Add the mint, pepper, and cheese and mix well, but carefully, and cook for 1 minute. Remove from the heat and transfer to a serving platter. Salt to taste, let the seviche come to room temperature, and serve with crusty bread or *crostini* (page 37).

Makes 12 servings

Zucchini Seviche

This Sicilian antipasto is typically served on a buffet table filled with other antipasti, *a table called the* tavola calda. *In Sicilian the dish is known as* cucuzzeddi fritti cu schibbeci, *which means, all said and done, "seviche." In Naples, they make a similar preparation called* cucuzielle 'a scapece. *It's important that you use a special, good-quality white wine vinegar, not some kind of distilled vinegar for everyday use.*

1 cup plus 2 tablespoons extra-virgin olive oil
2 large garlic cloves, lightly crushed
2 pounds small zucchini, peeled and cut into
  ½-inch-thick rounds
Salt and freshly ground black pepper to taste
¼ cup white wine vinegar
2 tablespoons finely chopped fresh mint leaves

1. In a large skillet, heat 1 cup of the olive oil over medium-high heat with the garlic; once the garlic begins to turn light golden, remove and discard, then cook the zucchini until golden, 6 to 7 minutes, turning once. Drain on paper towels and set aside. If you cook the zucchini in batches, which you probably will have to do so they are not crowded in the skillet, salt and pepper them abundantly once they come out of the oil.

2. Return the zucchini to the skillet, sprinkle with the vinegar and three-quarters of the mint, and cook over low heat until the vinegar evaporates, about 5 minutes.

3. Transfer to a serving platter using a slotted spoon, sprinkle with the remaining mint, drizzle with the remaining 2 tablespoons olive oil, let come to room temperature, and serve.

Makes 6 servings

How to Serve Italian Vegetable Antipasto

If you are serving a variety of vegetable *antipasti* as part of a buffet table—that is, more than four dishes—you don't need to accompany the preparations with anything. But if you are serving only one dish as an antipasto, then, depending on the kind of entertaining you're doing, you can serve the vegetables with *crostini* (page 37) or plain bruschetta (page 44).

Martha Rose Shulman's Marinated Broccoli Stems

My friend Martha Rose Shulman, author of Mediterranean Light *and many other cookbooks, always serves these delicious tidbits at her parties. They get gobbled up and everyone loves them. I finally asked her for the recipe since I believe they should be widely known.*

3 or 4 broccoli stems
½ teaspoon salt
1 large garlic clove, very finely chopped or pressed
1 tablespoon white wine vinegar
2 tablespoons extra-virgin olive oil (or use equal parts oil and vinegar)

1. Peel the broccoli stems and cut into $^1/_{16}$- to ⅛-inch-thick slices. In a medium-size bowl, toss the stems with the salt. Transfer to a jar, cover tightly, and refrigerate overnight.

2. In the morning, pour off all of the water that has accumulated in the jar through a strainer. Place the sliced stems in a bowl and toss with the garlic, vinegar, and oil. Transfer back to a jar and refrigerate for several hours. Serve at room temperature. These keep for a week or more, but the color will fade.

Makes 4 to 6 servings

Marinated Cauliflower Salad from Seville

The tapas bars of Seville are plentiful and extravagant in their offerings. This ensalada de coliflor *is a* tapa *I had once in Seville, and what I really love about these marinated vegetable salad tapas is how substantial they taste.*

Salt
1 head cauliflower (about 1½ pounds), trimmed of leaves

Dressing

6 tablespoons extra-virgin olive oil
2½ tablespoons sherry wine vinegar
2 teaspoons fresh lemon juice
1 large garlic clove, very finely chopped
1½ tablespoons salted or brined capers, rinsed or drained and chopped
1½ teaspoons mild Spanish paprika
¼ teaspoon cayenne pepper
Salt to taste

Garnishes

1 large hard-boiled egg, shelled and finely chopped
2 tablespoons finely chopped fresh mint or parsley leaves

1. Bring a large saucepan of water to a boil and cook the cauliflower with a little salt until tender when pierced with a skewer in the center of its stem, 10 to 12 minutes. Drain well and break into small florets. Place in a medium-size bowl.

2. Meanwhile, whisk the dressing ingredients together and pour over the cauliflower, tossing well. Leave to marinate overnight or for 8 hours, covered, in the refrigerator or at room temperature.

3. When you are ready to serve, toss with the chopped egg and mint.

Makes 6 servings

Marinated Carrot Salad from Seville

This tapa *is an* ensalada de zanahoria *that I once had in Seville and again in Ceuta, the*

Drinking in Tapas Bars

In the sixteenth century, the consumption of wine became widespread with the establishment of taverns outside the towns where the taxes on bottles were not charged. Low-quality wine became a cheap foodstuff, and its price fell every time grain became too expensive. Wine was a means of escape for the Spanish peasant, who still calls it *quita-penas*, "drowner of sorrows." Although Seville, a great center for tapas bars today, was the center of local wine production and international wine trade, it also had a brewery in 1542. For the most part, beer remained in northern Europe and Spanish wine drinkers mocked beer. In 1634, a Spanish soldier who fought at the Battle of Nördlingen in Germany against the Swedes during the Thirty Years' War had nothing but scorn for beer and would not touch it "because it always looks to me like the urine of a sick horse."

Spanish enclave on the Moroccan coast. I particularly like the freshly ground cumin, which I think elevated this tapa *to one of those memorable ones with vegetables that the Andalusians do so well.*

1 quart vegetable or beef broth
¾ pound carrots, peeled
Salt

Dressing
¼ cup extra-virgin olive oil
2 teaspoons white wine vinegar
1 large garlic, very finely chopped
½ teaspoon dried oregano
½ teaspoon freshly ground cumin seeds
½ teaspoon Spanish paprika

1. Bring to a boil enough broth to cover the carrots. Cook the carrots with a little salt until tender, 12 to 15 minutes. Drain and cut into ¼-inch-thick and 1½-inch-long sticks. Place in a medium-size bowl.

2. In a small bowl, whisk the dressing ingredients together. Pour over the carrots, tossing to coat everything, cover with plastic wrap, and leave to marinate overnight or for 8 hours in the refrigerator. Serve at room temperature.

Makes 4 servings

Marinated Carrots from Italy

There are many versions of this Italian antipasto called carote marinate. *Often it is served more as a* passatempo, *a little tidbit to be eaten with drinks, rather than as an antipasto. They are nice to snack on, too.*

3 cups water
6 tablespoons dry white wine

Carrots and the Reconquest

The Spanish Arab writer of the thirteenth century Abū Zakariyya drew up a list of the common vegetables of Moorish Spain, which included several varieties of Old World beans and peas, cabbage, carrot, cucumber, eggplant, endive, garlic, leek, lentil, melon, parsnip, gourd, spinach, radish, and turnip. On the whole, it was clear from much evidence that the portion of Spain still in Muslim hands in the fifteenth century was more abundantly supplied with produce than Christian Spain. The reward of a more varied diet must have been one source of inspiration for the Reconquest.

6 tablespoons white wine vinegar

¼ cup extra-virgin olive oil

1 large garlic clove, crushed

1 small bunch fresh parsley, tied together with kitchen twine

¾ teaspoon sugar

1 teaspoon salt

⅛ teaspoon cayenne pepper

¾ pound very young carrots, peeled and trimmed

1 teaspoon Dijon mustard

1 teaspoon finely chopped fresh basil leaves

1. In a medium-size nonreactive saucepan, bring the water, wine, vinegar, and olive oil to a boil with the garlic, parsley, sugar, salt, and cayenne; then cook the carrots until crisp-tender, about 10 minutes. Let cool in the saucepan. Arrange on a small serving platter.

2. Reduce the remaining poaching liquid over high heat to 1 cup. Stir in the mustard and pour 3 to 4 tablespoons over the carrots. Sprinkle with the basil and chill before serving.

Makes 4 servings

Marinated Mushrooms in the Tuscan Style

This marinated antipasto, called funghi in salamoia alla Toscana, *is still made by many families with the small white button mushrooms that are commonly sold in our markets, too. You may never have thought of making your own, given how common they are in supermarkets, where they are sold in jars. But this recipe is a little more personal and interesting than what you might be used to.*

2 pounds small button mushrooms, brushed clean

Juice of 1 lemon

1 cup champagne vinegar

4 large garlic cloves, crushed

1 bay leaf

Salt and freshly ground black pepper to taste

2 tablespoons extra-virgin olive oil

2 tablespoons tomato paste dissolved in 2 tablespoons water

1. Bring a large saucepan of salted water to a boil, then cook the mushrooms with half the lemon juice for 5 minutes. Drain and let cool.

2. In a medium-size nonreactive saucepan, bring the vinegar, remaining lemon juice, garlic, bay leaf, salt, and pepper to a boil; reduce the heat to medium and cook for 15 minutes. Pass this marinade through a strainer and cool the liquid. Once it is cool, stir in the olive oil and diluted tomato paste.

3. Transfer the mushrooms to a large jar and pour the marinade over them. Refrigerate 24 hours before using. Properly stored, they will keep for up to a year.

Makes 3 cups

Marinated Boiled Fennel and Olive Salad from Algeria

This recipe from Algeria is simply called salāṭat bisbās, *"fennel salad." Many salads in North Africa are served as a meze—what they call* qimiyya *in Algeria. This preparation is beguiling and although you will be happy to eat it alone, it is also an excellent accompaniment to grilled meat.*

2 Florence fennel bulbs (about 1½ pounds), stalks and leaves removed and saved for another purpose
Salt
2 garlic cloves, very finely chopped
3 tablespoons finely chopped fresh parsley leaves
½ cup pitted imported black olives, drained
3 tablespoons extra-virgin olive oil
1 teaspoon white wine vinegar
2 tablespoons fresh lemon juice

1. Quarter the fennel bulbs lengthwise. In a large saucepan, bring some lightly salted water to a boil, then cook the fennel until tender, about 20 minutes, drain, and let cool. Place the fennel on a serving platter and sprinkle with the garlic, parsley, and olives.

2. In a small bowl, whisk together the olive oil, vinegar, and lemon juice until it looks creamy yellow and pour evenly over the fennel. Serve at room temperature.

Makes 6 servings

Fennel in North Africa

Fennel seed is one of North Africa's favorite spices. There is a Muslim-Andalusi and Judeo-Andalusi influence in North African cooking that resulted from the expulsion of Muslims and Jews during the Christian Reconquest of Spain. The two great culinary centers of Algeria are Constantine and Tlemcen. Another favorite Algerian spice is cayenne pepper, a New World spice, while other common spices in Algerian cuisine are black pepper, cumin, ginger, caraway, aniseed, wild parsley, mint, cinnamon, and cloves. The popularity of fennel is evidenced in the number of words for fennel and the number of dishes featuring it. For example, *al-baraka ḥabba*, *basbās* (or *bisbās*), *jurjūr*, *rāznaj*, *rāziyānaj*, *sannūt*, *sūbr*, *shumr*, *shammār*, and *zarrīᶜat al-funūy* are all words for "fennel seed" in North Africa.

Red Bell Peppers Preserved in Olive Oil

This recipe, called filfil ākhḍar muṣabbar bi'l-zayt, *is from an Algerian friend, Necim Zeghlache, from whom I have learned a lot about Algerian cooking. Necim served this delicious red bell pepper preparation as part of a* qimiyya *table, what the Arabs of the Mashraq (eastern Arab world as opposed to the Maghrib, the western Arab world) call a meze, before he served a lamb and vegetable couscous.*

16 red bell peppers
Extra-virgin olive oil to taste
White wine vinegar to taste
2 large garlic cloves, finely chopped
Salt to taste
2 tablespoons finely chopped fresh parsley leaves

1. Preheat the oven to 450°F.

2. Roast the red bell peppers on a nonstick baking sheet until their skins are blackened, about 30 minutes, turning them as needed. Place 2 brown paper bags inside each other, put in a large pot (to reinforce the bottom of the bag), place all the peppers in, and close the bags so the peppers will steam.

3. After 10 minutes, remove the peppers and peel. Cut all the peppers into strips and place in a large bowl . Sprinkle with olive oil and vinegar to your taste and stir in the garlic. Sprinkle with salt and the parsley, and serve at room temperature. Properly stored in the refrigerator, they will keep for up to a month.

Makes 12 to 14 small servings

Celeriac Batons and Roasted Red Bell Peppers in Mustard Preserve

This preparation, called api-rabo à la moutardo *in the old Provençal language, derives from the* céleri-rave à la moutarde *found in J.-B. Reboul's classic nineteenth-century cookbook of the cuisine of Provence,* La cuisinière Provençale. *He calls for Spanish peppers, a recognition that the bell peppers grown in the Spanish region of Murcia are superior peppers. The recipe is quite old and traditional and not frequently seen.*

1 celeriac (celery root, about 1¾ pounds),
    peeled and cut into batons 1½ inches long and
    ¼ inch thick
½ cup champagne vinegar or white wine vinegar,
    heated to boiling
2 large red bell peppers, roasted (page 415),
    peeled, seeded, and cut into strips
2 tablespoons extra-virgin olive oil
2 to 3 teaspoons dry mustard, to your to taste

1. Bring a large saucepan of water to a boil, add the celeriac batons, and cook until tender, 6 to 8 minutes. Drain well. Place the celeriac in a heat-proof terrine or Pyrex or ceramic dish and cover with the boiling vinegar. Add the red bell peppers strips, let the mixture cool somewhat, cover with plastic wrap, and refrigerate until the next day.

2. Drain, saving the vinegar, and place in a wide-mouthed jar. In a bowl, whisk the olive oil and mustard together and dilute with the reserved vinegar until it looks like a vinaigrette. Pour this mixture over the vegetables and refrig-

erate for 24 hours before serving. Serve at room temperature.

Makes 8 servings

Celeriac

What's this, you ask? Celeriac is also known as celery root, and it is a form of celery where the lowest part of the stem, or corm, has been developed by growers into a swollen state. It is not the root. It was a popular vegetable in Egypt and was introduced to England in the mid-eighteenth century from Alexandria, Egypt. A traveler to Aleppo in Syria in 1536 reported that celeriac was eaten as a delicacy with salt and pepper. It can be found in your supermarket—just look for it. There will be a few of them, perhaps hidden next to other root vegetables. Look for one that feels heavy and doesn't look dried out.

Pan-Seared Marinated Pork Slices from Aragon

This tapa *from Aragon in the north of Spain is said to come from the town of Calatayud. It is called* lomo de orza, *an* orza *being an earthenware pan used to marinate the meat. This recipe is adapted from Penelope Casas's* Tapas.

1¼ pounds pork tenderloin, trimmed of any fat and silverskin and cut into 1-inch-thick slices
Salt and freshly ground black pepper to taste
1 cup extra-virgin olive oil

1 tablespoon fresh lemon juice
¼ teaspoon dried thyme
⅛ teaspoon crumbled dried rosemary
4 large garlic cloves, sliced

1. In a medium-size bowl, toss the pork slices with salt and pepper.

2. In a large skillet, heat 2 tablespoons of the olive oil over medium-high heat, then cook the pork until golden brown and crusty, about 3 minutes per side. Reduce the heat to low and cook until springy when poked, 12 to 15 minutes. Do not cook any longer, otherwise the meat will dry out.

3. Transfer the meat to a small earthenware or ceramic bowl or casserole, small enough so the meat fits snugly. Add the remaining ¾ cup plus 2 tablespoons olive oil, the lemon juice, thyme, and rosemary, and season with salt and pepper. Cover with plastic wrap and leave at room temperature for 24 hours. (The olive oil and lemon juice will protect the meat from bacterial growth.)

4. Cut the meat on the bias into ¼-inch-thick slices and arrange on a serving platter. Drizzle with the marinade and serve with cocktail toothpicks or on individual tapas plates.

Makes 6 servings

Preserved Fried Tuna

This preserved tuna dish is known as surra *in Sicily, where there has long been a vigorous tuna fishing industry. The word* surra *derives from the Arabic word meaning umbilical or "side of an animal." It refers to the belly*

Fishing in Sicily

The business of fishing in Sicily was already an ancient and well organized profession in the fourteenth century. At the end of that century and into the fifteenth century, many fishermen came from the island of Lipari. Between 1328 and 1390, the fishermen of western Sicily were very active, and many ways of preparing fish probably come down from that time, if not from the earlier Arab era. We know that the vernacular of Sicilian fishing is replete with Arabisms even today. The Sicilian *raysi*, or "tuna captains," is a term identical to the Arabic word for "captain." In the early fifteenth century, the fishermen and *raysi* of Trapani, Sciacca, and Marsala consisted of native Sicilians, but also a number of Catalan immigrants, a Corsican, a Maltese, and three people from Candia (modern Iráklion) on Crete. Very few fishermen and sailors came from interior towns, for these two worlds of the sea and the mountains didn't mix. Generation after generation of people from particular families engaged in fishing. But the most prestigious were the families of the *raysi* of the tuna crews who led the boats out to the *mattanza*, the tuna killing, set out the *madraga*, the complex of tuna nets, each to lead the tuna into the *camera di morte*, the chamber of death. The captain was responsible for setting the series of increasingly smaller rectangular net chambers that funneled the tuna into smaller areas, then into the final chamber where they were killed. Almost all of the *madraga* of Sicily in the fifteenth century, about 30 in all, were principally on the northwest coast of Sicily.

---

of the tuna, also called ventresca *in Italian, which is considered the choicest part. I like to serve this antipasto very simply without any garnishes or accompaniments other than crusty bread.*

2 pounds tuna, preferably sashimi-grade meat cut from the lower belly

1 tablespoon coarse sea salt

6 cups olive oil or olive pomace oil for frying

Extra-virgin olive oil for preserving

1. Cut the tuna into 2 x ½-inch slices. Lay the tuna on a tray and salt. Leave for 15 minutes.

2. Preheat the frying oil in a deep fryer or an 8-inch saucepan fitted with a basket insert to 365°F. Fry the tuna pieces until golden, about 90 seconds. Drain and arrange on a tray in the refrigerator, lightly covered with waxed paper, and leave for 24 hours.

3. Remove the tuna and place neatly and tightly in a large wide-mouthed glass jar as if you were packing sardines. Pour in enough

extra-virgin olive oil to cover completely. Store in the refrigerator and use after 48 hours, but serve at room temperature. Properly covered with olive oil, the tuna will keep for a year.

Makes 12 servings

Sfogi in Saòr

This famous marinated sole preparation from Venice traditionally made with baby sole or fresh sardines is a special preparation for the Festa del Redentore, on the third Sunday of July, when Venetians celebrate the Holy Redeemer with fireworks and food. The festival is connected with the thanksgiving for delivering Venice from the horrible plague of 1575–77, which left a quarter of the population dead.

Typically, baby sole are used for this dish, or sardines. If you can find neither, then use flounder, butterfish, porgies, small red snapper, or even smelts. The dish is almost always served as an antipasto.

1½ cups extra-virgin olive oil

All-purpose flour as needed

2 pounds fresh baby sole, sardines, sand dabs, butterfish, pompano, red snapper, or porgies, cleaned and gutted

Salt to taste

2¼ pounds white onions, very thinly sliced

1¼ cups white wine vinegar

¼ cup golden raisins, soaked in tepid water for 20 minutes and drained

¼ cup pine nuts

Pinch of ground cinnamon

1. In a large skillet, heat the olive oil over medium-high heat until 375°F or it begins to smoke. Meanwhile, flour the fish, tapping off any excess. Fry without crowding them in the hot oil until golden, about 1½ minutes per side for sardines (the other fish, such as sand dabs and porgies, will need 1 to 2 minutes per side longer), and drain. Place the fish on paper towels to drain some more and season with salt.

2. Reduce the heat to medium. Allow 10 minutes to pass for the temperature of the oil to reduce sufficiently. Once the olive oil has cooled, cook the onions until soft, about 30 minutes, stirring occasionally. The onions should still look white after they are cooked, although some people cook them until golden, or even brown. Pour off or ladle out ½ to ¾ cup of the frying oil. Increase the heat under the skillet to medium-high and add the vinegar, raisins, and pine nuts to the remaining oil, being careful about splattering oil, and cook for 5 minutes, stirring.

3. Arrange the fish in a large ceramic or glass baking pan. Sprinkle the cinnamon over the fish. Cover with the onions and all the liquid from the skillet. Cover with plastic wrap and refrigerate for 2 days. Remove from the refrigerator 2 hours before serving, transfer to a serving platter, and serve at room temperature.

Makes 6 servings

Swordfish Seviche

Pesce spada schibbeci from Sicily is a swordfish seviche that can be served as an antipasto. The word seviche *comes from the Spanish* escabeche, *also called* schebbeci *in Sicily, a word that means "marinated fish." The Arabs ruled both Spain and Sicily for centuries, and as a result the word* escabeche *can be traced to the dialectal Arabic word* iskibaj, *which the great Catalan lexicographer Joan Corominas, professor of Romance philology at the University of Chicago, described as deriving from the older* sikbāj, *meaning "a kind of meat with vinegar and other ingredients." This preparation is one I made nearly every August and September when I lived in Massachusetts and swordfish was in season. It also works well with shark.*

Juice from 5 lemons
1 large garlic clove, finely chopped
¼ cup finely chopped fresh oregano leaves
¼ cup finely chopped fresh parsley leaves
¼ cup finely chopped fresh mint leaves
¼ teaspoon red pepper flakes
Salt and freshly ground black pepper to taste
1¼ pounds very fresh swordfish steaks, sliced
    ¼ inch thick
¼ cup extra-virgin olive oil

1. Whisk together the lemon juice, garlic, oregano, parsley, mint, red pepper flakes, salt, and black pepper.

2. Arrange the slices of swordfish in a large glass or ceramic baking pan. Cover with the lemon juice mixture, cover with plastic, and let marinate in the refrigerator for 3 hours. The swordfish is ready when a small sliver tastes "cooked" rather than raw.

3. Remove the swordfish slices to a serving platter and cover with the olive oil. Taste a small sliver of marinated swordfish and correct the seasonings, if necessary.

Makes 6 servings

Perfumed Anchovies in the Sicilian Style

This Sicilian antipasto preparation for preserved anchovies is called ancióva sciavurúsi, *an unusual Sicilian name that means something like "perfumed anchovies." Remember that it can only be made with fresh anchovies, not canned or salted. Fresh anchovies are so fragile that taking the fillets off is extremely easy. Hold*

Nerves of Veal

In Venetian wine bars one might come across an antipasto made with veal nerves or spinal cord. They call these tapas-like foods *ciccheti* in Venetian, and they are a rare and unusual treat. Nerves, called *nerveti consi*, may not be to everyone's liking, so I don't provide a recipe. The *nerveti* are technically the nerves of veal or beef, but in reality it is a butcher's cut of tendon from the shin of calves or cows, or spinal cord. They require long boiling and the smell is not terribly pleasant. Once cooked, they are cut into strips, then cartilage, fat, and other junk are removed, and the meat is dressed with a marinade of tuna in oil, onion, anchovy, olive oil, and vinegar.

the head with the fingers of one hand and, with the other hand, run two fingers down the length of the spine starting right under the head, and the fillets are simply pushed off. But where can you find fresh anchovies? Well, believe it or not, they are common in American waters but used more often than not for bait. Occasionally, fish-mongers will carry them; when they do, buy a bunch of them.

1 pound fresh anchovies, heads and tails removed, washed, gutted, backbone removed, and patted dry with paper towels
¼ cup extra-virgin olive oil, plus more for topping
Sea salt to taste
1 small onion, finely chopped
1 large garlic clove, sliced
1 handful wild fennel or Florence fennel stalks and leaves, chopped
2 tablespoons finely chopped fresh parsley leaves
½ teaspoon dried thyme

1 small bay leaf
¼ cup dry white wine
Freshly ground black pepper to taste

1. In a large bowl, toss the anchovy fillets with 1½ tablespoons olive oil and salt. Leave for 15 minutes, then arrange in a pint-size glass jar, packed tight.

2. In a medium-size skillet, heat the remaining 2½ tablespoons olive oil over medium heat, then cook the onion, garlic, fennel, parsley, thyme, and bay leaf until the onion is softened, about 5 minutes. Pour in the wine, stir, and cook for 1 minute. Correct the seasoning with salt and pepper. Let cool, then pour into the jar with the anchovies and pour a thin layer of olive oil over the anchovies so they are not exposed to the air. Refrigerate for 2 weeks before using and serve at room temperature or cool. Properly covered with oil, these will keep for up to a year.

Makes 6 servings

Sauces,
Condiments,
and Spice Mixes

In any cuisine there are basics without which one cannot really begin to prepare countless other dishes. In this chapter are ten recipes that are used numerous times throughout the book and that you will have to make first if you want to prepare authentic Mediterranean little foods. None of them is hard to make and once made, most are quite content to live in the refrigerator, perhaps covered with a protective layer of olive oil as the recipe will instruct. For many Tunisian recipes you absolutely must have on hand Harīsa (page 468) and Tābil (page 471), both of which are simple preparations and are presented here. For Catalan foods, you'll be asked to make Allioli (page 466) or Romesco Sauce (page 467), and they, too, are easy to whip up. Pretty soon you will open the refrigerator and see the Preserved Lemons (page 469) you made six months ago that you need for the delicious Moroccan meze you noticed in another chapter.

Almond and Hazelnut Sauce

This all-purpose Catalonian sauce known as salsa de ametlla i avellana *is ideal for dipping fried or raw vegetables. Taste it and I'm sure you'll come up with other uses, too.*

½ cup hazelnuts, roasted and skins removed (see right)

½ cup blanched whole almonds, roasted in a 350°F oven until light golden

1 medium-size ripe tomato, cut in half, seeds squeezed out, grated against the largest holes of a grater, and skin discarded

3 large garlic cloves, pounded in a mortar with ½ teaspoon salt until mushy

Leaves from 3 sprigs fresh parsley

⅛ teaspoon cayenne pepper

½ teaspoon sweet Spanish paprika

3 tablespoons extra-virgin olive oil

2 teaspoons sherry wine vinegar

1. Place the nuts in a food processor and run until fine. Add the tomato, garlic, and parsley and process until liquidy. Add the cayenne and paprika and pulse a few times. With the machine running, slowly pour in the olive oil and vinegar through the feed tube.

2. Transfer to a serving bowl, cover with plastic wrap, and let stand 2 hours before using to let the flavors develop. It will keep in the refrigerator for up to 10 days.

Makes about 1 cup

Skinning Nuts

Almonds and hazelnuts are the two nuts most likely to have skin on. The skins are not pleasant to eat and so the nuts need to be blanched for cooking purposes. "Blanching" means to remove the skin. Almonds can be blanched by dropping them in boiling water for 5 minutes. Once they are drained and cool enough to handle, their skins can be pinched off with a squeeze of the thumb and forefinger. Hazelnuts are a little harder to skin. They must be roasted in a 350° to 400°F oven until they are dark brown, then once cooled, one rubs their skin off.

Tomato Sauce

This is an all-purpose sauce that I use for several recipes in the book. But I also use this sauce to quickly season some spaghetti, as well as spread it on a simple pizza or on top of a fried calzone. This is Pop's tomato sauce, made by my grandfather, who was from Campania, and who never used onions in tomato sauce.

6 cups crushed plum tomatoes (two 1-pound 12-ounce cans) or, if making it during the summer, 4 pounds ripe plum tomatoes, peeled, seeded, and crushed

Two 6-ounce cans tomato paste

3 large garlic cloves, finely chopped

¼ cup extra-virgin olive oil

1 teaspoon sugar (optional)

1 teaspoon dried oregano (optional)

1 leafy sprig fresh basil (optional)

3 bay leaves (optional)

3 tablespoons finely chopped fresh parsley leaves (optional)

Salt and freshly ground pepper to taste

1. Pour the tomatoes into a wide skillet with the tomato paste, garlic, and olive oil. Turn the heat to medium, and heat the sauce stirring; once the sauce is hot, reduce the heat to very low and simmer for about 2 hours or until dense, stirring occasionally. At some point during those 2 hours, add the sugar, oregano, basil, bay leaves, and parsley, if using.

2. Season with salt and pepper. Use the sauce right away or refrigerate or freeze. It will keep about 2 weeks in the refrigerator and a year in the freezer.

Makes 6 cups sauce

Mayonnaise

I often use a jar of Hellmann's when I need mayonnaise, and its quality is just fine. But since mayonnaise is not really hard to make, and because it is better tasting when homemade, I like to use this recipe. Mayonnaise is all about emulsifying egg and oil. The kind of oil you use will affect the taste of the final mayonnaise. I use a combination of oils, but you could use a straight extra-virgin olive oil for a very rich olive-tasting mayonnaise, which is quite nice with some of the Mediterranean recipes calling for it in this book.

¾ cup extra-virgin olive oil

¾ cup vegetable oil

1 large egg plus 1 large egg yolk

1 tablespoon fresh lemon juice or good-quality white wine vinegar

½ teaspoon very fine salt

½ teaspoon very finely ground white pepper

Mix the oils. Put the whole egg and egg yolk in a food processor and run for 30 seconds. Slowly pour in the oil in a very thin stream with the processor running, 5 to 6 minutes of pouring. Blend in the lemon juice for 30 seconds. Add the salt and pepper and continue to blend for another 30 seconds. Refrigerate for 1 hour before using.

Makes 2 cups

Allioli

In an arc from Valencia in Spain to the French Riviera, a special garlic mayonnaise predominates as a condiment for anything from rice dishes to fish soups. In Spain, allioli *is used on a variety of seafood-based tapas, especially those with cooked shrimp or lobster either atop canapés or in a dip. In Catalonia, probably its home, it is also known as* allioli *and appears to have an ancestry that goes back to the first century* A.D. *In Provence and Languedoc,* aïoli *and* aillade, *respectively, are made as a garlic mayonnaise, while the true Catalan* allioli *(*all, *"garlic,"* i, *"and,"* oli, *"oil") is prepared without eggs, using only garlic, olive oil, and salt. But today, cooks make it with eggs.*

5 large garlic cloves (about 1½ ounces), peeled

½ teaspoon salt

1 large egg
1 cup extra-virgin olive oil

1. In a mortar, mash the garlic and salt together with a pestle until mushy. Transfer the garlic to a food processor with the egg and process for 30 seconds.

2. With the machine running, slowly drizzle in the oil in a very thin stream through the feed tube until absorbed. Cover with plastic wrap and refrigerate for 1 hour before using to let the emulsion solidify a bit. Keep refrigerated for up to 3 months.

Makes 1½ cups

Romesco Sauce

Romescu *(in Catalan) sauce is said to originate in Tarragona in Catalonia. In Tarragona this preparation is as typical of the region as is paella in Valencia. Anton Gelabert, a painter from Barcelona, even wrote a tribute to* romesco sauce, *called* Llibre dels romescos. *It is not important as a dish on its own, but it is the sauce that goes with* suquet, *a famous fish stew.* Suquet *is actually a class of fish sauces and means, literally, culinary preparation. Romesco is a vinegary-almondy sauce that begins with a* sofregit, *a mixture of finely chopped onion, garlic, and tomatoes. I learned how to make this sauce at a demonstration held by the chef and owner of the Florian restaurant in Barcelona (Bertrand i Serra 20), Rosa Grau, and her sous-chef, Enrique Martin. They used a capsicum called a* guindilla *(finger) chile, which I've replaced with the mirasol or guajillo chile, which should be*

more widely available here. If it is not, then use a poblano (ancho) chile. Romesco Sauce is used in a couple of preparations in this book.

¾ cup extra-virgin olive oil, plus more if necessary
1 thick slice Italian or French country bread, crust removed
¾ cup blanched whole almonds, roasted in a 350°F oven until they turn color
4 medium-size onions, finely chopped
2 heads garlic
9 plum tomatoes (about 1¾ pounds), cut in half, seeds squeezed out, grated against the largest holes of a grater, and skins discarded
2 *guindilla* (finger), mirasol, guajillo, or poblano chiles, roasted (page 415), peeled, and seeded
4 large red bell peppers, roasted (page 415), peeled, and seeded
¾ cup good quality red and white wine vinegar (mixed)

1. In a small skillet, heat 1 tablespoon of the olive oil over medium-high heat, then cook the bread until golden on both sides. Place in a food processor along with the almonds and process until fine. Set aside in a bowl.

2. Put the cut-up onions in the food processor. Pull 6 cloves off one of the heads of garlic, peel, and place in the processor with the onions. Process both until very finely chopped.

3. In an earthenware casserole set over a heat diffuser, heat about 6 tablespoons of the olive oil over medium-high heat, then cook the *sofregit* of onions, garlic, and tomatoes until quite dense, about 1½ hours, stirring occasionally. (If

you are not cooking with earthenware and a diffuser, cook over medium heat and check for doneness sooner.)

4. Place the chiles and peppers in a medium-size saucepan or skillet with the vinegar and reduce by three-quarters over high heat. Pour into the casserole, add the ground almonds and bread, stir, and cook over medium-high heat until thick, about another 30 minutes.

5. Transfer the Romesco back to the food processor, in batches if necessary, and process as you drizzle in 4 to 6 tablespoons of the remaining olive oil, making sure that you do not process for more than 20 seconds. Romesco sauce will keep up to 2 weeks in the refrigerator.

Makes about 3 cups

Béchamel Sauce

The apocryphal story behind béchamel sauce attributes its invention to Louis de Béchameil, the steward of Louis XIV in France. That may be, but the sauce is nothing but a white sauce and white sauce can be traced to the ancient Greeks, as we know from the description found in the Greek antiquarian Athenaeus's (A.D. c.10–c.230) work on food citing the Alexandrian writer of scurrilous verse, Sopater of Paphos (c.300 B.C.), who mentions the use of white sauce.

2 tablespoons unsalted butter
3 tablespoons all-purpose flour
1½ cups hot milk
Salt and freshly ground white pepper to taste
Pinch of freshly grated nutmeg

In a medium-size saucepan, melt the butter, then stir in the flour to form a roux, cooking for 1 minute over medium heat. Remove the saucepan from the heat and whisk in the milk a little at a time until it is all blended. Sprinkle with salt and white pepper and the nutmeg. Return to the heat and cook, stirring almost constantly, until thick, 6 to 7 minutes.

Makes 1½ cups

Harīsa

Harīsa is the most important prepared condiment used in Tunisian and Algerian cooking and, in fact, you need to make this recipe and keep it in the refrigerator before attempting any other Tunisian or Algerian recipe. This famous hot chile paste is also found in the cooking of Morocco, Libya, and even western Sicily, where they use it in fish couscous. Harīsa is sold in tubes by both Tunisian and French firms. Although the Tunisian one is better, neither can compare to your own freshly made from this recipe. Be very careful when handling hot chiles, making sure that you do not put your fingers near your eyes, nose, or mouth. Wash your hands well with soap and water after handling chiles. If you can't find the chiles I call for, use 4 ounces of any whole dried red chiles.

2 ounces mildly hot dried guajillo chiles
2 ounces mild dried Anaheim chiles
5 large garlic cloves, peeled
2 tablespoons water
2 tablespoons extra-virgin olive oil, plus more for
  topping off

½ teaspoon freshly ground caraway seeds

¼ teaspoon freshly ground coriander seeds

1½ teaspoons salt

1. Soak the chiles in tepid water to cover until soft, 45 minutes to 1 hour. Drain and remove the stems and seeds. Place in a food processor with the garlic, water, and olive oil. Process until smooth, stopping occasionally to scrape down the sides.

2. Transfer to a small bowl and stir in the caraway, coriander, and salt. Store in a jar in the refrigerator, covering the surface of the paste with a layer of olive oil. As you use the *harīsa*, make sure to top it off with a little olive oil so that it is never exposed to the air to prevent spoilage. Properly topped off with olive oil so bacterial growth cannot occur, *harīsa* can be stored in the refrigerator for up to 6 months.

Note: To make *ṣālṣa al-harīsa*, or *harīsa* sauce, used as an accompaniment to grilled meats, stir together 2 teaspoons *harīsa*, 3 tablespoons olive oil, 2 tablespoons water, and 1 tablespoon finely chopped fresh parsley leaves.

Makes 1 cup

Variation: To make an even hotter *harīsa*, use 4 ounces dried guajillo chiles and ½ ounce dried de arbol chiles.

Parsley in Tahini Sauce

This sauce—called baqdūnis bi'l-ṭahīna *or sometimes* ṭaraṭūr *in Lebanon, Syria, and Palestine—can be used as a dip for Fried Kibbe* (page 363), *Fried Fish Balls in the Arab Style* (page 373), *or Falafel (page 388).*

8 large garlic cloves, peeled

1 tablespoon salt, or more to taste

½ cup tahini (page 59), stirred if oil has separated out

½ cup fresh lemon juice

¾ cup finely chopped fresh parsley leaves (from about 1 bunch)

1. In a mortar, pound the garlic with the salt until it is a creamy mush.

2. In a small bowl, beat the tahini and lemon juice together slowly. If it is too thick, add water—*never* more lemon juice. Stir the tahini-and–lemon juice mixture into the garlic and salt. Stir in the parsley and serve at room temperature. It will keep, covered, in the refrigerator for a month or two.

Makes 1½ cups

Preserved Lemons

In Morocco, preserving lemons is not only a magnificent way of conserving the bounty of the abundant lemon trees of this land, but it is also a most amazing condiment that enhances many dishes from meze to couscous. They're called ḥamaḍ muraqqaḍ *and are easy to prepare. If you are unable to find Meyer lemons, you can use regular supermarket lemons (usually the cultivar Eureka), but let them soak in water for three days. In the region around Safi, cooks add cinnamon sticks, cloves, and coriander seeds to their preserved lemons.*

2 Meyer lemons, washed well, dried well, and cut
    into 8 wedges each
⅓ cup salt
½ cup fresh lemon juice
Extra-virgin olive oil to cover

1. In a medium-size bowl, toss the lemon wedges with the salt, then place in a half-pint jar. Cover the lemons with the lemon juice, screw on the lid, and leave at room temperature for 1 week, shaking it occasionally.

2. Pour in the olive oil to cover, store in the refrigerator, where it will keep for up to 1 year.

Makes ½ pint

Bahārāt

Bahārāt *means "spice" in Arabic, derived from the word* bahār, *which means "pepper," so it is a mixed spice with black pepper. It is an all-purpose mix used in Lebanon, Syria, Jordan, and Palestine and found in many prepared savory dishes.*

Bahārāt *can be bought at Middle Eastern groceries and markets, but it is also quite easy to make fresh for yourself and keep stored in a spice jar. There are many different variations, all based on the basic ingredients of black pepper and allspice. Some mixes might include paprika, coriander seeds, cassia bark, sumac, nutmeg, cumin seeds, or cardamom seeds. This recipe is basic; if you like, you can fiddle with it by adding some of the other spices mentioned.*

¼ cup black peppercorns
¼ cup allspice berries

2 teaspoons ground cinnamon
1 teaspoon freshly grated nutmeg

Grind the peppercorns and allspice together and blend with the cinnamon and nutmeg. Store in a jar in your spice rack, away from sunlight. It will lose pungency as time goes by, but, properly stored, it will be good for many months.

Makes about ½ cup

Rās al-Ḥanūt

In spice shops in Morocco, the premier blend is known as rās al-ḥanūt, *literally "head of the shop." This blend may contain up to twenty-seven different spices, but each merchant has a different-tasting blend because measuring is inaccurate and the spices themselves can vary in intensity and flavor, depending on how old they are or where they came from.*

4 teaspoons ground cinnamon
2 teaspoons turmeric
½ teaspoon freshly ground black pepper
½ teaspoon freshly grated nutmeg
½ teaspoon freshly ground cardamom seeds
½ teaspoon freshly ground cloves

Optional spices, each added in ½-teaspoon
    increments:
Ground grains of paradise (page 471)
Ground mace
Ground ginger
Ground lavender flowers

Ground cassia
Ground black caraway (nigella) seeds

Mix all the ingredients and store in a spice jar. It will keep indefinitely but lose its pungency over time.

Makes about 4½ teaspoons

 ## Tābil

This all-purpose Tunisian spice mix is called tābil *(pronounced "table") in Tunisian Arabic. The word means "seasoning."*

2 large garlic cloves, chopped and left to dry in the open air for 2 days, or 2 teaspoons garlic powder
¼ cup coriander seeds
1 tablespoon caraway seeds
2 teaspoons cayenne pepper

In a mortar, pound all the ingredients together until homogenous. Keep in the refrigerator if using fresh garlic for up to 2 months or indefinitely, in a spice container, if using powdered garlic, although the pungency will decline as time goes by.

Makes about ¼ cup

Grains of Paradise

In the Middle Ages, black pepper was a most prized spice. But when it was in short supply in India from the fifteenth century onwards, European traders would replace it with a kind of ersatz pepper from the coast of Guinea in West Africa, known as *maniguette* or *malaguette*, which is also known as guinea pepper or grains of paradise. Grains of paradise are related to cardamom but have a hot peppery taste. The plant itself (*Aframomum melegueta*) grows like reeds and has trumpet-shaped flowers. In colonial America, grains of paradise were used in beer and mulled wine. Even today, the Sam Adams Beer Company of New England makes a summer ale with this exotic spice. Grains of paradise is used mostly in West and North African cooking. You will not find it in your local supermarket, but certain natural food supermarkets like Whole Foods do carry it.

Pastry Doughs
and Batters

This short chapter has your basics—basic bread dough, basic pizza dough, basic short dough, etc. If you make bread or pizza dough or short dough you have open to you a world of pizza and *pizzette*, of calzones and *panzerotti*, of empanadas and *empanadillas*, of pies and quiches, of turnovers and beignets. Once you can make some beignet batter, only your imagination will limit you. I don't provide recipes for phyllo pastry and puff pastry because I presume you will buy commercially made products, which are excellent and well-suited for the home kitchen.

Basic Bread and Pizza Dough

This basic bread and pizza dough can be used for all the empanada, pizzette, and calzone recipes in the book. For recipes calling for bread dough, just leave out the olive oil. For recipes calling for pizza dough, make sure to include the olive oil. To make dough in a mixer, see the box on page 474. The range of salt given is to your taste. This amount of dough will make five very thin 14-inch-diameter pizzas, the kind of pizza you are most likely to find in Italy.

One ¼-ounce package active dry yeast

1 cup warm water (105° to 115°F)

¾ to 1¼ teaspoons salt, to your taste

3½ cups bread flour or unbleached all-purpose flour, sifted

3 tablespoons extra-virgin olive oil (only add if making pizza)

1. In a large metal mixing bowl, previously warmed under hot running water, then dried, dissolve the yeast in the warm water. Let it rest for 5 minutes, then add the salt and shake gently.

2. Add the flour and olive oil (only if you are making pizza) and mix until you can knead it with your hands. The dough should stick a little bit for the first few minutes, but will then form itself into a ball with more kneading and folding. Once it is formed into a ball, dump it out onto a lightly floured surface and knead for exactly 12 minutes. If making bread, do not add flour or water, if needed, until at least the eighth minute of kneading.

3. Once the ball of dough is smooth, place it in a lightly floured or oiled bowl, cover with a clean dish towel, and let rise in a warm (80°F) place, such as inside a turned-off oven, for 2 hours.

4. Punch down the dough after 1 hour, cover, and let rise another hour. For more flavor, let the rising process go on longer: cover the dough with plastic wrap and place in the refrigerator overnight (this is called a cold rise), but let the dough return to room temperature before

Basic Bread and Pizza Dough in a Stand Mixer

Read the instructions to your mixer. This recipe was tested on a KitchenAid mixer.

One ¼-ounce package active dry yeast
1 cup warm water (105° to 115°F)
¾ to 1¼ teaspoons salt, to your taste
3½ cups bread flour or unbleached
  all-purpose flour, sifted

3 tablespoons extra-virgin olive oil (only
  add if making pizza)

1. In a large metal mixing bowl, previously warmed under hot running water, then dried, dissolve the yeast in the warm water. Let it rest for 5 minutes, then add the salt and shake gently.

2. Add 2½ cups of the flour and the olive oil (only if you are making pizza dough) and attach to the mixer affixed with the dough hook. Run according to the directions of the manufacturer, about 2 minutes, adding the remaining flour in ½-cup increments. Let the mixer run until the dough is pulled off the walls of the bowl and is being pushed by the dough hook.

3. Once the ball of dough is smooth, remove the mixer bowl and remove the dough from the bowl. Place it in a lightly floured or oiled bowl, cover with a clean dish towel, and let rise in a warm (80°F) place, such as inside a turned-off oven, for 2 hours. Proceed as the recipe instructs.

working it again. Now it is ready for making into a pizza. If you are making bread, go on to step 5, otherwise, use this dough for any recipe calling for Basic Bread and Pizza Dough.

5. Preheat the oven to 475°F. Transfer the dough to a baking stone, form into the shape you wish, and score with a razor blade or very

sharp knife. Place a pan of water in the bottom of the oven, then the loaf on the baking stone on the center rack. If you have another baking stone or baking tiles, you can line some in the oven for better tasting and textured bread. Reduce the oven temperature to 425°F and bake until golden brown on top, about 40 minutes, spraying it with water at first. Let cool on a wire rack before slicing.

Makes 2 thin-crust 16-inch pizzas,
5 very thin 14-inch pizzas, or
4 slightly thick 12-inch pizzas, 10 pizzette,
ten 4-inch empanada or calzone disks,
or 1 large round loaf bread

Variation: Use 6 tablespoons milk and ¾ cup water instead of 1 cup water for a richer flavor.

Basic Short Dough

Short dough is the name for the yeastless pastry made of flour and fat used for both sweet and savory pies, as well as a variety of pastries in the Mediterranean ranging from empanadas to some calzone-like pies. Short dough is known as pasta frolla *in Italian and* pâte brisée *in French.*

1¼ cups all-purpose unbleached flour, sifted
6 tablespoons (¾ stick) cold unsalted butter,
  cut into bits
2 tablespoons cold vegetable shortening or lard
¼ teaspoon salt
2 to 3 tablespoons ice water, or more as needed

1. Blend the flour, butter, shortening, and salt together in a large, cold mixing bowl using a pastry blender until the mixture looks like coarse meal. Add 2 tablespoons of ice water. Mix again until the water is absorbed. Add the remaining 1 tablespoon ice water if necessary to form the dough.

2. Shape the dough into a ball, handling it as little as possible (so do this quickly), then dust it with flour and wrap in waxed paper. Refrigerate for at least 1 hour before using, then let rest at room temperature for a few minutes before rolling out according to the recipe.

Makes enough for 1 double-crust 10-inch pie
or ten 4-inch empanada disks

Basic Puff Pastry Short Dough for Empanadas

This puff pastry–style short dough made with pork lard is adapted from one developed by Penelope Casas.

3 cups unbleached all-purpose flour
1½ teaspoons salt
1 cup ice water
4½ teaspoons white wine vinegar
2 large egg yolks
1 cup lard, softened

1. In a large bowl, mix the flour and salt, then mix in the water, vinegar, and egg yolks and knead until a dough can be formed. Wrap in plastic wrap and let sit for 30 minutes.

2. Roll the dough out on a lightly floured work surface until it is a 10 x 15-inch rectangle. Smear one third of the soft lard over the dough using a rubber spatula. Fold the dough into thirds as if you were folding a letter. Wrap in plastic wrap and refrigerate for 15 minutes.

3. Repeat step 2 two more times with the remaining lard. After the third time, refrigerate overnight.

4. When you finally roll out the dough, use a liberally floured work surface.

Makes enough for 40 pastries

Basic Beignet Dough for Baking

In French, this kind of beignet dough is called pâte à choux *or* pâte à beignets soufflés *or, more colorfully,* pets-de-nonne, *"nun's farts." It is made with flour and butter stirred into boiling water, with eggs then being incorporated one at a time. It is an ordinary cream puff pastry, the same kind used for making cream puffs and éclairs. Beignets are popular elsewhere in the Mediterranean, such as in Italy where* pastella per bignè *can also be called* pasta reale. *In Greece, beignet dough is called* sou. *There are two kinds of beignet dough, one for baking (this one) and the other used for deep-frying (opposite).*

1 cup whole milk
½ cup (1 stick) unsalted butter
¾ teaspoon salt
1 cup unbleached all-purpose flour
6 large eggs
Freshly grated nutmeg (optional)

1. Put the milk, butter, and salt in a large, heavy saucepan and turn the heat to medium-high. Once the butter has melted, add all the flour all at once. Stir with a wooden spoon until it creates a dough, pulls away from the sides of the saucepan easily, and the butter begins to ooze a little, 1½ to 2 minutes. Transfer to a bowl.

2. Preheat the oven to 400°F.

3. Beat the eggs into the flour mixture, one at a time, beating vigorously with a fork and making sure each egg is absorbed and the dough is smooth before you add the next one. Sprinkle with nutmeg, if desired.

4. Butter a baking sheet and, using a tablespoon, drop large tablespoonfuls of the dough in rows on the sheet 1½ inches apart. Each droplet of dough should be about 1 inch in diameter for smalls ones and 2 inches for medium-size ones. Bake until golden brown, 22 to 25 minutes. Do not be tempted to peek in the oven, and if you simply must, crack the oven door open slowly; otherwise, the puffs may collapse. They will look and seem done at 20 minutes, but they are not; continue to bake until they are firm when pressed down on top with your finger, another 2 to 5 minutes.

Makes 30 medium-size or 60 small beignets

Basic French-Style Beignet Batter for Frying

This is the master recipe for pâte à beignets, *the batter used for making deep-fried beignets as opposed to baked beignets.*

1 cup unbleached all-purpose flour, sifted
2 large eggs whole and 1 separated, white beaten until stiff peaks form
6 tablespoons light cream
¾ cup beer (lager)
1 tablespoon extra-virgin olive oil
1 garlic clove, very finely chopped
¼ teaspoon dried thyme
Salt and freshly ground black pepper to taste

Pour the flour into a medium-size bowl and make a well in the center. To the well, add the whole egg, egg yolk, cream, beer, and olive oil and beat with a fork to make a batter. Add the garlic, thyme, salt, and pepper. Mix well and check the seasonings. Incorporate the beaten egg white and fold it into the batter until homogenous. Refrigerate for 1 hour before using.

Makes 2 cups

Basic Italian-Style Beignet Batter for Frying

When Italian cooks batter-fry food, they use this pastella per bignè to coat the foods. The range in the amount of flour to use depends on the result you want. The more flour, the thicker the final product and the heavier the beignet taste.

½ to ¾ cup all-purpose flour, sifted

3 large eggs

¾ teaspoon salt, or more to taste

⅛ to ¼ teaspoon cayenne pepper, to your taste

½ cup light cream

1. In a medium-size bowl, combine the flour, eggs, salt, and cayenne until smooth. Pour in the cream in a slow stream, stirring as you do.

2. Cover with plastic wrap, refrigerate for 2 hours, and beat lightly before using.

Makes about 1½ cups

Suggested Party Menus

PASSED APPETIZERS FOR AN ELEGANT ITALIAN DINNER PARTY
Lobster Tomalley Canapés (page 21)
Red and Black Caviar Canapés (page 24)
Porcini Mushroom and Béchamel Crostini (page 43)
Smoked Salmon and Crab Rolls (page 397)
Barquettes with Lobster from the Languedoc (page 256)
Nantua-Style Shrimp Beignets (page 260)
Beluga Caviar Canapés (page 25)

PLATED APPETIZERS FOR AN ELEGANT ITALIAN DINNER
Sliced Tomatoes with a Mirepoix "Mask" (page 247)
Spinach Timbale with Shrimp Cream Sauce (page 148)
Vols-au-Vent Stuffed with Veal Sweetbreads and Black Truffles (page 258)
Potato Crispelle with Salmon Caviar and Mascarpone (page 397)
Cottage Fries Stuffed with Sour Cream and Salmon Caviar (page 223)
Belgian Endive Leaves Stuffed with Grilled Swordfish, Vegetable Mayonnaise, and
    Diced Beets (page 229)

PLATED ANTIPASTI FOR AN ITALIAN DINNER
Fried Mortadella (page 360)
Fried Dough with Fried Shrimp, Crispy Chard, and Zucchini Flowers (page 346)
Dressed Crab Venetian Style (page 369)
Sardinian Grilled Cheese (page 87)
Grilled Polenta with Artichoke Mascarpone Sauce (page 444)
Vegetable, Cheese, Bread, and Hazelnut Cake (page 179)

Antipasto of Asparagus with Freshly Grated Parmigiano Cheese (page 250)

Stockfish, Fava Bean, and Potato Stew from Liguria (page 159)

Scallops au Gratin in the Venetian Style (page 152)

Avocado Stuffed with Shrimp and Spicy Mayonnaise (page 216)

Baked Zucchini Stuffed with Beef, Olives, and Capers in the Sicilian Style
    (page 207)

Oven-Baked Stuffed Eggplant (page 217)

PASSED APPETIZERS FOR A SMALL DINNER PARTY

Puff Pastry with Roquefort and Walnuts (page 281)

Pistachio Canapés from Italy (page 33)

Pizza Sarde (page 301)

Fried Wontons Stuffed with Pork, Broccoli, Olives, and Walnuts (page 342)

PLATED ANTIPASTI FOR A SMALL DINNER PARTY

Fried Mozzarella in Tuna Sauce (page 93)

Golden-Fried Bread with Fontina Cheese Sauce (page 95)

Broiled Fresh Ricotta Cheese (page 87)

Polenta with Porcini Mushrooms (page 181)

Prosciutto and Peaches (page 394)

Boiled Asparagus with Maltese Mayonnaise (page 251)

Fried Soft-Shell Crabs with Light Tomato Dressing (page 153)

Fresh Anchovy in Orange Sauce (page 158)

Artichoke Bottoms Stuffed with Tuna (page 203)

Stuffed Fried Zucchini Blossoms (page 208)

Stuffed Escarole with Ground Beef, Pine Nuts, Raisins, and Olives
    as Made in Sicily (page 229)

ANTIPASTI FOR A SICILIAN BUFFET PARTY (DISHES WITH AN * CAN ALSO BE
SERVED AS A PASSED ANTIPASTO)

The Guards Who Came to Petralia (page 264)

Rustic Mountain-Style Calzone from Sicily (page 312)

Provolone and Mortadella Bombs (page 99)

Stuffed Fried Sicilian Pizza (page 347)

Arancini* (page 380)

Little Pricks* (page 382)

Panisse or Panelle* (page 385)

Sicilian Fried Eggplant "Sandwiches"* (page 378)

Ricotta, Potato, and Salami Cake (page 179)

Preserved Fried Tuna (page 458)

Swordfish Seviche (page 460)

Perfumed Anchovies in the Sicilian Style (page 461)

San Vito's Pizza* (page 298)

Pizza Ericina* (page 300)

Caponata (page 449)

A RUSTIC ITALIAN ANTIPASTO PARTY

Beet, Black Olive, and Chile Calzone from Basilicata (page 318)

Shrimp and Egg Canapés with Mustard Butter (page 21)

Artichoke and Mozzarella Crostini (page 42)

Pan Bagna (page 50)

Fried Sicilian Cheese Coins (page 344)

Fried Stuffed Olives from Venice (page 376)

Tuscan Tripe and Parsley Salad (page 132)

Pizza Rustica #2 (page 302)

Miniature Tomatoes and Chickpeas with Bottarga (page 248)

Baked Oysters in the Style of Taranto (page 417)

Sweet Bell Pepper Squares with Lebanese "Crushed" Cheese (page 233)

A COCKTAIL PARTY FOR WATCHING "THE GODFATHER"

Calzone Napoletana (page 319)

Mozzarella in Carrozza (page 94)

Crostini alla Napoletana (page 37)

Fried Escarole Calzone (page 348)

Ricotta-Stuffed Potato Croquettes (page 381)

Pizzette di San Gennaro (page 295)

Pizza Margherita (page 296)

Baked Oysters (page 418)

Clams Oreganata (page 419)

Clams Gratinate (page 419)

AN ITALIAN BUFFET PARTY

Lobster Salad with White Beans and Red Potatoes (page 405)

Prosciutto, Olive, and Mushroom Calzone from Venice (page 313)

Fontina Val d'Aosta Crostini (page 42)

Veal Scaloppine alla Milanese, Tomato, and Mozzarella Crostini (page 39)

Gorgonzola and Egg Fritter (page 98)

Fried Sausage, Provolone, and Tomato Empanada (page 351)

Potato, Prosciutto, and Scamorza Cheese Patties (page 383)

Spicy Grilled Eggplant "Sandwiches" (page 442)

Golden-Crusted Oven-Baked Zucchini, Tomato, and Fontina Cheese (page 187)

Pizza con Pancetta (page 303)

AN ITALIAN SUMMER SEAFOOD BUFFET PARTY

Roman Lobster and Squid Salad with Artichokes, Lupine Beans, and Grilled
Eggplant in Olive Oil (page 402)

Venetian Seafood Antipasto (page 402)

Fish and Tomato Calzone from Bari in Apulia (page 316)

Anchovy Empanada from Tuscany (page 355)

Shrimp, Mushroom, and Béchamel Croquettes (page 369)

Fish, Shrimp, and Parmesan Beignet Fritters from Modena (page 371)

Grilled Baby Squid on Skewers in the Sicilian Style (page 438)

Sfogi in Saòr (page 460)

Pizza Calabrese (page 303)

Prosciutto and Cantaloupe (page 395)

Peperonata (page 183)

Poor People's Summer Squash (page 188)

Spot Prawns in Tomato and Chile Sauce (page 145)

A SPRING ANTIPASTO PARTY

Antipasto Magro #1 (page 412)

Prosciutto and Five Cheese Calzone (page 311)

A SUMMER ANTIPASTO PARTY

A SIMPLE ITALIAN BUFFET PARTY WITH PASSED AND PLATED ANTIPASTI FOR 12
(CHOOSE 3 FROM THE FIRST GROUP AND 3 FROM THE SECOND GROUP)

Tiny Stuffed Onions with Ground Veal, Mushrooms, and Olives (page 225)
Cucumber Cups with Cream Cheese and Feta Cheese (page 232)

Genovese-Style Antipasto of Lemon-Flavored Rice (page 251)
Grilled Stuffed Squid in the Sardinian Style (page 439)
Grilled Eggplant from Sicily (page 441)
Stuffed Yellow Peppers in the Style of Bari (page 223)
Stuffed Eggplant from Sicily (page 221)

A WINTER BUFFET PARTY FOR 20
(CHOOSE 4 FROM THE FIRST GROUP AND 4 FROM THE SECOND GROUP)

Cucumber Cups with Lobster Salad (page 231)
Puff Pastry Squares with Botifarra Sausage and Mushrooms (page 278)
Spinach, Ricotta, Pine Nut, and Raisin Calzone in the Old Style (page 317)
Gruyère Half-Moons (page 87)
Crostini di Mortadella e Fontina (page 41)
Tuscan Chicken Liver Crostini (page 38)

French-Fried Pumpkin with Green Sauce from Naples (page 376)
Eggplant Ragout with Hazelnuts, Chocolate, and Raisins (page 196)
Pâté of the Two Sicilies (page 77)
Provençal Pine Nut and Bacon Quiche (page 265)
Stuffed Pork Crackling and Ricotta Pizza (page 304)
Pumpkin and Beans in the Calabrian Style (page 189)
Baby Octopus in Piquant Sauce (page 155)
Artichoke Bottoms Stuffed with a Macédoine of Vegetables (page 204)

PASSED APPETIZERS FOR A COCKTAIL PARTY FOR 20 (CHOOSE 6)

Barquettes with Crab and Mayonnaise (page 257)
Burgundian Cheese Puffs (page 85)
Four-Cheese Puff Pastry Roll in the Greek Style (page 274)
Puff Pastry Squares with Italian Sausage and Homemade Goat's Milk Ricotta
 (page 279)
Fried Lamb Cigars from Algeria (page 334)

Horseradish Canapés (page 33)

Duck and Chicken Liver Canapés (page 30)

Frico (page 92)

Veal Marrow Crostini from Lazio (page 40)

Caciocavallo and Anchovy Fritters from Sicily (page 97)

Prosciutto and Mozzarella Roll-ups (page 393)

Cucumber Canapés with Salted Sardine Mayonnaise (page 34)

PASSED APPETIZERS FOR ANOTHER COCKTAIL PARTY FOR 20 (CHOOSE 6)

Spanish Baked Cheese Marbles (page 86)

Pistachio and Emmentaler Cheese Sandwiches (page 50)

Fontina Val d'Aosta Crostini (page 42)

Crushed White Bean Crostini (page 44)

Croûtes of Cotechino Sausage and Marsala Wine (page 52)

Ham and Almond Beignet Fritters (page 362)

Leek Beignet Fritters from Corsica (page 387)

Panzerotti (page 345)

Sea Bass Kebabs from Alexandria (page 436)

Corsican-Style Pizza Flamiche (page 305)

Mortadella Roll-ups (page 396)

Stuffed Cherry Tomatoes with Mascarpone and Pancetta (page 212)

Cucumber Canapés with Scallions and Mascarpone (page 35)

Celery Sticks Stuffed with Taramasalata (page 232)

Martha Rose Shulman's Marinated Broccoli Stems (page 452)

Pizza Rustica #1 (page 301)

PASSED APPETIZERS FOR A COCKTAIL PARTY FOR 50 (CHOOSE 10)

Baked Scamorza, Ricotta, and Salami Pastry Coins (page 321)

Beignets with Smoked Salmon Mousse (page 261)

Puff Pastry Squares with Zaꞏtar and Feta Cheese in the Style of Damascus (page 277)

Cheese and Potato Cigars of the Tunisian Jews (page 334)

Lobster Canapés with Lobster Butter (page 19)

Gorgonzola and Walnut Canapés (page 31)

Anchovy Paste Canapés (page 26)

Corsican Anchovy and Fig Canapés (page 26)

Cucumber Canapés with Ricotta and Pancetta (page 35)

Parmesan Puffs (page 85)

Croûtes of Calf's Brain (page 52)

Two-Cheese Frittata (page 104)

Marinated Carrots from Italy (page 454)

Pissaladière (page 307)

Prosciutto Roll-ups Stuffed with Chicken, Pork, and Pistachio Pâté (page 393)

PASSED APPETIZERS FOR ANOTHER COCKTAIL PARTY FOR 50 (CHOOSE 10)

Breaded Fried Kashkaval Cheese of the Greek Jews (page 91)

Provolone and Pancetta Crostini (page 41)

Bruschetta with Tomatoes and Basil (page 45)

Cucumber Canapés with Tapenade and Walnuts (page 35)

Cucumber Canapés with Coriander Pesto and Hard-Boiled Egg Slices (page 36)

Croûtes Cardinal (page 51)

Brandade of Haricot Bean (page 72)

Artichoke Omelette (page 105)

Taleggio Cheese and Buckwheat Flour Fritters from Lombardy (page 99)

Chicken Croquettes from Emilia (page 366)

Herb Fritters from Corsica (page 387)

Fried Pizzas with Sweet Tomato Sauce (page 347)

Pizza from Egypt (page 308)

Spicy Fried Meat Empanadillas (page 352)

Marinated Mushrooms in the Tuscan Style (page 455)

Basṭurmā Roll-ups with Strained Yogurt (page 393)

A GREEK MEZE PARTY FOR 8

Lamb and Feta Pie from Cephalonia (page 267)

Feta Cheese Canapés (page 31)

Fried Feta Cheese and Black Olives with Oregano (page 90)

Four Young Greens Sauté (page 178)

Lamb Brain with Lemon and Dill Sauce (page 140)

Cheese Pie in Phyllo Pastry (page 271)

Pan-Fried Shrimp with Dill (page 144)
Mussels with Feta Cheese from Rhodes (page 149)

A GREEK COCKTAIL PARTY FOR 6
Kefalotyri Cheese Croquettes (page 101)
Greek Cocktail Meatballs in Sauce (page 138)
Spanakopita (page 268)
Phyllo-Wrapped Cheese Rolls (page 275)
Green Bean Salad with Lemon and Dill in the Greek Style (page 249)
Braised Lemony Chickpeas (page 164)

APPETIZERS FOR A GREEK DINNER
Mediterranean-Style Fried Small Fish (page 372)
Grilled Marinated Octopus (page 440)
Lamb Liver, Scallions, and Dill (page 141)
Zucchini and Cheese Pie from Greece (page 270)
Phyllo "Cigars" with Pastourma (page 291)
Carp Croquettes in Walnut Sauce in the Style of the Greek Jews (page 156)

A GREEK MEZE PARTY FOR 12 (CHOOSE 6)
Cheese Crescents from Crete (page 320)
Saganaki (page 91)
Eggplant Puree in the Greek Style (page 61)
Greek Rarebit (page 96)
Meat and Kefalotyri Cheese Croquettes (page 361)
Fried Cheese Pies from Lesbos (page 343)
Lamb Pies in Phyllo Pastry (page 290)
Wine-Braised Squid from Cyprus (page 154)
Baked Lima Beans in the Greek Style (page 168)

A MEZE PARTY IN THE STYLE OF THE OTTOMAN SULTANS
(CHOOSE 4 FOR 8 PEOPLE, 6 FOR 12 PEOPLE, AND 8 FOR 20 PEOPLE)
Eggplant, Yogurt, and Walnut Salad-Dip from Turkey (page 64)
Lamb Flank Kebabs in Yogurt and Tomato Sauce (page 433)

Circassian Chicken (page 126)

Turkish-Style Stuffed Mussels (page 416)

Scallops on Carp Roe Caviar (page 153)

Stuffed Tomatoes in Olive Oil (page 213)

The Imam Fainted (page 218)

Stuffed Eggplant with Rice, Currants, and Dill in Olive Oil (page 219)

Stuffed Grape Leaves with Rice, Currants, and Pine Nuts (page 228)

Stuffed Swiss Chard Leaves with Ground Lamb, Rice, and Parsley in Cool Yogurt (page 230)

Anatolian Creamy Eggplant and Almond Salad (page 63)

White Beans and Green Onions in Olive Oil (page 167)

Artichokes, Celeriac, and Potatoes in Olive Oil (page 206)

Celeriac in Olive Oil (page 199)

Fried Eggplant and Chiles with Yogurt and Garlic Sauce (page 191)

Smooth Walnut and Feta Cheese Dip (page 57)

AN EVERYDAY TURKISH MEZE PARTY
(CHOOSE 4 FOR 8 PEOPLE, 6 FOR 12 PEOPLE, AND 8 FOR 20 PEOPLE)

"Cigar" Börek (page 340)

Spinach and Feta Cheese Börek (page 341)

Poached Eggs in Garlicky Yogurt (page 121)

Fried Mussels from Antalya in Turkey (page 367)

Shish Kebab (page 431)

Grilled Chiles with Yogurt (page 443)

A Little Turkish Dish Called "Albanian Liver" (page 130)

Shrimp in Butter and Garlic Sauce as Made in Turkey (page 143)

Stuffed Bell Peppers with Rice and Currants (page 222)

Fried Eggplant, Pepper, and Tomato Salad from Turkey (page 193)

Pureed Eggplant, Tomato, and Bell Pepper Salad from Turkey (page 194)

Red Bean and Onion Salad with Dill (page 165)

Artichokes, Carrots, and Rice in Olive Oil (page 198)

Lentil and Bulgur Rissoles in Romaine Leaves (page 398)

Fried Pumpkin, Onion, and Dill Pancakes (page 36)

Turkish Shepherd's Salad (page 239)

Fava Bean Pods in Olive Oil with Dill (page 174)

Yogurt and Cayenne Dip from Turkey (page 56)

Smooth Feta Cheese Dip with Spices (page 57)

Carrot Slaw in Yogurt Sauce (page 247)

A TURKISH GRILL MEZE

(CHOOSE 4 FOR 8 PEOPLE, 6 FOR 12 PEOPLE, AND 8 FOR 20 PEOPLE)

Chop Shish (page 432)

Veal and Lamb Finger Kebabs from Anatolia (page 427)

Grilled Spiced Lamb Meatballs from Turkey (page 430)

Turkish-Style Grilled Marinated Swordfish (page 435)

Grilled Feta Cheese in Grape Leaves (page 89)

Pickled Stuffed Eggplant (page 448)

Whole Cauliflower with Pine Nut Tarator Sauce (page 189)

Eggplant and Tomato Marmalade from Istanbul (page 193)

White Bean and Red Onion Salad from Anatolia (page 166)

Speckled Beans with Carrot and Potato in Olive Oil (page 166)

Diced Vegetable Salad from Turkey (page 242)

Diced Chile and Tomato Salad (page 243)

Mashed Zucchini and Yogurt Salad (page 187)

Turkish Celeriac Slaw (page 245)

Cacık and Tzatziki (page 56)

Purslane and Yogurt Salad (page 242)

AN ARAB-STYLE MEZE TABLE FOR WINTERTIME

(CHOOSE AS MANY OR AS FEW AS YOU WISH)

Beans, Bulgur, and Lamb Salad from Lebanon (page 139)

Fried Artichoke Bottoms with Tarator Sauce (page 197)

Swiss Chard Stalk and Tahini Dip (page 73)

Batter-Fried Lamb Brains from Lebanon (page 366)

Sanbūsak (page 353)

Fried Fish Balls in the Arab Style (page 373)

Grilled Lamb's Tongue Marinated in Garlic and Lemon (page 435)

Kibbe with Yogurt (page 137)

Stuffed Eggplant with Lamb and Pine Nuts in the Style of a Sheik (page 220)
Baby Potatoes Stuffed with Ground Lamb, Pine Nuts, and Pomegranate Molasses
    (page 224)
Rolled Yogurt Balls (page 84)
Red Beets with Yogurt (page 190)

A SUMMER GRILL PARTY WITH ARAB MEZE FOR 12
Eggplant, Red Bell Pepper, and Tomato Salad from Egypt (page 195)
White Chickpeas with Lime Juice from Egypt (page 164)
Okra with Olive Oil in the Style of Homs (page 182)
Grilled Chicken Kebabs (page 423)
Grilled Spiced Chicken Hearts (page 423)
Grilled Kibbe with Pomegranate Syrup (page 427)
Lamb and Cherry Kebabs from Aleppo (page 434)
Artichoke Salad with Lemon and Mint (page 236)
Palestinian Shepherd's Salad (page 240)

THE CLASSIC ARAB MEZE TABLE
Olive Oil–Bathed Fava Beans with Tomato and Lemon Juice in the Palestinian Style
    (page 174)
Arab Spinach Pie Triangles (page 279)
Baba Ghannouj (page 60)
Hummus (page 68)
Fried Kibbe (page 363)
Falafel and Ṭaᶜmiyya (page 388)
Kibbe Nayya (page 76)
Ṣfīḥa (page 309)
Tabbouleh (page 238)
Stuffed Grape Leaves in Olive Oil (page 226)

A SIMPLE ARAB MEZE PARTY (CHOOSE AS MANY OR AS FEW AS YOU WISH)
Eggplant in Olive Oil in the Arab Style (page 194)
Lentils with Pomegranate Molasses, Garlic, and Cilantro in the Syrian Style (page 170)
Puff Pastry Fingers with Sesame Seeds and Feta Cheese (page 277)

Muḥammara (page 59)

Eggplant, Yogurt, and Garlic Dip from Syria (page 63)

Hummus with Olive Oil (page 69)

Stuffed Eggs with Thick Yogurt from Egypt (page 123)

Levantine Grilled Lamb Kafta (page 429)

Baby Meatballs in Spicy Tomato and Onion Ragout (page 136)

Palestinian Thyme and Sesame Seed Pizza (page 310)

Fattūsh (page 240)

AN ARAB-STYLE VEGETARIAN MEZE PARTY FOR 10 (CHOOSE 6)

Black-Eyed Pea and Cilantro Salad in Olive Oil (page 169)

Olive Oil–Bathed Artichokes from Syria (page 196)

Olive Oil–Bathed Green Beans and Tomatoes as Made in Nablus (page 171)

Chicory Leaves in Olive Oil (page 176)

The Monk's Salad (page 60)

Pumpkin Puree with Tahini (page 67)

Biṣāra (page 70)

Spinach with Garlic Yogurt on Fried Arabic Bread (page 176)

Pickled Walnut-Stuffed Baby Eggplants from Lebanon (page 448)

Cabbage Salad with Lemon and Garlic in the Syrian Style (page 236)

Lentil Salad in Olive Oil with Egyptian Spices (page 170)

Fried Eggplant with Yogurt and Cilantro in the Lebanese Style (page 192)

A MOROCCAN MEZE PARTY FOR 15

Beets with Orange Blossom Water and Moroccan Spices (page 190)

Moroccan Fish and Fresh Herb Turnovers (page 337)

Fresh Fava Bean Puree in the Moroccan Style (page 71)

Grilled Moroccan-Style Skewers of Spicy Ground Beef (page 424)

Grilled Moroccan-Style Skewers of Beef and Lamb (page 425)

Moroccan Chickpeas with Preserved Lemons (page 163)

Spicy Carrot Salad from Morocco (page 199)

A NORTH AFRICAN SUMMER MEZE PARTY (CHOOSE AS MANY OR AS FEW AS YOU WISH)

Radish Salad from Tunisia (page 244)

Brīk with Eggs (page 329)

Brīk "aux Fruits de Mer" (page 331)

Fried Peppers and Tomatoes with Beef Turnovers from Algeria (page 336)

Casse-Croûtes (page 48)

Eggplant Compote of the Tunisian Jews (page 65)

Lamb, Bean, and Parsley Frittata from Tunisia (page 118)

Marinated Boiled Fennel and Olive Salad from Algeria (page 456)

Curried Cucumber and Lamb Tongue Skewers (page 365)

Artichoke Bottoms Salad with Harīsa, Olives, and Capers (page 238)

Tunisian Salad (page 241)

Fresh Green Pepper Salad with Caraway and Olives from Tunisia (page 243)

A NORTH AFRICAN WINTER MEZE PARTY
(CHOOSE AS MANY OR AS FEW AS YOU WISH)

Brīk with Tuna and Egg (page 330)

Brīk with Brain and Egg (page 332)

Pumpkin Compote in the Style of the Tunisian Jews (page 66)

Carrot Compote of the Tunisian Jews (page 74)

Carrot Frittata from Tunisia (page 110)

Cauliflower and Parsley Frittata from Tunisia (page 111)

Potato, Onion, and Parsley Frittata from Tunisia (page 112)

Tunisian Lamb, Brain, and Fried Potato Frittata with Cheeses (page 119)

Potato and Bell Pepper Frittata in the Style of the Tunisian Jews (page 113)

Lamb, Onion, and Parsley Frittata from Algeria (page 120)

Cauliflower and Cheese Fritters from Algeria (page 384)

Braised Veal Tongue with Spicy Capers from Tunis (page 129)

Olives Stuffed with Ground Beef in Piquant Tomato Ragout (page 216)

A SEAFOOD MEZE PARTY FROM NORTH AFRICA
(CHOOSE AS MANY OR AS FEW AS YOU WISH)

Algerian Fish and Shrimp Cigars (page 337)

Tuna, Egg, and Cheese Canapés from Tunisia (page 28)

Sardine Canapés in the Algerian Style (page 28)

Tuna and Potato Frittata from Tunisia (page 114)

Tunisian Frittata with Grouper and Onions (page 115)

Smoked Herring, Potato, and Parsley Frittata from Tunisia (page 116)

Puff Pastry Squares with Veal, Ham, and Marrow from Provence (page 283)
Puff Pastry of Swiss Chard and Onion from Corsica (page 288)
Lamb Pastries in the Style of the Tunisian Jews (page 339)
Roquefort and Gruyère Canapés (page 32)
Mozzarella Fritta (page 94)
Bruschetta with Fresh Ricotta and Spinach (page 45)
Pizza-Style Frittata (page 104)
Miniature Focaccia with Tomato and Mushroom (page 306)

Baked Tomatoes and Peppers Provençal Style (page 186)
Baked Zucchini Stuffed with Shrimp in the Provençal Style (page 208)

A TAPAS PARTY (CHOOSE AS MANY OR AS FEW AS YOU WISH)
Puff Pastry Squares with Quail from Catalonia (page 248)
Puff Pastry Crescents with Saffron Chicken and Almonds from Spain (page 285)
Black Sausage, Raisin, and Pine Nut Canapés (page 30)
Dumpling Canapés of Chicken, Sausage, and Mushrooms with Garlic Mayonnaise (page 29)
Andalusian Spiced Mushrooms on Fried Bread (page 46)
Veal Roast and Sweet Pea Frittata in the Style of Granada (page 117)
Ham Fritters in the Andalusian Style (page 361)
Valencia-Style Empanadillas (page 356)
Crispy Fried Galician-Style Oysters on the Half Shell (page 368)
Chicken, Beef, and Ham Meatballs in Gravy (page 127)
A Tapa of Stewed Tripe and Sausage in the Style of Seville (page 131)
Chickpeas with Chorizo Sausage from Andalusia (page 135)
Shrimp and Garlic from Granada (page 146)

A CATALAN PARTY (CHOOSE AS MANY OR AS FEW AS YOU WISH)
Batter-Fried Spring Onions with Almond and Hazelnut Sauce (page 379)
Catalan Bread with Oil and Bread with Tomato (page 46)
Fried Stuffed Cabbage Bundles from Catalonia (page 375)
Fried Baby Potatoes in Allioli (page 179)
Pork and Pine Nut Meatballs in Romesco Sauce (page 133)

Veal Nuggets, Sweetbreads, and Squid in Tomato and Almond Sauce (page 128)
Bell Peppers and Zucchini with Garlic (page 185)
Shrimp in Garlic, Bell Pepper, and Hazelnut Sauce (page 147)

AN EASY AND QUICK TAPAS PARTY (CHOOSE AS MANY OR AS FEW AS YOU WISH)
Canapés of Lobster and Allioli (page 20)
Chicken Salad Canapés in the Style of Castile (page 28)
Andalusian Bruschetta with Olive Oil and Garlic (page 44)
Lettuce Frittata from Córdoba (page 109)
Olive Empanadillas (page 350)
Shrimp Fritters from Andalusia (page 371)
Mushrooms in Garlic from Spain (page 181)
Pan-Seared Marinated Pork Slices from Aragon (page 458)
Marinated Cauliflower Salad from Seville (page 453)
Marinated Carrot Salad from Seville (page 453)
Broiled Bacon-Wrapped Dates from Madrid (page 393)
Peppers and Tomatoes from Granada (page 186)
Mussels with Spicy Mayonnaise (page 417)
Baked Galician-Style Scallops on the Half Shell (page 152)

A TAPAS PARTY FROM THE ISLANDS (CHOOSE AS MANY OR AS FEW AS YOU WISH)
Lamb and Salami Empanadas from Majorca (page 323)
Puff Pastry Squares with Sobressada Majorcana (page 277)
Pastizzi—A Maltese Ricotta and Parsley Puff Pastry (page 287)
Minorcan Salt Cod, Spinach, and Lettuce Empanadas for Midday (page 324)

A SUMMER TAPAS PARTY (CHOOSE AS MANY OR AS FEW AS YOU WISH)
Red and Green Bell Pepper Empanada from Valencia (page 322)
Clam Salad Canapés (page 23)
Eggplant Frittata from Andalusia (page 106)
Fava Bean Frittata from Andalusia (page 107)
Green Bell Pepper and Manchego Cheese Frittata from Murcia (page 107)
Zucchini and Bell Pepper Frittata from Murcia (page 109)
Grilled Pork Kebabs from Andalusia (page 424)

Seviche of Artichoke Bottoms (page 237)
Chickpeas and Hazelnuts with Three Peppers (page 163)
Tomato and Avocado Salad from Andalusia (page 247)
Swordfish or Shark in Tomato and Saffron Sauce (page 156)
Valencia-Style Clams (page 150)

Sources

These are sources for food that I've referred to throughout the book. There are many other sources to try, but these are companies that I've ordered from in the past and am quite happy with.

F. Cappiello Dairy Products
115 Van Guysling Avenue
Schenectady, New York 12305
Phone: (518) 374-5064
Fax: (518) 374-4015
www.capiello.com

A source for Scamorza *cheese.*

Caseficio Gioia Mozzarella
9469 Slauson Avenue
Pico Rivera, California 90660
Phone: (562) 942-2663

A source for burrata.

La Española Meats, Inc.
25020 Doble Avenue
Harbor City, California 90710
Phone: (310) 539-0455
Fax: (310) 539-5989
www.donajuana.com

A Spanish food market, this is the place to find Botifarra sausage, Morcilla sausage, Spanish-style chorizo sausage, Sobressada Majorcana, *and Spanish paprika.*

Guerrero Foods
Consumer Affairs
P.O. Box 226706
Los Angeles, California 90022

Distributor of chicharrones, *or "pork cracklings."*

Kalustyan Corporation
855 Rahway Avenue
Union, New Jersey 07083
Phone: (908) 688-6111
Fax: (908) 688-4415
www.kalustyan.com

A source for many spices, including Aleppo and Turkish red peppers.

Ohanyan's Bastirma and
** Soujouk Company**
3296 West Sussex Way
Fresno, California 93722
www.shamra.com

As the name suggests, this is a source for basṭurmā *and* sujuk.

Penzeys Spices
19300 West Janacek Court
Brookfield, Wisconsin 53045
Phone: (800) 741-7787
Fax: (262) 785-7678
www.penzeys.com

Already offering over 250 spices, seasoning, and herbs, this spice store has recently begun carrying Aleppo red pepper.

Turkish Deli Inc.
6923 Bristol Pike
Levittown, Pennsylvania 19057
Phone: (215) 946-9461
www.turkishdeli.com

This online Turkish grocery store offers Aleppo and Turkish red peppers.

Zingermans.com, LLC
422 Detroit Street
Ann Arbor, Michigan 48104
Phone: (888) 636-8162
Fax: (734) 477-6988
www.zingermans.com

This company offers many varieties of gourmet food and gifts, including Aleppo and Turkish red peppers.

Index